TERRITORY · AUTHORITY · RIGHTS

TERRITORY · AUTHORITY · RIGHTS

From Medieval to Global Assemblages

Saskia Sassen

PRINCETON UNIVERSITY PRESS · PRINCETON AND OXFORD

© 2006 by Princeton University Press
Published by Princeton University Press, 41 William Street, Princeton, New Jersey
08540
In the United Kingdom: Princeton University Press, 3 Market Place, Woodstock,
Oxfordshire OX20 1SY

All Rights Reserved

Library of Congress Cataloging-in-Publication Data
Saskia, Sassen.
Territory, authority, rights : from medieval to global assemblages / Saskia Sassen.
p.   cm.
Includes bibliographical references and index.
ISBN-13: 978-0-691-09538-7 (cl. : alk. paper)
ISBN-10: 0-691-09538-8 (cl. : alk. paper)
1.   Social systems.   2. Social systems—History.   3. National state.
4. Globalization.   5. Jurisdiction, Territorial.   I. Title.
HM701.S26 2006
306.2'01—dc 22   2005048867

British Library Cataloging-in-Publication Data is available
This book has been composed in Goudy
Printed on acid-free paper. ∞
pup.princeton.edu
Printed in the United States of America

10   9   8   7   6   5   4   3   2   1

To Mara Van de Voort

An explorer of our world and her mind

with admiration.

Contents

Tables

Acknowledgments

ANY PROJECT that proceeds over years accumulates vast numbers of people and institutions to thank. I would like to begin with the Schoff Memorial Lectures Fund, which invited me to deliver three lectures on new work. Those lectures, delivered at Columbia University in 1995, were the first step into the subject of this book. Because these lectures were to be published, they ever so gently forced me to write, and there is no discipline like writing. Through this initial work I came to understand that I would need years of research, ruminations, and writing to do what I wanted to do. In addition to the fund I owe a large debt of gratitude to the late Dean Warren, to Kenneth Jackson, and to the many members of the Columbia community who came to all three lectures and provided support and valuable comments. Also special thanks to John Ruggie, Jagdish Bagwhati, and Katherine Newman, each one of whom introduced one of the lectures generously and with intellectual contributions of their own.

There are many great research assistants to thank, spanning my move from Columbia to Chicago. How to thank them for their intelligence, enthusiasm, support, reliability, and willingness to regularly do all-nighters–of which there were many at various junctures of the project. My appreciation goes to Giselle Datz, Rachel Harvey, Kathleen Fernicola, Harel Shapira, Chi-Chen Chiang, Shawna Davis, Lital Mehr, Sheldon Lyke, Joanna Woczjek, Geoff Guy, Nilesh Patel, Zachary Hooker, and many others. Colleagues both close to home and far away were an indispensable source of support and criticism. I owe many people a great thank you for intellectual support and great dinners. I wish I could name them all, but space constraints rule.

Funding was generously provided by various institutions directly and indirectly, among them the Ford Foundation, the Schoff Memorial Lectures Fund, the Volkswagen Foundation, and the Social Sciences Division Faculty Research Fund of the University of Chicago.

Princeton University Press was, as always, enormously supportive and helpful. I want to especially thank Ian Malcolm for his commitment, energy, and wisdom in moving the project along. Jennifer Backer was exceptionally helpful and precise in her copyediting. Meera Vaidyanathan was swift and very helpful in guiding the book through production.

At home, Richard Sennett and Hilary Koob Sassen made all the difference with their love and laughter.

TERRITORY · AUTHORITY · RIGHTS

1 INTRODUCTION

WE ARE living through an epochal transformation, one as yet young but already showing its muscle. We have come to call this transformation globalization, and much attention has been paid to the emerging apparatus of global institutions and dynamics. Yet, if this transformation is indeed epochal, it has to engage the most complex institutional architecture we have ever produced: the national state. Global-level institutions and processes are currently relatively underdeveloped compared to the private and public domains of any reasonably functioning sovereign country. This engagement cannot be reduced, as is common, to the victimhood of national states at the hands of globalization. The national is still the realm where formalization and institutionalization have all reached their highest level of development, though they rarely reach the most enlightened forms we conceive of. Territory, law, economy, security, authority, and membership all have largely been constructed as national in most of the world, albeit rarely with the degree of autonomy posited in national law and international treaties. For today's globalizing dynamics to have the transformative capacities they evince entails far deeper imbrications with the national—whether governments, firms, legal systems, or citizens—than prevailing analyses allow us to recognize.

The epochal transformation we call globalization is taking place inside the national to a far larger extent than is usually recognized. It is here that the most complex meanings of the global are being constituted, and the national is also often one of the key enablers and enactors of the emergent global scale. A good part of globalization consists of an enormous variety of micro-processes that begin to denationalize what had been constructed as national—whether policies, capital, political subjectivities, urban spaces, temporal frames, or any other of a variety of dynamics and domains. Sometimes these processes of denationalization allow, enable, or push the construction of new types of global scalings of dynamics and institutions; other times they continue to inhabit the realm of what is still largely national.

These are charged processes, even though they are partial and often

highly specialized and obscure. They denationalize what had been constructed
as national but do not necessarily make this evident. The institutional and
subjective micro-transformations denationalization produces frequently continue to be experienced as national when they in fact entail a significant historical shift in the national. Such transformations often need to be decoded
in order to become evident. These instantiations of the global, which are in
good part structured inside the national, do not need to run through the
supranational or international treaty system. Nor do they need to run through
the new types of global domains that have emerged since the 1980s, such as
electronic financial markets or global civil society. They include particular
and specific components of a broad range of entities, such as the work of national legislatures and judiciaries, the worldwide operations of national firms
and markets, political projects of nonstate actors, translocal processes that
connect poor households across borders, diasporic networks, and changes in
the relationship between citizens and the state. They are mostly particular
and specific, not general. They reorient particular components of institutions and specific practices—both public and private—toward global logics
and away from historically shaped national logics (including in the latter international operations, which are to be differentiated from current global
ones). Understanding the epochal transformation we call globalization must
include studying these processes of denationalization.

Much of the writing on globalization has failed to recognize these
types of issues and has privileged outcomes that are self-evidently global. Global
formations matter, and they are consequential. Yet even global regimes often
only become operative, or performative, when they enter the national domain.
This entry is predicated on—and in turn further strengthens—particular forms
of denationalization. The encounter between national and denationalizing processes is not an innocent event; it has multiple and variable outcomes. There is
a sort of invisible history of the many moments and ways in which denationalizing tendencies failed to materialize and succumbed to the powerful currents
of the national, still alive and well. In other cases denationalizing processes
feed nationalizing dynamics in separate though at times connected domains—
for example, the denationalizing of certain components of our economy and the
renationalizing in some components of our immigration policy. In brief, there
is much more going on than meets the global eye—or than highly recognizable global scalings allow us to understand. The transformation we are living
through is a complex architecture with many distinct working elements, only
some of which can easily be coded as globalization.

Both self-evidently global and denationalizing dynamics destabilize
existing meanings and systems. This raises questions about the future of crucial frameworks through which modern societies, economies, and polities

(under the rule of law) have operated: the social contract of liberal states, social democracy as we have come to understand it, modern citizenship, and the formal mechanisms that render some claims legitimate and others illegitimate in liberal democracies. The future of these and other familiar frameworks is rendered dubious by the unbundling, even if very partial, of the basic organizational and normative architectures through which we have operated, especially over the last century. These architectures have held together complex interdependencies between rights and obligations, power and the law, wealth and poverty, allegiance and exit. I will emphasize both negative and positive potentials associated with this destabilizing of existing arrangements.

HISTORICIZING ASSEMBLAGES OF TERRITORY, AUTHORITY, AND RIGHTS

In my reading of the evidence there are two distinct sets of dynamics driving globalization. One of these involves the formation of explicitly global institutions and processes, such as the World Trade Organization (WTO), global financial markets, the new cosmopolitanism, and the war crimes tribunals. The practices and organizational forms through which these dynamics operate are constitutive of what is typically thought of as global scales.

But there is a second set of processes that does not necessarily scale at the global level as such, yet, I argue, is part of globalization. These processes take place deep inside territories and institutional domains that have largely been constructed in national terms in much of the world. What makes these processes part of globalization even though they are localized in national, indeed subnational, settings is that they are oriented towards global agendas and systems. They are multisided, transboundary networks and formations which can include normative orders; they connect subnational or "national" processes, institutions and actors, but not necessarily through the formal interstate system. Examples are cross-border networks of activists engaged in specific localized struggles with an explicit or implicit global agenda, for example, human rights and environmental organizations; particular aspects of the work of states, for example, certain monetary and fiscal policies critical for the constitution of global markets now being implemented in a growing number of countries; the use of international human rights instruments in *national* courts; and noncosmopolitan forms of global politics that remain deeply attached to or focused on localized issues and struggles.

A particular challenge in the work of identifying these types of processes and actors as part of globalization is the need to decode at least some of what continues to be experienced and represented as national. The practices and dynamics listed above are not usually seen within global scalings. When the social sciences focus on globalization it is typically not on these practices and dynamics but rather on the self-evidently global scale. These instances are too often absorbed into conceptual frameworks that equate their location in a national setting with their being national, which obscures their global dimensions.

A key proposition that has long guided my research is that we cannot understand the x—in this case globalization—by confining our study to the characteristics of the x—i.e., global processes and institutions. This type of confinement is a kind of endogeneity trap, one all too common in the social sciences and spectacularly so in the globalization literature. The basic position in that literature is to explain globalization as growing interdependence, the formation of global institutions, and the decline of the national state; the most persuasive organizing fact in these descriptions is the power of transnational corporations (TNCs) to override borders and national governments or of the new telecommunications technologies to compress time and space. These various features of the global amount to a description but not an explanation of globalization.

Avoiding this endogeneity trap is one of the organizing efforts in this book. There are consequences to a type of analytics that posits that an explanation of x needs to be configured in terms of the non-x. For one, it demands a focus on the work that produced the new condition—in this case, globalization. How do we get from non-x to x? But we cannot confine this effort to tracking how a new condition—in this case, globalization—gets constituted. The "new" in history is rarely simply *ex nihilum*. It is deeply imbricated with the past, notably through path dependence, and, I will argue, through a tipping dynamic that obscures such connections to the past. The new is messier, more conditioned, and with older lineages than the grand new global institutions and globalizing capabilities suggest.

To avoid endogeneity and to historicize both the national and the global as constructed conditions, I have taken three transhistorical components present in almost all societies and examined how they became assembled into different historical formations. These three components are territory, authority, and rights (TAR). They assume specific contents, shapes, and interdependencies in each historical formation. The choice of these three rests partly on their foundational character and partly on the contingency of my fields of knowledge. One could, and I hope someone will, choose additional components or replace one or another of these.

Territory, authority, and rights are complex institutionalizations constituted through specific processes and arising out of struggles and competing interests. They are not simply attributes. They are interdependent, even as they maintain their specificity. Each can, thus, be identified. Specificity is partly conditioned by level of formalization and institutionalization. Across time and space, territory, authority, and rights have been assembled into distinct formations within which they have had variable levels of performance. Further, the types of instruments through which each gets constituted vary, as do the sites where each is in turn embedded—private or public, law or custom, metropolitan or colonial, national or supranational, and so on. Using these three foundational components as analytic pathways into the two distinct assemblages that concern me in this book, the national and the global, helps avoid the endogeneity trap that so affects the globalization literature. Scholars have generally looked at these two complex formations in toto and compared them to capture the differences. Rather than starting with these two complex wholes—the national and the global—I disaggregate each into these three foundational components. They are my starting point. I dislodge them from their particular historically constructed encasements—in this case, the national and the global—and examine their constitution in different historical configurations and their possible shifting across and/or insertions in various institutional domains. This also produces an analytics that can be used by others to examine different countries in the context of globalization or different types of assemblages across time and space.[1]

The dislodging of national capabilities that, I posit, is at work in constituting the global poses particular analytic difficulties. Critical here are the historical assemblage represented by the nation-state and the state-centric interpretation of history that has dominated the social sciences. In the modern

---

[1] I use the concept assemblage in its most descriptive sense. However, several scholars have developed theoretical constructs around this term. Most significant for the purposes of this book is the work of Deleuze and Guattari, for whom "assemblage" is a contingent ensemble of practices and things that can be differentiated (that is, they are not collections of similar practices and things) and that can be aligned along the axes of territoriality and deterritorialization. More specifically, they posit that particular mixes of technical and administrative practices "extract and give intelligibility to new spaces by decoding and encoding milieux" (1987: 504–5). Another significant contribution is that of Ong and Collier, for whom the proliferation of technologies across the world produces "systems that mix technology, politics, and actors in diverse configurations that do not follow given scalings or political mappings." Their concern is not with the broad structural transformations or new configurations of society and culture, but rather with "a range of phenomena that articulate such shifts: technoscience, circuits of licit and illicit exchange, systems of administration or governance, and regimes of ethics or values" (2004: 4; 9–14). These global assemblages are sites for the formation and reformation of "anthropological problems." There are many more elaborations around the concept assemblage, including not surprisingly, among architects and urbanists (vide the journal *Assemblages*). While I find many of these elaborations extremely important and illuminating, and while some of the assemblages I identify may evince some of these features, my usage is profoundly untheoretical compared to that of the above-cited authors. I simply want the dictionary term. I locate my theorization elsewhere, not on this term.

state, TAR evolve into what we now can recognize as a centripetal scaling where one scale, the national, aggregates most of what there is to be had in terms of TAR. Though never absolutely, each is constituted as a national domain and, further, exclusively so. Where in the past most territories were subject to multiple systems of rule, the national sovereign gains exclusive authority over a given territory and at the same time this territory is constructed as coterminous with that authority, in principle ensuring a similar dynamic in other nation-states. This in turn gives the sovereign the possibility of functioning as the exclusive grantor of rights. Clearly, then, globalization can be seen as destabilizing this particular scalar assemblage. Much attention has gone to the fact that the nation-state has lost some of its exclusive territorial authority to new global institutions. Now we need to examine in depth the specific, often specialized rearrangements inside this highly formalized and institutionalized national apparatus that enable that shift. It is not simply a question of policy-making. In overlooking such rearrangements it is also easy to overlook how critical components of the global are structured inside the national, producing multiple specialized denationalizations.

Today particular elements of TAR are becoming reassembled into novel global configurations. Therewith, their mutual interactions and interdependencies are altered as are their institutional encasements. These alterations take place both within the nation-state, for example, from public to private, and through shifts to the international and global level. What was bundled up and experienced as a unitary condition—the national assemblage of TAR—now increasingly reveals itself to be a set of distinct elements, with variable capacities for becoming denationalized. The disassembling, even if partial, denaturalizes what has often unwittingly become naturalized—the national constitution of territory, authority, and rights. These three building blocks are my navigators inside the two black boxes that are the national and the global. Each evinces the analytic capability for dissecting these two master categories.

FOUNDATIONAL TRANSFORMATIONS IN AND OF

COMPLEX SYSTEMS

At its most abstract, my question is about how to study and theorize foundational transformations in and of complex systems. Complex systems are not made *ex nihilum*. Critical to the analysis in this book is the possibility that some capabilities can be shifted toward objectives other than the original ones for which they developed. Also critical is that for this shift to happen a foundational reorientation in existing systems must occur. In part 1 of this book, that foundational shift is the constructing of the national in good measure through a repositioning of particular medieval capabilities. In part 2 this foundational reorientation is the construction of the global in good part through the repositioning of particular national capabilities. Part 3 then examines what assemblages might be forming though they may remain as yet barely legible, and what elements of the new organizational logic articulating territory, authority, and rights are getting locked in, thereby precluding other path dependencies.

When it comes to the analytics of historical transitions, knowledge about the dynamics shaping them can help raise the level of complexity through which we examine and understand current transformations. Rather than modeling the past or current periods to isolate a few causal variables, the effort here goes in the opposite direction. Recent scholarship has shown us the multifaceted rather than monocausal character of the earlier historical period that saw the emergence of territorial sovereign states. This is an important correction of the state-centric perspective that continues to dominate our understanding of the rise of territorial states and emerged partly as a function of the formation of national states. The effect has been a sort of capture by the nation-state frame of much of post-sixteenth-century history in the West.

This book uses particular historical conjunctures as a type of natural experiment. My analysis of such historical periods is not aimed at historical chronologies and evolutions. Though historical details are crucial and constitutive to my analysis, the effort is theoretical. Thus, going back to the earlier period of state formation is using history to illuminate possibilities and lock-ins rather than tracing an evolution. The fact that key dynamics of the current transformation tend toward disaggregation, in a reversal of the earlier period that saw the formation of the nation-state, is only one aspect of this inquiry. The main rationale is to use history as a natural experiment that has run its course and hence allows us to understand the character of discontinuities, to wit, that they can accommodate the transfer of old capabilities into new organizing logics. In developing this analytics of change, I specify three constitutive elements: capabilities, tipping points, and organizing logics. I introduce these briefly here; they recur throughout the book.

Capabilities

Capabilities are collective productions whose development entails time, making, competition, and conflicts, and whose utilities are, in principle, multivalent because they are conditioned on the character of the relational systems within which they function.[2] That is to say, a given capability can contribute to the formation of a very different relational system from the one it originates in. In using historical conjunctures as natural experiments to develop a more complex analytics of change, one can detect whether and how major transitions ushering novel arrangements, such as the shift from the feudal to the nation-state order, might depend on multiple capabilities of the older order. This "dependence" is not necessarily easy to recognize, as the new organizing logic can and will tend to alter the valence of a given capability.

This type of analysis makes legible the multivalence of capabilities and thereby helps explain some of the illegibility of major transformations in the making. It also signals that the capabilities needed to constitute complex structures are built over time, and that notions about major transformations entailing the destruction of the prior order are deeply problematic. But so are those who, accepting this proposition, then consider that there is nothing new in today's global era. My interpretation of the historiographies and the evidence about current developments points to an in-between dynamic: some of the old capabilities are critical in the constituting of the new order, but that does not mean that their valence is the same; the relational systems or organizing logics within which they then come to function may be radically different. The critical issue is the intermediation that capabilities produce between the old and the new orders: as they jump tracks they are in part constitutive and at the same time can veil the switch by wearing some of the same old clothes. In much of the book I seek to decipher particular historical configurations to understand this process of switching.

Much discussion about the ongoing role of the national state in today's global age evinces this type of confusion. First, it is not the national state as such, in its totality, but particular components that are undergoing denationalization; second, the valence of particular capabilities arises out of the organizing logics within which they are inserted.

This is made evident in, for instance, the rule of law and various components of the supranational system that were critical capabilities for the

---

[2] The concept of capabilities has been developed conceptually by a variety of scholars with different questions in mind. Most known and influential are probably the constructs developed by Sen (1999) and Nussbaum (2000). In both these elaborations there is a strong positive valence. My use of the term is simpler, more descriptive, and closer to the word as distinct from the construct. Further, in my use it is multivalent, in that I include what we might think of as negative capabilities normatively speaking: the capacity to destroy what ought not to be destroyed, such as human life or good cropland. Finally, I do not confine the term to individuals, but also include systems.

development of the nation-state and the interstate system but at a given confluence of dynamics can enable the formation of a global system. As they do,
they begin to neutralize some (not all) of the critical features of the nation-
state and interstate system. This illustrates one of the crucial dynamics I identify as part of foundational social changes. I mostly designated this dynamic
for shorthand as the fact that capabilities can jump tracks and become part of
new organizing logics.

Tipping Points

A second feature, then, of the methodology and heuristics developed
in this book is specifying the particular dynamics involved in capabilities
switching relational systems and/or organizing logics. That is to say, this type of
analysis can accommodate the fact of tipping, or the "event" in Sewell's sense,
rather than being confined to the outcome—a new whole or order.[3] A focus on
the outcome rather than the tipping point is typical of much of the literature
on globalization; this then leads to comparisons of the national and the global
and easily falls into the trap of assuming that if the global exists it is in spite of
the national. An analytics of capabilities and tipping points keeps us from having to posit that the ascendance of a new order necessarily means the end
of the old order. And it keeps us from having to accept the proposition that
the national state is still doing what it has long done and that not much
has changed.

I specify three distinct features of an analytics of tipping points.

First, for the types of questions raised in this book, identifying the
tipping point is a matter of extant historiographies and possibly novel interpretations. The central concern in this book is twofold: to develop an analytics that allows a more complex explanation of foundational change and to develop a better explanation of the foundational change we are living through
today. The critical historical tipping point of concern in this book is the one
that moves us from an era marked by the ascendance of the nation-state and
its capture of all major components of social, economic, political, and subjective life to one marked by a proliferation of orders. Correspondingly this is
also the most extensive analysis of a tipping point in the book, covering much

---

[3] The notion of tipping points first entered the public discourse in the United States
in discussions about white flight from inner-city neighborhoods in the 1960s where black residents had crossed a certain threshold as a percentage of the population (e.g., Crane 1991). Sociologists developed several models capturing these and other trends (e.g., Granovetter 1978;
Schelling 1971). Gladwell (2000) has once again brought the term into circulation.

of part 2. Detecting the transformations I am after, then, required moving inside the national state apparatus as it becomes the site for its own partial disassembling (chapters 4 and 5). Parts 2 and 3 address specialized instantiations of dynamics that construct the switch.

Second, because this analytics aims at capturing the transition from one order to another, it must accommodate the possibility of informal actors and practices as part of the pertinent processes, both of which may eventually become formalized. Among these dynamics informal practices are particularly important as they allow me to explore one of my hypotheses, to wit, that also the excluded make history. In terms of the analytics in this book, making history here can be identified as constructing capabilities. I explore this, among others, through the burghers of the Late Middle Ages—informal political subjects engaged in informal political practices—and their struggles to constitute themselves as carriers of formalized rights and obligations through the development of urban law (chapter 2). I also explore this through the case of minoritized citizens and unauthorized immigrants who through their informal practices can destabilize and blur formalized meanings of political membership as defined in today's modern nation-state (chapter 6).

Third, because it is about switching from one to another relational system and/or organizing logic, an analytics of tipping points needs to accommodate the distinction between that which is prevalent and that which is not yet is in the process of becoming dominant, that is, it is already producing systemic changes. What is already becoming dominant may as yet be incompletely formalized or basically informal.

Organizing Logics

Insofar as I use history to detect and deduce the character of organizing logics, the three major such instances of concern in this book are, respectively, the centrifugal scalings of the Late Middle Ages held together by several encompassing normative orders, the centripetal scaling of the modern nation-state marked by one master normativity, and the centrifugal scalings of the global that disaggregate that master normativity into multiple partial normative orders, thereby leaving open the questions as to its sustainability if we take history as a guide. In this regard then, the global is novel—different from earlier centrifugal scalings in that it also disaggregates normativity into specialized subassemblages.

Two components of the organizing logics arising in Europe as of the sixteenth century are the national state and the world political economy. This consideration entails a complicating element in that each needs to be positioned analytically both in the era of the formation of the national state and that of the global. Thus I posit that there are two critical components in the organizing logic of each the national and global era: the state and the empire—or, more analytically, a world scale for politico-economic operations. Central to the effort is, then, to distinguish the analytic positioning of the state and the world scale in, respectively, the national and global eras. Thus in examining the postwar Bretton Woods system I find that it is not part of the global era even though it developed capabilities that were to become crucial for the new global era. And I examine the national state today to argue that the executive needs to be distinguished as a strategic site for global operations.

Given the type of capabilities analysis developed in this book, foundational change need not entail the elimination of everything that constituted the preceding order. Hence, capabilities and tipping points are intermediations that allow me to capture, or deduce, this feature of foundational change because they disaggregate the whole into capabilities that die with the death of the old order and others that do not. In part 1 I examine how particular medieval capabilities fed the formation of a centralized state bureaucracy and the abstract notion of sovereign authority. A novel order is not an invention *ad novo*, and it does not necessarily announce itself as new, as radical strangeness—like science fiction or a futuristic account.

USING HISTORY TO DEVELOP AN ANALYTICS OF CHANGE

The scholarship on the earlier periods, with all its debates, produces a far more complex landscape than indicated by current models of social change, which are typically geared toward isolating key variables to create order where none is seen. Detailed historical accounts and debates open up the range of possibilities. Looking at this earlier phase is a way of raising the level of complexity in the inquiry about current transformations. Rather than a model, I am after a finely graded lens that allows me to disassemble what we have come to see as necessary aggregations and to track the formation of capabilities that actually have—whether in medieval times, the Bretton Woods era, or the global era—jumped tracks, that is to say, gotten relodged in novel assemblages. Thus, the divinity of the medieval sovereign represents the formation of an elusive capability whereby power is not just raw power but becomes legitimate authority; this capability in turn I interpret as becoming critical to the later formation of secular sovereignty, albeit with a switch in vocabularies and a novel rhetoricization. The internationalism that states developed through the setting up and implementing of the Bretton Woods agreement is a radically different type of world scale from that of the global era that emerges in the 1980s; nonetheless, critical capabilities for international governance and operations were developed in that process, which eventually became relodged into novel global assemblages.

This interpretive stance brings with it a methodological concern about including informal, or not yet formalized, institutional arrangements and practices in the analysis of change. That which has not yet gained formal recognition can often be an indicator of change, of the constituting and inserting of new substantive logics in a particular domain of the social—economic, cultural, political, discursive, subjective—which is thereby altered even though its formal representation may remain unchanged, or, alternatively, altered even though it remains informal, or is not yet formalized. These informal logics and practices, I argue, can be shown to have contributed to historical change even though they are often difficult to recognize as such. The fact that informal logics and practices are one factor in historical change also contributes to the lack of legibility that is frequently a feature of major social changes in the making.

This illegibility of social change is an issue that runs through the book and one for which history is a fruitful guide. The scholarship on "mentalities" has shown us, for instance, how difficult it is to apprehend such change. One of my concerns here is deciphering deep structural shifts underlying surface continuities and, alternatively, deep structural continuities underlying surface discontinuities. This then also rests on my conceptualization of certain conditions and dynamics as capabilities that can jump tracks and wind up lodged in path dependencies that diverge from the original ones. For instance, at a time when industrial capitalism was the new dominant logic, most people in England were still employed in agriculture and much of the economy and politics were centered in older social forms; industrial capitalism was dominant but not prevalent. I argue in part 2 of the book that we can make a parallel observation about denationalization today. We still do not recognize the precise locus of the epochal transformation we are living through and as a result cannot see its significance—what prevails in interpretation is the ongoing weight of national states and/or the self-evident scale of the global and its powers, leaving no room for the possibility of this third dynamic.

Two critical categories the book focuses on are the national state and the world scale. I use particular states as emblematic of the major changes in each of the eras examined. They are the French Capetian state in the Late Middle Ages, the British state in the development of industrial capitalism, and the United States in the post–World War II era. Focusing particularly on one state is a necessity given space constraints and the particular analytics I seek to develop in this book—that is, the need to understand major issues through detailed examinations of practices and discursive domains in ways that can accommodate both formal and informal processes and actors. This matters to the effort of capturing tipping points and the relocation of particular capabilities into a novel assemblage of territory, authority, and rights, one constituted through an organizing logic that differs from that of the preceding assemblage even as it captures some of its capabilities. Substantively, this is a way of specifying the character of the current transformation, to wit, my insistence that the national is one of its key locations. This type of interpretation of what is epochal about the transformation we are living through carries distinct policy implications when it comes to democratic participation and accountability.

The configuring of each of these states allows me to examine particular conjunctures when capabilities jump tracks. Specifically, in part 1 the focus is on the tipping points whereby capabilities shaped in the forging of decentered political systems are relodged into a national scalar assemblage; and, in part 2, on today's tipping points that relodge capabilities of national political economies into assemblages that denationalize and globalize nationally oriented capabilities. These capabilities come from both the public and private domains as constituted in the national era. Getting relodged into denationalizing and global organizing logics not only reorients these capabilities toward objectives other than those to which they were oriented, it also reconstitutes the construction of the public and the private, and of the boundaries between these domains.

One of my theses is that today's most developed form of globalization, economic corporate globalization, could not have happened without the use of highly developed capabilities of national economies. Further, precisely because they are highly developed, these capabilities functioned in the immediate past in ways that strengthened the national state. Through their typically partial denationalization they get relodged into globalizing dynamics. My reading of history then makes problematic the prevalent notion in the globalization literature that the new phase entails the elimination, or weakening, of what made the national state strong. I posit that such capabilities are collective productions whose development requires time, constructing, and conflicts; they are constitutive of assemblages, even as the latter in turn produce organizing logics that reposition those capabilities. For instance, the "rule of law" is a capability that was critical to the strengthening of national state authority to institute national economic protectionism. But today it is also critical to the global economy in order to open national economies. It is sufficiently developed that it can operate in a context of national protected economies and also become a key building block for the success of neoliberal deregulation and privatization—to some extent features that are the opposite of protectionism. But it can do so only by getting relodged in a new organizing logic.

In that sense, using history as a natural experiment can help illuminate some of these issues by providing the complexity of thick environments where multiple pressures and dissensions operate and by providing (rather than our having to forecast) the outcomes of these complex interactions. Game theoretic models would aim at simplifying, which can be a good thing, but they would do so at the cost of assuming we understand the organizing logic. The historical past can, ironically perhaps, provide us with a far more powerful analytic terrain than any model when we are confronting complex reconfigurations such as those we see today. Using particular historical configurations as a natural experiment also disciplines the researcher to avoid the risk of reifying crucial conditions, dynamics, and outcomes.

The second critical category in this book is the world scale. One of the theses I develop is that there are foundational differences between the world scale of several earlier phases of the world economy and today's global economy. The possibility of such foundational differences is critical to my thesis about the denationalizing of conditions historically constructed as national. I interpret these earlier world scales as constituted through the projection of emerging national territorial states onto the world for the purpose of developing national systems. This is an interpretation that corresponds to, and builds on, several strands in the scholarship about the emergence of capitalism, including Wallerstein's masterful contribution (1974) about the modern world system. However, in contrast to much of the current work that builds on historical studies, notably work with a world-system perspective, I interpret today's world scale as foundationally different in that it is constituted in good part through the insertion of global projects into a growing number of nation-states with the purpose of forming global systems. I include de facto as well as formalized projects that secure the development of global systems. Today it is, then, the foundational features of multiple global, rather than national, systems that get partly structured inside nation-states.

From this derives a second thesis about the world scale, one following up on the notion of capabilities. In earlier world scales we see considerable levels of development and institutionalization of capabilities, both administrative and economic, for what today we would consider global operations. Among these we can include already in the seventeenth century institutions such as the Bank of Amsterdam, the Bank of England, and stock markets that operated internationally, and toward the late 1800s, firms with affiliates across the world. What matters here are not the institutional features of these various entities, since these corresponded to conditions of that time, but the fact that they entailed capabilities for global operations. The Bretton Woods era represents an even more developed world scale.

Emphasizing the existence and development of these capabilities in earlier periods raises the analytical ante when it comes to my first thesis about foundational differences between earlier eras and today's world scale. In emphasizing a difference in spite of the fact that many of the features of today's world scale (firms with affiliates, global markets, cross-border administrative facilities) were present in the earlier phase, I position myself between the two main trends in the scholarship. Simplifying brutally, one of these trends posits a novel development, that is, globalization, and the other contests this notion. In much of the scholarship the earlier world scale has either not been addressed or been used to argue that nothing has really changed and we are living through a further development of what started in the sixteenth century as a capitalist world system.

At some very general level of analysis we can argue that today's global era is more of the same—yet another phase in the history of capitalism and/or the world system. But that is not the level of generality that interests me. I do make room for continuities by emphasizing the development of capabilities, but I diverge from the main strands in the scholarship in that I interpret key historical moments as the dislodging of at least some capabilities from an existing organizational logic and their insertion in a novel one. A key effort is, then, to emphasize analytically the extent of the institutional and operational development of the earlier world scale; this means, for instance, emphasizing the capabilities developed for extracting resources from colonies and imperial domination, rather than emphasizing extraction and domination as such. Herein then lies one point of divergence from what are key interpretations in the scholarship about the current phase and its relation to the past, which tends to emphasize either continuities or discontinuities. I examine to what extent both are flawed interpretations insofar as key capabilities developed in the earlier phase can become foundational to a subsequent phase but only as part of a new organizational logic that in fact also foundationally repositions those capabilities. The flaw, so to speak, I detect in much of this scholarship is an assumption that the sum of a given set of parts inevitably produces the same assemblage.

There are, then, two analytic issues that emerge out of this and might be seen as contradictory: one of them is the fact that much has changed, and the second is that the features of earlier periods need to be addressed for a deep and complex understanding of the current phase precisely because the earlier phase evinced some of the major capabilities that enable the current phase. One question that arises for me is why the current assemblage did not emerge at the earlier time since key capabilities for global operations were present then. Is it a matter of tipping points? That is to say, did those capabilities not reach the required thresholds in those earlier periods?

I argue that tipping points contributed to a far more foundational dynamic of sharp divergence between the organizing logics of the earlier and current phases. In earlier periods, including Bretton Woods, that logic was geared toward building national states; in today's phase, it is geared toward building global systems inside national states. One consequence (and an indicator) of that difference in the economic arena, perhaps still the most legible domain, is the fact that in the earlier period the development of the world scale and the growth of international rivalry were directly related while today they are inversely related. Today's formation of global systems has served to subject national differences to global economic logics insofar as the main actors are economic. One result is the formation of increasingly integrated systems both for the operational side of the emerging and expanding global economy and for its regulation and normative functions. These developments and tendencies depend on the collaboration, whether forced or willing, of "the community" of national states. The more the global economic system has expanded and developed in the 1980s, 1990s, and into the twenty-first century, the more these integrative features have strengthened and taken hold in other spheres as well. The opposite dynamic was at work in the development of the earlier world scale. Where today's global systems seek to override interstate military conflict, those of the late 1800s and early 1900s fed such conflicts. Further, as they grow stronger, today's global systems succeed more and more at diluting (or suppressing) rivalries among the major powers, while in the earlier period interstate rivalries became sharper as each of the major national powers grew stronger.

It is important to capture fully the extent to which states worked at developing the postwar international system and the extent to which the nature of this effort can be distinguished from the global era that began to take shape in the 1980s. For many the postwar period is one long phase building toward today's more extensive international economic system. I argue that it is indeed a phase where we see the development, building up, and formalizing of capabilities that allow states—at least some—to enter into a far broader range of formal international transactions and, in some cases, to assume international governing capacities. But the early Bretton Woods system aimed at protecting national economies from external forces, not at opening them up. Through a combination of dynamics, a tipping point was reached in the 1980s where these capabilities jumped tracks and became part of a new emergent organizing logic leading toward the constituting of a novel assemblage of key components. Not all world scales or international systems are articulated through the same organizing logic. The issue for me is to understand the particular type of organizing logic at work in these different phases. In this context, then, I also diverge from the literature that sees the state as evolving. Rather than merely seeing an evolving transformation of the state as it adapts to new conditions, I see the particular combination of dynamics that produces a new organizing logic as constitutive of foundational realignments inside the state. This is not merely a process of state adaptation; it is also constitutive of the new organizing logic.

There are, then, two key issues I extricate analytically from this thick and complex history since World War II. One is the character of the internationalism of this era, and the other is the character of the transformations inside the national state. Again, I use history but do not presume to do historiography, and again, I use one state, in this case the United States, the dominant and emblematic national state of the post–World War II era. One of the two central theses in this analysis of the Bretton Woods era is that the elements for entering the global age were there after World War II and into the 1970s. But because this was a world scale that had as its project the governing of the international system in order to protect national economies from external forces, it actually had more in common with the earlier world scale in some of its major systemic features than with today's global scale, no matter how modern and even contemporary its capabilities. The tipping point that would take us into the global age required vast mixes of elements, and these did not come together until the 1980s.

Thus I argue for a constitutive difference between that early post–World War II system and today's global system. One of the indicators of this is the internal transformation of the national state beginning in the late 1970s and strengthening in the 1980s, a transformation that partly enacts a novel globalizing project. It was marked by a significant shift of power to the executive, a loss of lawmaking capacities and public oversight functions by Congress, and, partly as a result, a new critical role for the judiciary in both public scrutiny of executive action and lawmaking. The intermediate variables that constitute the outcome are privatization, deregulation, and marketization of public functions and the associated rise in the number and power of specialized regulatory agencies within the executive that took over what were once oversight functions in the legislature.

However (and this is the second central thesis on the Bretton Woods era), the capabilities for state action on international transactions were present from earlier decades and were being further developed in this period, as was the disposition toward formalizing many of these capacities. These capabilities were developed through the work done by government and technical experts on multinational regulation of finance and trade, the transgovernmental networks that were formed in this work, and state officials' learning to negotiate the standardization involved in international governing so as to intermediate the enormous differences among participating governments and the political economy of their countries.

OUTLINE OF THE BOOK

Part 1 recovers the nationalizing of fundamental spatial, temporal, organizational, and rhetorical structures. The object is to understand how territory, authority, and rights became assembled into the modern nation-state. It took work to make society national—from generals fighting for yards of territory, to lawyers inventing new juridical frameworks and instruments, to the work of merchants and capital owners that strengthened the national scale in economic operations, to the work of schools and other "disciplining" institutions in the forging of a national citizenry. There was nothing natural, easy, or predestined about the national. The chapters in part 1 identify specific institutions and processes, historicize their features, and show to what extent their nationalizing was a novel and a "produced" project. By "produced" I mean that it took making. Similarly it takes much work to implement globalizing dynamics and some of this work, and probably most of it, requires an often deep engagement with the national institutionalizations of key building blocks and processes in the political economy. Examining the complexities of the earlier period of nation-state formation should expand the register of variables conceivably at work in such foundational transitions.

The particular assemblage of TAR we call the nation-state emerged out of a configuration profoundly different: the Late Middle Ages. However, I argue in chapter 2 that key capabilities constitutive of the nation-state were shaped during that medieval period. The critical analytical issue becomes then to understand how these medieval capabilities get relodged into a radically different assemblage articulated through an organizational logic that bears little resemblance to that of medieval times. This raises both the issue of differentiating the parts from the whole and the issue of historical transitions.

For example, the monetization of the economy declined sharply in the Middle Ages with the fragmenting of the political order into multiple units, each often with its own coinage and seigneurial power to coin and to design measures and weights. Monetization may thus not have advanced much at this time. But the matter cannot be reduced only to the actual extent and efficiency of monetization. It was also a capability that involved the acceptance of the idea of monetization. When national states emerge, monetization gets repositioned away from city-states and seigneurial domains to national treasuries. Money as a medium does not need to be invented from scratch, nor does the idea of monetizing transactions that had been taking place in kind or through barter. Rather, as a capability it can be seen as facilitating and partly constituting the more mediated economic organization characterizing territorial states.

Along these lines, I argue that the divine grace the French monarchy begins to invoke at a certain point in history in order to command autonomy from the papacy can be conceptualized as feeding eventually into the abstract notion of secular sovereignty. A variety of conditions and decisions established France early as a distinct entity and stimulated a specifically French identity, which included loyalty and patriotism. These developments allowed the formation of an abstract notion of sovereignty, which eventually becomes popular sovereignty, even though divine kingship was precisely the specific capability the French Revolution aimed at destroying. The divinity of the French kings can be interpreted as feeding the mythical character of the nation in the later secular period. Nationalism and patriotism can then be seen as capabilities developed through territorial kingship and its claim to divine origins. A godly source of authority destroyed by the revolution reemerges as a secularized capability—the founding myth of the nation.

Emblematic of what I am after is, for example, Strayer's (1970) interpretation that the papacy's declaration in the eleventh century of exclusive authority over ecclesiastical matters and autonomy from any secular authority in effect created a need for the forming of an entity such as the sovereign territorial state to give secular authority a base. Emblematic also is Berman's (1983) notion that our Western legal tradition originates partly in canon law even though it develops precisely as a contestation of the latter and has aimed at erasing that earlier form and the facts of that legacy.

This early history also offers us the possibility of seeing ex post the often considerable illegibility of foundational change. For example, there is scholarly consensus that at the end of the eleventh century it seemed incredible that feudalism, church, and empire would be challenged and come to be in many ways superseded by new logics of organization. By 1300 all three had started to give way to city-states, city leagues, and sovereign territorial states, even though these were not yet fully developed and recognizable as the dominant type of organization in the making. Yet one can find emergent capabilities. Thus the concept of national territory was preceded in the medieval west by an acceptance of the concept of patria, or fatherland (Kantorowicz 1957; Gottmann 1952: 34).[4] We can see herein one version of the notion that to implement sovereign territorial authority required imagining something that did not quite exist as a material reality (Ruggie 1993), unlike what is the case in, say, conquering a gold mine.

The development of territorial authority is crucial to the question of how the world scale emerging in the sixteenth century was part of the building of national states and national capitalism. Chapter 3 examines the interaction of these two major processes. The state bureaucracy for extracting revenue, particularly the capacity to implement increasingly standardized taxation, helped make the state the most significant economic actor at the time and the key organizer of world-scale economic operations. This strengthening of the state took place even as national unity was often unrealized; the development of state capabilities and of a world scale emerged as critical to the consolidation of national territorial unity. In addition, the temporal and spatial reframing of economic activity, which in turn produced new notions of time and space among those involved in these practices, eventually projected itself onto the larger social order. The past offers us the chance to examine the many micro ways in which these new spatial and temporal orders were achieved, often over a span of time involving many generations and hence not easily apprehended as a transformation.

Similarly, today there are reorganizations of temporal and spatial issues that are incipient and not easy to apprehend as such. Space-time compression, the feature that has received most of the attention, is not only a partial dynamic but also one that produces a penumbra around other issues that hence become difficult to recognize as part of the transformation. In that regard, examining these earlier processes helps us appreciate the complexities and different velocities and hence variable legibility of various components in these kinds of transformations.

The world scale that gets constituted in the sixteenth century diverges from that which existed through the trading networks of city-states and city leagues captured so well by Braudel. There had been far more long-distance trade in the earlier period than there was in the sixteenth century, when pillaging became the dominant practice. In turn, as the formation of

---

[4] For a discussion of the evolution of this term, see Kantorowicz (1957: 232–72).

the national state and capitalism proceeded through the seventeenth century
and onward through the twentieth century, the practices and projects that
constituted the world scale evolved and reached considerable diversification
of flows, institutionalization, and development of formidable administrative
capacities. However, the organizing logics remained geared toward building
national political economies.

Much of part 2 examines the partial, often specialized disassembling
of the national that becomes constitutive of the global. In my interpretation
the current phase of globalization consists at least partly of global systems
evolving out of the capabilities that constituted territorial sovereign states
and the interstate system. In other words, the territorial sovereign state, with
its territorial fixity and exclusivity, represents a set of capabilities that eventually enable the formation or evolution of particular global systems—itself a
partial condition—that require neither territoriality nor exclusivity. This runs
against the dominant interpretation which, whether explicitly or not, constructs the global and the national as mutually exclusive. Whether it is the
electronic global market for capital or the changed relationship of citizens to
their national states, we can begin to discern new alignments in the assembling of these constitutive elements. As already introduced above, chapter 4
concerns the international capabilities developed under the Bretton Woods
regime, which I interpret as still part of an older foundational logic but also
see them eventually feeding the formation of global systems. For this to
happen, however, they need to get relodged into a new foundational logic
marked by the denationalizing of what are historically national capabilities.
The same, I argue, holds for other national capabilities.

The level of complexity and specialization is high in these processes
and requires delving into distinct domains, each largely shaped and engaged
by the national. The effort here is to detect foundational shifts that may
still be functioning at the edges or be minor, albeit strategic, components
within each of several routinized institutional sectors. I address this transition
in chapter 5 through an examination of particular, highly specialized dynamics in the global political economy. First, I posit that the distinctive features
of the new, mostly but not exclusively private institutional order in formation
are its capacity to privatize what was heretofore public and to denationalize
what were once national authorities and policy agendas. This capacity to privatize and denationalize entails specific transformations of some of the components of the national state. Second, I posit that this new institutional order
also has normative authority—a new normativity not embedded in what has
been and to some extent remains the master normativity of modern times:
raison d'état. This new normativity comes from the world of private power

yet installs itself in the public realm and in so doing contributes to denationalize what had historically been constructed as national state agendas. Third,
I posit that particular institutional components of the national state begin to
function as the institutional home for the operation of powerful dynamics
constitutive of what we could describe as "global capital" and "global capital
markets." In so doing, these state institutions reorient their particular policy
work or, more broadly, state agendas toward the requirements of the global
economy.

These three dynamics raise a question about what is "national" in
these institutional components of states linked to the implementation and
regulation of economic globalization. National territory and national state
authority assume new meanings. The global, largely electronic market for
capital instantiates these dynamics sharply. But far less noted in the literature
is a feature I consider central to the foundational transformations afoot: it has
to do with the circulation of this market's operational logic through the public domain where it then emerges as state policy. In so doing, an examination
of the global market for capital also allows us to understand particular shifts in
the construction of the private and public domain.

Chapter 6, the final chapter in part 2, concerns changes in what remain the foundational subjects for membership in our societies: citizenship
and alienage. Although highly formalized, both are incompletely theorized
contracts with the state. Current foundational changes in the state and in its
positioning in a broader field of forces invite an inquiry as to how incompleteness can become activated today. I argue that we are seeing a blurring in
the distinctiveness of each subject in spite of the renationalizing of membership politics. This is perhaps most legible in specific formal transformations of
particular features of the institution of citizenship. They are not predicated
necessarily on deterritorialization or locations for the institution outside the
national state, as is crucial to conceptions of postnational citizenship. These
transformations are internal to the national state and hence to be distinguished from current notions of postnational citizenship. I will refer to them
as denationalized forms of citizenship.

In the context of significant but not necessarily absolute transformations in the condition of the national generally and the national state in particular, addressing the question of citizenship requires a specific stance. It is
possible to posit that at the most abstract or formal level not much has
changed over the last century in the essential features of citizenship. The theoretical ground from which I address the issue is that of the historicity and the
embeddedness of citizenship and the national state, rather than their purely formal features. Each—citizenship and the national state—has been constructed

in elaborate and formal ways. And each has evolved historically as a national bundle of what were often rather diverse elements, and with extreme correspondence between TAR, as in the national. Here I argue that some of the dynamics at work today are destabilizing these particular national bundlings and bringing to the fore the fact itself of that bundling and its particularity.

Part 3 examines dynamics and practices that constitute global digital assemblages which, I argue, are contributing to different meanings of territory, authority, and rights. To that end, chapters 7 and 8 examine a bundle of theoretical, methodological, and political issues that are part of the analytical effort to embed the digital in more complex conceptual and practical fields. Analytically this parallels the effort in part 2 aimed at the same type of embedding of the global—in that case, in the national. Doing this requires addressing how we as social scientists study these new technologies.

The chapters in part 3 are shaped by my particular theorization of globalization and digitization. When we consider globalization as partly endogenous to the national rather than as external (as is usually assumed or argued), the world scale is conceptualized as partly inhabiting the national. This has theoretical and political consequences. First, it implies that citizens can participate in global politics through the use of formal state instruments, not only global instruments. Second, denationalization is multivalent. It can function as a creative force rather than simply as a negative consequence of overwhelming external global power. Third, globalization is not simply growing interdependence—its typical definition—but the actual production of spatial and temporal frames that *simultaneously* inhabit national structures and are distinct from national spatial and temporal frames as these have been historically constructed. Out of this comes a highly dynamic and often combative interaction. Part 3 addresses each of these subjects through measures of time and space, of law and power, and of formalized versus nonformalized activity.

The transformations examined in parts 2 and 3 destabilize existing meanings and systems. We are seeing the formation of novel critical alignments in today's world scale. I examine some of these emergent, often informal, or not fully formalized dynamics in some detail. Specific and general transformations are denationalizing particular aspects of various domains arduously constructed as national. Globalization, digitization, the ascendance of human rights and environmental struggles, the unbundling of unitary normative frameworks, the transnationalizing of identities and experiences of membership—each of these is contributing to and enacting denationalizing outcomes. And each does so in particular and partial ways.

PART ONE • *ASSEMBLING THE NATIONAL*

In an abstract sense, the multifaceted political geography of the feudal order resembles today's emerging overlapping jurisdictions of national states, supranational institutions, and novel private global regimes. This is, indeed, one of the prevalent interpretations in the globalization scholarship. A second pertinent and prevalent interpretation, in this case in the scholarship on the origins of the national state, posits the foundational discontinuity of the national state's emergence with the preceding medieval period. Reading the historiography of the Late Middle Ages through the lens of medieval capabilities leads me to argue against, or at least to severely qualify, these prevalent positions in each of the two scholarships.

My concern is not historical evolution but developing an analytics of change using history. An organizing hypothesis in the following chapter is that particular medieval capabilities partly enabled the formation of the territorial national state and the notion of sovereign authority. This in turn brings to the fore the question as to where the tipping point lies that draws these capabilities into the new organizing logic represented by the territorially constituted sovereign state. There is a puzzle in this argument, to wit, that an entity whose exclusive authority and supreme power to grant rights derive from a territorial regime should have evolved partly out of the nonterritorial regimes of the Middle Ages and out of forms of authority centered in the divinity of rulers. Each of these is a distinct assemblage of territory, authority, and rights. What settles the puzzle is the thesis that critical capabilities built up in a given period can jump tracks and get lodged into new organizational logics that may diverge sharply from the preceding ones. The three key forms of political organization identified in the historiography of the Middle Ages—feudalism, church, and empire—all lacked territorial fixity and exclusivity. Each of these core assemblages of TAR in the Late Middle Ages contains and is constituted by specific capabilities. However, a given capability is not only specific to a formation but also relational vis-à-vis other capabilities in that formation and can thus, in principle, evince multivalence. That is to say, changes in key aspects of an assemblage can shift the valence of a capability.

In this sense, then, a capability can be regeared toward new logics and get lodged into novel path dependencies. I see this happening in the current global age when state capabilities historically constructed for the pursuit of national goals today get reoriented toward global projects.

In examining the European feudal order my interest lies in understanding whether the shift toward the territorial state as a dominant logic for assembling TAR also entailed as a critical constitutive element the reorienting of at least some of the existing medieval capabilities. There are two aspects I want to distill analytically from the thick and rich historiography of the period. One is how a given factor in the decomposition of an order, in this case the feudal order, can become a capability once it gets lodged in a novel organizing logic, in this case the new assemblage of TAR at the core of the national state. It is a notion I will return to when examining the current period. This analytic stance absolves the future—which at that time would have been the national state in the making—from having to invent or create *ad novo* all the capabilities that would come to distinguish it from its predecessor period. The second aspect I want to distill from the historiography of the period is in some ways the obverse of the first: how a factor that was constitutive of the critical elements in a given order can become a necessary capability in the novel order that rises out of the ashes of the former and, more important, might be the opposite of that former order.

Thus one of the hypotheses presented in chapter 2 is that the complex and abstract notion of the legitimate authority of the national territorial sovereign does not represent a radical innovation of the postfeudal order. Multiple medieval capabilities went into its making, from notions of divine authority to those of the secular and constitutional systems of law arising out of the formation of cities in the eleventh and twelfth centuries. These can, then, be conceived of as capabilities that can jump tracks and get lodged in novel logics, projects, or path dependencies. This in turn raises the issue as to the formation of an American national sovereign, given the absence of medieval lineages, a subject I address in chapter 3. How did an American centralized sovereign—a sovereign constituted as the source of authority and law—arise out of a loose confederacy of autonomous localities deriving their authority directly from common law and the Constitution?

A second hypothesis in chapter 2 that organizes my reading of the historiography of the period pertains to a distinct political economy of urban territoriality in the Late Middle Ages that contains dynamic tendencies toward the production of modern capabilities: secular authority, constitutional forms of government, and territoriality. My elaboration of the first two capabilities rests on the somewhat rare legal scholarship that has emphasized the importance of urban law. This is an aspect less noted in the general historiography of the eleventh and twelfth centuries, which tends to emphasize economic and political aspects, in particular the relationship of cities to lords, kings, and the church. The making of urban law entails a second, related dimension: the informal political practices of town dwellers inside the city, which contributed to constitute the burgher as a specific type of subject. With important exceptions, these two factors have not been given sufficient weight in the pertinent historiography. They are, however, critical to my capabilities analysis. The third critical urban element that has been insufficiently theorized concerns the implications of inter-city transactions for the construction of specific types of territoriality.

The question of territoriality has generally not been central to the historiography of cities, far more focused on their relations to various sources of power. When it has been emphasized, the focus has typically been on the cities themselves, conceived of as a type of territorial organization. In specifying a distinct political economy of urban territoriality I include the fact that these cities were not only nodal but also partly networked forms of territorial organization. Insofar as inter-city trade and the mobilities of particular corporate groups, notably the guilds, needed protections and rules for the crossing of territories, they produced a specific type of spatiality. This spatiality wormed its way into territories encased in multiple, formal, nonurban jurisdictions—feudal, ecclesiastical, and imperial—and set up a system of "urbanized" authorities over those routes. These authorities were mostly de facto and customary rather than formalized, and they were partial and from the ground up; in that sense they constituted a mostly informal type of territoriality.

The other major site for examination in this earlier time preceding the full-fledged establishment of the modern state is the formation of a world scale for economic operations that began in the sixteenth century, one of the subjects in chapter 3. Much historiography points to the importance of empire in the formation of the modern state. Both this early world scale and the second phase of empire from the late 1800s on are often used to argue or interpret the parallels with today's globalization. Insofar as the world scale of these two earlier periods fed the development of the national, it was a radically different constitutive element for the condition of the national state from what today's world scale is for today's national state. The possibility of such foundational differences is critical to my thesis about the denationalizing of conditions historically constructed as national. Simply to think that a world scale is a world scale reifies the matter. It is not simply a question of

scaling but also one of the organizing logics in play, the practices that constitute specific scalings, and the path dependencies those logics produce.

I interpret the earlier world scale as constituted through the projection of emerging national territorial states onto the world for the purpose of
developing national systems. This is an interpretation that corresponds to
and builds on several strands in the scholarship about the emergence of capitalism. However, in contrast to much of the current scholarship that builds on
those same historical studies, notably the world-system perspective, I interpret today's world scale as foundationally different from the earlier scale. Today's world scale is constituted in good part through the insertion of global
projects into a growing number of nation-states with the purpose of forming
global systems, from whence comes my hypothesis about today's denationalizing of particular state capabilities.

Going in what might appear to be a contradictory direction to the
above is a second organizing effort in my reading of the historiography on the
formation of a world scale: a capabilities analysis of the administrative resources
and coordination mechanisms developed in these earlier centuries for handling
what we would today consider global operations. This emphasis on capabilities
for global operations does raise the analytic ante when it comes to my hypothesis about foundational differences between that period and today's world scale.
The critical intervening variable is the organizing logic of each period briefly
mentioned in the preceding paragraph.

Beyond systemic shifts, two novel historic subjects emerged as agents
contributing to the shaping of a different organizing logic: the bourgeoisie
and the industrial workforce. Chapter 3 examines especially the formation of
the legal personae of a new type of legitimate owner of the means of production besides the Crown and the nobility, and of a new type of legally created
disadvantaged subject—the industrial worker.

2 TERRITORY, AUTHORITY, AND RIGHTS IN THE FRAMING OF THE NATIONAL

WHY THE NATION-STATE EMERGED out of feudalism is the subject of vast scholarly research and many debates. Revisiting these is not my purpose here. It is rather to engage particular issues and interpretations in this development so as to register its complexity. This should help in generating an analytic grid useful for understanding other foundational transitions, including current processes of denationalization.

A crucial feature in the analysis is the medieval political geography with its plural logics for the valuing of territory, authority, and rights. Three forms of political organization mark this period—feudalism, church, and empire.[1] The increasingly decentered geography of feudalism interacted with the distinct centralizing tendencies of church and empire. Yet the capabilities engendered, mobilized, and refined by each of these organizational logics in turn fed or accommodated yet other formations, including the explosion in the growth of towns that took place over a short period of ninety years or the

---

[1] Feudalism is an ambiguous, contested concept (see Bloch 1961 for a general treatment). The term was unknown to its medieval practitioners; it was first coined in the seventeenth century. It has been subject to enormous interpretation and theorization because it gets at foundational issues such as the origins of capitalism, the nature of constitutionalism, and the sequence of political evolution. Some historians argue that the term should no longer be used. (For discussions of different interpretations, see Strayer 1965; Cheyette 1975; and Berman 1983; for broad understandings, see Bloch 1961; Archibald Lewis 1974; and Saltman 1987.) For Duby (1978), feudalism proper originates after 1000, as it does for Strayer (1965), who sees fragmentation completed by 1000. For Weber (1958), the fact that military power is private stands out in feudalism, coming as it did after a "state"—the Roman Empire, the Holy Empire—had held that power (Gerth and Mills 1946: 47). For Spruyt (1994), feudalism is a valuable ideal type to structure the empirical environment of that period, characterized by a highly decentralized system of political organization based on personal ties. Thus Spruyt essentially follows Strayer in defining feudalism as a mode of political organization. For Strayer "the basic characteristics of feudalism in Western Europe are a fragmentation of political authority, public power in private hands, and a military system in which an essential part of the armed forces is secured through private contracts" (1965: 13).

amore patria that arose in the medieval period and is perhaps a first experience of "Europe."[2]

This chapter examines whether and how the shift toward the territorial state as a dominant logic for assembling TAR partly entailed a dynamic of reorienting existing capabilities, in this case medieval capabilities, rather than the more common interpretation that the latter had to be overcome and destroyed. The decomposition of the feudal order happened in a context in which a new order could be shaped, and this new order did not simply fall from the sky nor did it necessarily get created *ex nihilum*, even when the intense processes we describe as revolutions were part of the change. Wars and alliances, intermarriages, trade, and other types of economic transactions that helped shape and constitute the feudal order became instruments for its decomposition. Wars, alliances, and trade could, in this changed context, also become constitutive of a logic geared toward a different assembling of territory, authority, and rights—territorial kingship and towns. For the change in outcomes to happen, however, there had to be powerful dynamics reorienting processes toward new substantive rationalities or logics. I argue that contemporary denationalization similarly regears national capabilities toward the implementation of global projects. Examining the shift from feudalism to the national territorial state illuminates the complexities and possibly multiple modes of major historical transitions, in this case one fully executed.

DECIPHERING MEDIEVAL TERRITORY, AUTHORITY, AND RIGHTS

Each mode of politico-economic organization embodies specific features when it comes to territory, authority, and rights. In Europe the Middle Ages was a period of complex interactions among particular forms of territorial fixity, the absence of exclusive territorial authority, the existence of multiple crisscrossing jurisdictions, and the embedding of rights in classes of people rather than in territorially exclusive units.[3] In classic times, territoriality in

---

[2] The term "Europa" was extended to the north beyond Greece by 500 B.C.

[3] But this does not mean that exclusive territoriality and the systems of authority and rights that come with it in the modern state are the outcome of an evolutionary development in the West that begins with the absence of territorial exclusivity. In fact there had been forms of territorial politics, most notably the Greek city-states and the Roman Empire. Gottman (1973: 2) notes that the close association between the notion of political organization and the geographically defined concept of a territorial base begins very early in history, long before Aristotle. In the Old Testament territory is presented as a necessary condition for freedom.

the sense of exclusive territorial rule belonged to cities; ancient city-states were not only territorial but had exclusive authority over that territory.[4] The Roman Empire had territorial insertions and centralized authority but no fixed borders. The prevalent pattern in medieval times was one of crisscrossing jurisdictions, thus keeping territorial fixity from becoming exclusive territorial rule. Polanyi (1971) succinctly defines feudalism as marked by its multiple units, its economy in kind, and the emergence of personal ties. Of all conceivable origins, it is out of this configuration that the national territorial state emerged. But, then, feudalism had evolved out of a political geography shaped by what was once a centralized empire.

There was a kind of central authority during feudalism arising out of the church and the empire. But it was not based on territoriality—exclusive territorial authority. Their respective forms of authority could coexist with feudal jurisdictions, and with each other, albeit with frequent conflicts. Given their claims to universalism, church and empire could not admit any rival authority in their respective domains, but these domains were not centered in territoriality. There was thus ultimately no single source of overriding authority in feudalism. Yet there was, I emphasize, a discourse and a project about central authority in both the empire and the church, one that was eventually reconfigured by the Capetian kings as a foundational element in constructing the national territorial state and its sovereign authority.

Although exclusive territorial authority was not the defining trait of the political logic, social and political organizational forms had territorial insertions. Key actors controlled geographic spaces, such as the fiefs and the ecclesia, and in that regard we could describe the landscape as marked by scattered de facto mini-sovereignties in a vast system of often loose overlapping jurisdictions. But even where lords had jurisdiction over manors and lands granted them, they lacked exclusive territorial authority. In terms of political organization, when rewards were given in kind, notably land, political authority could easily become fragmented.[5] Yet this need not be the only outcome. Strayer (1965: 38) shows how vassalage was already in existence

---

[4] According to the *Oxford English Dictionary*, territory is "the land or district lying round a city or town and under its jurisdiction"; when this definition was eventually listed as obsolete, it was followed by one centered on the state, a usage dating back as far as 1494 (Gottman 1973: 16–17). Early discussions of territorial questions pertained to Greek city-states, to Roman cities, and then to medieval Italian cities such as Florence, Pisa, Genoa, Milan, and Venice. The territoriality of these city-states also entailed sovereignty. Theirs was a territorial sovereignty whereas the sovereignty of kings rested on allegiance of individuals and organized bodies, not territory.

[5] Though such service was often rewarded with a land grant—a fief—land was not necessarily a component of the system. Not all vassals owned land (Strayer 1965: 13–14).

at the start of the seventh century but political fragmentation did not prevail till the tenth century (see also Duby 1974).[6] The obligations that
bound lords, vassals, and serfs constituted a sort of barter system where military and economic obligations were in kind (Lattimore 1957). This relationship was constructed with specific duties and obligations for each side.
The fact that it was in kind, rooted in services, in rights and obligations in
situ fed the decentralizing of the political system, one that had originated in
a centralized empire with far higher levels of standardized monetization of
transactions.[7]

Even as rule was fundamentally nonterritorial, particular war technologies and the types of wars that led to feudalism did to some extent territo-
rialize certain features of authority, notably some aspects of war leadership. But
they did so in ways that differed from those of the Roman Empire and the Holy
Roman Empire. Notwithstanding different explanations as to its origins[8], there
is general agreement that feudalism historically evolved as a decentralized system of local defense in response to a decentralized set of aggressors as the Roman Empire disintegrated (Spruyt 1994: chapter 3). Decentralized attacks,
coming from multiple aggressors, could not easily be handled by standing
armies concentrated at the heart of the empire. There is a well-known and
important debate as to whether military technology is a crucial variable in
explaining the organization of power (Tilly 1975, 1990). The heavy shock
cavalry of the Franks was expensive and hence furthered dispersed concentrations of power in small military elites with the wealth to finance this type of
warfare and war technology. Fuhrmann (1986: 177) estimates that it may
have taken four hundred acres to maintain a single knight. Scholars who find
the origins of feudalism in other features of the military condition of the times,
particularly war leadership more so than war technologies, see in multiple

---

[6] This also led to the personalizing of political ties. But the locus of this personalizing
need not be the one evident in the Middle Ages, the lord's fiefdom. Charlemagne used personal
ties to set up an inspectorate and managed to engender an empire with centralized authority and
strong allegiances under conditions that included vassalage and decentralized economic and
political sites (Fesler 1962).

[7] This ideal-typical version of feudalism does not hold everywhere (Poggi 1978). Notable here are Italy's strong and rich city-states; these were quite self-sufficient when it came to
war. For instance, Genoa could call on 40,000 soldiers to defend itself against the French. These
cities did not tend to incorporate their surrounding populations, as did the German cities. One of
the sources of their greater wealth compared to that of the German cities was the prevalence of
long-distance trade, especially trade in luxuries, which produced high rates of profit—between 25
and 250 percent compared to 15 to 25 percent for Hanseatic League cities.

[8] These explanations variously emphasize political, economic, or military factors (see,
generally, Tilly 1995, 1975; Duby 1978; Strayer 1965; Saltman 1987).

dispersed battles the enablements for decentering the system into multiple territorial units.[9]

Nor was authority constituted through an abstract system of rule intermediated by formal law. Rather, authority in the Middle Ages was based on mutual ties, hierarchical but not clearly defined. For Bloch (1961), two sets of obligations shaped feudal authority and rights. One was based on reciprocal military obligations whereby the weaker could seek protection from the stronger in return for military service when required. The other was based on landholding. Though not all vassals had land (Strayer 1965), these were hierarchical and nonreciprocal obligations concerning the economy, particularly agriculture. Further, although localization was an organizing logic and helped produce a decentralized political system, inclusion in the feudal order was not defined by physical location; nor did territory determine identity and loyalty. An individual's or group's specific obligations and rights depended on position in a system of personal ties, not location in a particular area even when those personal ties might be concentrated in that locality. Even where there was some form of geographic rule, as in the manorial economy, it was not complete nor determinative, and only one of several systems of rule to which a locality might be subject; it was also largely constituted through personal relations between a lord and the manors. Overall, this system of obligations and rights was both an outcome and a feeder of particular economic and military configurations that enabled particular sources for legitimation.[10] This meant that feudal lords could become rivals to the types of central authority embodied by church and empire.

Crucial to a system of rights and authority centered in classes of people rather than territory are distinctions between those authorized to engage

---

[9] Thus for some scholars it is the character of the war technology, i.e., the Frankish heavy cavalry, while for others it is the fact of war leadership by knights that provides the foundation for decentralized authority among such knights (Gerth and Mills 1946; Lattimore 1957). Yet another explanation finds the influence of Germany, specifically the old Germanic chieftains who fought the Roman legions and were hence well situated to become feudal lords (Stephenson 1954). For Spruyt (1994), feudalism evolves out of the Frankish kings' military organization and the reciprocities marking Germanic alliances (see also note 11 below). An emphasis on military conditions leads to a perspective of feudalism as emerging out of already existing warrior elites who had served the emperor and had the capability to become decentralized military points of defense.

[10] The Frankish kings had a well-developed system of authority and rights around questions of allegiance in return for sustenance and a share of the spoils of war. Coming out of the old Germanic chieftains who had fought the Roman legions, leadership had emerged from war, making reciprocal relations with their followers critical. There were specific authorities and rights attached to this form of organization. If a king failed his knights, they could resign through a declaration in front of witnesses.

in reciprocal obligations and rights and those who are not.[11] This is a subject I return to later as today we see the formation of several cross-border regimes that unbundle some of the universalisms contained in liberal democracies and move toward specifying classes of people; for instance, we are seeing the formation of specialized cross-border regimes that grant protections to some classes of people (such as the regime for the cross-border movements of professionals that is part of the WTO and regional trade agreements) and withdraw protections from other classes of people (undocumented migrants who have lost many protections over the last decade and are now often constituted as semi-criminal subjects). From the eleventh century on the nobility asserted their distinctive character and the legitimacy of their claim to a privileged status. These claims were further elaborated in terms of the three established orders—clergy, warriors, and workers (Duby 1978). Warriors—the armed nobility—were the defenders of those who prayed, thereby articulating the division of people into three orders within the Christian realm. But there was also a secular legal ground for giving the nobility a special status (Berman 1983) with entitlements to certain holdings, which in turn gave rights of command and justice. Thus nobles could sit on courts with their peers and have armed retinues. Rule resided in the special legal status of the nobility and the particular legitimation of its authority.

Some see in these arrangements the formation of a caste. The right to bear arms differentiated those who were free from the servile. Notwithstanding the existence of significant differences in wealth and power—there were lesser lords and there were overlords—they all shared noble birth. Poggi (1978: 25) sees the nobility as a network of interpersonal relations, rather than linked by older forms of tribal affiliation. Rituals and symbolism reinforced this differentiation.[12] Thus the swearing of an oath was a right of the nobility and members of the clergy, not of servile people. Nobility married nobility, they were buried separately, and so forth. The superior status of the nobility did not, however, necessarily entail a clear hierarchy.[13] Hierarchical arrangements were often

---

[11] For an examination of how different types of authority can be constituted and how authority is to be distinguished from power, see, among others, Bourdieu (1977) and Sennett (1980).

[12] This again brings out the notion of some elusive quality that is part of the structuring of authority; it is not just a question of power (Sennett 1980).

[13] There was not a strict hierarchy but rather a diffuse web of "authorities." Those bearing arms and paying homage might have more than one overlord, again signaling the weakness of hierarchy in feudalism. Multiple overlords, including homage to weaker lords, were also not uncommon. It was only later, with Augustus, that the principle of *ligesse* (superiority of some types of homage over others) emerges in the form of fealty to the king as above all other forms of homage (Fuhrmann 1986: 29). Authority was also a more complex category than actual raw power.

vague and at times contradictory, and this pattern could hold even across kingdoms, including across France and England, which were often at war (Strayer
1965).[14] Thus a king could be indebted to his "inferiors."[15] Noblemen were
also often in service to lords who might become rivals or enemies. In brief, systemically, the locus of territory in the political organization enabled the possibility of decentered authority. And while there were systems of authority and
rights, these were foundationally nonterritorial even though they evinced
some kind of spatial dimension.[16]

A second concern in addition to the locus of territory in the organization of authority is detecting what could be described as proto-
capabilities for the formation of centralized and exclusive authority over a
given territory. Of importance in my interpretation here are the weight and
influence of such partly discursive capacities as the universalist claims of
church and empire—their insistence on each being the single source of ultimate authority in their respective domains. But so is the weight of the more
elusive and less institutionalized notion of *amore patria*; in this case we might
describe the latter as being performative. Further, I want to recover the material capabilities entailed by Charlemagne's earlier building of a territorially
centralized imperial administration, although it was never fully achieved and
was eventually overwhelmed by the decentralizing dynamics of feudalism.
His empire deployed existing capabilities—such as the personal ties that
would come to feed feudalism—in novel ways toward the construction of
administrative capacities. Later in chapter 3 I posit, along parallel lines of
analysis, that some of the capabilities built in the development of medieval
forms of organization fed into the formation of the nation-state and, similarly in part 2, that some of the capabilities for today's global systems come
out of the national state. In short, capabilities critical to a given period may
well have existed long before that particular period took off. Examining

---

[14] Thus at one point in time, the king of England was also duke of Normandy, and in
this capacity owed homage and tribute to the French king, even though the latter was much
weaker. Here we see, again, the building of authority through formalizations, not the simple exercise of power.

[15] It was not uncommon to have land from several lords, to all of whom one owed military service and economic tribute. One could simultaneously be the vassal of the German emperor,
the French king, and various counts and bishops, none of whom necessarily had precedence over
the others. Strayer (1970: 83) gives the example of the count of Luxemburg, a prince of the empire
accountable to the emperor, who also held a money fief (pension) from the French king. We see
here recognition of different superiors for different circumstances (Strayer 1970: 146ff.).

[16] European society was, in many ways, "too fluid and nomadic from the 5th to 12th
centuries to give any substance to a territorial concept" (Gottman 1973: 28). Individuals drew
their rights from the groups to which they belonged.

these earlier historical periods allows one to recover the complexity of these transitions and discontinuities rather than falling into causal models that seek to explain away the tensions, interactions, contradictions, and failures, thereby erasing much of history.

Thus, although there was no exclusive territorially determined authority in the Middle Ages, at least some of the multiple overlapping jurisdictions aspired to the status of single and superior authority. The universalizing claims of church and empire interacted with the increasingly decentered geography of feudal lords and ecclesia. Each of these crucial political actors had its own distinct organization of authority, albeit over a shared territory. The church's ecclesiastical territorial units mapped onto the old Roman Empire's units.[17] But the church as a community of believers recognized no geographic limits to its authority. As an organization it was centered both in this network of ecclesia or bishoprics and in a strong hierarchy headed by Rome. The collapse of the empire, the source of a universalizing secular authority, saw the church installed in the same geography constituted through a mix of religious-ethnic and administrative units. Like the imperial administration it partly replaced, the church's organization rested on an infrastructure of towns, key sites for the ecclesia or bishoprics.[18] While the church came to function in ways often similar to the empire before it,[19] this was a charged process, not simply a new administration replacing an old one. The Holy Roman Empire had not only claimed the same constituency as the church; it had also legitimated its power by a semi-religious status of its own.[20] There was, then, a kind

[17] Boundaries of the bishoprics were based on the perimeter of the old Roman territorial units of dioceses and civitas, the altar of the Roman city, now the place also for the bishop's church. Spruyt (1994: 28) constructs the correspondences somewhat differently.

[18] Mann (1986) observes that from the beginning there was an effective interaction of Christianity and the Roman Empire, with the former spreading throughout the empire rather fast; one reason for this was the Christian doctrine's appeal to traders and merchants who then spread the faith as they moved through the empire. Further, Christianity held particular appeal for artisans; as they tended to organize in local, usually urban congregations, the networks that connected them were another mechanism for spreading Christianity. Thus the church had a sort of network organization that, though distinct, could still be housed in that of the Roman Empire.

[19] The church took over functions previously performed by or installed in imperial administration (Pizzorno 1987). Spruyt (1994: chapter 3) notes that invading barbarians were absorbed into Christianity, which paralleled the earlier absorption of Germanic tribes into the empire, and that monasteries became local nodes for economic production. The church also became the repository of translocal knowledge, Latin, law, and cosmological interpretation (Pizzorno 1987). Indeed, Strayer posits that the eventual formation of the territorial sovereign state is "inconceivable without the Church" (1970: 22).

[20] This was epitomized by the emperor's claiming superiority over all other rulers: for example, "Frederick II, Lord of the World."

of isomorphism between church and empire and as the latter disintegrated, the church kept that older centralized organization going but on its own terms (Pizzorno 1987).[21]

The organizational architecture of this complex system might be interpreted as evincing modern imperial features. But for Wallerstein (1974), this decentered feudal geography interacting with two centralizing forms of authority—church and empire—did not constitute a world economy. Rather, he sees the Late Middle Ages in Europe as a Christian civilization with a core based on appropriation of the agricultural surplus produced in the manorial economy. For Morrall (1978: 10–11) "this fundamental dependence of society on a religious faith which it is assumed that all true citizens must share makes it legitimate to describe medieval society as a Christian Commonwealth."

For Strayer empire and church increasingly developed a theory of sovereignty insofar as they had each implemented a view of final authority (1970: 22ff.). But they were not territorial. Along with other scholars, Strayer sees the clash between the universalist modes of organization of church and empire as preceding and laying the basis for the emergence of sovereign territorial states. This type of interpretation is critical to my analysis in that capabilities for a future formation are developed through organizational forms and aims that diverge sharply with those of that future formation. Indeed, they would seem to be not only divergent but also incompatible. The return to "empire" (whether Charlemagne or the Capetian kings) worked for the church insofar as imperial organization fundamentally corresponded to the church's translocal multipolar organization and imperial secular authority was subject to church authority. In so doing the Christian ecumene also became a political organization, one at least partly dependent on the church. These interdependencies eventually led to conflict when emperors claimed their divinity made them rulers of the Christian realm, relegating church authority to that of vicar of Rome, or when the Capetian kings eventually claimed full authority over their territory. When Charlemagne was crowned in 800 in Rome, capital of the Christian commonwealth, the existence of the Frankish Empire was justified on religious terms (Bloch 1961: 390ff.). His authority became theocratic because he was the defender of the faith. The emperor became the vicar of Christ, and the pope the vicar of St. Peter, making the former the ruler of the Christian

---

[21] The tension between the idea of a Christian commonwealth and the legacy of the old Roman Empire fed strong interactions between them, which often led to conflict. It is only when the empire declined that Christianity flourished as a formal organization and took over many of the functions that had been performed by the Roman administration.

commonwealth. The pope was merely the bishop of the most important see in the Christian realm. The stage was set for conflict, even if practical matters may have made this an advantageous deal at that time for Rome. Thus the later Capetian move to claim full authority over a territory represented a sharp intervention in a longstanding condition where neither church nor empire had recognized territorial boundaries to their authority, even as both organizations were inserted in vast networks anchored in territorial units.

Today we think of the question of exclusive state authority as imbricated with territory and of nation-states as constituting equal jurisdictions. For both of these issues the question of territorial boundaries becomes critical. None of these was a significant factor in the political geometry of feudal lords, church, and empire. Even the Roman Empire's borders were not what we would consider borders today, particularly with regard to equal jurisdictions. Paul de Lapradelle usefully distinguishes between the self-imposed limitation of domain the Roman Empire carried out as a voluntary act and delimitation of territory by mutual agreement between two sovereignties. In Lapradelle's words, the problem of the modern frontier, a delimitation of equal jurisdictions, is inconceivable in the imperial stage of a powerful and solitary state. "At the confines of the empire there are the barbarians: so the policy is limitation, there is no possibility of a delimitation between equals. Neither the Roman Empire nor the Frankish Empire had any conception of the modern boundary. There was only a mere 'voluntary halting place' " (Lapradelle as translated and cited in Boggs 1940: 7).

Another feature of this period is the absence of a distinction between domestic and international politics. There was no sovereign source of ultimate authority and jurisdiction or the need to recognize the existence of other such sovereigns. In addition, none of the three modes of political organization that dominate this period—church, feudalism, and empire—is predicated on the notion that sovereignty implies recognition of equals (Kratochwil and Ruggie 1986). The frontier does not yet have a place in what we might think of as international public law. It existed only in internal imperial public law. Lapradelle observes that "delimitation is a Carlovingian institution. It was born, in a transition period, between Latin unity and feudal distribution, by the introduction of the Germanic principle of Frankish partition into the surviving framework of the Roman Universitas" (cited in Boggs 1940).

Even when there was an orientation toward ruling over a territory, as was the case eventually with the Capetian kings, such rule was problematic. Besides lacking exclusivity, the whole question of boundaries was undeveloped. Often the boundaries of the territory were not clear or continued to expand long after a king's rule.[22] Rule was over people rather than territory (Hallam 1980). Acquisition of authority over territory was often subject to the personal bonds that gave one such authority over a given geographic terrain.[23] Allegiance by individual and tribe to a sovereign and the church became the essential framework of social and political structure.[24]

TERRITORIALIZING AUTHORITY AND RIGHTS

The modern concept of national territory was still far from being developed in the Middle Ages. For Gottmann (1973: 34) it was preceded in the medieval West by an acceptance of the concept of patria (fatherland). Kantorowicz (1957) finds the origin of a territorial element in the *pro patria* starting in the thirteenth century, when it seems to have been discussed by lawyers and philosophers, especially at the University of Paris.[25] But it still had a strong association with community. By the fifteenth century territory and community begin to be associated with cities and a more material view. Tilly sees cities primarily as "containers" for the circuits of capital and states primarily as "containers" for means of coercion (1990: 51). Cities articulate two types of geography: first, a translocal urban network; second, a geography of centrality vis-à-vis a hinterland. A city accumulates surplus from the surrounding hinterland, which it can then distribute through the circuits of urban proto-capital (Harvey 1979). The state, with its means of coercion, can attempt to control this circulation to its own advantage, to pursue its own power projects both "internally" and "externally." In fact, for Tilly, this tension between state and capitalist power projects is fundamental for any understanding

[22] Hallam observes that in the early Capetian reign the kingdom lacked clear boundaries, and "rights of justice, tolls and taxes appear on a map as a network, more concentrated in some areas than others, rather than as a unit of land" (1980: 82).

[23] Some scholars (e.g., Fuhrmann 1986: 20) interpret rule as packages of rights of rulers, rather than authority over territory.

[24] There are objective conditions that help explain the western empire's inability to exercise full territorial authority. Pressure by the Barbarians led to the division into an eastern and western empire in AD 395; a few years later Visigoths invaded Italy and in 410 sacked Rome, which was then sacked again by the Vandalls in 455. Imperial authority lost its territorial base in the western empire. We see then a shift to using the cultural superiority of the empire and moral superiority of the church to convert Germanic and Slavonic tribes to Christianity and to reestablish a unified order based on the Christian faith.

[25] The evolution of this term has been examined by Kantorowicz (1957: 232–72). In ancient Greece and Rome it meant city of origin, and in the Middle Ages it still often meant home, but increasingly an individual could offer himself to many different lords. It could also mean the celestial city: "Heaven had become the common fatherland of the Christians" (Kantorowicz 1957: 475–76).

of the further development of state forms, and forms the basis of his distinction among capital-intensive, coercion-intensive, and capitalized-coercion
path to state building. In the formation of both cities and states, we can discern the possibility of a specific formation of territoriality. Arrighi (1994),
starting from the question of the formation of structures of the world system
and not of individual states, gives another perspective on this contrast
through his comparison of the capitalist logic of the Dutch and of the territo-
rialist logic of the British hegemonies. It is interesting to recall (Greenfeld
1992: 97) that the notion of *amore patria*—patriotism—was a fundamentally
Christian sentiment in the Middle Ages, both as heaven and as the land of
one's birth, or more precisely the province or locality of one's birth. During
the Middle Ages patria rarely designated the polity (Morrall 1980: 28).

What was to become a major innovation in the formation of boundaries and territoriality is a "three-cornered conflict" that appears profoundly
unrelated to what was about to happen (Morrall).[26] The empire positioned itself against the centralized authority of the papacy; the latter, in turn, wanted
centralized authority as the only way to reform itself so as to ensure that local
bishops and local secular clergy did not have too much power; and the ecclesia, which is to say the cities containing the bishoprics, wanted to preserve
their autonomy from the papacy. Simplifying, we might say that the overarching tendency may well have been the push of the papacy for centralization
and the attempt by the various others to get out of that centralized authority
of the papacy. "The Reformation . . . ended the medieval struggle to organize
the whole of western Christendom on the basis of a universally accepted interpretation of Christianity" (Morrall 1980: 136). Tilly (1990: 61) notes that,
with the exception of northern Italy, "Protestant Reformation concentrated
in Europe's city-state band, and at first offered a further base for resistance to
the authority of centralizing states." This could also work in a monarch's favor: "Elsewhere (in the Netherlands) Protestantism provided an attractive
doctrinal basis for resistance to imperial authority, especially authority but-
tressed by claims of divinely-sanctioned royal privilege. Confronted with the
spread of popular Protestantism, a ruler had three choices: embrace it, co-opt
it, or fight it" (Ibid). Because the pope and emperor each supported local particularistic forces that opposed their rival, Germany, which could count on
the pope, and Italy, which could count on the emperor, went toward fragmentation rather than centralization. The papacy eventually turned to territorial
rulers in its fight against the emperor. The weak French kings needed allies to

[26] "The Church and State problem in its modern sense of a tension between two separate societies with different aims did not exist in the eleventh century. The conflict was rather
one between different branches of one and the same society" (Morrall 1980: 28).

pursue the unifying of their kingdoms against the far more powerful feudal lords, and they found them in the church and in the towns.[27] In Germany, on the other hand, the need for domestic support led the kings to side with the nobility against the towns. The German kings curtailed the liberties of towns and surrendered Germany largely to the feudal lords, thereby diverging from the emerging pattern in France and England marked by the ascendance of territorial rulers. The split also formalized different modes of organizing and justifying rule. The papacy turned to canon law, while secular rulers invoked Roman law to justify their sovereignty.[28]

For many scholars the eleventh century marks the establishment of feudalism.[29] The estate had become a key framer for political and jurisdictional prerogatives. But it was also the beginning of a distinct phase of growth and consolidation in the European economy that brought about the ascendance of cities and city-states as core political economies in their own terms.[30] Growth took off in the twelfth century, driven by the expansion of long-distance and local trade, as well as the associated monetization of economic transactions. It all fed the rise and proliferation of towns.[31]

And it is the period when some of the key elements for the formation of territorial states came together. The economic transformations between 1000 and 1300 brought with them political innovations. Monetization, trade, and the growing wealth and numbers of towns altered the political organization of the times in that they weakened the system of in-kind transfers

[27] In contrast to the more common explanation of the emergence of territorial states out of warfare and war technologies (Tilly 1975, 1990), Spruyt (1994: chapter 5) emphasizes the existence of two weak parties—the kings and the towns—whose interests coincided and for whom an alliance was strategically useful given the enormous power of key sectors of the nobility. He notes that in regions where cities were strong, there was a different pattern, notably that cities did not need to ally themselves with the king.

[28] Henry IV already made that argument in the investiture conflict but lost. It took another century for this to be instituted.

[29] For Bloch (1961) this period is different from the earlier Middle Ages; it can be thought of as a second feudal age.

[30] From 1150 to 1300 there was geographical, economic, and demographic expansion in Europe within the frame of the feudal economy. It was followed from 1300 to 1450 by a contraction in all three variables.

[31] Trade and monetization encouraged division of labor, the growth of towns, and the founding of many new towns. For Pirenne (1925) the growth of trade from the eleventh century on created a merchant class with distinct interests. To protect their interests against feudal and ecclesiastic rule they often moved outside the old cities, which were often feudal fortifications, and founded new ones (newbourghs). In England and Holland *portus* (an entrepot for merchandise trade) came to be called burgers or poorters. They also created a series of new cities. In Germany the most important towns of the twelfth and early thirteenth centuries were created mainly by enterprising burghers of the old German towns (Rörig 1969). Those that did not originate then came from the time of the Roman Empire.

crucial to earlier feudal organization.[32] The rise of towns was a key political event; for Pirenne (1956) the growth in size and in the number of towns is crucial to subsequent European development, as it is for Braudel (1979).[33] It is also the period when territorial state sovereignty is invented, a type of state that for Wallerstein (1974), among others, is not a creation of the six-teenth century as is commonly asserted, but of the thirteenth century in western Europe. Yves Renouard (1958: 5–21) shows how the boundaries of France, England, and Spain were largely settled in a series of battles between 1212 and 1214. In addition it was at this time that the notion itself of boundaries was established. For Perroy this was the "fundamental change" in the political structure of Western Europe (1955: 369–70). He dates this transformation to mid-twelfth century and the beginning of the fourteenth, which is the height of the commercial and agricultural prosperity of the Mid-dle Ages.

The crucial agents in producing these innovations were France's Capetian kings.[34] Three features of this history matter to my analysis.[35] One is that these were initially weak kings, far less powerful than some of the lords in the kingdom-to-be.[36] This points to the difficulty of understanding transitions and the fact that it may well be the least likely actor who succeeds. For instance, I would argue that game theoretic models would emphasize the resources of the actor; working off these assumptions one would not have pre-dicted the trajectory of these initially weak kings. Familiar models may mask some of the contingencies resulting in major reversals. The second feature is that the Capetian kings eventually ascribed to themselves divinity and con-tested the authority of the papacy over them. It is then out of these self-apoth-eosized weak kings that the origins of the European sovereign territorial state

[32] Lords began to require money instead of military service to a ruler and demanded rent rather than in-kind produce from their peasants.

[33] Pirenne's thesis on the connection between cities' growth and trade has held up as the historiography has developed. For a series of debates on this thesis, see Havighurst (1976).

[34] Hugh Capet was elected to replace the disputed Carolingean lineage in 987, initi-ating the Capetian dynasty that lasted until 1328. The area under the Capetian kings' control after a century of civil war was tiny compared to that of the older, West-Frankish kingdom. Powerful dukes supported the installation of Capet, saw no threat in him, and considered it an elective monarchy.

[35] The analysis here is not centrally concerned with the history of the origins of the ter-ritorial state but with conditionalities and path dependencies. There is a large literature on the origins and a set of interpretations by various scholars as to how state formation happened: for ex-ample, through war, military technology, and protection bargains (see, among others, Tilly 1995).

[36] They gained kingship by consent from the barons after a long civil war; they were first among equals.

can be traced.[37] These kings succeeded in launching a territorial monarchic state that contested and then superseded the Christian commonwealth. By the time their dynasty ended they had claimed full authority over all inhabitants of the territory, within fixed boundaries, and held no claims beyond these.[38] Poggi (1978: chapter 3) notes that the rise of towns had a destabilizing effect on the feudal system of rule, ultimately favoring the territorial ruler over the feudatory system of rule (42). As towns gained power, their dealings with the monarch through the Estates came to represent not personal relations between lord and vassal, but rather the relations between a territorial ruler and a region of the kingdom's territory. The member of the Estate or Parliament came to the king as a representative of the town, signifying the town's willingness "to associate with [the ruler] in those aspects of rule that were understood as characteristically public and general" (43–44). The calling of Estates in this emergent system began to lose its particular reference to personal relations between lord and vassal, and began instead to represent the territory to the monarch (46–51).

A third feature worth emphasizing is that these French kings arose out of a context at the end of the tenth century when feudalism was fully entrenched in France[39]—that is to say, out of a context whose legitimating base was the superiority of warrior and priest; all others were inferior. At the time, power was often located at the level of the individual castle holder, down from the fifty-five dukes and counts (Barraclough 1984: 17); this decentralization was in turn strengthened by the localization of market exchange and legal procedures.[40] Thus the kings achieved territorial centralization out of extreme disaggregation. What matters here is that these weak kings gained control over a highly fragmented territory that was to become France and, further, managed to impose the principle of territorial exclusivity despite powerful and multiple lords and against the still very powerful papacy.

Contained in this shift is another major move, albeit one with several twists: the move from personal rule to public authority, embodied in the

---

[37] These initially weak kings' success in launching a major political innovation could not have been foreseen when they started. This is important to my analysis as it is a condition that recurs and is at work today.

[38] For Strayer, by 1300 the state had become the dominant form of political organization in Europe (1970: 57), but Spruyt (1994) notes that this is an excessive focus on France. See also Tilly (1975: 26–27). Strayer discounts Hanseatic League and Italian city-states; he is right in arguing that the royalist centralization had succeeded.

[39] At that time France was considered an area between the Loire and the border of Lotharingen, and sometimes even just the area around Paris (Dunbabin 1985).

[40] In fact, for Spruyt (1994) and Strayer (1970) the acquiescence of the privileged classes is a crucial factor. See note 38 above.

repositioning of the king as the fountain of law. This shift is further embodied in the acceptance of the Capetian concept of the king's exclusive authority over goods and land at the very same time as decentralized and overlapping feudal authority patterns had reached their apex. In late medieval
France the idea of sovereign authority became empowered and routinized.
Skinner (1978) has posited that one precondition for the modern concept of
the state is a distinct realm for politics separate from theology. The Capetian
kings implemented key elements of this history-making state project, but
they did so in good part by mobilizing medieval capabilities. They in fact
needed the pope to gain legitimacy and resources, and when they contested
the pope they invoked their own divine origins as a source of legitimacy.

The matter becomes more complex when we add to these struggles
for new types of authority the struggle to gain greater autonomy from the papacy. Succeeding at this entailed the emergence of a new type of authority or
at least a new component of authority, one distinct from the hierarchies of
the papal order.[41] The period from 1050 to 1150 saw an enormous transformation in the law of the church, with the pope claiming absolute jurisdiction
over ecclesiastical matters and full autonomy from secular authority in
church matters.[42] While it began earlier, it was Pope Gregory VII's assertion of
supreme authority over the entire Western church and of the independence
of the church from secular control that led to bloody wars over the next fifty
years. Only in 1170, almost one hundred years after that declaration, were
matters settled. This was a significant transformation, especially since it happened over a very short period of three generations (rather than, as has been
commonly interpreted until recently, more gradually over ten centuries)
(Berman 1983: part 1).

Strayer observes that this new concept of church authority "almost
demanded the invention of the concept of the State" (1970: 22) as a strong
autonomous base for secular authority. In the late eleventh and twelfth centuries the church for the first time acquired a legal identity independent of
emperors, kings, and feudal lords. It established a hierarchy of ecclesiastical
courts, as well as legal professionals and legal scholarship within the church.
Berman observes that even though all of this was new, it was predicated on a

---

[41] The separation into eastern and western Christian churches, paralleling the split
into eastern and western parts of the Roman Empire, was not formalized into a split until 1054.
During this time there was a movement to make the bishop of Rome the sole head of the church,
to emancipate the clergy from the control of secular authority—whether emperor, king, or feudal
lord—and to differentiate the church as a political and legal entity separate from secular polities.
This movement culminated in the Gregorian Reformation and the Investiture Struggle
(1075–1122) (Berman 1983).

[42] See Berman (1983: part 1).

preexisting community, the Christian commonwealth, which had taken shape in Europe between the fifth and eleventh centuries.[43] There are two things I want to point out here. First, a larger social body that enables the formalization of a legal order and, correspondingly, a legal order aspiring to logical consistency and systematic rules, both arise out of, and are even conditioned by, that preexisting community centered in custom and religion.[44] Second, and here I rely on Berman's interpretation, this body of law, new canon law, feeds the development of secular law.[45]

The systemic positions of the various actors produced different outcomes. The Capetian kings in France could use the church in furthering their struggles with the nobility and in their interest in written, codified law. England fought the church through Thomas Beckett and (eventually) replaced the church, though it took time; yet, as Innis (2004: 55–56) observes, the divine right of the papacy was replaced by the divine right of Parliament after the so-called Glorious Revolution of 1688–89.

Incorporating the transformation of authority into the various institutional domains that constituted the social order was complex and conflictual. It included clashes on collective versus private property; personal rule and public authority; divine versus secular law; and the challenge of territorial rule to those aspiring to universal authority. Roman law was one source of legitimacy for authority; it had been so for Roman emperors and the late medieval kings, and emperors reappropriated this body of law to enhance their position (Berman 1983: part 1). As a body of law it was oriented to overriding localized interests without necessarily promoting universal

[43] Though Europe was a collection of tribes, local units, and feudal lords, they came to share a common religious faith and a common military loyalty to the emperor and, outside the empire, to kings. The emperor or king was the sacred representative of the faith among all the peoples of his realm. "The preexisting community of faith and loyalty was not only a necessary precondition for the later emergence of the new separate legal identity of the church under the papacy; it was also a necessary foundation for that legal identity, since without it there would have been no underlying social reality to be legally identified" (Berman 1983: 362).

[44] Berman (1983: 51) finds that the Germanic folk law was (nonetheless) a necessary foundation for the secular legal systems that replaced it. The necessary foundation was, once again, the communitarian character of the society that the older folk law had helped maintain. This was a type of law that was basically tribal, local, and feudal, or protofeudal, based on blood feud, ordeals, and other procedures—all of which came under attack in the late eleventh and twelfth centuries.

[45] The influence of Roman law—as reappropriated in the changes of the eleventh and twelfth centuries—even on Anglo-Saxon law, is noteworthy. Maitland (1968) observes that British legal scholars have developed a historical interpretation that erases any presence of Roman law. Maitland (1968) and Berman (1983) hold that England's common law has far more elements of other continental European laws (both Roman and ecclesiastical) than legal historians in the UK ever recognize.

claims.[46] This made Roman law, aligned with royal justice, crucial for the establishment of public authority.[47] The Capetians succeeded at constructing a mode of organization not based on personal ties or universal domination as did the church and the Holy Roman Empire.[48] And they did it in opposition to feudal lords, some far more powerful than the original Capetian kings, as well as powerful actors such as the church (against whom the German emperor had failed). The later rise of the Estates (Standesstaatt) in much of Western Europe between the late twelfth and early fourteenth centuries further added an explicit territorial reference to the system of rule even as it confronted the king (Poggi 1978: 43–44, 48).

In this history of kings and church claiming to be the source of legitimate and autonomous authority, the Capetian kings played a strategic role in intermediating religious and secular authority. Not really Frankish, they appropriated and utilized the Frankish legacy, allowing them to claim to be the legitimate descendants of the Frankish kings and emperors, and hence heirs to their traditional function of defenders of the church and the papacy.[49] In the twelfth and thirteenth centuries the hereditary Frankish superiority in piety was seen as an attribute of both the kingdom and the king of France, but as we know, soon it was only "le roi" who was "très chrétien." The papacy—in need of the Capetian kings—eventually acquiesced and recognized that "God chose the kingdom of France among all other peoples"

[46] This possibility was partly embedded in key features of the Capetian administration as it provided the king with professional agents (Berman 1993) "who were less inclined to pursue their own interests than vassals who were remunerated in kind" (Spruyt 1994: 99), that is, with land. It helped promote the notion of public authority. Further, aligning the interests of professionals with the king's interests solved (at least partly) the problem of imperfect control over tax collection. And it worked as an antifeudal policy, further strengthening the public authority of the king.

[47] Property rights in Roman law were also important and could be aligned with exclusive territorial authority. In this regard Roman law can be conceived of as a protocapability for the development of the sovereign territorial state.

[48] Spruyt argues that the shift from personal rule to public authority was not part of the earlier medieval notion of the king's privileged position as first among equals (1994: 81). Thus he argues that we need to explain which "material interests and belief systems came together in order for the idea of sovereign, territorial kingship to become the system of rule in France" (82). In contrast, others, e.g., Reynolds (1984), argue that the notion of the kingdom as community had been a longstanding one (259).

[49] Greenfeld (1992: chapter 2) describes some of the many testimonials of the special place constructed for France in Christianity. In the literature on the Crusades, the Franks are represented as people who epitomize Christianity, are the most Christian, and are "chosen by God"; de Virtry in the thirteenth century declares, "There are many Christian nations, the first among them is France, the French are pure Catholics" (1992: 93n. 3).

and also made the king head of the Christian army. While there were mutual interests that could sustain this arrangement for a time, eventually the claim of the king's superior authority led to the rupture with the papacy.[50] The French kings did come to represent law as human, not divine, feeding into sovereign territorial rule and moving kingship away from ecclesiastical and into jurisprudential kingship— "Lex est Rex" (Kantorowicz 1957: 131ff.). Out of these struggles came a crucial component for the ascendance of sovereign territorial states and Western law.

One of the critical organizational forms for the Capets' success arose from their administrative practices: a state bureaucracy geared toward taxation. Taxation became a key mechanism for the development of a centralized administration. As Lockwood (1964) notes, there is a high interdependence between bureaucracy and taxation. The efficiency of a bureaucracy depends on the effectiveness of its taxation system, and vice versa (Braun 1975). But the obstacles to effective taxation in the Late Middle Ages were overwhelming. Net production was low, and the quantity of money was small. There was nothing resembling a bureaucracy to collect taxes, nor was there the needed recording capacity. Other means of obtaining revenue included confiscation, coinage debasement (e.g. D. Sinclair 2000), borrowing, and office selling. While these tactics may have solved short-term problems, they created long-term negative effects on rulers' strength (Wallerstein 1974: 30ff.). Tilly (1990: 137–43) provides an analysis of this "coercion-intensive" path to state building. Both this path and the "capital-intensive" path ultimately proved inferior to the "capitalized-coercion" path. Which path an incipient state takes, for Tilly, depends on what kinds of resources are available for a state-building project at the onset. Taxation was a challenge both as an idea and as an actual operation for collecting revenue. In the context of a highly fragmented political organization, scaling up this system to function as a centralized effective bureaucracy confronted major obstacles. The process of scaling up can be threatened by any decrease in taxation capacities and reach, pushing toward decentralizing

---

[50] The king's demands for full jurisdiction over his territory, including sovereignty in spiritual matters, led to rupture with Rome at the end of the thirteenth century; this rupture was between the papacy and Philip IV (le Bel), son of the crusader king the church had beatified as St. Louis. The church had never accepted the absolute territorial authority the king wanted, and the king could not accept the universal jurisdiction of the church in church matters and, ultimately, over secular rulers. Over the ensuing century jurists used several arguments in defense of the sovereign liberty of the king (Greenfeld 1992: 94), including religious arguments about the unequaled Christianity of the French. In fact, according to Hallam, the king's secular authority was continuously "encroaching on ecclesiastical jurisdiction" (1980: 310).

power.[51] And decreases in taxation can result from multiple conditions independent from effective taxation, including cyclical tendencies.[52]

It took some doing to get a taxation system going, but the Capetian kings succeeded. Although there was no direct tax over the whole kingdom at the end of the Capetian reign, these kings laid the foundation for a direct royal tax that was introduced shortly after their regime came to an end (Strayer 1970).[53] According to Strayer, Philip the Fair was the first king to impose general taxes (1970: 79, 394). An important component of the kings' success—and crucial to my analysis—is the fact that they did not operate in a historical vacuum. Their bureaucracy reflected similar administrative processes of the fifth-century Merovingian kings, as well as of the later Charlemagne.[54] But after Charlemagne the idea of a central administration disintegrated and feudalism proper established itself, with agents becoming counts and with hereditary positions. What is interesting here is that despite the general tendencies toward decentralization, the elements were put in place to develop a central territorial administration. It fell to the Capetians to reinstitute some of those older features and to develop a viable central administration.

One important dynamic furthering the Capetian project of taxation was that from the twelfth century on, monetization once again became significant. New uses of money developed into an increasingly important source of revenue, and agriculture's share declined (Lyon and Verhulst 1967: 94). The king or great lords to whom service was due would accept money instead of

---

[51] Intrinsic to an effective taxation system is ensuring that those in charge of taxation do their job. The issue during this period was ensuring that such officials would not appropriate what they should not since it meant that they could set up independent operations, or "feudalize." There were many factors that could cause a taxation system to fail, including the struggle of large landowners to escape taxation, or peasants being pushed into becoming dependent on large landowners to escape taxation. Lockwood (1964) argues that these centrifugal tendencies are both a cause and consequence of failures in mechanisms for maintaining effective taxation and central control.

[52] Lockwood argues that "the 'taxation' crisis of patrimonial bureaucracy is essentially analogous to the 'production' crisis of capitalism" (1964: 254).

[53] The achievement of the Capetian kings is notable given their weakness when they started. Indeed, when the royal tax became increasingly regularized from the 1380s onward, the church and the nobility were exempted. This was the French system for the next few centuries (Collins 1988: 27; Fryde 1983: 837, 858).

[54] These kings had sent out general field agents charged with taking care of fiscal, judicial, administrative, and military matters. They were often rewarded with land grants, since coinage became scarce after Rome's retreat, and eventually established themselves as counts, with the consequent decentralizing tendencies set in motion. Charlemagne reversed this process, reinstituting a centralized administration and reintroducing money. Field agents were paid rather than given land, and their posts were not hereditary (Dunbabin 1985: 6). The appointment of supervisors charged with ensuring that the king's authority was enforced also built up the central administration.

service.[55] As centralized authority developed, Philip the Fair established monetary rewards for various positions and pensions after service, thereby securing the interests and loyalty of middle- and lower-level nobility: it became an attractive source of employment. They performed administrative, judicial, military, and financial tasks for money, not for land.[56]

But the monetization of revenue sources was a highly conditioned process. It was at this juncture that towns emerged as critical sources of revenue for the Capetian kings.[57] These kings pursued a deliberate strategy of allying themselves with towns in their effort to centralize authority in the kingdom.[58] Hence they were willing to offer towns better deals than some of the dukes or counts might. As kings solidified territorial gains, two tactics that worked well were chartering new towns and granting burghers in both old and new towns generous privileges and liberties (Hallam 1980: 136, 186).[59] The expansion of towns produced a crucial infrastructure for the expanded monetization of transactions, a subject to which I will return later.

The fact that both kings and burghers had a strong vested interest in taxation was central to the Capetian success. The burghers in France were part of a very different trajectory from that which generated the bourgeoisie in England as a major force in industrial capitalism (Beaud 1981: 45–46). In subsequent centuries, the bourgeoisie was slow to develop in France and the state

[55] This also created the possibility for mercenaries, which in turn weakened and eroded the basis of power and legitimacy of the warrior aristocracy.

[56] Having troops with no need to give land, the king had less need of the powerful lords to serve militarily and bring troops to war. It is also doubtful whether the king had the power to demand service from the lords. According to custom they were the king's vassals, but they were more like rivals, and thus the king preferred getting military service via payment (Baldwin 1986: 265; Contamine 1984).

[57] The church was another critical source of revenue. The church had acquired considerable holdings throughout the Middle Ages; monasteries in Europe were centers for agricultural innovation, and the church earned revenue through its control over wills and marriages (it had exclusive jurisdiction because they required oaths under God); and people would leave legacies to the church to secure salvation. The clergy were de facto notaries, a professional element that also spilled over into other domains.

[58] In France, centralization was an indecisive process; in contrast, Anglo-Saxon England was forced to centralize after Hastings and the Conquest of Wales (Given 1990). France's local laws and customs remained in force and kings had to recognize them. This is one reason lower-level administrators were recruited from localities (Strayer 1980: 43–44). Indeed, much of the consolidation of the kingdom was through intermarriage and personal ties.

[59] "Recognizing the importance of the growing urban communities produced by the upswing of commercial activity in the early 12th century, these kings issued charters to towns throughout the northern half of France" (Baldwin 1986: 59). Philip Augustus chartered seventy-four towns during his reign (Hallam 1980: 141–42n.). Spruyt (1994: 86) posits that the emergence of towns permitted new social bargains, which allowed Capetian kings to centralize their authority.

played an enormous role in industrialization. The origins of this lie partly in the modest resources of towns in France and their alliance with the king. In turn, for the weak Capetian kings, towns were critical.[60] From the perspective of weak towns in the eleventh and twelfth centuries, harassed by a nobility and kings that would demand arbitrary exactions whenever they needed revenue, standardized taxation was a welcome development, not to mention employment in the king's administration.[61] Towns were interested in maximum independence, which meant they preferred the more rational, central administration of royal protection to that of lords (Tilly 1990). This eliminated cross-cutting obligations. Ecclesiastical lords were particularly disliked.[62]

The alliance between the king and the towns was key to the viability of a centralized administration and collecting taxes, especially given the history of abuse by kings and lords through the mostly arbitrary and willful demand of the *taille* (the cut).[63] The king's representatives who were in charge of securing collection were increasingly drawn from the burghers and lower nobility (Hallam 1980; Strayer 1980).[64] In the first phase beginning in the mid-eleventh century, the Capetians sent out provosts, who were field agents in charge of raising revenue, performing judicial functions, and keeping the peace. Interests of kings and provosts coincided because the income of the latter depended on what they collected. Both were keen to extend the taxable domain. The second phase, around the latter part of the twelfth century, saw the kings tighten the administration, adding supervisors to oversee field agents and establishing bailiffs (or seneschals) in the more recently acquired

[60] Because they were weak, these kings shared some proceeds from central authority with the powerful lords, including generous pensions and a share of the royal tax for the area of the lord. These lords were thus lulled into the royal orbit (Strayer 1980; Baldwin 1986).

[61] Burghers were hesitant to show they had wealth, not wanting to display their wares (though they needed to do so to be able to sell them) (Duby 1974: 228; Stephenson 1954: 41). There are many accounts of towns chasing and throwing out the collectors of the *taille* from various lords and kings. The multiple jurisdictions of feudalism meant merchants often paid taxes several times, and taxes were often collected arbitrarily—whenever the lords or the king needed revenue. It began to make more sense to pay the king's predictable tax than that of one or another local lord's irregular exactions. Poggi (1978) argues that towns preferred larger organizations to facilitate trade; lesser lords had less to offer.

[62] For some interesting examples of very aggressive tactics by towns to get rid of their ecclesiastical lords (including killing them or chasing them out) and to gain royal tutelage, see Beaud (1981: 45–46).

[63] There is not full agreement as to how long this alliance between the king and the towns lasted. Chevalier asserts that it lasted at least till 1550, but the wars for religion upset the balance (1988).

[64] It is important to recall that towns in France were not rich like Italian towns or as powerful as German towns and leagues. French burghers wound up serving in the king's administration, along with low-level nobles.

areas of the kingdom (Baldwin 1986: 126). This model was influenced by administrative notions derived from both the Norman and Carolingian experiences. The third phase in the extension of the royal administration, at the start of the thirteenth century, saw a sharp expansion of the centralized bureaucracy. Bailiffs were permanently stationed in particular areas to enhance their ability to supervise.[65]

The economic revival of the Late Middle Ages set the stage for these transformations. The growing wealth of towns made them attractive to kings, lords, and the church. This created incentives to allow the chartering of more towns, and it gave burghers bargaining power. Towns were granted specific protections, including better taxation arrangements—they were more institutionalized and regular, fitting the interests of burghers (Duby 1974: 225–28).[66] And burghers began to make important political claims. Burghers formed communes, which were sworn associations of equals, taxes were increasingly paid by the town as a whole, and burghers began to negotiate for the right to self-assessment (Strayer 1980: 106; Berman 1983: chapter 12).

But the historical transformation of towns went well beyond the particulars of the French case, where it enabled the development of a territorially centralized royal administration. The patterns evident in Germanic towns diverged sharply from those in French towns, and both diverged from those of Italian towns. English towns were in many ways the least autonomous. Yet in all cases towns emerged as significant actors in the formation of a distinct territorial regime.

THE POLITICAL ECONOMY OF URBAN TERRITORIALITY

With regard to territorial projects, most attention in the scholarship has been devoted to the territorial state that became a well-established type of political organization in Europe in the 1600s. But a second and in many

---

[65] The king's logic is interesting here: bailiffs were to control provosts, and several provostships were grouped into bailiwicks, which allowed bailiffs to claim jurisdiction over internal disputes among lords within the bailiwick. Fesler (1962) sees in this an explicitly antifeudal strategy. The bailiffs were generalists who duplicated the royal presence in the field. The number of bailiwicks doubled from twelve to twenty-four. Bailiffs were the highest authority outside Paris and represented the king. Their salaries were compatible with those of the king's advisors in Paris. Initially clergymen were important as royal administrators, but they could not be bailiffs since they lacked permissions for military functions and for instituting the death penalty. Bailiffs could not be from the nobility, since they were meant to be the king's instruments against the nobility. They were recruited from the bourgeoisie and lower nobility (Hallam 1980; Strayer 1980).

[66] One of the most important demands was a decrease in burdensome taxes and exactions. Those granted by King Louis VII in 1155 were imitated throughout northern France.

ways much older type of territorial organization is that of cities and city-states. One might take this further and argue that city-centered systems, such as the German leagues or the city-states that prevailed in northern Italy in the Late Middle Ages, already contained a notion of external limits aligned with the recognition of the mostly equal jurisdictions among city-states. This was a type of territoriality not characterized by a unitary proximate terrain. But it evinced mutual exclusivity among cities though it did not constitute an exhaustive organizational grid, as is the case with today's interstate system where just about all territory is encased in what are formally considered mutually exclusive states. There are exceptions, but they are few.

We might think of the political economy of urban territoriality in the Late Middle Ages as scattered territorialities—something akin to insertions in a larger and more vaguely constituted terrain with crisscrossing jurisdictions. Tilly (1990) points out that cities were located in at least three forms of territoriality: first, as the central place of a local economy; second, as a node in a translocal network of cities and capital circulation; third, as potentially subservient to a territorial state power. This third dimension is particularly important in determining the future course of state formation in Tilly's account, for the relative power of cities and states, the relative controls over means of coercion and capital, determine what combination of capital and coercion will factor into state building. By contrast, I emphasize the first two dimensions as a building block for "grounding" territory and territorial authority. Most of Western Europe lay outside these scattered territorialities and did not conform to them. Even where there were leading cities, they did not function as imperial authorities or overlords with regard to weaker cities. They may have been hegemonic in ways parallel to some states in today's interstate system, but just like these, leading cities were formally acknowledged as equal jurisdictions even when they may have had hegemonic power over other cities. Most towns in the Middle Ages did not necessarily have such hegemonic power and authority, though in the thirteenth and fourteenth centuries, with the explosion in new towns and in trade, several of them became enormously rich, powerful, and influential. An indication of this is that some of these towns were among the signatories to the Peace of Westphalia, one meant for national states.

Assemblages promoting exclusive authority over a territory cannot be confined to the sovereign state. While this may be self-evident to historians, in the social sciences there has been a sharp conflation of these two. It is yet another indicator of what has come to be referred to as the methodological nationalism of the social sciences (Beck 2001, Taylor 1994). I see today's global cities and high-tech districts as partly denationalized strategic territorializations with considerable regulatory autonomy through the ascendance of private governance regimes. It makes for lumpy geographies of sovereign control in both the past period and today.

It is a well-established fact that the expansion of trade, particularly long-distance trade, was crucial to the growth in the number and weight of cities (Pirenne 1956). This expansion resulted in part from the geographical expansion of the dominant political economy inside Europe that began in the eleventh century and continued until the crisis and economic contraction of the fourteenth century. One measure of this internal geographic expansion is the doubling in size of the Christian realm from the eleventh to the thirteenth centuries. In that period, western Europe "followed an almost classical frontier development" (W. A. Lewis 1955: 475) with the reconquest of Moor-controlled Spain; Christian Europe's recovery of the Balearic Islands, Sardinia, and Corsica; the Norman conquest of southern Italy and Sicily; and the Crusades' adding of Cyprus, Palestine, and Syria, and, later, Crete and the Aegean Islands. In northwest Europe, we see the English expansion into Wales, Scotland, and Ireland; and in eastern Europe, the German and Scandinavian conquest of Baltic and Slavic lands (W. A. Lewis 1955). A second frontier, and for Lewis the most important one, was internal: the marshes, moor, forests, swamps, and fen were settled and cultivated by Europe's peasants between 1000 and 1250 (476). Most European towns date from this period of geographic expansion, and those that do not date primarily from Roman times. The growth of new cities was particularly strong in frontier areas that were as yet relatively underdeveloped.[67] This period of internal expansion and colonization of marginal areas also engendered a series of new mobilities of traders, workers, displaced people, and footloose individuals and groups—pilgrims, crusaders, and growing numbers of uprooted people of all sorts. Many of these flows became increasingly articulated in inter-city networks, with some more institutionalized than others (Le Goff 1989). Much of this nomadic population was fed by the interaction of trade expansion, the explosive growth of towns over a very short period of time, the internal geographic expansion of the European political economy or, as it is more typically described, of the Christian realm, and the colonizing of unsettled marginal areas in Europe.[68]

[67] Even medieval Italy, which was already very urban, added about 2,000 settlements in this short period, though not all were towns (Becker 1981).

[68] The explosion in the number of towns was an important factor in generating what eventually became the guild-regulated migrations, which, in turn, fed more general migrations of craft workers and engineers. The later Tour de France and the Gesellenwanderung are emblematic of these types of migrations (Sassen 1999: chapter 2).

This form of territorial development was, at the aggregate level, a type of political economy. The founding of some of the new towns was guided by the struggle to avoid feudal and ecclesiastical rule. Merchants moved outside existing towns and created new ones, calling them newbourghs to differentiate from old feudal fortifications, and their inhabitants were called burghers (Hohenberg and Lees 1985; Le Goff 1989; Pirenne 1925). Rörig observes that the most important towns of the twelfth and early thirteenth centuries in Germany were created by enterprising burghers of the old German towns (1969: 35). The burghers forming these towns forfeited all political power upon exiting the only formally recognized structures for such participation at the time. However this urban growth represents the entrance of a new political force "which had to be reckoned with in the changing interdependence between territorial rulers and feudal lords, if only as a possible ally for one or the other" (Poggi 1978: 37).

The growth in the number of towns happened over a short period of time—eighty or ninety years. Though there is no consensus,[69] according to several scholars (Pirenne 1925; Le Goff 1989: 78; Verhulst 1989; Hohenberg and Lees 1985), the new social group, town dwellers—the burghers—came into existence beginning in the eleventh century. Important cities emerged out of the confluence of long-distance trade, the increased and often high specialization that accompanied it, and the large-scale financial capabilities such trade required.[70] Tilly, among others (Brenner 1998), notes the interdependence of the growth of the city and the growth of *commercial* agriculture: "substantial cities stimulated cash-crop agriculture in tributary areas reaching many miles into the countryside. Commercial agriculture, in its turn, generally promoted the prosperity of merchants, larger peasants, and smaller landlords while reducing the ability of great landholders to dominate the people in their rural surroundings" (1990: 48). This suggests that the dialectical relationship between city and countryside (see also Cronon) is deeply implicated in the emergence of state projects, both directly via the surplus economic resources available for their implementation, and indirectly through the formation of regional class structures. The disruption of rural class structures and the growth of a new urban class, in conjunction with the contemporary changes in warfare identified by Tilly [1990], parallels Skocpol's [1979] model

---

[69] Some scholars (e.g., Anderson 1974: chapter 4) argue that the towns continued to be part of the feudal order.

[70] This does not mean that agriculture disappeared. But Spruyt (1994) argues that the new urban classes improved their relative position and had an influence on the old economic and political order far beyond their objective share of the overall economy. In my analytic language it would mean that while not prevalent, they were foundational for the new emergent order.

of revolutionary situations, out of which a new translocal power structure can
be fashioned. This was also a period that saw the expansion of free labor and
new forms of peasant property, a renewal of commerce through commercial
fairs, reactivation of the artisan class through guilds, a renaissance of urban
life, and the formation of a commercial bourgeoisie. In this decomposition of
the feudal order, mercantile capitalism took root and developed.

The rapid proliferation of the towns of this period and the emergence of burghers as significant economic and political actors functioned in a
vast landscape that contained many other older social formations and moral
codes, notably those of kingships, fiefs, and the church. Neither the material
practices of town dwellers nor their belief systems fit the larger existing institutional and conceptual order (Berman 1983: chapter 12; Mundy and Riesenberg 1958; Clarke 1926; Stephenson 1933; Spruyt 1994: chapter 5). The incipient "middle class" of town dwellers did not fit the moral order of feudal
times centered on peasants and nobility (Pirenne 1980 [1925]: chapter 6).
Burghers had two preferences (Poggi 1978: 42): they wanted maximum
autonomy, given a condition where various actors with authority subjected
towns to often exploitative extractions of revenue or military service, and a
strong central authority that could protect them better from assault by various
parties—pirates, robbers, and feudal barons controlling transit points and demanding tolls and exactions—since their growth and prosperity depended on
translocal trade. A large, centralized state with effective authority over its territory would, under these conditions, be more effective than a series of feudal
lords. For some scholars (e.g., Spruyt 1994) it is out of this particular confluence that we can explain several key outcomes, notably new institutional orders such as the sovereign territorial state, city-states, and city leagues.

This was a far more patterned and lumpy political economy than the
notion of a clear position of towns against nobility suggests. First, it accommodated considerable variability in the economic situation of towns across
Europe; French towns were mostly weak and German and Italian ones were
mostly rich.[71] Further, the origins of the wealth also varied. Thus in German
towns wealth was a function of the high volumes of trade and the number
of cities involved. The Hanseatic League could be characterized as high-
volume and low-profit trading. In contrast, Italian cities such as Florence,
Genoa, and Venice engaged in much long-distance trade. Trading in luxury

---

[71] Because most of its cities' trade was regional, France remained deeply agricultural
and did not participate much in the long-distance trade. There were at least two ports (La
Rochelle and Bordeaux) that engaged in such trade. Eventually the monarch's enterprises did
much of the trading. Paris was the only large city in a context of modest urban development,
except in the north, especially in Flanders (Braudel 1979; Spruyt 1994).

goods was significant and highly profitable; it also encouraged an extensive division of labor. Except for the very rich cities in Italy, there was intense inter-city competition. Trading routes crossed many jurisdictions, with multiple tolls and many different types of coinage. No town could acquire a monopoly; even towns that were more important than others (for example, in Germany Lubbock and Cologne were leaders of the Hansa) still faced stiff competition. According to Tilly (1990: 52–53), likewise, no state was ever completely able to contain the entire geography of capital within its own geography of coercion. Those that came closest (the Hanseatic League, Venice, and Portugal) always ran the risk of their trading outposts being conquered by foreign territorial powers. Arrighi (1994) identifies a similar dynamic in the breakdown of hegemonies: the costs for the hegemon to maintain a territorial empire become excessive; and precisely what makes the leading state *hegemonic* is its ability to present itself as a legitimate leader, providing collective benefits for a larger community of states. This temporarily suspends destructive competition between states. The Hanseatic League was a response to this diversity of barriers and perhaps can be seen as a kind of free-trade zone, with assurances of fair trade and guarantees of contract. Because of their size, wealth, and enormous profits, Italian towns faced a very different situation. They could oppose political enemies alone and saw little need to collaborate or to develop city leagues.

Second, this political economy of urban territoriality contained diverse alliances and types of organization. French towns became the king's allies, Germans set up city leagues allying with neither king nor lords, and Italians set up autonomous city-states, some of which had their own vast armies.[72] Nonetheless, across this diversity we can detect a type of political economy of territory radically different from that of the territorial sovereign state. Both are, in turn, distinct from the nonterritorial regimes of feudal lords, church, and empire. Spruyt (1994) has examined this particular period in great detail and identifies it as a selective phase (competition, mutual empowerment, mimicry) that is strategic for the eventual ascendance of the sovereign territorial state, including cities, as the winning institutional form. He argues there were several potential competitors to the sovereign territorial state but that the change in the economic environment led to new forms of authority and new rules. Tilly (1990: 78) by contrast argues that as the Italian

---

[72] The systemic positions of each of these three types produced different political outcomes. As discussed earlier, in France weak kings aligned themselves with weak towns, in Germany the kings allied themselves with the nobility against strong towns, and in Italy the city-states were so rich and powerful that they were basically independent.

city-states were pulled into a larger European social system, they could no longer avoid their *land-based* wars. This neutralized the naval advantages of the city-states, while simultaneously enormously raising the costs of warfare. Armies had to be raised, supplied, and paid. Capital-intensive regimes were better equipped to raise money than coercion-intensive regimes; ultimately, however, the capitalized coercion path proved superior to both (90). A buildup of coercive capacities expanded a state's ability to extract resources from within its territory in order to wage a war, although at the potential price of citizen resistance (83). The development of capitalism domestically provided sovereign warmongers with easier credit. Like Tilly, Spruyt finds that city-states were no longer competitive given the changing forms and technologies of warfare; however, Tilly emphasizes the building up of internal state capacities and institutional structures. Arrighi (1994: 40) places more emphasis on the attempts of incipient capitalist states (Portugal and Spain) to capture the *sources* of Venetian wealth, that is, the circuits of long-distance trade. Rather than attempt to annex the city-states, they would control the seas: hence, the naval and navigation capacities of these states were highly important. As upstart entrepreneurs cut into the Venetian monopoly, the hegemony of Venice became insecure. Tilly acknowledges the importance of these naval wars but argues that "empire overseas did not build up state structure to the same extent as war at home. Nevertheless, the connection between state and empire ran in both directions: the character of the European state governed the form of its expansion outside of Europe, and the nature of the empire significantly affected the metropole's operation" (94). The waging of war abroad did not necessitate the buildup of domestic coercive capacities.

Unlike Spruyt's competition analysis, I read this period as building capabilities that were to be inputs for the formation of territorial states but not just through the circuits of capital emphasized by Tilly. This complex territorial regime implemented through the proliferation of towns is one active ingredient in the formation of the sovereign territorial state. It is not simply, as it is usually represented, a period merely preceding the development of territorial regimes; such a representation has the additional effect of reducing territorial regimes basically to one historical type, the sovereign state. What is important in this regard in Spruyt's work is that he views the ascendance of towns as a powerful "regime," though he does not necessarily identify or emphasize its territorial dimension as I do here.

What I seek to capture with the phrase "political economy of urban territoriality" is a somewhat submerged history in the historiography of the nation-state, one overwhelmed, it would seem, by the advent of the state itself. In the social sciences, the political economy of urban territory has been subsumed under models such as national urban systems conceived of as integrating national territory. Cities have been placed both administratively and theoretically in formalized scalar hierarchies running from the local to the urban, the regional, and then the national; all international traffic among cities is assumed to run through the administrative structures of the national state. In other words, there has been a strong push toward conceiving both the past and the present place of cities through the lens of the national state.

Medieval towns became the site for novel political and specifically legal cultures that thickened and institutionalized the urban territorial regime. In his examination of the historiography of cities at this time, Berman finds that notwithstanding the enormous diversity of cities across western and northern Europe, "they were all governed by a system of urban law" made by town dwellers (1983: 357).[73] This is significant if we consider that about five thousand of these cities were launched from the middle of the eleventh century to the beginning of the thirteenth century.

Different categories have been used to capture the notion that feudalism at large produced specific cultures that shaped human conduct and norms (Bloch 1961; Duby 1968; Le Goff 1989; Braudel 1980). Bloch was the first to develop the notion of a medieval mentality as a structure determining individual action. Spruyt uses the term "belief system" to distinguish a systematized way in which people aggregate and explain political phenomena (1994: 68–69) from an overencompassing concept of culture. Weber has given us some of the classic texts on the interactions of ideal and material interests and has elaborated these as they apply to medieval towns and burghers (1958). Perhaps one of the most significant versions of a shared medieval culture and mentality is that unearthed by Berman (1983). He argues that our Western legal tradition arose from a particular elaboration of canon law in

---

[73] The issue here is not that these were the first cities, but rather that in earlier periods cities had not had this degree of explicit representation of their "autonomy" as distinct entities from other formations. From the first to the fifth century the Roman Empire contained thousands of cities, but these had functioned as administrative centers for the empire. And the cities of ancient Greece had been independent city-states. While there were a few such administrative centers and there were some independent city-states, most of the cities of this medieval "urban era," in the eleventh and twelfth centuries, were neither. They were a different type of entity (M. Weber 1958). For Berman (1983: chapter 12) there was no continuity, except for a few cases such as Rome itself, between the former Roman cities and these medieval European cities, even when many arose at or near the old Roman sites. The cities that continued to be part of the ecclesiastical order (seats of bishoprics) had by then ceased being the metropolitan centers they had been and became towns that were more part of the countryside than they were urban.

the 1050–1150 period, a history largely erased from contemporary analyses of Western law that tend to locate its origins in the sixteenth century and in the formation of nation-states.[74] For Berman, the Western legal tradition developed continuously beginning in the eleventh and twelfth centuries, growing organically and knowingly building on itself. Thus reform itself is part of the tradition.[75]

Three critical components in this broadly conceived medieval culture are of interest to my proposition of a political economy of urban territoriality. One concerns the distinct politico-economic cultures that developed out of the ascendance of towns as a major territorial organization. A second one is the law, a mix of Roman, feudal, and Christian law, as well as a variety of specific laws, urban law in particular. These various systems of law had distinct institutional forms (that is, royal, feudal, urban) and operational insertions (the king, the nobility, the burghers) across Europe. A third one, which I develop later (chapter 8), concerns the more elusive transformations in the temporal and spatial framings of practices and norms—the embedding of time and space in a whole range of new institutions and discursive domains. The city emerges as a critical institutional environment for the embedding of novel spatial and temporal framings.

The Legal Order

There are two features of the legal order in medieval times that matter to the emerging political economy of urban territoriality.[76] Berman (1983) notes that perhaps the most important fact was the idea that law mattered.

---

[74] Berman posits that a definition of law in action would include legal institutions and procedures, legal values, and legal concepts and ways of thought, as well as legal rules. For Berman the purpose of the enterprise is not just the making and applying of rules but also other modes of governance—voting, issuing orders, appointing officials, and handing down judgments. Law is more than governance, as it facilitates voluntary arrangements through the negotiation of transactions. Law is, in brief, a living process of allocating rights and duties and thereby resolving conflicts and creating channels of cooperation. Berman posits that this broad definition is needed in order to bring into one framework the many specific legal systems that have existed in the West for centuries, and to understand the interactions of these systems with other political socioeconomic institutions, values, and concepts.

[75] This also holds, in Berman's analysis, for the great revolutions of the nineteenth and twentieth centuries, where he sees an eventual accommodating of particular prerevolutionary developments. The great revolutions he refers to are the French Revolution (1789), the American Revolution (1775–83), and the Russian Revolution (1917).

[76] This examination of urban law, while drawing on several sources, is largely based on Berman's (1983) analysis and interpretation.

What I want to emphasize here is that law mattered not just as an abstract norm, but as a capability that structured interests, and as such a capability it could carry over into subsequent periods even as the contents of those interests might change. The second feature concerns the plurality of sources of law. Multiple types of law arising out of different interests enabled specific politics of claim making (to use contemporary language). City dwellers used specific laws to gain justice and the freedoms to execute what we might refer to as the larger social, economic, and political project of the emergent urban order of the time.

The medieval legal order was a mix of church and "Roman vulgar law" as well as custom, including elements of folk law, developments such as the formalizing of the status of the nobility, and, over time, a variety of particular legal orders.[77] This mix varied in its outcomes across different areas, most notably between those that remained under a strong influence from Rome compared with those more shaped by the Germanic invasions.[78] The north wound up with unwritten customary law (droit coutumier) and the south with written law (droit écrit) (Bloch 1961). These differences meant, for instance, that in the north a plot of land could be owned by several individuals while this was not an option in areas under Roman law (e.g., Bloch 1961). Finally, across these differences in areas under written or unwritten law there was a growing intermediation in the relations and bonds among people, with money a key instrument in this process (Becker 1981; Spruyt 1994).[79]

How and where these features of the law became inserted in the institutions and practices of the time varied considerably. However, their insertion was distinct. Thus the vested interests of burghers aligned them with Roman law, which had well-developed theories of private property and the means of

---

[77] According to Berman (1983: part 1), in the eleventh and twelfth centuries there was a move to reappropriate classic Roman law, as well as Greek philosophy and the Old Testament. The actual version of Roman law in play was Romanist, rather than necessarily the classic version. After the decline of the Roman Empire, the influx of Germanic tribes had changed, if not driven out, the written Roman law. It had basically disappeared in the Germanic kingdoms with the final disintegration of the western Roman Empire in the fifth century. In northern Italy, Spain, and southern France some of the terminology and rules of Roman law survived, though it was a simplified Roman law. Even the most advanced legal collections of the time, such as that of the seventh-century Visigoth kings, lacked the conceptual unity of classic Roman law.

[78] In northern France, especially, invading Goths and Franks had diluted Roman law. Two sets of coexistent legal systems had evolved: laws that pertained to non-Romans (Lex Burgundium and Lex Visigothorum); and laws for the Romans. Law had become personalized.

[79] Becker (1981: 15) observes that in the area of Lucca and Florence before 1000, 80 to 85 percent of transactions, consisting mostly of land deals, took place through gift exchange and donations. By 1150, monetary sales accounted for 75 percent of all transactions.

ensuring compliance.[80] Burghers would also in principle be on the side of rulers who protected the right to private property and abolished trial by combat.[81] Burghers and towns favored a judiciary system centered in principles, in evidentiary procedures, and in courts, rather than the arbitrary exercise of power by lords and kings. It was in their interests that the law should become the domain of professionals. This put the towns in a sharply different systemic position toward the law from that of the nobility (Pirenne 1925; Berman 1983).[82] Through their vested interests, the burghers enacted a shift to instrumental, rational thought regarding property rights and juridical procedures (M. Weber 1958).

The vested interests of towns and burghers led to written, rational, evidentiary law which can be seen as a capability built into the systemic position of towns. It becomes a capability enabling the shift to a new political order. The fact that the systemic position of the Capetian kings should lead to a parallel project of finding value in such law is the added critical component that secures the shift to a new political order characterized by the aim of a centralized territorial administration.[83] Precisely because these kings were weak and confronted lords with far more power the law and a rational administration could intermediate between the king and the nobility.[84] These two medieval institutions—territorial kingship and medieval towns—both suffused in church authority could become agents in the project to develop and institute rational written law.[85]

[80] Christian doctrine objected to private property interest charges, where Roman law accepted both. Roman law granted an owner exclusive rights. Christian law objected to interest charges, while Roman law accepted this. Thus the adoption of Roman law had significant positive consequences for business. Further, as discussed above, the fight for property rights was a crucial one for burghers (M. Weber 1958).

[81] Recourse to the law helped burghers, since the nobility often presumed over burghers and, if there was a disagreement to be settled by trial, it had to be done through the use of arms, an option not available to burghers. Capetian kings in France, notably Louis IX in a set of ordinances, passed this regulation (1257–61) (Hallam 1980: 244).

[82] It is important to remember that the systemic position of the nobility varied across countries, as is evident, for instance, in the different relations of the nobility with the Capetian kings in France compared to that with the German kings.

[83] Critical is the shift from ecclesiastical kingship (law is divine, not made by mortals) (Holy Roman emperor) to jurisprudential kingship (law is made): Lex est Rex.

[84] This was by no means a perfectly executed project. The French kings were too weak simply to enforce the law. They could not fully tax all nobles, so they bought noble acquiescence by tax exemptions and direct payments, obtained through taxation on other parties. This is one reason why political representation in Parliament never became as important in France as in England: they had their tax exemption and their pension schemes. It also meant they did not much care about the economies of their estates, which may have led to their failures (P. S. Lewis 1962).

[85] Beaud (1981: 38–42) sees the alliance between the king and the towns at work in France at a time when England had the conditions in place for a forceful industrial bourgeoisie; for Beaud this then explains the late development of an industrial bourgeoisie in France.

The urban law of the eleventh and twelfth centuries can be described as communitarian, secular, and constitutional (Berman 1983: chapter 12). Its communitarian character was critical. Cities were often founded by a collective oath made by the full citizenry "to adhere to a charter that had been publicly read aloud to them" (393). The charter was a kind of social contract, and Berman posits that it must have been one of the sources of the modern contract theory of government; accepting the urban charter was a commitment to a permanent relationship.[86] Berman notes that this contract also took the form of a participatory relationship among the members (1983: 393).[87] Participation here was by no means akin to formal notions of modern democracy and equality. Rather, a small elite governed the community, with the latter actually consisting of a community of (mostly subordinate) communities. One's place in this hierarchical structure determined one's rights and obligations. The legal standing of individuals came through membership in one or more subcommunities. There were separate legal orders for the different artisans' and merchants' guilds. There was an overall recognition of the legal equality of citizens, but the poor generally were not included in various processes and there were multiple specific inequalities among the included, such as those between master and apprentice. Beyond the community of communities represented by the city, there was the larger entity of the Western Christian realm, a kind of master community of communities. Weber sees the communitarian social organization as a critical source of differentiation from the state. According to Weber, the medieval city was a "commune from the beginning of its existence"—even alongside development of the legal concept of "corporation," Weber argues, communitarian forms proved erosive of tribal or religious particularism, eventually promoting the general rights associated with urban law (1968: 234). In the medieval city clans lost importance as constituencies when cities became

[86] This is not to say that sworn confraternization between burghers was automatically treated as legitimate by the nobility. However, the legal defense of such rights worked to formally legitimize innovations. In 1112 Cologne, "city lords" would typically challenge the legitimacy of burgher association in a variety of ways. In answering charges that some law-finder or "alderman had not sworn an oath [of obedience]," "usurpatory" innovations found their formal legitimacy (M. Weber 1978: 1251). Further, in Cologne, the *Richerzeche* (guild of the rich), "which from the point of view of legitimacy was nothing but a private club of wealthy citizens, could successfully assert the right to confer citizenship—a quality which was legally quite independent from membership" in the guild (1251). The majority of medieval French cities, Weber adds, "obtained their urban constitutions in a similar way through acts of sworn confraternization of the burghers" (1251).

[87] This was reflected in legal obligations of mutual aid among citizens, mutual protection against outside attacks, and a series of mutual obligations to ensure the smooth functioning of the urban community.

"confederations of individual burghers" and even "clanless plebs accomplished ritualistic equalization in principle" (233). The burghers joined the citizenry and took oaths of citizenship as "single persons"—securing individual legal status based on personal membership in the "local association of the city" and not tribe or clan (1968: 236; 1978: 1246). Weber introduces a distinction between the communitarian nature of medieval cities and the "particularism" of more traditional arrangements.[88]

Second, the secular character of urban law partly positioned urban governments outside the hierarchies of ecclesiastical authority and enabled each city to develop its own variant of urban law. Urban law was one of several secular laws—royal, feudal, manorial, and mercantile—whereby no single law could claim exclusivity over cities, further strengthening the option of secularizing urban governance. This contrasts with the classic Greek and imperial Roman cities, each of which was responsible for a religious cult and the enforcement of its laws. In the cities of the eleventh and twelfth century, religion and its observances were serious matters but under the jurisdiction of ecclesiastical authority (Mundy and Riesenberg 1958). And though city charters invoked divine protection and authority, their mission "as cities, was defined as secular . . . primarily, to control violence and to regulate political and economic relations—that is, to keep peace and to do justice" (Berman 1983: 395). The city's secular mission was not a residual role but central to giving worldly goals a value independent of religious goals even as they were considered ordained by God. Finally, the fact that urban law was one of several secular laws and that it evinced autonomy from all of these other laws also contributed to the variability of urban law across cities, even as they shared foundational features: each urban law was a particular local system of rule over one aspect of urban residents' lives.[89]

[88] According to Weber, the *polis* of the medieval city tended toward an "institutionalized community" distinct from the state (1968: 234). Whereas legitimate association in the ancient city rested on "traditionalistic" forms such as the clan, medieval cities of central and northern Europe were political spaces in which exclusiveness, as embodied in cult associations, withered. The administration of public rituals, for example, which actually originates in the *ancient* city, forms precedents that achieve fuller expression during the medieval period. Conversely, the existence of totemic or magical taboo barriers, reinforcing clan associations, prevented confraternization and its consequent urban institutional forms (M. Weber 1978: 1243).

[89] Berman emphasizes how this also distinguishes medieval towns from Greek and Roman cities: the Greek city claimed exclusive rule over its residents while the Roman city was under Roman law, lacking a specific urban law. "The unique feature of the law of Western Christendom was that the individual person lived under a plurality of legal systems, each of which governed one of the overlapping subcommunities of which he was a member" (Berman 1983: 395).

Third, urban law was constitutional in that the authority of a written constitution was superior to enacted laws.[90] These cities were akin to modern states in that they had a full range of authorities—executive, judicial, and legislative, covering economic, military, and police matters—and were subject to formal constraints on these authorities. Urban law was founded, perhaps typically even if not always, on written charters, which included definitions of urban governmental authority and civil rights and liberties.[91] Even where there were no written charters, cities were considered to have a fundamental law establishing these basic constraints and rights. The rights and liberties of citizens included the right to participate in urban government generally.[92] Included also were exemptions from many feudal services and taxes and limitations on many others, as well as restrictions on royal prerogatives.[93] At the heart of these rights and liberties was the principle that citizens' obligations were to be set in advance and that citizens could not be taxed on whatever else they might have gained beyond those specific obligations. Finally, notwithstanding considerable diversity across cities, the forms of government shared critical aspects, notably government by popular assemblies of all citizens: their consent was needed for the election of officials and the introduction of new laws.[94]

[90] The concept of constitutionalism was invented in the late eighteenth and early nineteenth centuries to describe the American doctrine of the supremacy of the Constitution over enacted laws. But Berman argues that "the reality of modern constitutionalism, in the full sense of the word, was present first in the urban law systems of Western Europe in the eleventh and twelfth centuries" (1983: 396–98).

[91] For Berman these charters were the first modern written constitutions. The delineation of urban governmental authority and residents' rights and obligations had significant similarities with contemporary systems of constitutional government. Besides the division of power into modern-style branches, there were also periodic elections of various types of officers. Judges could be recalled by citizens. Laws were published. Civil rights included prohibitions on arbitrary arrest and the rule that imprisonment could only result from due legal process. In theory at least, the rich and the poor were to be judged alike. Citizens had multiple rights, including the right to carry arms and the right to vote. After a year of residence immigrants were entitled to the same rights as citizens. Outside ("foreign") merchants were to be given rights equal to those of merchant citizens.

[92] Berman sees in these conditions an element of constitutional theory "never fully accepted but never fully rejected, that political power was ultimately vested in the whole body of citizens" (1983: 397). England saw a weaker version of this democratic form of government and cities remained more dependent on the king than was the case in Italy, Germany, Flanders, and parts of France; even so, borough officials were often elected, and by the early 1200s the citizens of London could elect their mayor.

[93] Thus the city and the king often negotiated to set a fixed tax and the king was forbidden from imposing forced loans.

[94] As the twelfth and thirteenth centuries evolved, the trend changed toward setting up a council rather than a popular assembly and, eventually, less democratic forms of government.

Urban law also enabled growth and change. The governing bodies of cities as well as the various guilds regularly enacted and systematized ordinances and laws facilitating growth. Thus citizens were authorized to acquire land and buildings, and make use of their property, including selling, mortgaging, and leasing it.[95] Roman law was used to develop new legal ideas and principles for addressing new needs and to do so in a systematized way. This possibility of continuous development and systematization was, for Berman (1983: 398–99), partly rooted in the systematic character of Roman law and canon law, both of which functioned as sources for urban lawmaking.

Political Cultures of Towns

We can think of medieval towns, especially in the eleventh and twelfth centuries, as sites of commerce and production that promoted a distinct politico-economic culture. The medieval city accommodated practices that allowed burghers to set up systems for owning and protecting property and to implement various immunities against despots of all sorts.[96] Through these practices, incipient forms of citizenship were being constituted; the city can be seen as a key site for political innovation and work. Further, these were practices that eventually extended beyond the formal subject of the burgher—the member of the urban communitas—and fed into national forms of political membership. In this early process the burghers emerged as informal political actors demanding and instituting protections and guarantees that exceeded those that had been granted by higher authorities. Through their demands and work they constructed themselves as rights-bearing subjects.

Beyond the general historical explanations of the economic and social forces feeding the growth of cities, I want to emphasize three aspects that help illustrate the distinctiveness of this political economy of urban territoriality. First, urban settlements at the time were not politically and legally distinct units. In Pirenne's (1925) view, there were no cities in western Europe in the year 1000; there were "towns" living off the land that

[95] This bundle of legally established uses was similar to what came to be called "ownership" in the eighteenth century. But the strict regulation of urban economic activities by customary law and by guild rules meant that there were also restrictions in the eleventh and twelfth centuries on the private use of land and buildings that ceased to exist by the late eighteenth and the nineteenth centuries.

[96] In Russia, where the walled city did not evolve as a center of urban immunities and liberties, the meaning of citizenship diverged from concepts of civil society and cities—citizenship belonged to the state, not the city.

lacked a distinct status.[97] Unlike these, the cities of the late eleventh and twelfth centuries became sites for a new mode of production and distribution, and they increasingly constituted themselves as politically and legally identifiable entities. The second is the rapidly growing surplus population in agriculture given increases in productivity, which provided a supply for an "urban" population in the sense that their livelihood was no longer in the countryside. This condition created its own incentives for the types of political and economic innovation we see arise in these cities, and both fed and were nurtured by the explosion in trading of the eleventh and twelfth centuries.[98] Finally, multiple third parties—kings, lords, popes, bishops—could benefit from this growth in the number and economic weight of cities. They often chartered towns to secure military forces and economic resources.[99] While none of these conditions was new as such, they came together in the eleventh and twelfth centuries in a particularly dynamic and productive way. The coincidence of interests in cities also meant, however, that lords and kings often inserted clauses in cities' charters that enabled them to maintain control over the citizens, which the latter fought and sometimes succeeded at reducing.

What I want to distill from this is the specificity of the assemblage of territory, authority, and rights that materializes in the cities of the eleventh and twelfth centuries. These were the cities that Weber examined in his effort to specify the ideal-typical features constituting the city. In *The City*, Weber was interested in examining a kind of city that combined conditions and dynamics that forced its residents and leaders into creative and innovative responses and adaptations. Further, he posited that these changes produced in the context of the city signaled transformations that went beyond the city, which could have a far reach in instituting often fundamental transformations, eventually encompassing society at large. He did not see these possibilities in the modern industrial cities of his time.

[97] As has been remarked many times, Pirenne failed to note the importance of production for the constituting of urban economies and overemphasized commerce.

[98] It all made for much migration and socioeconomic mobility. Entire villages moved out and into the nearby town. Eventually, class inequalities grew, and much wealth and power were concentrated in merchant elites. But the image of the city as a place of opportunity held fast. Northern European cities of the eleventh century onward basically had no slavery, unlike those of ancient Greece and imperial Rome and the urban settlements before 1000.

[99] For a lord, towns often had military advantages over castles, as citizens had the right and the duty to carry arms; relying on rural populations meant dealing with peasants who did not have such rights and hence were less ready, while knights had to be paid for military service. Citizens were obligated to universal military service in defense of the city. As for economic resources, cities produced wealth and could be taxed.

There are two aspects of Weber's *The City* that are of particular analytic importance here.[100] One is under what conditions cities can be positive and creative influences on people's lives. For Weber cities are a set of social structures that encourage social individuality and innovation and hence are an instrument of historical change.[101] There is in this intellectual project a deep sense of the historicity of these conditions. For Weber modern urban life did not correspond to this positive and creative power of cities; he saw modern cities as dominated by large factories and office bureaucracies. My own reading of the mid-twentieth-century Fordist city corresponds in many ways to Weber's in the sense that the strategic spaces under Fordism were the government, through the social contract, and the large Fordist factory, both emerging as key sites for the political work of the disenfranchised.

For Weber, the towns of the Late Middle Ages combined the conditions that pushed urban residents, merchants, artisans, and leaders to innovate politically. These transformations could produce epochal change beyond the city itself: Weber tries to lay bare the complex processes accompanying the emergence of urban community, which for him are akin to what we might describe today in the language of governance and citizenship. In this regard struggles around political, economic, legal, and cultural issues centered in the realities of cities can become the catalysts for new transurban developments in all these institutional domains: markets, participatory government, rights for members of the urban community regardless of lineage, judicial recourse, cultures of engagement, and deliberation.

The particular analytic element I want to extricate from this aspect of Weber's understanding and theorization of the city is the historicity of the conditions that make cities strategic sites for the enactment of important transformations in multiple institutional domains. The argument developed in chapter 6 is that today a certain type of city—the global city—has emerged

---

[100] Mine is an analytic reading of Weber; the concern is less with the historical overview, which focuses on the gradual emergence and structuring of the force composition of the city in various geographic areas and under different conditions, and its gradual stabilization into a distinct form. My reading is centered in the historical details as he traces the changing composition of forces from the ancient kingships through the patrician city to the demos of the ancient world, from the Episcopal structures and fortresses through the city of notables to the guild-dominated cities in Europe.

[101] It is interesting that in the reading of Berman, a legal scholar, Weber fails to recognize the cities' dynamic character (e.g., 1983: 399–401). Weber fails to "explain why or how the twelfth-century city developed into the city of the sixteenth and twentieth centuries." The criteria invoked by Berman that allow him to see this evolution are ones that pertain to the city as a legal entity—a "corporation, endowed with legal personality, with capacity to sue and be sued, hold property, make contracts" (400)—and a political and economic entity with the rights and obligations this brings to the city as a corporation.

as a strategic site for innovations and transformations in multiple institutional domains, including the elements of a new political economy.

A second analytic element I want to extricate is the particular type of embeddedness of the transformations he describes and renders as ideal-typical features. This is not an embeddedness in what we might think of as deep structures because the latter are precisely the ones that are being dislocated or changed and are being opened to new arrangements. The embeddedness is, rather, in specific and contingent conditions, opportunities, constraints, needs, interactions, contestations, and interests. The aspect that matters here is the complexity, distributed character, and social thickness of the particular conditions and the dynamics he identifies as enabling change and innovation. It is the condition that urban merchants in general found themselves simply by being merchants and hence subject to the *taille*—to being taxed whenever a lord or the king needed revenue. The complexity and thickness of the conditions enabling or promoting change also produce ambiguities in the meaning of the changes and innovations. It is not always clear whether they are positive—meaning the creation or strengthening of some element, even if partial or minor, of equitable treatment—and in what time frame their positive effect would become evident. Weber finds contradictory and multivalent innovations in the cities of the Late Middle Ages. He dissects these innovations to understand what they can produce or launch.

Spruyt (1994) introduces a new dimension in the analysis by focusing on one particular aspect: the burghers' search as a social group for allies that could advance their preferred politico-economic order. Thus where Weber examines how the burghers became political actors through their practices aimed at gaining the right to protect their property, Spruyt examines the vested interests that guide their search for allies in this effort. These are not mutually exclusive analyses, but they do get at different issues. Spruyt, like Weber, emphasizes the interactions between material practices and ideal interests; the new coalitions enabled by shifts in material power also entailed conceptual shifts (1994: 67). But his main explanation is centered in the expansion of trade. The shift in belief systems in the late medieval period is an intermediate explanatory variable. For Spruyt this shift serves to justify alternative patterns of rule and simultaneously provide meaningful interpretations of new activities, even though belief systems fail to explain the decline of the medieval order and the many different ways in which this decline took place across Europe. In centering his explanation on the expansion of trade in the Late Middle Ages, Spruyt examines how "trade created new incentives and shifted the distribution of relative power in society," giving rise to new coalitions (67). This in turn could lead to redefining what was possible and to the development of new rules of authority. Here his analysis encounters Weber's examination of the political innovations brought about by burghers in their struggle to secure protections.

Weber's emphasis on certain types of innovation and change is important, particularly the construction of rules and norms precisely because deeper arrangements on which norms had been conditioned were being destabilized. Herein also lay openings for new political actors to emerge, as well as changes in the role or institutional locus of older norms, political actors, and forms of authority. This was a highly dynamic configuration where older forms of authority might struggle and succeed in reimposing themselves.[102] Along with the multiple forms of authority present in the Late Middle Ages and the diverse interactions they generated, there were contestations by commoners: notable here are the oaths villagers and townspeople took when forming communes in the eleventh and twelfth centuries since these were an act of defiance at a time when commoners were not allowed to take oaths (Duby 1968: 28). Burghers intent on securing protections and immunities extending beyond their practical and partly formalized condition were what I would today describe as informal political actors. Not being entitled formally or by customary rules did not keep them from contesting the arbitrary exercise of power by the nobility or by kings and the church. In this contestation by what were then relatively powerless commoners compared to the nobility, the church, and the kings lies an instance of what I conceive of as the complexity of the condition of powerlessness, even if in this case powerlessness was relative. It shows us that the practices of the excluded are one factor in the making of history. This is an important issue, and one that I return to in chapter 6 where I posit that there are conditions today that signal the possibility cities might once again function as such strategic sites.

CONCLUSION: MEDIEVAL CAPABILITIES AND THEIR CONSEQUENCES

In this chapter I identified four critical medieval capabilities for the development of the territorial state. The first one arises out of the fact of inferior power: the emerging territorial state was strengthened even as national unity was far from achieved and the state's authority was weak. It brings illegibility to the process of state formation insofar as the usual code does not yet

---

[102] Cf. Weber's examination of how these types of changes and innovations derive from his key concepts or categories for analysis: social actions, relations, and institutions; and his theory of the urban community.

apply. Seeing its origins at such a juncture allows us to capture the work it took to assemble the territories, authorities, and rights that would eventually coalesce into national units largely under the control of one sovereign, or into a unit over which the sovereign was in process of gaining full control. There is a counterfactual quality to this history in that it is the weak Capetian kings who succeeded. They implemented key elements of a centralized bureaucracy that created a grid for partial control over what was a sharply fragmented territorial and political organization with many actors far more powerful than the king.

The second capability arose out of the fact that at the heart of this process was the formation of a state bureaucracy for extracting revenue, particularly standardized taxation. The work of setting up a technocratic system entailed a development of capacities that made the state the most significant economic actor at the time. The later pillaging that marked the sixteenth century and fed into national capitalism was to a good extent organized and implemented by the one actor with the capacities to do so, the state.

The third capability involved the question of abstract forms of authority, to be distinguished from raw material power. The sovereign authority that would be critical for the national state was facilitated by the presumed divinity of the monarch, yet another elusive form of authority. The complex and abstract notion of the legitimate authority of the national territorial sovereign does not simply represent a radical innovation of the postfeudal order. Multiple medieval capabilities went into its making, from notions of divine authority to those of the secular and constitutional systems of law arising out of the formation of cities in the eleventh and twelfth centuries. Even when backed with material and identifiable power, authority is to be distinguished from raw power: sovereign authority introduces abstraction into the materialities of the sovereign's power. The medieval period makes clear the extent to which even at a time of brutal exercise of a ruler's material powers, the latter by itself did not suffice. In this regard the emergence of towns as complex political economies in their own right willing to contest powerful rulers and develop their own sources of political authority is interesting and illuminating, especially since most cities lacked armies.

The fourth capability arises out of the specific political economy of urban territoriality: the possibility of a unitary system with a citizenry that demanded and elaborated civil liberties, and developed secular and constitutional forms of government. Important to my conception of a political economy of urban territoriality is including not only the cities themselves but also a series of networks with highly variable territorial insertions and levels of institutionalization. These intercity networks can be conceived of as informal

insertions into a territory that was in principle under the jurisdictions of actors whose base of legitimacy was not the city: lords, kings, and the church.
Thus, I take this conceptualization beyond the notion of territoriality confined to the presence of cities in an ocean of multiple other organizational
forms, some increasingly territorial (the Capetian kingdom) and others not
(the church, feudal lords, itinerant society).

I posit that cities and intercity mobilities constituted a larger networked territorial formation, one arising from the ground up, which eventually functioned as a built-in capability for the emergent territorialities of national states. In the German case, it was a capability that produced a
distinctive territorial organization centered in strong subnational units, the
länder. Important to my analysis is the possibility that this complex medieval
territorial regime implemented through the proliferation of towns was one active ingredient in the formation of the sovereign territorial state. It was not, as
usually represented, a period merely preceding the development of territorial
regimes; one effect of this more common interpretation is the reducing of territorial regimes to one historical type, the sovereign state. More difficult to
disentangle is the notion that it represented a rival regime to that of the territorial state. This larger urban territorial formation was not marked by a unitary terrain, as is the case with the modern state. It was a particular type of
assemblage of territory, authority, and rights. One of the questions it raises is
to what extent a similar type of networked territoriality is being produced
through some of the contemporary dynamics I examine in parts 2 and 3.

3 ASSEMBLING NATIONAL POLITICAL ECONOMIES

CENTERED ON IMPERIAL GEOGRAPHIES

One point of entry into the question of the Western national state is through the particular features of its political economy. What stands out in this regard is the formation of a novel type of world scale beginning with pillage in the sixteenth century. Its eventual reinvention in the 1800s saw the formation of two novel historical agents in the emergence of the industrial capitalism that was to shape that later world scale. Continuing with the capabilities analysis of chapter 2, here I examine how some of these developments produced capabilities for global operations, but within an organizing logic that differs from that of today's global phase. This raises a question as to the features of the earlier organizing logic that kept these capabilities from constituting a global political economy. My argument is that the organizing logic of the world scale of the 1800s was foundationally different from today's global phase, and thus so was the relational system within which those capabilities functioned, no matter their shared modernity.

Why did the development and institutionalization of these potentially global capabilities not lead to the formation of global systems that could partly override or suppress national differences rather than, as it did, to intensified competing national colonizations, particularly as of the late 1800s? The answer I find most persuasive is that this was a world scale geared toward building national states and national capitalism.[1] There are multiple indicators of this. One is the fact itself that the growth of this world scale brought with it intensified national rivalries to the point of enormous war. The vast mobilization of internal material and ideational resources that were central to the building of national capitalism partly organized the building of the

---

[1] This interpretation is based on the extant historiography and scholarship, rather than new archival research. Further, as interpretation it arises from the perspective and in the light of current developments, rather than from the perspective of that historiography.

imperial geographies of each major European power. A second one is the central role of the state as the critical economic and military actor in the formation of the world scale both in the sixteenth century and in its redevelopment of the late 1800s; this role was constructed differently and evinced different organizing logics from those of the current post-1980s phase of the world scale.

The emergence of a world scale in the sixteenth century, and its later redevelopment in the late 1800s, was on the one hand conditioned on advances at the time (for example, in navigational techniques and in firearms) and, on the other, on capabilities developed in the prior phase, notably the significant expansion of merchant and banking capital and, crucially, the development of the state bureaucracy for collecting taxes. Wallerstein (1974: 348) argues that a distinguishing feature of the "modern world system" is the endurance of a world economy not contained within the boundaries of any single world empire. Wallerstein's definition of a world economy leans crucially on an analysis of trade and the division of labor; the structures of trade and power relations between core and periphery (states and colonial territories) vary within an essentially fixed world scale. That is, the fundamental mechanics of the world system in Wallerstein's analysis remain constant from the long sixteenth century to the present—basically military domination and unequal exchange. R. Brenner (1977) argues that Wallerstein ends up assuming that market/competition forces—the basic dynamic of the system—are present across history, and not just since the rise of capitalism. Similarly, Wallerstein seems primarily interested in the internal and generally constant contradictions in the capitalist world economy, leading to long cycles in global capitalism. Development and change in the world system is propelled by this contradiction: each new phase "solves" the problems of the earlier.

By contrast, I argue for a middle-range analysis grounded in local structures and practices, out of which the mechanics of the world system emerge. While Wallerstein's analysis can account for the form of a restructured world economy, its matching to an historically prior contradiction invites charges of a teleological analysis. I hope to recover some of the contingency and openness of the processes of restructuring, grounded in the work of states and state actors to restart accumulation. World systems remain capitalist not only because of the abstract necessities of a world economy, but also because of particular decisions by powerful political actors (Jessop 1999). There was also a more elusive dynamic at work that was both a capability developed in the prior era and an outcome of key developments in the sixteenth and seventeenth centuries. It involved the notion of national unity initially centered on the wealth of the prince as a public good that was eventually expanded to the notion of a public domain centered on the prosperity of merchants, bankers, and manufacturers.

This chapter examines these two phases in the formation of a world scale as part of the process of constructing the national territorial state. Thus this analysis is not unrelated to an earlier generation of underdevelopment studies, which argued that development in the core was contingent upon exploitation of the periphery, or Arrighi and Silver (1999: 63) who argue that British global power was basically financed by this plunder. I approach this dynamic differently. The concern is with analytical and theoretical questions rather than historiography per se; and, again, critical to the analysis is that capabilities can be shifted toward objectives other than the original ones for which they were developed. Such shifts require a foundational reorientation in existing systems. Here that shift is national construction through the development of imperial economic geographies, and the formation of two new historic subjects as legal personae that are agents in the making of the shift. They are a new class of legitimate owners of means of production where once the sovereign and the nobility had exclusive ownership, and a new class of workers legally constructed as disadvantaged, particularly though not exclusively in relation to their employers.

THE STATE AS THE CRITICAL ACTOR

Crucial to the formation of the world scale taking shape in the sixteenth century was the development of territorial authority as part of the building of national states and national capitalisms. The emergence of the state as the main economic actor capable of articulating global economic operations also carried with it the strengthening of territorial authority. The latter, in turn, was critical to the development of a notional public sphere centered on merchant capital.

There is a puzzle in this emergence of the state as the critical actor. In its aspiration to exclusive rule, the sovereign territorial state cannot be specified in terms of the web of interactions marking the Late Middle Ages.[2] As discussed in the preceding chapter, the forms of authority that prevailed in the Late Middle Ages were diverse and multisited: the personal bonds of

---

[2] There is an interesting parallel here with the history of U.S. state formation before the Civil War when the centrality, almost exclusivity, of local law and individual rights created a multisited confederation, a political form of organization not amenable to capitalism. After the Civil War we see a shift from common local law to centralized state law as part of the development of the strong federal state with a corresponding weakening of the confederate model.

feudalism and the special status of the nobility; the shared beliefs of Christianity as organized by Rome; and the sequence of holy empire followed by Germanic principalities and French territorial monarchy. The complex and often conflictive interactions among these three key types of authority contributed to the distinctiveness of each. Yet by the thirteenth century the state, as a form of organization, had acquired the capacity to gather far larger financial resources than those of any private person or community (Bloch 1961: 422).[3] The key mechanism was the state's bureaucracy, developed over the twelfth and thirteenth centuries, which was "strong enough to tax" and thereby finance a still stronger bureaucratic structure.[4] This capability was not evenly developed among the major powers in western Europe, nor was the institutional venue similar. Tilly (1990: 137–60), who emphasizes the differences for state formation of capital- and coercion-intensive paths, warns that a strong state apparatus for revenue extraction may, in the long term, be counterproductive as it tends to stifle local productivity while stimulating resistance to state initiatives. Evans (1995) identifies a similar dynamic in more modern times in his discussion of the predatory state.

France, above all other Western European countries, had a highly developed royal administration early on after three centuries of Capetian kings. This assumes added meaning when we consider that much of the fourteenth and fifteenth centuries saw economic contraction, crises, and much peasant revenue still winding up with the nobility. Gone were the great commercial and agricultural prosperity of the twelfth and thirteenth centuries that had supported the development of state bureaucracies, both civil and armed, and advanced the monetizing of the economy. Despite economic contraction, however, the French state's more effective bureaucracy secured a growing share of all revenues (Duby 1968: 331). This increased flow of funds to the king also weakened the nobility's source of revenue, further strengthening the state. The Late Middle Ages saw the shaping of increasingly complex interplays of interests in the various European states.

As states grew stronger, monetary manipulation became more profitable, and it became critical in the fourteenth and fifteenth centuries given

---

[3] Out of a century of conflict after the rupture between the French king and the papacy, the fifteenth century saw the consolidation of powerful rulers. These were "the great restorers of internal order" (Wallerstein 1974): Louis XI in France; Henry VII in England; and Ferdinand of Aragon and Isabel of Castille in Spain. The principalities of Germany can also be included here.

[4] Population growth, trade revival, and expanded circulation of money all laid the groundwork for state revenue through taxation, even though the fourteenth and fifteenth centuries did not evince the levels of economic growth of those of the twelfth and thirteenth centuries.

the financial crises of states involved in war and the low taxes derived from low-profit rural economies.[5] Wallerstein (1974) places great importance on the strained resources of feudal societies, including the organization of production and the overconsumption of small elites in a period of very low productivity. States had to find other sources of revenue. One easy and evidently attractive option in both France and England (D. Sinclair 2000) was debasement of the gold and silver in coins; but it was a short-term solution that led to inflation and hence a declining value of fixed revenues (Génicot 1966: 699). Tilly (1990: 84–91) calls attention to the importance of an emergent capitalist class capable of lending money to the sovereign for engaging in warfare. Initially, states were willing to borrow abroad, for example from the Fuggers. Eventually, states began to prefer borrowing from domestic capitalists, since they presumably proved easier to control than their foreign counterparts. "Around the time of Henry IV (1598–1610), France moved rapidly from dependency on other centers of capital (notably Lyon, a conduit for Italian capital) to Parisian financial dominance, from foreign to French financiers, and from negotiation to enforced payment of taxes" (Cornette 1988: 622–24 as quoted in Tilly 1990). Although insolvency threatened the Crown repeatedly during the following two centuries, that consolidation of fiscal power gave France an enormous advantage in the wars to come (Tilly 1990: 87). Insofar as the main recipients of fixed revenues were the feudal class, they were weakened vis-à-vis the prince or king.

It was the prince who embodied the emergent notion of the state in much of Europe—not just its bureaucratic capability but also its authority. The prince became recognized as such through a variety of mechanisms, including the growing distance between prince and subjects (Chabod 1958: 72).[6] The bureaucracy—the fourth estate—developed and emerged as a key ally to the prince, though it was an "ambivalent ally" (68–69, 72). In both France and England the burghers sought alliances with the king in their joint struggle against the nobility, and they were frequently incorporated into the state bureaucracy. But the nobility also used the state, both the bureaucracy and, especially in England, the various parliamentary bodies developed by kings to expand and legitimize taxation. These interactions around an increasingly

[5] Duby (1968) finds that agrarian recession and demographic collapse started before the fourteenth century. Epidemics, climate changes, recession, and collapse all came together in the fourteenth century to create crises.

[6] This is an issue I will return to in part 2 in examining the growing distance between the state and the citizen that is arising from some of the transformations, both formalized and not, brought on by globalization. That growing distance spells a possible reversal of one of the key emblematic achievements of the French and American revolutions, to wit, that the state and the people are one, a move that historically entailed a rejection of the specialness or divinity of the ruler.

strong state began to alter the nature of authority as both a concept and practice. Skocpol (1979) identifies an unintended consequence of the outcome of this struggle between bourgeois and nobility for control of the bureaucracy. Where it maintained control, the nobility was able to block agricultural reform and rationalization programs, ultimately impeding the state's ability to successfully engage in warfare. For Skocpol, declining competitiveness in war is one of the key triggers of a social revolution.

A second critical feature of this period is that the strengthening of the state took place even as national unity was often far from achieved. Tilly distinguishes among the territorial state, the nation-state, and the national-state for basically this reason. He defines *states* "as coercion-wielding organizations that are distinct from households and kinship groups and exercise clear priority in some respects over all other organizations within substantial territories." *National* states are "states governing multiple contiguous regions and their cities by means of centralized, differentiated, and autonomous structures." A *nation*-state is "a state whose people share a strong linguistic, religious, and symbolic identity" (1990: 2–3). At the time, the territorial state was the emergent actor, further fed by the development of empires. A focus on periods of transition brings out the actual work of assembling the territories, authorities, and rights that eventually coalesce into territorial units largely under the control of one sovereign, or over which the sovereign sought to gain full control.[7] These new assemblages of TAR were partly constituted through the decomposition of the feudal order, as monarchs consolidated greater kingdoms through various types of alliances, for example, intermarriages, and conquest through war. One organizing logic at work in these struggles to strengthen royal power was a search for greater autonomy from the papacy.[8] The decomposition of the feudal order and the exiting from papal authority, even if partial, also weakened the moral order of the Middle Ages. With its emphasis on the just price, prohibitions against lending at interest, and other strictures, the medieval moral order constrained the search for wealth and financial manipulation by the state, let alone by the merchant and banking bourgeoisies (Beaud 1982; M. Weber 1958).[9] Even though partial, the exit from the feudal moral order and autonomy from the papacy were

[7] It was also the period that established boundaries, which endure today, in some of the major continental countries (Renouard 1958: 5–21); for Perroy this was the "fundamental change" in the political structure of Western Europe (1955: 369–70).

[8] "Clamor for reforms became the Reform, which became a war machine against the papacy." (Beaud 1981: 20)

[9] The morality of the just price and prohibitions against lending at interest had already been seriously unsettled by the time Calvin argued that commercial success was a sign of divine election.

important conditionalities for the development of the new components of authority and novel types of rights.

This new type of authority was historically specific and increasingly formalized, embodying territorial jurisdiction and exclusive authority over that territory. The boundaries of sovereign jurisdiction became geographic.[10] This contrasts with medieval class-based jurisdictions, each comprising bundles of mutual rights and obligations, whereby an English king might owe service to a lesser French nobleman. The national territorial state became the final locus of authority rather than a monarch's divinity, a lord's nobility, or the claims of religious bodies. It repositioned the meaning of membership toward a territorial collectivity derived from a complex abstract authority that could not be reduced to a divine king or "superior caste" of the nobility. These were new concepts of authority and of the rights of membership. Early kingship was seen as deriving from the person, and the kingdom was represented as the king's personal possession: one was the other. There was no difference between the position and the person, or between the realm and the person of the king. In the Late Middle Ages, royal possessions and the larger realm were becoming separated. The increasing bureaucracy surrounding royalty, needed to assist in its management in territorial affairs, made this separation all the more apparent (Poggi 1978: 53). By the seventeenth century the foundational change had taken place: thus when Louis XIV sought to equate himself with the state in order to sell some public goods to finance the Hundred Years War, he was reminded that the king was now the protector, not the owner, of the common realm.

The transition from feudal lordship to territorial state required a change in the meaning of authority, as did the later move from a state dominated by the interests of the prince to those of the traders and manufacturers. The sovereign state needed to be imagined and personified before it could exist (Walzer 1985). Ruggie (1993: 162) posits that the transformation from feudal rule to sovereign territorial state involved an important epistemic shift, not merely a change in who exercised power. Later I return to this proposition in my examination of a similar dynamic in the current denationalizing of authorities that have historically been constructed as national. The Capetian project and its claim to divinity as a source of authority autonomous from the papacy was such an innovative epistemic shift and, thus a critical development

---

[10] This does not exhaust the definition of the modern state. The classic definitions are akin to Weber's: monopoly over legitimate means of violence. Tilly (1990: 127–43) adds a capital-intensive path to the coercion-intensive path to state building; he emphasizes that which path takes place depends on the types of resources available.

of capabilities for the national state, not merely a fight between those who wanted centralization and those who wanted decentralization.

In addition, sovereign territorial authority entailed recognizing a mutually agreed upon spatial demarcation of political authority. It demanded a principle of juridical equivalence. Thus the emergence of the sovereign territorial state and the interstate system is a critical component of that larger epistemic shift and also represents a cognitive shift. Ruggie (1993), Kratochwil (1986), and Holzgrefe (1989) all indicate that sovereignty brought about a change in the character of international transactions. This is more than the result of material practices: for instance, in other parts of the world with similar material economic growth, we do not see the emergence of a state system, and hence we need to consider that something else was at work in Europe. Wallerstein (1974: 355) argues that the emergence of a "partially autonomous" state is an outcome of material conflicts between bourgeoisie and aristocracy:

> [state managers and a state bureaucracy] emerge within the framework of a capitalist world-economy because a strong state is the best choice between difficult alternatives for the two groups that are strongest in political, economic, and military terms: the emergent capitalist strata, and the old aristocratic hierarchies. For the former, the strong state in the form of the 'absolute monarchies' was a prime customer, a guardian against local and international brigandage, a mode of social legitimation, a preemptive protection against the creation of strong state barriers elsewhere. For the latter, the strong state represented a brake on these same capitalist strata, an upholder of status conventions, a maintainer of order, a promoter of luxury.

Here the form of the state is basically a function of class conflict, which is itself a function of the capitalist mode of production. Defining the world system (world scale) exclusively in terms of economic categories (trade, division of labor, transportation technology, etc.) methodologically predisposes the analysis toward a reading of state form in terms of capitalist function. These categories express an abstract structural necessity to which state actors and representatives of various classes can only react. These structures, however, are embedded in the concrete practices of social interdependence, mediated by the value form of wealth (Postone 1993). States do not merely confront pregiven objective capitalist structures, but are actively engaged in their production and reproduction, and play crucial roles in the articulation of "accumulation strategies" (Jessop 1999). This constitutive function of states undermines one-sided materialist readings of state form, and opens up an analytic space for considering ideological dimensions. The extent to which labor (and, thereby, labor power) must be reproduced through the market instead of, for example, kinship or state welfare structures, or through self-subsistence based on ownership of the means of production, comprises one key axis along which states constitute these structures (Polanyi 2001; see also Esping-Anderson 1990 for a more contemporary analysis).

The territorial state, could, in principle, have been an institutional capability and/or home for a variety of socioeconomic orders. In western Europe it was the elements for the development of capitalism that were put in motion under the monarchical territorial state and city-states, both of which enabled the development of merchant and banking capital. These forms of capital were not enough by themselves to produce what eventually became the institutional apparatus for industrial capitalism, but they were necessary. Further, as with the feudal order, the development of capitalism evinced considerable variability across Europe. But beyond that variability one can detect an emergent new type of political, economic, and social order. What makes this order most legible is the formation of two new historic subjects—the industrial bourgeoisie and the industrial worker, to which I return later in the chapter.

CONSTRUCTING A WORLD SCALE

Two key dynamics in the history of the development of a world scale beginning in the sixteenth century matter to my analysis. The first is the tension between building up a national political economy and developing imperial geographies to enhance it. The second is the tension between securing the wealth of the prince and the emerging project of national wealth accumulation; the growing class of merchants and bankers in particular were interested in promoting the distinction between the public interest and that of the prince. We also see the formation of novel spatio-temporal (D. Harvey 1982) and moral orders (M. Weber 1930).

The world scale that began to take shape in the sixteenth century differed dramatically from the older one constructed by the practices and projects of city-states and city leagues. Where long-distance trade had marked the political economy of Germanic and Italian cities, long-distance pillaging marked the new era of explorations launched by Portugal and Spain. Both were attempting to capture the sources of wealth monopolized by the Italian city-states, in other words, to *conquer* the lucrative trade routes (Arrighi 1994: 40). Unable to militarily subjugate the European powers directly, military adventures turned to their imperial territories. Wallerstein (1974: 184–87) points out that by the end of the "first" sixteenth century, symbolically marked by the Treaty of Cateau-Cambresis (1559), it was no longer feasible for a single state to conquer the entire *European* world economy and to establish an empire within Europe. It had simply become too expensive, and states had not developed to a point where they were able to extract sufficient revenue to pursue such a project. In this "second" sixteenth century, military conflict would revolve more around direct conquest of periphery sources of wealth than around trade centers in the core: "The new system was to be the one that has predominated ever since, a capitalist world-economy whose core-states were to be intertwined in a state of constant economic and military tension, competing for the privilege of exploiting (and weakening the state machineries of) peripheral areas, and permitting certain entities to play a specialized, intermediary role as semiperipheral powers" (196–97; see also 179). But simultaneously, core states embarked on a specific process of building capacities for economic governance—creating import controls, monitoring the balance of trade and national production—in order to enhance their domestic financial capacities. This was, then, the beginning of a type of world scale that differed from the one constituted through the trading networks of cities such as Venice and Genoa (Braudel 1984). Indeed, there had been far more long-distance trade in the fifteenth century. Venice, for instance, was a key node in multiple geographies of trade that extended deep into Europe, the Mediterranean, and the Indian Ocean. What was different about sixteenth-century long-distance trade was the advent of pillaging on a world scale, especially in South America. The Spanish conquest and its search for gold and silver were a massive global state enterprise.[11] According to official Spanish figures, from 1521 to 1660, 18,000 tons of silver and 200 tons of gold were transferred from America (mostly Mexico, Peru, and to a lesser degree the Caribbean islands) to Spain (Beaud 1981: chapter 1). Other sources estimate that it was probably double that amount. It all came at a huge human cost in the pillaged lands. In a little more than a century, the Indian population was reduced by 90 percent in Mexico, falling from 25 million to 1.5 million, and by 95 percent in Peru. According to one estimate, more than 3 million people disappeared from the Caribbean islands between 1495 and 1503. As the priest and scholar Las Casas observed, "Who of those born in future generations will believe this? I myself who am writing this and saw it and know most about it can hardly believe that such was possible" (quoted in A. Frank 1978: 42). People were killed in war, used up in the mines and other work, and sent to Spain as slaves (Sassen 1988: chapter 1). If there are two

---

[11] In the sixteenth century Spain also gained considerable wealth through the production of sugarcane for rum, molasses, and sugar, and through the black slave trade.

master categories that mark the sixteenth century they are colonial pillaging and an organizing logic that aimed at increasing the wealth of the prince.[12]

The historical evidence (e.g., Wallerstein [1974]) indicates that the Italian city-states had played a crucial role in developing capacities for the ideational and material practices of long-distance navigation and trade. These city-states, especially Genoa, had long shown an interest in the harbors of Spain and Portugal and developed various operations there. In this regard, I would argue that some of the capabilities of city-states got inserted in what were radically different forms of political organization. Spain and Portugal shared little with the Italian city-states when it came to political organization. Yet some of these capabilities linked to long-distance navigation, including an associated discursive domain, reemerged to shape what were to become imperial geographies of pillage rather than trade. The reemergence of these capabilities points to a possibly important aspect of the constituting of world scales—a distinction between capabilities and the substantive rationalities organizing a system, including the nature of the utilities derived from deploying these capabilities on a world-scale (for example, long-distance trade versus pillaging). Although the practices and ideational projects were substantively different at this time from the earlier period so well captured by Braudel (1984), this did not preclude the insertion of capabilities developed in the earlier period into a radically different organizing logic.

A key element in the substantive rationality shaping Europe's major powers in the sixteenth century was increasing and maintaining the wealth of the prince—a type of wealth at the time embodied in reserves of gold and silver. This fed into mercantilist policies that became crucial in the construction of strong national states. Governments sought to prevent the export of gold and silver.[13] The wealth of the ruler was emphasized; the wealth of merchants and bankers was not, though eventually it would be central. Thus Machiavelli (1514) argues, "in a well-organized government, the state should be rich and the citizens poor." Although the link between the wealth of the state and the wealth of the merchants was not long in coming, it was not the central concern in the sixteenth century. The shift in both the territorial and moral orders and the development of new capabilities (transportation, manufacturing) contributed to a reorientation in the "power project" of the time: to search for

[12] In addition to the pillaging of the Americas, the crusaders to the east also amassed considerable fortunes.

[13] In Spain, exporting gold and silver was punishable by death (from the early sixteenth century on). France prohibited the export of coined money in 1506 and several times throughout the century. In 1546 and 1576 England attempted to place money dealings, even the trade in bills of exchange, under the control of government agents; both attempts were unsuccessful. (For more detail, see Beaud 1982: 23–24).

gold and silver wherever it could be found.[14] The Spanish monarchy embodied this particular phase.

For many scholars the sixteenth century marks the beginning of capitalism. Yet kings, nobility, and the church were the dominant actors, obscuring the fact that capitalism was in the making. The church opposed nontheological forms of thinking such as humanism and science; kings continued to reign and make war; the leisure of the noblemen was a fixture of society; and older forms of bondage continued in Europe (Beaud 1982: chapters 1 and 2). It was not until the seventeenth century that a bourgeoisie emerged as a political and economic force and that wealth takes on the form of value (see Postone 1993: 24–27 for the distinction between value and wealth). As economic production took on more and more of the properties we typically associate it with, wealth is measured progressively in terms of the socially necessary labor time for its production. Prior to the rise of capitalist production, wealth primarily took the form of accumulation of material goods. The mechanisms of surplus capture— or economic domination—similarly depended on direct and transparent relations of force and coercion. Along with the spread of value relations, we see the emergence of more mediated and abstract forms of economic domination expressed through the "necessities" of market competition. R. Brenner (1977) argues that prior to the emergence of capitalist social relations, the lavish expenditure of the aristocracy on luxuries and military goods was economically rational: since their capture of revenues depended on the unmediated exercise of force (the extraction of *absolute* surplus value), spending that would increase one's coercive power was logical. Expenditure that would rationalize production in the pursuit of *relative* surplus value would require far too much surveillance of the peasantry, making this path less optimal. It was in England, according to Brenner, that a class of "tenant capitalists" emerged between the aristocracy and the peasantry, close enough to local production to ensure the use of rational production and powerful enough to secure the additional returns of improved production. With this shift, itself contingent on the dispossession of the peasantry from their lands, wealth production would become structured by the dictates of the law of value.

Toward the middle of the sixteenth century, we see the elements for the formation of national unity through the development of a national market. These elements diverged from those at the heart of the feudal order. National unity through a national market, rather than mere pillaging, rested on a more complex notion of how to increase wealth. What we see take shape is

[14] The "great discoveries" can be seen as part of the project of trade and pillaging (A. Frank 1978), even when some of the explicit intentions of the explorers themselves might not have been.

the project of national production articulated around the figure of the monarch, captured in Bodin's instruction—"Build mills at home, don't import"—in *The Republic* (1576). National production meant not exporting metals, not importing goods (except for metals) if they could be made at home, and exporting what the kingdom did not need.[15] This also brought with it calls for greater control over internal labor supplies; one tract recommended bringing craftsmen living outside towns, who might hence feel freer to export, under the control of towns. In his 1581 *Discourse of the Commonweal of This Realm of England*, John Hales (1929) called for measures to ensure the protection of the national economy. In the sixteenth century the kings of Spain, England, and France all took steps in this direction: they created mills; granted monopolies or privileges to new products; instituted prohibitions of or tariffs against the entry of foreign goods; and forbade the export of raw materials (Beaud 1981: chapter 1). Although much of this was basically framed in terms of securing the wealth of the prince, both for himself and for financing wars, the bourgeoisie was emerging as a critical economic actor, already strong in the Low Countries and rising fast in England. Even in France, with its weak bourgeoisie, mercantilism and an emphasis on manufactures, albeit mostly royal manufactures, became key policies.

But we also see here the tension between this strengthening of a national scale and dependence on global circuits for resource extraction and trading, and thus the active formation of a world scale. Even the debates of the period capture this interaction. One of the central debates addressed the unsuccessful attempts by sovereigns to control sharp price increases and set wages.[16] For Jean Bodin (1576), prices rose because the supply of gold and silver was greater than it had been in the preceding four centuries, and these metals were used to measure the price of goods.[17] This explanation avoided other sources of inflation: the luxury demanded by kings and nobles, the cost of wars, and the burden of the indebtedness of rulers that led to succeeding revaluations.

[15] The policies developed in the mid-1500s were to prevent precious metals from leaving the country, stimulate their importation through growing demand at home, and to gain more control over internal labor supplies so that skilled workers, especially craftsmen, would not export metals or goods.

[16] In western Europe the average price of wheat, which had risen little between 1500 and the mid-1500s, quadrupled in the ensuing fifty years. In all the major countries at the time, prices generally more than doubled or tripled in a period of fifty years. Wages, on the other hand, fell by up to 50 percent, according to some estimates (Beaud 1982: 21).

[17] Bodin's explanation became generally accepted and prefigures the future quantitative theory of money; it was incompatible with another leading idea of the sixteenth century that posited it was the abundance of precious metals that created wealth in a kingdom.

There is a second tension, that between the aim of securing the wealth of the prince and the aim of securing the public good through such enrichment. While the dominant economic ideas of the period corresponded closely to the aim of enriching the prince, the increasingly mercantilist policies aiming at national production also led to the idea, albeit a rather narrow version, of public enrichment: "Each individual is a member of the commonweal and any trade lucrative for the individual can also be lucrative for whomever else wishes to practice it as well; what is profitable for one will also be profitable for his neighbor and consequently for everyone" (Hales [1581] 1929: 26). This set the stage for the idea that the wealth of the kingdom depended on the wealth of the merchants and manufacturers, which depended on global circuits for extraction and trading: the flow of precious metals from America and the development of production in Europe fed commerce. But the notion of the public was, of course, rather limited. Forced labor in America (especially in the production of sugar) and the decline of real wages in Europe linked to European inflation produced an additional surplus of labor. Enclosures in England added sharply to poverty and unemployment, making it clear that the public's well-being was not part of the public good (Sassen 1999: chapters 1 and 2).

I want to emphasize two key dynamics in this history. One is the emergence of a proto nation-state out of joining the imperial phase of pillaging with the project of building the wealth of the prince. This incipient nation-state was, in spite of a mercantilist stance, already partly dependent on global circuits, particularly for precious metals. The other dynamic is that although the sixteenth century saw one country, Spain,[18] dominate much of the pillaging, the world scale taking shape was being constituted through more than pillaging and by countries other than Spain. Cross-border systems were being set in place, particularly because the huge debts of the Spanish king meant the pillaged gold and silver recirculated through Europe.[19] The mechanisms shaping this recirculation were Spain's vast imports from markets in Italy, France, Holland, and England (A. Frank 1978: 50ff.). Pillaged wealth was recycled, at least partly, through systems other than just the elementary accumulation of

---

[18] By 1580 Spain had the vastest empire geographically. However, in 1588 the Invincible Armada lost, impoverishment set in with the huge debts of the monarch, and so forth. When Spain sank, Holland, England, and France rose in dominance. Austria, Spain's great ally through intermarriage, went down with it: occupied by the successive wars of the Thirty Years War, the major concessions in the Treaty of Westphalia in 1648 were the only way of getting out of the war.

[19] The metals passed from America to the royal treasuries of Portugal and Spain, to the coffers of the financiers of Genoa, Antwerp, and Amsterdam, and to the merchants. Even during the war between Spain and the Low Countries, Spain bought a great deal from the merchants of the Low Countries.

gold and precious objects.[20] This, in turn, required the development of customs operations, contracts, and an incipient lex mercatoria. In that regard, then, pillaging began to function as one factor in the formation of a type of capability we think of as modern: the apparatus to implement, organize, manage, and service cross-border economic transactions.

The construction of a scale where at least some of what had once been the wealth of the prince began to be represented as national opened up the possibility that the wealth of the kingdom could include and depend on the wealth of other economic actors, notably merchants, bankers, and manufacturers.[21] It also meant going beyond the moral order of the Middle Ages; and while this was already happening in France, England, and in the city-states, generally the papacy was still presumed to be the source of moral authority.[22] Eventually Calvinism's doctrinal assertion of commercial success as a sign of divine selection, emerged as a legitimate option to the medieval injunctions against greed and excess moneymaking. Merchants and bankers were encouraged to enrich themselves and to fight for the right to protect their property, the right to standardized taxation, and the right to trade, including foreign trade.[23]

CONSTRUCTING NATIONAL ECONOMIES CENTERED ON IMPERIAL GEOGRAPHIES

The major powers in Europe in the mid-sixteenth century shared a need for imperial geographies to build national political economies to accumulate national wealth. But there were significant differences among them in terms of how they went about it. These distinctive pathways to national capitalism can be used as an indicator of two features of this process. One is the national character of the process no matter how vast the imperial geography on which it depended. The specificities of the national economy, society, polity,

[20] This was mostly through trading and gold payments.

[21] Although the shaping of a world scale in the sixteenth century began with pillaging, it moved to colonial expansion and long-distance trade with Holland, France, and England.

[22] In the sixteenth century the church maintained an extremely rigid and regressive regime: Galileo was punished; the work of Erasmus put on the Index in 1559 and then banned; Giordano Bruno was burned as a heretic in 1600; and so on.

[23] The merchant and banking bourgeoisie became stronger in this context. Major cities grew in size, notably Antwerp, London, Lyon, and Paris. The bourgeoisie began to embrace the ideas of the Reform (commercial success is morally good), the affirmation of individual rights in the face of sovereign power, and, especially, the major expressions of humanist thought of the time, such as the work of Erasmus, Rabelais, and Montaigne. Michelangelo, Copernicus, and other major figures all entered the discursive domain of this emergent class, partly as a function of political development of a distinct position and aspiration (see also M. Weber 1958).

and culture mattered in shaping the outcome and were thereby partly strengthened rather than neutralized as the process proceeded, even as such national
specificities "modernized." This logic of accentuating differences in a context
of shared imperial aims reappears in my analysis of the current global phase—
the coexistence of globalizing and standardizing dynamics along with what we
might think of as the specialized difference represented by each national economy and polity, or each global city. The second feature is that particular capabilities already present in each of the countries were at work in the process of
developing a world scale. Thus these capabilities, shaped partly by the distinct
substantive rationalities of each prenational formation in medieval times,
could get dislodged from the older organizational logics and become part of
novel ones, in this case, logics constitutive of national capitalism. This conceptualization partly explains the distinctiveness of the national capitalisms that
ensued; it is, in good part, the insertion of older capabilities into the new organizing logic that accounts for the reproduction of the historical particularity
of each national capitalism and its corresponding imperial geography. In contrast, much of the treatment of the emergence of capitalism in the social sciences has emphasized the parallels among national trajectories. I do not deny
these parallels—the machine age and capitalist social relations had standardizing effects across countries. My effort here is to recover the reproduction of
national specificities beneath parallel developments. There is, in this effort, a
strong resonance with my conceptualization of current developments.

From its first formation, then, capitalism was both national and
global, shaped by key actors from both the private and the state sector. As has
been amply documented in the scholarship, the actual move toward capitalism took place over a long period of time and through many different, complex, and interlocking processes that produced rising levels of capital and
merchandise, better ships, and more powerful weapons.[24] While all these
served the expansion of commerce, discoveries, and conquests, capitalism was
not necessarily an inevitable outcome. It took a certain level and type of institutional and ideational development in the formation of banking and merchant bourgeoisies, in the appearance of nations and establishment of modern
states, in the expansion of trade and domination on a world scale, and in
advances in transportation and production; and it took the introduction of
new modes of production and new ideas, mentalities, and socialities.

[24] Commerce, banking, and finance developed strongly first in the Italian republics
of the thirteenth and fourteenth centuries, and then in Holland and England. In the second
half of the fifteenth century there were significant advances in the production of metals and
textiles, and in the development of cannons and firearms. Improvements in navigational techniques were critical for the expansion of maritime routes feeding into the trading, explorations,
and pillaging of the sixteenth century.

What I want to extricate from this rich scholarship about the ascendance of capitalism is the work of making the institutional, legal, discursive, ideational, and other capabilities required for implementing world-scale operations. This work of making, while often highly innovative, was partly shaped by the particular resources, cultures, dispositions, and ideational forms of each country and by the key actors whose interests shaped the process. It underlines the national specificities at play in the shaping of each national capitalism and its imperial geography.[25] The fact that the development of the world scale was deeply intertwined with the formation of national capitalisms is illuminated by a brief comparison of the making of these capabilities in the major European powers.

Long before any of the other major European powers of the time, the Low Countries began developing such capabilities in the early 1600s (industrial capitalism began in England a century later). The Low Countries[26] diverged sharply from the other major powers in Europe at the time: commerce was thriving, agriculture was modern, there was almost no nobility, and the bourgeoisie was strong and controlled the political economy. Holland in particular was known as a place that tolerated differences and became the destination of several well-known "heretics." The active and innovative merchant, banking, and manufacturing bourgeoisies were open to new ideas and possibilities, which fostered the development of each of these capitalisms.[27] Holland developed processing industries of all sorts, microscope construction, navigational instruments, terrestrial and maritime mapmaking, and book printing in all languages. But it did not quite develop industrial capitalism.

It took work to set up this type of political economy. The development of three major institutions became a capability for global operations: the Dutch East India Company (DEICO), the Bank of Amsterdam, and the merchant fleet. The process of setting up DEICO and the Bank of Amsterdam illuminates the development of a new institutional order in the Low Countries. DEICO was an elaborate institution made up of six distinct chambers and conceived as a vehicle to serve the common good.[28] Each chamber decided on

---

[25] The question of periodization is always subject to debate and revision. I chose Beaud's (1982: 115ff.) identification of three phases in capitalist industrialization on a world scale: 1780–1880, 1880–1950, and 1950 onward. Each of these phases is marked by specific sectoral and geographic dimensions.

[26] They received their independence from Spain in 1609 and declared themselves a republic in 1615.

[27] Marx saw Holland as the capitalist nation par excellence; it was a symbol of commercial and financial capitalism.

[28] Six chambers of merchants gathered in 1602 to form DEICO; this included seventy-three directors, all of whom were administrators of trading companies. Direction of common affairs rested with the College of Seventeen.

the business of its members: the purchases to be made in India, the amount of gold to be sent, and the sale of merchandise received. It decided on the organization of the fleets, their destination, and the price of the goods. The company enjoyed a monopoly of trade with India, and practiced *mare clausum* in its imperial geography, forbidding access to India by the English, Portuguese, and the French. It exercised regal rights in India[29] and deployed massive resources on the subcontinent.[30] Holland defended the *mare liberum* outside its colonies. Grotius brilliantly designed the mixed governance for empire (Sassen 1996: chapter 1). The Bank of Amsterdam was created in 1609— almost a century earlier than the Bank of England.[31] It offered security to depositors drawing on both Dutch and foreign currency. It was an "international" bank insofar as it was able to provide merchants with the money of any country, which permitted the purchase of merchandise of any origin and attracted foreign traders. The bank also carried out without charge all the merchants' payments, within the limits of their deposits, by simply transferring written notes and not moving any precious metals. To do this it used a currency with a stable value, the bank florin, which reassured its clients. It gradually became a credit bank, first giving credit to the city of Amsterdam in times of war and to DEICO; by the end of the century it also gave credit to private companies.[32] The third pillar was the merchant fleet.[33] One indication of its weight is the fact that in the early 1600s the Dutch fleet alone employed more sailors than the combined fleets of Spain, France, England, and Scotland. The Dutch, then, had a political economy dominated by a merchant and banking bourgeoisie, a sophisticated financial system in place, and a highly developed administrative capability to run a vast imperial geography, going as far as Japan to the east and the Americas to the west.[34] One might say that notwithstanding the loss of its empire, the Dutch never quite relinquished these massive capabilities for global trade and banking: what is today a very

---

[29] There are some parallels here with the IMF programs today.

[30] At its height the company had a land-based army in India of 10,000–12,000 troops, and a sea navy of 40–60 ships, which brought into Europe 10–12 million florins' worth of goods annually. DEICO gave dividends of 25 to 30 percent, so its stock value went from 3,000 florins to 18,000 in 1670.

[31] Moneychangers had been accused of monetary disorder, so the city of Amsterdam suppressed them, created a bank, and granted it a monopoly over exchange. It received all deposits in money or ingots greater than 300 florins.

[32] Impressive and well built, they industrialized production of these ships. They employed foreigners as sailors—the lowest level of work at the time (often English or French)—at lower wages than what natives were paid.

[33] A good indicator of this is the fact that, unlike what might have been the case with a nationalist monarch, the merchants supplied Spain with food even during the war between the two countries. Half of the gold and silver acquired by Spain ended up in Amsterdam.

[34] The Dutch also developed sugarcane cultivation in Java.

small country has surprisingly vast global operations and leadership in multiple specialized sectors, with a definite Dutch style.

England's rise in the early seventeenth century as a maritime and colonial power set the stage for the emergence of two critical dynamics. One was the increased rivalry with major European powers as each built its own massive imperial geography.[35] After fighting Spain at the end of the sixteenth century, England fought Holland in the second half of the seventeenth century, and France in the eighteenth century. Colonial expansion was a key feature of England's rise from the beginning of the seventeenth century. The bourgeoisie sharply expanded foreign trade, which rose tenfold between 1610 and 1640, and manufactures, leading to an enormous increase of the workforce. Second, the growth in commerce and manufacturing was also the beginning of a new political economy, with its need for specific types of protections and enablements. The rising bourgeoisie wanted both; while this was not unique to England's bourgeoisie, the process of attaining these protections and enablements took place in a complex setting marked by the vast powers of the monarch and the nobility, a condition radically different from that of Holland. While the monarchy wanted to maximize the accumulation of precious metals, the bourgeoisie was interested in maximizing the circulation of such metals in order to make them produce a profit. The prevailing deeply mercantilist and protectionist orientation could have been a powerful obstacle to developing free trade. The bourgeoisie in England wanted and fought for free trade, even as it was also mercantilist when this suited its interests. Through this struggle, it began to constitute itself as a distinct historic subject.

In this emerging political economy, English kings generally protected the interests of the bourgeoisie: they distributed privileges and monopolies; regulated and organized the control of manufactures; and prohibited the export of wool, ensuring adequate and low-cost supplies for manufacturers; and raised taxes on imported French and Dutch fabrics. The state's governing of the economy enabled the proliferation of monopolies and thwarted agricultural innovations even when they were technically justified. It was the nobility, positioned between the king and the bourgeoisie, who were losing their powers and privileges. Though I return to this issue in more detail in the next two sections, for now let me signal that in England the work of making the institutional and ideational infrastructure for the emergence of a national capitalism based in an English-dominated imperial geography followed a

---

[35] Empire decline is a complex matter. But wars, especially throughout the 1600s as well as the Spanish War of succession of 1702–14, and the economic depression of the second half of the seventeenth century put enormous pressures on Dutch capitalism. Heavy debts and a weakened economy contributed to the loss of Holland's dominant position.

rather different path from that of Holland, further contributing to the national specificity of capitalist development.

In France, where the absolutist monarchy exercised far more control over the economy than it did in England, the bourgeoisie allied itself with the king against the nobility, and mercantilism was imposed, though it largely served the interests of the state. While France and England both aimed at ensuring the wealth of the prince, from the beginning the bourgeoisie in England also wanted and fought for free trade. In France, the state's major and active role in developing commerce and manufacturing and in promoting mercantilism preempted the emergence of the bourgeoisie as a historic subject with a distinct project. The royal absolutist state strongly supported the development of manufacturing and worldwide trade; the French bourgeoisie was formed under its protection and would bear its imprint for a long time. But notwithstanding the far larger role of the state, English- and Dutch-style mercantilism also took shape in France (which included control of the seas, creation of a company for overseas trading, and the protection of monopolies). Mercantilism was at its height in France from 1663 to 1685.

The extent to which the formation of national capitalism was articulated with the development of an imperial economic geography became particularly legible in England when the revolution deposed the monarch and Cromwell brought power to Parliament. It is significant for my analysis that Cromwell, who was deeply nationalistic, did nonetheless want English imperial power. The difference was that he wanted to extend the benefits of the empire to English workers and the bourgeoisie.[36] The results of this mix of nationalism and imperialism were deeply mercantilist policies and control over maritime trade in mid-seventeenth-century England.[37]

[36] The compromise between the king and the bourgeoisie rested on enrichment of the state and of the merchants, mastery of the universe, and national greatness. This compromise was not enough, however, to overcome the strong popular rebellion: Charles I was decapitated, and Cromwell took over and proceeded to institute strong mercantilist policies and extensive controls over maritime trade to bring benefits to the English workers.

[37] The Navigation Acts passed by Cromwell sought to give enormous advantages to the English, demanding that the vast numbers of English ships and goods moving into various European countries had to be English. In the years prior to the Civil War, the government of the colonies was seen as the domain of the Crown. Immediately following the Civil War, however, Parliament passed a series of acts granting national control over colonial trade. In 1650, it passed an act forbidding trade with pro-Royalist colonies. In 1651 it passed the Navigation Act confining colonial export trade to English ships, enforced sporadically against Dutch carriers, and tightened up in 1660. Among other acts that were part of the Navigation Acts were the 1662 Frauds Act; the 1663 Staple Act; and the 1673 Plantation Duties Act (an attempt to control colonial trade by keeping the colonies solely in the position of a supplier to the home country). While the basic position in many of these acts was to resist the colonies' possible demands and claims (Ashley 1961: 225), they were mostly abolished by 1849 (Rubinstein 1998: 89).

The major transformations taking shape in the seventeenth and early eighteenth centuries were not immediately obvious. Even when the capitalist development of industry was taking over key economic sectors in England in the early nineteenth century, it was still far from prevalent. The industrial bourgeoisie was not yet a distinct social group; nor were wage workers. Older classes, such as the nobility, landowners, farmers, artisans, and shopkeepers, were the prevalent presence in the economic landscape. They were also the source of growing criticisms of the new order they sensed was coming, criticism often in the name of values of the past (Burke, Bonald, Maitre) or in the name of an alternative society ruled by norms of equity and reason (St. Simon, Goodwin, Owen, Fourier). But only a few decades later, by the mid-nineteenth century, the bourgeoisie had become the evident dominant class in England and the working class had become legible as a distinctly disadvantaged social group.

As a national bourgeoisie became a dominant political class, its economic project clearly remained linked to colonial expansion, maritime trade, and increased commerce with the empire.[38] With the rise of industrial capitalism and commercial growth, Britain began to follow a policy of territorial expansion from the 1820s on, including expansion to India and all of Canada. It also became a more flexible empire, adjusting to new realities, which included abolishing the East India Company after the revolt of the Sepoys in 1857. The articulation of national economic growth and enrichment with the fact of empire became stronger and more developed.[39] Thus, by 1870, one-third of all foreign invested capital went to the empire (Hobson 1938). Specialization and an international division of labor were evident in Britain's exports and increasingly in its imports. The conquest of foreign

[38] Yet another indication of the importance of the world scale for the building of national capitalism is that at the beginning of the nineteenth-century the British Empire, seriously reduced and disintegrating, launched a whole new phase of territorial imperial expansion at a time when capitalist development and the bourgeoisie were becoming dominant. National development continued to need empire.

[39] In this regard it is interesting to recall that, as Wallerstein put it, the capitalist farmers in the periphery would gladly have thought of themselves as an international gentry class. They willingly sacrificed local cultures for world cultures. But they needed the collaboration of the capitalist strata in core states, and this did not happen. The project of the capitalist classes in the major powers was one of building themselves as a national dominant force, albeit in need of colonizing empires and free trade. So increasingly these potential members of a sort of global propertied class became the snobbish hacenderos or "East European Nobility of later centuries, retreating from international class consciousness into local status solidarities"—all of which served the interests of the bourgeoisie in core countries (1974: 353). According to Wallerstein, these localized elites could also feel oppressed by the European bourgeoisies and see the advantages in seeking protections in their own nation-state, further promoting nationalisms.

markets was crucial for national capitalism.[40] In William Pitt's dictum, "British policy is British trade." Britain had the most advanced form of national industrial capitalism and was the most internationalized economy.[41] These and other features of the political landscape of the time point to the joint presence of elements that appear contradictory but are part of the formation of national capitalism: "monopoly and competition; state intervention and private initiative; world markets and national interest" (Beaud 1981: 55).

The illegibility of the dominance of industrial capitalism needs to be underscored, especially the fact that it remained so even as it was about to become very legible, or "explode" on the scene. This supports the argument that in its early phases, a new dominant economic logic may not necessarily be the prevalent social form. By 1870 industrial capitalism was the dominant logic in Great Britain, but it had only changed part of Great Britain and was firmly grounded only in bounded zones of western Europe and North America. However, it soon spread rapidly through the rise of new techniques and new industries, as well as ever larger and more powerful concentrations of capital whose field of action expanded to the world scale. Further, this expansion took place as the older state-controlled imperialisms declined, which, depending on one's interpretive categories, could easily be chosen to mark the period rather than the features of the new imperialisms. As industrial capitalism erupted on the scene, the enormously exploited national workforce became visible. This was also the moment of the rise and public recognition of a variety of workers' movements, as well as the development and implementation of new modes of domination over workers.

Even as it was reaching its zenith, Britain was already entering a phase of sharpened rivalries with ascendant powers that would challenge its position of dominance. Britain was losing out to Germany and the United States, even though it did not look that way at the time (Beaud 1981). The often problematic legibility of major transformations in the making is underlined by

[40] But British trade showed a deficit throughout this period: it bought more from the rest of the world than it sold. Its main partners were its own empire, Europe, and eventually America. This also fed the conflict between industrialists for whom cheap imports were a source of profits and farmers who could not compete with cheap imports of food and raw materials. What made the balance of payments positive was trade in services (insurance and brokerage, revenue from maritime transport, dividends, interest from abroad), which grew strongly in the second half of the nineteenth century.

[41] In the 1820s and 1830s Britain exported one-fifth of its production. In 1851 exports reached one quarter of all physical production, one-third in 1861, and two-fifths in 1871. Thus conquest of foreign markets was crucial for Britain's national economy. This also points to the significance of the debate between protectionists and free traders.

the fact that only in Great Britain had the bourgeoisie become the visible dominant class by the mid-nineteenth century, even as industrial capitalism was developing in what were to become other major powers.[42]

Notwithstanding the diverse trajectories and temporalities among the major European powers, they all point to the emergence of a specific historic subject in the construction of national capitalisms centered on imperial economic geographies. Although this historic subject eventually can be identified as the bourgeoisie in each of the countries, the state often played a crucial role in each and was, at the beginning, the critical actor. But its incidence and modes of institutional insertion varied. Simplifying complex configurations, we can say that in Holland the bourgeoisie was the critical actor from the start of the development of capitalism. In England it was the state, in the form of a king and a parliament in conjunction with the bourgeoisie, that jointly launched capitalism, and in France it was largely the state. When the bourgeoisie eventually emerged as the critical actor in the development of industrial capitalism it was a subject constructed differently in each of the major powers, both as a social actor and as a legal persona. This construction was critical to the shaping of a legitimate owner of means of production who was neither monarch nor nobility. The next two sections examine these issues with some detail, focusing largely on England.

CONSTRUCTING THE LEGAL PERSONA OF A NATIONAL BOURGEOISIE

There is an interesting tension in the historical development of a national bourgeoisie that needed national political institutions—notably Parliament in the case of the English bourgeoisie—to constitute itself even as its vested interests lay in imperial economic geographies. In this regard, England's development of industrial capitalism is a natural experiment for illuminating three sets of issues. The first is the articulation of foreign trade, global pillaging, and colonization with the growth and rise of a novel legal persona, the national bourgeoisie. The second is the lack of legibility of the fact that capitalism was dominant in the English economy at a time when it seemed kings and nobility were; as indicated earlier, this condition recurs in various historical phases across the centuries examined thus far in this book,

---

[42] Among the other major powers in Europe at the time, Holland had stabilized, Portugal and Spain were declining, and Russia continued its expansion toward Asia. During the Restoration France took possession again of its colonies, which had been neglected during the revolution and the empire. This neglect may partly have been connected to the fact that industrial capitalism was moving slowly, further signaling the importance of colonialism for capitalism. French colonial expansion was mostly military.

culminating with the illegibility of the dominance of industrial capitalism in the early nineteenth century. The third is the political economy that was constructed as the bourgeoisie carved out a legal persona for itself, a rights-bearing subject that began as a legal non-persona striving against absolutism and the nobility. The outcome is the construction of a novel subject—a legitimate owner of means of production and a legitimate bearer of the means for powerful controls over the workers it needs and depends on. This process, extended over a century, enacted a major historic switch, which if concentrated over a briefer temporal frame would be akin to what Sewell (1980) has described as "events" that disrupt existing structurations.

All of this was arising out of an older context where this history in the making was not particularly legible. Wallerstein (1974) notes that the sixteenth century was indecisive. The capitalist strata formed a class that survived politically but did not yet triumph in the political domain. The sectors benefiting from economic and geographic expansion of the capitalist system, especially in the core areas, tended to operate within the political arena as a group defined primarily by their common role in the economy. This group included farmers, merchants, and industrialists with an orientation toward profit making in the world economy. Other actors—the traditional aristocracy, guilds, owners of inherited farms—fought back to maintain their status privileges. But the major historical dynamic was toward novel class formation, even as all these other groups often seemed dominant and even as the veneer of culture led to a sense of unity.

By the seventeenth century the English bourgeoisie was strong enough to defy absolutism and to legitimate a new form of government. Locke gave them some of the instruments with his *Of Civil Government* (1690). It contained a justification for the overthrow of the sovereign in the name of freedom. For Locke, the protection of property was critical to the social contract: what establishes society and government (social contract) is the free consent of the citizens. If the sovereign were to take away property it would justify insurrection by the people. Locke rejects absolutism (which places the sovereign above the law and thus beyond civil society). But in Locke's work these principles were in fact confined to the "proper" classes—those who had won themselves the right to handle their affairs—especially enlightened landowners, commercial and financial bourgeoisies, the landed nobility, clergymen, and the gentry. He did not believe the working classes were capable of governing themselves. To cope with the poor he recommended force (1969: 34). All in all, the bourgeoisie found in Locke their theoretician. Locke's ideas were also a success among the ruling classes in England and Holland and, in the eighteenth century, among jurists and philosophers in France. They were the ideas for an enlightened bourgeoisie.

Locke offered a substantive rationality for major developments already in motion by the time his work was published. His ideas corresponded to the interests of the sectors of the bourgeoisie that saw in free trade the stimulus for a new expansion of commerce and production, and in Parliament the vehicle for politically legitimating their economic project. Operating at the world scale necessitated innovation in institutional infrastructure and operational capabilities. They used Parliament, which signaled the making of a new political economy, not just an elementary accumulation of capital.[43] The freedom to export grains, a means to encourage agriculture, was obtained in 1670. In addition to the establishment of the East India Company in 1600, several other such companies were founded, all aimed at furthering trade, notably the Hudson Bay Company in 1670 and the Royal Africa Company for slave trade in 1672. In 1694 the Bank of England was created.[44] It raised 1.2 million pounds in twelve days, an indication of the emergent power of capital owners. In return for loaning to the government, the bank became the first English joint stock bank and was permitted to discount bills (Carruthers 1996). The government did not have to repay but only serve up interest. The New East India Company was also founded in part to lend the government money (1698). Both the New East India Company and the Bank of England were controlled by Parliament, which increased its control over the Crown (Ashley 1961: 185) and thereby enhanced the political power of the bourgeoisie.

The growing power of Parliament contained a critical political shift that enabled the formation of the bourgeoisie as a rights-bearing subject. This shift was part of a long history of accumulating partial powers and claims in the emergent capitalist class. For instance, the 1624 Statute of Monopolies regularized patent law allowing the developer of an innovation to assert a right to revenues produced by its introduction, i.e. to assert "property rights over invention" whereas previously the Crown might have awarded prizes for innovation but granted no private returns to the innovator (North 1981: 164ff.; Hartwell 1971: chapter 11).[45] Another indication of accumulating "rights" was the resolution of a conflict surrounding the wool trade during the Stuart years concerning the extent of taxation; in the terms of the compromise the Crown

[43] Sir Dudley North wrote in his "Discourse upon Trade" (1691) in defense of free trade, which was clearly different from mercantilism. There is a strong correspondence between the ideas of political freedom (Locke) and the necessity for economic liberalism (North).

[44] The Bank of England was created by a group of financiers who promised to lend the Crown 1.5 million pounds to cover the expenses of the war against Flanders; in return they got the title of corporation, with the right to receive deposits and discount commercial bills.

[45] Previously patents had been caught up in a system of monarchial privilege and favors, dating back at least to 1331, whereby the Crown used the issuing of a patent or trade monopoly to expand its coffers. This came under attack during the second half of the sixteenth century (North and Thomas 1973: 147ff.).

received revenues, Parliament won the right to set taxation levels, and merchants got the monopoly of trade (North and Thomas 1973).

The capabilities developed in this extended and multifaceted politico-economic process of gathering advantages eventually became part of a system of private property protections, enablements for global operations, and the formalization of political decisions that began to concentrate advantages in the emerging bourgeoisie. Acts of Parliament, its enhanced taxation powers (Ashley 1961), and the enormous commercial expansion of eighteenth-century England were critical variables in this process.

In the eighteenth century long-distance trade became crucial to England's rapid development. Colonial domination, pillaging, and exploitation of native or imported workers, mostly through slavery, remained fundamental sources of enrichment, which contributed to trade and production. The effort included devious tactics, such as the 1700 prohibition on the import of Indian calicoes, a textile superior to anything made in England, which threatened domestic manufacturers. Commerce quintupled and national income quadrupled. Foreign trade was a major factor that enabled the sharp growth of the English port cities—Liverpool, Manchester, Bristol, and Glasgow.[46] But a sharp difference began to take shape. While state accumulation proceeded in the eighteenth century in the same domains as before (roads, waterways, harbors, fleets, administrative machinery), bourgeois accumulation took a new turn: even as it proceeded through an increase in private fortunes and stocks of merchandise, a growing share of capital became productive capital—raw materials, machines, and mills.

Quesnay (1757), Turgot (1795), and A. Smith (1976) saw this new logic: a net product could be extracted from productive labor that could enlarge or improve production. The principal agent was the bourgeoisie that had come from the merchant and banking sectors, from dealers and manufacturers, and, in England, from a portion of the nobility. This emergent new class articulated its economic and political project around the notion of freedom, something that held across the major powers of the time. In England, this class was involved with affairs of the state through Parliament: it sought and secured freedom of trade and production, freedom to pay labor at its lowest level, and freedom to defend against workers' alliances and revolts. In France, where the bourgeoisie were excluded from affairs of the

---

[46] The development of commerce required the development of transportation. In France and elsewhere on the continent this was done through corvée (a kind of bonded labor), but in Britain it was done through the initiative of local associations (large landowners, traders, shepherds, farmers) who financed the roads and collected the tolls. This strengthened the private sector; it also points to the different ways in which the division between public and private was constituted in Britain and in France, where the state undertook much of this work.

state, except as employees, they sought political freedom from the absolutist state, suppression of the privileges of the nobility, and a constitution promising equality.

The emergent notions of a liberal democracy gave the bourgeoisie an institutional form that enabled the "lawful" development of a "legitimate" system of laws and regulations that privileged the bourgeoisie and property as a criterion for granting rights.[47] It sought authority rather than simply the raw power of capital. This meant a government constituted through a social contract—rather than the divinity of the sovereign—and through political regimes. Where it once had taken shelter in royal authority against the nobility, liberalism now allowed it a variety of alliances in order to advance its own projects. Thus, at some point the notion of national unity ceased to be constructed in terms of the monarch and became a vehicle for alliances of the bourgeoisie and others against the monarch. While it remained allied with the monarch through a shared interest in colonial expansion and mercantilism, the English bourgeoisie knew how to use popular discontent in its fight against absolutism, which was also a battle to strengthen its own power.[48] By the end of the eighteenth century, the idea of the nation, connected to mercantilism, was used against the king; the French and American revolutions were the most prominent formulations of this shift.[49]

[47] It was the rich peasants, the dealers, the rich gentry and locally important men, the banking and trading bourgeoisie, the jurists, and the liberal professions who asked for parliamentary democracy (not necessarily in those words), freedom, and property. These groups represented an important new social force, underestimated by the monarchy reestablished after Cromwell's death. In a compromise the monarch agreed to respect a "Declaration of Rights" (1689), which asserted that the king could not suspend the application of the laws, collect taxes, or raise and maintain an army in times of peace without the consent of Parliament.

[48] National unity, originally established around the person of the king, could of course also function as a form of hypernationalism and intense warfare. (There was indeed a succession of wars.)

[49] Wallerstein (1974) notes that the bourgeoisie identified with the nation-state, but it could have identified with other entities, notably other bourgeois classes in other nation-states. The bourgeoisie became conscious of its position in a system but did so within the frame of the nation-state. There were other choices: they could have become conscious of themselves as a world class, and many groups pushed for such a definition. There were also capitalist farmers in the peripheral areas. At the height of Charles V's reign, many in the Low Countries, southern Germany, northern Italy, and elsewhere tied their hopes to the imperial aspirations of the Hapsburgs: these groups were a social stratum but could have become a class. The failure of the empire made the bourgeoisie in Europe realize that their fate was tied to nation-states. This points to the existence of possible alternative trajectories and thereby de-essentializes the historical record, and, more specifically, it points to contestations of the nation-state and thereby deessentializes the latter.

We see at this time the first instantiation of what was to become the liberal state: the development of a "legitimate" system of laws and regulations that privileged the owners of productive capital. The project of formalizing the rights of capital owners was most developed in England, but the trend was also evident in the other major powers of the time. Holland had long had a sort of embedded regime favoring merchant, banking, and manufacturing capitalists. The French Revolution, a far more complex and sudden event than the more extended struggles of the English bourgeoisie, eventually brought enablements to the French bourgeoisie, but these were only rendered fully effective in the 1850s through the alliance with the monarch, Napoleon III.

The foundational doctrines of this first phase of a liberal state incorporated ideas about individual freedom and the protection of bourgeois—as distinct from royal—property, as well as the colonization of foreign territories. All of these projects and interests were built as part of the doctrinal arguments for the political legitimacy of particular actors, even though often cloaked in notions of national unity and the common good. Hume in his "Essays on Economics" (1955) emphasizes the importance of foreign trade, rather than precious metals, as the source of wealth of subjects and as the way to increase the power of the state. He argues for the general advantages of foreign trade, both imports and exports.[50] Adam Smith, a disciple of Hume, sought to justify in his *Theory of Moral Sentiments* (1759) a social order based on the quest after individual interests.[51] What stands out in Smith's statements about the poor is the functionalism of poverty—language along the lines of, "If we did not have the poor, we could not have the ultimate experience, which is to give to them," or the poor are as happy as the rich, and so on. When Smith spells out the duties of the sovereign, he seems much closer to what we have come to understand as liberalism: to protect his country from invasion; to protect every member from the injustice and oppression of other members; and to erect and maintain certain public works. Smith also argues against mercantilism in the name of consumers' interests.[52] The world of Smith is that of manufacturing capitalism (mills, nails, pins); trades at the craft level; and shopkeepers, transporters, woodcutters, and shepherds. He emphasizes the importance of labor, the real measure of the exchangeable

---

[50] He also emphasizes that people have to be governed by their own interests, not by regulations and controls. From the multiple interests and egoisms, a new social harmony can arise—a form of liberal pluralism.

[51] He justifies the enjoyment of nobleness and wealth and the privilege of the few (it keeps mankind industrious, inventive, improving), and he advances the idea of the invisible hand (thereby justifying the fact that some have plenty and many have little.

[52] At the same time, civil government, so far as it is instituted to protect property, is for the defense of the rich against the poor.

value of all commodities.[53] Using the same ideas, the European descendants in the colonies began resisting European domination and clamoring for democracy and freedom, even as they used slave labor and massacred Indians.

The losers in this configuration were the nobility, small artisans, and, above all, the workers. The nobility, between the king and the bourgeoisie, saw their relative power and privileges decline. As for small artisans, even as they made claims against the landed nobility, a new mode of value extortion was the indirect domination by intermediaries and traders.[54] Poor artisans did not ask for democracy and freedom but for basic protections by regulation: better prices or wages, a shorter workday, and protection from foreign competition. The poorest layers of the peasantry were hurt badly by the new wave of enclosures in the mid-seventeenth century. Agricultural workers became destitute as both the earlier and later waves of enclosures expelled them from land. Various disciplining measures aimed at controlling workers and the poor generally in cities and towns all contributed to engender much discontent and agitation.

The enclosure movement continued strongly in the eighteenth century, especially after 1760, and increasingly took the form of laws passed by Parliament. The enclosure acts passed by Parliament illuminate the process of developing capabilities that gave the bourgeoisie economic and political instruments. In these acts Parliament formalized specific advantages for the owners of productive capital and enabled the formation of a particularly disadvantaged and vulnerable labor supply.[55] These acts also resolved the tensions between the Crown and the bourgeoisie to the advantage of the latter. Enclosures were not new to the modern period, dating back at least to the Statute of Merton (1236) (North and Thomas 1973: 151). At the heart of the concept was giving private rights to appropriate gains accruing from improvements to the land—"fatter rent rolls and larger profits." Enclosures were justified in terms of the positive consequences of private ownership rights for agricultural productivity (Thompson 1963: 217). Monarchies had diverse positions on enclosures (Polanyi 2001: 37–38). According to Briggs, "Between

[53] He was fundamentally against prohibitions—he was against anything that might restrain the right to work.

[54] Work at the craft level remained important for processing activity, even as other forms of production competed. Work at home for a merchant manufacturer now also became common for formerly independent artisans and peasant families. It was the main form of British manufacturing capitalism. Large manufacturing operations all under one roof were not common and did not become so.

[55] The modernization of agriculture and animal husbandry displaced a vast labor force that supplied mining and manufacturing companies. Modernization displaced or expelled the poor, the unemployed, squatters, orphans, and widows.

1761 and 1780 during the first phase of enclosure by Act of Parliament, 4039 Acts were passed: there were a further 900 between 1781 and 1800" (1959: 41).[56] The General Enclosure Act of 1801 rationalized the procedure.[57] The creation of this particular type of working class became a key resource for a dynamic that was expanding in England: producing more in order to produce more. The implementation of this project brought many changes in the organization of agriculture, mining, and processing. In the last third of the eighteenth century and the first third of the nineteenth century, this logic was extended to a growing number of sectors: clothing and textiles, machines, tools and metal domestic utensils, railroads, and armaments.

Perhaps the key analytic import of this type of relationship between workers and the bourgeoisie is that even as it progressed along different paths in the different major European powers of the time, it produced a similar outcome: a proletariat shaped both in terms of a systemic position in the emerging new economy and in terms of a particular type of legal persona through the passing of a variety of laws and regulations in each of the major countries—each with its own specifics. This was the making of a legal subject that lacked critical rights and enablements, in contrast to the propertied classes, which had been granted considerable rights. Both of these very different subjects were created as national, and as deeply embedded in and constitutive of a "national economy."

The articulation of this industrial project with a particularly disadvantaged working class might suggest the necessity of that disadvantage—the need for such a working class if industrial production was to proceed. While the historical trajectory might further reinforce this notion, the historical record also admits deeper complexity. In the royal manufactories of France this was not quite the case. One significant difference was that the French state was in charge of organizing production. Similarly, the Stuarts in England at times sought to resist or at least weaken the enclosure acts as a way of reducing the brutality and velocity through which the rural workforce was made into an urban industrial labor supply. Traditional liberal readings see the Crown as reactionary and impeding progress. But Polanyi (2001: 39) credits king and church with preventing enclosures from completely tearing the social

[56] Briggs (1984) gives 1,300 acts from 1760 to 1801, and another 1,000 from 1800 to 1820.

[57] Before 1801, "The procedure used was usually enclosure by act of parliament rather than by voluntary agreement or pressure. A successful Enclosure Act did not require local unanimity but it did require enough money to pay for the lawyers' and surveyors' fees and for fences, hedges, roads, and drainage after the bill had been passed. This was largely a formality since the Enclosure Commissioners appointed to survey the land invariably favored the parties wishing to enclose and so, too did Parliament" (Briggs 1984: 172).

fabric apart; this may have made an extremely destructive process into a somewhat more sustainable system of production and innovation. The king and church were anxious about rural depopulation and sought to impede the process of dislocation of agricultural workers; this brought them into conflict with the local lords and nobles. Parliament, by contrast, tended to favor enclosure. While Parliament seems to have usually been successful legislatively, the Crown did manage to implement the system of Poor Laws, discussed later, which were aimed at easing the transition and protecting local authority relations.[58] In this effort to slow down enclosures and give some protections to the disadvantaged, the state did also enable the industrial project by making life somewhat more manageable for the workers and the poor even as they were subjected to greater control.

Whatever paternalist protections the state may have provided for weaker groups overall, the state's major role in the process of industrial development was to strengthen the national capitalist project—through protectionist measures, the licenses and monopolies of mercantilist policies, and the laws and acts that protected the rights of the propertied classes and sharply weakened the status of workers. On the one hand, the state provided political and military support for commercial and colonial expansion. On the other hand, the state used the police and the law against the poor and to suppress workers' revolts. Parliament frequently aligned with the interests of the bourgeoisie and played a crucial role in this process. For instance, a 1769 law classified the voluntary destruction of machines and the buildings that contained them as a felony, and instituted the death penalty for those found guilty of such destruction and a 1799 law prohibited the formation of workers' associations that wanted wage increases, a shorter workday, or any other improvement in working conditions.[59]

The law was used to implement a massive assault on the poor and on workers. In this process the bourgeoisie began to take shape as a privileged legal persona. The new propertied classes mostly benefited from the state's interventions, and in that sense differed from the nobility, which was itself a propertied class but played a far smaller role in stimulating extensive and innovative state work, especially in the legal domain. The emerging bourgeois propertied class included a mix of social groups, both old and new: members of the nobility involved in commercial enterprises, farming, or mines; great merchants and financiers who displayed their success by purchasing estates;

[58] The reasons for intervention varied, but at the heart was a concern about the rising population (especially in the urban working population). In the late eighteenth century this increased the demand for cheap food, creating further pressure for agricultural improvement.

[59] Thus troops were sent to break up the riots in 1779 in Lancaster and in 1796 in Yorkshire.

merchants who became manufacturers and then established mills; and manufacturers and traders who became bankers. Together they handled the country's economy, and the state helped enable this.

We can see here the creation of what we now call the "rule of law." In this case, it legitimated private property, protected the rights of the emerging bourgeoisie from abuses of power by the king and the nobility, and sanctioned decisive control over workers as the legitimate right of these specific propertied classes. We see here the making of a rights-bearing subject that represents a contestation of absolutist power, opens up a space for the rights of novel actors, and institutionalizes overwhelming power over the workers it employs. It thus emerges as a historic subject in that it sets in motion a variety of processes shaping a new political economy. While this is only part of the formation of capitalism, it helped draw the key alignments in the emerging political economy. The developing practical and legal architecture enabled the formation of national economic projects that could accommodate foreign pillaging and trade, growing rights for the national bourgeoisie, and massive social divisions inside that national unit. And yet, the rights discourse was also to become a tool for the claims by the oppressed for expanded formal protections.

All of this took place against a context of a changing relationship between the bourgeoisie and the nobility. In the second third of the nineteenth century, Britain saw a decisive change in the composition of it's national capital: components linked to the development of capitalism (overseas securities, domestic railroads, industrial capital, and commercial and finance capital, including buildings) became dominant compared to traditional landed inheritance (estates and farms).[60] Throughout the nineteenth century the landed aristocracy lost its monopoly over political and local power. Many of the great reforms of this century benefited the rising bourgeoisie, not the old nobility, although they shared interests, were on the same side of the conflicts involving property, and were against the "masses." In the political arena, confrontation between conservatism (nobility) and liberalism (bourgeoisie) often masked the growing interactions and alliances between them.

The working class in Britain was not quite a political actor at this time. It had suffered from three centuries of abusive employers and had become weak. Thus the electoral reforms of 1832 that extended the vote to more social groups, including some factions of the working class, were acceptable to the aristocracy because they primarily benefited industrialists and traders, and only

---

[60] In 1819 there was what we might describe as a return to sound money (Briggs 1984: 201). The 1825 Bank Charter Act liberalized country banks; the 1826 Banking Act had deflationary effects; and so on. The 1844 Bank Charter Act established that only the Bank of England could issue paper bank notes. The 1844–61 corporation laws (McNeill 1986: 507) allowed all companies, except banks, to become limited liability concerns; banks were allowed in 1858.

raised the number of voters from 500,000 to 813,000. The reforms did not provide uniform voting rules, and generally only a few inhabitants of towns had the right to vote for borough representatives; property qualifications for voting for "knights of the shire" meant that the gentry controlled country elections (McNeill 1986: 449).[61] Radical tendencies in reform movements were chastened by the domestic counterrevolutionary fallout of the events of 1789 (Thompson 1963: 807), even though the issue of parliamentary reform was reopened in 1828. The nobility hastened to counterrevolution, and the industrial bourgeoisie tempered its claims and accommodated the status quo. But the predominantly working-class reform movement did become radicalized. In the crisis of 1831–32, massive popular demonstrations agitated for reform. E. Thompson suggests that the Whigs used the threat of a working-class revolution to attain reform limited to Whiggish interests, but they still needed to accomplish *something* in order to contain growing working-class agitation (1963: 809, 819). Ultimately, the middle-class Whig interests gained control of the emerging popular movement, containing its more revolutionary aspects. The worlds of the artisan and the unskilled worker remained too far apart for them to form a coherent political force, which fractured the movement and allowed it to fall under middle-class control (E. Thompson 1963: 814). McWilliam (1998) notes that enfranchisement helped break up the "crowd"—previously, the disenfranchised typically assembled in public places to make themselves heard; the Reform Act dispersed polling places, making such assembly more difficult. Even the repeal of the Corn Laws in 1846 was not a disaster for the landed property owners, who were forced to become better managers and mechanize, thereby increasing their earnings.[62]

But nineteenth-century England is marked by the rise of the bourgeoisie. The landed aristocracy did not necessarily recognize the epochal

---

[61] Key pieces of legislation here were the 1818–19 Sturges Bourne Acts, which restricted *local* voting to property owners. But there were a variety of "specialized" prohibitions, notably the 1828 repeal of the Test and Corporation Acts, which precluded Protestant Dissenters from being MPs; previously, "Indemnity Acts" were passed annually to allow Dissenters to hold office.

[62] The Corn Laws are a microcosm of political alignments in England at the time. The 1815 Corn Laws prohibited corn imports unless domestic prices reached 80 shillings per quarter (Briggs 1984: 201); it was the product of a "landed parliament" hit hard by immense harvests in 1813 and a poor quality harvest in 1814. Workers, ordinary people, and many commercial and industrial interests opposed the laws. The laws were revised in 1828: this meant that wheat could be imported free of duty if its price rose above 73 shillings per quarter, but it would have a stiff tariff if its price fell below 20 shillings per quarter (Rubinstein 1998: 77). In 1839 the Anti–Corn Law League was formed; in 1843 the Anti-League, which was pro–Corn Laws, was formed, with the support of the countryside and many Tories. The 1845 Irish potato famine was followed by the repeal of the Corn Laws in 1846.

transformation afoot and its displacement as a powerful political actor by the rising bourgeoisie, whom it could still force into disadvantageous positions through laws and decrees passed in Parliament, a body it could still control. Its displacement was further veiled by the ongoing weight of traditional economic institutions and activities, even though industrial capitalism was already the dominant form.

While the rise of industrial capitalism in England positioned the English bourgeoisie as emblematic of the formation of such a class, the other major powers had their own trajectories in this process. The fact of multiple trajectories is significant because they all eventually fed into the development of imperial geographies and thereby engraved national features and projects in the formation of the world scale. By the late 1800s, the national bourgeoisie in each country pursued the development of imperial geographies for trade and investment.

The rise of the bourgeoisie in France developed very differently from that of England. It remained a weak bourgeoisie even though the French Capetian kings had first created what was at its time the most accomplished version of the national sovereign state with its eventual weakening of the nobility. The French Revolution marked the defeat of the privileged—nobility and clergy—and in this regard benefited the capitalist bourgeoisie, the state bureaucrats (jurists, administrators, and local notables), and the peasantry, as well as the petty bourgeoisie of artisans and traders. After the fall of the empire, the bourgeoisie of bankers, manufacturers, and traders could no longer ally itself with the landed aristocracy, as had been the case in England.[63] An alliance with the nobility generally was out of the question given the politics of the revolution and the prevailing alignments of power. So the bourgeoisie had to depend on the peasants and petty bourgeoisie of artisans and traders in their conflicts with the industrial proletariat, as happened in 1830 and later. The binding elements of this alliance were ideas of freedom and democracy, as well as the right to and protection of private property. But this meant that in good part the condition for the alliance was the protection of the sectors that would have been destroyed by a rapid development of the capitalist bourgeoisie. It resulted in slow growth for industrial capitalism in France in the nineteenth century as protectionism, rather than free trade, and the slow use of new techniques were means to ensure the survival of agriculture and craft work.

The French case shows again how central a role the national state played in the rise of the bourgeoisie and national capitalism. After the 1789

---

[63] Beaud observes that eventually a large portion of the landed aristocracy "resigned itself to defeat, retiring to their estates or closing themselves up in their salons" (1981: 132n. 3).

revolution, the alliance between the king and the bourgeoisie was unsettled. The merchant wing of the industrial and banking bourgeoisie did not find support for development until Napoleon III. Sometimes this alliance failed, and sometimes it succeeded, as with the creation of banks during the 1830s and from 1850 to 1860; the development of railroads during the Second Empire; the digging of the Suez Canal; and the great urbanization projects inside France (Beaud 1981). But French society remained profoundly provincial, rural, and agricultural with much of the work still at the craft level. A good part of industrial and banking capitalism stayed provincial, and within each branch of industry there were agreements and consultations among key participants, leaving little room for market competition.

In Germany (more precisely Prussia, since a unified Germany did not arise until 1871), there was no bourgeois revolution. The 1848 movement and the consequent passing of a constitution by the king did not mark a major change in relations of production. Nor did it change the locus of political power, notwithstanding the Zollverein (customs union), which the merchants had already set up by then. The landed nobility retained political power, and the Prussian state remained dominated by feudal structures for a long time. Not until the state was led by Bismarck did the bourgeoisie rise to political domination, a development Marx and Engels (1949) saw as a revolution from above. Under Bismarck the state transformed itself from within, in the direction of capitalism. With the support of the state, capitalist industrialization, which had remained until then quite limited, intensified from the 1860s on. The bourgeoisie faced a working class that quickly became organized. Even when allied with the petty bourgeoisie, the bourgeoisie could not fight on two fronts—against both nobility and working class. It accepted the political domination of the coalition formed between the landed nobility and high-level state bureaucrats.

The United States at this point emerges as an interesting case, separately from the fact of its being on the way to becoming the major power in the world. Its development as an industrial capitalist political economy differed from that of France and Britain. It had no old feudal or agrarian society, as did Britain and France, and was originally a loose confederacy with a weak central state. It also lacked the medieval lineages of the legitimacy of a national sovereign that could become the source of law and authority.

One critical difference with England lies in the origins of the American political economy. While wealth in England had been grounded in landownership, the abundance of land made this system impractical in the colonies. Land distribution differed across the colonies, but it tended to benefit ordinary people. In New England, the Puritan colonies encouraged social cohesion by granting land to groups of settlers through townships and church congregations, which were then charged with its redistribution. Some of the colonies restricted the transfer of land and maintained common land: overall, however, they preferred individual ownership. Outside New England, a system of "head right" prevailed—land was awarded to each person immigrating to the colonies; some colonies offered this to indentured servants after their terms expired. Under this system, land could be purchased and sold, and many of the owners were formally required to remit a quitrent to the king or an overlord, although actual collection of these was spotty at best. This system lasted until the late seventeenth century.[64] After 1763, with the French and Indian War completed, the British Parliament sought to tighten imperial control over its colonies through stronger enforcement of the Navigation Acts and taxation. The closing of Boston Harbor in the early 1770s, which was seen as an assault on the economic liberty of Bostonians and an appropriation of private property without compensation or representation, shifted the colonies' relationship with England. In 1781 the Articles of Confederation were signed.

A second critical difference was a general disposition toward utility more than privilege. Thus, while generally enacting protections for private property, most colonies also enacted provisions requiring that land be productively used and developed. New England colonies frequently required either settlement or cultivation within a specified period of time. Ely (1992) provides a detailed yet concise overview of specific policies. Taxes were often levied to encourage development: the owner would have to derive revenue from the (improved) land in order to pay the tax. The risk of fire prompted the regulation of urban property. Throughout the eighteenth century, certain limited monopoly privileges were granted to improve transportation and develop technology. Many state constitutions in 1776–77 prohibited grants of monopoly and attempted to revise inheritance laws to prevent the maintenance of gigantic estates (through, for example, primogeniture). Before the drafting of the Constitution, each state had a slightly different articulation of property rights—some were embedded in a state's constitution, some in subsequent legislation. Generally, they included some form of protection of private property, some attempt to limit monopoly power, and some trade-off between eminent domain and compensation (Ely 1992: 30–32). A number of diverse conflicts and difficult problems led to growing support for the Constitutional Convention of 1787, which would more consistently protect property rights, regulate commerce, and restore public credit.

---

[64] It was most successful in Virginia, Maryland, and Pennsylvania; it was *completely* absent in New England, as residents resisted its feudal overtones (Ely 1992: 11ff.).

These conditions also created a different trajectory in the formation of the legal personae of the owner of production capital and the worker. To a large extent the making of a class of owners of productive capital, as distinct from inherited wealth or the agricultural economy of the South, was interwoven with the making of a strong federal state. I will argue that the latter was a critical variable in the possibility of securing vast concentrations of productive wealth given the strong distributive character of the earlier system.

CONSTRUCTING THE LEGALITY OF A DISADVANTAGED SUBJECT

One of the key dynamics at work in the shaping of industrial capitalism is that its formation entailed the establishment of a working class and the rise of a new ruling class. Each class was a mix of social groups, though eventually some of these became the majority or the marking group. Most, if not all, the groups within each class were, no matter how heterogeneous internally, on a particular side of the social conflicts of the epoch and the foundational economic relations taking shape. Yet the particular social, political, and legal trajectories through which the two groupings were constituted diverged significantly across countries even as key systemic features of the position of each were similar in an abstract sense.

My key analytic issue has received less attention than have the larger social and economic dynamics in the shaping of the working class. It is the active construction of the legal persona of the worker in juxtaposition to that of the owner of productive capital—that is to say, the class that ran the economy. We see in the laws and regulations the work of constructing distinct economic subjects/actors. There are rich debates about whether the law generally, particularly in the case of workers, is a derivative factor or can be constitutive (Bok 1970; Forbath 1991; Rogers 1990; Steinfeld 2001; Archer 1998). It is not my purpose here to engage, let alone settle, these debates. Rather, I want to focus on the law as one factor in shaping the disadvantage of workers, a factor sufficiently formalized and explicit as to render legible the work of constructing such a disadvantaged subject. Nor does this particular role of the law preclude the fact that the law was also used by workers and by third parties to claim rights for workers. What workers, their organizations, and political parties did with these laws varied depending on the conditions in their countries and the institutional channel through which this work proceeded. Where it was above all the Parliament in England, it was mostly the courts in the United States.

British legislation was clearly aimed at controlling workers. Engels (1892) and others at the time observed that the law and the actual conditions of workers had made the proletariat de facto slaves of the property-holding class, with the added advantage that employers could dismiss workers and need not be stuck with them, as was the case with slavery. Workers were subjected to severe regulations, repression by fines, wage reductions, or dismissal; unhealthy and unsafe workplaces; harsh work; and long workdays.[65] These conditions were the bases on which British industry developed in the nineteenth century. The relation between the emergent manufacturing working class and the owners of the factories was, at this point, a sort of primitive accumulation, where even minor profit differentials mattered and there were almost none of the intermediary structures that came later with the welfare state. By the mid-nineteenth century, the British industrial system was highly diversified and hence engendered a highly diversified working class. The previous system continued to exist through craftwork, homework, manufactories, and workhouses, as well as the mill system, which had appeared at the end of the eighteenth century. Handlooms remained dominant for cotton weaving until 1829–31. What did develop was the factory system. The emergence of the factory and putting-out systems signaled the emergence of a new logic. The latter was a new form of work in the home that put workers at a sharp disadvantage and engaged family labor to various extents; it gave employers full control over wage levels. In London in 1830, one-third of garments were produced through this system.

As had been the case with the Corn Laws, regulating factories became the site for playing out the opposing vested interests of agriculture-linked elites and manufacturing capitalists. A series of laws called the Factory Acts aimed to protect workers in key manufacturing sectors.[66] In general, Protectionist and

---

[65] Women and children were a large part of the workforce. In 1834 children under thirteen made up 13 percent of the workforce in the English cotton industry; 5 percent by 1850; and 14 percent in 1874.

[66] The manufacturing sector was quite diverse and included wool, silk, cotton, and flax spun or woven by steam or waterpower. Other sectors were knitwear, lace, printed fabric, bleachers, dyes, metal wares, pottery, and glass manufacture. And there was an agricultural and mining proletariat. The Factory Acts were passed to protect women and children, the more vulnerable workers, though this in turn engendered efforts among employers to limit these protections. The 1819 Cotton Factory Act prohibited child labor (under nine years old) in cotton factories and limited hours of work for ages nine to eighteen. The 1833 Factory Act required some schooling for children. The 1842 Mines Act prohibited girls, women, and boys under ten from working underground. The 1844 Factory Act limited the hours of work for children aged eight to thirteen and women in factories; a related bill mandated that the workday should begin at the same time every day (this was the first time Parliament regulated hours of work for adult males) and that clocks should be publicly visible, and it lowered the minimum working age from nine to eight (Rubinstein 1998: 80; Marx 1977: 394). In 1845, calico printing works were subjected to safety legislation (Rubinstein 1998: 80). The 1847 Factory Act-Ten Hours' Bill limited work for women and children to ten hours, and it de facto applied to men, since most factory work also required some child labor (McNeill 1986: 508).

Tory MPs were more likely to support factory legislation, while Radicals opposed the "improper" intrusion of the state (Rubinstein 1998: 80). The Tories' support was tied to their support for maintaining the Corn Laws: noting that most workers remained in agriculture, Tories argued that the best way to protect workers was to maintain agricultural protection, which would prevent the outflow of workers from the countryside to the city and avert high unemployment. There were other conflicts and alliances, often unrelated to concern for the actual conditions of workers, that steered the legislation.[67]

As English industrial capitalism accelerated, manufacturers sharpened their attempts to control workers. A supplementary compromise factory act was passed in August 1850, which lengthened the workday of women and children to ten and a half hours for the first five days of the week, and seven and a half hours on Saturday. Although England in 1848 was not marked by the sharp social uprisings taking place on the Continent, manufacturers used it as an excuse to clamp down on workers by eliminating meals at work, restoring night work for men, dismissing women and children, and so forth (Marx 1977: 398). This basically revived the "relay system" used by employers to evade the regulations by simply shifting young workers to another position in the factory (400–403). English courts had shown themselves to be unwilling to punish manufacturers for such practices; an 1850 decision by the Court of Exchequer ruled that these practices violated the spirit of the law but not its letter, effectively legalizing the practice. Throughout, class antagonism was continually flaring up, and factory conditions now varied widely across the country, depending on the sentiments of factory owners, enforcement of legislation, and other variables.

The traditional account of labor in this period identifies legal change as a type of natural, perhaps inevitable, outcome or as a change running parallel to the social and economic forces that shape a market economy.[68] Although English workers were "free" in the sense that they were not owned or bonded servants, the implementation of a formal apparatus for the control of workers and the possibility of the direct exercise of power by employers over workers make for a far more problematic account. One way into the bundle of issues is a focus on the rules that governed the treatment of British workers who breached their labor contracts in the nineteenth century. Steinfeld (2001) argues that the origins of what we currently call free labor (that is, the right to

---

[67] During this period the 1833 Emancipation Act was also passed, which abolished slavery or, rather, "administered freedom drop by drop" (Marx 1977: 392).

[68] In this account, workers were not free in the medieval period but gained legal freedoms in the late fourteenth and fifteenth centuries when Englishmen were allowed to work for wages. The law of the employer-employee was known as the law of "master and servant" for everyone except house servants and apprentices.

quit a job without penalty or other forms of pressure such as physical restraint or criminal punishment) did not emerge from market forces and the expansion of contractual social relations in the early nineteenth century, as is commonly assumed. Instead, he finds that "free waged labor" came out of "the restrictions placed on freedom of contract by the social and economic legislation adopted during the final quarter of the century" (10). Steinfeld uses court records, judicial opinions, parliamentary debates, and data about criminal and civil prosecutions of labor contract breaches between 1857 and 1873 to demonstrate that for much of the nineteenth century British workers were not free, in the sense of twenty-first-century notions of free labor.[69] If British workers left their employers before they completed their contracts, they faced a variety of nonpecuniary punishments including prison terms with hard labor and whipping.[70] For example, in 1860, 11,938 British workers were prosecuted for breach of contract, many of whom were coal miners and iron workers. A majority of these workers received criminal convictions. Steinfeld writes, "Of the 7,000-odd convicted, 1,699 served a sentence in the house of correction, 1,971 were fined, 3,380 received other punishments (wages abated and costs assessed, in all likelihood), and one person was ordered whipped" (2001: 81–81). The evidence shows a sharp expansion of penal sanctions in Britain between 1823 and the 1860s, indicating an increase in prosecutions during affluent moments in Britain's trade cycle. When unemployment was high, prosecutions tailed off, as happened between 1857 and 1873 though they stayed above 7,000 a year. Further penal sanctions also reached British workers indirectly through the threat of prosecution should the worker quit or refuse to comply with orders.

The timing of various repressive measures captures the accelerated and massive drive toward capital accumulation. The outlawing of trade unions and Jacobinal associations in the Combination Act (1799) coincided with the beginnings of the sharp expansion in the English economy (Rubinstein 1998: 20) and unintentionally brought these two groups into association (E. Thompson 1963: 500). The Combination Act that prohibited unions was repealed in 1824 but partly reinstated in 1825. The campaign in the 1820s to abolish the Combination Act found some support in Parliament (in Francis

---

[69] This is similar to arguments made by Steinfeld in his earlier work on the United States, in which he writes that the replacement of the unfree labor with free labor was not an inevitable by-product of eighteenth- or nineteenth-century capitalism. He argues instead that free labor resulted from struggles in which republicanism, the American Revolution, and the persistence of the increasingly odious institution of black slavery (1991: 137–46) impelled average American working men and women to act (123–27, 181).

[70] The ability of magistrates to penalize growing numbers of British workers derived from revisions of the Master and Servant Acts, which regulated the interactions between employers and employees.

Place and Joseph Hume, though Thompson qualifies this by arguing [517–18] that Place and Hume crushed more radical proposals) among those who argued that the act prevented the cooperation of workers and owners. The act's repeal in 1824 engendered a wave of strikes and riots, and a new parliamentary committee was set up to investigate the repeal. The new act in 1825 allowed "combination" only to discuss demands concerning wages and hours. Unionization was then not illegal as such, but it was still tightly regulated (Rubinstein 1998: 20ff.; E. Thompson 1963: 516ff.). Nevertheless, Thompson argues it was during these years (1799–1820) that union organization made its greatest advances (503–4). He further notes that sufficient legislation already existed to make any particular union activity illegal; the legislation was passed mainly to intimidate in sweepingly prohibiting *all* combination. He suggests that it was used much less against artisans than factory workers, although the threat of its use was probably common. Even in factories, however, the Combination Act was not often used to effect prosecution; rather, an older piece of legislation was often cited (504–7; Briggs 1959: 136). A "semi-legal" informal world of "combinations" (mutual benefit societies, trade clubs, and so on) was tolerated and created organizational infrastructure for the working class (E. Thompson 1963: 505, 508).

As a result of the 1825 act, if British workers did not give their employers one-month's notice of their intention to strike, they faced penal sanctions. The British historian D. C. Woods (1982) finds that 38 percent of criminal prosecutions in coal-mining districts between 1858 and 1875 were for unlawful strike actions rather than for unlawful quitting. If an employer signed a contract with a worker and then fired her, technically she could still collect wages on a "minimum" number of days of employment. Yet the Master and Servant Acts were rarely enforced against employers. For example, judges rarely forced employers to hire particular employees when trade was slow (Woods 1982: 165). Employers had "it both ways, criminally enforcing long agreements while at the same time disclaiming any responsibility for finding work during the term of the contract if fired or not hired" (107).

The developments in England launched a massive phase in the capitalist transformation of production. Production increased sharply, the system of wages was extended, the workforce grew, and workers' struggles multiplied. At the heart of this new type of economic logic were the mills and multiple technical inventions to promote increased production. Mills, typically housed in four-story brick buildings, employed hundreds of workers and were controlled like prisons. The exploited workers, many of whom were women and children, came from many different places and social groups, from farmers driven out of the countryside by enclosures to small artisans driven out of business by merchants. The working class that was taking shape was enormously diverse, but most workers were equally desperate.[71] This wide diversity of origins in the working class was constituted as the raw matter for the work process: its diversity was being reshaped by a particular type of logic. We see a parallel development today in the many different origins and statuses of the new workforces—immigrants, minoritized citizens, and various other marginalized groups, all coming together to constitute the labor force for particular types of work in large cities.

Just as the formation of the national state in the United States followed a distinct trajectory, so did the shaping of workers' disadvantage and the ensuing struggles by workers. In addition, there was no strong class-based political movement that could fight for workers' rights. As in England, employers used the state to formalize their advantage over workers, but instead of Parliament the United States had the courts. U.S. laws provided, as they continue to do, far fewer protections against abuse, injury, illness, and unemployment (e.g., Forbath 1991: chapters 1 and 5; Rogers 1990) than did European laws in response to workers' mobilization in the late 1800s and on. They covered, and continue to do so, a small share of all workers and fail to stipulate terms of employment that ensure basic protections (Bok 1971). While Europe's major powers saw the growth of labor organizations that took on broad class-based programs of reform and redistribution by the end of the nineteenth century, in the United States the American Federation of Labor rejected or avoided such broad programs (Forbath 1991; Bok 1971). Most of the scholarship explains this American difference or "exceptionalism" in terms of the conservatism and individualism of U.S. workers.[72] However, some scholars (Bok 1971) have seen the law and the courts, rather than workers' individualism, as critical in explaining U.S. workers' disadvantage. A few have consistently rejected the notion of American workers' "exceptionalism" (Katznelson and Zolberg 1986; Gutman 1976; Montgomery 1980; Sassen 1988, 1999), and lower rates of workers' organization than in European countries, notably France (Katznelson and Zolberg 1986).

Without reducing the weight of these diverse explanations, I want to isolate the one centered on the role of the law and its institutional orders

[71] Periods of major social transformation contain the possibility of major upheavals in people's lives and livelihoods, as well as a sharp increase in the level of desperation. The elimination of serfdom had a similar effect in Prussia. And, as I will argue later, the current formation of a highly mixed class of needed workers in major developed economies evinces similar patterns. One could use these features of the formation of a new workforce as an indicator of major transformations.

[72] There were other factors, such as the ethnic fragmentation of the American working class, that are often used to explain the failure to organize. For a critique of this factor, see Wilentz (1984). Further, the working classes in all the major European powers had immigrant workers in the 1800s (Sassen 1999), a fact that is not quite made part of "official" European history.

to see how the law has fed the construction of the disadvantage of workers
(Perlman 1928). For example, the U.S. government attacked the labor
movement so aggressively that by the end of the 1890s it had been seriously
weakened and, with few exceptions, opted for more moderate tactics. In Europe, by contrast, state attacks on workers had radicalized the large labor
unions. It was through the courts, including their policymaking, that the
U.S. state exercised this function, much more so than through legislative or
executive action (Bok 1971). Forbath (1991: chapter 3) documents how one
union was destroyed through the courts' outlawing sympathy strikes, ordering mass imprisonments, and putting armed force behind court decrees.[73]
Judges and courts played a critical role not just in judiciary action but also in
policy development, since the U.S. government throughout the nineteenth
century lacked a professional civil service, that is to say, a class of state workers that had tenure in the state bureaucracies and agencies, a key feature of
the major European states. The legal personae of the worker and of the
owner of productive capital were in good part established through a series of
major court decisions.

There is a specific American prehistory to these nineteenth-
century developments. Employment law in colonial America varied by location. But it was based on that of the Old World (Ray et al. 1999). The
prevalence of slavery meant that in the eighteenth century much of the labor force was not free; employers could be owners or masters who used slaves,
apprentices, and/or indentured servants.[74] Unlike British workers, roughly
after 1830 they generally experienced no civil or criminal penalties for labor

---

[73] Forbath observes (1991: 27) that the framers of the Constitution, concerned about
factionalisms, particularly the possibility of a factionalism of the poor that might lead to political
moves to forcefully redistribute wealth, placed matters of property and markets in a suprapolitical
realm of private right: these were then constituted as matters of law and not politics. I return to
these issues in the discussion of the constituting of the private and public domains (chapter 4).
From the perspective of contestation during the period of industrialization, the fact of a diffuse
federation made organization difficult, even if early on (by the 1830s) white men had the right to
vote: but "there was no unitary state to defend or transform" (Katznelson 1985: 273).

[74] In 1740 South Carolina declared slaves "to be chattels personal, in the hands of
their owners and possessors," and hence could be purchased, sold, inherited, taxed, or seized to
pay a master's debts (Ely 1992: 15). Although the law tended to distinguish between slaves and
other property—requiring the master to provide food and clothing, and forbidding him to kill or
overwork his slaves—enforcement was lax. Slave codes prohibited slaves from assembling, running away, owning goods or livestock, or using firearms; selling liquor to slaves was illegal, as was
teaching them to read and write. In the years before the Civil War, there was an expansion of
regulations on slave property that restricted the right of masters to free a slave, and slave patrols
could enter plantations without an owner's permission to punish slaves (Ely 1992: 61ff.). It was
not until 1808 that Congress prohibited the slave trade. In April 1862 slavery was abolished in
Washington, D.C.; in January 1863 the Emancipation Proclamation was passed; and in 1865 the
Thirteenth Amendment was ratified.

breaches.[75] This was due to the existence of chattel slavery in the United States and the vigorous efforts of Northern wage earners to abolish slavery—and any penal sanctions that evoked it—in Northern states where wages became common after 1820. The particular freedoms of American workers were not a result of capitalist market forces but reflected strong political and moral forces (such as the abolitionist movements of the North). Other legal historians discuss the persistence of coercion in the United States when free labor relations were supposed to be the rule of law. Writing about labor relations after the Civil War, Amy Dru Stanley (1998) notes that local laws against the poor worked to coerce transient individuals into the workforce, even though the Thirteenth Amendment to the Constitution abolished slavery. While American workers were free from penal sanctions (unlike British workers), they were coerced and regulated through a process called wage forfeiture. Under this practice, a worker who left a job before its completion would lose any unpaid wages to the employer. British judiciaries outlawed this practice, but in the United States employers used this practice as a method of controlling workers.

During the early nineteenth century, the traditional master-journeyman-apprentice system began to break down with increasing migration to cities and increasing division of labor in production. New journeymen found that they were competing for a decreasing number of traditional craft jobs and started forming organizations to advance their interests (Tomlins 1993: 112–14; Laurie 1997). Early labor organizers were typically attacked by employers through the courts under conspiracy charges drawn from English common law. The first such case was *Commonwealth v. Pullis* (1806, Philadelphia). The place of common law in the republic was already controversial; republicans wanted only legislatively enacted law to be binding and believed that the power of the police (administration of law) rested exclusively with the legislature and that just outcomes would emerge from a free market. Using the common law, the journeymen combinations (organizations) were seen as a conspiracy.

From 1806 to 1842, there were seventeen such trials. Judges typically handed down small fines, with threats of higher fines for repeat offenders; juries were typically composed of merchants and employers (Taylor and Witney

---

[75] Steinfeld (1991) also points out that while criminal penalties for employment breaches were not the norm in the United States, some American workers faced the same "unfree" labor environments as their British counterparts. Not all U.S. workers were free from penal sanctions after 1830. Steinfeld examines groups of workers who continued to face penal sanctions after 1830: sailors who were jailed if they quit; and Southern sharecroppers who faced punishments if they breached work agreements. He uses these (and other) examples to suggest that even in the comparatively free labor context of the United States, workers' actual freedoms were frequently at risk.

1992: 6–7; Tomlins 1993: 134). These cases tended to invoke the public welfare as a criterion for judging combinations: judges advocated common law as
the source of this welfare; radicals advocated the market. Through the 1820s
and into the 1830s, the emphasis shifted from forbidding combination as such
to the lawfulness of the means used and ends pursued (Tomlins 1993:
144–47). By the 1830s, conspiracy trials had become a flashpoint for working-
class discontent as workers became more aware of the decomposition of the
artisanal system (129, 153). Criminal charges and prosecutions were instrumental in breaking up work strikes, as most prosecutions led to conviction.
The last reported conspiracy prosecution was in 1842.[76]

The pertinent laws in the 1800s and early 1900s stated that the relationship between the American worker and her/his employer was simply a
matter of contract. This permeated the American legal landscape. Courts
conceptualized labor largely in terms of the right to contract, making it difficult for American workers to bargain for better work conditions. For example,
in a landmark case (*Lochner v. New York*), the U.S. Supreme Court ruled that
a New York state labor law—which regulated the number of hours a baker
could work—was unconstitutional because it violated an individual's fundamental right to engage in contracts.[77] The freedom to exchange labor was also

---

[76] This was an important case. In *Commonwealth v. Hunt*, 4 Met. (45 Mass.) 111
(1842), the Supreme Court of Massachusetts ruled that employers would have to show that
unions were pursuing unlawful ends or using unlawful means in order to secure a conviction
(Taylor and Witney 1992: 10; Tomlins 1993: 180); by dissolving the legal association between
unionism and conspiracy, membership in a union was no longer a crime in itself. Conspiracy
charges were still leveled against unions through about 1880 (Taylor and Witney 1992: 10). The
primary significance of *Commonwealth v. Hunt* was that it codified the application of conspiracy
charges; it basically summarized the content of decisions made over the prior decades (and hence
undercut accusations of judicial arbitrariness) (Tomlins 1993: 130, 215).

[77] In *Lochner v. New York* (1905) the Court threw out a statute restricting work in bak-
eries to ten hours a day or sixty hours per week because it violated the liberty of contract embodied
in the Fourteenth Amendment. The Court argued that long hours did not endanger the *health* of
workers; therefore, the New York legislation was intended to regulate labor relations, not protect
health. This decision embodied the laissez-faire libertarian outlook and provided the foundation
for stifling Progressive attempts at reforms in the states for the next thirty years (until the depression) (Ely 1992: 103). The Court remained open to cases where health and safety were obviously at
stake, for example, in mining and industrial accidents. Further, some restrictions in working hours
were allowed. For example, *Muller v. Oregon* (1908) allowed the limitation of working hours for
women in factories and laundries to ten hours per day, on the grounds of "special health needs"
(104). The Court struck down prohibitions of "yellow dog contracts," which stipulated that employees could not belong to a union, since these prohibitions would interfere in contracts (formal
equality as a screen for maintenance of inequality). Labor unsurprisingly saw this as confirmation of
anti-union bias in the courts (105). The courts were also reluctant to set minimum wages: *Adkins v.
Children's Hospital* (1923) overruled a D.C. statute establishing a minimum wage for women. Similarly, it struck down a Kansas compulsory wage arbitration system in *Charles Wolff Packing Company
v. Court of Industrial Relations of Kansas* (1923). Most of these decisions relied on contract logic.

part of the common law under the doctrine known as employment-at-will (Feinman 1976).

Because of the employment-at-will doctrine, many American workers did not receive remedy for workplace injuries. Many employers used defenses based on contract liberty to escape liability, including contributory negligence (the worker's actions contributed to the injury), assumption of risk (the worker assumed the risk of the danger he/she was engaged in), and the fellow-servant rule (Finkin, Goldman, and Summers 1989). The freedom to enter contracts also largely protected corporate employers to the detriment of American workers who assembled or organized to improve worker conditions (Forbath 1991).

Employers' use of labor injunctions as legal weapons was well established at the turn of the century. A court-issued labor injunction banned union activities (that is, picketing) during labor disputes. Injunctions also forbade individuals and groups from boycotting an employer. The injunction was an effective weapon through which those who violated the court order could be fined or sentenced to prison. In the 1870s, employers used the labor injunction to fight strike activity when it became prominent once again (particularly on the railroads). Courts recognized that individuals could withhold their own labor from employers, but they did not believe that individuals and groups could protest and intimidate other workers and customers. Courts used a theory that, no matter how peaceful, moral intimidation by workers and/or appealing to customers created hostile environments that interfered with employers' businesses. Conspiracy charges were becoming a less effective tool for employers as juries became more sympathetic to unions (both because there was more public support for unions and because workers were increasingly represented on juries). Employers began leaning more on injunctions against labor. The *Debs* (1895) case ruled this constitutional (Taylor and Witney 1992: 19ff.). This case originated in a dispute between the Pullman Car Company and the American Railway Union in 1894 over a wage cut and the dismissal of union leaders. When the strike failed, the union appealed to railroad companies to boycott Pullman cars; when the railroads refused, the strikes spread throughout the railroad industry. Since the railroads were involved in interstate commerce, an injunction was filed against the union.[78]

Employers also used antitrust laws to appeal to the courts to control the activity of labor unions. In *Loewe v. Lawlor*, the Supreme Court allowed

[78] By 1931, 1,845 injunctions were issued (Witte 1932: 234, as reported in Taylor and Witney 1992: 20). The *Debs* decision also upheld injunctions against people who might have aided workers in a labor dispute, that is to say, it applied to "all other people whomsoever" who were "interfering in any way whatsoever."

the Sherman Antitrust Act of 1890 to be enforced against unions that maintained unfair employer lists.[79] In an attempt to allow unions to organize without fear of antitrust suits, Congress passed the Clayton Act of 1914.[80] But
while under the Sherman Act only the *government* could file to obtain an injunction in an antitrust case, Clayton wound up being interpreted as extending this capacity to employers (Taylor and Witney 1992: 47). Since the 1840s
courts had fairly consistently been recognizing the right of unions to exist—
the question in courts had been whether their activities were "lawful." As
such, the Clayton Act did little good for labor, despite labor's initial enthusiasm and support for its passage. The Supreme Court narrowly interpreted the
Clayton Act and still granted an injunction to the manufacturers against the
unions in *Duplex Printing Press v. Deering* (1921). Unions had been working
with congressmen and supported Woodrow Wilson in the hope of getting legislation such as this passed, but when Wilson took office he tried to mend
fences with business and lost interest in the more radical possibilities embodied in the Clayton Act.

However, as industrial capitalism became an increasingly massive
process, the workforce of citizens and immigrants became a force to be reckoned with as well. Both in the major European powers and in the United
States, notwithstanding their different trajectories of labor organizing and of
employers' uses of the state to control workers, the 1900s saw significant
victories for workers' causes. In the United States, the New Deal and its

[79] The Sherman Antitrust Act declared illegal every contract or combination in restraint of trade among the states. Sherman was applied to unions as well: the clauses in the act
outlawing combination and targeting monopolists did not specifically *exclude* labor, so the Court
applied the act to unions (Taylor and Witney 1992: 37). The first application to a union came in
Louisiana in 1893; the Court found that the interruption of trade resulting from a strike constituted a restraint of trade, forbidden under the act (38). The Supreme Court declined to determine whether the act applied to unions in 1895 (*In Re Debs*), but found that it applied to unions
in the *Danbury Hatters* case (*Loewe v. Lawlor* 1908). In this case, the United Hatters brought
pressure on Loewe & Company by organizing a successful nationwide boycott; a circuit court
found for the union, but the Supreme Court reversed the decision. A second case in 1915—
Lawlor v. Loewe—ruled that damages could be recovered from the union and its membership.

[80] The Clayton Act (1914) was an attempt to outlaw specific types of competitive behavior that were thought to result in monopoly conditions (Fligstein 1990: 25), for example purchasing competitor's stock, predatory pricing, and tying unrelated products together. The
Supreme Court interpreted this act narrowly in four cases through the 1920s, and businesses
managed to maintain merger activity by purchasing assets prior to purchasing stock (Fligstein
1990: 27). In relation to labor (Taylor and Witney 1992: 45ff.), section 6 states that "the labor of
a human being is not a commodity or article of commerce. Nothing contained in the anti-trust
laws shall be construed to forbid the existence and operation of labor, agricultural, or horticul-
tural organizations, instituted for the purpose of mutual help . . . nor shall such organizations, or
the members thereof, be held or construed to be illegal combinations or conspiracies in restraint
of trade, under the anti-trust laws."

accompanying legislation created a revolution in American labor law. Many of the legal tools from the nineteenth century discussed above were changed. Eventually, employers' widespread use of labor injunctions resulted in the 1932 Norris-LaGuardia Anti-Injunction Act—an attempt to give workers more protections. Congress intended for the act to strengthen workers' rights to assemble and stop courts from prohibiting union organization, strikes, and assembly. Some courts remained hostile to workers' activities and continued issuing injunctions during labor disputes (A. Cox 2001: 17–51). In 1935, Congress passed the Wagner Act (currently known as the National Labor Relations Act [NLRA]), which gave workers the right to organize and engage in collective bargaining or other orchestrated activities; it also formed the National Labor Relations Board (NLRB) to prohibit employers' unfair labor practices and to require workers' compensation.

THE AMERICAN STATE: MAKING A NATIONAL SOVEREIGN OUT OF A CONFEDERATION

The United States emerges as an interesting case because it enters this phase of rapid capitalist industrialization as a federation with a weak central state and little politico-social and ideological infrastructure for implementing a strong central state. The other historical cases crucial to the development of industrial capitalism are marked by strong centralized states with powerful administrative bureaucracies. In principle, the United States could have shown us that another mode of organizing state power and administration could also have accommodated industrial capitalism and the modern state. While much of the attention in the scholarship on the American state in this period has focused on its emergence as a major power, my focus is on how this powerful central state evolved out of a loose confederation—eventually a federation—with extensive decentralized powers residing at local levels, with a culture of local self-government, and with strong notions of participatory democracy—all of it often represented as a laissez-faire political system that contrasts sharply with the history of major European states.[81] In contrast to the European configuration whereby the sovereign was the source of

---

[81] Beneath these general alignments lies a somewhat complex history. In 1781, the thirteen former colonies ratified the Articles of Confederation. The articles maintained that each of the thirteen states were sovereign and independent (article 2). There was no unified government, and the articles served more as a treaty. The confederated government did not have the power to set and collect taxes, provide a uniform currency, or regulate interstate or foreign commerce and trade.

authority and law, in the earlier American confederation and the later federation, the source of authority was common law, which meant the localities and
the citizenry.[82]

    This raises the question as to whether this decentralized state was
compatible with the development of industrial capitalism and its historically
associated formation of imperial geographies. Was there another way of doing
it in a New World that had not inherited medieval capabilities, such as centralized bureaucracies, or the elusive notion of sovereignty derived from the
earlier divinity of monarchs? The pre–Civil War United States in this regard
clearly represents a social infrastructure for an alternative concept of the
polity and of government. Three sectors came to provide the infrastructure
for its political economy: a rural society based on plantation slavery and cotton in the South; industrial capital in the Northeast; and family farming in
the Midwest. The first dominated what was at the time a confederate state apparatus since its formation. The industrial capitalist class we see emerge in
England and, albeit under different modalities, elsewhere in Europe only became dominant in the United States after the Civil War. The Civil War was
both an occasion for and a factor in the growth of industrial capitalism.[83]

    Nonetheless, it is important to recognize that what we might call the
American difference does not quite lie in the timing of the formation of a
strong central state. It was not until the late nineteenth century that many of
today's leading states, notably Germany and Italy, were established in their
modern unified forms. Further, the main institutions of property ownership
were formally modernized in the major capitalist states only as of this time.
The difference of the American case lies in the fact that its eventual modern
centralized state emerged out of a decentered polity with a powerful
ideational structure that provided the substantive rationality for this organization. It is at this juncture that we can see the American case as a natural
experiment. The victory of the northeastern industrial capitalist sector in

[82] For various reasons, the confederation was unable to accommodate critical emergent needs. While the independent states feared a strong central government, they recognized
that a central government had to have power to perform tasks that individual states were unable
to—particularly with respect to taxes and the regulation of trade and tariffs. A new, federal constitution was drafted in 1787 and went to the states for ratification. The debates that ensued in
each state between the Federalists (supporting the new central government) and the Antifeder-
alists (opposing the new central government) illuminate critical conjunctures in the history of
the United States. By 1788 the U.S. Constitution was ratified, and in 1789 the United States of
America was born.

[83] The Civil War and its aftermath brought power to the industrial Northeast, prevented the secession of the South, and contributed to the elimination of slavery, the economic
base of the landed upper class of the South. For a non-American perspective on this history, see
Debouzy (1972).

a context of a decentered political system and political culture could have evinced a different trajectory from that of the other major powers of the time.

The evolution of a powerful central state out of federated decentralization and traditions of self-government raises three issues. The first is the nature of the work of constructing a powerful central state in a context of rapid capitalist industrialization. There is a sort of embeddedness in that the need for centralized state power in capitalist industrialization has historically been deeply connected to the development of nationwide infrastructures: markets, interstate commerce, transport systems, contracts and guarantees for property, and so on. But this embedding entailed complex government work executed in interaction with often powerful localities. The second issue concerns a set of more elusive categories, particularly the reconstruction of sovereign authority given the pre–Civil War understanding of the relation between the law and sovereign authority. Third, the development of national capitalism in the major powers evolved as part of international, that is, imperial, frameworks set up by national states. The United States has a long, strong, and varied history of isolationisms in relation to European states, even when colonization dressed as manifest destiny was foundational to its formation. It might thus illuminate distinct aspects about this combination of national and international components. The interstate system emerging in a context of a world economy and several major rising powers in the late nineteenth century pushed toward convergence. Escaping the internationally pertinent framings prevalent at the time may not have been an option even for the United States.

Formally, the making of a strong central American government took place from 1877 (the year that marks the formal end of Reconstruction) to 1937 (the year of the formal implementation of the New Deal).[84] This entailed a radical shift from nineteenth-century traditions of self-government, local citizenship, and a weak central state to the development of a powerful federal government that accumulated significant new rights and old rights previously held by the states and localities. The capabilities entailed in this shift had been in the making for a long time. The strength of the central federal government had been repeatedly exercised by Congress and confirmed by the U.S. Supreme Court in two landmark cases, *McCulloch v. Maryland*

---

[84] There was never a constitutional amendment associated with Roosevelt's New Deal, but the U.S. Supreme Court held that a number of New Deal acts passed constitutional muster. For example, the Court discarded the doctrine of freedom of contract in order to uphold state minimum wage laws. It also approved the NLRA.

(1819) and *Gibbons v. Ogden* (1824).[85] Even following these cases, however, states still worked to advance their power under the states' rights doctrine. Eleven southern states wanted to preempt national government regulation of slavery and argued they had the right to secede. The defeat of the Southern Confederacy in the Civil War not only ended the debate over secession but also established that states could not "nullify" federal acts on a theory of (subnational) state sovereignty. As for Reconstruction, it did not necessarily mark a radical shift from a weak federal government to a strong one, but it did solidify and reaffirm the standing of the federal government. It was the process of admitting the former "rebel states" of the Civil War back into the Union (made possible by Congress through the Reconstruction Acts of 1867) that substituted military control for civilian governments in the ten southern states that initially refused to rejoin the Union. The Fourteenth Amendment (1868), which gave former black slaves national citizenship, and the Fifteenth Amendment (1870), which gave black men the right to vote, added to the weight of the federal government.

This period saw the establishment of basic governing institutions, the acquisition and distribution of new territory, the promotion of national and international commerce, the development of a powerful national defense and a formalized yet flexible national legal system, and the growth of aggressive policies of regulation, administration, and redistribution. This historical transformation has been called the "era of reform" (Hofstadter 1955), a response to industrialism (Hays 1957), "a search for order" (Wiebe 1967), and "federal centralization" (W. Thompson 1923). Its interpretation is dominated by notions of an exceptional American development, marked by the struggle of some state institutions to shape a strong welfare state being obstructed by others, notably the courts and the Supreme Court, which were beholden to the interests of big business. My concern is not to settle these debates but to use law-making as one critical dimension of the shift.

The role and uses of the law in building up this new central state, particularly the statecraft involved in the more foundational aspects of this shift, is important here. Lawmaking may at times have little to do with the underlying realities. Yet the radicalness of the historical shift meant that lawmaking had to become part of it and to some extent would have to reflect

---

[85] In *McCulloch*, the state of Maryland tried to tax the national bank. The Supreme Court ruled in favor of the national bank (federal government), thus reaffirming federal power. In *Gibbons*, the Court ruled that under the commerce clause of the Constitution, the federal government had the power to regulate commerce between states.

organizing notions about statehood and rights.[86] In the previous section I briefly examined how lawmaking served to construct distinct legal personae in the process of industrial capitalism, with a growing number of specific rights accumulating to property holders and few rights to workers. Further, struggles around the law and lawmaking illuminate broader social alignments, notably workers' struggles contesting the rights granted to employers (property owners) and the absence of workers' rights. Some uses of the law can create new capabilities.

Novak (1996) uses lawmaking in this period to contest what is still a prevalent interpretation about the formation of the American state. Much historical analysis has centered on particular phases of the Supreme Court, notably the early obstructions to Roosevelt's New Deal legislation.[87] But there is also a historiography that finds a majority of cases approved by the Supreme Court and a positive role for law. The much cited laissez-faire constitutional cases *E. C. Knight*, *In Re Debs*, and *Lochner v. New York* have fed this prevalent view of the judiciary as obstructing the formation of a strong central state, specifically a welfare state along social-democratic lines. Novak argues that there is a largely unstudied mass of laws concerning regulatory, administrative, corporation, utility, tax, eminent domain, policing, health, insurance, telecommunications, monetary, and fiscal issues that have played a crucial creative role in building the American liberal state.[88] Skowronek similarly emphasizes the power of nineteenth-century courts and parties: "The early American state maintained an integrated legal order on a continental scale; it fought wars, expropriated Indians, secured new territories, carried on relations with other states, and aided economic development" (1982: 19). My purpose here is not to argue that one or the other side of this interpretive divide is right but to use lawmaking heuristically to understand the making of a centralized state apparatus. Novak (1996) reexamines these various materials and finds that the law played a largely positive role in the construction of the American state and that courts, including the Supreme Court, upheld the vast majority of

[86] For instance, in the post–Civil War period we see in the United States the invention of a new legal conception of privacy, featuring a prominent concern for the protection of personality and personhood; we see the transformation of the notion of civil rights from a free person's guarantee to a corporate bill of rights to civil liberties to the social rights of the early American welfare state. According to Novak (1996), such rights were an indispensable part of the new balance struck in the pursuit of public order and the protection of private liberty by the American liberal state.

[87] A few decisions, notably *Lochner*, have dominated the interpretation of this period.

[88] See previous section in this in this chapter for a description of some of these cases.

decisions that were considered. Novak contests the Progressive interpretation of the law as obstructing the formation of a welfare state in the United States.[89]

While I see problems with some of the indicators Novak uses, I find his central concern with the recovery of lawmaking through the judiciary important. The European cases discussed in this and the preceding chapter all signal the critical role played by the law in transforming raw power into authority and in negotiating conflicting vested interests. "Law" played an important role in constructing authority and rights, two categories far more complex and elusive than the mere fact of the power to impose one's will. Even with strong coercive power, a ruler will need some sort of legitimation, even as the sources for the latter are not historically constant. This brings up another issue that is constitutive of statehood, one illuminated by the formation of a strong central state in the United States, to wit, the question of the source of law. The medieval lineage of the major European states contained an original source of legitimacy in the divinity of the monarch—itself derived from an earlier church-linked divinity—and thereby made sovereignty the source of law. But this did not hold for the American republic. A loose confederacy centered on local self-government lacked a sovereignty that could be the source of law. If anything, this early polity found in the law the source of its own legitimacy—in this case the preeminence and high regard held for common law. Constitutional law, which replaced the common law (Willrich 1998), can then be seen as the final authority on the legitimacy of state power, but not necessarily as the source of law.[90]

Perhaps because lawmaking was accommodating and enacting a major structural shift, many of the legal ideas of the period were put into practice

[89] The significance of constitutionalization for modern civil rights is well documented. But three other crucial elements of legal-constitutional development have been "comparatively neglected in histories of the late 19th century and early 20th" (Novak 1996: 266): legal positivism, administrative law, and federal police power. (See also W. Thompson 1923.)

[90] Charles Warren, actually a Progressive himself, was interested in why *Lochner*—one of the emblematic cases always cited in the Progressive literature to show how the Court obstructed the effort to build a social democratic welfare state—was an omnipresent citation in the Progressive critique of law and a key case for the argument that the Court had obstructed the making of law. He examined the constitutional fate of state regulatory legislation between 1887 and 1911. Warren found that of 560 Fourteenth Amendment cases, only three state laws relating to social justice were overturned (including *Lochner*), and thirty-four laws relating to private property were turned back, primarily on the grounds of taxation or eminent domain. An overwhelming majority of state regulatory laws in Warren's catalogue were upheld by the court, including state monopoly laws; anti-lottery laws; antitrust and corporate monopoly laws; liquor laws; food, game, and other inspection laws; laws pertaining to the regulation of banks and telegraph and insurance companies; cattle health and quarantine laws; laws pertaining to the regulation of business, as well as to water, gas, electric light, railroad (not interstate), and other public service corporations; segregation laws; and labor laws (Warren 1913: 695).

in twentieth-century economic and social policymaking. The financial and banking sectors capture some of this and reveal policymaking to be at the intersection of powerful vested interests and popular expectations; the history of the organization of these sectors is deeply connected with that of economic and political centralization. No matter how powerful the interests of key banking and financial sectors, customary and widespread normative notions about justice and localism continued to play a significant role (along with local vested interests) in the organization of these sectors even as the power of the central state grew and it could conceivably have imposed a new banking regime. The deep suspicions in the culture about centralization extended, not surprisingly, to banking and finance.[91] Thus banking in the United States remained largely decentralized, while the banking system in Britain became centralized with the Bank of England playing a central role in the political economy of the country. In contrast, in the United States there was a proliferation of local banks through the first half of the nineteenth century—a decentered system paralleling political decentralization and a weak central government.[92] There was a laissez-faire system of issuing banknotes, whereby each bank issued its own until about 1863 (Zelizer 1997). The first "central bank" in the United States, First Bank of the United States, was allowed to lapse in 1811, and the next one, the Second Bank, chartered in 1816, had its official status rescinded in 1836. It was only with New Deal legislation that an effective central bank was set up.

However, banks and capital markets began to play an important role in the rapidly growing U.S. economy.[93] As had happened in Europe's major powers, financial centralization grew in sectors where the United States was a leader: agricultural exports after the Civil War and industrial

[91] The foundational work of Burgess (1890), Willoughby (1896), Freund (1904), and Goodnow (1911) gives a sense of the character and scope of this legal revolution.

[92] During and immediately following the Industrial Revolution, banking in Britain and in the United States took place mostly through small banks, located close to the users of capital. Larger city banks and merchant banks also emerged, both as places where the smaller country banks could deposit some of their reserves or make loans and to service urban centers and interregional and international trade.

[93] The establishment of the national banking system with National Bank Act of 1863 was not meant to lead to bank concentration but was based on "free banking" principles, which basically meant that it was very easy to set up a little bank and most banking was unit banking—banks without branches. The number of commercial banks peaked at 30,000 in 1921, then steadily declined, and fell sharply after 1929. There were some large national banks but these were not allowed to set up branches until 1922. There were multiple constraints through state policy on intrastate branching, a condition that in one form or another remained in place until recently. In Europe banks rapidly consolidated as industrial and financial internationalization proceeded in the late nineteenth century.

production beginning in the 1880s. These and other conditions secured the consolidation of a small number of very powerful banks involved in economic circuits that differed sharply from those of the thousands of small banks. The late nineteenth and early twentieth centuries also saw the strengthening of the central government. In this period the U.S. financial system evolved and diversified, consisting of the older forms of "free banking" throughout the country, but also a developing securities market, the emergence of finance capital through large investment banks, and a stronger monetary and regulatory role for the federal government, culminating eventually with the establishment of a central bank.[94] Notwithstanding its multiple isolationisms, this period also saw a growing interpenetration of the U.S. economy and its financial markets with the world of international high finance, a factor pushing the United States toward international convergence in finance and state form.

The financial and banking system and the role of government in monetary policy brought with them political conflict in the late nineteenth century. Throughout there was strong populist suspicion of finance, as well as disagreements in various banking and financial sectors regarding the need for currency inflation in a context of increasing tensions from the international gold standard. Monetary reform became a major issue in Congress and in the 1912 presidential election, and it was one of the first concerns of Woodrow Wilson when he became president. In December 1913 Congress passed the Federal Reserve Act—a compromise between those who feared too much Wall Street control and those who feared too much federal government control, which meant banking regulation never approached the level of centralization typical in the major European powers (Sassen 2001: chapters 4 and 5).[95] In some ways, the development of the banking and financial sectors from

[94] The Civil War and its aftermath was also a key period in the development of securities markets, which complemented rather than competed with the commercial banking system. There were over two dozen exchanges below 14th Street. The New York Stock Exchange (one of several competing exchanges in Manhattan) had already developed the closed corporate character, which was to become the norm for a "self-regulating" market: traders would only trade with each other; exclude outsiders; and charge fixed rates for their services (Cerny 1996). Even during the period of rapid industrialization in the later nineteenth century, the securities markets were mainly the exclusive sphere of the traders themselves and of the large investments banks and commercial banks, which had developed in the urban centers, especially around Wall Street. The investment banks, besides trading government securities, were crucial middlemen in underwriting stocks and bonds for many of the huge new corporations dominating America, especially railroads and public utilities.

[95] The uneven rates among these elements were shaped by a series of booms and slumps, notably the Panic of 1907, eventually culminating in the 1929 crash (Cerny 1996; Beaud 1982: chapter 5).

a highly decentralized into a far more centralized system evokes the larger history of the state and the law.

At the heart of this evolution lies the old question of the legitimacy of the power of the state. The European states discussed in the preceding chapter secured legitimacy through various medieval capabilities, notably the posited divinity of the monarch and the fact of nations. These eventually also evolved into capabilities for developing statehood and imperial geographies. The reshaping of the central government in the United States and its growing accumulation of powers also raised the question of its relation to the law. What enabled it to function as a sovereign, specifically as the source of law? The formation of a centralized state entailed the unifying of the loose American federation into a union and a nation. The language of union and nation became critical.[96] With it came the need to downplay the original significance of compact, contract, states' rights, and, significantly, of constitution in the creation of state authority. Instead, legal and political discourse came to emphasize and defend the overriding prerogative of nation, union, and national government. In the post–Civil War period there was much concern about saving the union at all costs. Some posited that all antebellum efforts to derive the nature of sovereignty from constitutional standards were, in Hurd's (1881: 97) words, futile: sovereignty could not be an attribute of law, law flows from sovereignty; law becomes possible by the pre-existence of sovereignty.[97] This was all well captured later in Woodrow Wilson's declaration about law as the direct command of the sovereign.[98]

We see then, in this formative process of an American sovereign, a distinct road from a decentralized polity whose legitimacy derived from "law" to a centralized national state that became the source of law. This was a critical

[96] Administrative units like such as a central bank or the 1914 Federal Trade Commission were created during a wave of Progressive support for an expert-run administrative state. By putting nonpartisan experts in charge of the administration of domestic policy, the hope was to garner the advantages of the expertise and flexibility in the rational control of business activity (Ely 1992: 110) to put regulation above politics. The Court's consistent protection of contract and property led reformers to see the federal judiciary as an obstacle to reform. It was a semi-decentralized organization, with twelve regional federal banks. The federal government took greater control of the currency, reshaped the system of financial markets and institutions, and established a more complex regulatory system. It was only with the 1929 crash that the sector was fully reorganized.

[97] Legal and constitutional scholars first began to rethink the nature of the American nation-state during the Civil War. The immediate post–Civil War saw a flood of treatises that drew on and carried forward the nationalist oratory of Webster and Lincoln, advocating a strong nationalist theory of the state and a constitutional defense of the Union (Novak 1996).

[98] Charles Merriam describes this "new national school" as one that disregarded the doctrine of the social contract and emphasized the "instinctive forces whose action and interaction produces a state" (1915: 296).

question in a broad debate about the legal personality and authority of groups, where the state is the highest form of legal personality (Gierke 1887; Maitland 1968; Laski 1917). The crisis of conceptions of nationhood produced by the Civil War became the basis of a new political science and jurisprudence that repositioned the state, sovereignty, and public law away from the nineteenth century's emphasis on local authority, self-government, and participatory democracy (Novak 1996). The focus shifted to the nation-state and its sovereign powers (Willoughby 1896: 180).[99] Willoughby saw state sovereignty linked to a conception of "law as wholly a product of the State's will." From the 1870s on, American courts produced legal doctrine to accommodate the need for greater federal regulation. Notwithstanding multiple sources of resistance, federal constitutional law displaced local common law as the preeminent law in post–Civil War America. The postwar constitutional amendments further made law national: what had been the domain of local, state, and common law interpretations became the domain of the U.S. Supreme Court.[100] What we see in the making is a type of modern state that could not function within the framings of the common law tradition. Through its jurisprudence the Court established foundational criteria that were to hold for the whole country—notably boundaries between private and public right and state and federal power. There were particular changes in legal doctrine and practice underlying the transformation of American public law.[101] These innovations captured a fundamental rethinking of the nature of the state and state power in late nineteenth- and early twentieth-century America.[102]

A critical component of the expanded powers of the federal government was public administration. What the Capetian kings developed in the Late Middle Ages America got to in the late nineteenth century. The rise of the administrative state in the United States in the early twentieth century

---

[99] Woodrow Wilson (1890: 634–35) defines law as the command of an authorized public organ, acting within the sphere of its competence. What organs are authorized and the sphere of their competence are determined by the organizing law of the state; this law is the direct command of the sovereign.

[100] According to Willoughby, "however confederate in character the Union may have been at the time of its creation, the transformation to a Federal State was effected" (1896: 33). The foundation of that state was not a compact or natural rights or constitutional limitations, but sovereignty—the source of all law, but not itself founded upon law.

[101] For instance, the governments police power was constitutionalized in the late nineteenth and early twentieth centuries with the national reframing of old regulatory issues through hundreds of Supreme Court cases.

[102] Novak (1996) emphasizes four sets of jurisprudential innovations: a) the new legal definitions of state and sovereignty represented in the work of Burgess (1890); b) new conceptions of constitutional and positive law captured in the work of Willoughby (1896); c) expansion of legislation and police power symbolized by the work of Freund (1904); and d) invention of a centralizing administrative law as articulated by Goodnow (1911).

has received much attention in the scholarship (Novak 1996; W. Thompson 1923; Rohr 1986; Cook 1996; Stillman 1998). Critical in turn to the rise of the administrative state and the shift from nineteenth-century notions was, first, a reconceptualization of the relation of officeholding and self-government and, second, the problem of the constitutional separation of powers (Goodnow 1911). Like the common law generally, nineteenth-century conceptions of the legal nature of officeholding and administration assumed general continuity between ruler and ruled, officeholder and citizen, all implied in the nature of local self-government (Sandel 1996). In contrast, modern administrative law and theory distinguishes the professional officeholders from the citizens as political subjects. The constitutional doctrine of the separation of powers—in contrast to nineteenth-century conceptions of local self-government—called for a balance of powers among executive, legislative, and judicial branches, and between the federal government and the states. This did not facilitate the effort to centralize administrative power in the executive branch given resistance from the other branches of the federal government and from states and localities. Goodnow (1911) criticized the tendency to emphasize the rights of states and individuals for resulting in a constitutional tradition that does not grant the federal government powers that it ought to have the constitutional power to exercise.[103] Further, Goodnow called for a centralized and professional bureaucratic corps insulated from popular politics,[104] a notion that was, again, incompatible with nineteenth-century notions of local self-government. We see here, then, the remaking of the nineteenth-century articulation among the state and the people.

The United States came to have a central state with the sovereign authority to make laws and the administrative right and capability to govern the economy and society. For some, for example, Arnold Paul, the legal developments that were launched in the late nineteenth century were a "massive judicial entry into the socioeconomic scene . . . effecting a conservative oriented revolution in the name of concentrated private property" (1960: 69–70; Harris and Milkis 1996). Others argue that these developments eventually enabled the public goods orientation of the New Deal, making social

---

[103] So-called commonwealth historians have established the active role of the nineteenth-century state through law in establishing, promoting, and regulating the nation's socioeconomic infrastructure through public works, subsidies, corporate charters, public land policies, eminent domain, mixed enterprises, and police power (Handlin and Handlin 1947; Hartz 1948).

[104] In *Social Reform and the Constitution* (1911), Goodnow attempted to create jurisprudential room for the expansion of administrative power through a critique of an overly rigid constitutional understanding of federalism and the separation of powers. He called on courts to continue to "abandon certainly the strict application of the principle of the separation of powers whenever the demand for administrative efficiency would seem to make such action desirable" (1911: 11, 221).

welfare the object of a national administration increasingly committed to guaranteeing social rights (Novak 1996). What I want to extricate from these conflicting perspectives is the multivalence of this massive administrative capacity, a subject I return to later in the book.

HYPERNATIONALISM AND IMPERIALISM

The late nineteenth century, more than any preceding one, makes legible the fact that the world scale at the time was largely constituted through the projection of national capitalisms onto foreign geographic areas. Colonization and foreign trade remained crucial components in the process of building national capitalism. Indeed, they expanded at various times from the second half of the nineteenth century into the twentieth century. With each major power aiming at exclusive control over its dominions, intercapitalist rivalries strengthened. As the four major European powers developed and their national capitalisms grew so did the chances for intercapitalist wars. Rivalries and wars in turn stimulated further wars, which in turn stimulated nationalism. The United States followed a different trajectory, but only to the extent that its imperial geography did not engage intra-European rivalries. At the time, U.S. interventions in Hawaii, Puerto Rico, Samoa, the Philippines, and Panama shaped a distinct American imperial geography.

A second feature of the late nineteenth century was that national states began to develop various forms of international economic coordination, producing many agreements and launching various international codes. The internationalization of capital in the nineteenth century increasingly took place inside an emerging interstate system; it was not then, as it is not today, a purely economic process. A key to its shaping was the internationalization of a framework of state structures, which guaranteed the internationalized ownership of capital mostly through the legal persona of the corporation. Although the framework's primary unit was the territorially defined state, the international system was not merely an aggregation of compartmentalized units but a network of loose and overlapping jurisdictions (Picciotto and Mayne 1999).

Thus the world scale in the late nineteenth century, while still led by Britain, evinces several key differences with the preceding period marked by absolute British domination. There was domination, overt annexation, and colonization. But under capitalism economic competition and cooperation assumed a far more foundational role than it had before. This led to the rapid development of interstate agreements as well as a kind of convergence, driven largely by private interests, in some aspects of national corporate law and regulations. The world scale of this period was marked by a mix of separate imperial geographies being built by the major powers and the growth of interstate coordination. We see the emergence of nationally based but internationally coordinated corporate capitalisms. There were, then, strong parallels with the contemporary global scale—a fact that raises the analytical ante for my argument about constitutive differences between that period and today.[105]

A) NATIONAL EMPIRES AND INTERNATIONAL CONVERGENCE.

In the late 1800s and early 1900s a few national capitalisms accounted for much of the world-scale economy. The century that ran from 1780 to 1880, the first world scale of industrial capitalism, saw four countries (Britain, France, Germany, and the United States) account for between three-fifths and two-thirds of the world's industrial production. At this time the new capitalisms of Germany and the United States experienced the types of growth that allowed them to prevail over the old capitalisms of Britain and France. According to some interpretations (e.g., Beaud 1981: 123), Britain's decline began in the first third of the nineteenth century, even though in absolute terms, Britain kept growing. But the deep structures of capitalism had changed.

The great depression of the nineteenth century (1873–95) marked the beginning of a period with several crises interspersed with short periods of prosperity that lasted until 1914 (Suter 1992). It was a period of accelerated industrialization, modernization, the "development of underdevelopment" (A. Frank 1966), as well as the multiplication of national imperialisms (Hobsbawm 1975; 1977). The expanding imperial geographies of the major powers brought an expanded mobilization of dominated people into processes of capitalist production. This mix of national and imperial dynamics rested on the increased exploitation of native and foreign workers at home, and on the domination of peoples in colonized territories (Sassen 1988: chapters 1 and 2; 1999: chapters 5 and 6). In this period two crucial issues were the strengthening of the working class and the growing rivalries among different national capitalisms, with the rise of German and U.S. capitalism confronting Britain's hitherto undisputed dominance.[106] From 1880 onward the working

---

[105] I return to this issue in chapter 4 in the discussion of the growth of executive power since the 1980s, which parallels some of these issues though in a radically transformed context—the deregulation and privatization of public functions and the associated power this brings to specialized regulatory agencies in the executive.

[106] During the first half of the nineteenth century, Britain found its main partners for exports and investments in Europe and then in America. Britain also benefited from the industrializing of these countries, and sold engines, machines, and other such goods to them.

classes in the major countries strived for certain rights and variously succeeded in getting new social legislation. It was the beginning of a new phase
of capitalism, marked by declining profitability and sharp competition in the
old sectors of the first industrialization, resistance to workers' demands, and
multiple pressures to remain competitive.[107]

The different meaning of these crises for each of the major powers
suggests the extent to which this period of crises in a vastly expanded and diversified world scale was rooted in the development of national economies. For
Britain the prolonged period of crisis signaled the waning of a once dominant
form of capitalism. In the United States and Germany the crises arose partly
out of the rapid growth of new leading sectors: railroads, steel, coal, and naval
construction. In 1871, and even in 1880, Britain produced more coal than the
United States and Germany together. But by the end of the century they were
beginning to surpass Britain. While the most conspicuous indications of each
of these crises occurred either on stock exchanges or among banks, detailed
historiography suggests these crises were really rooted in more fundamental
economic and social conditions. Beaud (1981: 119) argues that it is a mistake
to analyze them separately from these deeper conditions.

A fundamental transformation of capitalism had begun: concentration and centralization of industrial capital, formation of trusts and national
monopolies, and expansion on a worldwide scale for all the leading capitalisms
by means of trade and capital export, multinational groups, finance capital,
and colonization. As exports increased from capitalist countries, international
competition became even more severe, leading to similar reactions by the major powers. Protective tariffs were imposed by Germany in 1879 and again in
1902; in the United States in 1857; and in France in 1892, 1907, and 1910.
The exception was Britain, whose strength lay in its preeminence in open
world markets—at least in some sectors. Protective tariffs were followed by
cartels and trade agreements inside countries. These were particularly numer-
ous and well organized in Germany but certainly present in the other countries
as well. In the United States, a variety of such internal agreements were made
in several sectors, especially railroads, gunpowder, tobacco, and oil.

In this period we see a form of "regulated capitalism," and the differences among the main capital countries were determined by their historical
characteristics. With its strong state and banking system, Germany favored
state-sanctioned or state-supported cartels; Britain's liberal heritage rested on
informal controls by both the state and "public opinion." In the United States a
new form of corporate liberalism developed, initially coalescing around private

---

[107] While the right to strike existed, it was increasingly not recognized. Further, there
were attempts to increase control over workers.

bodies such as the National Civic Federation and eventually leading to the establishment of the great regulatory commissions (Kolko 1988; Weinstein 1968; Sklar 1988). The cartels and conglomerates were often international.

Part of the solution to the multiple crises of this period was the expansion of capitalism on a world scale. Although the major contradictions leading to the great crisis operated at the national level, they intensified the search for foreign outlets for goods and investment.[108] In this process a second powerful wave of colonization took place, which was accompanied by rivalries, conflicts, and wars.[109] The moral economy was centered in the notion of "civilization" and/or religion, as well as certitude of the superiority of Western culture. Yet when "necessary," whole populations were massacred. Alongside the protectionisms described above, there was a sharp rise in exports further signaling the complex national-global interactions of the period. In Germany exports rose fourfold in 1875–1913 and fivefold in the United States. These growth rates were much higher than those of Britain, even though in absolute figures British exports were very large and represented a high share of its national production of goods. Among the key destinations for all these exports were the new countries that were industrializing, urbanizing, and equipping themselves.[110] This in turn sharpened the rivalries among the major national capitalisms and raised the ante in terms of the degree of risk and the possibility for profit. It also increased the competition between national and foreign capital. The complexity and financial character of investments at the time was yet another feature of the world economy that evinces strong parallels with today's global economy.[111] Capital was exported and overseas holdings and affiliates were created.[112] Further, the structure of exports and imports

---

[108] The same fundamental crisis as present in each of these crises: a mix of conditions leading to declines in profitability and difficulties in profit realization, which in turn led to stiffening competition and increasingly precarious positions of companies in any sector. At that point a crisis can be triggered by anything: a stock exchange rumor, a lost market, or a company or bank discontinuing payment, precipitating an uncontrollable chain reaction (Beaud 1981; Suter 1992).

[109] To which some added the export of unemployment; thus Cecil Rhodes proclaimed that moving "our unemployed to the colonies is good for everybody."

[110] Much of this was represented as good for the national economy and good for the dominated peoples. There is a parallel here in the form, though not in the content, with how neoliberal policy has represented its benefits today.

[111] Britain reoriented its investments partly to Latin America and the Commonwealth. The United States mostly exported and invested in the Americas, particularly Canada, Mexico, and Cuba.

[112] Finance capital became a major factor at this time (Arrighi 1994; Suter 1992). For Hilferding, finance capital is the unification of industrial, trading, and banking capital, under the direction of high finance. Thus it obliterates the specific character of capital and makes capital a unitary power (1981: 111–38). Hilferding sees imperialism as necessarily linked with finance capital; Bukharin and Hilferding both argue that the policy of finance capital is imperialism. (See Arrighi 1994 for a variety of arguments on finance capital.)

of capital underscored the extent to which the major powers were key sources and destinations, not unlike some of the features of today's global economy. Yet the orientation was toward the building of national capitalism pointing to a different organizing logic. Foreign assets assumed many different forms: subscriptions to public loans (that is, treasuries, government bonds); government loans; loans to banks and firms; shares (equities) in the various sectors publicly listed; and setting up affiliates in the case of large conglomerates and trusts.[113]

Expansionism brought rivalries but also the need for alliances and international coordination, as well as the growth of various kinds of internationalism. There were deep structural tendencies in this mix of national and international trends. All the major powers saw sharp capital concentration in their economies, which in turn led to another type of structural convergence: mass mobilization of workers. The process of capital concentration and centralization was not smooth or orderly. Attempts to control labor's power on a large scale were contested by new forms of labor organization (mass unions and socialist, anarchist, or Marxist political parties). The concentration of capital also led to a series of international debates about the growth of big business and cartels. The greatest concern was in the United States, where the process of concentration had started first and strongest after the Civil War and had led to populist agitation against the "trusts" and to the passing of antitrust legislation. The German imperial government also issued a report on cartels (Fennema 1982: 11–20). But both public pressures and the legal restrictions on conglomerates simply led to more outright mergers that bypassed alliances and cartels. The next section examines the variety of internationalisms arising from these synergies and tensions.

B) INTERIMPERIAL COORDINATION.

One of the key features of this period, in contrast to earlier phases of the world scale, was an emerging orientation toward interstate coordination through both national legislation and international agreements. In terms of

[113] The export of capital assumed a growing importance at the end of the nineteenth century (Suter 1992: part 2; Beaud 1981: chapter 4). British foreign investment flows doubled from 1880–84 to 1890–94, and quadrupled between 1890–94 and 1910–13; Germany's doubled from 1883 to 1893, and doubled again from 1893 to 1914; France's tripled from 1880 to 1914. Together these three countries represented over three-fourths of the capital invested abroad in 1914: Britain, 43 percent; France, 20 percent; Germany, 13 percent; the United States, 7 percent. Europe received 27 percent of all FDI; North America was next with 24 percent; Latin America, 19 percent; Asia, 16 percent; Africa, 9 percent; Oceania, 5 percent.

national legislation, there were several ways of achieving the types of conver-gence needed for the internationalization of capital in a context of multiple dominant powers. The English Companies Act of 1862, the French Loi sur les Sociétés of 1867, and the German Aktiensrechtsnovelle of 1870, while spe-cific to each country, facilitated the internationalization of capital. The devel-opment of this legislation depended to a great extent on the means devised by entrepreneurs and their advisors (Picciotto and Mayne 1999).[114] The govern-ments of these countries did not resist international competitive pressures; they could, in principle, have refused to authorize some of the options devel-oped in these regulations for firms, such as the possibility of one-person com-panies or corporate subsidiary networks. The growth of international cartels was another national condition that often required state backing and states acting in concert, or even states acting within a private or public interna-tional organization.[115] This sort of convergence in national economic legisla-tion was also furthered by the export of capitalist legal systems through colo-nization and military domination. Finally, we see the ascendance of a norm for "modernization" centered on the legal systems being developed in the major capitalist countries and their partial adoption by countries seeking to modern-ize. The case of Meiji Japan stands out, but we also see this in Latin America.

In terms of international economic coordination, we see the develop-ment of agreements and the formation of new international private and public organizations. All played a significant role in coordinating the development of a regulatory framework for corporate capital and its enforcement. Crossborder infrastructures for world markets and investments, such as transport and com-munications, produced a range of international organisms: the International Telegraph Union of 1865, the Universal Postal Union of 1875, and the Inter-national Meteorological Organization of 1878 (Hobsbawm 1975: chapter 3). "Nevertheless international standardization and unification . . . remained fee-ble and partial" (1975: 66). One important agreement in the context of capital internationalization was the Paris Convention of 1883 and the Union of States for the Protection of Industrial Property (Noble 1977).[116] The principles estab-lished in the convention would govern the debates over international control

---

[114] It is worth noting the network of affiliates of major firms at the time (Beaud 1982).

[115] Although the legal framework for incorporation played a small role in the early pe-riod of capitalist industrialization, it provided the basis for the institutionalization of corporate ownership in the form of giant enterprises based in the main capitalist states that developed in the period 1885–1914.

[116] Notwithstanding the heightened nationalism preceding World War I, by 1914 there were 114 international cartels, including 29 in coal production and metallurgy, 19 in chem-ical industries, and 18 in transportation.

of technology well into the twentieth century.[117] One example of international state coordination was the Permanent Sugar Commission of 1902, which restructured subsidized sugar-beet production in favor of sugarcane producers.[118]

The emergence of a nationally based but internationally coordinated corporate capitalism raised important questions for the many popular movements of this period, further feeding the internationalism of the time. Notable here is the much debated analysis of Kautsky that international economic cartelization could lead to international political cartelization and international class struggles. The fact that this appeared right before World War I, a deeply nationalist war, easily led to the flat dismissal of Kautsky's thesis by Lenin, among others. (But it does resonate with current developments of supranational systems and their enabling a variety of political transnationalisms.) Many at the time saw the need and possibility for an international working-class alliance to destroy all capitalist states and resisted class alliances inside nations aimed at gaining state power at the national level.[119] The historical record does suggest that Lenin's analysis was closer to the truth[120] but that Kautsky's might be closer to today's reality. The dominant politics at the time was something along the lines of controlled capitalism. It was nation-based and protectionist—but within an international framework—and based on state support for or involvement in the extensive network of international cartels with the purpose of regulating them. Indeed, these

[117] An international movement for the modernization and harmonization of intellectual property laws emerged. Stimulated early on by Prince Albert at the Great Exposition of 1851, it was strengthened by the wave of international interest in scientific innovation and in using science to pursue some of the interests of corporate capital (Noble 1977). This culminated in a decade of negotiations and disputes.

[118] This meant that the large corporations of dominant powers controlled the markets, whereas beet production was more likely to be in the hands of small local producers.

[119] World War I was devastating to the internationalism of these movements. It exposed the international contradictions of social democracy, particularly the bureaucratization of its institutions and the division over the dilemmas of social reform versus revolution. In becoming national and orienting its efforts toward demanding protections and entitlements from the national state, social democracy made a trade-off between accepting capitalism and getting some security. World War I was predicated on hypernationalisms; it nationalized struggles that might once have been internationalist. Gaining control over the national state became critical.

[120] Lenin's well-known critique (following Bukharin) was that the growth of firms and links among them was much denser inside countries than between countries, making international political cartelization unlikely and hence underscoring the need for national struggles. Lenin further developed his thesis by emphasizing that monopoly did not preclude competition; if competition were regulated, it would lead to the decay of many of the monopolies. Lenin argued that capitalist alliances were unstable because the system could not ensure an even development among the various major sectors (banking, trusts, different branches of industry, etc.). Hence uneven development and the unstable alliances it entails create different political conditions within states; there is no common political condition across states that might enable political cartelization among the working classes of these countries. For Lenin, then, national political struggles were crucial.

extensive networks rather than protectionism held back the growth of transnational corporations in the 1930s (Picciotto and Mayne 1999). Finally, the integration of labor into the state through social legislation in all the major powers was not a purely national process; it entailed the interaction of national and international processes.

The expansionism of this era did bring alliances, but they were against a background of nationalisms of all sorts. International fairs and expositions proliferated, but they were about nation building. At the same time expansionism brought with it a renewed role of the state through social legislation, expanded public works projects, territorial expansion, and militarism. Military spending increased, feeding the industrialization of the major capitalist countries. Beginning in the twentieth century a "new capitalism"—called imperialism by many—emerged. Hobson (1938) characterized the new imperialism by the ascendance of multiple imperialisms and hence competition, all in the name of national aggrandizement and commercial gain, and, second, by the dominance of financial over mercantile interests. For Hilferding (1981: 142), among others, the ever-increasing power and "greatness" of the state was a key dynamic for subordinating individual interests to a higher general interest. Something crucial was thereby achieved: the joining of a nation that stands outside of or separates from the state, and the state. The national idea becomes the driving force of politics. Class antagonisms disappear and are transcended in the service of the collectivity. The common action of the nation, united by a common goal of national greatness, replaces class struggle.

This is one way of explaining why the leadership of major labor unions failed in boycotting the nationalist wars of their governments, which meant going to war against the working classes from other countries. Nationalism trumped internationalism, securing the national capitalist project and destroying the internationalist working-class project.[121] The imperial expansion of national capitalisms at the turn of the century in a context of international capitalist rivalries, competition, frictions and confrontation, and the feeding of patriotisms all combined to produce World War I, which killed millions of people, mostly from the urban and rural working classes.[122]

---

[121] For the nonrevolutionary left, which argued that political power was to be obtained through parliaments, a focus on the national state was inevitable. A key objective became the nationalizing of major firms as a way to develop a social democratic state. The extensive involvement of states in industry through direct price-fixing and control of outputs taking place in all major countries during the war was seen as a step toward full nationalization.

[122] There is a vast historiography examining the causes of World War I. My key concern here is the mix of international and national developments that may show World War I to be about nation building even as the international system developed. Elsewhere I have examined

In sum, the hypernational era that took off in the late 1800s and continued for much of the 1900s was a complex outcome of multiple dynamics. But perhaps the key one was the building of national capitalisms in a world of major powers that both competed and interacted in an emergent twentieth-century world economy. The various colonizing efforts took place within the frame of the domestic and imperial expansion of national capitalisms. The economic internationalism of cartels and markets, backed by interstate coordination, was geared toward building national capitalisms. In many ways the Keynesianism of the 1930s that was to come functioned as an enlightened version of nationalism. Its key features were a genuine effort to recognize the claims of national economic actors, including national workforces and populations, from whence came the rights granted to workers and the entitlements granted to consumers through investments in national collective consumption. The combination of conditions at the turn of the century launched what would be the greatest period of systemic nation building over the next seventy years. This period would see a variety of internationalisms in the capitalist world, but they were primarily geared toward national capitalism.

It is from within this thick, complex, highly formalized national context, marked by strong cultural formations, that the processes of denationalization I examine in part 2 began to take shape in the late twentieth century. The nationalism centered on imperial geographies is the background for arguing that the current global economy represents a starkly different project. Emerging in the late 1800s and growing through much of the twentieth century, it stands in sharp contrast to the current global phase, where intercapitalist rivalries are addressed in the economic rather than military domain, and through increasingly formalized public and private institutional mechanisms. Political nationalism may still prevail rhetorically and make these deep structural transformations illegible. But it needs to be distinguished from structural tendencies that make international competition today function primarily as a mechanism for denationalizing capital, while in the earlier phases it functioned as a logic for strengthening national capital and developing political nationalism.

---

the period surrounding World War I from the perspective of actions by states and international organs toward displaced people, refugees, and migrants (1999: chapter 4; for the best historical analysis of this aspect at the time I am aware of, see Marrus [1985]). This particular angle into the history of this period also confirms the picture of national governments and economic actors in the business of nation building; even when engaged in developing international systems to govern the flow of refugees and displaced people, the purpose was to protect nation-states.

PART TWO • *DISASSEMBLING THE NATIONAL*

FOUNDATIONAL changes in the organization of territory, authority, and rights are one critical element in forming the new organizing logic that was to take us into the global age launched in the 1980s. To explore this thesis, I use the state, the global economy, and citizenship for in-depth analyses of, respectively, authority, territory, and rights. The state is the most complex and developed instance of authority. Citizenship is such an instance for rights. Exploring the question of foundational change in the organization of territory requires an additional analytic operation, as territory is deeply imbricated with both authority and rights in the case of the modern national state. I use the global economy, especially its electronic components, as a counterfactual in that it can be understood to test the limits of the state's territorial authority. Today's global economy is constituted through an increasingly institutionalized space for operations that is both electronic and territorial, and simultaneously supra-, inter-, and subnational, thereby evincing multiple types of territorial insertions. Using this space for global operations as a heuristic for understanding changes in the organization of territory illuminates both the limits of state authority over its territory and the fact of necessary interactions of global economic operations and territory. In brief, although territory, authority, and rights are interdependent, their analytical disaggregation helps illuminate the thesis of the emergence of a new organizing logic within which old capabilities are repositioned and new ones shaped.

The earlier world scale of the turn of the nineteenth century had reached considerable levels of complexity and operational and administrative development. The presence of such capabilities then raises the question as to why the earlier period did not produce global systems that could have overridden or suppressed national differences rather than, as it did, intensify competing national colonizations. National rivalries grew to the point of devastating wars among the major powers precisely because it was a world scale constituted through the extraterritorial projection of several major national capitalisms and geared toward building national states rather than global systems.

The world scale entered a whole new phase after World War II. This is especially evident in the intense and extended effort to implement the Bretton Woods agreements, which were designed to form a supranational system for governing cross-border transactions. Many scholars see this postwar period as one long phase building toward today's more extensive global system.

One of the questions I examine in chapter 4 is the extent to which the Bretton Woods phase should be distinguished from the global era that began to take shape in the 1980s. If such a distinction is indeed warranted and we are dealing with a novel type of world scale today, then we need to allow for the possibility that it brings with it new forms of articulation with national states and foundational realignments inside the state and between the public and private realms as historically constituted.

Three central theses organize chapter 4 and to some extent chapter 5. The first is that critical capabilities for entering the global age were in place in the first two decades after World War II and into the 1970s. The Bretton Woods system is a phase of the development, build up, and formalization of capabilities that allowed states—at least some states—to enter into a far broader range of formal international transactions and, in some cases, to assume international governing capacities. But in the postwar decades and well into the 1970s, this was a world scale designed to govern the international system in order to protect national economies from external forces. In this sense, some of the major systemic features of the Bretton Woods era had more in common with the earlier world scale than with today's global scale.

The second thesis is that the tipping point that would take us into the global age arose out of a combination of dynamics in the 1980s that made these capabilities jump tracks and become part of a new, emergent organizing logic. Not all world scales or international systems are articulated through the same organizing logic. I use the lens of territory, authority, and rights to decipher this process. The purpose here is to understand the particular type of organizing logic at work in these two different phases—the world scale of the Bretton Woods era and that of the current global era.

The third thesis is that the particular combination of dynamics that produces a new organizing logic is partly enacted through foundational realignments inside the state and, thereby, between the state and the private realm. This realignment is constitutive, which also means that the state is partly constitutive of the new organizing logic. In this context, then, I diverge from the scholarship that sees the state as merely evolving and adapting. In positing foundational realignments inside the state, I do not preclude the presence of adaptive processes when it comes to other components of the state from those I focus on, but these need to be distinguished from constitutive ones. This thesis is critical to my larger argument about denationalization. It matters for a full specification of today's epochal transformation, to wit, that one strategic locus lies deep inside the national. This interpretation of what is epochal about the current transformation carries distinct policy implications for democratic participation and accountability in that it shows the national is one site for global politics.

As I have done in the preceding chapters, I use one state, in this case the American state, as emblematic of the critical changes of an era, though not necessarily representative of statehood in that era. The Capetian state in the Late Middle Ages and the British state in industrial capitalism were emblematic states of the two eras examined in part 1, even though neither was representative of statehood in its time. What we can detect in each of the three cases examined in this book is a form of statehood in the making that eventually spreads to other countries, albeit "imperfectly." Selecting one state for empirical specification of key dynamics is a function of the particular analytics I seek to develop in this book—that is, the need to understand major issues through detailed examinations of practices and discursive domains in ways that can accommodate both formal and informal processes and actors. This matters to the effort of detecting tipping points and deciphering the relocation of particular capabilities into novel assemblages of territory, authority, and rights.

The American state is an illuminating site for apprehending the internal transformations of the national "liberal" state beginning in the 1980s. I argue that these internal transformations are part of the constitutive difference of today's global era. The mix of policies we usually describe as privatization, deregulation, and marketization of public functions in their aggregate effected a significant shift of power to the executive, a loss of lawmaking capacities and political participation by Congress, and, partly as a result, a new critical role for the judiciary in public scrutiny of executive action and in lawmaking. Further, the globalization of a growing range of economic actors and processes brings with it an increased inequality in the power of different parts of the government, sharpening whatever inequalities may have long existed. Thus, in contrast to the common thesis of the decline of the state due to globalization, I have long argued that the U.S. Treasury and the Federal Reserve gained significant powers precisely because of globalization. Here I extend that argument to other components of the executive branch. While each state is different, the internal redistribution of power away from the legislature and toward the executive is becoming evident in a growing number of states worldwide. Further, through these changes a major realignment is effected in the historically constructed and highly formalized divide between the public and the private realms, with the latter increasingly absorbing forms of authority once exclusive to the state. This privatizing of particular public authorities is also part of the tipping point that ushered the global age.

Today states confront and endogenize new geographies of power. One of these is internal to the state: the shift of power to the executive branch and away from the legislature examined in chapter 4. The other is external: a field of forces that includes a far broader array of nonstate actors than ever before and the rise of new normative orders beyond that of the nation-state. Both geographies entail a particular set of dynamics that profoundly alter the constituting of the private and public domains, a rupture in an old history that dates back to the origins of the liberal state. In chapter 5 I examine this new external geography of power and argue that it entails a far more differentiated process and a more transformative process of the state than is indicated by notions of an overall decline in state significance. I use both the global economy (especially the largely electronic financial markets) and emergent forms of global law as sites for investigating the limits of state authority. These transformations in the state's positioning are partial and incipient but strategic. The field of power within which national states now function is constituted not only by the community of states but also by the formation of a new private institutional order linked to the global economy and by the rise of institutional orders comprising NGOs and human rights organizations.

These significant, though not necessarily absolute, transformations in the condition of the national generally and the national state in particular raise the possibility of significant shifts in the architecture of political membership, the subject of chapter 6. Citizenship, the foundational institution for membership in the modern state, has long been deeply articulated with the national state. A key element in the evolution of citizenship has been the will of the state to render national major institutions that might well have had a different trajectory and to some extent did for most of recorded Western history. The construction of political membership as a national category is today mostly experienced as an inherited condition. The degree of institutional formalization and sociocultural thickness makes it difficult to experience the historicity of this construction. It is easily naturalized. And yet, as part 1 examined, for most of Western history territory was subject to multiple systems of rule—the king, the local lord, the church—and so was membership. The nationalizing of territory and allegiance entailed encasing geographic territory into an elaborate institutional system: territory became state territoriality, and identity became nation-based citizenship.

Some of the main dynamics at work today are destabilizing these particular arrangements and bringing their historical particularity to the fore—not necessarily producing their downfall but making legible that other arrangements are possible. Among these dynamics are globalization and electronic networks, both as material processes and as imaginaries. In multiple ways these bring about changes in the formal and informal relationships between the national state and the citizen, and in the relationship between the formalized apparatus for politics and both old and new informal types of politics. Among the latter are a range of emergent political practices often involving hitherto silent or silenced peoples and types of struggles. Through their destabilizing effects, globalization and electronic networks are producing operational and rhetorical openings for the emergence of new types of political subjects and new spatialities for politics. More broadly, the destabilizing of national state-centered hierarchies of legitimate power and allegiance has enabled a multiplication of nonformalized or only partly formalized political dynamics and actors. We are seeing the possibility of various types of rights-bearing subjects beyond the citizen, even though they are more partial and thinner than the latter."

These trends signal not only a deterritorializing of citizenship practices and identities, as is usually argued, but also their partial denationalizing. Specific transformations inside the national state have directly and indirectly altered particular features of the institution of citizenship, including discourses about loyalty and allegiance. These transformations are not predicated necessarily on deterritorialization or locations for the institution outside the national state, as is the key to conceptions of postnational citizenship.

4 THE TIPPING POINT

Toward New Organizing Logics

THE CAPABILITIES for entering the global age were long available. This is perhaps particularly so after World War II when major states were developing international regimes and the requisite institutional infrastructure. For many this is when the global age begins. But I argue that the larger organizing logic was one centered in international regimes aimed at protecting national economies from external economic forces rather than at forming a global economy. Though international, this period was geared toward building the national economy and protecting the national interest. No genuinely global system was set in place; thus the first phase of the Bretton Woods system assumes added significance insofar as its first twelve years did aim at something approaching genuine global governance for the common good. But the United States was both then and later a reluctant participant in this larger effort and consistently sought to pursue its own advantage. It moved Bretton Woods toward the development of state capabilities for enabling private global actors, which in practice meant particularly U.S. firms since these were dominant at a time when other major powers were dealing with massive war destruction. These other major powers were far more disposed toward thinking in terms of an international system that would ensure balance.

Much had to come together to reach the major tipping point for a new organizing logic that reoriented state capabilities toward global projects. The strong unilateral pursuit of global dominance for its firms by the United States was not enough and was a different type of project from that of shaping and furthering today's global economy. Even the U.S. push for a system dominated by markets and firms and their interests was not enough to get to the tipping point. But these capabilities were to become critical for the implementation of a global economy.

Methodologically this entails distinguishing the particular components from the larger whole. Among these components are a series of capabilities involving both state and nonstate actors. For instance, the existence of cross-border financial flows is not enough to secure the existence of a global financial market, nor are cross-border trade flows enough to create a global trading system. The particular assemblage of territory, authority, and rights wired into the formation of today's global financial market or global trading system differs sharply from that of earlier international systems for handling cross-border flows, a subject I develop in the next chapter and in part 3. However, some of these older capabilities were critical to the novel organizing logic even as the larger assemblage within which they functioned has been foundationally transformed. Focusing on territory, authority, and rights provides three alignments along which to examine capabilities and the possibility of their positioning in two different organizational logics. Further, this type of disaggregation allows me to detect distinct trajectories for each of the three, as well as distinct institutional insertions—thus, for instance, the repositioning of territory in the case of a global financial market is a process we can distinguish from that undergone by authority or rights in that market.

The first section examines the character of the internationalism of the Bretton Woods period compared with that of today's global era. There is a constitutive difference between these two periods, an issue that brings up the question of tipping points, the subject of the second section. One of the indicators of this constitutive difference is the internal transformation of the national state beginning in the late 1970s and especially in the 1980s, the subject of the third section. The corresponding reconfiguration of the relationship between the private and the public domains associated with these transformations inside the state is the subject of the fourth section. Chapter 5 returns to the division between a private and a public domain from the perspective of new forms of private authority in the global economy.

VARIETIES OF INTERNATIONALISM

An infrastructure of laws and customs for interstate collaboration and cross-border transactions has been in place for well over a century. National states, especially major powers, have participated in a variety of internationalisms across history, especially during the immediate post–World War II period. This is one indicator that internationalism per se was not enough to move us into the type of world scale evident today. It is too general a feature: the modern capitalist state was born within an international framework.

The major powers of the late nineteenth and early twentieth centuries had broad jurisdictions to prescribe regulations for their citizens given that the nexus between the modern market-centered state and the subjects of its laws could be very loose (for a variety of angles, see Picciotto and Mayne 1999; Murphy 1994; Suter 1992). Reciprocal arrangements such as extradition and judicial assistance were already developed by the late nineteenth century. While the executive power to enforce such regulation was, and in most regards remains, essentially territorial, the mobility of people and firms, and the interlinking of ownership and world markets have meant that, in principle, state authority has long had considerable scope beyond its national territory (e.g., Brilmayer 1989; Walker 1993). This is especially true of powerful states. In principle, a state's laws can be enforced against any person who can be found or even brought within the territory (even by kidnapping or by invasion and extraction), or against assets or goods present or passing through, or even by denying access to markets.

The particular history of internationalism arising out of imperial Britain's role in maintaining order in the world economy through the gold standard demonstrates the making of modern global governance capabilities (e.g., Cain and Hopkins 1986, 1987). When the United States became the dominant world power, notwithstanding its strong isolationism in some spheres, it continued to build up some of these capabilities eventually institutionalized in the dollar's role as leading currency. But it also developed new ones. Thus, in terms of my capabilities analysis, the American multinational corporations that emerged at the end of the nineteenth and early twentieth centuries transformed international trade and the relationship between private and public sector institutions, marking the beginning of a specific type of international economic history to be distinguished from that of Britain. The new American firms were based on technical changes in strategic sectors: metallurgy, mechanical engineering, chemistry, and the generation of electricity. Most important were the changes that transformed transportation and communication. Yet notwithstanding their differences, both British- and U.S.-based economic internationalisms were predicated on nationalisms. Woodrow Wilson's internationalism had as its cornerstone self-determination and guarantees of territorial integrity and political independence—a formulation later embodied in the UN Charter.

Micro-internationalisms also proliferated. The diffusion of institutional models and practices was one mechanism through which this took place.[1] The late nineteenth and early twentieth centuries had seen the cross-border adoption and direct transplants of legal institutions for the ownership and transfer of property, including the liberalization of the corporate form and

---

[1] See the work by Meyer et al. (1997) for a definitive treatment of these mechanisms in specialized domains such as education and economic development.

the ideology of contractual freedom.[2] In the preceding chapter I discussed international economic coordination among the major powers in the late nineteenth and early twentieth centuries, and less formalized cross-border networks and organizations. Formal international economic coordination among major powers addressed issues important to an international economic system; thus the granting of patent monopolies, for instance, was already handled in a coordinated way among the major powers in the late nineteenth century. We can identify additional types of cases in this diffusion of institutional models and practices. For instance, the classical tripartite structure for regulating industrial affairs through cooperative consultation among representatives of business, labor, and the government, which is part of the constitution of the International Labor Organization (ILO), influenced many national structures.[3] Picciotto and Mayne (1999; Picciotto 1990) find that the institutional framework for corporate capitalism in the United States that developed from the end of the Civil War to World War I was shaped through a process of international debate and emulation. The late nineteenth and early twentieth centuries saw an explosion in the growth of nonstate international organizations, as well as a proliferation of what today we might call transgovernmental networks (e.g., Slaughter 2004). These micro-internationalisms included multiple fora for scientific, cultural, and business communities, and the formation of international private organizations. The number of formally recognized nongovernmental organizations, many of them small, grew rapidly from 330 in 1914 to 730 in 1939, and 6,000 by 1980 (Jacobson 1996), that is, before the tipping point into the current global era. The agendas deployed in these various internationalisms did not only include the interests of governments and firms. For instance, the creation of the ILO reflected the internationalizing of labor struggles, directly and indirectly.[4]

---

[2] Picciotto and Mayne (1999) emphasize the mutual influence among the main capitalist countries in formulating legislation; measures such as the freedom of incorporation and its limits, if any, were embodied in legislative formulations and interpretations responsive to international competition.

[3] This was a model transplanted from the United States, developed in the Progressive Era, to the ILO (Picciotto and Mayne 1999).

[4] It was particularly to counter the Labour Charter of the International Federation of Trade Unions (IFTU) that the Paris Peace Conference's Commission for International Labour Legislation, headed by Samuel Gompers, drew up the ILO's most daring proposal, the eight-hour-day. It made little headway when it came to actual ratification by member states. Setting up the ILO was one component in the effort toward international liberalization promoted by Woodrow Wilson. One reading is that it represented a response to Bolshevism and any independent labor internationalism (see Silver 2003). This was a thick and complex period when it came to international politics. The formation of the ILO cannot be completely separated from the fact that a revived Socialist International and the new IFTU met in Geneva in 1918 in the months during which the Paris Peace Conference was in preparation.

This increasingly complex grid of macro- and micro-internationalisms involved the major state and corporate actors of the time as well as less formalized actors. In brief, the consolidation and extension of the national state and of nationalism in the twentieth century took place in a far more dynamic international context than later state-centered narratives of the past make visible.

The Bretton Woods system is perhaps the most accomplished capability for international coordination among national states before the global age launched in the 1980s. The true players in the shaping of the system were Britain and the United States,[5] even though forty-five countries participated.[6] It is useful to distinguish two phases before the breakdown of the early 1970s. In its first twelve years, and in its framers' concept, the Bretton Woods system was a supranational authority for protecting national governments.[7] Eventually it evolved into a market-centered system dominated by private banks, particularly U.S. banks. Neither of these phases was akin to the current global economic system.

There are two critical conditions for framing the character of the postwar world scale. The first is the role played by the state in the Bretton Woods era. The U.S. federal government that emerged out of the New Deal and carried over into the post–World War II period was by then a powerful and significant entity, a whole new type of state from what it was in the pre– and immediate post–Civil War era.[8] The New Deal was a critical vehicle in the process of consolidating the authority of the federal government. There is a particular combination of dynamics that comes together and enables the federal government to play a specific role in the postwar period. We can identify three of these. The first is the growing role of the federal government in economic management as government spending brought money into the economy, and government borrowing and taxation brought private money into the government. The second one is the very different role that the financial markets played at this time compared to their role in the 1980s and onward: until the 1950s financial policy was cautionary, regulatory controls were in place,

---

[5] The Bretton Woods conference in 1944 was the last stage of a process initiated by Britain and U.S. Treasury officials working on the rules for a postwar monetary and trade regime, as well as the conditions for countries' participation.

[6] This number includes the Danish delegation.

[7] We see considerable shifts in the balance between internationalists and nationalists in the postwar years. Thus, in 1948 Congress rejected the International Trade Organization (ITO), which the executive had worked hard to change and negotiate, because it would have undermined state sovereignty. The ITO was not all bad: it gave Less Developed Countries (LDCs) some preferential treatment in the development of finance and commodity agreements, which were not included in the later General Agreement on Tariffs and Trade (GATT); thus after Congress rejected the ITO, the LDCs felt little incentive to join GATT.

[8] Please refer to chapter 3 for a discussion of this subject.

and the stock market was relatively inactive. While it is not easy to disentangle the causal interactions between policy and stock markets, the government kept these policies in place even as growth resumed and stock markets revived in the 1950s; suggesting that policies could govern stock market growth, unlike what is the case with the post-1980s changes. The third dynamic is the relative protection of the financial system from international competitive and exchange rate pressures; this insulation was the norm in the world economy of that time (Eichengreen and Fishlow 1996).[9]

The other major framing condition concerns a critical difference between the Bretton Woods's international economic system and the current global economy. The post–World War II international system had managed exchange rates and controls on international capital flows.[10] This was a different type of world scale than today's global economy. In the postwar period all the major powers supported systems for domestic economic management—including the United States, which seems incompatible with today's dominant policy orientation, or at least its rhetoricization. The most familiar of these policy systems are Britain's Keynesian welfare state, West Germany's "social market," France's "indicative planning," and Japan's Ministry of International Trade and Industry (MITI) model of systematic promotion of export industries. There was a trade-off in the early Bretton Woods phase between, on the one hand, embedded liberalism in the international trading and production order and, on the other, increased domestic economic management aimed at protecting national economies from external disruptions and shocks. This was the Bretton Woods formula for internationalism. In his examination of the making of a postwar economic system, Kapstein finds that "postwar leaders resolved to build a global economy that would be far more institutionalized and constitutionalized than it was in the 19th century, and they would do so in the interests of political stability, economic growth and social justice—all inextricably linked in the minds of postwar leaders" (1994: 93).

These two framing features radically distinguish the postwar Bretton Woods system, especially in its first decade, from the current world scale, even if some of the Bretton Woods rules may have remained the same.

---

[9] In their history of finance, Eichengreen and Fishlow (1996) confirm that one key difference between the earlier phases of finance and today is that national economies were more protected. Today's greater capital mobility has brought on more crises. For an excellent examination of these various conditions, see Cerny (1996).

[10] This involved setting the dollar officially as the primary reserve currency, through the gold exchange standard and a fixed exchange rate system. It also involved the export of U.S. capital—through the Marshall Plan, Korean War boom, and U.S. multinational corporations (MNCs) investing abroad. This all promoted international expansion both in the sense of growing markets for U.S. firms and a growing role for the U.S. financial sector.

This difference is captured in the fact that in the immediate postwar years the central policy issue was unemployment, not free trade or global finance, as it became in the 1980s. In fact unemployment was seen as resulting *from* free trade.[11] Thus while the early phase of the Bretton Woods project involved the making of a global system, it was not of the kind that began to emerge in the 1980s. This then raises two questions: what type of a system would it have been, and why did it not prevail.

The type of global system that could have emerged from the early phase was principally designed by Britain. Britain's position promoted strong multilateral regulatory agencies and respect for the view that national sovereignty took precedence over international capital mobility. The logic underlying this policy stance was a concern with the redistributive effects of capitalist economies. Critical for Keynes was his proposal for making debtor and surplus countries work at returning the international system to balance—a position the United States, then the leading surplus country, rejected.[12] Keynes (1932) proposed that surplus countries pay interest above a certain level, which would stimulate imports to rebalance the world system and thereby offer deficit countries a chance to pursue employment growth policies. Keynes wanted easier borrowing for debtor nations (by then Britain was a debtor nation) and prevention of capital flight.[13] The United States did partly accept a multilateral system compatible with the requirements for domestic stability, encouraging a sort of international division of labor that would minimize disruption and national economic and political vulnerabilities, yet allow a role for comparative advantages (Ruggie 1998: 265). The

[11] There was neither strong opposition to free trade nor much serious consideration of it. Viner (1958) notes at the time that no one was addressing the question of free trade or, indeed, even talking about it.

[12] The United States insisted that surplus countries not be penalized. Eventually the United States became far less competitive and a massive debtor; nonetheless its hegemonic position allowed it to escape the disciplining—through the supranational system and market dynamics—that other debtor countries were subjected to (Sassen 1996: chapter 2). Paralleling Britain at its time of world dominance, in the postwar period the United States sought an open trading system, while most other countries sought protections under national developmentalist regimes. There is a vast scholarship on the postwar asymmetry between the United States and most other countries that traces in enormous detail the consequences for different actors of having an open trading system under U.S. dominance versus the advantages for development of nationally protected economies; it is quite different from the scholarship that emerges in the 1980s and 1990s. It is impossible to do justice here to that postwar scholarship. (I have discussed it at some length in Sassen 1988.)

[13] Tabb (2004: chapter 5), among others, finds that there is a strong case to be made that the high costs borne by the more vulnerable components of the world community could have been avoided if Keynes's position (that surplus countries had as much responsibility as debtor ones to reestablish equilibrium) had prevailed.

U.S. position was a weak guarantee compared to Keynes's proposal. The actual regime adopted was quite different from what Keynes had envisioned (Tabb 2004: 112).

Several scholars have noted that later interpretations and debates about the Bretton Woods system focus largely on the private side of the issues, where each state conducts itself as a private actor with private interests, rather than focusing on the shared commons of the international community of states. The larger issue at work is what we might formulate as a distinction between institutions serving private interests and those serving the public interest. While liberal democratic theory would posit that the former wind up being in the public interest as well, the distinction is helpful in understanding the Bretton Woods founding documents and the evolution of their interpretations. For instance, in his research on the constituting of GATT, Abbott (1992) finds that most of the analyses and even debates have focused on what could be referred to as the "private" side of GATT, neglecting the "public" institutions side of the agreement. Most discussions of GATT as an institution—particularly those relating to rule making, dispute settlement, enforcement, and such—are organized around dichotomies representing opposing conceptions of the process or the institution. Two of these dichotomies dominate the literature, though there are variants. The most common is legalism versus pragmatism.[14] The other dichotomy is John Jackson's (1997) rule-oriented versus power-oriented procedures and diplomacy. Abbott proposes an additional dichotomy for thinking about GATT: institutions and procedures designed to serve private interests and those designed to serve the public interest. Public refers here to the common interests of the nation-states forming the world trading community; private refers to the particular interests of the individual states, the contracting parties to GATT. This distinction leads to intellectual connections that are not usually made; it provides perspectives on the nature of GATT as an institution (both under its traditional arrangements and the reforms negotiated in the Uruguay Round) that differ from—though they intersect with—the traditional legalist and pragmatist positions. Indeed it reveals, according to Abbott, that both positions operate largely on the private side of the dichotomy.[15]

The process of shaping and implementing Bretton Woods can be seen as a strategic site in two senses. First, its provisions addressed foundational

[14] We can find this in the work of such major figures as Dam (1970) and Hudec (1987).

[15] For instance, the private interest argument provides a strong and consistent rationale for many of the Uruguay Round dispute settlement reforms. The question then is how would such dispute mechanisms look if they were also shaped by the public interest side of the founding documents of GATT?

issues for a world system of governance. Second, these provisions elicited considerable debate and attempts to block the agreement inside the two main framing countries, the United States and Britain. These debates made legible the range of political interpretations of what global governance might have entailed. U.S. isolationism was able to accommodate a global system insofar as it was ruled by open markets, specifically, open to U.S. goods, services, and investment. The combination of isolationism with an option on open markets is perhaps only available to a hegemonic power.[16] What matters here to my analysis is that they coexisted and that they indicate the disposition in key U.S. government sectors and at least some business sectors toward developing a world economy no matter how isolationist the political climate.[17] It was not certain Congress would accept the IMF. The League of Nations had failed to win approval in Congress and isolationism was strong. Neither the business community nor the financial community supported government-managed exchange rates or the IMF. Treasury officials worked hard to persuade the financial community and others that the IMF was essential for domestic prosperity in that it would expand the market for U.S. goods and investment abroad. Britain also had its divisions, to some extent centered on policy options regarding its currency, once the standard for the world economy.[18]

The configuring of the tipping point that took us from rich contradictions of the Bretton Woods era into the global age entailed a new alignment of critical aspects of territory, authority, and rights.

[16] For instance, in the context of postwar isolationism domestic politics and economic imperatives came together in the forming of the International Bank for Reconstruction and Development, later called the World Bank: the absence of popular support for foreign aid was overcome by the support of internationalist corporate interests and an appeal to ethnic communities for aid to the "home" country.

[17] Many influential congressmen, senators, and businessmen did not want any restrictions on U.S. capital flows and hence objected to the IMF provisions (Tabb 2004). They also later objected to the restraints in the ITO (fear of foreign competition) (Aronson 1997).

[18] One sector wanted an overvalued currency at an outmoded gold value (opposed by Keynes), which required a very tight monetary policy, one that had kept Britain in a depression through the second half of the 1920s when the United States was booming. Tight monetary policy had contributed to high unemployment and industrial stagnation but had benefited financiers. It also brought with it a strong contagion effect when Britain finally devalued its currency in September 1931 because it put pressure on other countries to stop trying to defend their own gold parities. Eichengreen (2003) notes that as each nation tried to produce a positive outcome in its foreign accounts, all kinds of collapses occurred—of trade and banks, protectionism, etc.—to the collective detriment. Given this experience, the key concern of many of those gathered in Bretton Woods was to have instruments that could provide controlled flexibility in establishing a postwar financial regime.

THE TIPPING POINT

There is a particular moment in the thick, complex post–Bretton Woods years that I find illuminating. By the mid-1970s the U.S. government had lost significant financial and military power, in both material and symbolic terms. The average U.S. household had lost buying power, and firms in many different sectors were not posting profits. The massive and powerful federal administration developed in the New Deal period confronted a fiscal crisis (O'Connor 1973). It was also the specific juncture when U.S. transnational banks had emerged as perhaps the most powerful actors in the international system, in good part fed by the oil crisis and their role in recycling petro dollars.[19] For many observers the rise of the transnational banks in the mid-1970s signals the move into the global era. In my reading this is not the case.

The rise and growing power of the transnational banks in the 1970s was instead the last hurrah of a type of organization that, if anything, was blocking the move into the global era. It was the crisis of this type of banking system that provided one of several critical elements that fed into the tipping point. What matters is the partial "evacuation" of this particular banking system from the U.S. capital markets and from the international financial system partly due to the so-called Third World debt crisis of the early 1980s. This opened up a vast global space for new types of actors and corresponding new alignments in the relation between the state and banking/finance. The crisis of the transnational banks in a larger context of economic stagnation created operational space for finance and contributed to the rapid spread of the financializing of a growing number of economic sectors.[20] Among the new types of actors were the comparatively smaller financial services or non-bank banks—typically referred to as investment banks in the United States and merchant banks in Britain—and a new generation of offshore financial markets. These firms and markets operated under a very different regime from that of banks, one that was much more flexible, tied to fewer regulations, able to convert broad sectors of fixed capital and of debt into financial instruments, and thereby into new modes of capital mobility.

---

[19] The power of the transnational banks jumped orders of magnitude thanks to the rise in the price of oil, which contributed to the loss of earnings in households and profits in firms in many countries in the world, including the United States. The power of the large commercial banks and the enablements for transnational operations ensured by the U.S. government's insistence within and after Bretton Woods set up the conditions for their sharp rise and eventually their crisis in the early 1980s.

[20] I have examined this in some detail (see Sassen 2001: chapters 4 and 7).

There are two bundles of critical elements in the complex mix of processes that took us to a tipping point and into a new organizing logic. The combination of these two bundles of elements provides the missing pieces in the larger international configuration that launched the global era. One of the bundles consists of the development of a variety of capabilities which at specific junctures tip into a novel organizing logic operating at the level of the system; the transformation of banking and finance described above is one of these capabilities. Understanding this tipping process requires distinguishing between the system and its component parts, in this case between the international system at the time of Bretton Woods and the fact that in this process both the U.S. government and leading U.S. firms and markets developed capabilities, institutionally and in terms of practices, that would serve them well later in the global age. At issue here is a set of processes that enact, accommodate, or constitute the track jumping of capabilities. In this intersection lies the tipping point that would launch a new organizational logic for the deployment of these capabilities. I see this tipping point as produced by an accumulation of conditions, dynamics, and dispositions among key actors in combination with the systemic weight of the United States and its strong support for the international operations of U.S. firms. The result is a redeployment of the capabilities for Bretton Woods internationalism, including the rather distinct U.S. internationalism, into an emergent new assemblage—today's global era.

The other bundle concerns the American state. The weakened U.S. government of the 1970s enabled a reorientation in important policy alignments. That is to say, the much noted crisis of the American state at that time does not preclude the fact of a particular type of agency—or power—in that state, and thereby the possibility of internalizing the project of the new economic actors that were beginning to supersede the older ones, thereby internalizing and contributing elements of the new organizing logic. The state—more precisely particular components of the state—worked at developing a novel alignment between state and economy, one furthering the development of a new or sharply changed type of relation between state regulation and powerful economic actors.

Why Was Bretton Woods Not the Tipping Point?

There are multiple elements that have led observers to consider Bretton Woods the beginning of the global era. These include micro trends such as the rise of the transnational banks alluded to earlier and the establishment of various multilateral systems for economic operations, including the IMF and the World Bank, which continue to be central organizations in the current global era. Further, key demands by the United States in the framing of the Bretton Woods system were akin to the later neoliberal policies of the 1980s and 1990s, making it easy to argue that the current global phase had already begun then or, alternatively, that there is nothing distinct about the global phase of the 1980s onward. For some scholars, the 1980s and 1990s are a period when states are simply negotiating what they have always negotiated—the self-interest of their constituencies, albeit with changing contents and distributive effects (e.g., Krasner 2003). For Eichengreen (2003), the Bretton Woods financial system is the only radical change in the modern Western history of finance, implying that the developments of the 1980s do not represent a major innovation.

IMF conditionality, already introduced in the 1940s and 1950s, illuminates some of the differences between the Bretton Woods era and the current era. As it does today, also then the United States demanded structural adjustments from debtor nations among which Europe was prominent. In the case of Europe, securing needed foreign investment was partly conditioned on opening markets, including the capital market, which, again like today, led to capital flight. But implementation and, more important, the wider project entailed by IMF conditionality bear little resemblance to today's IMF. Even though IMF conditionality was one of the U.S. policy preferences and hence had its full backing, European states kept far more state coordination of the economy in the postwar decades than the United States wanted. Nor did the United States implement these measures extensively in its own economy. Further, several developing countries withdrew their requests for assistance to avoid the imposition of IMF conditionality. This type of resistance and withdrawal represents a scenario that would be almost inconceivable today, partly because market openness and conditionality are embedded in and constitutive of the fabric itself of the national and international political economies (global financial markets, global firms, deregulation, privatization). The disbelief encountered when Malaysia went its own way after the 1997 Asian crisis or when Argentina refused to pay debt service in 2001 and opted for sovereign bankruptcy signals a difference in the current world system from what was the case in the immediate postwar decades. These unilateral decisions by Malaysia and Argentina, each a singular event, confronted the IMF with "novel" conditions within the framing of policy that had evolved in the 1980s and into 2000.

Scholars working in a variety of theoretical lineages see the transition from the Bretton Woods era to the current global era as an evolution or adaptation of either the state (e.g., Weiss 1998; Krasner 2003) or the international system (Wallerstein 2001; Hirst and Thompson 1996) to new conditions. In this regard several scholars, among them Krasner (2003) and Weiss (1998), emphasize the tendency today to exaggerate the power of the state in earlier periods, as if there was once a time when states were not subject to external forces obliging them to many accommodations. The postwar high-growth period can easily be interpreted as reflecting the past power of states to set macroeconomic policy stimulating high growth and high government revenues. For Weiss, it was internal state dynamics rather than globalization that led to the ensuing economic stagnation of the 1970s; the particular difficulties of national governments with macroeconomic management (for example, balancing budgets, mobilizing sufficient revenue to fund government programs, and so forth) had more to do with internal fiscal difficulties caused by recession than with the onset of globalization. Thus recessions and fiscal weakness are phases, as are growth and fiscal plenty: a return to sustained growth can then again enable governments' macroeconomic policymaking.

Did the rationales and aims of Bretton Woods represent the formation of, or aspiration to, a global system? For many, the fact that Bretton Woods was a multilateral system to handle world markets makes it part of the history of globalization. It is a system that developed state capabilities for multilateral coordination. But this level of generality does not help. There are differences that can only be captured at a far greater level of detail. This can be illustrated by focusing on the character of the international financial system. The Bretton Woods system proposed that a government agree "not to accept or permit deposits or investments from any member country except with the permission of the government of that country" (Helleiner 1994: 38). This provision gave debtor countries some protections and gave governments considerable control over international capital flows. Early plans for the IMF gave it the authority to block changes in exchange rates and other related conditions.[21] Keynes did not want the reestablishment of the gold standard, which he had come to regard as a "barbaric relic," or any other regime that would limit the autonomy of member countries to follow their own monetary policy and to pursue full domestic employment. But he did want a strong global central bank. The formation of such a bank would include a new international currency for states to use in their international transactions. The extent and content of government control made for a substantively different international financial system from what gets launched in the 1980s (Sassen 1991: chapter 4).

[21] These provisions together with Keynes's support for self-sufficiency for national economies and social engineering were a direct response to the failure of free markets to move countries out of the instability and suffering of the European economies in the 1920s and 1930s (Crotty 1999).

The U.S. government played a critical role throughout the postwar period in putting in place some of the conditions that would bring about the tipping point of the 1980s and, in this regard, a critical role in producing the confusions about the meaning of Bretton Woods for our current global era: that is, globalization as Americanization. The United States wanted the dollar as the global settlement currency—which would keep debtors from easy access to other sources of credit—and wanted to abolish exchange controls. It won on the first demand over Britain and the other major powers of the time that wanted a new international currency for settlement operations, but it lost on exchange controls.[22] Though less transparent than in the Bretton Woods debates, U.S. policy preferences were also at work in the Marshall Plan and the activities of large American multinational firms. But, I will argue in the next section, the type of government in place in the United States at the time could not have secured that tipping point.

At the international level, it is important to recognize that the multilateralism of the Bretton Woods era is very different from that of today, even though institutions such as the IMF and World Bank are still key actors. Two features differentiate the multilateralism of the earlier period with that of today; states a) developed capabilities for multilateral action and did so to protect their national economies from international forces, and b) worked for a stronger multilateral system and did so without relinquishing policies calling for governments to manage their economies and function as significant economic actors. That is to say, multilateralism did not preclude state economic coordination or national protectionisms. The overall organizing logic of the international system in the 1940s and into the 1960s was marked by much state work to develop, implement, and govern a multilateral system. Further, and albeit it with different modalities across the world, states were significant economic actors running large public sectors with often strong state-led coordination of economies and welfare. Even in its highly international and multilateral components, this work was aimed at building the national economy and polity. The project was governing the international system in order to protect the national interest, no matter the definition of the latter.

In this context the United States was the major innovator critical for reaching the tipping point, which has led to easy interpretations that globalization is Americanization. I will argue in chapter 5 that it is only at a

[22] As the leading creditor nation at that time, the United States took the position that Britain had taken in the pre–World War I and interwar periods—a push for open markets and a gold standard represented by its currency.

very high level of generality that we can equate globalization with American-ization, and that we can interpret the United States as already having put in place before the 1980s the system that we now call neoliberal globalization, either internationally or nationally. When one leaves this level of generality and enters the particular domains that constitute the political economy of nation-states and of the international system, there are significant differences between the Bretton Woods era and the current global era. These differences are partial, not total or absolute. Crucial here are internal national policy and state coordination. Thus in the earlier period and into the 1960s, even the United States implemented domestic policies that are best seen as a variant of Keynesianism rather than neoliberal, such as the expansion of the welfare state, massive national planning projects, and extensive regulation in major economic sectors, notably finance and banking, which still reflected New Deal regulation. This was a kind of new Keynesianism that was uncomfort-able with or critical of an excessively strong financial sector, one seen as driven by speculation and harmful to the productive development of the real economy of manufacture and services. In addition, several economic sectors and political constituencies in the United States wanted increasing govern-ment participation through macroeconomic demand management and the welfare state. In brief, the United States of the early Bretton Woods era was marked by a mix of national orientation, a search for expanding international markets for American exports, and a particular kind of differentiation of pol-icy domains. In the 1980s the U.S. state ceased to be the type of significant economic actor it had been since the New Deal and well into the postwar de-cades, and it altered its strategic relation to the economy from one of produc-tion and physical planning to one that ran through the financial system. The explosive growth in U.S. treasuries captures this. The massive U.S. debt built up during the Reagan administration emerged as a key input for the financial markets of the mid-1980s with the development of multiple new instruments centered on debt. Thus my interpretation differs from that common in the scholarship on globalization, which sees the changes in the relation of the state to the economy beginning in the 1980s as either an adaptation that ensures the state's survival or as the decline of the state in a global world, and further, interprets the United States' pressure on other states to get out of being eco-nomic actors and out of protecting their economies, as more state adaptation.

But these changes do not simply mean a loss of power and they are far more foundational than the notion of adaptation and that of globalization-as-Americanization might suggest. In the United States the state tightened its power function through a rise in executive power, even as other parts of the government lost power. And, although the United States projected its

agenda onto the world, it took work on the part of the other states to implement that agenda, and hence points to possible internal state transformation
toward strengthening the executive branch. The depth of the new global
transformation is greater than imperial imposition of U.S. preferences might
suggest. Though not representative of statehood in the 1980s, the United
States may well turn out to be emblematic—and the extreme case—of statehood in the global era. Some of the most developed liberal states in the global
north are beginning to evince similar trends: a rise in executive power and a
loss of congressional or parliamentary functions and authority.

Beyond the more general differences between the Bretton Woods era
and today's global age discussed earlier, there are also specific differences by
country. In the case of the United States, I identify two as critical. The first is
the particular forms of authority embedded in, respectively, the strong U.S. federal government of the postwar period and today's sharp power gain of the executive over Congress and over globalization-linked policy implementation.
We might also want to include the increasingly unchecked power of the executive over matters of war. Second, economic management by the federal government in the postwar period was partly enabled by the somewhat inactive stock
market, whereas in the 1980s a whole new financial phase emerges, characterized by innovation, aggressive trading, and high levels of speculation. The type
of power held by the state and the character of the financial system are critical
variables for understanding the difference between these two periods.

The United States: Shaping Systemic Capabilities for the Tipping Point

There are, then, two issues that the Bretton Woods case brings to
the fore in terms of these types of questions. The first concerns the development of capabilities for the neoliberal project that became dominant in the
1980s in the United States along with a handful of other major economies,
and worldwide, in the 1990s. The second one is the question of what is and
what is not legible, and hence the heightened role of interpretation in historiographies about the period.[23]

---

[23] One line of interpretation is Tabb's (2004: chapter 7), which emphasizes the consistent and unitary project of the U.S. government to support its key economic actors—MNCs and
financial firms; he does not differentiate the 1980s from the postwar period. The difference for
Tabb, and I agree with this part of his interpretation, is that the first twelve years of the Bretton
Woods system should be distinguished from what followed in the 1960s. Even as the United
States got what it wanted throughout, in the second period the system shifted increasingly toward the U.S. agenda.

We can begin to address these two issues by focusing on a particular aspect of the position of the United States in both the framing of the Bretton Woods system and the development of systemic conditions that contained capabilities for tipping into a new organizing logic. U.S. demands that countries in its orbit reduce their government's role in the economy and promote market openness may have seemed less significant in the first decade of the Bretton Woods system because of overall high growth, which obscured the longer term negative consequences potentially arising from these demands. Fighting against U.S. demands seemed perhaps less pressing. Yet, and especially for LDCs, the drawbacks of ceding to the demands for less government and more open markets turned out to be multiple. The drawbacks included new governmental practices, such as central banks around the world accepting the dollars the United States forced on them, thereby tying their economic policies to surplus dollars. These practices also contributed to reorient various institutions susceptible to these policies. Thus welfare systems had to function on reduced resources as financial openness shrank the autonomy of states in the U.S. orbit. These policies also contributed to diminish the viability of national firms that could not compete with U.S. firms, either through their exports to or direct production in these countries.[24] This was the buildup of a sharp asymmetry: financial and market openness as a threat to less powerful economies and as an advantage for U.S. finance capital as it could benefit from the lower taxes and freedom to pursue profitable opportunities globally.

These costs became fully evident in the 1970s. Freer capital markets had reduced the efficacy of domestic monetary and fiscal policies worldwide, even as key financial sectors thrived on this insofar as it disciplined governments to be more attentive to markets. A combination of conditions at this point was fraught with the potential for crisis: a) U.S. insistence on making the dollar the standard currency combined with the U.S. production of an oversupply of dollars relative to actual international demand for dollars, and b) U.S. willingness to force dollars on central banks around the world. For this mix of trends to work, including for the United States, required that the U.S. economy have high growth, high revenues, a stable dollar, and the capacity and will in the U.S. government to buy those dollars back as it had promised. Although the United States enjoyed high growth for a good

[24] Once the dollar was the standard currency, the United States had the privilege of seigneurage: every printed dollar gave it command over real resources in the world economy (Cohen 1998). Thus in the 1960s when it printed more dollars than were in demand it forced central banks of other countries to hold dollars, thereby bringing a built-in inflationary bias to the international system. This put countries at the mercy of destabilizing monetary flows they could not control.

number of years, when economic growth slowed and the government lacked the resources and was unwilling to borrow in order to buy back the dollars it had promised to buy back, the situation became unsustainable.[25] In addition, the United States refused to allow a negotiated arrangement that could have minimized the crisis this combination of trends represented for many countries, especially the less developed ones. Finally, when the dollar could no longer be propped up, the U.S. government unilaterally devalued it, thereby creating massive hard currency losses for countries that could ill afford it.[26] The fact that this coincided with the oil shocks helped camouflage the actual longer-term origins of the crisis.[27] The two oil shocks added to the crisis but were not the cause of the crisis. It took time for the negative outcomes of the norms guiding the U.S. position in the postwar decades to become legible; they only did when the structural shift had taken place. At that point there was considerable irreversibility in the system.

There was a normative transformation afoot in the postwar period that was worked out through the policy proposals of the U.S. government in the Bretton Woods system. The changes that began to emerge in the 1970s were not simply an outcome of a set of new U.S. policies. They are one outcome of an older history of the United States building capabilities for global operations by its government and its firms. Further, besides using the Bretton Woods system to push for open markets and less government, the U.S. government also pursued these objectives through the Marshall Plan.

Two outcomes of the Marshall Plan that are far less noted than its growth effect (e.g., Krueger 1993) are important here. First, the Marshall Plan

[25] By the late 1960s the dollar shortage became a dollar glut. The U.S. government did not have the gold reserves to back all the dollars held by governments worldwide that it had promised to buy back whenever those governments wanted to sell them. U.S. policies also contributed to domestic problems: the Vietnam War carried high economic and political costs but the government was reluctant to raise taxes or cut domestic programs. Instead it increased borrowing, which in turn led to inflation. We see here, once again, the militarism so present in the politics of major countries (Mearsheimer 2001).

[26] In 1971 Nixon announced unilateral suspension of dollar gold convertibility at the fixed exchange rate. This meant that that both foreign government and private holders of vast amounts of dollars and dollar-denominated instruments overseas were hit hard; the U.S. government had abruptly reneged on its promise and shown its willingness to end the Bretton Woods system. The U.S. government in 1970–71 faced demands for aiding development and for greater exchange flexibility, but it would not adjust the U.S. economy, even though it had contributed to the crisis (McKinnon 1993: 39). In so doing it was willing to sacrifice the most successful international monetary system the world had seen.

[27] The inflation and general financial disarray of the 1970s is usually attributed to OPEC. But the large rise in oil prices can more easily be traced to the instability in international relations and the inflation pressures that arose after the devaluation, itself the result of U.S. unwillingness to control dollar printing. See Triffin (1979) on enormous increases in prices before the 1973 OPEC interventions.

turned out to be a critical instrument for strengthening the norm of open market policies pushed by the United States through Bretton Woods and, second, the plan was a critical factor in the build-up of capabilities for a new type of intermediate economy that would contribute to the financializing of economic activity of the 1980s and on.[28] At the heart of the plan were measures designed to open up the European economies and institute more market-directed and less state-directed development. This enabled, if not caused, large capital flight out of Europe; indeed, in the immediate postwar period capital flight was larger than U.S. aid. Under policy arrangements that would have allowed more protective measures than the open system required by the Marshall Plan, controls on capital flight would have diminished the need for the investment capital brought in through the plan. U.S. financial and banking firms handled both capital flight out of Europe (going mostly into the United States) and capital inflows under the plan. In so doing they built up capabilities for a new type of intermediate economy that became a critical component of today's global economy (Sassen 2001: chapter 4).

There were foundational normative differences between the protectionism preferred by most European governments and citizens, including variable degrees of state-coordinated development, and the market-dominated framing of the Marshall Plan.[29] In Europe many saw the United States as the problem: it held half the world's gold and currency reserves and ran vast payments surpluses. The United States, on the other hand, saw the state-directed European economies and the high costs of their social democracies as the problem. If capital controls had been in place as Keynes had called for, the Marshall Plan would have been much smaller, taken far less out of the U.S. government's tax revenue, European capital would have stayed in Europe, Wall Street would have profited much less, and Europe's state-led economic policy would have remained in place to a larger degree than it did.[30]

The United States needed markets for its vast production capacity built up through the demands of a multicountry, multiyear war. Transforming the reconstruction of war-destroyed economies in Europe and elsewhere into

---

[28] In his extensive review of the literature on the Marshall Plan, Tabb (2004: chapter 5) finds that attention and interpretation of the plan has tended to be confined to its growth effect, but that its normative aspects regarding the political economy are perhaps the more enduring legacy.

[29] The majority of the European population did not want the United States to be so present and influential in their countries: "the statist regimes in Europe were dismantled under the umbrella of U.S. generosity" (Tabb 2004: 115).

[30] Both U.S. public opinion and an isolationist Congress opposed the plan. It was sold by the administration as a vehicle for opening up markets for U.S. firms and farmers and for containing communism, which was becoming a major issue in U.S. political discourse.

markets for U.S. goods was a major goal of U.S. policy. Europe was rebuilding its economies and would have continued to do so, albeit more slowly, without the massive capital inflow of the Marshall Plan. The plan can be seen as an intervention that reoriented European reconstruction away from state-led, European capital-based development. The Marshall Plan ensured accelerated reconstruction and the development of open markets for trade and finance, which included the outflow of European capital to the United States. The plan also could be used to show the world that trade and financial liberalization worked. It neutralized the critics of the plan at the time, who emphasized that this type of financial liberalization would generate sharp economic cycles and financial crises.[31]

Some of the problematic outcomes in the 1970s for the United States were a result of the economic growth in the 1950s and 1960s. That growth led U.S. banks and financial investors to search for ways to get around the walls built into the banking and financial sectors to protect them from the types of reverberations that had characterized the 1929 stock market crash (Strange 1986; Cerny 1996). This search contributed to the formation of the offshore markets discussed briefly in the preceding section. Economic growth also made domestic economic policy instruments less effective at "fine-tuning" the economy: high growth reduced the immediate consequences of government spending and borrowing. Spending and reflation, rather than generating economic growth, became the issue for government policy. Further, the power of the large U.S. commercial banks along with their expanding transnational operations enabled by the U.S. government's insistent backing within and after Bretton Woods helped their sharp rise in the 1960s and eventually their crisis in the early 1980s.

One way of reading this mix of outcomes is that U.S. policies through Bretton Woods and the Marshall Plan a) weakened the other players (Western European states) by raising their interdependence/dependence vis-à-vis the United States, forcing or pressuring them to adopt policies they did not necessarily want; b) obscured the negative effects on these countries and the world system in that high growth resulting from postwar reconstruction made any economic and policy development look good; and c) contributed to the conditions for the financial and fiscal crises of the 1970s and early 1980s.

A foundational transformation was beginning to take place. The indicators cannot be confined to the policy level. Critical here are the longer

---

[31] Coming from the opposite direction, some critics argue that the slower growth characterizing much of Western Europe is partly a function of the failure of European states to fully dismantle their economic management apparatus.

and deeper histories that had built up a variety of capabilities that then went into this strategic switch. In a very short period of time—from the 1970s into the 1980s—basic structural realignments began to consolidate. To think that the United States had already undergone this transformation in the Bretton Woods period given its incipiently neoliberal policy positions is to underestimate the depth and radical character of the transformation that ushered in the global era.

REDISTRIBUTING POWER INSIDE THE STATE

The internal redistribution of power in the American state that began in the late 1970s and took off in the 1980s illuminates critical issues about the state in the current global age. Today elements of this shift are evident in a growing number of states around the world, but at the time it was, and today remains, perhaps the sharpest in the United States. The competition for influence among the three branches of government in the United States is an old story, but at different times "one or another has come to the fore and asserted at least a comparative primacy in setting the direction and influencing the outcome of administrative process. . . . [T]his time, that institution is the Presidency" (Kagan 2001: 2246ff.). The shift of power to the executive took off during the Reagan administration. It was a distinct departure from the immediately preceding period (Aman 1992, 2004; Kagan 2001; Scheuerman 1996).

This raises at least three questions about the state as one of the critical institutions for both the tipping point and the constituting of a new organizational logic. The first concerns the character of the growing power of the executive, especially in a context where most of the scholarship on globalization holds that the overall power of the state has declined. The second question is in what ways this accumulation of powers in the executive launched by the Reagan administration is any different from that of the New Deal; that is to say, is the character of this power shift different for each of these two specific periods. The third question concerns the implications of the executive's growing power for the other branches of government and, more generally, for the character of the formal political apparatus in the liberal democratic state, notably the formalized division between a public and a private domain.

A common interpretation in the scholarship on the state and globalization that cuts across many different theoretical positions is that states have, willingly or not, relinquished functions through deregulation, privatization, and marketization. Whether this is interpreted as resulting from external or internal forces, there is a generalized recognition that something has changed. The theoretical starting points for this common understanding and the derived implications vary considerably. They include those who posit that globalization exists and those who argue it does not; those who posit nothing new has really come about, and those who allow for something new; those who emphasize the weight of internal dynamics, and those who emphasize external forces. The shared understanding that something has changed also holds among researchers with very different empirical foci—for example, finance, industrial policy, or the welfare state.

For some, including scholars from different theoretical stances and empirical foci, the transformations in the role of the state are an indicator of the strength of the state because they demonstrate its capacity to evolve and adapt (Krasner 2004; Wallerstein 2001; Cerny 1997; Robinson 2004; Slaughter 2004) and, at the limit, signal that the state will play a bigger rather than smaller role in the world economy as both keep evolving (Weiss 1998; Krasner 2004), or a smaller role but will remain the key player (Hirst and Thompson 1996; Helleiner 1994; Wade 1990). For others, the state has been deeply diminished by deregulation, privatization, marketization, and the corresponding ascendance of private authority where once public authority reigned (Cutler 2002; Ferguson and Jones 2002; Ferguson and Mansbach 1996; Hall and Biersteker 2002) and by the growing contestations to state authority for failing to fulfill its obligations to the citizenry (see Gills 2000; Rupert 2000).

One aspect neglected in this rich scholarship has to do with the type of administrative capability represented by the state and the differential weight of particular state components in the process of globalization. These are two areas that the highly diverse scholarship on globalization and the state has addressed only haphazardly or in terms of the overall adaptability of states. The internal structuration of the state has been sidelined, given the prevalent foci for consideration in the scholarship. One strong tendency is to emphasize the homogenizing and standardizing impact of globalization. In this regard, my concerns are closer to the scholarship that emphasizes the adaptability of the state, but even here detailed examinations of the internal shifts of power within the state brought about by globalization are missing. The tendency in the state adaptability scholarship is to consider the state as a whole or to focus on a particular ministry or agency, with a corresponding emphasis on differences among states rather than within states. The emphasis on state adaptability brings to the fore the many differences, both old and new, that characterize states, including differences among the states of the leading economies; these differences point to the need for detailed research about the internal structuration of states as part of the globalization research agenda.

I am less persuaded by this scholarship's prevalent explanation of trends toward policy convergence (for example, neoliberal policies regarding fiscal and
monetary issues) as resulting largely from similar internal pressures or from
the state's mediating of external forces. International pressures matter but I
also emphasize the power of global markets and global firms to institute their
needs inside particular state components, such as central banks and ministries
of finance, and the resulting power shifts. As a consequence, even as this
scholarship underscores the variability of states and their responses to the
same set of external and internal forces, it still tends to focus on one or another ministry, agency, or policy and does not particularly address structural
shifts inside the state; more important, explanation does not rest on these internal shifts. In my analysis, these internal shifts are partly produced by and
partly constitutive of globalization and are, thus, critical for understanding
the global age.

The work of legal scholars as varied as Ackerman, Aman, and Kagan
underlines the internal redistribution of power toward the executive, even
though the questions guiding their research vary sharply. Aman has perhaps
most directly and pointedly addressed this shift in the context of globalization
(1992, 1995, 1998, 2004). A particular variant of this scholarship is one that
examines the growing weight of the judiciary, a subject I return to later; it includes classic texts such as Jackson (1941) but also a variety of contemporary
analyses that address various pertinent questions (e.g., Rittich 2001; Rajagopal 2003), though not necessarily the question of the redistribution of
power inside the state. Outstanding in this regard is the work of Dezalay and
Garth (2002a), which focuses on the shift of power away from lawyers to
economists in the major states in Latin America. The work of scholars such as
Cox (1987, 1997), Panitch (1996), Gill (1996), and Rosenau (1992), while
not addressing the issue of the redistribution of power per se, is critical to the
more general subject of the internal transformation of the state. There is, of
course, a vast technical literature that examines the Reagan and subsequent
administrations, focusing particularly on major policy changes aimed at reducing the role of the government in various domains and the implications
this carried for the organization of the Reagan administration.[32] Though not
necessarily concerned with the shifts of power inside the state, this literature
does document the policy components and legal underpinnings of that shift.

The redistribution of power within the state is a consequence of
changes in both the national and international political economy but is also

---

[32] It is impossible to discuss this vast literature here and to do justice to it.

constitutive of those changes. I first focused on this in the early 1990s through the lens of global finance, specifically the work of states in the development of a global financial system (Sassen 1996: chapter 2). My question at the time was whether state work in this domain involved redistributing power within the various agencies of the executive branch of government, focusing primarily on the United States. My hypothesis was that state participation in the work of implementing the global economy would redistribute power inside the state, increasing the weight of certain components of the government, notably the Treasury, the Federal Reserve, and finance-related specialized regulatory agencies. The ascendance of these agencies within the government was particularly due to the higher level of strategic importance and complexity of their tasks in a global economy. For the same reasons such shifts took place in a growing number of countries as they globalized their economies.

Here I extend this argument and posit that the increased complexity and technicality of the economy, whether national or global, is a key factor in the internal state redistribution of power. Oversight functions increasingly shift out of Congress and into specialized government agencies and the private sector. One way of addressing the question of the internal transformation of the state is to focus on these internal shifts of power. I have found the legal scholarship especially helpful (Aman 1992, 1998; Picciotto and Mayne 1999; Kagan 2001; Ackerman 2000), as well as the scholarship that focuses on legal issues even if not from a legal perspective (Hall and Biersteker 2002; Cutler, Haufler, and Porter 1999; Sell 2003).

With regard to the first of the three questions raised at the beginning of this section, the legitimate power of the president over the administration of government is a complex matter subject to different interpretations by constitutional legal scholars, and subject to different types of criteria in those interpretations, partly depending on the body of law being considered, such as constitutional or administrative law. One kind of interpretation among constitutional scholars posits the constitutional basis for a "unitary executive" (see, e.g., Lessig and Sunstein 1994), where all administrative activity is controllable by the president.[33] On the other hand, Kagan (2001), who carefully documents the growth of the executive and does not necessarily object to it, does not accept the proposition of a "unitary executive." Critical for me is the actual growth in presidential control of the administration, an issue

---

[33] Thus, in this interpretation, Congress has deprived the president of his powers by creating the so-called independent agencies, i.e., the president cannot remove these agencies' heads.

that has not been at the center of the debate about the relationship of the president to the administration (Kagan 2001). For administrative law scholars, it is important to preserve the distinctive administrative authorities of, respectively, the president and independent agencies; this eventually emerged as an issue when it became clear that the changes instituted by Reagan were beginning to erode agency independence (Aman 1992). The growth of executive power over the administration is at the expense of congressional power insofar as the erosion of agency independence is a form of erosion of congressional oversight powers.

In brief, constitutional and administrative law scholars each raise distinct, though not unrelated, issues. The pertinent issue, addressed by both, is the change in the relationship between the president and the administration of government beginning with the Reagan administration. This change concerns me also insofar as it brings about a transformation in the relationship between the president and Congress. No matter their different foci of analysis, both of these scholarships (see, respectively, e.g., Kagan 2001; Aman 1992, 2004) document a change that began with the Reagan administration and continues today regardless of which political party holds the executive.[34]

As for the second of the three questions raised above, the character of the accumulation of powers in the federal government that took place through the New Deal is different than that of the current period. In both periods, the accumulation of power was enormous and at least partly discontinuous with their preceding eras. The transformations of the New Deal involved Congress as a key player after initial "obstructions" by the Supreme Court, whereas today's shifts of power inside the state mostly do not. Indeed, today's accumulation of powers is concentrated in the executive and has reduced the political participation of Congress. I argue that this erosion of congressional authority begins with the deregulations that began with Reagan, and have continued since, and is fed partly by the rising complexity in the work of a growing number of agencies (just about anything having to do with finance, telecommunications, and other sectors at the heart of the emerging deregulated and globalizing economy). Deregulation and complexity have had autonomous effects in shifting oversight power out of Congress and toward specialized "regulatory" commissions; putting them together only heightens that effect. Though coming from a very different angle and with different questions

---

[34] Deregulation began with the Carter administration's deregulation of the airlines industry. However, deregulation became an overall objective and a doctrine during the Reagan administration.

in mind, the work of Ackerman is critical here. In his detailed comparison of U.S.-style presidentialism and other forms of organizing the democratic liberal state, Ackerman documents the democratic deficits in the U.S. model arising out of the excessive power of the presidency (2000: esp. 643–70).[35] This internal redistribution of power tends to be overlooked in most of the social science scholarship on the state and globalization, regardless of the theoretical stance or empirical focus, and no matter whether the state is seen as continuing to be a key player or as a variously diminished actor.

When it comes to the third question raised above, the implications of this shift for other branches of government and the formal political apparatus, there is an increasingly sharp difference between Congress and the judiciary. Aman (1992) points out that the vast accumulation of powers in the federal government through the New Deal was not really challenged at the time, and that the issues of constitutional import this often entailed were not the subject of extensive debates when they could have been. The Supreme Court was willing to let Congress handle the economic crisis.[36] But, Aman continues, the accumulation of powers in the executive did become an issue forty years later. In the late 1970s and early 1980s, a series of constitutional issues were raised concerning the structure and place of administrative agencies in the federal system. Aman notes that these constitutional challenges coincided with a general policy shift at the federal level toward deregulation and greater reliance on the market and market-based forms of regulation.[37]

---

[35] Ackerman finds that "although the American system has been quite successful in fostering an independent and professional judiciary, the same cannot be said of its impact on the bureaucracy" where the competition for control among the congressional branches and the president has deeply politicized the administration, "transforming the executive branch into an enemy of the rule of law" (2000: 641). Indeed, Ackerman proposes a model of "constrained parliamentarism" as the one most likely to ensure the checks and balances so central to liberal democracy.

[36] This stands in stark contrast to the notorious decisions by the Court referred to in chapter 3, notably the emblematic *Lochner* case. In fact the Court made several key decisions that directly contested congressional involvement, but these may have had the indirect effect of strengthening power via the ruling on the autonomy of agencies, and soon enough the Court deferred to Congress in the handling of the economic crisis.

[37] Several trends are at work here. Notable are the increasingly active role of the Supreme Court in the 1960s and 1970s, a period when Congress passed a series of major regulatory acts and the Court assumed the role of enforcer, and second, the Court's enforcement of deregulation in the late 1970s and taking off in the 1980s and onwards. The Court had also allowed the executive considerable leeway. This changed drastically in the 1960s when the Court began to take strong review positions, eventually holding all parties, including the executive, to the new acts passed by Congress, and moving into the current period into holding the executive under review.

Aman (1992) examines why these constitutional and deregulatory issues reemerged in the late 1970s and 1980s with such force: "What factors made relevant once again legal and policy arguments that had been essentially dormant for over fifty years?" (1992: xii). Aman finds that it is not a matter of party politics and ideology, even though these played a role in the processes of change in the U.S. public law system. He identifies a deeper level in that these regulatory changes corresponded to patterns of change that originated far beyond the politics of the Reagan administration. This would then also explain why a socialist president such as Mitterrand in France also adopted some of the same policies, notably in finance and banking (see Sassen 2001: chapters 4 and 7). For Aman the return of these issues is an indication of the emergence of a new era and the transition from a primarily national to a global economy. Other indications are evident in the language, legal interpretations, and politics of legislators, executive officials, agency decision makers, and courts.

Let me elaborate on the two arguments introduced above. One of them is whether the implementation of major changes and the appearance of constitutional battles about presidential power after a long silence of forty years is a coincidence or whether these are systemic manifestations of the same underlying transformation. Reagan's presidency is key because it instituted many of the changes. To a large extent the framing of this transformation is within the domestic rather than international realm: deregulation is seen as an opportunity for state and local governments to reclaim some of the decision-making authority they had ceded to the federal government. After all, as Novak puts it, the shift of powers from the states and local governments to the federal government in the first half of the twentieth century is one of the "most significant expropriations of political power in American history" (1996: 270). It included areas of business, labor, transportation, morals, health, safety, and education. With the Reagan administration, the federalization of issues was reversed. This then became a venue for reopening many of the constitutional issues that had not been pursued since the New Deal. These constitutional questions carried implications for both the structure and status of federal administrative agencies.

Although these issues played out within the domestic domain, some of the particular types of deregulation and power shifts involved eventually became strategic in the shaping of the regulatory apparatus for participation in the global economy (for example, opening up to foreign firms and investors). The banking and financial sectors illustrate some of these issues. Deregulation was oriented, inevitably, to the domestic system. The multiple separate domains that characterized the banking and financial regulatory structure of the New Deal began to be dismantled.[38] The neutralizing of some of the older divisions greatly helped major players in an increasingly global-ized financial system and had devastating consequences for the more tradi-tional, domestic-oriented sectors.[39] Much of the dismantling did not go through legislative acts, as had happened in the New Deal implementation of regulations, but simply took place through ad hoc regulatory arbitrage: regula-tory agencies began to give their constituencies what they wanted (Cerny 1996). Key factors in this change were a mix of economic stagnation, the breakdown of the post–World War II international financial regime, and an attempt to capture the rapidly growing capitals and opportunities of the off-shore markets, which were a response to the rigidities and impediments of the New Deal financial and banking regulations (Sassen 1991: chapter 4).

The many deregulations launched by the Reagan administration and executed via regulatory commissions rather than new legislation in Congress carried far deeper implications than often recognized. Insofar as Congress was marginalized and the new agencies were formed using old statutes and laws, the executive got involved where Congress would once have been in charge.[40] This brought with it a considerable loss of oversight functions by Congress, which in turn entailed a decline in public scrutiny where the electorate, in principle, plays a role through its representatives. It promoted a proliferation of specialized regulatory agencies and commissions (Aman 1992), and it led to considerable growth in the public bureaucracy (Ayers and Braithwaite 1992). Deregulation on the scale launched by the Reagan administration also brought a shift of functions to the private sector and an associated development of new forms of private authority. Finally, this shift of authority to the executive cre-ated a growing role for the judiciary, which emerged as one of the sites for scrutiny in cases where previously Congress might have been the critical actor.

The role of the executive in initiating various deregulatory reforms

---

[38] After the crash of 1929 and up to the 1970s, we see what amounts to a great experi-ment in keeping the pluralism but creating legal separations in terms of function (different types of markets), enforced through a new system of regulation aimed at avoiding the diffusion of the crisis throughout the economy that had happened after the crash. Some scholars (e.g., Beaud 1981) do not view the crash as the cause but rather the most acute site of the crisis, the crisis be-ing one that involved fundamental aspects of the economy.

[39] There is a vast literature on this, which I discuss in Sassen 2001: chapter 4.

[40] Thus, regulatory agencies themselves did much of the deregulatory law reform. As Aman (1992) notes, often the same agencies were the villains to those seeking deregulation; by taking charge of the deregulation they also became the heroes of deregulation. Most deregulation at the agency level took place within the statutory frameworks originally meant to regulate what-ever the sector involved. This clearly was much easier than changing the statutes (see Calabresi 1982 on the difficulties of repealing statutes).

changed the relationship of the executive to administrative agencies, the legislature, and the courts. Under Reagan, it was not only the substance of regulations that changed but also the forms and formalizations of change. One outcome was the doctrine of presidential deference and litigation aimed at redefining the constitutional relationships among courts, agencies, the executive, and Congress. "These developments were often at odds with a deliberative conception of administrative law, one that emphasizes incremental legal change based on reasoned decision making that reflects regulatory policy goals enunciated or at least implied by Congress" (Aman 1992: 2).[41] The overall lack of comprehensive involvement by Congress has meant that pressure for and initiation of regulatory change has largely come from the executive branch. Aman (2004) finds a long-term trend of increasing executive power over the administrative process. Kagan (2001) shows how this has evolved across subsequent administrations since Reagan. According to Kurland (1986: 607–10), the need for executive coordination increased as the policymaking power of the bureaucracy increased. In addition, as courts exercise oversight functions they need a justification; the latter has increasingly been centered in market efficiency, where once there might have been a very different norm, something closer to the public good in a Keynesian frame (Rittich 2001). To survive judicial review of such reforms, agencies must often justify the market values and results of deregulation as simply another form of regulation.[42]

With the George W. Bush administration, we see yet another phase in the accumulation of powers in the executive.[43] To some extent this is a function of a national security emergency due to the administration's declaration of

---

[41] The conception of administrative law underlying deregulatory change often differs in at least three ways from a more deliberative change: It favors more abrupt change; it is initiated by the president and the executive branch rather than Congress and the courts; and it tends to rationalize change in terms of political power and executive accountability rather than agency expertise or reasoned agency deliberations.

[42] Public choice theory has been influential in the development of strong rationales for deregulation and marketization. It was "the prevailing wisdom in the Reagan Administration" (Dempsey 1989: 26). For Dempsey, proponents of "the public choice theory embrace the normative conclusion that we would be better off with less regulation and less government . . . politicians often . . . magnify rather than eliminate market imperfections" (26n. 47). Dempsey sees public choice theory at work in all the major deregulations in the Reagan administration (reduction of environmental regulation; decimation of the Federal Trade Commission's antitrust regulatory staff; repeals of regulations in the Federal Communications Commission; and the approval by the Secretary of the Department of Transportation of all airline mergers proposal submitted to the agency under Elizabeth Dole.

[43] The current executive has asserted that the presidency has been losing power for the last thirty years (Dean 2004). The Watergate Commission set up by Congress thirty years ago was one of the last great assertions of authority by Congress.

a global War on Terror. But against the longer-term trends discussed above, we can detect a deeper development as well. The continuing decline in the political power of Congress is both systemic and willful. This is illustrated by the outcome of the October 2003 congressional vote to end the Total Information Awareness (TIA) Act, a Pentagon plan designed to analyze vast amounts of information on all persons in the United States so as to detect patterns of terrorist activity. At the time it seemed a great victory for privacy after all the highly visible post–September 11 privacy losses.[44] However, congressional refusal to fund the program did not apply to the Pentagon's classified budget,[45] so the Pentagon can execute this program under its classified budget. The choices from the perspective of Congress and the public interest are limited: to approve the program and make it subject to congressional oversight or to reject it and lose the option of public scrutiny.[46] Federal programs to collect and search vast computer databases for security purposes continue to grow in the Pentagon as well as in other agencies. Further, Congress is part of the state's war against terror. Thus it has directed the Department of Homeland Security to develop "data mining and other advanced analytic tools to access, receive and analyze data, detect and identify threats of terrorism against the United States" (D. Cole 2003: 51). Congress also authorized some of the federal funding for the U.S. government's participation along with several other governments in the Multistate Antiterrorist Regional Information Exchange (MATRIX) System, which links law enforcement records with other government and private databases to identify suspected terrorists.[47]

[44] It would have meant security and military agencies continuously checking on people. The Pentagon did not help itself; its office for public affairs came up with that name and announced a logo of a pyramid topped by a large digitized eye and the Latin motto: Scientia Est Potentia. Further, John Poindexter, who headed the Pentagon's Defense Advanced Research Projects Agency (DARPA), which developed the plan, had been convicted of lying to Congress in the Iran-contra affair; his conviction was overturned on appeal on a technicality. Finally, DARPA floated an idea to create a market for betting on terrorist attacks and other disasters. Although Congress's rejection did not stop the Pentagon's plans, it was significant in that it showed that Congress was willing to stand up to the executive.

[45] The Pentagon explained that TIA was not the tip of the iceberg but "one small specimen in a sea of icebergs."

[46] Congress is not in an easy position when it comes to the power of the executive branch not only in the War on Terror but also to do undercover work in criminal cases. For instance, President Bush invoked executive privilege to block a congressional subpoena related to the FBI's use of informants in Boston-area criminal investigations (Anthony Lewis 2004).

[47] The private firm that is running MATRIX, Sesint, based in Florida, had earlier compiled a "terrorist index" of 120,000 persons using all kinds of indicators, including age, gender, ethnicity, credit history, information about pilot and driver licenses, and connections to dirty addresses known to have been used by other suspects. Thus data mining remains a central instrument in the government's response to the threat of terrorism.

An instance of willful nonparticipation can be seen in Congress's reluctance to constrain executive overextension regarding the conditions under which prisoners from the War on Terror are held at Guantánamo. It was the Supreme Court, which has shown considerable support for this executive, that rejected the Bush administration's assertion of broad unchecked authority to lock up individuals indefinitely without trial or hearing.[48] Congress did not move to confront the executive on its treatment of and assertions of authority over the six hundred Guantánamo prisoners. There are multiple instances that point to a lack of will on the part of Congress to confront the executive.[49]

This contrasts sharply with how Congress conducted itself in the 1960s and 1970s when confronted with undue demands by the executive. A good case in point is how Congress handled the abuses of power by the executive during the Nixon administration. It renewed privacy protections of individuals and strengthened public oversight over the executive. In 1974, after the Watergate process, Congress enacted the Privacy Act, which strictly limited federal collection and use of information about citizens, and at the same time expanded the Freedom of Information Act, giving citizens access to information about their government.[50] When President Nixon resigned, he entered into an agreement with the Administrator of General Services that

[48] In November 2001, President Bush signed an order decreeing that suspected terrorists may be tried in military tribunals instead of regular courts—a policy that kept secret the identities of more than seven hundred detainees. Many experts, as well as organizations such as the ACLU, did not agree with the executive's position on this matter. Various cases were filed in court, but in June 2003 a federal appeals court sided with the Justice Department and ruled that the government did not have to disclose the names of the detainees.

[49] For instance, even in a case where Congress was aligned with widespread public and media support—the September 11 investigative commission—it failed to confront the executive on the infamous twenty-eight pages the Pentagon withheld from the joint report that was to be distributed to the public and to the media. The congressional investigation concerned a matter of national interest: how to learn from the mistakes and inadequacies that may have contributed to the September 11 events so as to prevent its recurrence. The commission was charged with looking into intelligence failures, particularly the failure to foresee the attacks. The authors of the bipartisan report asserted that most of the pages did not need to be classified, but when the executive refused Congress accepted this reversal without much of a fight. According to Steve Aftergood, director of the Federation of American Scientists' Secrecy Project, this is a representative case of how Congress has conducted itself and he finds it a "disgrace." Further, in this process "not only was crucial information withheld" from the public but "false information, whether knowingly false or otherwise, was introduced into the mix" (National Public Radio, On the Media, interview, December 26, 2003).

[50] The Supreme Court reaffirmed these rights of citizens to information. Justice Lewis Powell defended the "essential role of privacy in a democracy" in a landmark decision in 1972 invalidating warrantless domestic security wiretaps and reaffirming the importance of private dissent and public discussion as essential to a free society.

would have given him possession and control over his papers and tape recordings. Congress responded by passing legislation seizing those materials and creating a commission to study how best to handle the papers of future presidents. The commission's work eventually led to the passage of new legislation, the Presidential Records Act of 1978. But these congressional and judiciary protections have not fully survived the erosion of privacy rights and the growing secrecy of the executive evident in the last twenty years. On November 1, 2001, President Bush issued a sweeping order under which "former presidents and vice presidents, or representatives designated by them or by their surviving families, could bar release of documents by claiming one of a variety of privileges: military, diplomatic, or national security secrets, presidential communications, legal advice, legal work or the deliberative processes of the president and the president's advisers" (Clymer 2003).

Secrecy has become one of the key forms through which the Bush administration has accumulated powers in the executive. This is deeply connected with, and enabled by, the issue of national security. Compared to the deregulation of the economy so central to the Reagan and Clinton administrations, national security concerns can more easily be used to legitimate sharp increases in government secrecy. The attacks of September 11, 2001, and the warnings of more attacks are real. The question is whether the extent and content of this accumulation of powers are necessary or point to an overextension, becoming possibly an illegal overextension of executive power. In what follows I briefly take the case of this sharp growth in government secrecy to examine a particular aspect of the growth of executive power in the current global age.

The Executive's Privatizing of Its Own Power

There are two important issues in the rise of government secrecy. The first is how the shift of power to the executive is articulated with the sharp increase in government secrecy. The growing literature on the decline of public authority and the rise of private authority tends to deal with the state as a whole; yet the sharpened differences of power inside the state signal that this may not be adequate. The focus here is on how the executive is not only gaining power but also gaining "privacy." The second is how the shift of power to the executive and the rise in government secrecy are articulated with the erosion in the privacy rights of citizens that protect them from excessive state power.

The evidence shows a growth of secrecy along with an erosion of privacy rights. This came together powerfully in the so-called Patriot Act, the package of anti-terrorism measures approved by Congress after the September 11, 2001, attacks.[51] It was passed overwhelmingly on October 25, 2001, after only a few weeks of congressional deliberation. For some the Patriot Act "represents the most radical change in police powers in decades, and codifies counterterrorist measures previously rejected by Congress as too intrusive" (Donohue 2002: 157). Through the Patriot Act and various executive initiatives, the government has authorized official monitoring of attorney-client conversations, wide-ranging secret searches and wiretaps, the collection of Internet and e-mail addressing data, spying on religious services and the meetings of political groups, and the collection of library and other business records. All of this can be done without probable cause about the guilt of the people searched—that is to say, the usual threshold that must be passed before the government may invade privacy has been neutralized. This is an enormous accrual of powers in the administration, which has found itself in the position of having to reassure the public that it can be "trusted" not to abuse these powers. But there have been abuses.[52]

Beyond abuse of the formal provisions of the Patriot Act, several of the formal provisions themselves contain what many legal experts would consider an abuse of well-established rights of citizens under the Constitution. Some of the most controversial provisions in this regard give the government investigative powers that are by definition secret: this makes it impossible for abuses to be reported. For instance, two provisions of the act radically expand

[51] Its full title was clearly meant to produce the acronym PATRIOT: Provide Appropriate Tools Required to Intercept and Obstruct Terrorism (PATRIOT) Act. The title suggests that opposition to it is unpatriotic.

[52] Here are a couple of examples. Sami Omar al-Hussayen, an Idaho student, was charged under the act for aiding terrorism because his Web site had links to sites that included speeches endorsing terrorism. The government never alleged, let alone proved, that he had terrorism-furthering intentions. Under the government's decision, any Web link to a site advocating terrorism is a violation of the Patriot Act's ban on assistance or expert advice to "designated terrorist organizations." The New York Times has such links on its Web site for educational purposes, including one to an Osama bin Laden recording. The weakness of the government's case and the abuse of its powers led a jury in Idaho to acquit in June 2004. In another case, involving the same Patriot Act provision, the government held the Humanitarian Law Project, a human rights group in Los Angeles, liable to face criminal prosecution for advising a Kurdish group in Turkey on protecting human rights; the group's aim is precisely to discourage violence and promote respect for lawful ways of pursuing Kurdish rights. The administration claims it can prosecute such human rights advocacy as "material support of terrorism" even though it is speech and not aimed at violence. As of late 2004 the courts had ruled that the Patriot Act's application to such activities is unconstitutional, but the Bush administration appealed. For details, see the ACLU Web site on the abuses of the Patriot Act.

the government's ability to obtain personal business records without showing probable cause.[53] The act also expands the authority of the government to conduct wiretaps and searches under the Foreign Intelligence Surveillance Act (FISA) without having to show probable cause of criminal activity (EPIC 2001; EFF 2004). A government report shows FISA searches have grown sharply since the Patriot Act was passed and for the first time now exceed the number of conventional wiretaps authorized in criminal cases. Since everything else about FISA searches and wiretaps is secret, no information is available as to how these provisions have been used and how many people have been affected. The target of a FISA search is never notified unless evidence is subsequently used in a criminal prosecution, and even then the defendant is not allowed to see the government's explanation for the search, and thus cannot raise questions as to its legality in court. In conventional criminal wiretaps, the attorney general must file a detailed report providing the legal grounds for each wiretap, its duration, and whether it resulted in a criminal charge or conviction. None of this is required under FISA.[54]

Thus it is not even possible to provide examples of the government's new authorities because of the legal requirements for secrecy about government searches, seizures, and wiretaps. When the House and Senate Judiciary Committees have requested general information about how the act has been used, the executive has refused to provide it. The position of the government is that since September 11 a growing number of citizens must be open to scrutiny, and a growing number of the government's operations must be kept secret. This inverts a foundational aspect of liberal democracy: individual privacy must be protected and the government must be subject to public scrutiny.

A second major set of issues concerns the sharp increase in the extent to which the government is classifying information and restricting access to unclassified information. For example, in 2003 the federal government—actually the executive and the administration's agencies—spent $6.5 billion to classify over 14 million government documents and to secure their secrets

---

[53] Before the passage of the Patriot Act, the government had to limit its inquiries to a specific set of financial, phone, and travel records, and these could only be obtained if the target was "an agent of a foreign power." The act expanded the definition of records that may be seized; it now includes library and bookstore records and medical files. It eliminated the requirement that the target be an agent of a foreign power; now the government can get anyone's records. Further, the government's authority is protected: it is a crime for the target to tell anyone about the request. The act does not require the government to notify people whose records have been reviewed and does not require that any report of its activities be made available to the public.

[54] The annual report detailing use of criminal wiretaps authority is over one hundred pages long; the FISA report is a one-page letter.

(D. Cole 2003).[55] This is more than the government spent in any single year in the last decade to classify documents. The 14 million documents represent a 60 percent increase over 2001[56] and several times more than the annual average for the 1990s; for example, in 1995, 3.6 million documents were classified. It cost the government over $450 to classify a document and its accumulated secrets in 2003. This information on costs and quantity of documents classified excludes data from the CIA, whose volume of classified information is secret. In addition, agency heads are shifting taxpayer dollars from declassifying to classifying documents. In 2003, agencies spent $120 on maintaining already classified documents for each $1 spent on declassifying, compared to an annual average of $20 for each dollar from 1997 to 2001.

The content and the forms under which this increase in secrecy have taken place vary considerably. The appendix to this chapter gives a sense of the range of issues involved though it is not meant to be an exhaustive listing. Some of the objects of this secrecy clearly go beyond the question of national security. In some cases this is very clear, such as the decision to stop releasing data on mass layoffs by U.S. firms, also a move by the former Bush administration of 1988–92 at a time when terrorist attacks were not an issue but reelection was. The case for invoking national security concerns is at best tenuous in other decisions to classify information, such as the newly imposed restriction on access to Reagan's presidential records; these were to be made available to the public in 2001 following the provisions of the Freedom of Information Act (FOIA) passed by Congress in 1966. Before this order by President Bush, the archivist of the United States could reject a former president's claim of privilege. Finally, less tenuous cases for secrecy but, perhaps, excessive nonetheless are other measures instituted after the 2001 attacks. Since September 11, 2001 three new agencies were given the power to stamp documents "Secret"—the Environmental Protection Agency, the Department of Agriculture, and the Department of Health and Human Services. Also in this category is the March 2002 Defense Department draft regulation concerning possible limits on publication of unclassified research it finances and sharp restrictions on access by foreign citizens to such data and research facilities.

---

[55] See OpentheGovernment.org (info@openthegovernment.org), August 26, 2004. The data are for fiscal years, so they end on September 30 of the calendar year named. The data for 2003 include expenditures and classification by forty-one federal agencies.

[56] It should be noted that the 2001 fiscal year includes nineteen days of classification of documents after the terrorist attacks; it is likely that there was above-average classifying during that period, making the figures for 2001 higher than they would have been without the post-attack days. Thus the extent of the increase in classification as shown by comparing 2003 with 2001 may well be an underestimate.

Another indicator of whether national security concerns are at issue is a set of differences across presidencies. Since the Reagan administration, regardless of the party in the presidency, we have seen an accumulation of powers in the executive, but this does not preclude some variation in how this power is deployed (Kagan 2001). During the Clinton presidency, the Department of Labor reinstituted the tracking of mass layoffs. Further, in October 1993, Attorney General Janet Reno dispatched a memorandum revamping the way FOIA would be administered to standardize the rules of disclosure. Reno decreed that in the event of FOIA-related litigation, FOIA officers should apply a presumption that the Justice Department would no longer defend an agency's withholding of information merely because there was a "substantial legal basis" for doing so. This contrasts with the memo—in the works long before the terrorist attacks—issued in October 2001 by Attorney General John D. Ashcroft assuring agencies that "when you carefully consider FOIA requests and decide to withhold records . . . you can be assured that the Department of Justice will defend your decisions."

These transformations inside the state illuminate critical issues that mark a discontinuity and hence are part of the tipping point that moves us into a new era. Some of these changes have entered the more general debate about globalization and the state through the concept of the democratic deficit, rather than through a focus on internal state redistribution of power. I agree that we are seeing a growing democratic deficit. But confining the analysis to this deficit easily leads to the notion of the decline of the liberal state confronted with the power of global firms and global markets or to a malfunction of the liberal state. This is also taking place. But as a source for a democratic deficit it needs to be distinguished from deficits brought about by a disproportionate concentration of power in the executive branch of government and a partial hollowing out of Congress. The period that takes off in the 1980s sees a type of presidential "lawmaking" through the often extreme reinterpretation of old laws rather than allowing Congress to make new laws. Legislatures slow down the political process: they are the site for public deliberation, often moving into public brawls, allowing the average citizen to catch up. In principle, when the government institutes major changes, new lawmaking is required. But this has barely happened. The role of Congress was marginalized by the decision to reinterpret existing laws instead of making new laws (Aman 1992). There is something extreme, to the point of a possibly illegal overextension, in reinterpreting New Deal laws—which were originally meant to raise government participation in social and economic domains—to deregulate, privatize, and marketize government functions. In principle, the kinds of major restructurings that took place required the participation of Congress—that is, the power of Congress to pass new laws authorizing major changes as the act of a body more fully representative of the electorate than the executive. Passing new laws in Congress is a far more visible event than are the executive's decisions. When these amount to "lawmaking," we can begin to speak of a serious democratic deficit at the heart of the liberal state but one resulting from the accumulation of powers in the executive.[57] The public deliberations and public oversight typical of congressional debates are absent in executive decision making. Such public deliberations would have helped make evident to the average citizen, and politician, the depth of the changes that were being instituted.[58]

My argument can be summarized, albeit it a bit sharply, as a move toward a privatized executive vis-à-vis the people and the other branches of government along with an erosion of citizen's privacy. Partly through these dual trends, and partly through the policies of deregulation, privatization, and marketization that also contributed to the changed position of the executive, there is a reconstruction of the public-private divide.

RECONSTRUCTING THE PUBLIC-PRIVATE DIVIDE

The historically constructed and formalized division between a putatively apolitical private market domain and a public political realm has been one of the constitutive elements of national capitalism and a highly valued norm of liberal democracies (Walzer 1985).[59] The central category in question for my analysis is public authority—that particular combination of power and

[57] Kagan (2001: 2281–5) notes that even as this shift to presidential power also took place under Clinton, he handled it differently: he put himself up front, thereby making the power of the executive public and more subject to examination, at least in the court of public opinion. Further, where the Clinton attorney general encouraged government agencies to declassify, the first-term Bush attorney general encouraged classification and promised the full support of his department.

[58] It would also have reduced the possibility for the executive, especially in countries other than the United States, to claim that it could do little to avoid such changes given the power of global firms and markets. This assertion raises several issues about the extent to which it also holds for the United States itself and, further, about the extent to which U.S. firms and markets reduced the power of the executive branch of government in other countries.

[59] Included here is also the designation of the household as part of the private sphere where "politics are absent," a representation that neutralizes the power inequalities between men and women, and adults and children, and the fact that the household has variously served as one of the infrastructures for the growth of capital—whether the household as ensuring the survival of low-cost plantation and factory workers, or the household that becomes one of the sites of industrial production. It is impossible to do justice to these issues here; for a discussion of some of these points, see Sassen (1996).

legitimacy for which state authority has long been the emblematic instance.[60] The logic of the transformation at issue is that forms of authority once exclusive to the public domain are now shifting to or being constituted in the private sphere of markets with the corresponding normative recoding. This then raises anew the question of the nature of the private-public divide, the location of this divide, and in what specific ways these changes are—or not—part of the tipping point that ushered in the current global age. A critical variable in this discussion is the historicity of the construction of these domains, the character and location of the divide, and the legitimating norms. Thus the modern western evolution in the formalizing of two distinct spheres largely expanded and valued the public realm, even as it developed the private as a sphere marked by neutrality and the absence of politics; the development of the sphere of the market was enabled by a strong public realm and a strong concept of the national interest.[61]

Do the character and content of this division change with the post-1980 developments in the nature of capitalism and of the liberal state? My answer is a qualified yes. Qualified, because many of the critical capabilities for the distinction between a private and public sphere, shaped during the preceding two centuries, remain in place; they are not especially engaged in the new organizing logic that marks the current era. This fits into my argument that globalization is a partial, not absolute development: it does not encompass all components of society. A second reason for this qualified yes is that the administrative capability represented by the national state remains a critical agency for the instituting of the new organizing logic of the global age and thereby for the reconstructing of the public-private divide, including for the expansion of the private domain. It remains so in a manner akin to the role of the state in the development and enablement of markets over the last two centuries, though the forms and contents as well as the location of the divide are often radically different across time-spaces. Again, this is a partial rather than absolute or total condition: only some components of the state function as such critical agents. Indeed, other components, notably the expanded authority of the executive over citizens, function in opposite ways.

---

[60] This is a foundational norm in liberal democratic theory; its normative character, at the same time, shrouds the actual operations of authority and power that might take place in the private sphere (Shklar 1964). Thus, returning to the issue raised in the preceding footnote, critical feminist scholarship has laid bare this shrouding in the case of the household and the family (e.g., Pateman 1989; Minnow 2002).

[61] There is a large critical scholarship that has documented the historicity of the division and shown us its variability and the fact that the domain of the private is political and far from neutral. It is impossible to do full justice to this scholarship here.

This transformation, albeit qualified and partial, in the private-public divide is part of the bundle of dynamics constituting the tipping point that ushered in the current global age. I see this transformation as formed through three major processes. The first is the reversal in the centuries-old trend that saw the growth and the strengthening of a formalized public domain. Beginning in the 1980s we see the private domain expand and gain power through the absorption of particular state authorities and through the formation of new types of private authority; I add to this argument the dynamic interaction between a "privatizing" executive and the erosion of citizens' privacy rights. These various trends hold especially for the United States, although the growth of private authority in the 1990s is evident in a growing number of countries in the global south and with much milder variants in the rest of the developed world. The second process is the formation of new public-private arrangements (privatization and marketization of public functions) that blur particular components of the public-private divide. One example of this blurring is the difficulty the U.S. Supreme Court had in establishing whether guards in privatized prisons have the same federal rights as those in government-run prisons. The foundational change lies in the details—these become heuristic in that they illuminate the difficulties of or the need for adjusting the existing machinery to these mixed forms. Accommodating these new public-private forms requires further elaboration of legal and regulatory matter. The third process is the change in the character of the private interests that insert themselves in public policymaking and thereby shape possibly critical components of the domain of the public. While private interests may long have shaped components of the public domain (for instance, the state's enabling of a market economy that was the project of the emerging bourgeoisie of the 1800s in England), the specific interests in play have varied, as has the extent to which the opposing interests of capital owners and workers succeeded in shaping the public domain. Today, economic globalization has brought with it a new formalization of the private sphere, including a strengthening of its representation as neutral and technical, and of the market as a superior ordering from that of governments. Much of what circulates through the public domain today is geared toward setting up the infrastructure for global operations of markets and firms, as well as for shedding the responsibilities of the social wage that are part of the preceding era. This is, clearly, a highly variable project across countries, and one imperfectly executed.

One question this raises is in what ways the public sphere might also today, as it was in the past, be critical to the viability of the new types of markets and emerging types of private authority, rather than simply a victim of the growth of the private domain. In the past, an expanding public sphere took on many of the externalities of markets, including workers' demands, insufficient consumption capacity, or environmental damage. The Fordist contract and Keynesian policies are perhaps the strongest examples of the public sphere's compensating for the costs, or responding to the needs, of the private economic sphere. Today both the character of economic globalization and the power shifts inside the state evince strong associations or correlations with the increased prominence of the market and the law and with their renewed formalization as neutral. This in turn strengthens the legitimacy of the private domain. The current sharpened emphasis on the neutrality of the market can easily obscure the historicity of the private-public distinction—it has been constituted differently across time and across countries, as well as across different types of markets. Its historicity signals it is not a neutral, purely technical division. It is constructed and in this regard reflects different interests and the differential power of actors. Who benefits from the distinction can vary. Further, today's new and increasingly formalized public-private arrangements blur the distinction, as is suggested by my thesis of the privatizing of executive power at the heart of the public domain. This blurring assumes specific forms depending on the type of domains involved. In brief, both the location of that division and what it is that gets arrayed on each side are variable and, in a growing number of cases, ambiguous. Markets are not all the same and neither is the relationship between the public and the private, suggesting the division is internal to the political economy of a period and a place. Also internal to the political economy is the formalization of the private as a distinct and separate domain where political power supposedly plays no role, a foundational element of liberal democratic theory.

In what follows I first examine the variability in the articulations of the public and the private, and then the increasingly developed relationship of the public domain to markets.

The Variable Articulations of Private and Public Authority

Governments have long shared regulatory authority with private actors. Hadfield notes that "from the Middle Ages to the infant digital age, there are examples of law developed and administered by private entities with varying degrees of state involvement" (2001: 41). Nonetheless, the broad trend over the last two centuries has been to incorporate what were once private regimes or informal regimes into national law, in effect nationalizing regulation and leading to the emergence of the regulatory state. Thus the current expansion of the private sphere, particularly through the privatization and marketization that took off in the 1980s in some countries and worldwide in the 1990s, is a novel turn in the history of the national state. That does not mean that the overall state apparatus is shrinking, even if some components are, notably those linked to the social wage. Deregulation has actually expanded various parts of the public administration as has the growing shift toward executive coordination of the latter.

Today's trends represent a partial rupture with the history of much of the last two centuries in the major Western powers. The distinction between a private and a public sphere in the modern state is one historically constructed under specific conditions and alignments.[62] One critical dynamic in the formation of a distinct private sphere was the strengthening of merchant capitalism in the Late Middle Ages, its later scaling to a world level, and hence the need for a flexible law that gave merchants freedom of contract and guarantees in their dealings with parties worldwide. But the consolidation of the modern state included the development of capabilities to regulate the economy and reduced the autonomy of merchants compared to what it had been in the Late Middle Ages. The ascendance of the national state brought with it development of the public realm. What is easily forgotten in the current representation of this divide is that the state was the major economic actor in the period of colonial pillaging and the subsequent centuries of commercial and military imperialism. What had once been private merchant law and private dispute settlement outside the state's reach became public. One crucial feature of this process was the incorporation into state law of market regulation. As the state's capabilities and its regulatory project evolved, it also reduced the formal autonomy of the early industrial capitalists even as these became an increasingly developed legal persona. This was not necessarily against the interests of the capitalist class; on the contrary, since the geographic expansion of commercial transactions raised the difficulties and costs of contract enforcement and guarantees. The complex interactions between private and public authority are also legible in the fact that because merchant law was a significant capability, its incorporation into national law strengthened the latter in both its private and public forms. This incorporation of the

---

[62] As I discussed in chapters 2 and 3, in medieval times there was no public sphere as we have come to understand it—there was a vaguely defined private sphere and there was the realm of divine authority of the church and the emperor. The public sphere was rudimentary—the nobility had the authority to command military service and to sit as judges. The formal recognition of a distinction between the interests of the king and those of the public realm is a major step in this evolution of a public domain. But it took a specific mix of dynamics to produce a full-fledged distinction between a public and a private realm.

jurisdiction of merchant courts into national law made national judicial enforcement increasingly prevalent (Cutler 2001: 488).[63]

An interesting compensatory dynamic is that as merchant law became absorbed into national legal systems and thereby particularized, there was a growing need for a new system to handle cross-border transactions: international law (J. Paul 1995; Ruigrok and van Tulder 1995; Sell 2003). The proliferation of national differences as the modern nation-state evolved over the nineteenth and much of the twentieth centuries brought with it a shrinking realm for the more standardized law merchant. Where the latter had been an instrument allowing international commercial transactions to be guided by a set of "universal" criteria, albeit typically imposed by the dominant power(s), its insertion into the distinct laws of each national system particularized merchant law (Cutler 2001: 482).[64] International law was developed to accommodate international commercial transactions in the emerging interstate system. Critical to the project of international economic expansion of major powers was reducing legal barriers to exchange and securing contract guarantees, both of which reduced the costs of contracting. In the case of Britain, the interest in enabling cross-border transactions went back centuries; in the case of the major powers that arose in the late nineteenth century this interest strengthened in the twentieth century, with sharp ups and downs due to wars and economic crises. Over that century, the division between the private and public and the contents of the specific interests involved varied markedly.[65]

At the heart of the formalization of this distinction lies the proposition that the market is not political and hence deserves to fall under a specific

---

[63] Cutler has one of the best analyses of this historical evolution. In this period when states became the strongest economic and political actors, national adjudication and enforcement became the norm, as conflict between private and public was resolved in favor of public. But as a norm national regulation was only moderately strong given the continuing recourse to private arbitration in some jurisdictions.

[64] Cutler, Haufler, and Porter observe that a distinct social block emerges around the interest of developing international private law for cross-border business transactions, consisting of a mix of groups interested in the expansion of capitalism across borders, enabling the mobility of capital, and promoting international commerce: an elite group of merchants, trade lawyers, trade associations, and government officials working in combination with intergovernmental efforts to unify commercial law and practice (1999: chapter 1).

[65] The Bretton Woods discussion captured some of these differences, especially as they concerned the United States vis-à-vis the other major powers. In its first decade, the Bretton Woods system actually strengthened the power of each national state over its economy as part of the international agreement: Bretton Woods called for a system that would protect countries from external influences. The profound asymmetry between the United States and the other major powers devastated by war created a very different setting from that of the turn of the nineteenth century, when exports and colonial trading systems were major objectives for each of the leading powers.

legal regime.[66] In this neutral private sphere the law is meant to ensure participants freedom to enter contracts and guarantees of contract. In fact, in its origins the development of a distinct sphere of private law served to construct the legal persona of the bourgeoisie and to endow it with a broad range of rights, all of it represented as the neutral requirements of the market. More generally, this development of private law has enabled the formation of a variety of economic actors depending on the period and the place. Cutler (2001) posits that the distinction between a public and a private realm enables the formation of social blocs that vary over time, each with specific interests, but always represented as neutral, natural, technical, and efficient.[67] Cutler emphasizes that the attribution of neutrality and naturalness to the private domain of exchange obscures significant differences across the various phases in the character of the beneficiaries of the recognition of a private realm (2001: 481). Thus the private and public domains have changed as historic blocs have vested them with different contents and as these blocs themselves have evolved and assumed specific contents across different countries and economic eras in the last two centuries. As I discussed briefly in chapter 3, industrial capitalism got constituted in often markedly different ways in the major powers of the time even as in each case the distinction between a private and a public domain was crucial. Industrial capitalism succeeded in developing the private domain in Britain. In comparison, in France the state remained a key player in the evolution of industrial capitalism, thereby producing a rather different division between the public and the private.

Today, in the context of the formation of a global economy, the privatization of public sector activities, and the deregulation of national economies, the private-public distinction and its particular beneficiaries get constituted in yet other ways. It has become clear after twenty years that the formation of a global economy has brought enormous advantages to some and has been

---

[66] In the United States the Constitution highlights the distinction, and although it is not completely clear, the division remains an important part of constitutional jurisprudence, and hence there long has been a need to distinguish the public from the private for some issues (Aman 1998: 771n. 39), and it continues to be relevant even though under globalization the state functions in different ways.

[67] This obscures the conflicts possible between state elites and society, thereby also obscuring the distinction between state and society. They do not explain why political elites found it useful to regulate dispute settlement in the second phase of the regime but not in the third. This type of argument is incapable of accounting for the influence of national power and state interests, because heuristic and analytic issues are reduced to efficiency concerns. On how international relations scholarship has had difficulty accommodating non-state actors in the transformation of the public-private divide, see Haufler 1997 on private actors providing public goods.

devastating for other sectors of national capital. Furthermore, the distinction between private and public gets constituted differently from what it was in other economic phases of the development of capitalism, most notably the Keynesian period of the recent past. There is not only an expansion of the domain of markets but also a repositioning of markets, as these are increasingly represented as optimal for the execution of erstwhile public state functions. Finally, cross-border processes require new approaches for determining the character and location of the distinction between these domains. In addition, there is a sharply increased role of the law as a neutral agent and source of criteria in the economy, which is also further strengthening the private domain.

The current globalization of major firms and markets that began in the 1980s and sharpened in the 1990s has created specific objectives in terms of freedom of contracts and guarantees. It includes states worldwide expanding such freedoms and guarantees for foreign firms and it includes states collectively eliminating legal, accounting, and technical barriers to cross-border transactions. Insofar as these objectives are construed as pertaining to the private realm, the putative neutrality of the latter can be seen as a major help in instituting the requisite changes inside each pertinent nation-state. Today the efficiencies assumed to be associated with markets reinforce belief in the superiority of private regulation (see Posner [1997] for an elaboration; Aman [1998] for a critical examination). Yet the different locations for the division and contents of each realm across time and place suggest that the efficiency argument is highly conditioned by historical junctures or periods. Efficiency explanations do not accommodate the differences across nation-states within a given historical period and the shifting construction of the division within a given nation-state across time.

Efficiency-centered analyses need to historicize efficiency to accommodate the fact that the period of formation and development of the nation-state brought with it a growing role of the state in regulating commerce and investment when today the equivalent economic actors seek to privatize multiple public regulatory functions. One might argue that it is all efficiency centered—why should efficiency be the same in the Stone Age as it is today, or in the Middle Ages as it is at the time of nineteenth-century commercial empires? But there is a risk in these arguments of a spurious correlation, one evident in today's common assumption that where there is a "free" market, outcomes can be interpreted as delivering efficiency.[68] On the other hand, even if one were to accept a historicized definition of efficiency sufficiently

---

[68] There is a vast literature documenting the failures of markets to deliver efficient outcomes (see Noble 1977).

general to account for enormous variance across time and place, such a level of generality is not useful for my purposes, as it is precisely the specific contents of the private and public domains that concern me. The content of efficiency for dominant groups evolved, thereby signaling the changing weight of particular interest groups. To situate today's concept of market efficiency we need to factor in both the historical specificity of each particular social bloc for a given time and place and the fact of often sharp variance across countries and historical periods. Perhaps more today than in past periods, this historicity and variability of efficiency is easily overlooked in technical analyses of market neutrality, to which we can now add the supposed efficiencies derived from implementing Western-style legal codes.

While there may be sharp disagreements in the scholarship as to the efficiency and neutrality of the private market domain, there is little disagreement concerning the overall growth of private authority since the 1980s. Where preceding centuries saw the growth of the national public realm, the last few decades have seen a sharp reversal in this trend. Again, the particular component of the private sphere at issue is the growth of private forms of authority around matters once exclusive to the state and the public domain. The private and the public can be articulated in variable ways even within a given historical period and country, notably the United States since the 1980s, and the variable ways in which private authority gets constituted. We can identify several distinct dynamics in the recent growth of private authority. The first is the proliferation of private agents who originate rules and norms to handle domains once exclusive to governments. The second is the marketizing of public functions both at the domestic and international levels. The third is the growing weight of private agents in internationalizing political authority.

There are two additional, rarely recognized variants of the privatizing of forms of authority once exclusive to the public domain. Both are highly mediated and elusive, far from the self-evident quality of the three mentioned above. One is the circulation of private norms and aims through the public domain of national states where they get represented as "public" when in fact they are private (Sassen 1996: chapter 2). While this is not new, today it has assumed a far sharper form and is happening in a context with highly developed rationales as to the superiority of markets. The other is the shift of public regulatory functions to the private sector where they reemerge as specialized corporate services: accounting, legal, and other such "order maintenance" services. In this process their utility logics shift from servicing the "public good" to servicing a private good, mostly a very particular private good (Sassen 2001: chapters 1 and 5).

In my schema, and acknowledging the limitations of all classifications, the private and public domains today get articulated through two distinct sets of dynamics. The first set involves a shift of authorities out of the state. It includes all the familiar variants of private authority recognized in the scholarship about the current period, as well as the far less noted shift of specialized regulatory capabilities to the private sector I identify above—part of the global city syndrome. The second set of dynamics does not entail a shift of authority out of the state but a denationalizing of particular components of the public domain. In what follows I elaborate on the first set of dynamics; I will return to the second one in chapter 5.

The growth of these trends since the 1980s has brought an increased variability in the meaning of private authority. Not all forms of government delegation to private regulators are the same and neither are all markets. In a helpful classification, Schwarcz (2002) broadly identifies four variants in the relation of government authority to private actors according to the extent of governmental participation. These range from rules of law originating with and put into force by the government to rules (both domestic and international) adopted by private actors without government sanction. Within these two extremes he identifies two additional variants: rules originating with private actors but put into force by governments; and rules originating with and put into force by private actors "pursuant to government delegation." Except for the first, the rest represent privatization, albeit in varying degrees.[69]

The reemergence of commercial arbitration since the 1980s captures some of these dynamics (Carbonneau 2004; Kauffman-Kohler 2003). It frees firms engaged in domestic or cross-border business transactions to agree on what legal instruments are to be used in case of a business dispute, which allows them to avoid the uncertainty of whatever the requirements of the domestic law of the forum or jurisdiction within which the transaction takes place. For their part, national states have increasingly come to represent the shift away from national courts to solve business disputes as a practical solution to the inability of judicial systems to deal with the increased volume and complexity of commercial transactions and the widespread use of courts to settle commercial disputes (Carbonneau 1990, 2004). When it comes to cross-border business transactions and dispute resolution, international commercial arbitration has become the norm; it eliminates the risk of winding up in a jurisdiction or forum with the "wrong" types of laws. Over the past twenty years, international commercial arbitration has been transformed and institutionalized as the leading contractual method for the resolution of transnational commercial disputes

---

[69] When governments delegate authority to private actors to originate and enforce rules we are "squarely in the domain of private authority" (Schwarcz 2002). A good example is that of major credit rating companies; these are private firms that can issue credit ratings and thereby decide the status of a firm or government in the capital market (T. Sinclair 1994). Here the government regulates, i.e., authorizes, the private actor, but not the rule it originates.

(Dezalay and Garth 1996). Cutler, Haufler, and Porter (1999) see in the rise of arbitration the consolidation of an historic bloc premised on the "liberal myth of the natural, apolitical, consensual and efficient nature of private economic regulation," which insulates global capital from national regulation.

There is a strong tendency to see in the rise of international commercial arbitration the resurgence of the medieval lex mercatoria, a return to an international law of business independent of national laws (Carbonneau 1990, 2004; de Ly 1992; Hermann 1998). Insofar as American-style law is now dominating international commercial arbitration, the prevalent practices are moving such arbitration away from academic law and lex mercatoria. In their major study on international commercial arbitration, Dezalay and Garth (1996) find that the administration of international commercial disputes is delocalized and decentralized, connected by more or less powerful institutions and individuals who are both competitive and complementary. It is not a unitary system of justice, nor is it centered in an overarching lex mercatoria.

Two features of this brief examination matter to my analysis. The first is that the current forms of international commercial arbitration constitute a different type of capability from that of the old medieval law of merchants. As Cutler, Haufler, and Porter (1999) note, merchant autonomy in the medieval period operated largely due to the absence of a state. Today's international commercial arbitration operates precisely because there are national states with the power to enforce laws. The second feature is that international commercial arbitration operates with the endorsement and support of states (Schwarcz 2002).

Two additional features about the shift in authority from what is formally represented as the public to the private sphere are evident in international commercial arbitration and other transnational institutions and regimes for governing the global economy. Both point to far deeper changes in the relationship between states and the governance of global economic processes than is suggested by interpretations that see all of this as a pragmatic response to new types of difficulties. One is a novel type of spillover effect from fairly established forms of private authority enabled by governments: for instance, the work of credit rating agencies today goes beyond rating particular firms and governments to establishing whether they should be subjected to more stringent regulations, becoming a de facto standard setting for the financial industry as a whole (Schwarcz 2002). The other is that the shift of authorities from the public to the private also contains a shift in the capacity for norm-making (Sassen 1996: chapter 2). Today, the private sphere is originating the critical standards and norms for its governance. In that sense we can see the formation of a new type of social bloc reorganizing the private sphere.

Private actors are shaping new forms of authority that go beyond the familiar private forms and mixed public-private forms. They are also shaping insufficiently recognized new forms of public authority. The international domain is particularly active here: partly because it has never been as regulated as the national domain and today, in the context of privatization, deregulation, and marketization, the international domain becomes increasingly transnational as the community of states, or community of national authorities, encompasses relatively fewer cross-border transactions, as the latter become increasingly economic. The proliferation of private regimes not delegated by governments can be seen as indicating that markets need more regulation than common notions of market neutrality suggest. The current moment makes this legible in a way that is not always the case and is in that sense a heuristic moment. "Soft law" becomes increasingly present because it deals with the issues that hard law cannot accommodate, especially in the international setting.

The role of private actors in internationalizing political authority (interests related to globalizing capital markets, trade, and property rights) has become a key factor in shaping the domain of international regulation. The most familiar form is the role of private agents in the elaboration of particular supranational and intergovernmental institutions and norms seen as necessary for a global economy; the aim is to set up global systems for governing trade, capital, services, and information flows through intergovernmental agreements on critical requirements such as financial reporting standards, the private property rights regime, or the global trading agreement.[70]

Here the private-public distinction easily operates in ways that veil the fact that it is often the utility functions of private actors in the global political economy that are shaping public policy. This can also happen in the domestic economy, where the utilities of global private actors can get enacted through the vocabularies of public policy and the national interest. Thus, private logics circulate through public institutional domains, even as private authority as such also increases in importance. The delegation of authority to private actors, domestically, internationally, and transnationally, is reconfiguring political space (Picciotto and Mayne 1999).

We see at work in these various developments a new importance and formalization of the distinction between the private and the public marked by the ascendance of markets and a sharply increased role of the law as a putatively neutral agent and setter of criteria in the economy.

---

[70] A different set of issues is raised by the development of capabilities among nonstate actors to deliver public goods, once the domain of the state or interstate organizations (e.g., Haufler 1997).

The Rise of Markets and the Law in Reshaping the "Public Interest"

The shifting location of the public-private divide toward expanding the latter raises questions about the role of older notions of a national public interest, the latter critical to the normativity of the state. When the expansion of the private sphere occurs internationally, that is to say, in a context where national states have always had weaker governance capabilities than in their national polities, we add yet another dimension to the problematic of the national public interest. The void seems to have been filled through the expanded privatization and marketization of public sector functions in a growing number of countries around the world: the result is a global concept of regulation as efficiency. With efficiency as its sole aim, privatization becomes legitimate in domains once exclusive to the state. The neutrality attributed to markets makes them critical to attaining efficiency and hence to the overall public benefit.[71] As efficiency becomes the objective, it tends to replace or function as a stand-in for the public interest. The ideal of the regulatory state has given way to that of the competitive state whose new norm is to maximize efficiency.[72]

But the private sphere has never operated in a neutral and consensual manner as posited by liberalism. There are, to start with, two practical issues. The first is that some processes cannot be reduced to market-based understandings of efficiency. They might entail other types of criteria, such as distributive effects.[73] Second, private mechanisms may not produce the greatest efficiency. Beyond these two types of issues, there is the fact that given competition with other countries in the global economy, a race-to-the-bottom effect is likely and thereby the further extension of deregulation, possibly going beyond what is efficient and even including illegal overexten-

---

[71] From a market perspective, regulation carries costs and thereby reduces competitiveness and adds unnecessary costs for consumers. However, this proposition clearly accommodates a variety of qualifiers. Markets require regulations, such as antitrust enforcement (mostly referred to as competition policy outside the United States), to ensure the existence of free markets. Further, there are highly regulated markets, e.g., those for medicines that ensure the competitive success of products.

[72] Schwarcz (2002) finds that few legal scholars mention goals other than efficiency for commercial regulation. The focus is primarily on whether regulation is necessary to correct market failures (monopolies, externalities, bargaining power problems, and information problems) in order to increase efficiency. Schwarcz questions whether efficiency is the only goal of commercial regulation.

[73] Further, there are limits to what markets can achieve—though the discourse on the efficiencies of deregulation may not always help us understand what the limits might be in particular domains. Thus markets do not necessarily secure the public goals they are meant to achieve. Further, the actual market moment does not include all the parties affected by the transaction (Harden 1992).

sion.[74] Deregulatory dynamics do not necessarily produce a sort of golden mean and can easily produce cumulative causation in one direction, that is, deregulatory excess.[75] A fourth feature is what we might describe as the stickiness of existing harmonized multilateral frameworks (for example, for trade), which, once established, will tend to leave little if any room for incentives to see alternatives as preferable to the existing arrangement (Stephens 2002), even if they would increase market efficiency. Thus, if such an agreement contains deregulatory implementations, the tendency will be for these to stick and to continue to set the norm—a sort of built-in bias.

Public aspects of private activities are becoming increasingly unregulated and unaccountable (Hall and Biersteker 2002). The deregulation of the economy and the privatization and marketization of public functions not only expand the private sphere but also remove economic activity from public scrutiny and accountability. This matters because privatized and marketized public functions often retain public aspects. It is further accentuated by the fact, as discussed earlier for the United States, that where there are specialized regulatory commissions these are mostly within the executive branch of government and escape routine public oversight by the legislature. Increasingly the private economic sphere functions outside the scope of most forms of public accountability and scrutiny beyond basic compliance with the law.

Economic globalization and its emphasis on state competitiveness has promoted the advantages of markets over governments also in the provision of a broad range of public services and products once delivered through the public sector. The emphasis on market efficiency easily slides into notions of the advantages of getting the government out as a way of maximizing the public good. Shifting public sector activities to the market can indeed reduce government costs; it can also contribute to a kind of de facto "regulatory harmonization" in that market conditionalities enter the picture when a firm is operating in more than one jurisdiction. Market-driven regulatory harmonization is efficient for the firm, but this does not guarantee efficiencies for the public. Aman (2004: 10–12) observes that it is critical to establish whether the efficiencies realized are those of private providers rather than those of the public, in which case the challenge becomes how to achieve better matches.

---

[74] Public functions such as regulation raise the weight of local factors as local jurisdictions are pulled into the competition for global industries. The possibility of moving from one to another jurisdiction based on lower regulatory demands puts downward pressures regarding regulations across all jurisdictions. This also extends to the international level.

[75] Aman (2002) raises the issue of privatizing prisons that save money for a particular government but do so at the expense of the constitutional rights of the prisoners, an overall cost to a society under the rule of law. Another case with a similar implication is that of savings to consumers (an overall gain to a particular society) through imports from countries that use child labor, a violation of law.

The marketizing of public functions can take on different forms depending on whether it involves existing markets or creates a market where there was none before. The deregulation of market-based industries is by far still the most common form of the growth of market dynamics replacing government regulation. The making of a new market to handle public functions, for example, the privatizing of prisons, is in many ways a novel development. A more common version in this second case is the public-private partnership, one that has tended to involve sectors where there is a market. The evidence (see Aman 2004) suggests that the globalization of the economy has pushed states to marketize both types of public functions.[76] It is part of the overall trend in a growing number of countries to shift government-centered ways of handling regulatory problems at all levels of government to markets. An examination of the use of markets for what were once functions of the public sector also illuminates some of the issues discussed earlier on internal state redistribution of power. The shift to markets and market authority is a far more complex dynamic than terms such as deregulation suggest. Privatization, deregulation, and marketization have reduced the role of Congress but added to the role of the executive through the setting up of specialized commissions and the power they have assumed. In addition, this is a shift that is beyond party politics (Kagan 2001: 2344).

This shift of public functions to markets raises several questions, notably about the advantages of market versus government regulation and, more generally, whether all markets are the same and hence equally susceptible to market discipline. We are seeing new mixes of private and public powers in the marketizing of public functions. Today we see public-private partnerships for mixed public-private goals that result in entities that are neither fully public nor fully private, with all the added governance challenges this may entail. These novel mixes cannot be analyzed adequately in terms of traditional categories for such partnerships. Markets and market approaches can vary sharply, with different problems regarding fairness, transparency, and the degree of public participation. There is growing evidence that market discipline, or "regulation," does not necessarily improve public services. There are many examples, including some in highly developed countries with well-functioning market economies that show mixed results at best. For example, the British government has had to resume control over key components of privatized rail travel. It makes clear that not all markets are the same. Some markets are effective at providing some types of public services, but we cannot generalize on either the market or services side.

This shift to markets also raises questions as to the effects on citizens'

---

[76] But public-private partnerships and use of private entities did not result from but rather predated globalization.

rights. Some public services involve rights; when such services are marketized, citizens' rights may get lost (Aman 2004: 99–101). Schwarcz (2002), in his work on the privatization of prisons, observes that rights subject to markets are no longer rights. But he goes on to argue that we can use economic ends for non-economic means, for instance, to provide affordable housing for all (see Sandholtz 1999). In some ways, when the government creates markets where there are none, we are seeing the formation of markets that are neither wholly public nor wholly private. Three questions that need to be asked (Aman 1992) concerning the privatizing of public services are: 1) what are the political values that the use of markets seeks to achieve; 2) what is the impact of the power exercised by entities involved in these markets on the individuals involved: customers, citizens, consumers; and 3) what procedures can best ensure the kind of public participation and transparency necessary for political legitimacy. Thus markets in public goods where citizens can decide through their legislature what a good is worth in terms of national resource allocation, for instance, are not simply a private domain involving private actors.[77] These types of issues also bring out the constructed character of the private-public division.

   Related to the notion of market efficiency and its neutrality is the presumption built into legal systems that the contracting parties have equal bargaining power. While this is an accepted view in much of the liberal Western world, it is not accepted everywhere (Rittich 2001; Rajagopal 2003). The assumption of equal bargaining power holds for some situations, but it rarely does in transactions involving states with asymmetries in economic, technological, and legal capabilities. This is one issue raised by poorer states with little bargaining power and obstacles to market access (Thomas 1999). While there have been efforts to correct this outcome, foundational norms remain untouched (Rittich 2001: 942–43). Legal rules have distributive effects and thus may determine who has access to which markets, goods, and services and on what terms. This has been further exacerbated by the developments of the 1990s onward. We see a blurring of the distinction between the private and public domains today in some global regimes, such as trade, in the form of a multiplication of alliances between public and private agents, and between elites from the government and the corporate private sector. These alliances are grounded in a shared commitment to the expansion of capitalism through the promotion of private regulatory authority (Wendt 1995; Cutler, Haufler, and Porter 1999).

   Further, freedom to enter contracts often entails accepting contract

---

[77] When privatization through markets is a cost-cutting measure and these markets are seen as private, transparency decreases. This can undercut public participation around the issue involved. More important, the information that would make public participation meaningful ceases to be available when public services are marketized. New procedural approaches are necessary to make some markets accountable to citizens.

specifications that come out of highly developed economies and presume various types of capabilities. There are many cases that illustrate this particular asymmetry, and one need not come at it from a highly critical perspective of the global economy. In his study of IMF standards and their workability, Eichengreen (2003: 9–11) finds that many debtor countries in the global south simply lack the legal, accounting, and technical financial capabilities and resources to handle IMF-imposed programs, even if they wanted to fulfill all the requirements. These contracts are enormously complex and presume resources and technical proficiencies typical of rich global north countries. A different type of example is the process at the Doha Round of the WTO that secured some concessions from large pharmaceuticals on their intellectual property rights in recognition of the desperate health situation, notably AIDS, in many poor countries. But even here, as soon as the meeting was over, the lawyers representing the pharmaceuticals went to work, chipping away at many of the negotiated gains of the poor countries, which lacked the resources and enough legal talent to fight back.

Another trend that increases the power of private actors and works to the disadvantage of poorer countries is the marked shift beginning in the 1990s in the global south toward U.S.-style economics at the highest levels of national governments (Dezalay and Garth 2002a; Babb 2001; Fourcade-Gourinchas and Babb 2002) and the shift toward private corporate law and away from traditional public law as a source of norms. In the case of Latin America this meant a shift away from the dominance of traditional nation-state oriented lawyers (Dezalay and Garth 2002a). With the rise of the economists and the growing role of the IMF came a shift to a Western-style legal discourse in international development institutions which often served to justify what the economists were proposing: to enhance economic corporate globalization, corporate transparency to assure investors, privatization, and marketization of erstwhile public functions. Even as economists displace (traditional) public law lawyers in a growing number of governments in the global south, private corporate law is now increasingly used in the development discourse to justify the turn to the market. Markets now dominate where before the government was the main actor, promoting—often, but never completely, as a rhetorical contribution—the public interest, safety of citizens, provision of basic needs, and so on; the evidence shows that since the 1980s there have been massive cuts in nearly all countries in the global south of basic needs budget items, as well as a general decline in economic development objectives.[78] Today in international finance

[78] This new project today displaces the concerns that marked the first phase of the postwar development project and endured in the second, the import substitution phase. A move from development-based to adjustment and policy-based lending in the 1980s by the international finance institutions led to a sharp interest in the failure of states, government institutions, and practices, and hence gave an entry point for legal reform. The transition states were the occasion for

and development, law and legal discourse play a particularly important role in the representation and legitimization of reforms. Rather than poverty allevia-tion and economic growth the emphasis is on contract guarantees, rights of firms, intellectual property rights, and the notion that legal criteria are neutral, technical, and transparent. "Good governance . . . is [made] synonymous with sound development management" (Rittich 2001: 932). Law here serves to make this project recognizable and acceptable as a new ideology for develop-ment. It places securing entitlements, honoring obligations, and limiting risk for investors at the forefront of the legal reform agenda.[79] For Klare (1982: 1358) this is indicative of the broader role of law as promoting the idea of the rational and the natural: the law as legitimating ideology makes the histo-rically contingent appear necessary. In that sense legal discourse keeps us from considering new modes of democratic self-government (Rittich 2001; Rajagopal 2003).

Reports and policy statements by the major developmental institu-tions are replete with references to the benefits of the rule of law and the need for "good governance." In its recent (2001) "comprehensive development framework" the World Bank attempts to set out a template for the pursuit of de-velopment, emphasizing good and clean government and an effective legal and justice system are identified as the first elements of sustainable growth and poverty alleviation. For the World Bank the successful separation of law and politics, putting law on the side of economics, is crucial. Governance efforts can be justified if they are on the side of economic concerns; if they are linked to politics they are more problematic (see World Bank 2001: n. 20). In con-trast, as recently as 1997 (World Development Report 1997) the World Bank reconsidered the role of the state in fostering growth in a globalized economy. Now the World Bank is developing a new major project for a comprehensive framework for legal and judicial reform.

In the case of the global south, law emerges as a solution to a broader set of problems. First, failures of economic development have come to be seen as a function of state interference in the economy, various vested interests which

---

this given their preceding period as centrally planned economies and hence supposedly especially in need of international institutions to help in the transition. The ongoing decline and stagna-tion in large parts of Africa, on the other hand, was explained in terms of failed states. In both cases the project became one of helping these states adjust to the rules of the global economy. Law is seen as a remedy to stalled development.

[79] The law that matters to neoliberal legalism is a core of private law rules and other laws and regulations that enhance efficiency and support investment. Rittich observes that at the heart of what motivates legal reform is the aim to promote private sector growth. There are foun-dational laws for market economies to function: laws pertaining to the protection of property and enforcement of contract rights, augmented by corporations and bankruptcy law, banking and securities regulations, intellectual property protection laws, and competition laws.

distort markets, and large social demands on the state. Much of the strong insistence on the rule of law is to eliminate these "distortions"—when in fact both public and private law operate within a mode of production (Wood 2003). Second, law is seen as the counterweight to politics. In fact, law can itself be subject to politics in the narrow sense of the term, both in its practice and original design. The rule of law provides transparence, but transparence is itself a constructed and conditioned outcome that often is in the interests of certain actors, for example, corporate investors, even as other parts of the law can protect individuals against the state and other powerful actors. Third, many laws and regulations about state involvement in economic development—for example, in development or welfare projects—no matter how democratically derived or sanctioned, are represented as undesirable "state interventions" or excessive regulations and thus as bad economic practice. In brief, law is a means to protect boundaries: between the state and the individual, and the private and public where boundaries are seen as weak. Law can protect the markets from the state and political interests, and is thus identified with efficient markets. Finally, law is represented as separate from power, where power may in fact be at work both in the use and in the formulation of law (Duncan Kennedy 1997). One critical outcome is that the law is increasingly divorced from distributional issues and social conflict even as it assumes a growing role in the economy. As the development discourse increasingly is formulated in the vocabularies of the law, many of the institutional and value choices entailed by market reform and development projects disappear behind the supposedly neutral technical language of the law.

At the heart of this process of rendering the vested interests of powerful actors invisible lies a particular view of the nature of law and adjudication. Rittich raises critical questions that allow us to understand the drastic nature of this shift in the role of law. "How does law come to be seen at the side of economics rather than politics? The instrument of efficiency rather than distribution, the guardian of private right rather than the instrument of democratic will? The domain of experts rather than the concern of the public? What is the conception of the practice of adjudication and the figure of the judge behind the new master notion of the benefits of the law?" This type of neoliberal conception of law as promoting neutrality and efficiency obscures the fact that there are political choices "in the very design and implementation of the legal regimes underpinning market centered development" (2001: 931).[80]

---

[80] Beyond the matter of the character of the law, there is a second aspect critical to this attribution of neutrality to the private sphere: the notion that the application of the law is a neutral process. Mainstream legal thinking posits that lawmaking and law application belong to two

Although there is a role for the state in implementation and enforcement, "these entitlements are conceived as the individual rights of natural or juridical persons, techniques for keeping the state and the collectivity at bay and ways to ensure that investors can calculate risk and avoid interference with returns on their investments. The determination of the good law of the market, then, is not fundamentally a question of politics" (Cutler, Haufler, and Porter 1999: 935). Certain laws are simply necessary to markets because they promote growth and efficiency. The proposition that the market knows best dragged the law into its orbit and legitimated much of this. Often it is bureaucrats or private parties who apply the law because it is seen as merely a matter of getting the application right, when in fact it may well involve interpretation that is likely to be partly shaped by politics or interests.

With economic globalization it has become increasingly common for rules originated by private actors to be eventually enacted by governments. One incentive for this type of regulation is that it can overcome the lack of collaboration among governments. For Schwarcz (2002), this type of privatization of regulation is not particularly handicapped by legitimacy problems: insofar as it is enacted by governments it can be assumed to have been scrutinized and sanctioned by the enacting government. Some of these rules, however, can be and have been criticized for capturing only the interests of particular types of countries, especially highly developed ones. This has been the case with some of the WTO rules, financial and accounting rules, and capital requirement rules, even when each member country processes the incorporation of the rules into its national law and institutional frame, which I interpret as denationalized state work.

The overall effects of these various forms of privatization on democratic accountability and participation in the current global age are problematic. There is a tendency toward decreased transparency when it comes to public accountability even as corporate transparency grows. Perhaps at the heart of the issue is not so much contesting all forms of privatization but ensuring greater transparency and accountability of the private domain, not presenting it as neutral.

---

different domains. Judges apply the law. But according to some scholars (e.g., Duncan Kennedy 1997), far from being neutral, the process of application of the law—adjudication and interpretation—is a critical site for the elaboration of legal norms. Kerry Rittich (2001) uses Duncan Kennedy's argument (1997) that far from being the neutral technical moment of application of rules, adjudication is charged with politics and ideology because it is ambiguous and open-ended. An essential aspect of the practice of judging is the denial of the very large degree of choice and agency a judge faces in reaching a decision and developing the reasons that support it. Decisions are not simply the result of mechanical applications of the pertinent rules and doctrines to the case.

Violations of the Freedom of Information Act (FOIA)

Executive Action and Background	Instance(s) of Secrecy	U.S. Precedent	Institutional Reaction[1]	Some Consequences
The Freedom of Information Act (FOIA) was passed in 1966 and went into effect in 1967. It was amended several times, most significantly in 1974 when Congress gave the courts power to review agency decisions. It is grounded in the belief that a democracy functions best with an informed public. It was again amended in 1996 by the Electronic Freedom of Information Act, which requires that agencies create "electronic reading rooms." The law gives citizens the right to petition agencies for information and offers nine exemptions, including the need to protect national security, trade secrets, deliberative processes, and personal privacy. In addition, there are 142 different statutes that	A memo issued in October 2001 by Attorney General John D. Ashcroft is an indication of the Bush administration's drive to restrict access to information. The memo—in the works long before the terrorist attacks—assures agencies that "When you carefully consider FOIA requests and decide to withhold records, in whole or in part, you can be assured that the Department of Justice will defend your decisions unless they lack a sound legal basis or present an unwarranted risk of adverse impact on the ability of other agencies to protect other important records" (http://www.usdoj.gov/oip/foiapost/2001foiapost19.htm). Classification actions in 2001 increased by 44 percent to 33,020,997 (Nelson 2003b). Since September 11, three new agencies were given the	Openness in government was considered as a democratic value when President Wilson was inaugurated in 1913. That radically changed with World War I. Much of today's structure of secrecy took shape in about eleven weeks in the spring of 1917 while the Espionage Act was being debated by Congress and war hysteria predominated. Wilson called for legislation that would make it a crime to disclose defense secrets to unauthorized persons. The Espionage Act has been amended several times over the years. Since 1950, penalties have been added for the violations of the statute. Under a 1978 executive order by President Carter, government officials for the first time were ordered to consider the public's right to know in classifying information and were instructed to use the lowest level	On the Cheney energy task force case: The General Accounting Office (GAO) filed a lawsuit to enforce a subpoena it had issued for information about the task force's activities. In this suit, the administration argued that the GAO, as a legislative branch agency that reports to Congress, has no standing to enforce its requests for information against the executive branch. The GAO lawsuit resulted in a stinging defeat for the GAO when a federal district court in Washington, D.C., accepted the administration's argument. In a second lawsuit prompted by the Judicial Watch and the Sierra Club, the administration has argued that it would violate executive privilege for the vice president even to have to respond to the plaintiffs' discovery requests. In the summer of 2002, the district	What now are "temporary" emergency orders will hold for twenty years—as was the case with the cold war restrictions for years after it was over. The lack of openness impedes the ability to create public pressures to solve issues of relevance to the population. For example, when risk analyses of chemical plants were available on the Internet, people could pressure companies to do better or move away. (Graham 2002). This is no longer the case. It is important to note many of the withdrawals in information (particularly from the Web) mirrored efforts industry had been making for years to prevent the spread of information.

permit withholding infor-
mation.

In 2003, the Homeland
Security Act added a pro-
vision prohibiting disclosure of voluntarily pro-
vided business information
relating to "critical infrastructure." FOIA's management is decentralized. The
Justice Department pro-
vides some guidance and
training for agencies (Banisar 2004).

Although committees
formed to advise the gov-
ernment on policy matters
that include persons who
are not government em-
ployees are required to
comply with the Federal
Advisory Committee Act
(FACA), which, among
other things, requires bal-
anced membership and
open meetings, this has
not been the case. One example is Vice President
Cheney's closed-door en-
ergy negotiations.

power to stamp documents
"Secret"—the Environmental
Protection Agency, the Department of Agriculture, and
the Department of Health and
Human Services. (Some material that has been removed
from Web sites is still available, though obviously to
fewer people, in government
reading rooms.)

In March 2002, the Defense
Department issued a draft regulation concerning possible
limits on the publication of
unclassified research it finances
and sharp restrictions on access by foreign citizens to such
data and research facilities. On
June 20, 2005, the ACLU issued a report charging the
Bush administration with plac-
ing "science under siege" (the
title of its report on the issue).
The ACLU accused the ad-
ministration of tightening restrictions on information, individuals, and technology so as
to compromise academic freedom and scientific inquiry in
the name of homeland security
(American Civil Liberties
Union 2005).

of clearance when in doubt. In
1982, President Reagan signed
an executive order rescinding
these provisions and encouraging more classification of materials (Nelson 2003b). In October 1993, to better standardize
the process and create more
openness in government, Attorney General Janet Reno dispatched a memorandum re-
vamping the way FOIA would
be administered. FOIA officers
should "apply a presumption of
disclosure." Reno decreed that
in the event of FOIA-related
litigation, the Justice Department would no longer defend
an agency's withholding of information merely because there
was a "substantial legal basis"
for doing so.

In 1995 President Clinton issued an executive order aimed
at holding classification to
a minimum and promoting
as much declassification as
possible.

The increased secrecy in the
United States comes at a time
when governments around the
world are trying to establish

court denied the administration's motion to dismiss the
claims under FACA, and, later
in the fall, it firmly rejected
the administration's con-
tention that executive privilege excused the vice president
from even having to respond
to the plaintiffs' discovery requests for the documents necessary to resolve the FACA issue. Although such rulings are
normally not applicable, and
the district court denied the
government's request that it
specially certify the case for
appeal, the administration has
attempted to appeal anyway.
Both the district court and the
appellate court denied the
government's motion for a stay
of discovery pending the appeal, and the case was argued
before the U.S. Court of Appeals for the D.C. Circuit in
April 2003.

On April 1, 2004, a federal
judge ordered several federal
government agencies to release
documents concerning their
work on Vice President Cheney's energy task force or provide a legal reason for with-

The National Resources
Defense Council, an envi-
ronmental advocacy
group, and Judicial Watch,
a government watchdog
organization, have been
trying for three years to
obtain the records from
the energy task force meetings. The organizations
claim the documents will
show the extent to which
the task force staff met se-
cretly with industry executives to craft the Bush administration's energy
policies, such as drilling
for oil in the Arctic Na-
tional Wildlife Refuge and
weakening power plant
pollution regulations. A
disclosure of such deci-
sions is of crucial interest
to the public, even beyond
U.S. borders.

In the 2003 fiscal year, for
every $1 the federal gov-
ernment spent declassify-
ing documents, it spent an
extraordinary $120 main-
taining the secrets already
on the books. In total,
the government spent

(continued)

Violations of the Freedom of Information Act (FOIA) (Continued)

Executive Action and Background	Instance(s) of Secrecy	U.S. Precedent	Institutional Reaction[1]	Some Consequences
In 2002, there were over 2.4 million requests made to federal agencies under FOIA and the Privacy Act, the highest number ever. Law enforcement and personal privacy were the most cited exemptions for withholding information (Banisar 2004).	Critics of the efforts of the president and vice president to withhold from the public information about the membership of the National Energy Policy Development Group (known as the Cheney Energy Task Force) have charged that representatives of the energy industry were given preferential access to the deliberations of the task force as compared to representatives of environmental groups, consumer advocates, and others whose agendas differed from those of Enron and Exxon, among others. Note: The Executive Order on Classified National Security Information requires that all information twenty-five years and older that has permanent history value be automatically declassified. Within five years unless it is exempted. Individuals can make requests for mandatory declassification instead of using FOIA. Decisions to retain classification	the precedent of openness and disclose information. More than fifty countries now have guaranteed their citizens the right to freedom of information. More than half such laws passed in the last decade, according to a global survey posted by the virtual network of openness advocates (freedominfo.org and developed by Banisar 2004). While the majority of the cases involve developed countries, in Asia, nearly a dozen countries have adopted freedom of information laws or are on the brink of doing so. In South and Central Asia and the Caribbean, six countries have adopted such law and approximately twelve are considering them. Openness has started to emerge in South Africa where the Promotion of Access to Information Act was approved by Parliament in 2000. Members of the Commonwealth in South and Central Africa are following this lead.	holding them. U.S. District Judge Paul L. Friedman rejected arguments by Bush administration lawyers that employees from the Department of the Interior and Department of Energy can claim special confidentiality privileges for the period when they worked for the task force, which held private meetings with energy industry representatives as it crafted a national energy policy. Other general issues regarding secrecy and FOIA: With the many reports on government secrecy being published by media channels, Congress has begun to respond. A bipartisan collection of senators—Ron Wyden (D-Oreg.), Trent Lott (R-Miss.), Bob Graham (D-Fla.), and Olympia Snowe (R-Maine)—introduced the Independent National Security Classification Board Act of 2004 (S. 2627) in late July	$6.5 billion in 2003 creating some 14 million new classified documents (Craig 2004).

are then subject to the Interagency Security Classification Appeals Panel. Between 1995 and 2001 over 950 million pages out of 1.65 billion pages were declassified. The executive order was amended, however, in 2003 to restricted release. The Information Security Oversight Office (ISOO), a division of the National Archives, has policy oversight of the government-wide security classification system. ISOO's 2002 report states that classification by government agencies is increasing while declassification has slowed down (Banisar 2004).

Other (selected) cases: *Bosnia and Herzegovina*: The Freedom of Information Act was adopted in October 2000; *Kosho*: The Law on Access to Official Documents was approved on October 16, 2003; *Mexico*: The Federal Transparency and Access to Public Government Information Act was unanimously approved by Parliament and then signed by President Fox in 2002; *Pakistan*: President Musharaff promulgated the Freedom of Information Ordinance in October 2002; *Panama*: The Law on Transparency in Public Administration was enacted on January 22, 2002; *Poland*: The Law on Access to Public Information of Public Interest was approved in October 2001; *Tajikistan*: The Law on the Republic of Tajikistan on Information was signed by President Rahmonov in May 2002; *Thailand*: The Law on the Right to Information went into effect in April 2004 (Banisar 2004).

2004. This legislation seeks to create a board in the executive branch that would review current classification policies, make recommendations for reform, and "serve as a neutral forum for reexamining disputed classification decisions." A companion bill (H.R. 4855) to the Senate version has also been introduced in the House (Craig 2004).

(*continued*)

Secrecy about Presidential Records

Executive Action and Background	Instance(s) of Secrecy	U.S. Precedent	Institutional Reaction[1]	Some Consequences
The Presidential Records Act of 1978 provides that presidential (and vice presidential) records are public property. The law requires all presidential and vice presidential records to be turned over to the National Archives when an administration leaves office, so that the archives may prepare them to be made available to the public. The law permits an outgoing president to impose a twelve-year restriction on access to records that contain confidential communications with and among his aides, but requires that such materials be made available to the	On November 1, 2001, President Bush passed a sweeping order under which former presidents and vice presidents, representatives designated by them, or by their surviving families could bar release of documents by claiming one of a variety of privileges: "military, diplomatic, or national security secrets, presidential communications, legal advice, legal work or the deliberative processes of the president and the president's advisers."	Until the Nixon administration, presidential records were treated as private property and presidents would make those papers available voluntarily after they left office. When President Nixon resigned, he entered into an agreement with the Administrator of General Services that would have given him possession and control over his papers and tape recordings. Congress responded by passing legislation to seize those materials and create a commission to study how best to handle the papers of future presidents. The commission's work eventually led to the passage of new legislation, the Presidential Records Act of 1978.	The order was promptly attacked in court and on Capitol Hill. Scott L. Nelson of the Public Interest Litigation Group sued on behalf of historians and reporters, maintaining that the new order allowed unlimited delays in releasing documents and created new privileges to bar release. House Republicans were among the order's sharpest critics. On December 30, 2002, the White House sought to silence the complaints by announcing that nearly all of the 68,000 pages of the Reagan records were being released. Legislation introduced to undo the order never made it to the House floor, where leaders had no interest in embarrassing the	Same as above.

public on request after twelve years have expired (except for materials that are classified as national security or are within a small number of other exempt categories).

Before the order by President Bush, the archivist of the United States could reject a former president's claim of privilege. This is not the case anymore.

president. A lawsuit challenging the order languishes in Federal District Court before Judge Colleen Kollar-Kotelly.

Public Citizen has filed suit in federal court in Washington, D.C., to block implementation of the order. However, the lawsuit also revealed that additional Reagan documents were being withheld as a result of the order, and on April 24, 2003, the White House announced that President Reagan had asserted executive privilege to seventy-four pages of documents as well as a number of videotapes. Under the executive order, the archivist is now forbidden to release those materials unless President Bush overrules President Reagan's claim of privilege, which is not likely.

(*continued*)

Legal Secrecy and the Patriot Act

Executive Action and Background	Instance(s) of Secrecy	U.S. Precedent	Institutional Reaction[1]	Some Consequences
The Patriot Act is the controversial package of anti-terrorism measures approved by Congress after September 11, 2001. It was passed overwhelmingly by Congress on October 25, 2001. According to Levy, from its initial draft to its final adoption, the USA Patriot Act, elaborated in six weeks, contradicted much of the Fourth Amendment—in far less time than Congress typically expends on routine bills that raise no constitutional concerns (2001). In this case, Congress's so-called deliberative process took place in closed-door negotiations. that is, no conference committee, no committee reports, or final hearing at which oppo-	The Patriot Act allows for (increasing) secrecy in many areas of the federal government. Most notably, and perhaps rightly commented on by the press, has been the lack of information regarding detainees (non-U.S. as well as U.S. citizens). Allegations about detainees being "enemy combatants" (which would warrant different treatment as they would be subjected to military tribunals) have not been backed up by serious evidence or much official effort. As the Patriot Act was being signed many individuals were detained without being charged, much less tried, yet the number of people in U.S. custody, the charges against them, the status of their cases, and the circumstances under which they were being held were not known. The Justice Department refused to provide this	During the Carter administration, Congress passed the Foreign Intelligence Surveillance Act (FISA), which created a new federal court to approve electronic surveillance of citizens and resident aliens alleged to be acting on behalf of a foreign power. Until now, the FISA court granted surveillance authority if foreign intelligence was the primary purpose of an investigation. This no longer is the case.	While the government's policy in the immigration cases has suffered some judicial setbacks, appeals and stays have allowed it to remain in effect. In November 2001, President Bush signed an order decreeing that suspected terrorists may be tried in military tribunals instead of regular courts—a policy that kept secret the identities of more than seven hundred detainees. In June 2003, a federal appeals court sided with the Justice Department and ruled that the government did not have to disclose the names of the detainees. One month later, President Bush invoked executive privilege to block a congressional subpoena related to the FBI's use of informants in Boston-area criminal investigations. Levy explains that "the negligible legislative	The Patriot Act, perhaps most explicitly than any other of the "instances of executive secrecy" listed here makes clear that unchecked authority on the part of the executive sets civil liberties as part of a trade off scheme with national security, where the latter seems to win out. Ample literature exists to make clear the serious treat an unchecked executive—and hence the serious damage of balance of power—is to a free society. Much more problematic is now the case in which the U.S. uses national security as a permission pass to the deterioration of individual freedom, which—most ironically—it professes as being the (rhetorical) key commitment of the Bush administration to the

nents could testify were carried out. Legislators hardly had a chance to read the 131 single-spaced pages about to become law. At the time of these developments, the House and Senate were closed because of the anthrax threats (Levy 2001).

information and even to explain why it would not give it. By June 2002, the Justice Department had still not identified many detainees. Fewer than 400 were then still in custody—74 for immigration violations, 100 who had been criminally charged, 24 as material witnesses, and 175 awaiting deportation. They had been denied legal counsel, access to their families, and details of pending charges, if any (Levy 2002).

record will make it difficult for courts to determine the intent of Congress. And because legislative intent matters to some judges—for example, Supreme Court Justices Stephen Breyer and David Souter—the USA PATRIOT statute might ultimately be invalidated as unconstitutionally vague. Ironically, Congress' rush job, which facilitated passage of the bill, could be the cause of the bill's downfall" (Levy 2001).

On September 29, 2004, a federal judge in New York ruled that a key component of the Patriot Act is unconstitutional because it allows the FBI to demand information from Internet service providers without judicial oversight or public review. In a 120-page ruling, U.S. District Judge Victor Marrero found in favor of the ACLU, which filed a lawsuit on behalf of an unidentified Internet service provider challenging the FBI's use of a type of administrative subpoena

world, as its foreign policy. In his 2005 inaugural speech, President Bush stated, "In a world moving toward liberty, we are determined to show the meaning and promise of liberty" (*http://www.whitehouse.gov/inaugural*).

(continued)

Legal Secrecy and the Patriot Act (Continued)

Executive Action and Background	Instance(s) of Secrecy	U.S. Precedent	Institutional Reaction	Some Consequences
			known as a national security letter. Such letters do not require court approval and prohibit targeted companies from revealing that the demands were ever made. The judge ordered the Justice Department to halt the use of the letters but delayed the injunction by ninety days to allow for an appeal. Moreover, in a legislative effort that seeks to modify aspects of the Patriot Act, the Bush administration lobbied hard in early July 2004 to defeat a proposed amendment strongly supported by the library and bookseller communities that would have restricted the government's ability to seize library and bookseller records under the act. After contentious debate at the House, the amendment was defeated by one vote" (Craig 2004).	

On February 14, 2005, during his speech at the inauguration of Attorney General Alberto Gonzales, President Bush urged for the reauthorization of the Patriot Act. Some of its provisions come up for renewal at the end of 2005.

Note: According to many, Gonzales has been involved in designing several secrecy initiatives at the White House" (Shaw 2004, citing Lucy Dalgleish, executive director of the Reporters Committee for Freedom of the Press).

On June 15, 2005, the House defeated President Bush's effort to preserve the broad powers of the Patriot Act, voting to curtail the FBI's ability to seize library and bookstore records for terrorism investigations. Under the House change, officials would require search warrants from a judge or subpoenas from a grand jury to seize records about a suspect's reading habits (Allen 2005).

(continued)

Secrecy on Layoff Data

Executive Action and Background	Instance(s) of Secrecy	U.S. Precedent	Institutional Reaction[1]	Some Consequences
According to the Bureau of Labor Statistics' final monthly report, U.S. employers initiated 2,150 mass layoffs in November 2002, affecting 240,028 workers. A mass layoff is defined as any firing involving at least 50 people. California had by far the most employees given the boot—62,764, primarily in administrative services. Wisconsin was a distant second with 15,544, followed by Texas with 14,624. Between January and November, 17,799 mass layoffs were recorded and nearly 2 million workers were handed their hats by businesses (Clymer 2003). Produced by the Mass Layoff Statistics Program, the statistic on layoffs by U.S. companies was issued monthly and closely watched by hard-hit Silicon Valley, serving as a key parameter for corporate America's financial health.	On December 31, 2002, the Bush administration ended funding to the Mass Layoff Statistics Program, a Department of Labor Department program that tracked mass layoffs by U.S. companies. No extra money was found to finance the production of these statistics, even though the Labor Department was given a total budget of $44.4 billion in 2002, up from $39.2 billion in 2001.	In 1992 President George H. W. Bush canceled the Mass Layoffs Statistics program amid election-year charges that he had bungled the handling of the economy. The program was resuscitated two years later by the Clinton administration.	None.	The nonproduction of crucial data on the labor market may serve electoral purposes but masquerades important economic numbers that paint a real picture about the state of the economy.

Secrecy about Possible Prisoner Abuse, and Executive Reactions to Move beyond Human Rights Law

Executive Action and Background	Instance(s) of Secrecy	U.S. Precedent	Institutional Reaction	Some Consequences
The Third Geneva Convention requires that any dispute about a prisoner's status be decided by a "competent tribunal." American forces provided many such tribunals for prisoners taken in the Persian Gulf war in 1991. But President Bush has refused to comply with the Geneva Convention. He decided that all the Guantánamo prisoners were "unlawful combatants"—that is, not regular soldiers but spies, terrorists, or the like.	The *Wall Street Journal* and other newspapers obtained copies of a Pentagon report that concluded that some methods of torture were legal, including sleep deprivation and so-called stress positions. The April 2003 report said Mr. Bush had the constitutional power to authorize torture—which is against U.S. law—if American lives were in danger. The memo that dates from August 2002 looks at the sections of the legal code (2340–2340A) that implement the UN Convention against Torture. It was written by Jay S. Bybee, the assistant attorney general in charge of the Office of Legal Counsel at the Justice Department.	President Bush's military order of November 13, 2001, which denies prisoner-of-war status to captives from Afghanistan and allows their detention without charge or access to a lawyer at Guantánamo was the first such directive since World War II. The Constitution gives Congress power to "make rules for the government and regulation of the land and naval forces." This contradicts claims of untrammeled presidential authority. When Harry Truman tried to seize Youngstown Sheet and Tube in 1952 to prevent a steel shortage during the Korean War, the Supreme Court stopped him.	On June 29, 2004, in three separate opinions, the Supreme Court reined in the Bush administration's claims of exclusive power over prisoners captured in the War on Terror. The administration had said that it, and only it, could decide if and when legal protections applied to such prisoners. The Supreme Court disagreed, reaffirming the fundamental principle that the courts have the power to say when the president has gone too far. Two of the cases, *Hamdi v. Rumsfeld* and *Padilla v. Rumsfeld*, involve American citizens—one captured in Afghanistan, where he was suspected of fighting on behalf of the Taliban, and the other caught in Chicago and suspected of involvement in a plot to set off a "dirty bomb" in the United States. Unilaterally labeled	See consequences of violations regarding FOIA.

(continued)

Secrecy about Possible Prisoner Abuse, and Executive Reactions to Move beyond Human Rights Law (Continued)

Executive Action and Background	Instance(s) of Secrecy	U.S. Precedent	Institutional Reaction	Some Consequences
			"enemy combatants" by the Bush administration, Yaser Hamdi and Jose Padilla are being held indefinitely at a naval brig in Charleston, S.C. They have never received any formal charges or any legal proceedings. The remaining two cases, which were consolidated in a single court opinion, followed a similar pattern. In *Rasul v. Bush and Odah v. United States*, the administration claimed that it could indefinitely detain at Guantánamo Bay any foreign nationals captured abroad in connection with the war on terror, and declared it was under no obligation to charge the prisoners or to provide them with any legal process.	

Contending with the Media and the Cases of Leaks

Executive Action and Background Instances:	Instance(s) of Secrecy	U.S. Precedent	Institutional Reaction	Some Consequences
Pentagon-produced "news"; legal prosecution against journalists refusing to name sources; eventual official "leaks" of information in line with the administration's strategies; and White House press passes contingent on "friends or foes" clearance.	CNN reported that the Pentagon produces Web sites with "news" articles intended to influence opinion abroad and at home, but one has to look hard for the disclaimer: "Sponsored by the U.S. Department of Defense." The agencies spent $88 million on these activities in 2004, as well as with P.R. contracts (cited by Dowd 2005).

In a civil suit filed against the federal government by nuclear scientist Wen Ho Lee, Judge Thomas Penfield Jackson has held five reporters, including Bob Drogin of the *Los Angeles Times*, in contempt and fined them $500 a day for refusing to reveal their confidential sources. In Providence, R.I., U.S. District Judge Ernest Torres has found Jim Taricani, a television reporter for the local NBC affiliate, in contempt | Despite heavy lobbying by President Wilson, Congress dropped the anti-leaks provision before passing the Espionage Act in 1917. According to this act, the government must prove intent to harm the United States or benefit a foreign power in order to detect a violation. That is hard to prove.

Even before September 11, proponents of tougher anti-leak laws were successful in their efforts. In 2000, for the first time in history, Congress passed a bill allowing the unauthorized disclosure of all forms of classified information. "Only an unprecedented, last minute lobbying campaign by media executives and a late flood of editorial columns and news articles persuaded President Clinton to veto the measure, which his administration | An unprecedented group of government and press representatives—called "Dialogue"—meets periodically in off-the-record sessions to discuss ways to protect the most sensitive national secrets without eroding the public's right to know what the government is doing. Working without public notice, this group contributed to Attorney General Ashcroft's decision not to seek a more sweeping anti-leaks law in 2002.

On October 20, 2002, Senator Bob Graham (D-Fla.), then Senate Intelligence Committee chairman, accused the Bush administration of selectively disclosing classified information that corresponded more closely to its political agenda than to national security concerns (Nelson 2003b). | The discussion of the evolution of media sources in a time of Internet blogs is beyond the scope here. Yet, it is clear that trying to "maneuver" the media via the "production" of information or the coercion of journalists and sources is possibly one of the most dangerous tools in the arsenal of unrestricted executive discretion.[2] |

(continued)

Contending with the Media and the Cases of Leaks (Continued)

Executive Action and Background Instances:	Instance(s) of Secrecy	U.S. Precedent	Institutional Reaction	Some Consequences
	because he refused to name the person who gave him a videotape of a city official accepting an envelope filled with cash (Shaw 2004). According to senior PBS journalist Bill Moyers, "we are witnessing new barriers imposed to public access to information and a rapid mutation of America's political culture in favor of the secret rule of government." His statement about the issue is worth quoting in length: "[N]ever has there been an administration like the one in power today—so disciplined in secrecy, so precisely in lockstep in keeping information from the people at large and, in defiance of the Constitution, from their representatives in Congress. The President's chief of staff orders a review that leads to at least	had supported" (Nelson 2003b: 3). Reporters in thirty-one states are protected by shield laws that generally enable them to refuse to disclose—even in a court of law—the identity of sources to whom they have promised confidentiality. Shield laws exist so that sources with important information can come forward without fear of exposure or reprisal—and so reporters can avoid being seen as participants or partisans in any litigation. However, these laws are not absolute (Shaw 2004). In 1972 the Supreme Court ruled that requiring journalists to testify before a grand jury did not necessarily abridge the First Amendment guarantees of freedom of the press. The court ruled, 5–4, that freedom		

6000 documents being pulled from government websites. The Defense Department bans photos of military caskets being returned to the U.S. To hide the influence of Kenneth Lay, Enron, and other energy moguls the Vice President stonewalls his energy task force records with the help of his duck-hunting pal on the Supreme Court. The CIA adds a new question to its standard employer polygraph exam asking, "Do you have friends in the media?" (Moyers 2004).

Secrecy is a maneuvering tool that at times goes in the opposite direction: Nelson reports that the administration has followed tradition and leaked national security secrets to serve policy purposes. It has repeatedly leaked classified information to the media about plans for war with Iraq and to paint a positive picture about its War on Terror (Nelson 2003a).

of the press had to be weighed case by case against the requirements of the criminal justice system. Thus, the court left it up to individual states to create their own shield laws. A number of states had such laws, and about twenty subsequently enacted them. That is why the recent increase in subpoenas to reporters has come in federal court, not state courts. Although shield laws vary by state, most afford more protection than the First Amendment, and in federal court, its the less protective First Amendment that prevails (Shaw 2004).

(continued)

Contending with the Media and the Cases of Leaks (Continued)

Executive Action and Background Instances:	Instance(s) of Secrecy	U.S. Precedent	Institutional Reaction	Some Consequences
	A bizarre case: A man covering the White House with the name of Jeff Gannon was found to be James D. Guckert, who was linked to the GOP (not to mention more salacious personal links that were disclosed about him). Despite not being a journalist and not using his real name, Guckert was a regular in the White House press briefing room, free to question President Bush and his press secretary on a regular basis. This event rightly raised questions about press clearance for positions of privileged access to the White House if not the president directly. For example, Maureen Dowd, columnist for the *New York Times*, revealed she was rejected for a White House press pass at the start of the Bush administration. One of the most widely debated questions has been			

Guckert's access to the White House, which is usually limited to well-established news organizations and off limits to paid political workers. Some reports mention that former White House press secretary Ari Fleischer was concerned with Guckert's possible ties to the Republican Party, but he was still asking the president questions after Fleischer left the White House, something Guckert started doing possibly as early as February 2003.

[1] Since the intention here is to capture the inflated power of the executive over the legislature and eventually the judiciary, the several and significant reactions prompted by NGOs and other "watchdog" types of organizations are not systematically listed. However, these are many and mostly a result of serious work by a variety of professionals. For example, dozens of organizations including the American Association of Law Libraries, the American Library Association, the Federation of American Scientists, the Reporters Committee for Freedom of the Press, and the National Coalition for History have joined together in a new coalition—OpenTheGovernment.org. See also the Coalition of Journalists for Open Government, at *http://www.cjog.net/.*

[2] See Allen (2004, 2005); American Civil Liberties Union (2005); Banisar (2004); Clymer (2003); Craig (2004); Dowd (2005); Eggen (2004); Froomkin (2005); Graham (2002); Hathaway (2004); Leonnig (2004); Levy (2002); C. Lewis (2004); Anthony Lewis (2004); Moyers (2004); Nakashima (2002); Nelson (2003a, 2003b); Safire (2003); "Shameful Revelations" (2004); Shaw (2004); Symons (2003); Stevenson (2004); "Transcript" (2005); U.S. Department of Justice (2001).

5 DENATIONALIZED STATE AGENDAS AND

PRIVATIZED NORM-MAKING

STATES today confront new geographies of power.[1] The associated changes in the condition of the state are often described as an overall decline in the significance of the state, especially its regulatory capacities. Economic globalization has brought strong pressures for the deregulation of a broad range of markets, economic sectors, and national borders and, furthermore, for the privatization of public sector firms and operations. Although this is correct, it is far too partial an analysis of the foundational transformations taking place inside the state and in the field of external forces within which it functions.

The work of states or raison d'état—the substantive rationality of the state—has had many incarnations over the centuries. Each transformation has had significant consequences. Today the conditionalities for and the content of specific components of the work of states have changed sharply compared to the immediate post–World War II decades or the longer multi-centuries frame discussed in part 1. Some of these changes are typically captured today through notions such as the neoliberal or competitive state, to be distinguished from the welfare state of the postwar era.

In chapter 4 I emphasized the importance of the redistribution of power inside the state, with growing power shifting to the executive and away from the legislature, and the judiciary's assumption of new strategic functions. In this chapter I focus on the larger context within which states function today. I develop three arguments in an attempt to get at the critical and strategic features of that larger context. First, and most generally, I posit that the marking features of the new—mostly but not exclusively—private institu-

---

[1] Many scholars coming at the subject from a variety of angles would agree, even though they might use other vocabularies. See, e.g., Hobsbawm (1994); Tilly (1995); Jessop (1999); Hardt and Negri (2000); Robinson (2004). See also various chapters in the following collections to get a cross-section of critical perspectives: Mittelman (1996); Olds et al. (1999); Smith, D. et al. (1999); and Calabrese and Burgelman (1999), to cite English-language literature.

tional order in formation are its capacity to privatize what was heretofore public and to denationalize what were once national authorities and policy agendas. Scholars have focused mostly on the rise of private authority, including the privatizing of domains once exclusive to the state. The growing range of such forms of private authority constitutes a critical component of the new field of power within which states have to function today. I add capabilities to privatize and denationalize that are internal to the state itself, such as specific policymaking capacities in ministries of finance and central banks that can reorient some parts of the state to global agendas. In brief, the rise of private authority is not simply an external force that constrains the state. It is partly endogenous to the state.

Second, as a new growing scholarship has shown, it is important to recognize such private authority in domains once exclusive to the state, a subject introduced in the preceding chapter. I extend this argument in two ways that develop the issues raised in a more abstract fashion. On the one hand I posit that this type of private authority represents a new normative order, one that exists outside what has been and to some extent remains the master normativity of modern times, raison d'état. On the other hand, I argue that key elements of this new normative order enter the public realm where they get represented as part of public policy or public objectives; this contributes to denationalize what had historically been constructed as national state agendas. Particular components of the national state begin to function as the institutional home for the operation of powerful dynamics constitutive or critical for "global capital." In so doing, these state institutions reorient their particular policy work or broader state agendas toward the requirements of the global economy even as they continue to be coded as national.

Third, what is the meaning of "national" in institutional components of states linked to the implementation of economic globalization? National territory and state authority assume new meanings under these conditions. I examine these issues through the specifics of the global market for capital. The reconfiguring of this market since the 1980s and the corresponding ascendance of financial norms as criteria for economic policy instantiate this unsettling of existing meanings. The research to date does not adequately address a central feature of the foundational transformations afoot: it is the fact that the utility logic of the global capital market actually increasingly circulates through the public domain where it eventually emerges as state policy (Sassen 1996: chapter 2). In so doing, an examination of the global market for capital also allows us to understand particular shifts in the construction of the private and public domains, including the de facto blurring of the distinction even as it is formally strengthened.

The chapter concludes with a discussion of the character and emergent formalization of a complex, multisited institutional order that entails a dislodging of various types of norms and authorities, both private and public, from their traditional encasements in national domestic and international law. This signals that such formalizations are possible outside the sphere of law of the national state. At its most developed this is becoming a form of global law (Teubner 2004). At its most elementary it consists of a variety of partial and autonomous systems of rule for governing specialized sectors. In both cases, it amounts to a proliferation of partial, often internetworked assemblages of specific and always partial elements of TAR.

The particular transformations inside the state, the new emergent privatized forms of authority for governing a growing range of specialized domains, and the circulation of private utility logics inside the public domain are all partial and incipient but strategic developments. They have the capacity to alter possibly crucial conditions for the liberal state and for the organizational architecture of international public law, its scope, and its exclusivity. In this sense they have the capacity to alter the scope of the formal authority of states and of the interstate system, the crucial institutional domains through which the "rule of law" is implemented. How do these trends engage the larger questions about the current global age and democracy, as well as the sources for the "legitimacy" of claims and norms?

VARIABLE INTERPRETATIONS OF STATE POWER IN THE GLOBAL ECONOMY

A key issue in the scholarship on the contemporary state and globalization is the power of global capital to constrain and even force national states to adopt particular policies. One line of argumentation on both the left and the right of the political spectrum is that this leads to more fiscally conservative policies, notably the trimming of social programs, and to pressures for greater openness to international trade and investment. These trends are often represented as evidence of the rise of a new global capitalism that renders states powerless to make real policy choices: transnational markets have constrained states to adopt increasingly similar economic, social, and fiscal policy regimes. The result is a convergence on neoliberalism: growing state acceptance of U.S. ideals of low taxes, market-based policies, shrinking welfare states, and elimination of industrial policy (Brenner and Theodore 2002; Fourcade-Gourinchas and Babb 2002). Another line in the scholarship rejects this (Helleiner 1999; Weiss 1998; Krasner 2004), albeit with variable levels of recognition of the extent of globalization. For some the above thesis is incorrect both empirically, that is, the data show far less support for strong globalization that reduces state powers (Evans 1997; Mann 1997), and theoretically, that is, there is nothing new about this since states have long been interdependent (Krasner 2004). An elaboration of this line posits that even if economic integration were far more advanced than it is presently, the predicted generalized emasculation of state powers would not necessarily come about. The reason is the effects of economic integration on governing capacities would not be uniform since states can adapt and manage challenges differently. Thus Weiss (1998) finds considerable state adaptability and variety in both their responses to change and their capacity to mediate and manage international and domestic linkages, particularly the articulation of business and government. Continued divergence can also be expected because in some key instances globalization is being advanced through the nation-state and hence depends on the nation-state for its meaning and existence (Helleiner 1995; Pauly 2003).

Among those who think globalization has been highly exaggerated, some find that the state remains an important locus for accumulation and that along with international actors they will continue to structure economic space (Wade 1990; Mann 1986). Others see state powers as much more circumscribed through the shedding and shifting of traditional responsibilities (Hirst and Thomson 1996; Panitch 1996; Swyngedouw 1992) and the diminishing of the state's traditional role as economic manager and sovereign power. For these, the state maintains its role as a key agent that can legitimate and delegate authority to powers above and below the national level; further, its territorial centrality and constitutional legitimacy assure the state's continuing key role in an international world economy even as conventional sovereignty and economic management powers lessen. Nation-states should no longer be seen as the sole governing powers; they are now one class of several types of powers and political agencies in a complex system of power from the global to the local level (Hirst and Thomson 1996: 190; Brenner 2004; Kelly 1999; Swyngedouw 1992).

For Weiss (1998) states will matter more and this will advance rather than retard development of the world economy, a view that rests partly on her emphasis on state adaptability rather than a view that emphasizes the decline of state functions. In this regard very diverse scholars (e.g., Krasner, Weiss, Mann, Evans) emphasize the tendency to overstate the power of the state in earlier periods—that this type of argument suggests that there was once a time when states were not subject to external forces that required or imposed accommodations. Postwar high economic growth can easily be interpreted as reflecting a past power of states to set macroeconomic policy stimulating high growth and plenty of revenues for the government to spend. In this light the ensuing economic stagnation of the 1970s that reduced the fiscal resources of states and led to the need to raise taxes can then be attributed to the emerging global economy. But for these scholars (e.g., Weiss) the particular difficulties of national governments with macroeconomic management (for example, balancing budgets or mobilizing sufficient revenue to fund government programs) have more to do with internal fiscal difficulties caused by recession than with globalization. Fiscal crises are phases and so are periods of growth: a return to sustained growth can then again enable governments' macroeconomic policymaking.

Another major bundle of issues in the scholarship concerns the standardizing and homogenizing effects of globalization. An important body of literature has demonstrated that there is enormous variability among nation-states. This literature criticizes the notion that because of globalization all governments follow fiscally restrictive policies and evolve institutionally toward convergence. The deregulations of the 1980s and 1990s affected many advanced industrial countries but they also evinced policy divergence (e.g., Vogel 1995; Sassen 2001).[2] Most cases of deregulation reflect governments' combining liberalization (introducing more competition into markets) with re-regulation—the reformulation of old regulatory rules and the creation of new ones. There is much debate about the extent of domestic changes. The subject of welfare decline is one issue here: it illustrates the need to distinguish the internal state reorganization of service provision from the level or extent of such provision. Pierson's study of Britain, Germany, the United States, and Sweden finds little evidence of radical change (1996): despite changes in how delivery is organized, welfare service provision regimes are stable (Clarke 2003; Taylor-Gooby 2004; Esping-Andersen 1990 and 1996). These changes can thus be interpreted as more connected to the evolution of the welfare state since its inception fifty years ago than as the result of global market pressures (e.g., Weiss 1998: chapter 5). Yet more recently, there is evidence of less regime stability (Clarke 2003, Taylor-Gooby 2004).

The empirical evidence showing considerable variability in policy responses and states' broader macro- and microframing is crucial as a counterbalance to easy generalizations about the powerlessness of national states con-

---

[2] Vogel's comparison of regulatory reforms in Britain and Japan shows that governments have responded to similar market pressures in remarkably different ways, reorganizing rather than abandoning control of private sector behavior. See also Sassen 1991.

fronted with global markets, global firms, and their homogenizing powers. Such firms and markets are powerful and they can standardize key aspects of the various countries they enter, but this is not the full story. Once global firms and global markets enter national institutional spaces they confront considerable national specificity. Empirically I add the existence of "national" systems whose operational features are de facto global as a result of the denationalizing of particular national policy frames; these systems are then to be distinguished from imperial systems of earlier phases of the world economy, which were de facto national.

I agree that the tendency to expect institutional convergence and the failure to recognize state variety are two sides of the same coin (Weiss 1997: 4). Both are based on a policy instrument theory of state capacity in which the relevant instruments are somehow predetermined and fixed in character. Any decline in a particular policy is read as state loss of power. State specificity is crucial, and not recognizing it can lead to spurious inferences. But this perspective leaves out the fact that global systems insert themselves in national domains where they once were nonexistent. The outcome of this negotiation between standardizing global systems and the thick environments of the national can easily be packaged as national even though its actual content pertains to new global systems. In this regard I find Cox's thesis that strong states act as midwives, not victims of internationalization, compelling (1987: 204). Failure to differentiate state capacities, both across countries and inside a given national state, easily can keep globalization scholars from considering, let alone examining, how states may at times facilitate globalization.

State involvement needs to be differentiated. Some forms of such involvement actually correspond to the national/world economy interaction of preceding periods rather than the denationalization I identify as critical for many features of the current era. In this light, I would interpret the 1997–98 Asian financial crisis and Japan's prolonged economic crisis of the 1990s as global systemic disciplining, even punishment for pursuing their own type of policies aimed at keeping their economies under firm control by national capital owners and to some extent the state. By the late 1990s we see in both of these countries a forced denationalizing of control over their economies. Rather than seeing the imposition of further "liberalization" and deregulation on their economies made possible partly by the "crises" of these economies, as state adaptability to the global era, I would interpret these crises and the ensuing liberalizations as an imposed systemic adjustment to the current global economic regime. The high levels of regulation and of national capitalist control over their economies well into the 1990s is, then, more akin to contesting a particular model of participation—that represented by the United States—in the global economy. The crises—financial in South Korea and economic in Japan—are not failures of these governments but the outcome of global systemic disciplining. This would then raise a question as to how long these states can pursue their own distinctive model of economic growth, still marked by considerable state coordination and powerful national capitals.

My interpretation raises two specific analytic questions. They concern the distinction between policy vocabularies, which may well still be national and may still diverge considerably across countries, and what it is that is in fact taking place. Thus a particular state policy orientation may well be represented as national but in fact no longer be national in the sense in which it was historically constructed. In a later section in this chapter I examine the implications of the policies of the 1980s and 1990s promoting privatization, deregulation, and marketization—briefly, they are national policies but they are effecting a foundational change that alters the notion itself of the national. It raises a question as to the character of such national policy and criteria, and the possibility that we are actually dealing with a globalizing dynamic functioning through state policies—that is to say, denationalized state work. This in turn brings up a second analytical distinction, that between a capability (for example, states that can still command enough taxes to have strong welfare states) and the assemblage within which it is positioned (a different organizing logic may well be at work). For example, larger public investing into raising school standards in the United States may now be connected to shaping a "competitive" labor force for a global world. This would be a different project and purpose from the original concept of educating one's population as a matter of civic and social rights. The scholarship on the state tends to conflate what happens inside the national state with "the national"—in the historically constructed sense of the last centuries. From here it is easy to fall into the dualisms of the global and national as mutually exclusive, or a reifying of the global as external and the national as internal (for a critical analysis of this duality, see, for example, Walker 1993).

In brief, the interpretation developed in this chapter thus builds on the current scholarship about economic globalization and the state yet differs from it in significant ways. When it comes to the debate about the impact of globalization on the state, I build on the scholarship that has documented the ongoing significance of state participation, whether willing or enforced. The state participates in and enables the formation of global markets and a global space for the operations of firms and markets. I also build on the scholarship that has documented how the state has evolved in these processes and adapted to new enabling and constraining conditions.

But my work differs from this scholarship in two specific lines of analysis. One is my thesis of a major tipping point that launches a new organizing logic in the assemblage of state capabilities for international action and collaboration. This means that while particular older capabilities may still be there the larger assemblage within which they function has been foundationally transformed. Methodologically this entails distinguishing the particular components from the larger whole. For instance, cross-border financial flows are not enough to have a global financial market, nor are cross-border trade flows enough to establish a global trading system. We have had both types of flows for centuries, but not the systems that they constitute today. The particular assemblage of territory, authority, and rights entailed by the formation of a global financial market or a global trading system differs sharply from earlier international systems for handling cross-border flows. Analytically, a focus on TAR provides three alignments along which to examine capabilities and the possibility of their positioning in two different organizational logics. Further, this type of disaggregation allows me to detect distinct trajectories for each of these three, as well as distinct institutional insertions. For instance, the repositioning of territory in the case of a global financial market is a process we can distinguish from that undergone by authority or rights.

Second, I emphasize the internal transformation of the state and that this transformation is itself constitutive of the new organizing logic, a proposition introduced in the preceding chapter. This contrasts with the more common notion that globalization comes from the outside and forces the state to adapt to a new set of external factors. I find myself far closer to some of the legal scholarship on the state than with the International Political Economy (IPE) scholarship on globalization, which has not really examined the internal transformations of the state in great detail and deals with "the state" as a unitary category. These details are critical to my synthesizing interpretation of a denationalizing dynamic and of an epochal transformation for which the state is a strategic site. Further, in much of the scholarship that does emphasize a role for the state in the context of globalization, often a critical one, the global and the national are still posited as two separate domains. My argument is that while some aspects of state participation are in fact instances of states adapting to and participating in the global, other components of the national state and of the larger nation-state are themselves strategic sites for the structuring of the global and in this process undergo foundational change.

This conceptualization brings up another key issue. As the national becomes a more complex site for the global, the specific and deep histories of a country become more, rather than less, significant and hence produce distinctive negotiations with the new endogenous and external global forces. This will then exacerbate the differences between weak and strong states, as well as the differences among various institutional domains inside a given state.

DENATIONALIZED STATE AGENDAS

One of the longstanding roles of the state vis-à-vis international economic transactions has been to negotiate the intersection of national law and the activities of foreign actors in its territory as well as the activities of its national actors in foreign countries. These actors can be individuals, firms, markets, or supranational organizations.[3] While this is not a new role, it has been transformed and expanded in the current global age, especially in the case of economic actors. In all countries now incorporated in the global economic system, governments have issued legislative measures, executive orders, and court decisions enabling foreign firms to operate in their territory and their markets to become international.

Are there particular conditions that make executing this role in the current phase distinctive and unlike what it may have been in earlier phases of the world economy? While this is in many ways a question of interpretation, in the preceding chapter I argued that there is indeed something distinctive about the current period compared with the earlier world scale examined in chapter 3 and the immediate post–World War II international system examined in chapter 4. By the 1980s there was an enormously elaborate body of law developed in good measure over the preceding hundred years that secured the exclusive territorial authority of national states to an extent not seen in earlier centuries. But there has been a considerable institutionalizing, especially since the 1990s, of the "rights" of non-national firms, the deregulation of cross-border transactions, and the proliferation of privatized systems of law internal to specialized fields, most notably the reinvented lex mercatoria and the new lex digitalis. These are systems of private rules to govern specialized domains. Except for the most powerful, states today also find their work constrained by the growing influence and power of several supranational organizations, particularly the IMF and the WTO. If securing these rights, options, and powers entailed an even partial relinquishing of components of state authority as constructed over the last century and more, this signals a necessary engagement by national states in the process of globalization,

---

[3] I examine the case of noneconomic actors in chapters 6 and 7.

even as this same process also enables the formalization of nonstate normative orders where the state once had exclusive authority.

This raises a question as to the nature of this engagement by the state in processes of globalization, and how it might vary for different types of states.[4] Is the role of the state simply one of reducing its authority (for example, as suggested with terms such as deregulation and privatization, and generally "less government"), or does it also require the production of new types of work by states—notably regulations, legislative items, court decisions, and executive orders, all amounting to the production of a whole series of new "legalities"?[5] Some states, that is, the United States and Britain, are producing the design for these new legalities and are hence imposing these on other states given the interdependencies at the heart of the current phase of globalization. Yet even so, participating states need to develop the specific instruments in terms of their own politico-economic arrangements.[6] That is to say, legislative items, executive orders, adherence to new technical standards, and so on will have to be produced through the particular institutional and political structures of each of these states, incorporating the new norms into each state's specific policy and legal vocabularies.[7] In this regard, the state can be seen as incorporating the global project of its own shrinking role in regulating economic transactions (Cox 1987; Panitch 1996; Gill 1996; Helleiner 1995).

[4] Even as I confine this discussion to what are described as states effectively functioning under the rule of law, we must allow for considerable differences in the power of these states. As has been said many times, the U.S. government can aim at imposing conditions on the global markets and on participating states that, for instance, the government of Argentina cannot— even as it revealed itself capable of unsettling the IMF when it refused to abide by its demands after the 2001 crisis by deciding to go into sovereign default.

[5] I use this term to distinguish this type of production from lawmaking and jurisprudence (Sassen 1996: chapter 1).

[6] This dominance assumes many forms and affects more than poor and weak countries. France, for instance, ranks among the top providers of information and industrial engineering services in the world and has a strong though not outstanding position in financial and insurance services. But it has found itself at an increasing disadvantage in legal and accounting services because Anglo-American law and standards dominate international transactions. Anglo-American firms with offices in Paris service the legal needs of firms, whether French or foreign, operating out of France. Similarly, Anglo-American law is increasingly dominant in international commercial arbitration, an institution grounded in continental traditions of jurisprudence, particularly French and Swiss.

[7] The guarantee of the rights of capital arises historically out of a particular type of state, a particular conception of the rights of capital, and a particular type of international legal regime (see ch. 3). Thus today it is largely Western notions of contract and property rights developed by some of the most developed and most powerful countries in the world that dominate. To this we now need to add the new legal regimes aimed at furthering economic globalization, e.g., the push to get countries to support copyright law.

Thus the emergent, often imposed consensus in the community of states to further globalization is not merely a political decision of accepting (or rejecting) that consensus. It entails specific types of *work* by a large number of distinct institutions in each of these countries, and thereby partly shapes the actual work of states. My argument is, then, that the state emerges as one of the key sites for developing and instituting the conditionalities of corporate economic globalization; the working state can be conceived of as a technical and administrative capacity that cannot be fully replicated at this time by any other institutional arrangement. And it is a capacity backed by military power, with global power in the case of some states (Hirst and Thompson 1995). While in this interpretation the state matters, it does not do so on the terms posited by those who argue that globalization has not really altered the centrality of state power. The accommodation of the interests of foreign firms and investors under conditions where most of a country's institutional domains have been constructed as "national" entails a negotiation. The negotiation in the current phase has tended toward the denationalizing of several highly specialized national institutional components. The hypothesis is then that some components of national institutions, even though formally national, are not national in the sense in which state practice has constructed the meaning of that term in the West since the emergence of the so-called regulatory state in the late 1800s and early 1900s. A good illustration of this is the Keynesian regime, the high point of the regulatory state. Though imperfectly implemented and often excluding national minorities, it aimed at strengthening the "national" economy and "national" consumption capacity, as well as raising the educational level of "national" workforces. There are, clearly, enormous variations among countries in terms of the extent to which such a national policy project existed, its features, and the actual period of time of its implementation. Many of the European states were and remain far more developed in this regard than the United States. The policies that emerge in the 1980s and 1990s to accommodate the global projects of some firms and some markets partly unbundle this notion of the national and target particular places, economic sectors, and workforce segments.

But this work of states has an ironic outcome insofar as it has the effect of destabilizing some aspects of state power itself. Thus the U.S. government as the hegemonic power of this period has led and sometimes forced other states to adopt these obligations toward global capital and, in so doing, has contributed to strengthening the forces that can challenge or destabilize what have historically been constructed as state powers, including its own.[8]

---

[8] See, e.g., the argument by Arrighi (1994); see also the debate in Davis (1999).

One of the ways in which this becomes evident is that while the state continues to play a crucial, though no longer exclusive role in the production of legality around new forms of economic activity, at least some of this production of legalities is increasingly feeding the power of a new emerging authority structure marked by denationalization in some of its components and by privatization in other components. An important, insufficiently noted mediation in this process is precisely the rise and partial privatizing of the power of the executive branch in government (chapter 4). Among liberal democracies this is sharpest in the United States and the United Kingdom. From the perspective of firms operating transnationally, the objective is to ensure the functions traditionally exercised by the state in the national realm of the economy, notably guaranteeing property rights and contracts. How this gets done may involve a range of agents. To some extent national states are producing the necessary instrumentalities that enable new forms of authority. These instrumentalities may include national legislative acts or measures that are in one way or another extranational yet need to be enforced inside national economies. This holds also for what is considered to be the first instance of global economic law, the Trade Related Agreements on Intellectual Property Rights (TRIPS) implemented in 1995; this is a specific form of international economic law to be distinguished from the international law of states. Further, to an increasing extent this work of guaranteeing is becoming privatized, as is signaled for instance by the growth of international commercial arbitration and other forms of private authority, yet even so needs to secure accommodations by national states, that is, that a state will not use military power to support one of its national firms that may have lost its case in an international commercial arbitration.

Many of these trends come together in the strategic role played by central banks today. These are national institutions that address national matters. Yet over the last decade they have become the institutional home within the national state for monetary policies that are necessary to further the development of a global capital market and, indeed, more generally, a global economic system. One key element of the new conditionality of the global economic system that needs to be met for a country to become integrated into the global capital market is the autonomy of central banks.[9] This facilitates instituting a certain kind of monetary policy, specifically, one privileging low inflation over job growth even when a president may have preferred it the other

---

[9] This autonomy is taken for granted in the United States and in most EU countries (though before the formation of the European Central Bank France's central bank, for instance, was not considered as quite autonomous from the executive). But in many countries the executive or local oligarchies have long had undue influence on central banks—albeit not always to the disadvantage of the disadvantaged.

way around, particularly at reelection time. While securing central bank autonomy has certainly cleaned up a lot of corruption, it has also been a key vehicle through which national states accommodate the requirements of the
global capital market. A parallel analysis can be made of ministries of finance
(or the U.S. Treasury) which impose certain kinds of fiscal policies as part of
the new conditionalities of economic globalization.

      We generally use terms such as deregulation, financial and trade lib-
eralization, and privatization to describe the changed authority of the state
when it comes to the economy. The problem with such terms is that they
only capture the withdrawal of the state from regulating its economy. They do
not register all the ways in which the state participates in setting up the new
frameworks through which globalization is furthered, nor do they capture the
associated transformations inside the state—a subject introduced in chapter 4
and developed in this chapter. This means capturing and conceptualizing a
specific set of operations that take place within national institutional settings
but are geared toward non-national or transnational agendas where once they
were geared toward national agendas. There is a set of strategic dynamics and
institutional transformations at work here. They may incorporate a small
number of state agencies and units within departments, a small number of
legislative initiatives and executive orders, and yet have the power to institute a new normativity at the heart of the state; this is especially so because
these strategic sectors are operating in complex interactions with private,
transnational, and powerful actors. Much of the institutional apparatus of the
state remains basically unchanged. The inertia of bureaucratic organization
suggests continuity and easily obscures the fact of foundational changes in key
state sectors.

      Submerged in what has been constructed as national legislative his-
tory, it is possible to find in many of the national states that participate in the
global economy a series of legislative items and executive orders that can be
read as accommodations on the part of these states to the demands of global
firms and global markets. Even more significant is the accelerating history of
executive branch work to deregulate, privatize, and marketize public sector
functions. These accommodations had to be produced and in that sense represent the active participation by these states in working out the conditions
for economic globalization. This is a history of micro-interventions, often
minute transformations in regulatory or legal frameworks. It is clearly not a
new history, not for the United States or other Western former imperial powers (for example, the "concessions" to trading companies under British,
Dutch, and other colonial regimes). Yet, we can identify a new phase, one
that has very specific instantiations of this broader feature.

This is a particularly developed microhistory in the United States where it clearly facilitated the expansion of the cross-border operations of U.S. firms. Among the first in a long sequence of legislative measures, and perhaps among the best known, are the tariffs passed in the mid-1960s to facilitate the internationalization of manufacturing, which exempted firms from import duties on the value added of re-imported components assembled or manufactured in offshore plants. In the case of the United States, I date the beginning of this microhistory of legislative and executive interventions to the mid-1960s, with a full crystallization of various measures facilitating the global operations of U.S. firms and the globalization of markets in the 1980s, and work continuing vigorously in the 1990s. The Foreign Investment Act of 1976, the implementation of International Banking Facilities in 1981, the various deregulations and liberalizations of the financial sector in the 1980s, and so on are but the best known landmarks in this microhistory.

Yet another aspect of this participation by the state in the implementation of a global economic system can be found in the new types of cross-border collaborations among specialized government agencies concerned with a growing range of issues emerging from the globalization of capital markets and the new trade order. These often build on long-standing networks (H. K. Jacobson 1984). Slaughter (2004) identifies three types of such government networks. One functions within international organizations in terms of issue areas. It involves the national ministries or agencies charged with the particular issue area: trade ministers in GATT, finance ministries in the IMF; defense and foreign ministers in NATO; central bankers in the Bank for International Settlements. A second type consists of government networks within the framework of an executive agreement. These are transgovernmental networks that emerge outside a formal international institution, even though members operate within a framework agreed on at least by the heads of their respective governments. Examples are transatlantic governmental interactions specifically authorized and encouraged by executive agreement.[10] A third type consists of spontaneous government networks, a development of the current era. These networks arise outside formal intergovernmental agreements, whether treaties or executive agreements: the Basel Committee of the Bank for International Settlements (BIS) is a leading example. They are networks that lack a foundational treaty and nothing they do purports to be legally binding on the members. Another example is agreements among

---

[10] Pollack and Chaffer (2001) examine several such executive agreements between U.S. and EU commission presidents to foster increased cooperation, including the Transatlantic Declaration of 1990, the New Transatlantic Agenda of 1995 (with a Joint U.S.-EU Action Plan attached), and the Transatlantic EC Partnership agreement of 1998.

domestic regulatory agencies of two or more countries. The last few decades have seen a vast increase in these, with agreements that can be implemented by the regulators themselves, without further approval by national legislators. These have grown far more than traditional treaty negotiations.

There are multiple instances of this highly specialized type of convergence in regulatory issues concerning telecommunications, finance, the Internet, and so on. In some of these sectors there has long been an often elementary convergence, or at least coordination, of standards. What we see today is a sharp increase in the work of establishing convergence. For instance, we see an intensification of transactions among central bankers, necessary in the context of the global capital market. While central bankers have long interacted with each other across borders, we can clearly identify a new phase in the last ten years. The world of cross-border trade has brought with it a sharpened need for convergence in standards, as is evident in the vast proliferation of ISO items. Another example would be the institutional and legal framework necessary for the operation of cross-border commodity chains and value-adding chains.

In what follows I examine two aspects of these new or reinvented forms of state work. One is the WTO's intellectual property rights law, the first instance of a new type of international economic law. The other is a particular type of intergovernmental network of specialists in competition policy, one of the critical building blocks for the corporate global economy; competition policy, or antitrust policy, is a good example of this work of states aimed at achieving global convergence of standards and rules.

Antitrust Policy: From Extraterritoriality to a Global System?

The 1980s launched a period of reinvigorated antitrust activities, with rapid acceleration in the 1990s.[11] Economic globalization put pressure on governments to work toward convergence in antitrust regulations in a situation where countries tended to have diverse competition laws or enforcement practices. The end of the cold war and the reinsertion of the so-called Eastern bloc countries into the market system further added to this new importance of competition policy. This convergence around specific antitrust issues by regulators in a growing number of countries frequently exists in an ocean of enormous differences among these countries in all kinds of laws and

---

[11] For a detailed study of these developments, especially the intensification of cross-border interactions among competition policy regulators, see Portnoy (1999).

regulations covering components of the economy which do not intersect with globalization. It is then a very partial and specialized type of convergence among regulators from different countries who often begin to share more with each other than they do with colleagues back home in the larger bureaucracies within which they work.

Competition policy is one key area for the changing relation between the private and the public in the context of globalization and for the competition between different models, notably those of the United States and Europe. While many countries have had some version of competition policy, there has been a sharp increase in those that have adopted such policies or reinvigorated inactive ones. By the late 1990s more than seventy countries had something resembling Western antitrust rules, compared to forty in 1970 (Portnoy 1999).[12] The reactivation of existing antitrust laws is also important. Thus the Netherlands, Great Britain, Denmark, Portugal, and Greece have had to overhaul some of their laws especially in relation to the European Commission (EC) and the development of a European competition regime. The leadership of the EC played a crucial role in this shaping phase, notably under Competition Policy Commissioners Sir Leon Brittan and Karel van Miert.

The enormous change in the international organization of business makes it difficult to apply the old norms of what a desirable competition policy might be. We see new forms of cross-border cooperation among firms, including the growth of business alliances (Dunning 1997) and complex patterns of subcontracting and short-term partnerships (Dieter Ernst 2005). In addition we are seeing the emergence of new industries that do not fit existing patterns and evince an increasingly complex relation to the intellectual property rights regime (S. Weber 2005). The deregulation of markets and industries and the new technologies make designing competition policy a difficult task because it is not even clear what the new competitive structure should be in dynamic industries operating in cross-border markets or functioning through global firms. More theoretically, perhaps, the shifting boundary between private and public authority when it comes to regulatory capacity (for instance, the growth of self-regulatory efforts in some industries) further complicates matters. To these challenges one can add the efforts in the EU to achieve agreement on specific EU company types—legal entities not based on or created through national legislation. This also illustrates the difficulties of

[12] Much of the growth in the 1990s came from developing countries and transitional economies in central and Eastern Europe, reaching over 100 countries by 2000. Among developed countries there were fewer than 10 in 1950, 20 in 1975, and 29 by 1998 (including the developed countries from central Europe).

convergence efforts: It took over thirty years for an agreement on a European Company (Societas Europaea) to be reached.[13] Among the reasons that agreement was so difficult regarding the creation of entities such as a European firm is the fact that not all member states have the legal forms entailed by the proposals, or if they do, their features may differ significantly. If this is a difficulty within the EU, it is easy to imagine the difficulties present in broader cross-border configurations.

One can see a degree of convergence in regulatory responses to global economic pressures, particularly market liberalization and the growth of cross-border business activity. The relation between competition policy and trade policy, that is, anti-dumping provisions, is a central issue here. According to one line of analysis, this convergence is basically a form of Americanization of competition policy.[14] Countries have adopted different versions of American antitrust, but perhaps an even bigger effort in many countries is toward harmonizing their legal systems with EU policy in a sort of Europeanization of antitrust law (Portnoy 1999: chapter 4).[15] According to Wallerstein (1974), U.S. antitrust law is not very exportable to other countries because it was developed under very specific historical, political, and industrial conditions not found elsewhere. Further, in view of the many different interpretations of the Sherman Act, Wallerstein argues that it is not clear what aspect of the Sherman Act might be exported. At the same time, the current internationalization of antitrust may have reinvigorated U.S. antitrust law. In his research, Portnoy (1999) finds that the better explanation of the spread and convergence of antitrust law lies in the formation of transnational networks of regulators who increasingly interact and collabo-

[13] Features of the agreement (in force October 2004) include European Company (SE) formation, state/firm relations, and structures (Hannigan 2003). What does not fall under the agreement is subject to the governance of the state. Proposals for the European Mutual Company, European Cooperative Company, and others are now being considered. Despite the passage of this agreement, its reliance on member states company law has raised questions about whether it represents a true unification of company law. The development of further Company Directives (the 3rd and 10th) relating to cross-border movements might undermine this agreement (Hannigan 2003: 58–59).

[14] Portnoy (1999) disagrees with this interpretation and notes that it was only with the general acceptance of extraterritoriality and the emergence of international antitrust cooperation that antitrust regimes proliferated in the late 1980s and 1990s. American power was great for many decades before this and yet did not impose antitrust on countries where it had undue influence—except for Japan and Germany in the immediate postwar period where it was not subsequently much enforced. In the 1980s antitrust had become a lame regime in the United States.

[15] For instance, the countries of central and Eastern Europe have been more likely to adopt the administrative form of European competition policy. This is understandable since they come from traditions where state bureaucracies are used to dealing with the economy.

rate. He identifies the growing number of organizations and occasions where this interaction and cooperation take place. The International Competition Policy Advisory Committee (ICPAC) is one key site for these processes. Some of these are public sector entities, others are private sector entities, and still others are hybrids.[16]

In terms of the role of the state, we are seeing a shift from supporting strategic or basic industries to establishing conditions for competitiveness in a global economy, a shift from macro- to microeconomic issues. And it is a shift from Keynesian policies of general national welfare to the promotion of enterprise, innovation, and profitability in both private and public sectors (Cerny 1997: 260). Again, in these shifts we can also detect a change in the boundaries between the private and the public domains (e.g., Cutler 1997).

The issues of convergence and diversity in antitrust rules come to the fore in merger policy. Most countries have not had merger regulations. It is only in recent years that this has changed: over fifty countries now have merger rules; most of this increase is due to developing countries instituting such rules (Shelton 1999). When it comes to substance and procedure, much effort has gone into rationalizing merger control systems in the EU. The EU developed a two-tiered system in 1989: large mergers go to the EU merger control regime, while smaller ones are regulated by the national agencies. The result has been unification of a significant and growing portion of all European merger regulation.[17] The most important interregional merger market is the

---

[16] The OECD Competition Law and Policy Committee has operated since 1994, the U.S.-Japan Structural Impediments Initiative Talks (1989–91), and the bi-annual U.S.-EU Dialogue, operating since 1997. Among the private entities are the International Chamber of Commerce (ICC); the International Antitrust Section of the American Bar Association; the Business Industry Advisory Committee of the OECD; various industry associations; transnational law firms such as Skadden Arps and Covington Burling; and the Trans-Atlantic Business Dialogue. Among the hybrid entities are the U.S. International Policy Advisory Committee (1997–99); the U.S. Federal Trade Commission Global Competition hearings, operative since 1995; the EC Group of Experts (1993–95); the Global Forum for Competition and Trade Policy (World Bank/IBA); and private consultants such as antitrust experts (Portnoy 1999: chapter 4).

[17] One agreement—on December 12, 1989 the Council of Ministers adopted the European Community Merger Regulation (ECMR), with two significant amendments in March 1998 and May 2004. The ECMR has sought to develop procedures for mergers, resolve jurisdictional matters, and create tools for judging what counts as concentration in an industry. Another related area concerns the development of a EC takeover code. A Takeover Directive was finally passed by the European Parliament in December 2003. It took almost fifteen years for the passage of this Directive to occur. Its eventual passage was made possible by market developments (Hannigan 2003), such as the convergence of the Directive with United Kingdom's own Takeover Code and the establishment of takeover codes in several countries (i.e. Belgium, Germany, Netherlands) that modeled the United Kingdom's code (the effectiveness of the Directive, however, is subject to debate, e.g. Novarese 2004).

North Atlantic. Mergers and acquisitions between North America and Europe totaled $256.5 billion in 1998, up from $69.4 billion in 1995. There have long been significant differences between the U.S. and Western European merger control models. The latter is more likely to define relevant markets more narrowly, to find competition threatened at lower market-share thresholds, to take much greater account of the well-being of individual competitors rather than generalized effects, and to adopt a more expansive definition of unlawful dominant firm behavior (Kovacic 1998: 1086). These differences are beginning to weaken and there is growing convergence between the EU and the United States, especially in the area of single-firm and oligopolistic dominance.[18]

Disagreements remain on the question of efficiency as a reason for clearing a proposed merger; the EU continues to be more concerned about broader conditions such as the unemployment effects of a merger. The areas of convergence continue to exist in national contexts that are enormously diverse, including differences in the institutionalizing and implementing of antitrust rules, that is, judicial versus administrative institutionalization.

International Economic Law: Autonomous from But Inserted in National Law

The interstate system, in its various incarnations across the last 150 years, has worked hard at securing intellectual property rights. The solutions developed over time have been centered in mutual recognition of different territorial systems.[19] The Paris and Berne conventions of 1887 and 1886, respectively, provided a legal framework for intellectual property. The Berne Convention epitomizes this effort.[20] However, the basic architecture of the Berne Convention cannot easily accommodate the growth of emergent global economic systems, the consequences for property rights arising out of the

[18] Simply put, it could be said that to oligopoly coordination, long a major concern in U.S. antitrust policy, U.S. agencies have now added greater attention to single-firm dominance, long the central focus of EC merger review. Conversely, the EU has moved toward the U.S. approach to market definition, going beyond the measure of market share.

[19] See the discussion in chapter 3 on the emergence in the late 1800s of a series of efforts to govern patents, notably the Paris Convention.

[20] The nature of the protection granted can be found in article 5 of the convention: "Authors shall enjoy, in respect of works for which they are protected under this Convention, in countries of the Union other than the country of origin, the rights which their respective laws do now or may hereafter grant to their nationals, as well as the rights specially granted by this Convention." Teubner (1988) finds that there were efforts to establish harmonized copyright law, but they did not succeed.

development of digital technologies and the new possibilities for transmission of copyrighted materials, or the globalization of a variety of scientific, artistic, and other creative sectors.[21] The World Intellectual Property Organisation (WIPO) is the modern institution through which states have sought to administer almost all multinational agreements on intellectual property. They have done so by means of the Agreement on TRIPS concluded during the GATT Uruguay Round in April 1994,[22] through various cooperation efforts between the WTO and WIPO,[23] through the European Convention relating to questions on copyright law, through "WIPO Internet Treaties," and by means of a variety of European measures concerning copyright (Teubner 2004).

An international economic law emerged when the Marrakesh agreement, which implemented WTO in 1994, came into effect in January 1995. It established the public legal regime of trade rules among nations that are members of WTO,[24] which accounts for 97 percent of world trade. At the heart of this international economic law are the provisions in the WTO (2003) agreements that spell out a regime for international property rights (IPRs). For some (e.g., Yueh), these provisions are a break with past international custom and treaty law, which had long been centered on the principle of the state's exclusive territorial authority principle. For others, this type of law remains centered on old territorial national law (e.g., Dinwoodie 2000; Bermann 2000; Teubner 1987, 1988). Fischer-Lescano and Teubner (2004: 1020) find no harmonized international copyright since territorially bound and nationally divergent copyright guarantees remain determinative: international agreements simply mediate between different protection standards and establish reciprocal national entitlements to the implementation of minimum levels of protection.

TRIPS rests on the norm that the harmony or uniformity of laws is the ideal for the free flow of goods and services globally. This makes states key

---

[21] The two major doctrines under public international law concern territoriality (property rights are to be protected under each state's rules) and independence (the rules under which property holds in one state are not to be forced on another state). But after World War II, an increasing concern for innovation and the benefits of diffusion, especially to LDCs, led to challenges to this legal norm. Yueh (2003) finds that enabling development in LDCs seemed to justify a reduction of benefits to the innovator. The two doctrines were seen as having lost relevance with the implementation of the WTO TRIPS provisions. Since 1995 LDCs have been compelled to adopt TRIPS, which gives inventors some monopolistic rights so as to ensure that innovation takes place, and includes provisions that recognize some of the issues of concern to LDCs.

[22] This has been in force since January 1, 1995.

[23] The Agreement between WIPO and WTO (December 22, 1995) provides WIPO resources to WTO members. The TRIPS agreement specifies a continuing role for WIPO, including in the periodic reviews of TRIPS implementation.

[24] As of April 2003.

implementers of this new regime: they must do the work that it takes to implement WTO international standards protections. These will go into national
law.[25] In this regard, some of the implications of WTO law are the denationalizing of specific components of national law. For several scholars the difficulties
of enacting WTO and of achieving harmonization and effective implementation point to the difficulties of overcoming national territorial criteria for protections and the need to do so in today's global age. Thus Dinwoodie (2000)
and Berman (1993) argue that moving away from territoriality (and adopting
functional regime affiliation) would mean that the division of jurisdictional
competencies and the normative preconditions for substantive decisions
could no longer be inferred from each local legal order involved. For Dinwoodie the "facade of copyright rules based upon territoriality needs to be
stripped away, and a new approach constructed. Some uncertainty is an inevitable, but worthwhile, short-term cost" (2000: 469, 573). Underlying
these propositions is an understanding of global law as centered on a multiplication of global but partial regimes that address the needs of specialized
sectors. Teubner's work is a brilliant examination of such an alternative conception of global law. He posits that a move toward property rights protections that would work in today's world would require a reorienting away from
conflicts between national legal orders, and their refocusing upon conflicts
between sectoral regimes, such as is the case in the context of collisions
among WIPO, WTO, EU, and national laws. From my perspective, there
are two sites for the making of global law. One is along the lines posited by
Teubner. The second is the state, but in its denationalized mode. The implementation of WTO law is a good example. Unlike Teubner, I do not see the
coexistence of these two sites for the making of international economic law
and more generally global law as contradictory, a subject I return to in the last
section of this chapter.

A NEW INSTITUTIONAL ZONE OF PRIVATIZED AGENTS

A critical and growing component of the broader field of forces
within which states operate today is the proliferation of specialized types of

---

[25] The conditions take account of the variable capacities of countries depending on
level of development. Developing countries are granted a one-year transition to adjust their national law to these new requirements. Countries coming out of centrally planned economies are
given five years. Countries lacking product patent protections in a particular domain would have
ten years to do so; the exception is pharmaceutical and chemical-agricultural products, where they
must recognize and protect intellectual property rights from the day of filing for WTO admittance.

private authority. These include the expansion of older systems, such as commercial arbitration, into new economic sectors, and they include new forms of private authority that are highly specialized and oriented toward specific economic sectors, such as the system of rules governing the international operations of large construction and engineering firms. The proliferation of self-regulatory regimes is especially evident in sectors dominated by a limited number of very large firms. These trends indicate the extent to which the global economic system needs governance, though of a different sort from that associated with the older normativity of the Keynesian state. These and other such transnational institutions and regimes raise important and difficult questions about the relation between the state and economic globalization. As Rosenau (1992) has noted, because so many processes are transnational, governments increasingly are not competent to address some of the major issues confronting our societies; this is not the end of sovereignty but an alteration in the "exclusivity and scope" of the competence of governments.[26]

One system that captures the proliferation of private authority in the global corporate economy is international commercial arbitration, today's leading contractual method for the resolution of transnational commercial disputes.[27] It allows each party to avoid being forced to submit to the courts of the other and to maintain the secrecy of the process. Such arbitration can be "institutional" and follow the rules of institutions such as the International Chamber of Commerce in Paris, the American Arbitration Association, the London Court of International Commercial Arbitration, the World Bank's International Center for the Settlement of Investment Disputes, and others. It can also be

---

[26] There is a wider systemic process here that needs to be distinguished from the effects of globalization. It is a worldwide and apparently growing distrust of governments and bureaucracies. Already earlier Shapiro (1993) found that this had contributed to the emergence of certain commonalities in law, notably the growing importance of constitutional individual rights that protect the individual from the state and other organizations. The particular hallmark of American constitutionalism is constitutional judicial review, which now has also emerged endogenously in Germany and Italy, and to some extent even in France (where there now is an active constitutional court and a constitutional bill of rights). The Court of Justice of the EU has evolved into a constitutional court (which entailed that constitutions and rights had to come about in Europe) (Sassen 1996: chapters 2 and 3).

[27] It represents one mechanism for business disputes. The larger system includes arbitration controlled by courts, arbitration that is parallel to courts, and various court and out-of-court mechanisms such as mediation. The following description of international commercial arbitration is taken from Dezalay and Garth (1996); for these authors, today "international commercial arbitration" carries a different meaning from what it did twenty years ago. It has become increasingly formal and more like U.S.-style litigation as it has become more successful and institutionalized. Today international business contracts for, e.g., the sale of goods, joint ventures, construction projects, or distributorships typically call for arbitration in the event of a dispute arising from the contractual arrangement.

ad hoc, typically adopting the rules of the UN Commission on International Trade Law (UNCITRAL). The arbitrators are private individuals selected by the parties; usually a case uses three arbitrators. They act as private judges: they hold hearings and issue judgments. There are few grounds for appeal to courts, and the final decision of the arbitrators is more easily enforced among signatory countries than would be a court judgment (under the terms of the widely used 1958 New York Convention).

The ascendance of this system as economic corporate globalization grew is indicated by the sharp growth in the number of arbitration centers over a short period of time in the 1990s, when a large number of countries became "integrated" into the global economy. Excluding those concerned with maritime and commodity disputes—an older tradition—there were 120 centers by 1991, with another seven created by 1993; among the more recent centers are those of Bahrain, Singapore, Sydney, and Vietnam. There were about 1,000 arbitrators by 1990, a number that had doubled by 1992 and seems to have stayed at that level.[28] There has been a sharp growth in arbitration cases and a sharpening competition among arbitration centers to get the business. The development of the market for multinational legal services has further sharpened the competition as the large law firms can choose the centers that work best for their clients. In Europe there has been a reinvigorating of arbitration laws beginning in the 1980s, mostly oriented toward the interests of firms seeking international arbitration. In the United States such a revision was brought about through the Supreme Court in 1985 (Carbonneau 1990). The overall trend has been toward strengthening international arbitration and further freeing it from the regulation of national court systems. One open-ended question is whether the formation of new structures, notably WTO, NAFTA, and the EU, will require some new legal elements in the international arbitration world.

The reasons for the Americanization of international commercial arbitration are somewhat interrelated: the rationalization of arbitration know-how; the ascendance of large Anglo-American transnational legal services firms; and the emergence of a new specialty in conflict resolution (Dezalay 1992).[29] The large Anglo-American law firms that dominate the international market

[28] Smit and Pechota (2004); Dezalay and Garth (1996); Aksen (1990). Yet the international arbitrators are a tight community, with relatively few important institutions and limited numbers of individuals in each country who are the key players both as counsel and arbitrators. There is a kind of "international arbitration community," a "club," and arbitration has become big legal business (Salacuse 1991; Carbonneau 2004). Dezalay and Garth (1996) found that the large English and American law firms have used their power in the international business world to impose their conception of arbitration and, more largely, of the practice of law.

[29] Anglo-American practitioners tend not to support the continental, highly academic notion of a lex mercatoria. The so-called lex mercatoria was conceived by many as a return to an international law of business independent of national laws (Carbonneau 1990; de Ly 1992).

of business law include arbitration as one of the array of services they offer—a kind of litigation that uses a different forum than courts. Specialists in conflict are practitioners formed from the two great groups that have dominated legal practice in the United States: corporate lawyers, known for their competence as negotiators in the creation of contracts; and trial lawyers, whose talent lies in jury trials. The growing importance from the 1980s onwards of such transactions as mergers and acquisitions, antitrust, and other litigation contributed to a new specialization: knowing how to combine judicial attacks and behind-the-scenes negotiations to reach the optimum outcome for the client. Dezalay and Garth (1996) note that under these conditions judicial recourse becomes a weapon to be used in a situation that will almost certainly end before trial.

Another example of a private regulatory system is debt security or bond-rating agencies, which have come to play an increasingly important role in the global economy.[30] Thus in the mid-1980s Moody's and Standard and Poor had no analysts outside the United States; ten years later they each had about one hundred in Europe, Japan, and Australia. Three ratings agencies dominate the international market: Moody's, Standard and Poor, and Fitch Rating.[31] Sinclair posits that these agencies function as mechanisms of "governance without government": they have leverage because of their distinct gate-keeping functions on investment funds sought by corporations and governments. In this regard they can be seen as a significant force in the operation and expansion of the global economy.[32] And as with business law, their

[30] There are two agencies that dominate the market in ratings, with listings of $4 trillion each. They are Moody's Investors Service, usually referred to as Moody's, and Standard & Poor's Ratings Group, usually referred to as Standard & Poor. The European-based Fitch Ratings is the third largest credit rating agency in the world. IBCA bought Fitch in 1997, creating Fitch IBCA, which in 2001 became Fitch Ratings. Fitch Ratings is part of the Paris-based company Fimalac, S.A. While there are several rating agencies in other countries, these are oriented to the domestic markets.

[31] This is from Sinclair (1994), picking up on Rosenau (1992). The growing demand for ratings has given them increasing authoritativeness, which for Sinclair is not well founded given the processes of judgments that are central to it. These processes are tied to certain assumptions, which in turn are tied to dominant interests, notably narrow assumptions about market efficiency. The aim is undistorted price signals and little if any government intervention. Sinclair (1994: 143) notes that transition costs such as unemployment are usually not factored into evaluations and are considered outweighed by the new environment created.

[32] Their power has grown in good part because of disintermediation and the globalization of the capital market. The functions fulfilled by banks in the capital markets (i.e., intermediation) have lost considerable weight in the running of these markets; insofar as banks are subject to more government regulation than what has replaced banks, the lesser role of banks inevitably brings with it a decline in government regulation over the capital markets. Rating agencies, which are private entities, have taken over some of the functions of banks in organizing information for suppliers and borrowers of capital. An important question here is whether these agencies and the larger complex of entities, such as those represented by Wall Street, has indeed formed a new intermediary sector (cf. Thrift 1987; Sassen 2001: chapter 5), one largely not regulated the way the banking sector is.

expanded influence overseas is to some extent both a function and a promoter of U.S. financial orthodoxy, particularly its short-term perspective. The two large European rating agencies have also grown in importance.

A third type of private authority can be seen in the so-called lex constructionis. This combines the notion of an autonomous system of rules internal to a sector with the fact of a few large firms having disproportionate control over a sector, which thereby facilitates the making of such private systems of rules. It is a combination of rules and standard contracts for cross-border construction projects. The sector is dominated by a small number of well-organized private associations: the International Federation of Consulting Engineers (FIDIC), the International European Construction Federation (FIEC), the British Institution of Civil Engineers (ICE), the Engineering Advancement Association of Japan (ENAA), and the American Institute of Architects (AIA). In addition, the World Bank, UNCITRAL, UNIDROIT, and certain international law firms also contribute to developing legal norms for how the sector is meant to function. Because of the nature of large construction and engineering projects, this case also illuminates the ways in which having an autonomous system of rules and having the type of power that large global firms have does not mean that these firms can escape all outside constraints. Thus, these firms increasingly "need" to address environmental protection. The way this issue gets handled in the lex constructionis is also emblematic of what other such autonomously governed sectors do: largely a strategy of deference that aims at externalizing the responsibility for regulating the environmental issues arising out of large scale construction projects. The externalizing is to the "extra-contractual" realm of the law of the host state, using "compliance" provisions that are today part of the standard contract.

These and other such transnational institutions and regimes signal a shift in authority from the public to the private when it comes to governing the global economy. They also contain a shift in the capacity for norm-making and in that regard raise questions about changes in the relation between state sovereignty and the governance of global economic processes. International commercial arbitration is basically a private justice system, credit rating agencies are private gate-keeping systems, and the lex constructionis is a self-regulatory regime in a major economic sector dominated by a limited number of large firms. Along with other such institutions, they have emerged as important governance mechanisms whose authority is not centered in the state.

But for all of this to happen, it took a broader normative transformation in matters concerning the substantive rationality of the state—matters concerning raison d'état. In good part this normative transformation is enacted outside the state and originates outside the interstate system. Further, there are multiple private agents, some minor, some not so minor, that ensure and execute this new normative order. Nowhere is this transformation as developed and influential as in the normative weight gained by the logic of the global capital market in setting criteria for key national economic policies. In this sense, the global capital market is a heuristic space for understanding the normative power evinced by what are represented as private formations notwithstanding their norm-making capacities in the public domain. This is the argument I develop in the next section.

THE GLOBAL CAPITAL MARKET: POWER AND NORM-MAKING

In the many negotiations between national states and global economic actors we can see a new normativity derived from the *operational logic* of the capital market that has imposed itself on important aspects of national economic policymaking in the 1990s. Some of the more familiar elements are the new importance attached to the autonomy of central banks, privileging anti-inflation aims over employment growth, exchange rate parity, and the variety of items usually referred to as IMF conditionality.[33] In this new normative order, certain claims and criteria for policymaking emerge as legitimate. In addition, other types of claims are delegitimated—generally expenditures concerning the well-being of people at large, which are now often evaluated as making states "less competitive" in a normative context where states are expected to become more so.

I try to capture this normative transformation with the notion of a privatizing of capacities for making norms, capacities we have associated with the state in our recent history. This brings with it strengthened possibilities of norm-making in the interests of the few rather than the majority. In itself this is not novel. What is novel is the formalization of these privatized norm-making capacities and the sharper restricting of who might benefit, two features that evince sharp divergence from the prior Keynesian phase of many Western states. This process also brings with it a weakening and even elimination of public accountability in domains of norm-making which when in the public sector were, at least in principle, so subject. Again, while in practice this might not appear to be much of a difference, it is the formalizing of this withdrawal from the sphere of public accountability that is important.

---

[33] Since the Southeast Asian financial crisis there has been a revision of some of the specifics of these standards. For instance, exchange rate parity is now evaluated in less strict terms.

The formation of a global capital market represents a concentration of power capable of systemically influencing national government economic policy and, by extension, other policies. The key concern here is the fact that the global financial markets are not only capable of deploying raw power but also have produced a logic that now is seen as setting the criteria for "proper" economic policy. IMF conditionality has some of these features. In a way these markets can now exercise the accountability functions formally associated with citizenship in liberal democracies: they can vote governments' economic policies out or in; they can force governments to take certain measures and not others. The issue here is not so much that these markets have emerged as a powerful mechanism where those with capital can influence government policy.[34] It is rather that the overall operation of these markets has an embedded logic that calls for certain types of public sector economic policy objectives. Given the properties of the systems through which these markets operate—speed, simultaneity, and interconnectivity—the orders of magnitude they can produce signal a politico-economic situation where the outcome is much more than the sum of the parts. This weight can be exercised on any country integrated into the financial markets, and this is a rapidly growing number.

The issue of the power of today's global market for capital, its features, and its premises raises two critical questions. One of these is whether today's global capital market is different from earlier ones; the other, whether it is in fact a larger market than that of earlier global eras. My answer to the first question is yes, and that this difference matters as we seek to understand the power of this market when it confronts states and national economic actors. My answer to the second question is that whether it is larger or smaller than previous world markets, as counted in value, is of secondary importance to the character of its globality—that is, under what conditions it is articulated with national states and economies. The size of the market does matter in a relational sense: can it overwhelm national central banks, national investors, and national capital markets?

Distinguishing Today's Market for Capital

There has long been a market for capital and it has long consisted of multiple, variously specialized financial markets (e.g., Eichengreen and Fishlow

---

[34] See, e.g., Arrighi (1994).

1996; Helleiner 1999). It has also long had global components (Arrighi 1994; Eichengreen 1996). Indeed, a strong line of interpretation in the literature is that today's market for capital is nothing new and represents a return to an earlier global era at the turn of the century and, then again, in the interwar period (Hirst and Thompson 1996). However, all of this holds at a high level of generality, and when we factor in the specifics of today's capital market some significant differences emerge with those past phases. There are two major sets of differences. One has to do with the level of formalization and institutionalization of the global market for capital today, which is partly an outcome of the interaction with national regulatory systems that themselves gradually became far more elaborate over the last hundred years (see Sassen 1991 and 2001: chapters 4 and 5). The second set of differences concerns the transformative impact of the new information and communication technologies, particularly computer-based technologies (henceforth referred to as digitization). In combination with the various dynamics and policies we usually refer to as globalization they have constituted the capital market as a distinct institutional order, one different from other major markets and circulation systems such as global trade.

Two sets of interrelated empirical features of these markets can function as preliminary or elementary indicators of rapid transformation since the 1980s.[35] One set concerns the accelerated growth of finance over the last two decades, partly as a result of the electronic linking of markets—both nationally and globally—and of the sharp rise in innovations enabled by both financial economics and digitization. The second set concerns the sharp growth in the use of a particular type of financial instrument, the derivative, a growth evident both in the proliferation of different types of derivatives and in its becoming the leading instrument in financial markets.[36] This diversification and dominance of derivatives has raised the complexity of operations and has further facilitated the linking of different financial markets. I argue that together these two sets of empirical features partly distinguish the financial markets emerging in the 1980s.

Beginning in the 1980s, finance functioned on a different growth curve from other globalized sectors that have also grown sharply. Since 1980,

[35] There are other factors that are significant, particularly institutional changes, such as the bundle of policies usually grouped under the term deregulation and, on a more theoretical level, the changing scales for capital accumulation. For a full analysis of these issues, see Eichengreen (2003) and Eichengreen and Fishlow (1996) on deregulation and re-regulation in the financial markets today; on new scales for capital accumulation, see Dicken (2003) for one of the most exhaustive analyses of all major economic sectors involved.

[36] See p. 350 in chapter 7 for a brief description.

the total stock of financial assets has increased three times faster than the aggregate GDP of the twenty-three highly developed countries that constituted the Organisation for Economic Cooperation and Development (OECD) for much of this period; and the volume of trading in currencies, bonds, and equities has increased about five times faster and now surpasses aggregate GDP by far. The worldwide (notional) value of traded derivatives, which accounts for most financial market transactions, was $30 trillion in 1994, over $65 trillion in 1999, over $80 trillion by 2000, $97 trillion by 2001, and $220 trillion by 2004, for a 120 percent increase as of 2001, pointing not only to higher levels in values traded but also to an increase in the growth rate (BCBS 2005b: 21). To put this in perspective it is helpful to compare it to the value of other major components of the global economy, such as the value of cross-border trade ($11 trillion in 2004) and global foreign direct investment stock ($6 trillion in 2000 and $8.2 trillion in 2003 [WTO 2005: 3; UNCTAD 2005: 9]). Annual foreign exchange transactions were ten times as large as world trade in 1983 but seventy times larger in 2004, even though world trade also grew sharply over this period.[37] In 2001, the average daily turnover in foreign exchange markets was $1.3 trillion and in 2004, $1.8 trillion (BCBS 2005b), equal to almost one-fifth of the total annual value of world trade in 2003.[38]

In many ways the international financial market from the late 1800s to the interwar period was as massive as today's if we measure its volume as a share of national economies and in terms of the relative size of international flows. This fact is critical to scholars who argue that globalization is not new (e.g., Hirst and Thompson 1996). The international capital market in the earlier period was large and dynamic, highly internationalized, and backed by a healthy dose of Pax Britannica to keep order. The extent of its internationalization can be seen in the fact that in 1920, for example, Moody's rated bonds issued by about fifty governments to raise money in the American capital markets (T. Sinclair 1994). The depression brought on a radical decline in the extent of this internationalization, and it was not until very recently that Moody's was once again rating the bonds of about fifty governments. Indeed, as late as 1985, only fifteen foreign governments were borrowing in the

---

[37] The foreign exchange market was the first one to globalize, in the mid-1970s. Today it is the biggest and in many ways the only truly global market. It has gone from a daily turnover rate of about $15 billion in the 1970s, to $60 billion in the early 1980s, and an estimated $1.3 trillion in 1999 and $1.8 trillion in 2003. In contrast, the total foreign currency reserves of the rich industrial countries amounted to about 1 trillion in 1999 and 3 trillion in 2004.

[38] WTO (2003) and BCBS (1999); author's calculations.

U.S. capital markets. Not until after 1985 did the international financial markets reemerge as a major factor.[39]

One type of difference concerns the growing concentration of market power in institutions such as pension funds and insurance companies. Institutional investors are not new, but what is different beginning in the 1980s is the diversity of the types of funds and the rapid escalation of the value of their assets. There are two phases in this short history, one going into the early 1990s and the second one taking off in the later 1990s. Focusing briefly on the first phase and considering pension funds, for instance, their assets more than doubled in the United States from $1.5 trillion in 1985 to $9 trillion in 1993. Pension funds grew threefold in Britain and fourfold in Japan over that same period, and they more than doubled in Germany and Switzerland. In the United States, institutional investors as a group came to manage two-fifths of U.S. households' financial assets by the early 1990s, up from one-fifth in 1980. As table 5.1 shows, by 2001 these assets had reached $19.2 trillion. Further, the global capital market became an increasingly necessary component of a growing range of types of transactions, such as the diversity of government debts that began to get financed through the global market—kinds of debt that were thought to be basically local, such as municipal debt, are now entering this market. The overall growth in the value of financial instruments and assets also held for U.S. institutional investors whose assets rose from 59 percent of GDP in 1980 to 136.3 percent in 1993, and 191 percent in 2001.

While all of these trends continued in the second phase that took off in the 1990s, it is the rise of hedge funds that stands out. Hedge funds are among the most speculative of financial institutions; they sidestep certain disclosure and leverage regulations by having a small, private clientele and, frequently, by operating offshore. While they are not new, the growth in their size and their capacity to affect the functioning of markets grew enormously in the 1990s and they emerged as a major force by the late 1990s. According to some estimates they numbered 1,200 with assets of over $150 billion by mid-1998 (BCBS 1999), which exceeded the $122 billion in assets of the total of almost 1,500 equity funds as of October 1997 (UNCTAD 1998). By 2002 they numbered over 8,000 and global hedge funds assets stood at a reported $600 billion (BCBS 2005b: 79). Both types of funds need to be distinguished from

---

[39] Switzerland's international banking was, of course, the exception. But this was a very specific type of banking and does not represent a global capital market, particularly given basically closed national financial systems at the time (I have examined this difference in Sassen 1991: chapter 4).

TABLE 5.1
Financial Assets of Institutional Investors, 1990–2001, Selected Countries (bn USD)

	1993	1999	2001
Canada	435.9	757.3	794.3
France	906.3	1691.1	1701.3
Germany	729.8	1529.0	1478.4
Japan	3610.7	4928.2	3644.8
Netherlands	465.2	799.3	722.3[2]
United Kingdom	1543.6	3321.3	2743.3
United States	9051.7	19274.0	19257.7
Percentage of OECD[1]	90.6	87.2	86.3

Source: Based on OECD, *Institutional Investor Statistical Yearbook*, 2003, table S.1, p. 20.
[1] Percentages based on author's calculation.
[2] Netherlands' figure for 2001 excludes non–life insurance.

asset management funds, of which the top ten are estimated to have $10 trillion under management.[40]

A second set of differences has to do with the properties that the new information technologies bring to the financial markets. Two sets of properties need to be emphasized here. A first set concerns the technical features of these technologies: instantaneous transmission, interconnectivity, and speed. The second concerns the increased digitization of transactions and the associated increase in capacities to liquefy assets. The new technologies have enabled the electronic linking of markets inside and across countries, and the technical properties mobilized have enabled sharp increases of transactions within a given time frame. The digitization of financial instruments has meant that many more than just the cognoscenti can derive advantages from the accelerated innovation and increased complexity in the instruments involved. This holds especially for derivatives, now the main instrument in financial transactions.

The particular properties of the new interactive and digitization technologies explain to a significant extent some of the key empirical fea-

[40] In that same period, assets of insurance companies increased by 110 percent (from $1.6 trillion to $3.3 trillion), assets of commercial banks grew by 100 percent (from $3.5 trillion to $7 trillion), and deposits of commercial banks increased by 79 percent (from $2.5 trillion to $4.5 trillion) (Investment Company Institute 2003: 1–2n. 4). The level of concentration is enormous among these funds, partly as a consequence of mergers and acquisitions driven by the need for firms to reach what are de facto the competitive thresholds in the global market today.

tures of these markets today, specifically, empirical features that distinguish them from earlier phases. These properties—instantaneous transmission, interconnectivity, and decentralized access—are partly interrelated, but it is useful to isolate their effects on markets. Vast computer networks enable the first two features, and both of these, in turn, assume a whole new potential in the context of the third feature, insofar as the latter raises the number of participating investors. The combination of these three features leads to growth in the amount of capital mobilized by raising the number of transactions that can be executed within a given time frame, and it leads to an increase in the velocity at which a given set of transactions can produce a given amount of value added as compared, for instance, with instantaneous transmission between only two points. This clearly also raises the potential for total value lost in the case of a financial crisis. The ability to realize (or lose) value from a transaction happens at a larger scale and faster, thus raising the value gained (or lost) and decreasing the time span between investment and realized profit (or loss). As each transaction can in principle be completed in increasingly shorter intervals, as long as the majority of investments yield a profit, more value is produced in less time. It signals a kind of built-in potential for exponential growth in value added through the multiplication of transactions. This is a capability that other major sectors in the economy, such as trade and direct investment, lack. When it comes to the instruments traded in this environment, the key technical condition that contributes to distinguish today's derivatives from past instantiations of this type of instrument is digitization.

The impact of decentralized access on the market for capital has been conditioned on a set of distinct policy changes in each country that has become integrated into this market. Since the late 1980s, a growing number of financial markets have become globally integrated. This integration was, and continues to be, based on a crucial conditionality, the adoption of a bundle of policies generally referred to as economic deregulation. At the same time, the possibility of decentralized access greatly facilitated the direct incorporation and simultaneous participation in the global market for capital by a rapidly growing number of national financial markets.

As for the digitization of instruments, it has been critical for the possibility of simplifying the use of complex instruments. This possibility takes on its full import if we consider that one of the marking features of the financial era that began in the 1980s is its drive to produce innovations and raise the level of complexity of instruments. In fact, a key feature of the global financial markets today is accelerated innovation. The multiplication of types of instruments and the intensity of transactions is one feature distinguishing today's derivatives trading markets from their historical predecessors.[41] Digitization has enabled innovations, and derivatives are the key type of instrument on which innovation has centered.[42] Innovations, in turn, have been crucial in raising the supply of financial instruments that are tradable.[43] One way of interpreting this drive toward innovation is the push to raise the level of liquidity in the system given the sharply increased thresholds of capital needed for executing a growing number of large transactions, for example, mergers of large firms or privatizations of huge, once public utilities. In addition, a crucial incentive for innovation is the push to liquefy forms of wealth hitherto considered non-liquid.[44] This can require enormously complex financial instruments and has driven much innovation.[45] The possibility of using computers has not only facilitated the development of such instruments but also has enabled the widespread use of these instruments insofar as much of the complexity can be contained within the software. Use does not require full understanding of the financial mathematics or the software algorithms involved.

The properties of interactive and digitization technologies assume added meaning because they enable a multiplication of the number of transactions that can be executed within a given time frame. This multiplication of transactions is evident in the lengthening distance between the financial instrument and actual underlying asset, that is, the increased number of intermediate transactions, each of which can produce a profit (or a loss). The values of cross-border transactions in bonds and equities as the percentage of GDP capture this at the macro-level (table 5.2). Table 5.2 also shows the recency of the accelerated increase. For instance, the value of such transactions represented 4 percent of GDP in 1975 in the United States, 35 per-

[41] A key component of innovation over the last two decades has been the increase in speculation, a fact that has added to the complexity of instruments. The 1990s also saw the proliferation of institutional investors with speculative investment strategies.

[42] While currency and interest rates derivatives did not exist until the early 1980s, and represent two of the major innovations of the current period, derivatives on commodities, so-called futures, existed in some version in earlier periods. Amsterdam's stock exchange in the seventeenth century—when it was the financial capital of the world—was based almost entirely on trading in commodity futures.

[43] There are significant differences by country. Securitization is well advanced in the United States but only began to take off in the late 1990s in most of Europe and Japan.

[44] Perhaps the most familiar case is the invention of instruments that represent real estate (Real Estate Investment Trusts [REITs]) and that became a major source of innovations in the 1980s.

[45] For instance, after the Mexico crisis and before the first signs of the Asian crisis, the leading financial services firms negotiated a large number of innovative deals that further expanded the volumes in the financial markets and incorporated new sources of profit, thereby ensuring liquidity even in a situation of at least partial crisis. Typically these deals involved novel concepts of how to sell debt and of what is a saleable debt.

TABLE 5.2

Cross-Border Transactions in Bonds and Equities* as Percentage of GDP, 1975–2002 (Selected Years)

	Percentage of GDP				
	1975	*1985*	*1995*	*2000*	*2002*
United States	4	35	135	229	292
Japan	2	62	65	96	106
Germany	5	33	172	447	464
France	—	21	187	398	430
Italy	1	4	253	782	—
Canada	3	27	187	241	311

Source: Bank for International Settlements, Annual Report 1999, April 1, 1998–March 31, 1999, table VI.5; IMF 2004, table A.3.

* Denotes gross purchases and sales of securities between residents and nonresidents.

cent in 1985 when the new financial era was in full swing, had quadrupled by 1995 and risen to 292 percent by 2002. Other countries show even sharper increases. In Germany this share grew from 5 percent in 1975 to 464 percent in 2002; in France it went from 5 percent in 1980 to 430 percent in 2002. In part, this entails escalating levels of risk and innovation driving the industry. We have seen this acceleration only over the last decade and a half.

Today, after considerable deregulation in the industry, the incorporation of a growing number of national financial centers into a global market, and the sharp use of electronic trading, we might think that the actual spatial organization of the industry would reflect increasingly market-driven locational dynamics, unlike what may have been the case in the earlier highly regulated phase.[46] This should hold especially for the global market given the earlier prevalence of highly regulated and closed national markets. There has, indeed, been geographic decentralization of certain types of financial activities, which has been aimed at securing business in the growing number of countries becoming integrated into the global economy. Many of the leading investment banks have operations in far more countries than they had twenty years ago. The same can be said for the leading accounting, legal, and other

---

[46] Beginning in the 1980s there has been growing worldwide deregulatory pressure by key state and nonstate actors involved in the global capital market across the political spectrum; the aims are market linking, global integration, and intersectoral mobility within finance. Thus London saw its "big bang" of 1984 and Paris saw "le petit bang" two years later under governments as diverse as the Tories in England and the Socialists in France.

specialized corporate services whose networks of overseas affiliates have seen explosive growth (Taylor, Walker, and Beaverstock 2002; see generally GAWC). And it can be said for some markets. For example, in the 1980s all basic wholesale foreign exchange operations were in London while today these are distributed among London and several other centers (even though their number remains far smaller than the number of countries whose currency is being traded).

But empirically what stands out about the global financial markets after two decades of deregulation, worldwide integration, and major advances in electronic trading is the extent of locational concentration and the premium firms are willing to pay to be in major centers (Sassen 2001: chapters 4 and 7). Large shares of many financial markets are disproportionately concentrated in a few financial centers. This trend toward consolidation in a few centers also is evident within countries. Further, this pattern toward the consolidation of one leading financial center per country is a function of rapid growth in the sector, not of general decay in the losing cities.

The sharp concentration in leading financial markets can be illustrated with some empirical data. London, New York, Tokyo (notwithstanding a national economic recession), Paris, Frankfurt, and a few other cities regularly appear at the top *and* represent a large share of global transactions.[47] This holds even after the September 11 attacks that destroyed the World Trade Center (though this was largely not a financial complex) in New York and were seen by many as a wake-up call about the vulnerabilities of urban agglomerations and concentration in a few sites. Table 5.3 shows the extent to which pre–September 11 levels of concentration in stock market capitalization in a limited number of global financial centers continued to hold after the attacks. The top twelve exchanges accounted for 90 percent of global market capitalization. Table 5.4 shows foreign listings in major markets have sharply higher numbers than most markets, further indicating that location in the leading markets is one of the features of the global capital market. London, Frankfurt, and New York account for an enormous world share in the export of financial services. London, New York, and Tokyo account for over one-third of global institutional equity holdings. For instance, London, New York, and Tokyo account for 58 percent of the foreign exchange market, one of the few truly global markets; together with Singapore, Hong Kong, Zurich,

---

[47] For regular updated figures see the International Bank for Settlements; IMF national accounts data; specialized trade publications such as the *Wall Street Journal*'s WorldScope, and MorganStanley Capital International; *The Banker*; data listings in the *Financial Times* and in *The Economist*; and, especially for a focus on cities, the data produced by Technimetrics, Inc. (now part of Thomson Financials) and the World Federation of Stock Exchanges. These and additional names of standard, continuously updated sources are listed in Sassen (2001).

TABLE 5.3

Major Markets by Capitalization for Top 12 Markets for 2000–2004 (bn USD)

	2004 Market Capital- ization	2004 Percentage of Members Capitaliza- tion	2002 Market Capital- ization	2002 Percentage of Members Capital- ization	2000 Market Capital- ization	2000 Percentage of Members Capital- ization
NYSE	12,707.6	34.2	9,015.3	39.5	11,534.5	37.1
NASDAQ	3,532.9	9.5	1,994.5	8.7	3,597.1	11.6
Tokyo	3,557.7	9.6	2,069.3	9.1	3,193.9	10.3
London	2,865.2	7.7	1,856.2	8.1	2,612.2	8.4
Euronext	2,441.3	6.6	1,538.7	6.7	2,271.7	7.3
Osaka	2,287.0	6.2	1,491.9	6.5	[1]	[2]
Deutsche Borse	1,194.5	3.2	686.0	3.0	1,270.2	4.1
Toronto	1,177.5	2.8	570.2	2.5	766.2	2.5
Spanish Exchange	940.7	2.5	461.6	2.0	[1]	[2]
Swiss Exchange	826.0	2.2	547.0	2.4	792.3	2.5
Hong Kong	861.5	2.3	463.1	2.0	623.4	2.0
Italy	789.6	2.1	477.1	2.1	768.4	2.5
Percentage of Total World Capital- ization		89.3		92.7		90.8[2]

Source: World Federation of Exchanges Annual Statistics (2001: 92; 2002: 80; 2003: 82), year-end figures with calculations of percentages added.

Note: Data on market capitalization exclude investment funds, and include common and preferred shares, shares without voting rights, otherwise stated. Euronext includes Brussels, Amsterdam, and Paris.

[1] The top 12 for 2000 did not include Osaka or the Spanish Exchanges (BME). The Spanish Exchanges did not exist in 2000. Instead Spain (which preceded the Spanish Exchanges) was eleventh with market capitalization of $504.2 billion and Australia was twelfth with market capitalization of $372.8 billion.

[2] This figure indicates the percentage represented by the top 12 exchanges in terms of market capitalization for 2000 (including the exchanges in Spain, 1.6%, and Australia, 1.2%).

Geneva, Frankfurt, and Paris, they account for 85 percent in this, the most global of markets.

The trend toward consolidation in a few centers, even as the network of integrated financial centers expands globally, is also evident within countries. In the United States, for example, the leading investment banks are concentrated in New York; the only other major international financial center is

TABLE 5.4
Foreign Listings in Major Exchanges, 2000–2004

	2000		2002		2004	
	Number of Foreign Listings	*Percentage of Foreign Listings*	*Number of Foreign Listings*	*Percentage of Foreign Listings*	*Number of Foreign Listings*	*Percentage of Foreign Listings*
NASDAQ	488	10.3	445	11.0	340	10.5
NYSE	433	17.5	461	19.2	459	20.0
London	448	18.9	409	17.5	351	12.4
Deutsche Borse	241	24.5	235	23.9	159	19.4
Euronext[1]	—	—	—	—	334	25.1
Swiss Exchange	164	39.4	149	36.2	127	31.1
Tokyo	41	2.0	38	1.8	30	1.3

Source: World Federation of Exchanges (2001: 86; 2002: 96; 2000: table 1.1), with calculations of percentages added.

Note: 2000 figures are year-end figures.

[1] Euronext Amsterdam, Euronext Brussels, and Euronext Paris each had separate listings. After 2000 Euronext accounts for Brussels, Amsterdam, and Paris.

Chicago. Sydney and Toronto have equally gained power in continental-sized countries and have taken over functions and market share from what were once the major commercial centers, Melbourne and Montreal, respectively, as have Sao Paulo and Bombay, which have gained share and functions from Rio de Janeiro and New Delhi, respectively. These are all enormous countries and likely could sustain multiple major financial centers.[48]

There is both consolidation in fewer major centers across and within countries *and* a sharp growth in the numbers of centers that become part of the global network as country after country deregulates its economy. This mode of incorporation into the global network is often at the cost of losing functions that these cities may have had when they were largely national centers. Today the leading, typically foreign, financial, accounting, and legal services firms enter their markets to handle many of the new cross-border

[48] In France, Paris has larger shares of most financial sectors than it did ten years ago and once important stock markets like Lyon have become "provincial," even though Lyon is today the regional hub of a thriving cross-border economic area. Milano privatized its exchange in September 1997 and electronically merged Italy's ten regional markets. Frankfurt now concentrates a larger share of the six financial centers in Germany than it did in the early 1980s, as does Zurich, which once had Basel and Geneva as significant competitors.

operations.[49] Incorporation in the global market typically happens without a gain in their global share of the particular segments of the market they are in even as capitalization may increase, often sharply, and even though they add to the total volume in the global market.

Why is it that at a time of rapid growth in the network of financial centers in overall volumes and in electronic networks there is such high concentration of market shares in leading global and national centers? Both globalization and electronic trading are about expansion and dispersal beyond what had been the confined realm of, respectively, national economies and floor trading. Indeed, one might well ask why financial centers matter at all. I return to these particular issues in part 3 as a way of specifying the limits of capital mobility and implications for governance in the public interest from this ongoing territorial insertion. That the global capital market is partly located in these specific terrains needs to be distinguished from the notion that it is encased in national territories: the institutional arrangements and professional practices involved in the operations of these markets may well have the effect of denationalizing the financial centers and hence constitute a spatiality that is distinct from that of national territoriality.

Governments and the Global Market for Capital

What are the mechanisms through which the massive growth of financial flows and assets and an integrated global capital market can shape states' economic policymaking? A global capital market could be simply a vast pool of money for investors without conferring power over governments. That it can discipline government economic policymaking is a distinct power, one that is not ipso facto inherent in the existence of a large global capital market. There are several mechanisms through which the global capital market exercises its disciplining function on national governments and pressures them to become accountable to the logic of these markets. The power of governments over their economies in market-centered systems has traditionally been based on the ability to tax, to print money, and to borrow. Before the deregulations that took off in the 1980s for several major developed countries and in the 1990s for most of the world, governments had considerable control over the amount of bank lending through credit controls and ceilings on interest rates, which made monetary policy in principle more effective than it is today.

---

[49] This also holds for highly developed countries that do not have Anglo-American legal systems.

The global financial markets have affected all three sharply. With deregulation of interest rates in more and more highly developed countries, central banks now have to rely simply on changes in interest rate levels to influence the level of demand in the economy. They can no longer use interest rate ceilings. But the impact of interest rates on the economy, in turn, has been diminished by the widespread use of derivatives. Derivatives (futures, swaps, options) are meant to reduce the impact of interest rate changes and thereby can be seen as reducing the effectiveness of interest rate policy by governments on the economy.[50] Indeed, an estimated 85 percent of U.S. Fortune 500 firms make some use of derivatives to insulate themselves from swings in interest rates and currency values, as do public sector entities, exemplified in the notorious case of the municipal government of Orange County in California. Most of these derivatives are actually on interest rates, which means that as their use expands, the power of central banks to influence the economy via interest rates will decline further, no matter how much significance the media attribute to central bankers making a change in rates.[51] At the same time, insofar as many firms and sectors now operate with levels of capital far larger than they were in the past, interest rate changes can represent massive amounts of money in absolute terms.

In addition to the reduced impact central banks can have through interest rate policy, the power of governments to influence interest and foreign exchange rates and fiscal policy can be severely reduced, if not neutralized, by the foreign exchange markets and bond markets. For example, the markets can respond to a cut by the U.S. government in interest rates by raising the cost of loans to the U.S. government through an increased yield in long-term bonds. This has

---

[50] Since these derivatives entail a redistribution of interest sensitivities from one firm or sector to another in the economy, one could argue that the overall sensitivity to interest rates in the economy remains constant. But the fact is that different firms may have different sensitivities to changes in interest rates; we can assume that the risk is being shifted from highly sensitive firms to less sensitive firms, thereby reducing the overall impact of interest rates on the economy. Through the use of derivatives, interest rate sensitivity is switched to less sensitive sectors.

[51] Media coverage of heads of central banks, notably Alan Greenspan in the United States and, earlier on, Hans Tietmeyer in Germany, portrays them as extremely powerful. The suggestion is the whole country is hanging on their every word. The stock market is sensitive to their decisions on interest rates. Further, in such gatherings as the World Economic Forum, held annually in Davos (Switzerland), which offers an opportunity for the CEOs of the 1,000 largest corporations in the world to mix with central bankers (and presidents and prime ministers), one central banker after another will hold forth at length about his bank's autonomy from government and the financial markets. But it is not at all certain that just because central bankers find themselves in this increasingly strategic position that their autonomy from the financial markets is the same as the power to contest the logic of the latter. (See Sassen 1996 for a further discussion.)

emerged as a standard procedure.[52] The channel through which central banks have traditionally carried out their monetary policies is the banking sector. However, in the United States for instance, its role is shrinking because of the new financial institutions and instruments. Changes in the industry due to consolidation have further reduced the significance of this role of banks. Thirty years ago banks provided three-fourths of all short- and medium-term business credit; by 1995 this was down to 50 percent (*The Economist* 1995). By 1999 the share of commercial banks in total financial assets was less than 20 percent (*The Economist* 1999).[53] The rise of electronic cash further reduces the control capacity of central bankers over the money supply. Electronic money moves through computer networks, bypassing the information-gathering system of central banks.

All of these conditions have reduced the control central banks have over the money supply. It is certainly a matter of thresholds, since this control was never total, but now it is seriously partial, given the rules of the game under which central banks operate. Clearly these outcomes vary in severity depending on the country's banking structure. Overall the impact of financial deregulation and innovation has made the effect of a change in interest rates on a national economy more uncertain and increased the opportunities for mistakes.[54] A perhaps important countervailing tendency is the increasing convergence among central bankers in terms of policy, which we have seen over the last decade, along with the increasing acceptance of central bank autonomy.

Private firms in international finance, accounting, and law, the new private standards for international accounting and financial reporting, and supranational organizations such as the IMF all play strategic non–government centered governance functions in the global capital market. The events following the well-documented Mexico crisis provide some interesting insights about these firms' role in changing the conditions for financial operation, about the ways in which national states participated, and the formation of a new institutionalized intermediary space.

---

[52] There is the famous case of George Soros and his Quantum fund, which made $1 billion in profits on Black Wednesday in 1992 by helping to push the British pound out of the European Exchange Rate Mechanism.

[53] Another issue is the currency markets. Governments with large debts are partly in the hands of investors—whether foreign or national—who can switch their investments to other currencies, and increasingly in the hands of so-called vulture funds that will now take governments to court, breaking the tacit rules that have governed sovereign debt (see appendix to this chapter). Governments and their central banks have been losing control over long-term interest rates. This is no minor matter if one considers that 60 percent or more of private-sector debt in the United States, Japan, Germany, and France is linked to long-term interest rates.

[54] There is a separate discussion to be had about who benefited from the earlier period, for example, in the United States when the Federal Reserve had greater control. Even though many were excluded, the beneficiaries were a far wider spectrum of workers, communities, and firms than they are today.

J. P. Morgan worked with Goldman Sachs and Chemical Bank to develop several innovative deals that brought investors back to Mexico's markets.[55] Further, in July 1996, a large $6 billion, five-year deal that offered investors a Mexican floating rate note or syndicated loan—backed by oil receivables from the state oil monopoly PEMEX—was twice oversubscribed. It became somewhat of a model for asset-backed deals from Latin America, especially oil-rich Venezuela and Ecuador. Key to the high demand was that the structure had been designed to capture investment-grade ratings from Standard and Poor and Moody's. This was the first Mexican deal with an investment grade. The intermediaries worked with the Mexican government, but on their terms—this was not a government-to-government deal. This secured acceptability in the new institutionalized privatized intermediary space for cross-border transactions—evidenced by the high level of oversubscription and the high ratings. It allowed the financial markets to grow on what had been a crisis and remained a crisis for much of the economy.

This period saw many innovative deals that contributed to further expand the volumes in the financial markets and to incorporate new sources of profit, that is, debts for sale. Typically these deals involved novel concepts of how to sell debt and what could be a saleable debt. Often the financial services firms structuring these deals also implemented minor changes in depository systems to bring them more in line with international standards. The aggressive innovating and selling on the world market of what had hitherto been thought to be too illiquid and too risky for such a sale further expanded and strengthened the institutionalization of this intermediary space for cross-border transactions operating partly outside the interstate system. The new intermediaries have done the strategic work, a kind of "activism" toward ensuring growth in their industry and overcoming the potentially devastating effects of financial crises on the industry as a whole and on the notion of integrated global financial markets.

Central banks and governments appear to be increasingly concerned about pleasing the financial markets rather than setting goals for social and economic well-being. One is reminded of the Argentinean and Brazilian

[55] The $40 billion emergency loan package from the IMF and the U.S. government and the hiring of Wall Street's top firms to refurbish its image and find ways to bring it back into the market helped Mexico "solve" its financial crisis vis-à-vis the global market for capital; it did not solve the crisis of middle-class mortgage owners and devastated economic sectors. Goldman organized a $1.75 billion Mexican sovereign deal in which the firm was able to persuade investors in May 1996 to swap Mexican Brady bonds collateralized with U.S. Treasury bonds (Mexican Bradys were a component of almost all emerging market portfolios until the 1994 crisis) for a thirty-year naked Mexican risk. This is quite a testimony to the aggressive innovations that characterize the financial markets and to the importance of a whole new subculture in international finance that facilitates the circulation, i.e., sale, of these instruments (Sassen 2001: chapter 7).

governments after the Mexican crisis, which promised not to devalue their currencies and to do whatever it took to avoid this—including plunging the lower-middle classes into poverty. Governments try to guard perhaps excessively against inflation, in a trade-off with job growth. It also holds for developed countries, as was evident in the critiques leveled by the middle sectors in Germany against Hans Tietmeyer, the much-admired head of the German Central Bank in the 1990s. It could be argued that there may be some positive effects as well: if national debts become too large, bond holders will demand higher yields (that is, raise the cost of a loan to governments) and lower the value of a national currency, as was clearly the case with the dollar in the United States from the mid-1980s to the early 1990s.[56] In the past, inflation was a way of coping with growing debt. But today the bond markets will raise the yields and hence the cost of loans to governments, thereby sometimes terrorizing governments into keeping inflation under control.

These conditions raise a number of questions concerning the impact on states of this concentration of capital in markets that enable rapid circulation in and out of countries. How does this affect national economies and government policies? Does it alter the functioning of democratic governments? Does this kind of concentration of capital reshape the accountability that has operated through electoral politics between governments and their people? A critical question is whether the citizenries of the pertinent countries want the global capital market to exercise this discipline over their governments and impose such criteria for national economic policy and to do so at all costs—jobs, wages, safety, health—and without a public debate.[57] The

[56] This happened only after more than a decade of excessive spending on defense by the Reagan administration. Indeed, the money to pay for the added debt was extracted from the mix of state expenditures on the social wage, on infrastructure, on public housing construction, school buildings, parks, etc. The dollar had plunged by 60 percent against the yen and German mark since the mid-1980s; this could be seen as a verdict on U.S. economic policies on borrowing at the time.

[57] Further, the global financial markets discipline governments in a somewhat erratic way: they can fail to react to an obvious imbalance for a long time and then suddenly punish with a vengeance, as was the case with the Mexico crisis, the Asian crisis, the 1998 Russian crisis, and more recently the 2001 Argentine crisis. The speculative character of many markets means that they will stretch the profit-making opportunities for as long as possible, no matter what the underlying damage to the national economy might be. Investors threw money into Mexico even though its current account deficit was growing fast and reached an enormous 8 percent of GDP in 1994. Notwithstanding recognition by critical sectors in both the United States and Mexico that the peso needed a gradual devaluation, nothing was done. A sudden sharp devaluation with the subsequent sharp departure of investors threw the economy into disarray. The nationality of the investors is quite secondary; an IMF report says it was Mexican investors who first dumped the peso. Gradual action could probably have avoided some of the costs and reversals. Even in late 1994 many Wall Street analysts and traders were still urging investment in Mexico. It was not until late 1994 that ratings began to change.

ongoing embeddedness of the global capital market in a network of financial centers operating within national states, not offshore, is crucial to understanding regulation and the role of the state in the global capital market. But it will take different types of regulatory interventions from those premised on older notions of state territorial authority (Sassen 2003a).

THE PARTIAL DISEMBEDDING OF SPECIALIZED STATE

OPERATIONS AND NONSTATE ACTORS

One outcome of these various trends is the emergence of a strategic field that entails a partial disembedding of specific state operations from the broader institutional world of the state geared to national agendas. It is a fairly rarified field of cross-border transactions among government agencies and business sectors aimed at addressing the new conditions produced and required by economic globalization. The transactions are strategic, cut across borders, and entail specific interactions with private actors. They do not entail the state as such, as in international treaties, nor are they confined to the types of intergovernmental networks examined by Slaughter (2004). Rather, these transactions consist of the operations and policies of specific subcomponents of the state (for instance, technical regulatory agencies, specialized sections of central banks, such as those in charge of setting particular monetary policies), components of the supranational system linked to the economy (IMF, WTO), and private nonstate sectors. These are transactions that cut across the private-public divide and across national borders in that they concern the standards and regulations imposed on firms and markets operating globally. In so doing these transactions push toward convergence at the level of national regulations and law aimed at creating the requisite conditions for globalization.

There are two distinct features about this field of transactions that lead me to posit that we can conceive of it as a disembedded space in the process of becoming structured. The transactions take place in familiar settings: the state and interstate system for officials and agencies of governments and of the supranational system; the "private sector" for nonstate economic actors; and so on. But the practices of the agents involved are constituting a distinct assemblage of bits of territory, authority, and rights that function as a new type of field for operations. In this regard it is a field that exceeds the institutional world of the interstate system. Insofar as interactions with private actors provide substantive public rationality, it is a field of practices within which denationalized state agendas get defined and enacted. This field of transactions entails a partial and often highly specialized unbundling of the condition of state bundling preceding the current period. This unbundling is also one element in the broader dynamic of a changed relation between state authority and national territory.

The stickiness of multilateral agreements (Stephen 2002) illustrates some of these issues. It produces a kind of disembedding from the context of national lawmaking; this effect is further strengthened if the multilateral agreement is constructed through top-down lawmaking. Stephan (2002) notes that the adoption of a general norm through multilateral agreements, if done consistently, leads to "legal stickiness." Once in place, these agreements typically require unanimity for their modification or replacement, which Stephan finds functions as a barrier to adjustment and evolution. We see at work here a kind of cumulative causation in a given direction within specialized domains, a dynamic I have found in several of these domains. Stephan further finds that "[w]idespread adherence to a difficult-to-change set of legal rules may produce an evolutionary dead end, rather than a clear and optimal regime" (2002: 311). He argues that given lawyers' built-in bias for harmonization in the context of multilateralism, and given the enormous diversity across national legal systems, supranational institutions are the ones legal analysts will see as preferable further reinforcing "legal stickiness."

The other feature of this field of transactions is the proliferation of rules that begin to assemble into partial, specialized systems of law. Here we enter a whole new domain of private authorities—fragmented, specialized, and increasingly formalized but not running through national law per se.

Toward Global Law Systems: Disembedding
Law from Its National Encasement

Over the last two decades we have seen a multiplication of cross-border systems of rule that evince variable autonomy from national law. At one end are systems clearly centered on what is emerging as a transnational public domain and at the other are systems that are completely autonomous and private. Some scholars see in this development an emergent global law. We might conceive of it as a type of law that is disembedded from national law systems. At the heart of the notion of global law lies the possibility of a law not centered in national law and thus distinct from international law, and going beyond harmonizing the different national laws. Much of the supranational system that addresses economic globalization, environmental issues, and human rights does not go much beyond such harmonizing. Autonomous highly differentiated systems of rule have grown rapidly.

For some scholars this multiplication does not amount to global law: whatever might approach global law is actually a site where multiple competing national systems interact. The project is then one of harmonizing differences through conflicts, law, or force. Much of the scholarship on global governance comes from this type of perspective. Dezalay and Garth (1996) note that the "international" is itself constituted largely from a competition among national approaches; there is no global law (Shapiro 1993).[58] Thus the international emerges as a site for regulatory competition among essentially national approaches, whatever the issue—environmental protection, constitutionalism, human rights, and so forth.[59] From this perspective "international" or "transnational" has become in the most recent period a form of "Americanization," an outcome of regulatory competition.[60] The most widely recognized and general instance of this is of course the notion of a global culture

---

[58] Shapiro, writing in the early 1990's (1993) notes that there is not much of a regime of international law, either through the establishment of a single global law giver and enforcer or through a nation-state consensus. He also posits that if there was, we would be dealing with an international rather than global law. Nor is it certain that law has become universal—i.e., that human relations anywhere in the world will be governed by some law, even if not by a law that is the same everywhere. Globalization of law refers to a very limited, specialized set of legal phenomena, and Shapiro argues that it will almost always refer to North America and Europe and only sometimes to Japan and other Asian countries. There have been a few common developments and many parallel developments in law across the world. Thus, as a concomitant of the globalization of markets and the organization of transnational corporations, there has been a move toward a relatively uniform global contract and commercial law. This can be seen as a private lawmaking system where the two or more parties create a set of rules to govern their future relations. Such a system of private lawmaking can exist transnationally even when there is no transnational or supranational court.

[59] Charny (1991); Trachtman (1993). There are two other categories that may partly overlap with internationalization-as-Americanization, but are important to distinguish, at least analytically. One is multilateralism and the other is what Ruggie (1988) has called multiperspectival institutions.

[60] None of this is a smooth lineal progression. There is contestation everywhere, some of it highly visible and formalized, some of it not. In some countries, especially in Europe, we see resistance to what is perceived as the Americanization of the global capital market's standards for the regulation of their financial systems and standards for reporting financial information. Sinclair (1994) notes that the internationalization of ratings by the two leading U.S. agencies could be seen as another step toward global financial integration or as an American agenda. There has clearly been resentment against U.S. agencies in Europe for many years, as became evident on the occasion of the 1991 downgrading of Credit Suisse and, in early 1992, the downgrading of Swiss Bank Corporation. It is also evident in the difficulty that foreign agencies have had in getting SEC recognition in the United States as Nationally Recognized Statistical Rating Organizations. There have been reports in the media, for example in the *Financial Times*, about private discussions in London, Paris and Frankfurt about the possibility of setting up a Europe-wide agency to compete with the major U.S.-based agencies.

that is profoundly influenced by U.S. popular culture.[61] But, though less widely recognized and more difficult to specify, this has also become very clear in the legal forms that are ascendant in international business transactions.[62] Through the IMF and the World Bank as well as GATT/WTO this vision has spread to—some would say been imposed on—the developing world.[63] There is a distinction to be made here between international law (public or private) that is always implemented through national governments and the policies generated by entities such as the WTO and the IMF that aim to further globalization. Yet both may reflect legal elements of particularly powerful countries. The competition among national legal systems or approaches is particularly evident in business law where the Anglo-American model of the business enterprise and competition is beginning to replace the continental European model of legal artisans and corporatist control over the profession.[64]

[61] For a discussion of the concept of globalization, see King (1990); Robertson (1992). Robertson's notion of the world as a single place, or as the "global human condition," is addressed to a particular type of issue—the possibility of a novel subjective condition. I would say that globalization is also a process that produces differentiation, but the alignment of differences is of a very different kind from that associated with such differentiating notions as national character, national culture, and national society. For example, the corporate world today has a global geography, but it isn't everywhere in the world: it has highly defined and structured spaces and is increasingly sharply differentiated from noncorporate segments in the economies of the particular locations (a city such as New York) or countries where it operates.

[62] Shapiro (1993: 63) finds that law and the political structures that produce and sustain it are far more national and far less international than are trade and politics as such. He argues that the U.S. domestic legal regime may have to respond to global changes in markets and in politics far more often than to global changes in law; for the most part, national regimes of law and lawyering will remain self-generating. However, he adds that they will do so in response to globally perceived needs. This last point may well be emerging as a growing factor in shaping legal form and legal practice.

[63] The best-known instance of this is probably the austerity policy imposed on many developing countries. This process also illustrates the participation of states in furthering the goals of globalization, since these austerity policies have to be run through national governments and reprocessed as national policies. In this case it is clearer than in others that the global is not simply the non-national; global processes materialize in national territories and institutions.

[64] U.S. dominance in the global economy over the last few decades has meant that the globalization of law through private corporate lawmaking assumes the form of the Americanization of commercial law (Shapiro 1993). Certain U.S. legal practices are being diffused throughout the world, e.g., the legal device of franchising. Shapiro notes that it may not only be U.S. dominance but also a receptivity of common law to contract and other commercial law innovations. He posits that (in the late 1980s and early 1990s) it was common in Europe to think that EC legal business goes to London because its lawyers are better at devising legal innovations to facilitate new and evolving transnational business relations than is the civil law of the continent. "For whatever reasons, it is now possible to argue that American business law has become a kind of global *jus commune* incorporated explicitly or implicitly into transnational contracts and beginning to be incorporated into the case law and even the statutes of many other nations" (Shapiro 1993: 39).

This holds even for international commercial arbitration. Notwithstanding its deep roots in the continental tradition, especially the French and Swiss traditions, this system of private justice is becoming increasingly "Americanized."

For other scholars, global law is emergent and is centered on the development of autonomous partial regimes. The Project on International Courts and Tribunals (PICT) has identified 125 international institutions in which independent authorities reach final legal decisions.[65] These range from those in the public domain, such as human rights courts, to those in the private sector. They function through courts, quasi-courts, and other mechanisms for settling disputes, such as international commercial arbitration (see, e.g., Alford 2003). They include entities as diverse as the international maritime court, various tribunals for reparations, international criminal courts, hybrid international-national tribunal instances, trade and investment judicial bodies, regional human rights tribunals, convention-derived institutions, as well as regional courts such as the European Court of Justice, the EFTA Court, and the Benelux Court.[66] The number of today's private systems reflects sharp growth in the last decade.

Strictly speaking, the formation of global regimes is not premised on the integration, harmonization, or convergence of national legal orders. In this sense, then, it goes beyond the type of international economic law arising out of the WTO TRIPS agreements. Most prominently, Teubner (1987) sees a multiplication of sectoral regimes that is an overlay on national legal systems. The outcome is a foundational transformation of the criteria for differentiating law: not the law of nations or the distinction between private and public but the recognition of multiple specialized segmented processes of juridification, which today are largely private. "Societal fragmentation impacts upon law in a manner such that the political regulation of differentiated societal spheres requires the parceling out of issue-specific policy-arenas, which, for their part, juridify themselves;" in this perspective, global law is segmented into transnational legal regimes, which define the "external reach of their jurisdiction along issue-specific rather than territorial lines, and which claim a global validity for themselves" (Teubner 2004: 41).[67]

---

[65] See *http://www.pict-pcti.org*. PICT was founded in 1997 by the Center on International Cooperation (CIC), New York University, and the Foundation for International Environmental Law and Development (FIELD). From 2002 onward, PICT has been a common project of the CIC under the Centre for International Courts and Tribunals, University College London.

[66] PICT has gathered good documentation on legal frameworks and explicatory literature. See Shelton on the area of human rights (1999); on hybrid courts, see Dickinson (2003: 295).

[67] For instance, the Internet Corporation for Assigned Names and Numbers (ICANN) is one of these specialized transnational regimes. See Lehmkuhl (2002: 61–78, 71ff.).

CONCLUSION

The issues addressed in this chapter engage above all the relation between the state's territoriality and the emergent and increasingly institutionalized territoriality of the global economy. The ascendance of diverse forms of private authority and the incipient development of global law are producing institutional encasements of a space of operations for global firms and global markets. But I argued that part of the territoriality for global firms and markets is produced inside the nation-states articulated with the global economy. To illustrate this I used the case of the global, largely electronic, capital market, precisely one of the most extreme instances of the ability to transcend the geographic jurisdictions of the national state. I showed that it is simultaneously global and in need of multiple insertions in national territories. In this regard it can be seen as a natural experiment that tests the limits of both the state's exclusive territoriality and global capital's transnational jurisdictions.

While the state participates in enabling the expansion of the global economy, it does so in a context increasingly dominated by deregulation, privatization, and the growing authority of nonstate actors, some of which assume new normative roles. In many of these new dynamics and conditions, the state continues to play an important role, often as the institutional home for the enactment of the new policy regimes we associate with economic globalization. This institutional home within the state has evolved sharply over the last two decades and today consists largely of the executive branch and a proliferation of regulatory agencies. Another key component of the national as institutional home for global processes and actors exists in the private economic domain, through the corporate economy and the formation of strategic spaces for global operation, including global cities and, on a more micro level, financial centers.

My concern with unpacking this particular issue stems from the embeddedness of much of globalization in national territory under conditions where national territory has been encased in an elaborate set of national laws and administrative capacities. The new geography of global economic processes and the strategic spaces for economic globalization had to be produced, both in terms of the practices of corporate actors and the requisite technical and institutional infrastructure (that is, global cities), as well as in terms of the work of the state in producing or legitimating new legal regimes. This signals a necessary participation by the state, including in the regulation of its own withdrawal. The question then becomes one of understanding the specific type of authority/power this participation gives to the state or attaches to various institutions of the state, as might be the case with some of the increasingly specialized technical regulatory agencies.

The mode in which this participation by the state has evolved has been toward strengthening the power and legitimacy of privatized and denationalized state authorities. The outcome is an emergent new spatio-temporal order that has considerable governance capabilities and structural power. This institutional order strengthens the advantages and the claims of certain types of economic and political actors and weakens those of others. It is extremely partial rather than universal, but strategic in that it has undue influence over wide areas of the broader institutional world and the world of lived experience yet is not fully accountable to formal democratic political systems. While partially embedded in national public and private institutional settings, it is distinct from them. Insofar as it is partly installed in national settings, its identification requires a decoding of what is national in what has historically been constructed as the national.

These developments have consequences for certain features of the state and the interstate system, and in this regard inevitably perhaps for liberal democracy as well as for international law and the modes of accountability therein contained. First, the growth in cross-border activities and global actors operating outside the formal interstate system affects the competence and scope of states and of international law, as these have been constituted historically. Second, this domain is increasingly being institutionalized and subjected to the development of private governance mechanisms, which affects the exclusivity of state authority and the (albeit always partial) exclusivity of international law. Third, the growing normative powers in this private domain affect the normative power of international law. Fourth, the state's participation in the re-regulation of its role in the economy and the incipient denationalization of particular institutional components of the state necessary to accommodate some of the new policies linked to globalization transform key aspects of the state. In so doing this participation by the state also alters the organizational architecture for democratic accountability inside states and the organizational architecture for the interstate system and for international law.

My emphasis on the multiple ways, including very minor ones, in which the new regime for the implementation of the global economy is constituted in good part through the work of states is predicated on a critical understanding of the public-private division as constructed in liberal democratic discourse. But it also aims at understanding the possibilities for constructing new forms of state authority under current conditions. This would include forms of state authority that would not be confined to furthering economic globalization but aim at greater equity and accountability. In this regard, then, my position is not comfortably subsumed under the proposition that nothing has much changed in terms of state power. Nor can it be subsumed under the proposition of the declining significance of the state. It aims rather at mapping an intermediate zone marked by great possibilities for changing current alignments—a highly dynamic intermediate zone with different outcomes depending on the types of political work that get done.

VULTURE FUNDS AND SOVEREIGN DEBT: EXAMPLES FROM

LATIN AMERICA (NOVEMBER 2004)

Brazil

1. Case involving vulture fund(s): Dart Container Corp., with some $1.4 billion in Brazilian debt, threatened to derail Brazil's efforts to restructure its foreign debt in the early 1990s. Dart ultimately failed because it did not have the 5 percent in debt holdings needed to stop Brazil's deal with other creditors.

2. Debt situation: The value of Brazilian foreign debt in 1998 reached 29 percent of the country's GDP.

3. Social factors: In 1990, 17.4 percent of the population lived below the poverty line. In 1997, 17.4 percent of the population lived on less than $2 a day. Public expenditure on education has gone up from 3.6 percent of GDP in 1980 to 5.1 percent in 1997. Public spending on health between 1990 and 1996 was 3.4 percent of GDP.

Panama

1. Case involving vulture fund(s): In October 1995, the New York fund Elliott and Associates L.P. purchased approximately $28.7 million of Panamanian sovereign debt for about $17.5 million. In July 1996, Elliott brought suit against Panama seeking full repayment of the debt. The fund obtained a judgment and attachment order, ultimately receiving over $57 million in payments with interest included.

2. Debt situation: The value of Panamanian external debt in 1998 was 78 percent of the country's GDP.

3. Social factors: In 1997, 37.3 percent of the population lived below the poverty line. From 1980 to 1997 public expenditure on education increased only modestly from 4.9 percent of GDP to 5.1 percent.

Peru

1.   Case involving vulture fund(s): Elliott and Associates also bought Peruvian debt in 1996. Although the fund bought $20.7 million in debt for $11.4 million, after suing the Peruvian government, it managed to collect $58 million. The U.S. Court of Appeals in New York City reversed the prior verdict in Peru's favor.

2.   Debt situation: The value of the debt of Peru was 55 percent of the country's GDP in 1998.

3.   Social factors: In 1997, 49 percent of the population lived below the poverty line. Public expenditure on education decreased from 3.1 percent of GDP in 1980 to 2.9 percent in 1997. Public expenditure on health from 1990 to 1998 was 2.2 percent of GDP.

Ecuador

1.   Case involving vulture fund(s): Gramecy Advisors, whose sole mission has been to collect Ecuadorian and Russian defaulted debt, has emerged as one of the loudest defenders of "bond holder's rights." They are a fund of small creditors of Ecuador, holding $10 million in debt. Although they did not sue the government of Ecuador, traditionally bit players in major debt workouts tend to drive the hardest bargain because governments will pay off a small claim to facilitate a large deal with major creditors.

2.   Debt situation: Foreign debt payments consume half of Ecuador's tax revenues. The total of foreign debt nearly equals its $14.5 billion annual output. The value of the debt in 1998 was 75 percent of the country's GDP.

3.   Social factors: In 1994, 35 percent of the population lived below the poverty line. Government expenditure on education decreased from 5.6 percent of GDP in 1980 to 3.5 percent in 1997, while public expenditure on health from 1990 to 1998 reached 2.5 percent of GDP.

Argentina

1.   Case involving vulture fund(s): (i) On February 5, 2004, a Maryland federal district judge, acting on behalf of Argentine bond holders, temporarily seized four Argentine military stockpiles in the United States valued at $3 million. On January 31, 2004, a U.S. District Judge in New York had

cleared the way for bond holders to identify state-owed commercial assets that could be subject to seizure. Argentina's government hired a group of attorneys to claim diplomatic immunity for the assets seized. (ii) Argentina initiated its official debt restructuring process in early 2005. The offer was accepted by 76.15 percent of the country's creditors. Two hedge funds who did not participate in the exchange decided, instead, to sue the Argentine government. The funds were EM Ltd.—a fund linked to the (in) famous investor Kenneth Dart—and MNL Ltd., a Cayman Islands–based fund linked to Elliott Associated (the hedge fund that sued Peru for $58 million in 1996). The Argentine debt restructuring settlement was held up while deliberations in New York City were underway, delaying the exchange of old bonds into new ones—a distressing outcome for a government that had finally reached a restructuring agreement with the majority of its creditors on debt in default for almost four years. Finally, in May 2005, the panel of the Second Circuit Court of Appeals in Manhattan decided to uphold an earlier decision by Judge Thomas Griesa on March 31, 2005, against the creditors. Griesa deliberated that the creditors could not seize $7 billion in Argentine bonds until the debt exchange had been completed, because they were owned by the bond holders, and hence were to be considered liabilities of the Argentine government, not its assets. After the debt swap, the bonds would be canceled under the terms of the exchange, leaving them without value to the plaintiffs. This was considered a significant victory by the Argentine government, not only because it made the exchange finally viable, but because it made evident to other (potential) vulture/holdout creditors that litigation was not to be considered a lucrative avenue in dealing with their defaulted bonds.

2.   Debt situation: After defaulting on over $80 billion worth of debt in 2001, in February 2005 Argentina offered bond holders about $41 billion in new bonds in exchange for the $102.6 billion outstanding in principal and interest. This was considered the biggest loss of principal taken on by creditors of a sovereign government of any sovereign debt restructuring in modern times.

3.   Social factors: The crisis that culminated with the decision to default on sovereign debt was the worst the country has faced. Already high levels of unemployment (18.3 percent in October 2001) jumped to 21.5 percent in May 2002 (six months after the announcement of the suspension of payments on sovereign debt owed to private creditors). Job loss was sharp, especially in the formal sector where employment fell 10.5 percent since June 2001 (as of November 2002). World Bank estimates for twenty-eight

urban centers indicate an increase in poverty rates from 38.3 percent in October 2001 to a peak of 58 percent by the end of 2002. The number of people living below the indigence line doubled in the same period. Income distribution worsened, suggesting that the poorest segments of the population suffered more than the more well off. This dramatic context has had a strong impact on the health and education sectors where there is a growing evidence of deterioration in service delivery. Violence has increased. As of July 2003, spending targeting the poor had increased by 21 percent from the pre-crisis level. However, the large increase in the number of impoverished during the crisis means that real spending per poor person has actually declined by 16 percent.

4. Economic Developments: Despite these great difficulties, Argentina achieved a 9 percent real GDP growth in 2004. Also, the government managed to run a fiscal surplus of around 3.2 percent of GDP (as of mid-2005) that pleased international investors and especially credit rating companies. For example, Standard and Poor's upgraded Argentine swapped bonds, making those increasingly more attractive to international investors looking for relatively high returns (of approximately 16 percent annually in mid-2005) at a time when interest rates in developed countries remain low (approximately 4 percent annually). Nevertheless, keeping the fiscal surplus will remain a challenge for the Argentine government, which faces increases in spending, especially linked to debt repayment.

Nicaragua

1. Case involving vulture fund(s): A group of U.S. investors is suing the government for full repayment of defaulted commercial bank debt from the 1980s, plus accrued interest. Eight years ago, Leucadia National Corp., a troubled New York–based conglomerate, and Van Eck, a New York investment fund, bought the debt for a few cents on the dollar. If they get their way, their Nicaraguan investment will repay spectacularly. Van Eck alone bought about $50 million in face value Nicaraguan loans, which would be worth $250 million if it were to collect on the full debt and accrued interest.

2. Other factors: Nicaragua is a poor country that has suffered civil wars, natural disasters, and a series of corruption scandals that have led to the detention in jail of former president Arnaldo Aleman. The present government states that it is trying to end corruption, reduce poverty— average incomes are just $500 a year—and qualify for debt relief under the

Highly Indebted Poor Country Initiative (HIPC), sponsored by the World Bank.[1]

[1] Giselle Datz, "Whose Problem? Globalization's Expanding Spheres of Accountability and the Case of Foreign Debt in Developing Countries" (Master's thesis, University of Chicago, 2001); InterPress Service News, "Steadfast against Impatient IMF: Hovering Vulture Funds," February 12, 2004; "Inhiben mas bienes argentinos en EE.UU," *La Nación*, February 10, 2004; "Argentina reclama a EE.UU. por las inhibiciones de bienes del Estado," *Clarín*, February 11, 2004; Ariel Fiszbein, Paula Ines Giovagnoli, and Isidro Aduriz, "Argentina's Crisis and Its Impact on Household Welfare," World Bank Office for Argentina, Chile, Paraguay, and Uruguay, Working Paper No. 1/02, November 2002; "Argentine President Berates Bondholders," *Financial Times*, February 9, 2004; "Feast of the Vultures," *Latin Finance*, December 2003; "La Justicia de EE.UU Dio Luz Verde al Canje de la Deuda," *La Nación*, May 14, 2005; "Para S&P, La Argentina Salió del Default," *La Nación*, June 2, 2005; "La Situación Económica Mejoró, Pero Surgen las Preguntas," *La Nación*, June 19, 2005; "Argentina's Debt Program Seen as Exception to the Rule," Reuters, May 13, 2005; "NY Court Lifts Argentine Bond Freeze," *Financial Times*, May 14, 2005; Michael Massa, "Global Economic Prospects: Slower but Still Solid Growth in 2005," Institute for International Economics, 2005; World Bank-Poverty Reduction and Economic Management in Latin America and the Caribbean Region, "Argentina—Crisis and Poverty 2003," Report No. 26127-AR, July 24, 2003.

6 FOUNDATIONAL SUBJECTS FOR
POLITICAL MEMBERSHIP
Today's Changed Relation to the National State

FEW, if any, modern institutions are as emblematic of rights as citizenship. In this regard, the construction of citizenship over the last several centuries and its current partial deconstruction illuminate critical issues about rights and the formation of a rights-bearing subject. The rights articulated through the subject of the citizen are of a particular type and cannot be easily generalized to other types of subjects. Yet the complexity and multiple tensions built into the formal institution of citizenship make it a powerful heuristic for examining the question of rights more generally.

Building on this complexity and these tensions, the organizing thesis in this chapter is that citizenship is an incompletely theorized contract between the state and its subjects.[1] Further, it is meant to be incomplete, given the historically conditioned meaning of the institution of citizenship. This incompleteness makes it possible for a highly formalized institution to accommodate change—more precisely, to accommodate the possibility of responding to change without sacrificing its formal status. Incompleteness also brings to the fore the work of making, whether it is making in response to changed conditions, to new subjectivities, or to new instrumentalities. It is at this point of incompleteness that I position my inquiry. In chapter 2 I used this lens to examine the forming of a citizen-subject in medieval times out of the active making of urban law; and in chapter 3, to examine the making in England and the United States of a fully enabled property-owning citizen (epitomized by the industrial bourgeoisie) and a disadvantaged subject (the factory worker), an inequality formalized in the law. Through civil and workplace

---

[1] With other questions in mind, Sunstein (1993) develops the notion of an incompletely theorized contract. My use of this notion takes liberties with Sunstein's formulation. I first used this in an examination of immigration policy, arguing it should be conceived of along these lines (1996: chapter 3) given the complexity and multiple tensions involved in the bundle of processes we designate as "immigration." Here I extend this analysis to the question of citizenship.

struggles, disadvantaged subjects fought for and gained formal rights, and these struggles for remaking citizenship continue. Yet all along, the formal institution has remained in place; it was not toppled. In this chapter I examine how the institution confronts today's changes in the larger social context, in the law, in political subjectivities, and in discursive practices.

A key element bringing these various histories together and in some ways securing the durability of the institution of citizenship has been the will of the state to render national major institutions that might well have followed a different trajectory and to some extent did for most of recorded Western history. Political membership as a national category is today an inherited condition, one experienced as a given rather than as a process of making a rights-bearing subject. And while its making arose out of the conditions of the cities of the Late Middle Ages, today it is generally understood to be inextricably articulated with the national state (Himmelfarb 2001). Yet today's significant, even if not absolute, transformations in the condition of the national generally and the national state in particular help make visible the historicity of the formal institution of citizenship and thus show its national spatial character as but one of several possible framings. Citizenship becomes a heuristic category through which to understand the question of rights and subject formation and to do so in ways that recover the conditionalities entailed in its territorial articulation and thereby the limits or vulnerabilities of this framing. At the most abstract or formal level not much has changed over the last century in the essential features of citizenship unlike, for example, the characteristics of leading economic sectors. The theoretical ground from which I address the issue is that of the historicity and the embeddedness of both citizenship and the national state. Each has been constructed in elaborate and formal ways. And each has evolved historically as a tightly packaged national bundle of what were often rather diverse elements.

Some of the main dynamics at work today are destabilizing these national bundlings and bringing to the fore the fact of that bundling and its particularity. The work of making and formalizing a unitary packaging for diverse elements comes under pressure today in both formalized (for example, the granting of dual nationality and recognition of the international human rights regime) and nonformalized ways (for example, granting undocumented immigrants in the United States the "right" to own homes and access mortgages). Among the destabilizing dynamics at work are globalization and digitization, both as material processes and as signaling subjective possibilities or imaginaries. In multiple ways they perform changes in the formal and informal relationships between the national state and the citizen. There are also a range of emergent political practices often involving hitherto silent or silenced population groups and organizations. Through their destabilizing effects, these dynamics and actors are producing operational and rhetorical openings for the emergence of new types of political subjects and new spatialities for politics. More broadly, the destabilizing of national state-centered hierarchies of legitimate power and allegiance has enabled a multiplication of nonformalized or only partly formalized political dynamics and actors.

Today's unsettlement helps make legible the diversity of sources and institutional locations for rights, as well as the changeability and variability of the rights-bearing subject that is the citizen, notwithstanding the formal character of the institution. This chapter's deconstruction of the institution gets at this diversity and changeability through two analytic processes: a redeployment of specific components of citizenship across a wide range of institutional locations and normative orders; and a detecting of sites where formal or experiential features of citizenship generate instability in the institution and hence the possibility of changes. The particular foci for analysis are of two kinds, one pertaining to the formal apparatus of citizenship as an institution and the other to domains outside that formal apparatus and in that sense akin to informal citizenship as far as the institution is concerned. Among the first foci for analysis are the changing relationship between citizenship and nationality, the increasingly formalized interaction between citizenship rights and human rights, the implications for formal citizenship of the privatizing of executive power along with the erosion of citizens' privacy rights, and the elaboration of a series of standards and entitlements for citizens engaged in novel types of formal cross-border arrangements.

Among the second foci for analysis is a range of incipient and typically nonformalized developments in the institution that can be organized into three types of empirical cases. One of these is processes that alter a status and involve both informal and formal institutional environments. Two examples illustrate the range of possible instances: the fact that international human rights enter the national court system through an often rather informal process that with time can become stabilized and eventually made part of national law; and the fact that undocumented immigrants who demonstrate long-term residence and good conduct can make a claim for regularization on the basis, ultimately, of their long-term violation of the law. These types of dynamics are a good example of one of the theses that runs through the book: excluded norms and actors are one of the factors in the making of history, even though they only become recognized when formalized. A second type of empirical case is the variety of components usually bundled up along with the formal rights even though their legal status is different. A possible way of categorizing these components is in terms of practices, identities, and locations for the enactment of citizenship. This allows me to focus on subjects who are by definition categorized as nonpolitical, such as "housewives" or "mothers," but who may have considerable political agency and be emergent political actors. Another example is political subjects not quite fully recognized as such, notably undocumented immigrants, but who can nonetheless function as bearers of partial rights (for example, the right to wages for work done) and, more generally, as part of the political landscape. One of the critical institutional developments that gives meaning to such informal political actors and practices is the notion developed in this chapter that the formal political apparatus can accommodate less and less of the political in today's world.

I organize these various issues through the proposition that insofar as citizenship is at least partly and variably shaped by the conditions within which it is embedded, conditions that have changed in specific and general ways, we may well be seeing a corresponding set of changes in the institution itself. These changes may not yet be formalized and some may never become fully formalized. The national state is one of the strategic institutional locations for both the larger contextual changes and the more specific changes pertaining to citizenship. Thus I argue that citizenship, even if situated in institutional settings that are "national," is a possibly changed institution if the meaning of the national itself has changed. The empirical examination, then, addresses the question as to whether the changes brought about by globalizing dynamics and by denationalizing the territorial and institutional organization of state authority, are also transforming the institution of citizenship. One question then is whether this transformation is occurring even when citizenship remains centered on the national state, that is, barring postnational versions of citizenship.[2] The empirical examination aims at detecting and deciphering formal and informal changes in the rights of citizens, in citizens' practices, and in the subjective dimensions of the institution; by including nonformalized "rights," practices, and subjectivities the analysis can grasp instabilities and possibilities for further change. I interpret these types of changes as a partial and often incipient denationalizing of citizenship.

A concluding section argues that many of the transformations in the broader context and in the institution itself become evident in the sphere of informal politics. Perhaps the most evolved type of site for these transformations is the global city, which concentrates the most developed and pronounced instantiations of today's larger systemic changes; in this

---

[2] Bosniak (1996: 29–30) understands this when she asserts that for some (Sassen 1996; Jacobson 1996) there is a devaluing of citizenship but that the nation-state is still its referent and in that regard is not a postnational interpretation.

process it is reconfigured as a partly denationalized urban space that enables a partial reinvention of citizenship as practice and as project. These are spaces that can exit the institutionalized hierarchies of scale articulated through the nation-state. Practices and informal politics can take the institution away from questions of nationality narrowly defined and toward the enactment of a large array of particular interests, from protests against police brutality and globalization to sexual preference politics and house squatting by anarchists. I interpret this as a move toward citizenship practices that revolve around claiming rights to the city. These are not exclusively urban practices. But it is especially in large cities that we see simultaneously some of the most extreme inequalities and the conditions enabling these citizenship practices. In global cities, these practices also contain the possibility of directly engaging strategic forms of power, which I interpret as significant in a context where power is increasingly privatized, globalized, and elusive. Where Max Weber saw the medieval city as the strategic site for the enablement of the burghers as political actors and Lefebvre saw the large modern cities as the strategic site for the struggles of the industrial organized workforce to gain rights, I see in today's global cities the strategic site for a whole new type of political actors and projects.

CITIZENSHIP AND NATIONALITY

In its narrowest definition citizenship describes the legal relationship between the individual and the polity. This can in principle assume many forms, in good part depending on the definition of the polity. In Europe one of the key definitions of the polity was originally the city in both ancient and medieval times. But the configuration of a polity reached its most developed form with the national state, making it eventually dominant worldwide. The evolution of polities along the lines of state formation gave citizenship in the West its full institutionalized and formalized character and made nationality a key component of citizenship. Today citizenship and nationality both refer to the national state. While essentially the same concept, each term reflects a different legal framework. Both identify the legal status of an individual in terms of state membership. But citizenship is largely confined to the national dimension, while nationality refers to the international legal dimension in the context of an interstate system. The legal status entails the specifics of whom the state recognizes as a citizen and the formal basis for the rights and responsibilities of the individual in relation to the state. International law affirms that each state may determine who will be considered a citizen of that state.[3] Domestic laws about who is a citizen vary significantly across states as do the definitions of what it entails to be a citizen. Even within the increasingly formalized European Union, let alone worldwide, there remain marked differences in how citizenship is articulated and hence how noncitizens are defined notwithstanding the trend toward harmonization (Hansen and Weil 2002).

The transformation of citizenship into a national state institution and away from one centered on cities and civil society was part of a larger dynamic of change. Key institutional orders began to scale at the national level: warfare, industrial development, and formal educational and cultural institutions. These were all at the heart of the formation and strengthening of the national state as the key political community, and the one crucial to the socialization of individuals into national citizenship. It is in this context that nationality became a central constitutive element of the institution of citizenship in a way that it was not in the medieval cities described by Weber.

The evolution of the meaning of nationality makes some of these transformations legible. Historically, nationality is linked to the bond of allegiance of the individual to the sovereign. It dates from the early European state system, including some of its more elementary forms, and described the inherent and permanent bond of the subject to the sovereign captured in the prescription, "No man may abjure his country" (Turner 2000). This bond was seen as insoluble or at least exclusive. But while this bond was defensible in times of limited individual mobility, it became difficult in the face of large-scale migration, which was part of the new forms of industrial development. Insoluble allegiance was gradually replaced by exclusive (hence changeable) allegiance as the basis of nationality. Where the doctrine of insoluble allegiance is a product of medieval Europe, the development of exclusive allegiance reflects the political context in the second half of the nineteenth century, when state sovereignty became the organizing principle of an international system—albeit a system centered on and largely ruled by Europe.

This is evident in how nationality was conceived and how it has evolved. The aggressive nationalism and territorial competition between states in the late nineteenth and much of the twentieth centuries made the concept of dual nationality generally undesirable it was incompatible with individual loyalties, and it destabilized the international order. Indeed, we see the development of a series of mechanisms aimed at preventing or counteracting the common causes for dual nationality (Sassen 1999: chapters 4 and

[3] The critical document is the 1930 Hague Convention on Certain Questions Relating to the Conflict of Nationality Laws. Nationality is important in international law in a variety of contexts. However, various treaties and conventions in turn impact nationality.

5; Marrus 1985). There were no generalized or generic international accords on dual nationality; the latter was only an option under exceptional conditions. This is in sharp contrast with the 1990s, which have seen a proliferation of states allowing dual nationality.[4] The negative perception of dual nationality continued well into the 1960s and even 1980s in many countries, and even today its granting often rests on a sort of informal acceptance that a citizen may also acquire a second nationality. This reluctance is partly structural, as the main effort by the international system has historically been to root out the causes of dual nationality by means of multilateral codification of the law on the subject (Rubenstein and Adler 2000). The institution of citizenship centered on exclusive allegiance did not reach its high point until the twentieth century. And it was only toward the late 1900s that larger transformations once again brought conditions for a change in the institution and its relation to nationality, thereby also changing the legal content of nationality. States began to accommodate formal and informal options that diluted that particular formalization: nationality began to move to more flexible forms. The long-lasting resistance to dual or multiple nationality shifted toward a selective acceptance. According to some legal scholars (Rubenstein and Adler 2000; Spiro 1997), dual and multiple nationalities will become the norm. Insofar as the importance of nationality in international law is a function of the central role of states in the international law machinery, a decline in the importance of this role will affect the value of nationality. There is a parallel here with the partial devaluation of nation-state based sovereignty.

Some of the major transformations occurring today under the impact of globalization may give citizenship yet another set of features as it continues to respond to the conditions within which it is embedded. The nationalizing of the institution that took place over the last several centuries may give way to a partial denationalizing. A fundamental dynamic in this regard is the growing articulation of globalization with national economies and the associated withdrawal of the state from various spheres of citizenship entitlements, with the possibility of a corresponding dilution of loyalty to the state. In turn, citizens' loyalty may be less crucial to the state today than it was at a time of intense warfare and its need for loyal citizen-soldiers. Troops today can be replaced by technology and citizen-soldiers with professionals. Most important, in the highly developed world, warfare has become a less significant event partly because of economic globalization. Global firms and global markets do

---

[4] Soysal (1994, 1997) and Feldblum (1998) interpret the increase in dual nationality in terms of postnational citizenship rather than a mere devaluing of national allegiance. I would argue that it is a partial denationalizing of citizenship (see my response to Bosniak in Sassen 2000).

not want the rich countries to fight wars among themselves. The "international" project is radically different from what it was in the nineteenth and first half of the twentieth centuries. This became evident in the debates leading up to the invasion of Iraq in 2003, an event that renationalized politics. Except for highly specialized sectors, such as oil and war-linked supplies and services, global firms in the United States and elsewhere were basically opposed to the invasion. The position of the citizen has been markedly weakened by states' concern with national security, even though done in the name of citizen's security. Where before nationality could determine designation as a suspect resident citizen, for example, Germans and Japanese in the United States during World War II, today all citizens are, in principle, suspect in the United States given the government's War on Terror (See 'Nervous Borders' conference, http://cgsigmu.edu/nervousborders).

Many of the dynamics that built economies, polities, and societies in the nineteenth and twentieth centuries contained an articulation between the national scale and the growth of entitlements for citizens. This articulation was not only a political process; it contained a set of utility functions for workers, for property owners, and for the state. These utility functions have changed since the 1970s. During industrialization, class formation, class struggles, and the advantages of employers or workers tended to scale at the national level and became identified with state-produced legislation and regulations, entitlements, and obligations. The state came to be seen as a key to ensuring the well-being of significant portions of both the working class and the bourgeoisie. The development of welfare states in the twentieth century resulted in good part from the struggles by workers whose victories contributed to actually make capitalism more sustainable; advantaged sectors of the population, such as the growing middle class, also found their interests playing out at the national level and supported by national state planning, such as investment in transportation and housing infrastructure. Legislatures (or parliaments) and judiciaries developed the needed laws and systems and became a crucial institutional domain for granting entitlements to the poor and the disadvantaged. Today, the growing weight given to notions of the "competitiveness" of states puts pressure on the particular utility functions of that older phase, and new rationales are developed for cutting down on those entitlements, which in turn weakens the reciprocal relationship between the citizen and the state. This weakening relationship takes on specific contents for different sectors of the citizenry. The poor and low-waged workers are perhaps the most visible case (Munger 2002), but the impoverishment of the old traditional middle classes evident in a growing number of countries around the world is also becoming increasingly visible. Finally, the intergenerational effects of these trends signal more change. Thus the disproportionate unemployment among the young and the fact that many of them develop only weak ties to the labor market, once thought of as a crucial mechanism for the socialization of young adults, will further weaken the loyalty and sense of reciprocity between these future adults and the state (Roulleau-Berger 2002).

As these trends have come together at the turn of the twenty-first century they are destabilizing the meaning of citizenship as it was forged in the nineteenth and most of the twentieth centuries. The growing emphasis on notions of the "competitive state" and the associated emphasis on markets have brought into question the foundations of the welfare state broadly understood, that is, that the state bears responsibility for the basic well-being of its citizens, and that the state's utility function is to be distinguished from that of firms. For Marshall (1977) and many others the welfare state is an important ingredient of social citizenship; the reliance on markets to solve political and social problems is seen as a savage attack on the principles of citizenship (Saunders 1993). For Saunders, citizenship inscribed in the institutions of the welfare state is a buffer against the vagaries of the market and the inequalities of the class system. Citizenship in the modern state has typically been based on an individual obligation to contribute taxes to a state system of provision. This was a key ingredient of the postwar Keynesian reconstruction. It was based on assumptions about full employment, the preeminence of the nuclear household, and exclusive heterosexual relations. These were the assumptions of the dominant model of Marshallian citizenship. They have been severely diluted under the impact of globalization and the ascendance of the market as the preferred mechanism for addressing more and more social issues.

The nature of citizenship has also been challenged by the types of changes discussed in chapter 4, for example, the erosion of privacy rights, as well as by a proliferation of old issues that have gained new attention. Among the latter are the question of state membership of aboriginal communities, stateless people, and refugees.[5] All of these have important implications for human rights in relation to citizenship (Benhabib 2004; Brysk and Shafir 2004). These social changes in the role of the nation-state, the impact of globalization on states, and the relationship between dominant and subordinate groups also have major implications for questions of identity. Ong (1999: chapters 1 and 4) finds that in cross-border processes individuals actually accumulate partial and often contingent rights, a form she calls flexible citizenship.

"Is citizenship a useful concept for exploring the problems of belonging, identity and personality in the modern world?" (Shotter 1993: ix). Can such a radical change in the relation between the state and citizen leave the institution itself unchanged? This question takes on added meaning when we

[5] See, for example, Knop 2002; see also Sassen (1999: chapter 6).

consider the weight of civil society in the shaping of citizenship and the cultural and historical specificity of both concepts of civil society and citizenship in Western social and political theory (Turner 1993; Benhabib 2002). Insofar as the new conditions alter the meaning and content of civil society, they may well thereby alter citizenship. Global forces that challenge and transform the authority of nation-states may give human rights an expanded role in the normative regulation of politics as politics become more global. If citizenship is theorized as necessarily national (Himmelfarb 2001), then, these new developments are not fully captured in the language of citizenship.[6] An alternative interpretation would be to suspend the national, as in postnational conceptions, and to posit that the issue of where citizenship is enacted should be determined in light of developing social practice (Bosniak 2000a).[7]

The scholarship on citizenship and its transformations has contributed to a number of novel types of distinctions and alignments, some centered on the nation-state and others not. In the brief review that follows, which cannot do full justice to this rich scholarship, it becomes evident that narrow formal definitions are increasingly inadequate. While this has, of course, always been the case to some extent, the scholarship points to the notion that current conditions—globalization, growing diversity, claims by the excluded—are sharpening this dynamic.

DEBORDERING AND RELOCALIZING CITIZENSHIP

Scholars from many different disciplines and armed with different questions have contributed to a renewed elaboration of the subject of citizenship and the many theoretical distinctions it elicits. Yet more often than not,

---

[6] Thus for Karst, "In the U.S. today, citizenship is inextricable from a complex legal framework that includes a widely accepted body of substantive law, strong law-making institutions, and law-enforcing institutions capable of performing their task" (2000: 600). Not recognizing the centrality of the legal issues is, for Karst, a big mistake. Postnational citizenship lacks an institutional framework that can protect the substantive values of citizenship. Karst does acknowledge the possibility of rabid nationalism and the exclusion of aliens when legal status is made central.

[7] E.g., Soysal 1994; Jacobson 1996. There is a growing literature that is expanding the content of citizenship. For example, some scholars focus on the affective connections that people establish and maintain with one another in the context of a growing transnational civil society (see generally *Global Civil Society Yearbook* 2002; J. Cohen 1995; Lipschutz and Mayer 1996). Citizenship here resides in identities and commitments that arise out of cross-border affiliations, especially those associated with oppositional politics (Caglar 1995; for a legal elaboration, see Hunter 1992), though it might include the corporate professional circuits that are increasingly forms of partly deterritorialized global cultures.

the nation-state is the typically implicit frame within which these distinctions are explored. In this sense, much of this literature cannot be read as postnational even when it seeks to locate citizenship in areas that go beyond the formal political domain. Nonetheless, this deconstruction of citizenship has also fed a much smaller but growing scholarship, which begins to develop notions of citizenship not based on the nation-state, whether understood in narrow political terms or broader sociological and psychological terms. The growing prominence of the international human rights regime has played an important theoretical and political role in strengthening postnational conceptions even as it has emphasized the differences between citizenship rights and human rights. Later in this chapter I juxtapose these postnational conceptions to denationalized framings for these transformations.

A brief examination of some of the key issues emerging from the vast scholarly literature is helpful in mapping the sharply expanded terrain through which the question of citizenship and rights is being constructed today. Over the last two decades there have been several efforts to organize the various understandings of citizenship: citizenship as legal status, as possession of rights, as political activity, and as a form of collective identity and sentiment (Kymlicka and Norman 1994; Carens 1996; Benhabib 2002; Vogel and Moran 1991; Conover 1995; Bosniak 2000b). Further, some scholars (Young 2002; Turner 1994; C. Taylor 1994; see also generally Van Steenbergen 1994) have posited that cultural citizenship is a necessary part of any adequate conception of citizenship, while others have insisted on the importance of economic citizenship (Fernandez Kelly 1993; Sassen 1996: chapter 2). Still others emphasize the psychological dimension and the ties of identification and solidarity we maintain with other groups in the world (Conover 1995; Carens 1996; Pogge 1992).

While many of these distinctions deconstruct the category of citizenship and are helpful for formulating novel conceptions, they do not necessarily cease to be nation-state based. The development of notions of postnational citizenship requires questioning the assumption that people's sense of citizenship in liberal democratic states is fundamentally characterized by nation-based frames. These questions of identity need to be taken into account along with formal developments such as EU citizenship and the growth of the international human rights regime. Insofar as legal and formal developments have not gone very far, a focus on experiences of identity emerges as crucial to postnational citizenship. In this regard, a focus on changes inside the national state and the resulting possibility of new types of formalizations of citizenship status and rights—formalizations that might contribute to a partial denationalizing of certain features of citizenship—should be part of a more general examination of change in the institution of citizenship. Distinguishing postnational and denationalized dynamics in the construction of new components of citizenship allows us to take account of changes that might still use the national frame yet are in fact altering the meaning of that frame.

The scholarship that critiques the assumption that identity is basically tied to a national polity represents a broad range of positions, many having little to do with postnational or denationalized conceptions. For some, the focus is on the fact that people often maintain stronger allegiances to and identification with particular cultural and social groups within the nation than with the nation at large (Young 1990; C. Taylor 1994). Others have argued that the notion of a national identity is based on the suppression of social and cultural differences (Friedman 1973). These and others have called for a recognition of differentiated citizenship and modes of incorporation predicated not only on individuals but also on group rights, often understood as culturally distinct groups (Young 1990; Kymlicka and Norman 1994; C. Taylor 1994; Conover 1995). As Torres (1998) has observed, the "cultural pluralist" (Kymlicka and Norman 1994) or multiculturalist positions (Spinner-Halev 1994) posit alternatives to a "national" sense of identity but continue to use the nation-state as the normative frame and to understand the social groups involved as parts of national civil society. This also holds for proposals to democratize the public sphere through multicultural representation (Young 1990; Kymlicka 1995) since the public sphere is thought of as national. Critical challenges to statist premises can also be found in concepts of local citizenship, typically conceived of as centered in cities (e.g., Magnusson 1990, 2000; Isin 2000), or by reclaiming for citizenship domains of social life often excluded from conventional conceptions of politics (Bosniak 2000a). Examples of the latter are the recognition of citizenship practices in the workplace (Pateman 1989; Lawrence 2004), in the economy at large (Dahl 1989), in the family (Jones 1998), and in new social movements (Tarrow 1994; Magnusson 2000). These are more sociological versions of citizenship, not confined by formal political criteria for specifying citizenship. While some of these critical literatures do not go beyond the nation-state and thereby do not fit in postnational conceptions of citizenship, they may fit in a conception of citizenship as partly or increasingly denationalized.

Partly influenced by these critical literatures and partly originating in other fields, a rapidly growing scholarship has begun to elaborate notions of transnational civil society and citizenship. It focuses on new transnational forms of political organization emerging in a context of rapid globalization and proliferation of cross-border activities of all sorts of "actors," notably immigrants, NGOs, first-nation people, human rights, the environment, arms control, women's rights, labor rights, and rights of national minorities (Smith and Guarnizo 1998; Keck and Sikkink 1998; Bonilla et al. 1998; Wapner 1996; Brysk and Shafir 2004). For Falk (1992) these are citizen practices that go beyond the nation. Transnational activism emerges as a form of global citizenship, which Magnusson describes as "popular politics in its global dimension" (1996: 103). Wapner sees these emergent forms of civil society as "a slice of associational life which exists above the individual and below the state, but also across national boundaries" (1996: 312–33).

Questions of identity and solidarity include the rise of transnationalism (Torres 1998; R. Cohen 1996; Franck 1992; Levitt 2001) and translocal loyalties (Appadurai 1996: 165; Basch et al. 1993). Bosniak (2000a: 482) finds at least four forms of transnationalized citizenship identity. The first is the growth of European-wide citizenship developing as part of the EU integration process and beyond the formal status of EU citizenship (Jacobson and Ruffer 2003; Soysal 1994, 1997; Benhabib 2002; Howe 1991; Isin 2000; Delanty 2000). Turner has posited a growing cultural awareness of a "European identity" (2000). Second, people establish and maintain affective connections with one another in the context of a growing transnational civil society (J. Cohen 1995; Lipschutz and Mayer 1996; GCS 2002). Citizenship here resides in identities and commitments that arise out of cross-border affiliations, especially those associated with oppositional politics (Falk 1992), though it might include the corporate professional circuits that are increasingly forms of global cultures with distinct territorial insertions in global cities (Sassen 2001: chapter 5). Third is the emergence of transnational social and political communities constituted through transborder migration. These begin to function as bases for new forms of citizenship identity to the extent that members maintain identification and solidarities with one another across state territorial divides (Levitt 2001; Portes 1995; Basch et al. 1993; R. Smith 1997; Soysal 1997; Caglar 1995). These are, then, citizenship identities that arise out of networks, activities, and ideologies that span the home and the host society. Fourth is a sort of global sense of solidarity and identification, partly out of humanitarian convictions (Slawner and Denham 1998; Pogge 1992). Notions of the ultimate unity of human experience are part of a long tradition. Today there are also more practical considerations at work, as in global ecological interdependence, economic globalization, global media, and commercial culture, all of which create structural interdependencies and a sense of global responsibility (Falk 1992; Hunter 1992; Held 1995; Sassen 1996; Hoerder 2000).

In brief, through different vocabularies and questions these diverse literatures make legible the variability of citizenship. In so doing, they also signal what we might think of as the incompleteness of citizenship, one inherent to the institution given its historicity and embeddedness. In this incompleteness also lies the possibility of its transformation across time and place.

DECONSTRUCTING CITIZENSHIP: A LENS INTO THE
QUESTION OF RIGHTS

These empirical conditions and conceptual elaborations of the late twentieth century together produce a fundamental question. What is the analytic terrain within which we need to place the question of rights as articulated in the institution of citizenship (Sassen 1996: chapter 2)? The history of interactions between differential positionings and expanded inclusions signals the possibility of further change. The new conditions of inequality and difference evident today and the new types of claim making they generate may well bring about further transformations in the institution of citizenship. For instance, although it has an old history[8], the question of diversity assumes new meanings and contains new elements. Notable here are the globalization of economic and cultural relationships and the repositioning of "culture," including cultures embedded in religions that encompass basic norms for the conduct of daily life.[9] It is clear that republican conceptions of citizenship are but one of several options, even though they can accommodate diversity via the distinction of public and private spheres.[10]

There are three aspects I want to examine as a first step in deciphering conceptual parameters that capture the complexity of citizenship today and, more generically, the formation of rights-bearing subjects. One of these can be captured through the proposition that citizenship is partly produced by the practices of the excluded; this opens up the terrain for rights to nonformalized actors and issues especially if the grip of the nation-state on questions of identity and membership is weakened by major social, economic, political, and subjective trends. Second, by expanding formal inclusions, the

[8] The challenge of negotiating the inclusion of citizens and the question of diversity is an old one. Saxonhouse (1992) observes that ancient Greece confronted the problem of diversity and thereby produced political theory—we might add, to rationalize exclusion.

[9] For example, it is becoming evident that in the Muslim world the sphere of the public is being affected by current dynamics, notably the growing use of the Internet, which is enabling the formation of a transnational Muslim public sphere (Eickelman and Anderson 1999).

[10] This has been the official position of the French, explicated in the case of the demand by some Muslim sectors in France for girls to wear veils to school: they can be worn at home but are prohibited in public spaces, including public institutions.

national state itself contributed to legitimate conditions that eventually facilitated key aspects of post- or transnational citizenship, particularly in a context of globalization. Third, insofar as the state itself has undergone significant transformation, notably the changes bundled under the notion of the competitive state and the quasi-privatized executive, the chances that state institutions will do the type of legislative and judiciary work that has led to expanded formal inclusions is likely to diminish.

These three dynamics point to the absence of a lineal evolution in the institution and the debordering of formal citizenship, albeit with great variations across countries. We cannot assume the continuation of the progressively expanding inclusions that took off in the United States in the 1960s; on the contrary, we now see a loss of rights and entitlements. At the same time, those formal expansions produced novel trajectories in the development of citizenship; they enabled a variety of actors to make claims. The formalizing of inclusions has contributed to the centrality of equality to citizenship, now a visible and named norm that creates new types of claims. With this, tension between the legal status and the normative project of citizenship has also grown. For many, citizenship is now a normative project whereby social membership becomes increasingly comprehensive and open-ended. Globalization and human rights contribute to this tension, thereby furthering the elements of a new discourse on rights. Though in very different ways, both globalization and the human rights regime destabilize the existing political hierarchies of legitimate power and allegiance.

Though often talked about as a single concept and experienced as a unitary institution, citizenship actually describes a number of discrete but connected components in the relation between the individual and the polity. Current developments are bringing to light and accentuating the distinctiveness of these various components, from formal rights to practices and subjective dimensions, and the tension between citizenship as a formal legal status and as a normative project or an aspiration. The formal equality that attaches to all citizens rarely embodies the need for substantive equality in social terms. Finally, the growing prominence of an international human rights regime has produced synergies between citizenship rights and human rights, even as it has underscored the differences between these two types of rights.

Insofar as citizenship is a status that articulates legal rights and responsibilities, the mechanisms through which this articulation is shaped and implemented can be analytically distinguished from the status itself. In the medieval cities examined in chapter 2, urban residents themselves set up the structures through which to establish and thicken the rights and obligations of the citizen, and they did so through a codification contributing to a specific type of law, urban law, that constructed them as rights-bearing subjects. Today it is largely the national state that articulates the subject of the citizen. With the major transformations afoot inside the state (chapter 4) and beyond the state (chapter 5), as well as the ascendance of human rights, this articulation may well begin to change once again, as might the actual content and shape of citizens' rights and obligations.

Some of these issues can be illustrated through the evolution of equal citizenship. Equal citizenship is central to the modern institution of citizenship; the expansion of specific types of equality among citizens has shaped a good part of its evolution in the twentieth century. Yet insofar as equality is based on membership, as a criterion citizenship status forms the basis of exclusive politics and identities. This exclusiveness can be seen as essential because it provides the sense of solidarity necessary for the development of modern citizenship in the nation-state (Walzer 1995; Bosniak 1996). In a country such as the United States, the principle of equal citizenship remains unfulfilled, even after the successful struggles and legal advances of the second half of the twentieth century. Groups defined by race, ethnicity, religion, sex, sexual orientation, and other "identities" still face various exclusions from full participation in public life. This is especially so at the level of practices even in the face of changes in the formal legal status, and notwithstanding formal equality as citizens. Feminist and race-critical scholarship has highlighted the failure of gender- and race-neutral conceptions of citizenship, such as legal status, to account for the differences of individuals within communities (Benhabib et al. 1995; Crenshaw et al. 1996; Delgado and Stefancic 1999; Benhabib 2002). In addition, because full participation as a citizen is conditioned by a (variable) minimum of material resources and social rights (Marshall 1977; Handler 1995), poverty can severely reduce participation.[11] In brief, legal citizenship does not always bring full and equal membership rights because these rights are often conditioned by the position of different groups within a nation-state.

Yet when we use a sufficiently long time span, we can see that there have been critical instances where it is precisely the outsider position of these different groups that has engendered the practices and struggles that forced changes in the formal institution of citizenship itself. Although it is not possible to generalize this outcome, it is nonetheless the type of dynamic that warrants the status of a proposition in the framing developed in this book. The work of formalizing the inclusions brought about by the struggles of the groups affected is typically in the hands of distinct entities—legislatures and courts.

---

[11] Even in a rich country such as the United States, old and unreliable voting machines and difficult-to-access polling stations can reduce participation.

This by itself can be seen as a factor making the role of claimants in the outcome illegible. It is likely to be easier to register the formalizing moment within a formal institutional setting than the often invisible struggles by the powerless. This is not to minimize the formalizing of rights—it is critical. There is debate as to what brought about the expanded inclusions of the Civil Rights Acts of the 1960s. For some (e.g., Karst 2000), national law has been crucial in promoting measures that recognized and sought to eliminate exclusions: it was national law that "braided the strands of citizenship"—formal legal status, rights, belonging—into the principle of equal citizenship. Most recently, this took place through a series of Supreme Court decisions and acts of Congress beginning with the Civil Rights Act of 1964. Karst emphasizes how important these constitutional and legislative instruments are and that we cannot take citizenship for granted or be complacent about it. However, the importance of the formalizing moment does not preclude the role of the powerless themselves in making history through their claim making, bringing these claims to legislative and judiciary fora.

Where citizenship is a lens into the question of rights, immigration is a lens through which we can understand the strains and contradictions in nation-state membership. It gets at the constitutive tensions of liberalism (Benhabib 2002). Immigration is the core of the second major institution for membership in the modern nation-state: alienage. Unlike the "citizen," the immigrant or, more generally, the alien, is constructed in law and through policy as a partial subject. The immigrant and immigration have been made into solid realities, and as words they are charged with content. In this tension between a thin formal subject—the alien—and a rich reality lies the heuristic capacity of immigration to illuminate tensions at the heart of the historically constructed nation-state (Sassen 1996: chapter 3). These tensions are not new (Sassen 1999), but as with citizenship, current conditions are producing their own distinct possibilities. Further, the changes in the institution of citizenship itself, particularly its debordering of formal definitions and national locations, carry multivalent implications for the definition of the immigrant. Confronted with postnational and denationalized forms of citizenship, what is it we are trying to discern in the complex processes we group under the term immigration?[12] On the other hand, the renationalizing of citizenship narrows the definition of the

[12] At some point we are going to have to ask what the term immigrant truly means. People in movement are an increasingly strong presence, especially in cities. Further, when citizens begin to develop transnational identities, it alters something in the meaning of immigration. In my research I have sought to situate immigration in a broader field of actors by asking who are all the actors involved in producing the outcome that we then call immigration. My answer is that it's many more than just the immigrants, whereas our law and public imagination tend to identify immigrants as the only actors producing this complex process.

citizen and thereby that of the immigrant. As a subject, then, the immigrant filters a much larger array of political dynamics than its status in law might suggest.

THE MULTIPLE INTERACTIONS BETWEEN

LEGALITY AND RECOGNITION

Working with the distinctions and transformations discussed thus far, I want to explore the possibility of two somewhat stylized subjects that destabilize formal meanings and thereby illuminate the internal tensions of the institution of citizenship, specifically the citizen as a rights-bearing subject. On the one hand, we can identify a type of informal citizen who is unauthorized yet recognized, as might be the case with undocumented immigrants who are long-term residents in a community and participate in it as citizens do. On the other hand, we can identify a formal citizen who is fully authorized yet not fully recognized, as might be the case with minoritized citizens and with subjects engaging in political work even though they do so not as "citizens" but as some other kind of subject, for example, as mothers.

Unauthorized Yet Recognized

Perhaps one of the more extreme instances of a condition akin to informal citizenship is what has been called the informal social contract that binds undocumented immigrants to their communities of residence (Schuck and Smith 1985). Thus, unauthorized immigrants who demonstrate civic involvement, social deservedness, and national loyalty can argue that they merit legal residency.

Citizens can move among the multiple meanings of citizenship. So can undocumented immigrants, albeit among a far narrower range of these meanings. Undocumented immigrants' daily practices in their community—raising a family, schooling children, holding a job—over time can earn them citizenship claims in just about all developed countries, including the United States. There are dimensions of citizenship, such as strong community ties and participation in civic activities, that are enacted informally through these practices. They produce an at least partial recognition of immigrants as full social beings. In many countries around the world, including the United States, long-term undocumented residents often can gain legal residence if they can prove their long-term residence and "good conduct." This can then be seen as evidence of the existence of such an informal social contract. For instance, prior to the new U.S. immigration law passed in 1996, individuals who could prove seven years of continuous presence, good moral character, and that deportation would be an extreme hardship were eligible for suspension of deportation and thus U.S. residency. At the macrolevel, the evidence of such informal social contracts can be seen in group-specific or national amnesties. An example of the former is the 1997 Nicaraguan Adjustment and Central American Relief Act (NACARA), which created an amnesty for 300,000 Salvadorans and Guatemalans who were unauthorized residents in the United States to apply for suspension of deportation.[13]

The case of undocumented immigrants is, in many ways, a particular and special illustration of a condition of effective, albeit partial, citizenship. One way of interpreting this dynamic in light of the discussion in the preceding sections is to emphasize that the multiple dimensions of citizenship engender strategies for legitimizing informal or extra-statal forms of membership (Soysal 1994; Coutin 2000; Ngai 2004; Carens 1989). The practices of undocumented immigrants are a form of citizenship practices, and their identities as members of a community of residence assume some of the features of citizenship identities. This could hold even in Walzer's communitarian model, where the community can decide whom to admit and whom to exclude, but once admitted, proper civic practices earn full membership.

Further, the practices of migrants, even if undocumented, can contribute to recognition of their rights in their countries of origin. During the 1981–92 civil war, Salvadoran migrants, even as citizens of Salvador, were directly and indirectly excluded from El Salvador through political violence, enormous economic hardship, and direct persecution (Mahler 1995). They could not enjoy their rights as citizens. After fleeing, many continued to provide support to their families and communities. Further, migrants' remittances became a key factor for Salvador's economy—as they are for several countries around the world. Post–civil war governments of El Salvador began to support emigrants' fight for residency rights in the United States, even joining U.S.-based activist organizations in this effort (Coutin 2000). The Salvadoran government was thus supporting Salvadorans who were formerly excluded citizens—they needed the remittances and they needed the emigrants to stay out of the Salvadoran workforce, given high unemployment. Thus the participation of undocumented migrants in cross-border

---

[13] This is an immigration remedy that had been eliminated by the Illegal Immigration Reform and Immigrant Responsibility Act in 1996. See Coutin (2000).

communities, as well as family and political networks, has contributed to increasing recognition of their legal and political rights as Salvadoran citizens (Coutin 2000; Mahler 1995; see also Vogel and Moran 1991).

According to Coutin (2000) and others, moving between membership and exclusion, and between different dimensions of citizenship, or legitimacy and illegitimacy, may be as important for disadvantaged actors as redefinitions of citizenship itself. Given scarce resources the possibility of negotiating the different dimensions of citizenship may well represent an important enabling condition. Undocumented immigrants develop informal, covert, often extra-statal strategies and networks connecting them with communities in their native countries. Hometowns rely on their remittances and their information about jobs in the United States. Sending remittances illegally can be seen as an act of patriotism, and working as an undocumented can be seen as contributing to the host economy. Multiple interdependencies are thereby established, and grounds for claims on the receiving and the originating countries can be established even when the immigrants are undocumented and laws are broken. In this mix of contradictions, a subject takes shape (Spivak 1994).

Authorized Yet Unrecognized

At perhaps the other extreme of the undocumented immigrant whose practices allow her to become accepted as a member of the political community are those who are full citizens yet not fully recognized as such. Minoritized citizens who are discriminated against in any domain are one key instance. This is a familiar and well-documented condition. However, a very different case is the citizen who functions as a political actor even though she is not recognized as such. This is a condition I see emerging all over the world and read as signaling the limitations of the formal political apparatus for a growing range of political projects. In an enormously insightful study of Japanese housewives, LeBlanc (1999) finds precisely this combination. Being a housewife is a full-time occupation in Japan and restricts Japanese women's public life in many important ways, both practical and symbolic. A "housewife" in Japan is a person whose very identity is customarily that of a particularistic, nonpolitical actor. Yet, paradoxically, it is also a condition that provides these women with a unique vehicle for other forms of public participation, ones where being a housewife is an advantage, one denied to the professional politician or to those who might be seen as having the qualifications for higher-level political life. LeBlanc documents the housewife's advantages in the world of local politics or the political life of a local area: her evaluation of a political candidate can be trusted precisely because she is a housewife, she can build networks with other housewives, and hers is the image of desirable public concern and of a powerful—because believable—critique of mainstream politics.

There is something extremely important in this condition, which is shared with women in other cultures and vis-à-vis different issues. For example, women emerged as a specific type of political actor during the brutal dictatorships of the 1970s and 1980s in several Latin American countries. It was precisely their condition as mothers that gave them the clarity and courage to demand justice and bread, and in a way protected them from attack by the armed soldiers and policemen they confronted. Mothers in the barrios of Santiago during Pinochet's dictatorship, the mothers of the Plaza de Mayo in Buenos Aires, and the mothers regularly demonstrating in front of the major prisons in Salvador during the civil war were all driven to political action as mothers—by their despair over the loss of children and husbands and the struggle to provide food in their homes.

Further, there is an interesting parallel between LeBlanc's capturing of the political in the condition of the housewife and the status of immigrant women in the United States as critical agents in the process of immigrant settlement even though they are easily seen as subordinate to the men in their communities. There is growing evidence that immigrant women are more likely to want to stay than their husbands. Their culturally specified subordinate role to men in the household notwithstanding, employment gives immigrant women greater personal autonomy. But for immigrant men it represents invisibility and losing ground compared to what their status as men had been in their cultures of origin. Precisely because they are in charge of the household, women are responsible for dealing with public services such as schools, health clinics, and police, making them the public actor in the household (Hondagneu-Sotelo 1994). They usually handle the legal vulnerability of their families in the process of seeking public and social services. This greater participation by women suggests that they may emerge as more forceful and visible actors than immigrant men and make their role in the labor market more visible as well. It gives them a chance to become incorporated in the mainstream society, albeit in often very informal ways and typically as their household mediators in this process. It is likely that some women benefit more than others from these circumstances; we need more research to establish the impact of class, education, and income on these gendered outcomes. The incorporation of women in the migration process strengthens the settlement likelihood and contributes to greater immigrant participation in their communities and vis-à-vis the state.

These are dimensions of formal and informal citizenship and citizenship practices that do not fit the indicators and categories of mainstream academic frameworks for understanding citizenship and political life. The subject that is the housewife or the mother does not fit the categories and indicators used to capture participation in public life. Feminist scholarship in all the social sciences has had to deal with a set of similar or equivalent difficulties and tensions in its effort to constitute its subject or to reconfigure a subject that has been flattened. The theoretical and empirical distance that has to be bridged between the recognized world of politics and the as yet unmapped experience of citizenship of the housewife—not of women as such, but of women as housewives, only one of the many subjects any woman is, recurs in many types of inquiry. Bridging this distance entails both an empirical research strategy and a theorization.

NEW GLOBAL CLASSES: IMPLICATIONS FOR POLITICS

The articulation of global systems with the possibility of experiencing citizenship through multiple rights and practices has enabled the emergence of global "classes."[14] Their formation points to dynamics that partly disaggregate the national state from the inside and weaken the grip of national politics over the particular groups that constitute these global classes. At the same time, the particular features of these classes, especially their ambiguous position between the global and the subnational, point to the limits of the meaning of global class. Conceived this way, we can also contest the widespread notion that global classes will tend to be cosmopolitan and outside the reach of the national.

Most of the attention in the emerging scholarship on global classes has gone to a new stratum of transnational professionals and executives (Sklair and Robbins 2002; Robinson 2004; Van der Pijl 1998; Palan 2003). But I see at least three other global classes in the making. The first arises out of the proliferation of transnational networks of government officials. Among these networks are those formed by experts on a variety of issues critical to a global corporate economy, by judges having to negotiate a growing array of international rules and prohibitions that require some measure of cross-border standardization, by immigration officials needing to coordinate border controls, and by police officials in charge of discovering financial flows that support terrorism. The second one is an emergent class of activists, including key sectors of global civil society and particular kinds of diasporic networks; I examine

---

[14] I use the term classes rather loosely here and more as a designator than a theoretical construct.

these in the context of electronic networks in chapter 7. And the third emergent global class consists of mostly disadvantaged low-wage workers, including members of transnational immigrant communities and households.

In the early twenty-first century, the various transformations examined in this book generate something approaching global classes only in particular domains. It is largely at the top and at the bottom of the social system that the national state has weakened its grip in shaping the experience of membership and identity. Vast middle sectors—workers, firms, or places—have not been particularly affected by the processes of transformation in the developed world.[15] Similarly, most of the work of governments has not been affected either, even though there is a specific type of government official at the forefront in the work of developing the technical infrastructure for corporate globalization and key aspects of global governance.

There are a variety of economic, political, and subjective structures underlying the formation of these four global classes. Global networks with variable degrees of formalization and institutionalization are evident for each class. Further, contexts such as the global corporate economy or the international human rights regime also play critical roles in the proliferation of global networks. These and other globalizing dynamics have weakened the exclusive authority, both objective and subjective, of national states over people, their imaginaries, and their sense of belonging. This facilitates the entry of nonstate actors into international domains once exclusive to national states. Economic, political, and civic processes confined largely to the national sphere can now go global, even when this is only an imaginary or a subjective disposition rather than a daily reality for many of these actors.

And yet, none of this presupposes a move to postnational citizenship, nor does it necessarily preclude such a move. The global networks involved are not seamless as is often thought. They are lumpy: they contain nodes (global cities, major supranational institutions, and particular activist networks) where much of the global action gets done. There are, then, national insertions for each of these global classes. In this regard, for now at least, these global classes evince strong features that might be characterized as partly denationalized rather than postnational citizenship. This also raises a question about the notion that global classes must be cosmopolitan.

It is easy to equate the globalism of the transnational professional and executive class with cosmopolitanism. A more careful examination of this class raises some doubts about its cosmopolitanism. This is also the case with

---

[15] The impact has in fact been far more extensive, including vast middle sectors, in developing countries (Sassen 2003b).

the other global classes. All of them evince forms of globality that are not necessarily cosmopolitan. Each remains embedded, in often unexpected ways, in thick, localized environments: financial and business centers, national governments, the localized microstructures of daily civic life and struggles, and the translocal insertions of immigrants. And each of these classes is guided by a single logic rather than the multiple logics at the heart of genuine cosmopolitanism: profits in the case of the new professional elites (no matter how cosmopolitan their tastes for, say, culture); specific and narrow governance issues in the case of government networks; and specific local struggles and conflicts in the case of global civil society, diasporas, and immigrant networks.

The fact of global classes that are not necessarily cosmopolitan and that remain partly embedded in localized environments does not diminish the potential for destabilizing the national as historically constructed. Through their daily practices and imaginaries they partly reconstitute the meaning of the national. One way of thinking about them is as bridging the thick national environments within which most politics, economics, and civic life still function with the global dynamics that are "denationalizing" particular components of those national settings.

Thus the emergent global classes I focus on here are partial and specific outcomes. They can be, but are not necessarily new social forms as such; they can also arise out of a subjective, self-reflexive repositioning of an old social practice or condition in a transnational framing. For instance, transnational immigrant households have long existed, but today this condition assumes a whole new meaning and the immigrants themselves know it and act on it. Similarly, an international class of powerful elites has long existed, but in today's context it carries novel implications. It is partly their objective systemic position and partly this subjective interpretation that give the new global classes their political import. One of the crucial dynamics at work here is a process of incipient denationalization, a changed attachment to the national rather than a full exit from it.

The new global professional class evinces three features pertinent to the concerns of this chapter. First, the driving force in the emergence of this cross-border domain bears little resemblance to the forces driving and constituting cosmopolitanism in the rich sense of the word. While this new transnational professional class may open up to diverse cuisines and urban landscapes, the particular condition that constitutes it as a global class is a rather narrow utility logic—the drive for profits. In itself, this is not a cosmopolitan drive, even though it may help these professionals become worldlier. Second, through its work this new global class shapes an increasingly significant change in its relation to the system of national states. As a class it does not have the same systemic position as that of a country's national business community, even though particular individuals may circulate in both. The third feature is that this class and its work are partially embedded in national settings—most conspicuously the network of global cities. To be global and hypermobile this class needs a state-of-the-art infrastructure in a growing number of these cities. From here then comes a particular type of engagement and partial dependence on national states, which is easily obscured by the language of the new cosmopolitanism and hypermobile capital. Another condition for this class is setting in place the systems and subcultures necessary for a global economic system. The network of global cities produces what we could think of as a new subculture, a move from the "national" version of international activities to the "global" version of such activities (Sassen 2001: chapter 7).[16] A key feature, then, of this new global class is its intermediate position between the subnational and the global.

The second type of global class, transgovernmental networks of government officials, has existed for a long time. But novel types of networks in the 1980s and 1990s (chapter 5) connect corporate globalization and the globalizing of governmental responsibilities and aims, for example, regarding human rights, the environment, and the fight against terrorism (Slaughter 2004).[17] What is critical about these transgovernmental networks as an emergent global class is the change brought on by globalization that began in the 1980s when a tipping point was reached. This is no longer the post–World War II Bretton Woods decade of intergovernmental collaboration. The aim is not simply intergovernmental or international communication and collaboration but a deregulatory project to denationalize the components of state work that are necessary for corporate globalization (or, in other settings, for implementing global treaties about the environment, human rights, and other

[16] The longstanding resistance in Europe to mergers and acquisitions, especially hostile takeovers, and East Asia's resistance to foreign ownership and control are indications of national business cultures that are somewhat incompatible with the new global economic culture. Global cities and the variety of global business meetings (such as those of the World Economic Forum in Davos and other similar occasions) contribute to partly denationalize corporate elites (as well as government elites). Whether this is good or bad is a separate issue, but it is one of the conditions for setting in place the systems and subcultures necessary for a global economic system.

[17] The key actors are government officials from the pertinent national ministries or agencies. Transgovernmental regulatory networks can be found among trade ministers in GATT, financial ministers in the IMF, defense and foreign ministers in NATO, and central bankers in the Bank for International Settlements, as well as various efforts within the OECD and the EU Council of Ministers. These are often enormously powerful networks of government officials in charge of critical work in the development of a global corporate economy.

noneconomic efforts). In the early Bretton Woods period the project was global governance to protect national economies; by the 1980s the goal was opening up national economies and creating hospitable and institutionalized environments for global firms and markets. This brought a proliferation of highly specialized transgovernmental networks, including the worldwide efforts to institute compatible competition policies, accounting standards, and financial reporting standards. The work of the pertinent, typically highly specialized government officials began to be oriented toward a global project. One consequence has been an increased commonality among officials within each transnational network and a growing distance with colleagues from the national bureaucracies back home. In this sense, then, we can speak of an incipient global class that occupies, again, an ambiguous position between the global and the subnational in that they represent a specific, often highly specialized component of the national government.

As for the third and fourth types of global classes, there is a distinct global formation comprising a mix of individuals, population categories, and organizations. Notwithstanding sharp internal diversity and mostly lack of interaction, there are shared objective conditions and subjective dynamics. It cannot be thought of as equivalent to global civil society, even though part of it is at specific times, and even though the imaginary about such a global civil society is a significant subjective condition shared by some of the people and projects involved. Most of them, including civil society activists, are not part of a traveling transnational class or the new global civil society international elites. What is of particular interest here is that most of the people involved are immobile. Yet they are either objectively or subjectively part of specific forms of globality, a subject I return to in chapter 7.

There are five issues that arise out of these conditions. The first concerns the forms of politico-civic engagement that are made possible for the disadvantaged in global cities; these are at least partly enabled by globalization and the human rights regime. The second is that the presence of immigrant communities produces specific transnational forms of engagement, including the formation of globalized diasporas. For instance, we see a growing number of immigrant networks concerned with specific struggles, such as exposing illegal trafficking groups and brides-by-mail organizations, which partly reorient these communities away from a one-to-one relationship to their home countries and toward other immigrant communities in the city or co-nationals in other immigration countries. The third is the modes of engagement made possible in the global city between the disadvantaged and global corporate power, for instance, anti-gentrification struggles or fights against transforming industrial districts into luxury office districts. The fourth is the extent to which access to the new media, specifically the Internet, allows and/or induces various types of groups to transnationalize their efforts (for example, poor women's organizations, environmental activists, or human rights activists). Many of these groups have begun to connect with other such groups in other countries where previously they were purely local. The binding is through the shared objectives rather than through travel and meetings. The fifth concerns the extent to which these multiple activities and engagements denationalize the global city and thereby enable more global forms of consciousness and of membership and belonging even among the disadvantaged. These are all elements that are part of the localized microstructures of global civil society.

The large numbers of people from all over the world who often encounter each other for the first time in the streets, workplaces, and neighborhoods of today's global cities produce a kind of transnationalism right there in situ. These encounters can include encounters with co-ethnics who are in highly professional jobs (that is, a class encounter). We see an emergent recognition of globality, often shaped by the knowledge about the recurrent struggles and inequities in city after city. This knowledge enabled by both global media and the rapidly spreading use of the Internet among activists, functions both as fact and as subjective formation. This subjective dimension increasingly enables the disadvantaged and the localized to recognize the presence of the global in these cities and their participation in it; the global becomes visible. This then also produces an ambiguous position for these mostly activist, disadvantaged, and localized actors between the subnational and the global.

TOWARD POSTNATIONAL AND DENATIONALIZED CITIZENSHIP

The transformations discussed in this chapter thus far raise questions about the proposition that citizenship has a necessary connection to the national state insofar as they significantly alter the conditions for that articulation.

Posing the question this way denaturalizes conventional political thought and parallels the argument about the historicity of both the institution of citizenship and that of sovereignty, especially as these are brought to the fore through the new conditions introduced by globalization. Some scholars (e.g., Bosniak 2000b) argue that there is no objective definition of citizenship to which we can refer authoritatively to resolve any uncertainties about the usage of the term. The discussion in the preceding section showed the extent to which the institution of citizenship has multiple dimensions, many of which are under contestation.

These developments have increasingly been theorized as signaling the emergence of postnational forms of citizenship (Soysal 1994; Jacobson 1996; see multiple chapters in Isin 2000 to mention just some of the rapidly growing literature on this notion of citizenship). The emphasis in this formulation is on the emergence of locations for citizenship outside the confines of the national state. The European Union passport is, perhaps, the most formalized of these. But the emergence of a reinvigorated cosmopolitanism (Turner 2000; Nussbaum 2000) and of a proliferation of transnationalisms (Brysk and Shafir 2004; GCS 2002; Smith and Guarnizo 1998; Held 1995; Levitt 2001) have been key sources for notions of postnational citizenship. Bosniak states that there is a reasonable case to be made that "the experiences and practices we conventionally associate with citizenship do in some respects exceed the boundaries of the territorial nation-state—though the pervasiveness and significance of this process varies depending on the dimension of citizenship at issue" (2000a: 460). Whether it is the organization of formal status, the protection of rights, citizenship practices, or the experience of collective identities and solidarities, the nation-state is not the exclusive site for their enactment. It remains by far the most important site, but the transformations in its exclusivity signal a possibly important new dynamic.

There is a second dynamic becoming evident that shares aspects with postnational citizenship but is usefully distinguished in that it concerns specific transformations within the national state that directly and indirectly alter specific aspects of the institution of citizenship. These transformations are not predicated necessarily on locations for the institution outside the national state, which are key to conceptions of postnational citizenship. The albeit minor changes in the law of nationality described later in this section capture some of these transformations inside the national state and further indicate a valuing of effective over purely formal nationality. Other internal changes are the loss of formal citizens' rights and protections. The scholarship on postnational citizenship often overlooks some of these formal changes in the relationship of citizens to the state.

The context for both dynamics is defined by the transformations in the national state since the 1980s and the emergence of multiple actors, groups, and communities enabled and willing to voice their dissatisfaction with automatic identification with a nation as represented by the sovereign. Many of today's major developments, such as globalization and the rise of information technologies, have played important roles in producing these outcomes, even though the latter cannot be reduced to these developments. Again, the growth of the Internet and linked technologies has facilitated and often enabled the formation of cross-border networks among individuals and groups with shared interests that often represent highly specialized or particularized political projects. This has engendered or strengthened alternative notions of membership in a community. These new experiences and orientations of citizenship can be seen as overdetermined outcomes, often the result of long gestation or features evident, albeit with different contents, since the beginning of the formation of citizenship as a national institution.

Distinguishing Postnational and Denationalized

We are dealing with two distinct dynamics rather than simply the emergence of locations for citizenship outside the frame of the national state. I distinguish what I would narrowly define as denationalized from non-national or postnational, the latter the term most commonly used and the only one present in the broader debate. I see the potential for capturing two—not necessarily mutually exclusive—possible trajectories for the institution of citizenship in the differences between these dynamics. These trajectories are embedded in some of the major conditions that mark the contemporary era; that we can identify two possible trajectories contests easy determinisms about the impact of globalization, and they signal the potential for change in the institution of citizenship.

Their difference is a question of scope and institutional embeddedness. The understanding in the scholarship is that postnational citizenship is located partly outside the confines of the national.[18] In considering denationalization, the focus moves on to the transformation of the national, including the national in its condition as foundational for citizenship. Thus it could be argued that postnationalism and denationalization represent two different trajectories.[19] One has to do with the transformation of the national, specifically through global and denationalizing dynamics that tend to instantiate inside the national. The other has to do with new forms that we have not even considered and might emerge out of the changed conditions in the world located outside the national rather than out of the earlier institutional framework of the national. Both are viable, and they do not exclude each other. Thus Soysal's focus on the EU (1994) is capturing an innovation located both in and beyond the national.

---

[18] See notably Soysal's (1994) trend-setting book; see also Bosniak (2000a) who, while using the term denationalized, is using it to denote postnational, and it is the postnational concept that is crucial to her critique as well as to her support of some of the aspirations signaled by the term postnational.

[19] In this regard, Bosniak's (2000a) conclusion contains both of these notions but conflates when she asks whether denationalized citizenship can ultimately decouple the concept of citizenship from the nation-state.

The key issue in positing a novel condition for citizenship cannot be confined to its taking place necessarily beyond the confines of the national state, as in postnational conceptions. My concern is to specify the particular ways in which the development of a global economy necessitates a variety of policies that have to be implemented in national economies through national institutions and can thus have an impact on citizenship. With denationalization I seek to capture something that remains connected to the national, as constructed historically, and is indeed profoundly imbricated with it but is so on historically new terms of engagement. Incipient and partial are two qualifiers I usually attach to my use of denationalization. From the perspective of nation-based citizenship theory, some of these transformations might be interpreted as a decline or devaluation of citizenship.

There are multiple conditions suggesting that citizenship, even if situated in institutional settings that are "national," is a possibly changed institution if the meaning of the national itself has changed. One of the empirical questions organizing this chapter is if important features of the territorial and institutional organization of the political power and authority of the state have changed, then we must consider that key features of the institution of citizenship—its formal rights, its practices, its subjective dimension—have also been transformed even when it remains centered on the national state. This territorial and institutional transformation of state power and authority has allowed operational, conceptual, and rhetorical openings for nation-based subjects other than the national state to emerge as legitimate actors in international/global arenas that used to be confined to the state (e.g., *Indiana Journal of Global Legal Studies* 1996). Further, among the sharpest changes in the condition of citizens are the new security measures discussed in chapter 4, which in this context can be seen as a stimulus for particular citizens to want to go global to make claims, notably human rights courts.

The national remains a referent in my work on citizenship. But clearly it is a referent of a specific sort: it is, after all, its change that becomes the key theoretical feature through which it enters my specification of changes in the institution of citizenship. Whether this devalues citizenship, as Jacobson (1996) might posit, is not immediately evident at this point, partly because I read the institution of citizenship as having undergone many transformations in its history precisely because it is to variable extents embedded in the specifics of each of its eras.[20]

---

[20] In this regard, I have emphasized the significance (1996: chapter 2) of the introduction in the new constitutions of South Africa, Brazil, Argentina, and the central European countries of a provision that qualifies what had been an unqualified right (if democratically elected) of the sovereign to be the exclusive representative of its people in international fora.

We can identify three formal types of elements that signal this particular way of using the national as a referent for capturing changes in the institution of citizenship. First, it was through national law that many of the expanded inclusions that enabled citizens were instituted (Karst 1997), inclusions that today are destabilizing older notions of citizenship.[21] This pluralized meaning of citizenship partly produced by the formal expansions of the legal status of citizenship is helping explode the boundaries of that legal status even further, for example, the increasing number of states that now grant dual nationality, EU citizenship, and the strengthening of human rights. If we assume that "the enjoyment of rights remains as one aspect of what we understand citizenship to be, then we can argue that the national grip on citizenship has been substantially loosened" (Bosniak 2000a: 447), perhaps most especially by the emergence of the human rights regime (Soysal 1994; Jacobson and Ruffer 2003). This transformation in nation-based citizenship is not only due to the emergence of non-national sites for legitimate claim making.[22] The meaning of the territorial itself has changed (see chapter 5; Sassen 1996: chapter 1), and, further, digital space enables articulations between national territorial and global spaces that deborder national encasements for a variety of activities from economics to citizenship practices.[23] All of these have been interpreted as loosening the "national grip" on citizens' rights.

The second critical element is the strengthening, including the constitutionalizing, of rights that allow citizens to make claims against their states and to invoke a measure of autonomy in the formal political arena that can be read as a lengthening distance between the formal apparatus of the state

[21] One example comes indirectly through changes in the institution of alienage. In Karst's interpretation of U.S. law, aliens *are* "constitutionally entitled to most of the guarantees of equal citizenship, and the Supreme Court has accepted this idea to a modest degree" (2000: 599; see also 599n. 20, where he cites cases). Karst also notes that the Supreme Court has not carried this development nearly as far as it could have (and he might wish), thereby signaling that the potential for transforming the institution may well be higher than the actual disposition to change it. Neumann (1996) has provided what is perhaps the most developed and in-depth account of the status of immigrants and aliens generally in the Constitution. A significantly transformed institution of alienage would have some impact on changing at least some features of the meaning of citizenship. For a very different type of examination, see Schuck and Smith (1985). For an extraordinary account of how the U.S. polity and legal system has constructed the subject of the immigrant, in this case the Asian American, see Palumbo-Liu (1999).

[22] This interpretation then also affects my reading of a literature that centers on location as a criterion for specifying citizenship (e.g., Bosniak 2000a). This criterion is rendered problematic insofar as I argue that some components of the "non-national" are embedded in the national and hence we would need to decode what is national about the national. Moreover, the increasing relocation of significant activities associated with "national" territory to digital space compels reconsideration of what is meant by the "territorial base" itself (Bosniak 2000a).

[23] See, e.g., Teubner's (2004) argument about a right of access to digital space as part of a larger argument about decentered constitutionalism.

and the institution of citizenship. The political and theoretical implications of this dimension are complex and in the making: we cannot tell what the practices and rhetorics that might be invented and deployed will be. Certainly the erosion of citizens' privacy rights is one factor that has sharpened the distance with the state for some citizens and has caused some citizens to sue the government.

Third is the critical issue of whose claims are legitimate. The granting of multiple "rights" to foreign actors, largely and especially economic actors—foreign firms, foreign investors, international markets, and foreign business people—also constructs these as a rights-bearing legal persona (Sassen 1996: chapter 2).[24] Increasingly the claims of such non-national entities are legitimate vis-à-vis the national state, and their utility logics can alter existing national law. In this sense these entities have gained economic "citizenship" rights. Admittedly, this is not a common framing. It comes out of some of the issues examined in chapters 4 and 5 and their impact on the relationship between the state and foreign economic actors. I see this as a significant, though not much recognized, development in the history of claim making. How citizens should handle these new concentrations of power and "legitimacy" that attach to global firms and markets is a key to the future of democracy. Detecting the extent to which the global is embedded and filtered through the national is one way of understanding whether therein lies a possibility for citizens to demand accountability of global economic actors through national institutional channels, rather than having to wait for a "global" state (Sassen 2003a).

Thus, while accentuating the national may appear as a handicap in terms of democratic participation in a global age, it is not an either/or proposition precisely because of this partial embedding of the global in the national. There is indeed a growing gap between globalization and the confinement of the national state to its territory. But it is inadequate simply to accept the prevailing wisdom that, wittingly or not, presents the national and the global as two mutually exclusive domains for theorization and for politics. This is a highly problematic proposition even though I recognize that each domain has specificity. It is enormously important to develop forms of participatory politics that decenter and sometimes transcend national political life, and to learn how to practice democracy across borders. In this I fully support the political project of postnational citizenship. We also can engage in democratic practices that cross borders and engage the global from within the national and through national institutional channels.

[24] See Sassen 1996: chapter 2.

The international human rights regime may eventually become an acceptable and effective alternative to specific cases of judicial enforcement of citizens' rights. In the United States, for instance, it would mean the Bill of Rights and the Fourteenth Amendment. In Europe some of this is already happening. Accession to the European Convention on Human Rights and various EU treaties has produced important substantive changes in the domestic law of member countries, enforced by domestic courts (e.g., Jacobson and Ruffer 2003). But in most of the world, human rights are enforced through national law or not at all. Critical here is Koh's (1997) argument that human rights norms get incorporated into national law through an at times slow but effective process he calls "transnational legal process." Two major changes at the turn of the millennium are the growing weight of the human rights regime on states under the rule of law and the growing use of human rights instruments in national courts both for interpretation and adjudication. This is an instance of denationalization insofar as the mechanisms are internal to the national state—national courts and legislatures—while the instruments invoke an authority that transcends the national state and the interstate system. (The arguments I develop in chapter 5 signal that one could examine the case of WTO law along the same lines.) The long-term persuasive powers of human rights are a significant factor in this context. It is important to note here that the human rights regime, while international, deals with citizens inside a state. It thereby destabilizes older notions of exclusive state sovereignty articulated in international law, which posit that matters internal to a country are to be determined solely by the state. The human rights regime subjects states to scrutiny when it comes to treatment of individuals within its territory.

Toward a Partial Repositioning of Nationality

Given its highly formalized status in international law, nationality provides an interesting lens and a register for establishing some of the ambiguities in the institution of citizenship. If the national state is being transformed by current developments, we might posit an impact on the legal status of nationality and on its functionality as a legal and social instrument. Various developments of international law principles within the current system reveal incipient tensions that will need to be addressed in nationality law. Among these developments are recent decisions by entities such as the International Court of Justice, the European Human Rights Court, the UN's Compensation Commission, the Iran-U.S Claims Tribunal, and the Human

Rights Committee under the International Covenant on Civil and Political Rights.[25]

For example, according to Sadat and Carden (2000) the adoption of the International Criminal Court (ICC) statutes represents a major, albeit not yet recognized or actualized, (constitutional) innovation in international law. It alters some features of sovereignty, even though it does not go as far as it could have.[26] The ICC is the last great international institution of the twentieth century. According to Sadat and Carden, its creation "has the potential to reshape our thinking about international law." Even though the tenacity of Westphalian sovereignty is wired into it (for example, the court's enforcement jurisdiction is limited and weak), "there are elements of supranationalism and efficacy (in spite of the complementarity principle) that could prove powerful: state and non-state actors are placed side by side in the international arena, and the Court will put real people in real jails" (2000: 385). It tends to blur the lines between international law and world order, insofar as international law is centered in national states and their Hobbesian international project (cf. Koh 1998). The implementation of the ICC suggests that established political structures accept the necessity of an ICC as part of the normative system of international law, pace the quite specific objections of the United States in an effort to escape lawsuits resulting from its major role in much international conflict. State acceptance is no minor matter since ratification will require many states to amend their constitution or/and enact complex implementing legislation. Critical is the decision to establish the court as a free-standing institution outside the UN system, an instance in a larger trend toward the type of nonstate centered global law discussed in chapter 5.

A second type of instance can be identified in a mix of issues pertaining to the authority of international law in national (domestic) courts. Several international law cases (Knop 2000; Rubenstein and Adler 2000; Koh 1998) show changes in the interactions between international norms and national law, even though "case law is necessarily restricted to justiciable disputes in a given field" (Rubenstein and Adler 200: 533). These cases represent a small and often possibly unrepresentative cross-section of practice in a given area (Knop 2000). This is particularly so when it comes to nationality in international law, based as it is on the assumption of sovereignty and hence the fairly unilateral power of the state to determine under its own law who its

[25] The formation of this last committee indicates change in the features of nationality under current conditions compared with earlier periods (see Sassen 1999: chapter 4).

[26] The adoption of the ICC statutes is the result of over seventy-five years of hard work and false starts. See Bassioni (1997), who eventually was appointed chair of the Drafting Committee at Rome; see also Sadat and Carden (2000) and Wexler (1996).

nationals are. As a result there are only a limited number of cases where supranational tribunals have cause to comment on issues of nationality.

There are two broad categories of cases when it comes to nationality: standing cases and human rights cases (Knop 2000). Standing cases require international arbitration because they involve a conflict between two states over the nationality of an individual. What a state does to its own national is not subject to international law, but what it does to a national of another state can be if the state to whom the individual belongs takes issue on behalf of the citizen. The leading case, and one it is difficult to avoid in this subject area, is *Nottebohm vs. Guatemala* (1955) (Knop 2000; Rubenstein and Adler 2000). The International Court of Justice's decision was grounded on the concept of allegiance and a reluctance to recognize nationality without allegiance. The case represented, then, the old version of nationality as allegiance, further suggesting the extent to which the mid-twentieth century may well have been a high point in the development of nation-based citizenship. But since that 1995 case, including more recent times, there "has been some movement towards reducing the force of this type of unfettered sovereignty" (Rubenstein and Adler 2000: 535; Knop 2000). One case shows a dilution of nationality as a legal tool for resolving international law dilemmas involving a person's connection to the nation-state, thereby emphasizing nationality as a progressive or normative project rather than as formal status. In the cases before the Iran-U.S. Claims Tribunal and the UN Compensation Commission-Claims against Iraq, allegiance played less of a role and dual nationality was granted more weight.

The weakening of unilateral sovereignty is also evident in various cases based on human rights law. "Whereas the standing cases present nationality as a preliminary issue, the human rights cases consider the rights of citizenship or nationality in a substantive sense" (Rubenstein and Adler 2000: 538). Rubenstein and Adler review a series of cases showing that in both the standing and human rights cases, the formal status of nationality in international law lacks precision. These are primarily cases in which an individual lacks the protection of citizenship, and hence are a way of strengthening her claims. They can also be cases where an individual wants to escape the consequences of unwanted nationality. Human rights are an instrument for individuals to seek "the protection of principles associated with nationality, when nationality is lacking" (2000: 539). There are different ways of interpreting these cases. Knop (2000) provides a detailed examination of the question of interpretation in the use of international law in domestic courts. One interpretation is that they produce a distinct form, one that can be characterized as "relational nationality." This is a type of status whereby the nationality of women and children is determined by broader family criteria that are invariably gendered. Another type of interpretation emphasizes how these decisions show a distinction between nationality based on formal admission to a state and nationality acknowledged on the social facts of an individual's participation in the life of a community. Rubenstein and Adler's (2000) distinction between formal nationality and effective nationality captures a departure from the decision in *Nottebohm*, which emphasized an older understanding of nationality as allegiance and of the place of nationality in international law. It strengthens citizenship as a category, precisely because of its greater flexibility and fluidity (Bosniak 2000); at the same time, the more fluid standing of nationality in international law produces a potentially fruitful convergence (Sassen 2003a).

Nationality can no longer be easily deployed as a singular condition and in this regard may well evolve into an instance of Benhabib's (2002) notion of constitutive tensions in liberal democracies. For the immigrant who is naturalized, it may be a useful instrument that allows more access to her country of origin rather than a matter of switching allegiance. In the United States, the 1996 Immigration Act has sharpened differences between legal residents and citizens and hence raised the value of nationality as a strategic resource for those who have transnational lives and family arrangements. The constitutive "tension" in this instance revolves around the desire to counter exclusion and to have family access more so than to demonstrate allegiance.

Immigration policy illuminates particular aspects of these often slippery changes in the standing of an individual's nationality in international law. This is particularly the case in the EU, given its considerable level of formalization of a transnational domain even as member states continue to exercise considerable authority, especially over immigration policy matters. Jacobson and Ruffer (2003) argue that we are seeing a complex shift in the locus of the individual as a result of the ascendance of the judiciary in the Europeanization of rights. They find that this shift and the role of the judiciary take the current condition beyond the common interpretation of tensions between the EU level and its national member states. In this regard they see the struggle between the judiciaries and the executive and legislatures as a struggle between an increasingly individual-centered form of the political and the state's republican national project. The authors find that the growing role of the judiciary in this process is predicated in good part on the increasing density of the law, which promotes rights and prerogatives.[27] The judiciary mediates

---

[27] For example, to mention just one of the more recalcitrant EU members, in 2000 Britain incorporated the bulk of the European Convention on Human Rights into domestic law. The British Parliament adopted the Human Rights Act of 1998 in November 1998; it became effective in Britain in October 2000.

and adjudicates this web of law, at national and regional levels, for both domestic and international law. In this shift toward the judiciary the authors see the rise of a form of agency that is individual centered. Further, Jacobson and Ruffer find much significance in the transfer of the coordination of immigration policy from the third pillar in the EU to the first pillar: "Legal provisions emanating from the third pillar are not part of community law; they are norms regulated by public international law. In contrast, legal instruments emanating from the first pillar become part of European Community law and are binding on each member state." Moreover, given that "individuals have the legal capacity to invoke first pillar laws and bring them to bear against member states, the changes of the Amsterdam Treaty may give the judiciary, here the European Court of Justice, more control over immigration policy" (2003: 80). Similarly, the now formal commitment of the EU to human rights under the Amsterdam Treaty may enhance the European Court of Justice's authority in such matters over member states.

In addition, there is in all of this the making of a global scale from which to understand the character of law and its dominant national framing. In a detailed examination from a distinct perspective, Rajagopal (2003) argues that insufficient attention has been paid to the complex relationship between international law and the Third World during the twentieth century. He suggests that it is impossible to obtain a full understanding of this complex relationship unless one factors in two conditions: a focus on development discourse as the governing logic of the political, economic, and social life in the Third World; and an appreciation of the role of social movements in shaping the relationship between Third World resistance and international law. Common approaches to international law are, according to Rajagopal, deficient because they neither take development discourse to be important for the very formation of international law and institutions nor adopt a subaltern perspective that enables a real appreciation of the role of social movements in the evolution of international law. "The central concern then is: how does one write resistance into international law and make it recognize subaltern voices? Substantial parts of the architecture of international law—international institutions—have evolved in an ambivalent relationship with this resistance; second, the human rights discourse has been fundamentally shaped—and limited—by the forms of Third World resistance to development" (2003: 1). His focus on these two areas of international law—international institutions and human rights—responds to the centrality of these areas of law in modern international law, that is, from the League of Nations. By showing that the central aspects of modern international law cannot be understood without taking due account of the impact of development and Third World social movements, Rajagopal

challenges traditional narratives of how international legal change has
come about and how one might understand the place of law in "progressive
social praxis." He then argues that international law "needs to be fundamentally rethought if it is to take the disparate forms of Third World resistance seriously" (2003: 1).[28]

The partial and specialized unbundling of national state territoriality
has the perhaps ironic effect of instantiating some of the issues raised by Rajagopal in what we might think of as strategic spaces—the global cities that
are the centers of power for global corporate capital.

CITIZENSHIP IN THE GLOBAL CITY

The particular transformations in the understanding and theorization of citizenship discussed thus far bring us back to some of the earlier historical formations around questions of citizenship, most prominently the crucial role played by cities and civil society. The loss of power at the national
level produces the possibility for new forms of power and politics at the subnational level. The national as container of social process and power is
cracked, opening up possibilities for a geography of politics that links subnational spaces. Cities are foremost in this new geography. One question this
engenders is how and whether we are seeing the formation of new types of
politics that localize in these cities.

The large city of today emerges as a strategic site for these new types
of operations.[29] It is one of the nexuses where the formation of new claims materializes and assumes concrete forms. It does not necessarily represent a majority situation but is rather a sort of frontier zone for novel, perhaps merely
incipient, forms of the political, the economic, the "cultural," and the subjective (Abu-Lughod 1989; Watson and Bridges 1999; Yuval-Davis 1999;
Clark and Hoffman-Martinot 1998; Allen, Massey, and Pryke 1999).[30] Today
global cities especially are the terrain where multiple globalization processes

---

[28] See also the discussion about Rittich's analysis (2001) along these lines in chapter 4.

[29] For George Simmel cities produced new mentalities and identities: the stranger and
blasé attitudes, Benjamin's *flanneur*. Today, Turner (2000) argues, these somewhat negative attributes become positive: irony, emotional distance, cosmopolitan irony, and the multicultural
tensions of global cities become the citizen virtues in a global city.

[30] See here the difference with the transformation of the Enlightenment and aspirations to cosmopolitanism (e.g., Kant) into exclusionary nationalist paradigms of citizens with
the development of the nation-state. Thus Friedrich Meinecke's notion of cosmopolitanism is a
critique of Prussian nationalism. In the twentieth century the critics of cosmopolitanism were
generally also critics of liberalism.

assume concrete, localized forms. These localized forms are, in good part, what globalization is about. Thus they are also sites where some of the new forms of power can be engaged. Much of the organizational and command side of the global economy is located in a network of about forty global cities, forming a strategic geography of power. Another localization of the global is immigration, a major process through which a new transnational political economy and translocal households are being constituted (Portes 1995; Bhachu 1985; Mahler 1995; Hondagneu-Sotelo 1994; Boyd 1989; Georges 1990) largely in major cities. Most immigrants, certainly in the developed world, whether in the United States, Japan, or Western Europe, are disproportionately concentrated in major cities. Immigration is one of the constitutive processes of globalization today (Sassen 1998: part 1; Skeldon 1997), even though it is not recognized or represented as such in mainstream accounts of the global economy.

If we consider that large cities concentrate both the leading sectors of global capital and a growing share of disadvantaged populations—immigrants, poor women, people of color generally, and, in the megacities of developing countries, masses of shanty dwellers—then cities have become a strategic terrain for a series of conflicts and contradictions. We can thus think of cities also as one of the sites for the contradictions of the globalization of capital even though, heeding Katznelson's (1992) observation, the city cannot be reduced to one dynamic. Recovering cities along these lines means recovering multiple presences in this landscape.

The significance of the city today is as a setting for engendering new types of citizenship practices and new types of incompletely formalized political subjects. While citizenship originated in cities and cities played an important role in its evolution, we cannot simply read some of these current developments as a return to that older historical condition. Nor does current local city government have much to do with earlier notions of citizenship and democracy described for ancient and medieval cities in Europe (Isin 2000: 7). Here I would like to return to the fact of the embeddedness of the institution. What is being engendered today in terms of citizenship practices in the frontier zone that is the global city is quite different from what it was in the medieval city of Weber. Today's citizenship practices have to do with the production of "presence" of those without power and a politics that claims rights to the city. What the two situations share is the notion that through these practices new forms or elements of citizenship are being constituted and that the city is a key site for this type of political work being, indeed, partly constituted through these dynamics. After the long historical phase that saw the ascendance of the national state and the scaling of key economic dynamics at the national level, the city is once again a scale for strategic economic and political dynamics.

The historicity of this process rests in the fact that under Keynesian policies, particularly the Fordist contract, and the dominance of mass manufacturing as the organizing economic dynamic, cities lost strategic functions and were not the site for creative institutional innovations.[31] The strategic sites were the large factory and the processes of mass manufacturing and mass consumer markets, as well as the national government where regulatory frameworks were developed and the Fordist contract instituted. The factory and the government were the strategic sites where the crucial dynamics producing the major institutional innovations of the epoch were located. With globalization and digitization, and the specific territorial and organizational rearrangements, global cities emerge as such strategic sites. As several of the key components of economic globalization and digitization instantiate in this type of city they produce dislocations and destabilizations of existing institutional orders and legal/regulatory/normative frames for handling urban conditions. It is the high level of concentration of these new dynamics in these cities that forces creative responses and innovations.[32] While the strategic transformations are sharply concentrated in these cities, many are also enacted (besides being diffused) in cities at the lower end of national urban hierarchies. Furthermore, particular institutions of the state, such as the executive branch and the Treasury, also are such strategic sites even as other components of the state lose significance through deregulation and privatization.

Current conditions in global cities are creating not only new structurations of power but also operational and rhetorical openings for new types of political actors that may have been submerged, invisible, or without voice. A key element here is that the localization of strategic components of globalization in these cities means that the disadvantaged can engage the new forms

---

[31] As already discussed in chapter 2, much of Weber's examination in *The City* focuses on the gradual emergence and structuring of the force-composition of the city in various areas under different conditions and its gradual stabilization into a distinct form. He traces the changing composition of forces from the ancient kingships through the patrician city to the demos of the ancient world, from the Episcopal structures and fortresses through the city of notables, to the guild-dominated cities in Europe. He is always trying to lay bare the complex processes accompanying the emergence of urban community, which for Weber is akin to what today we might describe in terms of governance and citizenship.

[32] An important element in Weber's work on cities, discussed in chapter 2, is his emphasis on certain types of innovation and change; the construction of rules and norms precisely because deeper arrangements on which norms had been conditioned are being destabilized. Herein also lie openings for new political actors to emerge, as well as changes in the role or locus of older norms, political actors, and forms of authority. This is a highly dynamic configuration where older forms of authority may struggle and succeed in reimposing themselves.

of globalized corporate power and, further, that the growing numbers and diversity of the disadvantaged in these cities under these conditions become heuristics in that they become present to each other. It is the fact of such "presence," rather than power per se, that generates operational and rhetorical openings. Such an interpretation seeks to make a distinction between powerlessness and invisibility/impotence, and thereby underlines the complexity of powerlessness. Powerlessness is not simply the absence of power; it can be constituted in diverse ways, some indeed marked by impotence and invisibility, but others not. The fact that the disadvantaged in global cities can gain "presence" in their engagement with power but also vis-à-vis each other does not necessarily bring power, but neither can it be flattened into some generic powerlessness. Historically this is different from the 1950s–70s in the United States, for example, when white flight and the significant departure of major corporate headquarters left cities hollowed out and the disadvantaged abandoned.[33] Today the localization of the global creates a set of objective conditions of engagement whereby local struggles, such as those against gentrification, are actually instances of a larger conflict about rights to the city in a context where global capital needs these cities for some of its strategic organizational operations and a growing mass of disadvantaged and minoritized people find in these same cities the possibility for survival and for access to space, whether that is housing or a shanty.[34]

The conditions that today make cities sites for political innovation in turn destabilize older systems of organizing territory and politics (Caldeira 2002; Drainville 2004). The rescaling of the strategic territories that articulates the new politico-economic system contributes to the partial unbundling or at least weakening of the national as the container of social process (Taylor 1994). Insofar as citizenship is embedded and in turn marked by its embeddedness, these new conditions may well signal the possibility of new forms of citizenship practices and identities, particularly enabled and made visible in cities.

The impact of the multiple transformations discussed in the chapters in part 2 of this book has been significant in creating operational and conceptual openings for other actors and subjects to enter domains of activity once exclusive to national sovereigns. Other actors, from NGOs and minority

---

[33] The ghetto uprisings of the 1960s were short, intense eruptions confined to the ghettos and causing most of the damage in the neighborhoods of the disadvantaged themselves. In these ghetto uprisings there was no engagement with power.

[34] The expanded demand for developing office, commercial, and residential space for top-end users encroached on minority and disadvantaged neighborhoods and commercial districts and led to growing numbers of homeless beginning in the 1980s in the major emerging global cities—New York, London, Paris, Tokyo, and so on.

populations to supranational organizations, are increasingly emerging as actors in international relations.

The ascendance of a large variety of nonstate actors in the international arena signals the expansion of an international civil society. This is clearly a contested space, particularly when we consider the logic of the capital market—profitability at all costs—against that of the human rights regime. But it does represent a space where other actors can gain visibility as individuals and as collectivities, and come out of the invisibility of aggregate membership in a nation-state exclusively represented by the sovereign.

The category of global civil society is, in a way, too general to capture the specific transboundary networks and formations connecting or articulating multiple places and actors. A focus on these specifics brings "global civil society" down to the spaces and practices of daily life, furthered by today's powerful imaginaries around the idea that others around the world are engaged in the same struggles. This begins to constitute a sense of global civil society that is rooted in the daily spaces of people rather than on some global stage. It also means that the poor, those who cannot travel, can be part of global civil society. I include here cross-border networks of activists engaged in specific localized struggles with an explicit or implicit global agenda and noncosmopolitan forms of global politics and imaginaries attached to local issues and struggles that are part of global horizontal networks containing multiple other such localized efforts, a subject I return to in chapter 7. A particular challenge in the work of identifying these types of processes and actors as part of globalities is decoding at least some of what continues to be experienced and represented as national. These types of practices and dynamics are constitutive of globalization even though we do not usually recognize them as such. The global city is a specific type of site for the emergence of new types of transnational social forms. It endogenizes global dynamics and thereby transforms existing social alignments. And it enables even the disadvantaged to develop transnational strategies and subjectivities. Often this enablement is at heart a *prise de conscience*. What I mean here is that it is not always a new social form as such but rather a subjective, self-reflexive repositioning of an old social practice or condition in a transnational framing. Transnational immigrant households, and even communities, are perhaps emblematic of these new types of micropolitics and subjectivities.

There are two strategic dynamics I seek to isolate here: the incipient denationalizing of specific types of national settings, particularly global cities; and the formation of rhetorical and operational openings for actors other than the national state in cross-border political dynamics, particularly the new global corporate actors and the collectivities whose experience of membership has not been subsumed fully under nationhood in its modern conception, for example, minorities, immigrants, first-nation people, and many feminists.

There is something to be captured here. In the context of a strategic space such as the global city, the types of disadvantaged people described here are not simply marginal; they acquire presence in a broader political process that escapes the boundaries of the formal polity. This presence signals the possibility of a politics. What this politics will be will depend on the specific projects and practices of various communities. Insofar as the sense of membership of these communities is not subsumed under the national, it may well signal the possibility of a transnational politics centered on concrete localities.

CONCLUSION

If there is one theme that brings together today's many different citizenship dynamics it is the lengthening distance between the citizen and the state. Many microtransformations have shaped this process. In their aggregate they spell a historical reversal of the phase that began most emblematically with the French Revolution. Where the French Revolution made the people the sovereign, thereby neutralizing the difference between people and rulers prevalent in preceding periods, today's trends again lengthen the distance. Central to the argument in this chapter is the proposition of this lengthening distance and its construction through the multiple, often minor changes discussed in this chapter, and their accumulation and often extended and diffuse consequences. Second, because citizenship, while highly formalized, is marked by incompleteness it can accommodate such micro-changes. In that regard we can think of citizenship as a type of natural experiment for observing how a highly formalized institution can undergo significant transformations without going under.

These micro-changes have assumed many different shapes. Among the more familiar transformations is the shrinking welfare state that is part of the neoliberalizing of liberal states: in eliminating a range of citizens' entitlements, it reduces the number of relations/interdependencies between citizens and their states. That is to say, it is not just a matter of shrinking social rights and shrinking state obligations. It is also a question of a reduced set of interactions between citizens and the state: they have less to do with each other. Another such instance is the growing acceptance of dual nationality, which alters the exclusive allegiance of citizens to one state, long a basic norm of national statehood and thereby of the interstate system. Again, this is not simply a matter of more passports and the option to live and work in more countries.

I argued in this chapter that this creates a diffuse shift away from citizenship as exclusive allegiance to one state and toward a more practical understanding of citizenship on the part of both states and citizens. The emerging trend toward professional armies rather than citizens' military service dents hallowed notions such as citizens' willingness to die for their state and, obversely, that a state's wars are the people's wars—the state and the people are one. While the chapter focused largely on the United States, where these processes began in especially legible ways in the 1980s, by the 1990s some of these trends became evident in a growing number of developed and developing countries.

To these familiar trends I add some that are more elusive and difficult to nail down but contribute to that lengthening distance. I focused particularly on the somewhat diffuse consequences of the emergence of global classes whose allegiances are more distributed than those of the typical citizen, the emergence of informal political actors who function outside the channels of the formal political system even when they are citizens, and the multiplication of political vocabularies beyond the two major formal paths open to citizens—voting and taking one's government to court. The shift away from citizenship as exclusive allegiance to a state and the willingness to die for that state are conditions that feed into these more diffuse informal political subjectivities and actions. We also need to include here the erosion of the privacy rights of citizens along with a privatizing of executive power discussed in chapter 4, which entails changes in the relationship between the citizen and the state, at least in its formal aspects and for a majority of citizens in the United States, beyond the de facto abuses of the privacy rights of some segments of the citizenry have long existed in the United States.

I was particularly interested in recovering whether and how dynamics internal to the national are contributing to this growing distance between the state and the citizen. The hypothesis was that given the embeddedness of citizenship in key political structures, notably the national state, at least some of the transformations in the latter would induce changes in the relationship of state and citizen. That is to say, I distinguished these changes from the more familiar ones subsumed under notions of postnational citizenship, transnational identities, and the formalized innovations that are the European passport and the increasingly institutionalized human rights regime. The argument was that citizenship can undergo significant transformations without needing to be dislodged from its national encasement. I argued that this holds even when there is a transnational entity at work. For instance, in the case of the human rights regime, it is not human rights as an external regime that are at play here, but rather as a set of norms that gradually and often somewhat informally get wired into national law and therewith transform the rights-bearing subject that is the citizen; these processes are underway even if they may not be completely legible or recognized. My effort in this chapter was, then, to expand the analytic terrain within which we place the question of rights without necessarily leaving the domain of the national state.

Again, the critical assumption here is that citizenship is inevitably an incompletely specified contract between the state and the citizen, and that in this incompleteness then lies the possibility of accommodating new conditions and incorporating new formal and informal instrumentalities. Periods of change make this incompleteness operational and legible, whether in the contesting of discrimination, aspirations to equal citizenship, the decision by first-nation people to go directly to international fora and bypass the national state, or the claims to legal residence by undocumented immigrants who have met the requisite formal and informal criteria. I also interpreted this growing distance between the state and the citizen as the emergence of a type of political subject that does not quite correspond to the notion of the formal political subject that is the voting and jury-serving citizen, notably citizen women who center their political claim-making in the subject that is the mother or housewife rather than citizen. The multiplying of informal political subjects points to the possibility that the excluded (in this case from the formal political apparatus) also can make history, thereby signaling the complexity of powerlessness. Many of these dynamics become legible in cities. Through the thickness of daily life and local, mostly informal politics, cities can accommodate and enable the unbundling of the tight articulation of the citizen and formal state politics. These various trends resonate with the case of the burghers in medieval cities: they were informal actors who found in the space of the city the conditions for their source of "power" as merchants and for their political claim making. In my interpretation, complex cities today also function as such a productive space for the very different types of informal political actors and their claim-making. Whether this is a productivity exclusive to cities or whether cities simply make these processes more visible is, at this point, an empirical question.

PART THREE • *ASSEMBLAGES OF A
GLOBAL DIGITAL AGE*

THE CHAPTERS in part 2 decipher the variable weight of different national domains in today's epochal transformation. These chapters show it is inside the national where much of the work of disassembling the historically constructed nation-state gets done. This disassembling is in good part endogenous to the national rather than the consequence of external "attacks." In this process the national is not necessarily eliminated, but some of its components are given different meanings by new organizing logics.

Among these new logics are those that constitute a variety of global digital assemblages and novel spatio-temporal framings for social activity broadly understood. A common and, in my view, deeply flawed understanding represents digital technology as eliminating territory and functioning outside national jurisdictions, autonomous from state authority, and hence potentially subversive of state authority. This type of representation also leads easily to the assumption that digital space is a global and not national domain and capability. But these notions need to be interrogated. How autonomous are these global digital assemblages? What is their relation to the historical nation-state and to the particular spaces inside the latter that have been newly denationalized? Can we simply interpret these global digital assemblages as postnational or is that far too general given the elaborate specificities that characterize them.

We can think of digital assemblages as a sort of theoretical frontier for understanding the character of the global, even though the global is both more and less than the new electronic world. In this third part I examine a bundle of theoretical, methodological, and political issues that are part of the analytical effort to embed the digital in more complex conceptual and practical fields. Analytically this parallels the effort in part 2 aimed at an equivalent type of embedding of the global. Doing this requires addressing how we as social scientists study these new technologies, a task that has begun but is far from finished. A good part of chapter 7 deals with this question. Armed with reasonably effective analytic tools developed in the first part of the chapter, I then move to detailed examinations of two major domains for which the new technologies have been critical and constitutive—global electronic financial markets and global activist networks.

The argument I develop is that while the digital is specific and in many ways irreducible in the sense of nonfungible, it does nonetheless evince often complex imbrications with the nondigital. I use the concept imbrication to accommodate both interdependence and this irreducibility of each the digital and the nondigital. That is to say, their interdependence does not necessarily make them hybrids. The detailed examination of these two particular domains aims at establishing the limits of the autonomy of the digital from the social, paralleling the effort to establish the limits of the autonomy of the global from the national in part two. This detail is necessary to destabilize the master categories through which digital space has been conceptualized and interpreted; those categories tend to confine the import of these new technologies to their technical capacities and to assume that outcomes will reflect those capacities.

In this examination, the questions of territory, authority, and rights are revisited through the lens of the formation of digital domains we easily think of as not territorial, not subject to conventional state authority, and not involving any formal rights to speak of. Neither the territory nor the kind of territoriality that became a key component of the nation-state and of exclusive state authority are at work in the types of networks I will focus on. Nor is this a territoriality that resembles that of the urban political economy of the Late Middle Ages. Yet, I explore the possibility that territory plays a specific role and, further, that a particular kind of territoriality gets shaped via imbrication with these global digital assemblages.

These assemblages are basically informal in that they cannot be captured in terms of a specific legal persona. Even when a proprietary financial digital network can be constituted as a legal persona, the more complex assemblage within which it functions and gains its meaning, cannot. Further, these technologies are only one factor that facilitates political engagement on the part of "actors" arising out of or constituted as digital networks: typically these are not formal political actors. Thus the formal persona that is an incorporated market, firm, or financial network, is a private economic one, not a political one. Both in terms of the issues raised in chapter 5 and in terms of political "work" the new technologies are facilitators. For instance, the additional power they have brought to financial markets can translate into added political power over governments. In this sense, they enable new types of political actors—networked assemblages—which while informal evince particular forms of power, and in turn, these actors through their practices partly build and shape those assemblages. Global capital and the new global activisms discussed in chapter 7 are two such actors. The formalizing apparatus of the state is caught up in a different, much slower, temporal frame than that of digitized transactions; the state may succeed in formalizing some features of these assemblages but it might not catch up with others or with the assemblage in toto.

Two critical consequences of these particular interactions between digital and historically constructed national conditions are that the latter become inflected with digitally enabled temporal and spatial orders, and secondly, that their constituting as assemblages brings with it the emergence of a multiplication of partial, often highly specialized novel spatio-temporal orders and sub-orders that are often radically different from national ones. Chapter 8 begins to examine these developments and how they in turn might shape questions of territory, authority, and rights.

7 DIGITAL NETWORKS, STATE AUTHORITY, AND POLITICS

THE RAPID PROLIFERATION of global computer-based networks and the digitization of a broad array of economic and political activities that now can circulate in these networks raise questions about the effectiveness of current framings for state authority and democratic participation. In a context of multiple partial and specific changes linked to globalization, these forms of digitization have enabled the ascendance of subnational scales, such as the global city, and supranational scales, such as global markets, where previously the national scale was dominant. These rescalings do not always parallel existing formalizations of state authority.

The overall outcome might be described as a destabilizing of older formal hierarchies of scale and an emergence of not fully formalized new ones. Older hierarchies of scale dating from the period that saw the ascendance of the nation-state continue to operate; they are typically organized in terms of institutional size and territorial scope: from the international down to the national, the regional, the urban, and the local. But today's rescaling dynamics cut across institutional size and across the institutional encasements of territory produced by the formation of national states. At its most general these developments raise a number of questions about their impact on the regulatory capacities of states and about their potential for undermining state authority as it has come to be constituted over the last two centuries. More analytically we might ask whether these developments signal new types of imbrications between authority and territory, and more specifically, place.

This chapter examines these questions by focusing on how digitization has enabled the strengthening of older actors and spaces and the formation of novel ones capable of engaging the competence, scope, and exclusivity of state authority. The particular empirical cases examined to get at these larger questions are global finance and the new types of cross-border activist politics, in both of which digitization has been transformative. To some extent these outcomes are overdetermined in that they entail multiple causalities and contingencies. By focusing on digitization I do not mean to posit a single causality. On the contrary, digitization is deeply caught up with other dynamics that often shape its development and uses; in some cases it is completely derivative, a mere instrumentality of these other dynamics, and in other cases it is constitutive of new domains.

One key assumption here is that understanding the imbrications between digitization and politico-economic processes requires recognizing the embeddedness of digital space and resisting purely technological readings of the technical capacities entailed by digitization. One of the subjects this chapter needs to address is the as yet underdeveloped analytics for understanding digital technology from a social science perspective. Much of the social science work done in this field sees these technologies either as all-powerful or as more of the same, only faster. Both views are deeply flawed and have produced many incorrect forecasts. Developing analytic tools that allow us a better grasp of the conditionalities not even these technologies can escape is critical for the types of questions I raise in this book.

This chapter develops these issues through an examination of four subjects. I begin with a general introduction of some of the questions and debates concerning the relationship between state authority and the rapid growth of the Internet and private digital networks. This is a necessary introduction to a subject weighed down by assumptions about the built-in capacities of the Internet to override existing relations of law to territory, notably the much noted fact that firms, individuals, and NGOs can elude government control when operating in cyberspace. This first section also briefly introduces the questions that can be addressed through the two empirical cases developed at greater length later in the chapter. A deeper development of the question of digitization, authority, and territory requires conceptual elaboration. In the second section I discuss critical conceptual aspects, with a particular focus on computer-centered interactive technologies, that remain underdeveloped in what we might refer to as the social science of digital technologies. The third section examines the relation between state authority and the global capital market, particularly the fact that this market is not only largely electronic and de facto supranational but also enormously powerful. The fourth section examines the formation of types of global politics that run through the specificities of localized concerns and struggles yet can be seen as expanding democratic participation beyond state boundaries. I regard these as noncosmopolitan versions of global politics that in many ways raise questions about the relation of law to place that are the opposite from those raised by global finance.

STATE AUTHORITY CONFRONTS DIGITAL NETWORKS

The condition of the Internet as a decentralized network of networks has contributed to strong notions about its built-in autonomy from
state power and its capacity to enhance democracy from the bottom up via a
strengthening of both market dynamics and access by civil society.[1] At the
core of the Internet are a series of components that are infrastructural: Internet exchanges, national backbone networks, regional networks, and local
networks. These infrastructures are often privately owned. Thus while in
principle many of the key features of the Internet do indeed have the capacity
to enhance democracy, its openness and its technology also contain possibilities for significant indirect control and limitations on access, including once
inside the Internet. Furthermore, a large share of electronic networks are private and inaccessible to non-members, among which wholesale financial
electronic networks are perhaps the most significant example. There are,
then, limitations on what many have considered the inherently democratic
character of digital networks.

A distinct issue concerning the relation between the state and digital networks is the possibility for the average citizen, firm, or organization operating in the Internet to escape or override most conventional jurisdictions
(Post 1995; Jones 1998). Even where this might be the case it does not necessarily imply the absence of regulation. Much of the literature on this issue operates at two very different levels. One general, still rooted in the earlier emphasis on the Internet as a decentralized space where no authority structures
can be instituted. The other is a rapidly growing technical literature, in good
part stimulated by the growing importance of issues such as Internet addressing and surveillance, with the associated legal and political issues.

---

[1] What constitutes the Internet is continuously changing (WIO 2002). Some years
ago it could still be described as a network of computer networks using a common communication protocol (IP protocol). Today networks using other communication protocols are also connected to other networks via gateways. Further, the Internet is not only constituted by computers
connected to other computers: there are also point-of-sale terminals, cameras, robots, telescopes,
cellular phones, TV sets, and an assortment of other hardware components that are connected to
the Internet. On October 24, 1995, the U.S. Federal Networking Council made the following
resolution concerning the definition of the Internet: " 'Internet' refers to the global information
system that i) is logically linked together by a globally unique address space based on the Internet
Protocol or its subsequent extensions/follow-ons; ii) is able to support communications using the
Transmission Control Protocol/Internet Protocol (TCP/IP) suite or its subsequent extensions/fol-
low-ons, and/or other IP compatible protocols; and iii) provides, uses, or makes accessible, either
publicly or privately, high level services layered on the communications and related infrastructure described herein" (*http://www.itrd.gov/fnc/Internet_res.html*).

Generalized commentaries about the Internet continue to overlook what are at least three factors that constitute a de facto management of the Internet. One is governmental authority through technical and operational standard setting for both hardware and software. The second is the growing power of large corporate interests in shaping an orientation of the Internet toward privatizing capabilities. And the third is the fact that there has long been a kind of central authority overseeing some of the crucial features of the Internet concerning addresses and numbers granting, as well as the domain name system. These three conditions do not signal that regulation is ipso facto possible. They merely signal that the idea that the Internet escapes all authority is simply untrue.

Boyle (2000), among others, has examined how the built-in set of standards that constitute the Internet undermines claims that the state cannot regulate the Internet. Indeed, he argues that the state's regulatory agenda is partially contained in the design of the technologies. Thus the state can regulate in this case even though it is not via sanctions. Boyle notes that privatized and technologically based rule enforcement would take policing away from the scrutiny of public law, freeing states from some of the constitutional and other constraints restricting its options. This can be problematic even for states that operate under the rule of law, as examples of abuse of power by various U.S. government agencies make clear.[2]

The second de facto "regulatory" condition is the power of private corporate interests in shaping the activity space of the Internet. The question of democratic governance goes far deeper than the types of bodies set up to govern. Beyond governance, the actors shaping the development of the Internet diverge sharply, ranging from the original group of computer scientists that developed the open and decentralized features of the Internet to multinational corporations concerned with intellectual property rights protection (Latham 2005). Most recently, there has been a strengthening of civic and political groups concerned with the extent to which private corporate interests are shaping Internet access and development (Lovink 2002).

One central issue that captures these divergent interests is the fact that the leading Internet software development efforts since the mid-1990s have been in firewalled intranets for firms, firewalled tunnels for firm-to-firm transactions, identity verification, trademark protection, and billing. The rapid

---

[2] The power of the U.S. government to engage in multiple forms of surveillance, including surveillance of corporations in countries run by governments who are strong and long-term allies, was illustrated in the alleged use by the U.S. government of its Echelon surveillance system to spy on European corporations (WIO 2002: chapter 6).

increase of this type of software and its use in the Internet does not necessarily strengthen the publicness of the Internet and risks orienting much of the collective capability it represents toward corporate and more broadly commercial interests. This is especially significant if there is less production of software aimed at strengthening the openness and decentralization of the Internet, as was the case in its earlier phases. Since 1995–96 political and technical developments have brought about what may be interpreted as an increase in controls (see, generally, Lessig 2000). Prior to 1995 users could more easily maintain their anonymity while online and it was difficult to verify user identity, thereby ensuring better privacy protection. The architecture of the Internet inhibited "zoning"—any technique that facilitates discrimination in access to or distribution of some good or service.[3] This has changed with the drive to facilitate e-commerce: the architecture of the Internet now facilitates zoning.[4] These conditions inevitably play a role in current efforts toward Internet governance.

The third factor is the existence of an originally informal and now increasingly formalized central authority governing key functions of the Internet.[5] The nature of this authority is not necessarily akin to regulatory authorities but it is a gate-keeping system of sorts and raises the possibility of oversight capacities, albeit of a sort that will increasingly demand considerable innovation in our concepts about what constitutes regulation.[6] The establishment in the summer of 1998 of the Internet Corporation for Assigned

---

[3] Lessig (2000) labels the architecture of the Internet "code," by which he means the software and hardware that constitute it and determine how people interact or exist in this space.

[4] Elsewhere I have made a similar argument using the notion of the emergence of cybersegmentations (Sassen 2002). One of my concerns was to argue that the notion of a digital divide should not be confined to access to the technology. Even if one has access, once inside the Internet, there are multiple other digital divides.

[5] This centrally managed function of the Internet involves the control and assignment of the numbers that computers need to locate an address. It therefore can instruct all the top "root servers" of the Internet—the computers that execute address inquiries—and these will accept these instructions. This is, clearly, a power of sorts. As is well-known, the particular function of assigning addresses is crucial and was for many years under the informal control of one scientist who named this function the "Internet Assigned Numbers Authority." More generally, the community of scientists who have worked on making the Internet workable and have had to reach many agreements on a broad range of technical matters have long been a sort of informal central "authority." In most other cultural settings they would probably have become a formal, recognizable body—with, one might add, considerable power. There is an interesting sociology here.

[6] There are also more specific issues that may affect the regulation of particular forms of digital activity through a focus on infrastructure (Latham 2005). There are different types of infrastructure for different types of digital activities, for instance, financial markets versus consumer wireless phones.

Names and Numbers (ICANN), now the group charged with overseeing the Internet's address system, represents a formalization of the earlier authority.[7] It was started as a group of insiders with fairly loose and ineffective by-laws. By early 1999 it had implemented conflict-of-interest rules, opened up some board meetings to the public, and worked toward developing a mechanism to elect board members in an effort to build in more accountability.[8] Setting up ICANN has by no means solved all problems.[9] Today ICANN is the subject of growing debate among various digital subcultures. Many see ICANN as a deeply undemocratic regulatory apparatus largely dominated by U.S. interests, notably large corporations.[10]

These trends demonstrate the existence of Internet management. They also show the necessity for fair governance if we are to ensure that public interest issues also shape Internet development. Market forces alone will

---

[7] With the growth of business interest in the Internet, the de facto authority of the early pioneers and their logic for assigning addresses began to be criticized. To cite a familiar case, firms found that their names had already been assigned to other parties and that there was little they could do; the whole idea of brand names and intellectual property rights over a name was not part of the early Internet culture.

[8] Since October 2000 the board of ICANN has been the final decision-making authority on standards. But there is a complex web of organizations involved in various aspects of the operation of the Internet. The Internet Society and its subsidiary organizations—the Internet Architecture Board, the Internet Engineering Steering Group, the Internet Engineering Task Force, and the Internet Research Task Force—are responsible for the development of communications and operational standards and protocols that allow users to communicate with each other over the Internet. The Internet Societal Task Force is responsible for naming Internet policy issues. The copyright on the protocols is held by the Internet Society. Other organizations such as the WWW Consortium specialize in the development of standards for certain services of the Internet.

[9] The U.S. government's earlier "Framework for Global Electronic Commerce," a blueprint for Internet governance, argues that because of the Internet's global reach and evolving technology, regulation should be kept to a minimum. It also suggests that in the few areas where rules are needed, such as privacy and taxation, policy should be made by quasi-governmental bodies such as WIPO or the OECD. One of the issues with this type of proposal is the absence of transparency and the problems it brings with it. These became evident in one of the first big Internet policy dilemmas: cybersquatting (private speculators seizing valuable corporate brand names on the Internet and selling them back, at an enormous price, to the firms carrying those names). Internet addresses are important for establishing an identity online, so companies want to establish a rule that they are entitled to any domain names using their trademarks. But the Internet is used for more than e-commerce, so consumer advocates say this rule would unfairly restrict the rights of schools, museums, political parties, and other noncommercial Internet users. However, in the deliberations that have taken place at WIPO, it is primarily the large firms that are participating in meetings that take place mostly behind closed doors. This privatizes the effort to design regulations for the Internet.

[10] See, e.g., Nettime (1997) and Lovink (2002) for summaries and analyses of the debates.

not ensure that the Internet contributes to the strengthening of democratic institutions. As the Internet has grown, become more international, and gained economic importance, there is growing concern in specialized circles that we need a more organized and accountable system.

The debate about the Internet and its governance is somewhat divided on the question of whether it can be governed at all.[11] Simplifying what is a partially overlapping set of positions, for some the Internet is an entity that can be subjected to a governance mechanism while for others there is no such entity but rather a decentralized network of networks that at best can lend itself to coordination of standards and rules.

Among those who consider the Internet a single entity, much of the concern has focused on the establishment of a system of property rights and other such protections and the means for enforcing them. The disagreement has centered on how to administer and enforce such a system. For some (e.g., Foster 1996) it would be necessary to attach such a system to a multilateral organization, notably ITU or WIPO, as long as there is no global trademark law, only national law, while the Internet is a global entity. This would ensure recognition from member governments. For others, the mechanisms for governance would come from the institutions of the Internet itself. Gould (1996), for example, argues that there is no need for outside institutions to be brought in but rather that Internet practices could produce a sort of constitutional governance pertaining exclusively to the realm of the Internet. A third type of proposal was developed by Mathiason and Kuhlman (1998), who suggested the need for an international framework convention agreed upon by governments; such a framework convention could parallel the UN Framework Convention on Climate Change.

On the other hand, the experts who consider there is no such entity as the Internet, only a decentralized network of networks, argue that there is no need for any external regulation or coordination. Further, the decentralized nature of the system would make external regulation ineffective. But there tends to be agreement with the proponents of governance as to the need for a framework for establishing a system of property rights. Gillett and Kapor (1996) argue for the functionality of diffused coordination mechanisms; further, the authority of such coordination, they posit, could be more easily legitimated in distributed network environments as is the Internet, and increasingly so given a stakeholder community that is becoming global. Mueller (1998) strongly argues against an Internet regulatory agenda and

---

[11] The distinctions noted here partly follow Pare's classification and research on the subject (2003: chapter 3).

against the policing of trademark rights. He is critical of the very notion of the term governance when it comes to inter-networking as it is the opposite of what ought to be the purpose: facilitating inter-networking. He argues that too much debate and effort has focused on restricting the ability to inter-network.

In one of the most systematic examinations of these various perspectives, Pare (2003) argues that neither approach offers much insight into the processes actually shaping the governance trajectory of the Internet; he focuses particularly on the addressing system. Nor, argues Pare, can these approaches account for the operational structures of the organizations currently responsible for managing the core functions of inter-networking (at both the national and international level) or the likelihood of their survival.[12] One important issue is the role of the actual features of the technology in shaping some of the possibilities or forms of governance or coordination (Lehmkuhl 2002). Post (1995) and Johnson and Post (1996) argue that transnational electronic networks create a set of different jurisdictions from those of territorially based states, and hence there is little purpose in trying to replicate regulatory forms of the latter for the Internet. These authors maintain that various dimensions of inter-networking, including Internet addressing, could be governed by decentralized emergent law that eventually could converge into common standards for mutual coordination. For others emphasizing the technology question, the Internet has been a regulated environment given the standards and constraints built into the hardware and software. Reidenberg (1998) agrees that the Internet undermines territorially based regulatory governance. But new models and sources of rules have been and continue to be created out of the technical standards and their capacity to establish default boundary rules that impose order in network environments (see also Lessig 2000). Technical standards can be used as instruments of public policy, and in this regard Reidenberg posits the emergence of a lex informatica.

But the Internet is only one portion of the vast new world of digital space, and much of the power to undermine or destabilize state authority attributed to the Internet comes, I argue, from the existence of private dedicated digital networks, such as those used in wholesale global finance.

---

[12] Pare (2003) calls for and develops another kind of approach in the study of these questions of governance and coordination. He argues that an emphasis on results and optimal governance strategies produces analytical blind spots. A crucial issue is the need to understand the dynamic relationship between the institutional forms delivering technology and the network structures that emerge over time. See also Lessig (2000) and Latham (2005).

Distinguishing Private and Public-Access Digital Space

Many assertions about digital dynamics and potentials are actually about processes happening in private digital space and have little to do with the Internet. I consider this a serious, though fairly common confusion. Most wholesale financial activity and other significant digital economic activities take place in dedicated private digital networks.[13] Private digital networks enable forms of power other than the distributed power associated with public digital networks. Key instances are wholesale financial markets, corporate intra-nets, and corporate networks bringing together lenders and borrowers in a private domain rather than the public domain of stock markets.

In chapter 5 I examined how the digitization of financial markets and instruments played a crucial role in raising the orders of magnitude, the extent of cross-border integration, and hence the raw power of the global capital market. These conditions raise a number of questions concerning the impact of this concentration of capital in global markets that allow for high degrees of circulation in and out of countries. As I argued in chapter 5, the global capital market now has the power to "discipline" national governments, that is to say, to subject at least some monetary and fiscal policies to financial criteria where before this was not quite the case. How does this affect national economies and government policies more generally? Does it alter the functioning of democratic governments? Does this kind of concentration of capital reshape accountability? Does it affect national sovereignty? Do these changes reposition states and the interstate system in the broader world of cross-border relations? These are some of the questions raised by the particular ways in which digitization interacts with other variables to produce the distinctive features of the global capital market. While the scholarly literature has not directly raised or addressed these questions, we can find more general responses, ranging from those who find that in the end the national state still exercises the ultimate authority in regulating finance (e.g., Helleiner 1999; Pauly 2002) to those who see in the larger global economy an emergent power gaining at least partial ascendance over national states (Panitch 1996; Gill 1996). In my analysis, developed in chapter 5, the vastly expanded global capital market that takes off in the 1980s has the power and necessary organizational articulations with national economies to make its requirements weigh in national economic policymaking, and to do so

---

[13] Retail investment and stock trading use the Internet, as does direct online investment, which is mostly retail and represents a minor share of the overall global financial market. Even factoring in its expected tripling in value over the next three or four years will not give it the type of power characterizing the wholesale global financial market I am discussing here.

dressed as desirable for the national economic interest.[14] The *operational logic* of the capital market provides some of the norms for national economic policy-making going far beyond the financial sector as such. In this sense, the global capital market functions as an informal political "actor."

Seen this way, digitization emerges as a variable whose significance goes beyond its technical features. While digitization of instruments and markets was critical to the sharp growth of the global capital market and thereby enabled the financializing of economic criteria, this outcome was shaped by interests and logics that typically had little to do with digitization per se, even though it was crucial. The logic of use at work is not that of the technology as such but that of finance, one to be distinguished no matter how important those technologies have been for its growth and its character. This makes clear the extent to which digitized markets are embedded in complex institutional settings. In addition, while the raw power achieved by the capital markets through digitization also facilitated the institutionalizing of certain finance-dominated economic criteria in national policy, digitization per se could not have achieved this policy outcome.

One crucial implication of this particular type of embeddedness of global finance is that the supranational electronic market space, which partly operates outside any government's exclusive jurisdiction, is only one of the spaces for finance. The other type of space is one marked by the thick environments of actual financial centers, places where national laws continue to be operative, albeit often profoundly altered laws. The embeddedness of private economic electronic space entails the formation of massive concentrations of infrastructure, not only worldwide dispersal, and a complex interaction between digitization and conventional communications infrastructure—the latter far more subject to direct state authority. The notion of "global cities" captures this particular embeddedness of various forms of global hypermobile capital—including that of financial capital in actual financial centers.[15] In the case of private digital spaces such as those of global finance, this embeddedness

---

[14] Returning to the discussion in chapter 5, I try to capture this normative transformation in the notion of privatizing certain capacities for making norms that in the recent history of states under the rule of law were in the public domain. (I am not concerned here with cases such as the Catholic Church, which has long had what could be described as private norm-making capacities but is of course a private institution or meant to be.) Now what are actually elements of a private logic emerge as public norms even though they represent particular rather than public interests. This is not a new occurrence in itself for national states under the rule of law; what is perhaps different is the extent to which the interests involved are global.

[15] For instance, the growth of electronic trading and electronic network alliances among major financial centers is allowing us to see the particular way in which digitized markets are partly embedded in these vast concentrations of material resources and human talents represented by financial centers. (See Sassen 2001: chapters 4, 5 and 7.)

carries significant implications for theory and politics, specifically, for the conditions through which governments and citizens can act on this new electronic world.

In brief, I argue that the private digital space of global finance intersects in at least two specific and often contradictory ways with the world of state authority and law. One is through the introduction of new types of norms, reflective of the operational logic of the global capital market, into national state policy. The second one is through the partial embeddedness of even the most digitized financial markets in actual financial centers, which partly returns global finance to the world of national governments, though conditioned on denationalized policy components. Global digitized finance makes legible some of the complex and novel imbrications between law and territory and the fact that it is not simply an overriding of national state authority even in the case of this most powerful of actors. It consists, rather, of both the use of that authority for the implementation of regulations and laws that respond to the interests of global finance, and the renewed weight of that authority through the ongoing need for financial centers.

A Politics of Places on Cross-Border Circuits

Perhaps the opposite kind of imbrication of law and territory from that of global finance is evident in a domain that has been equally transformed by digitization but under radically different conditions. The key digital medium is the public-access Internet and the key actors are largely resource-poor organizations and individuals. As discussed in chapter 6, the Internet has enabled a new type of cross-border politics that can bypass interstate politics. As even small, resource-poor organizations and individuals can become participants in electronic networks, it signals the possibility of a sharp growth in cross-border politics by actors other than states. This produces a specific kind of activism, one centered on multiple localities yet connected digitally at scales larger than the local, often reaching a global scale.

Through the Internet *localized* initiatives can become part of cross-border networks and move from being subject to specific national/local laws to a global scale where these laws almost cease to be operative; what rules is the collective presence of whatever national or local norms are in play. One question this raises is what kind of a "territory" is constituted through such a network of multiple localities in matters of law.

Current uses of digital media in this new type of cross-border political activism broadly suggest two types of digital activism by place-centered activist groups focused on local issues that connect with other such groups around the world. Much of the evidence shows that the types of places are mostly, though not exclusively, cities.[16] Activists can develop networks for circulating not only information (about environmental, housing, political, and other matters) but also for executing political work and deploying strategies of engagement. The first type consists of new kinds of cross-border political work centered on the fact that specific types of local issues recur in localities across the world. By being part of such a global network, place-based activists concerned almost exclusively with local issues have gained something vis-à-vis their local or national governments, or other entities they are aiming at engaging or addressing for claim making. What they have gained is not money or power per se, but perhaps something akin to political clout through the often suggestive power of global networks and the particular political subjectivity it can engender. This represents one of the key forms of critical politics that the Internet can make possible: a politics of the local with a difference—these are localities connected with each other across a region, a country, or the world. It also makes evident that the fact a network is global does not mean that it all has to happen at the global level; however, the network's globality can function as a political support and resource for the localities that constitute that network.[17]

The second type of digital network-centered politics is one that does most of its work in the digital network and then may or may not converge on an actual terrain for activism. The extent to which the work and the political effort are centered on the transactions in the digital network will vary. Organizing against the Multilateral Agreement on Investment was largely a digital event. But when these digital political actions hit the ground, they can do so very effectively especially in the concentrated places that cities are. This is well illustrated by what is considered to be one of the first of such global events, the 1989 Seattle anti–WTO demonstrations, the first in a continuing series of demonstrations organized by the anti- and alter-globalization networks in cities hosting meetings of the major members and institutions of the supranational system. This is a different type of digital activism from hacktivism (Denning 1999) because it is partly embedded in nondigital environments that

---

[16] It is not clear that if these organizations were located in rural areas this would make a difference generally speaking. However, a more fine-grained analysis suggests that it does. For an analysis of the distinctiveness of digital (and other) networks centered in rural communities, see Garcia (2002).

[17] I see parallel features in the cases where use of the Internet has allowed diasporas to be globally interconnected rather than confined to a one-to-one relationship with the country or region of origin. (See, e.g., *Global Civil Society Yearbook* 2002; Axel 2004)

shape, give meaning, and to some extent constitute the event. It would also have to be distinguished from cyberwar (Der Derian 2001).

These forms of activism contribute in multiple microlevel ways to an incipient unbundling of the exclusive authority, including symbolic authority, over territory and people we have long associated with the national state. The unbundling of national state authority may well happen even when the individuals involved are not necessarily problematizing the question of nationality or national identity. This can be a de facto unbundling of formal authority, one not predicated on a knowing rejection of the national. Among the more strategic instantiations of this unbundling is, again, the global city. The growing intensity of transactions among these cities is creating a strategic cross-border geography that partly bypasses national states (e.g., Taylor, Walker, and Beaverstock 2002; GAWC) and increasingly includes a broad range of types of actors, not only global corporate ones. The new network technologies further strengthen these transactions, whether they are electronic transfers of specialized services among firms or Internet-based communications among the members of globally dispersed diasporas and interest groups.

The new network technologies have amplified these possibilities and have, to some extent, given activists the essential vehicle necessary for the outcome. But, again, technology by itself could not have produced the outcome. The possibility for cities and global digital networks to emerge as nodes in these types of transboundary politics is the result of a complex mix of institutional developments. Perhaps crucial among these are globalization, both as infrastructure and as an imaginary, and the international human rights regime. These have contributed to create formal and informal operational openings for nonstate actors to enter international arenas that were once the exclusive domain of national states. Various, minor developments signal that the state is no longer the exclusive subject for international law or the only actor in international relations. Other actors—from NGOs and first-nation peoples to immigrants and refugees who become subjects of adjudication in human rights decisions—are increasingly emerging as subjects of international law and actors in international relations. Nonstate actors can gain visibility as individuals and as collectivities, and come out of the invisibility of aggregate membership in a nation-state exclusively represented by the sovereign.

EMBEDDING THE DIGITAL

One of the themes running through the preceding section is the need to recognize that the weight of technical capabilities in the shaping of social outcomes (as distinct from, for example, engineering tests) is variably affected by the substantive rationalities that guide users.[18] The implication is that we cannot simply infer the impact of these technologies—on state authority, on democratic participation, on global finance—by considering their technical capabilities. The latter interact with the diversity of substantive rationalities organizing different social domains. And this means that some of these capabilities may not get used at all or may get underused. This perspective also helps explain why so many forecasts based on all that these technologies can do, technically speaking, turned out to be partly or completely wrong.

A second theme is that of the embeddedness of these technologies in nondigital environments or contexts. This embeddedness consists partly of the preceding theme: what these technologies deliver depends partly on how and for what they get used. Thus finance has known how to use these technologies to an extent not present in many other sectors. There are other elements making for embeddedness, notably the material conditions necessary for the deployment of these technologies, or the fact that much of the meaning of what happens in digital space comes from nondigital settings. Digital networks are embedded in both the technical features and standards of the hardware and software, as well as in actual societal structures and power dynamics (e.g., Castells 1996; Latour 1991; Lovink and Riemens 2002; Mackenzie and Wajcman 1999; Avgerou 2002).[19] There is no purely digital economy and no completely virtual corporation or community. This means that power, contestation, inequality, and hierarchy inscribe electronic space and shape the criteria for what types of software get developed.

These observations hold particularly for the types of interactive digital domains that concern me here, and are parts of social life and, particularly, social change. These are domains that involve people, firms, and organizations

---

[18] Beyond these issues of intentionality and use lies the question of infrastructure and access (e.g., NTIA 1998; Petrazzini and Kibati 1999; Shade 1998; Sassen 1998: chapter 9; Thomas 1995; Latham 2005). Electronic space is going to be far more present in highly industrialized countries than in the less developed world and far more present for middle-class households in developed countries than for poor households in those same countries (Jensen 1998; Harvey and MacNab 2000; Hoffman and Novak 1998). However, there are very cheap ways of delivering access to the Internet, far cheaper than the standard telephone system, and once such access is secured, the opportunities for low-income households and communities, especially in the global south, can increase enormously (e.g., ITU 1998; Nadeau et al. 1998).

[19] Although using a different vocabulary, Latour (1991) makes a radical statement in this direction. Lovink and Riemens (2002) give us a detailed account of the multiple nondigital conditions (including neighborhood subcultures) that had to come together to create the enormously successful city-wide digital inter-network called Digital City Amsterdam.

that are intensive users with defined objectives, rather than, for instance, computer scientists and engineers working on the technology itself, or online shoppers merely clicking into existing options. As social scientists we need to avoid focusing exclusively on the technical capabilities; we cannot overlook the social environments in which they get used. Neither can we disregard the specificity of these technical capabilities which enable the formation of whole new interactive domains. We need analytical tools that allow us to examine these and constitute them as objects of study. These technologies cannot be reduced, as is common, to the status of "independent variables," which confines the matter to its impact on existing conditions. As Judy Wajcman (2002) points out, many social scientists see technology as the impetus for the most fundamental social trends and transformations.[20] To this I would add, first, a tendency to understand or conceptualize these technologies in terms of what they can do and assume that they will do; and second, a strong tendency to construct the relation of these technologies to the social world as one of applications and impacts.

Thus the difficulty analysts and commentators have had specifying and understanding the relation between digitization and multiple social conditions can be seen as resulting from two analytic flaws. One of these (especially evident in the United States) confines interpretation to a technological reading of the technical capabilities of digital technology. This is crucial for the engineering side, but it is problematic for a sociological understanding. Such a reading inevitably neutralizes or renders invisible the material conditions and practices, place-boundedness, and thick social environments within and through which these technologies operate.[21] The second flaw is the continuing reliance on analytical categorizations that were developed under other spatial and historical conditions, that is, conditions preceding the current digital era. Thus the tendency is to conceive of the digital as simply and exclusively digital and the nondigital (whether represented in terms of the physical/material or the actual, all problematic though common conceptions) as simply and exclusively nondigital. These either/or categorizations filter out alternative conceptualizations, thereby precluding a more complex reading of

[20] For critical examinations that reveal particular shortcomings of technology-driven explanations, see, e.g., Loader (1998); Nettime (1997); Hargittai (1998); and, more generally, Latour (1991); Munker and Roesler (1997); Mackenzie (1999); Mackenzie and Wajcman (1999).

[21] Another consequence of this type of reading is to assume that a new technology will ipso facto replace all older technologies that are less efficient or slower at executing the tasks the new technology is best at. We know that historically this is not the case.

the interactions between the digital and the nondigital, notably place-bound conditions.

Understanding the place of these new technologies from a social perspective requires, then, avoiding a purely technological interpretation and recognizing the embeddedness and the variable outcomes of these technologies for different social orders. They can indeed be constitutive of new social dynamics, but they can also be derivative or merely reproduce older conditions. In addition, this perspective calls for categories that capture what are now often conceived of as contradictory or mutually exclusive attributes. The challenge is to develop analytic categories that allow us to capture the imbrications of the digital and the nondigital moment in the often complex processes wherein these new technologies get deployed. The issues introduced in the first section of this chapter point to the enormous capabilities of these technologies but also to their limitations. They will not necessarily allow users to escape state authority nor will they necessarily ensure their democratic rights. They will not inevitably globalize users and eliminate their articulation with particular localities, but they will make globality a resource for these users. The outcomes are not unidirectional and seamless, as the most common representation would have it. They are mixed, contradictory, and lumpy.

Castells has laid the foundation for a social science of information technology in his recent work (1996). His is a synthesis of a vast array of conditions, dynamics, and actors. It is a macrolevel account of the challenge that the development of these new types of technologies brings to the social sciences. Here I develop a set of meso- and microlevel analyses that are part of the challenge to analyses that seek to capture the specificity of the technical and the social, where the technical is recognized to be partly society frozen but assumed to have its own specificity once frozen.

In what follows I develop these questions about analytic strategies for capturing the embeddedness of the new technologies by focusing on three critical components of that embeddedness: the complex interactions between digital and nondigital domains; the destabilizing of existing hierarchies of scale made possible by these technologies; and the mediating cultures that organize the relation between these technologies and users. I confine my focus to computer-centered interactive technologies (henceforth, digital technologies) and to interactive domains that are part of social life, rather than game-theoretic or fictive virtual environments. In the second half of the chapter I examine these analytic issues as they get instantiated in the two substantive social arenas briefly introduced above: the interactions between capital fixity and capital mobility in the case of global finance, and the emergence of a new politics of places on global networks.[22] The organizing concern here, as throughout this chapter, is with the implications of these technologies for questions of state authority, territory, and rights.

Digital/Nondigital Imbrications

Hypermobility and "dematerialization"[23] are usually seen as mere functions, or capabilities, of the new technologies. This understanding ignores the fact that it takes multiple material conditions to achieve this outcome. Once we recognize that hypermobility (of a financial instrument, or the digitization of an actual piece of real estate through its incorporation into a digital financial instrument) had to be *produced*, we introduce nondigital variables in our analysis of the digital. Obversely, much of what happens in electronic space is deeply inflected by the cultures, the material practices, and the imaginaries that take place outside electronic space. Much of what we think of when it comes to cyberspace would lack any meaning or referents if we were to exclude the world outside cyberspace. The digital and the nondigital are not simply mutually exclusive conditions. The digital is embedded in the larger societal, cultural, subjective, economic, and imaginary structurations of lived experience and the systems within which we exist and operate. At the same time, through this embeddedness, the digital can act back on the social so that its specific capabilities can engender new concepts of the social and of the possible.

For instance, producing capital mobility takes capital fixity: state-of-the-art environments, well-housed talent, and conventional infrastructure—from highways to airports and railways. These are all partly place-bound conditions, even when the nature of their place-boundedness differs from what it may have been a hundred years ago when place-boundedness was far more likely to be a form of immobility. But digitization also brings with it an amplification of capacities—often part of fixed capital, such as computer hardware—that enable the liquefying of what is not liquid, thereby producing or raising the mobility of what we have customarily thought of as not mobile or barely so. At its most extreme, this liquefying digitizes its object. Once digitized, it gains hypermobility—instantaneous circulation through digital networks with global span. It is important to emphasize that the hypermobility gained by an object through digitization is but one moment of a more complex condition.

---

[22] See, respectively, Sassen 2001: chapters 2 and 5, and 2002.

[23] Dematerialization is often used to capture what digitization does to physical objects such as a book. Strictly speaking it is incorrect as a designation for digitization, since the latter is merely a different type of materiality.

Representing such an object as hypermobile is, then, a partial representation since it includes only some of the components of that object, that is, those that can be digitized at a given time. Much of what is liquefied and circulates in digital networks and is marked by hypermobility is only one component of a larger entity that remains physical in some of its components.[24]

In turn, much place-boundedness is today increasingly—though not completely—inflected or inscribed by the hypermobility of some of its components, products, and outcomes. More than in the past, both capital fixity and mobility are located in a temporal frame where speed is ascendant and consequential. This type of capital fixity cannot be fully captured through a description confined to its material and locational features, that is, through a topographical description (Sassen 2001: chapters 2 and 5). The real estate industry illustrates some of these issues. Financial firms have invented instruments that liquefy real estate, thereby facilitating investment in real estate and its "circulation" in global markets. Even though the physical remains part of what constitutes real estate, it has been transformed by the fact that it is represented by highly liquid instruments that can circulate in global markets. It may look the same, it may involve the same bricks and mortar, it may be new or old, but it is a transformed entity.

We have difficulty capturing this multivalence through our conventional categories: if it is physical, it *is* physical; and if it is hypermobile, it *is* that. In fact, the partial representation of real estate through liquid financial instruments produces a complex imbrication of the physical and the digitized moments of that which we continue to call real estate. And so does the partial endogeneity of physical infrastructure in electronic financial markets. I use the term imbrication to capture this simultaneous interdependence and specificity of each the digital and the nondigital. They work on each other but they do not produce hybridity. Each maintains its distinct irreducible character.

The Destabilization of Older Hierarchies of Scale

The many imbrications of the digital with the nondigital brings with it a destabilization of older hierarchies of scale and often dramatic rescalings.

---

[24] Much of my work on global cities (2001) has been an effort to conceptualize and document that the global digital economy requires massive concentrations of material conditions in order to be what it is. Finance is an important intermediary in this regard: it represents a capability for liquefying various forms of non-liquid wealth and for raising the mobility (i.e., hypermobility) of that which is already liquid.

This functions on at least two levels, one politico-administrative and the other, more theoretically, through the reconstituting of territorialities.

As the national scale loses specific components of the state's formal authority, other scales gain strategic importance, especially subnational scales, such as the global city, and supranational scales, such as global markets. This does not mean that the old hierarchies disappear but that various practices and institutional arrangements produce a rescaling of at least some of the old hierarchies of scale. These new rescalings can often trump the latter.

Existing theory is not enough to map today's multiplication of non-state actors and forms of cross-border cooperation and conflict, such as global business networks, NGOs, diasporas, global cities, transboundary public spheres, and the new cosmopolitanisms. International relations (IR) theory has had the most to say about cross-border relations. But current developments associated with various mixes of globalization and the new information and communications technologies point to the limits of IR theory and data. Its models and theories remain focused on the logic of relations between states and the scale of the state at a time when we see a proliferation of non-state actors, cross-border processes, and associated changes in the scope, exclusivity, and competence of state authority over its territory, many partly enabled by these new technologies.

The transformations in the components of international relations and the destabilization of older hierarchies of scale can also be seen, more theoretically, as producing new types of territories. More precisely, these are territorialities in that they entail specific political, operational, or subjective encasements, including some that might be formalized and some that might remain informal. For example, much of what we might still experience as the "local" (an office building, a house, or an institution in our neighborhood or downtown) is something I would rather think of as a microenvironment with global span insofar as it is deeply inter-networked. Such a microenvironment is in many senses a localized entity, but it is also part of global digital networks, which give it immediate far-flung span. To continue to think of this as simply local is not useful. More important, the juxtaposition between the condition of being sited and having global span captures the imbrication of the digital and the nondigital and illustrates the inadequacy of a purely technological reading of the technical properties of digitization, which would lead us to posit the neutralization of the place-boundedness and thus of precisely what enables the condition of being sited, yet having global span.

A second example is the bundle of conditions and dynamics that marks the model of the global city. To single out one key dynamic: the more globalized and digitized the operations of firms and markets, the more their central management and coordination functions (and the requisite material structures) become strategic. It is precisely because of digitization that simultaneous worldwide dispersal of operations (whether factories, offices, or service outlets) and system integration can be achieved. And this combination raises the importance of central functions. Global cities are strategic sites for the combination of resources necessary for the production of these central functions. The cross-border network of global cities emerges as one of the key components in the architecture of "international relations."

Mediating Cultures of Use

There are multiple ways of examining the interactions between the new digital technologies and their users. There is a strong tendency in the literature to conceptualize the matter of use as an unmediated event, as unproblematized activity; the problematic moment, if it exists, is conceived of as having to do with access, technical competence, and interface design. In contrast, a longstanding concern with what I have called analytic borderlands[25] has led me to try to detect the mediations in the act of using the technologies. I have found that use is constructed or constituted in terms of specific cultures and practices through and within which users articulate the experience and utility of electronic space. Thus my concern is not with the purely technical features of digital networks and what these might mean for users, nor is it simply with its impact on users. The concern is, rather, with this in-between zone that constructs the articulations of cyberspace and users.

This conceptualization clearly rests on the earlier proposition that digital space is embedded and not a purely technological event. Thus this space is inflected by the values, cultures, power systems, and institutional orders within which it is embedded. If we were to explore these issues in terms of, for instance, gendering, or specifically the condition of the female subject, we would then posit that insofar as these various realms are marked by gendering, this embeddedness of cyberspace is also gendered at least in some of its aspects and, further, that so is cyberspace itself.[26] This is so even though there

---

[25] I develop the notion of analytic borderlands in chapter 8.

[26] Much of what has been described for cyberspace in the specialized and general literature is explicitly or implicitly far more likely to be about particular groups of men because these have thus far dominated usage and produced many of the cybercultures (e.g., Holloway and Valentine 2001). Thus we also need more information about men who do not fit those particular groups.

is enormous variability in this gendering by place, age, class, race, nationality, and issue orientation; at the same time, there are likely to be various situations, sites, and individuals not marked by gendering or by hybrid or queered genderings.

The second consequence of this embeddedness is that the articulations between electronic space and individuals—whether as social, political, or economic actors—are constituted in terms of mediating cultures; it is not simply a question of access and understanding how to use the hardware and software. Of interest here is the finding (Eickelman and Anderson 1999) that traditional scholars of the Koran can be far more sophisticated users than modern Muslim youth. When the former use the Internet for reading and interpretation they can hyperlink their way through a variety of annotated texts and add annotations, while the latter use it in a more elementary fashion, similar to most youth in the West (for checking Web sites, participating in chat rooms, shopping, and so on). The mediating culture present in the case of these traditional scholars leads them to use more of the technical capabilities available on the Internet. The "traditional" actor turns out to bring a more sophisticated culture of use to the new technologies than the "modern" actor.

NEW INTERACTIONS BETWEEN CAPITAL FIXITY

AND HYPERMOBILITY

Perhaps the most extreme example of how the digital might reveal itself to be indeed free of any spatial and, more concretely, territorial conditionalities is the case of complex derivatives trading markets. The mix of speed, interconnectivity, and enhanced leverage evinced by these electronic markets produce an image of global finance as hypermobile and placeless. Indeed, it is not easy to demonstrate that these markets are embedded in anything social.

The possibility of an almost purely technical domain autonomous from the social is further reinforced by the growing role played by academic financial economics in the invention of new derivatives, the most widely used instrument today. It has led to a growing notion that if anything these markets are embedded in academic financial economics. The latter has emerged since the 1980s as the shaper and legitimator, or the author and authorizer, of a new generation of derivatives (Callon 1998; MacKenzie 2002). Formal financial knowledge, epitomized by academic financial economics, is a key competitive resource in today's financial markets. Thus formal academic work in financial economics also represents the "fundamentals" of the market value of formal financial knowledge, that is, some of these instruments or models are more popular among investors than others.[27] Derivatives, in their many different modes, embody this knowledge and its market value.

But here I will argue that these technical capabilities along with the growing complexity of instruments produce a need for cultures of interpretation in the operation of these markets. (For a full development of the technical issues, see Sassen 2004.) Thus, and perhaps ironically, as the technical and academic features of derivatives trading markets and instruments become stronger, these cultures become more significant, in an interesting trade-off between technical capacities and cultural capacities. We can then use the need for these cultures of interpretation as an indicator of the limits of the academic embeddedness of derivatives and therewith recover the social architecture of derivatives trading markets. More specifically, it brings us back to the importance of financial centers—as distinct from financial "markets"—as key nested communities enabling the construction and functioning of such cultures of interpretation. The need for financial centers also, then, explains why the financial system needs a network of such centers. This need, in turn, carries implications for territorially bounded authority and signals the formation of a specific type of territoriality, one marked by electronic networks and territorial insertions. I see here an interesting parallel with the notion developed in chapter 2 about a medieval political economy of urban territoriality centered on trading networks and cities.

Developing these issues requires a somewhat detailed and technical examination of features of derivatives trading markets that are not commonly part of the representation of these markets as hypermobile and placeless, and as consisting of digital networks and digitized instruments. Much of this detail reads somewhat like a detour from the main issues that concern me in this

---

[27] Thus the model designed for Long Term Capital Management (LTCM) was considered to be not only a significant innovation but brilliant. It engendered many followers who adopted similar arbitrage strategies, despite the fact that LTCM did its best to conceal its strategies (MacKenzie 2003). In MacKenzie and Millo's (2003) discussion of the success of the theory of option pricing (Black-Scholes) in the Chicago Board Options Exchange, they argue that this model was empirically successful because of two factors. First, the markets gradually changed so that the assumptions of the model became increasingly realistic. The empirical world was shaped by changes such as alterations of Regulation T, the increasing acceptability of stock borrowing, and better communications, to name a few. Second, interlocking cultural and economic processes gradually reduced different barriers to the model's widespread use. As MacKenzie stresses, the performativity of this model was not automatic but "a contested, historically contingent outcome, ended by a historical event, the crash of 1987" (2003: 138).

book. But it is necessary to bring to light what might be some of the limits, frictions, and lumpiness in this apparently seamless space of circulation. Chapter 5 began to address some of these issues from an institutional perspective. Here I focus on the technical aspects of market operation and supervision as a way to get at what is at the heart of my concern here: the extent to which and the ways in which global finance has a far more complex interaction with territory and state authority than is captured in mainstream representations.

A New Generation of Markets and Instruments

The electronic linking of markets (both nationally and globally), the accelerated rise in innovations enabled by both financial economics and digitization, and the sharp growth in the use of a particular type of financial instrument, the derivative, have come together in ways that have launched a new phase in financial markets. The diversification and dominance of derivatives has raised the complexity of operations and has further facilitated the linking of different financial markets. Just to give a sense of orders of magnitude, in 2001, the average daily turnover in foreign exchange markets was equal to almost one-fifth of the total value of world trade for that whole year.[28] The possibility of digitizing complex financial trading instruments has brought with it at least three distinctive capabilities. First is the capability to reduce the instrument to a piece of software (softwaring, for short), which means that use can be far more widespread than if it required detailed knowledge about financial economics and the technicalities of electronic networks. The software itself embodies the theory of academic financial economics and the code contains the technicalities of the software. Second, softwaring has, in turn, enabled a second capability in that increases in the complexity of the instrument do not constitute a barrier to use. It allows users who might not fully grasp either the mathematics or the software design issues to be effective in their deployment of the instruments. This fosters increasingly greater uses of these instruments, including newly integrated participants from around the world. Third, the increased use of derivatives, in turn, has facilitated and furthered the linking of diverse national markets by making it easier to exploit price differences (that is, arbitrage) between different financial instruments, thereby enabling an incentive (or utility function) to take on the added complexities of trading across markets. As these markets have globalized,

---

[28] WTO 2003; BCBS 1999. Author's calculations.

derivatives have continued to be the key instrument used for an increasingly diverse set of market operations. Derivatives are specifically designed to manage risk and thus are a key instrument in the functioning of today's financial markets. In an environment of electronically linked and globalized markets and rapid innovations, risk and uncertainty assume specific meanings and weight. This, in turn, partly explains why derivatives have become the most widely used financial instrument. Such an environment raises the demand for the development of new, often increasingly complex types of derivatives to handle risk and uncertainty.[29]

There are two features about derivatives that matter for my argument here. The first, frequently overlooked both in general commentaries as well as in more academic treatments, is that the distinctive feature of derivatives is not so much that they reduce risk, as is commonly believed, but that they transfer it to less risk-sensitive sectors in the economy. This aspect is easily lost in academic fields centered on firms. Insofar as firms remain central to a model, it makes sense to confine observation to the fact that firms use derivatives to hedge and thereby reduce their risks. This is correct, but only partially.

What has been left out of this picture, I argue, is that in the context of electronically linked markets and an absolute predominance of derivatives as the instrument of choice in today's financial markets, the transfer of risk by individual firms becomes a collective transfer of risk to the market. In so doing derivatives trading produces a network effect that is a new type of risk: market risk. This is the second feature that matters for my analysis here.

The crucial contextual variable contributing to this network effect is that derivatives are used by firms in all financial markets and account for the vast majority of financial transactions. As individual firms export risk via the use of derivatives in a context of the widespread use of these instruments and of electronically interconnected markets, the result is market risk. This type

---

[29] The growing importance of academic econometric modeling produces, in turn, a new type of risk. Thus today a good part of risk management involves what has come to be called "model risk," that is risk associated with modeling. It first appeared in the mid-1990s, as a component of a new generation of financial risk management systems for the financial derivatives industry. Indeed, a New York–based financial consultancy Capital Market Risk Advisors recently estimated that 40 percent of total derivatives related trading losses were due to modeling errors, which amounted to $2.7 billion in 1997 (Stix 1998: 97). Model risk has been defined as a kind of financial risk that "results from the inappropriate specification of a theoretical model or the use of an appropriate model but in an inadequate framework or for the wrong purpose" (Gibson-Asner et al. 1998: 5). In other words, it involves the particular risks and uncertainties associated with formal scientific work (modeling, estimating, and testing) in the economics of financial markets activity.

of risk is not bounded by a firm as in credit risk, the major category of risk in much economics and in economic sociology. It can affect all firms via the network. That is to say, market risk produces a distinct type of interdependence, one not associated with or conceptualized for producer markets and their interfirm networks: financial firms are part of a network within which they as individual firms transfer risk to the network but collectively experience the aggregate effects of risk transfer as market risk.[30] The management of risk becomes, then, crucial both for firms and for markets.

Managing Risk in Global Financial Markets

Insofar as market risk is an increasingly important feature of financial markets and is in good part an outcome of the aggregate decisions by firms to transfer risk, the regulation of finance has partly been reoriented to supervising how firms manage risk (rather than regulating a firm's capital reserves and debt levels). At the same time, the rise in value at risk in the globally integrated market for capital, the added velocity of transactions, accelerated innovation, and rising complexity of the academic models involved in major financial instruments have all made external supervision increasingly challenging. Supervision in this context requires vast resources and enormous numbers of talented financial economists— who can of course reap far larger rewards by working for firms instead of external supervisory agencies. By expanding the possibilities for accommodating academic financial economics in widely used instruments, digitization has, in turn, added to the challenges of external supervision.

One overall consequence has been the considerable instability in the regime for external supervision over the last decade. An indication of the challenges for external supervision engendered by the increasing use of these instruments in the 1990s was the inability of the existing regime to cope with

---

[30] Insofar as producer markets become increasingly articulated with capital markets directly or indirectly (via the financializing of their operations, i.e., their use of complex derivative packages to hedge the firm's risk), they also can experience this network effect. An example of this articulation occurs with gold mining companies and gold markets (R. Harvey 2003). Producers will engage in hedging in order to lock in a favorable price for future output (this hedging can vary from 10 to 20 percent of future production; some companies hedge 100 percent of their production). This hedging can be a significant source of profit. In 1990, for instance, gains from hedging accounted for nearly a third of mining company profits. Some analysts argue that hedging depresses the current gold price. As this example shows, the securitization of gold (such as the use of gold forwards or futures) allows producer and financial markets to be increasingly interwoven.

its supervisory functions and the consequent need for restructuring. The earlier, more traditional system for external supervision was well embodied in the 1988 Basel Capital Accord (BCA), which called for harmonizing national banking capital standards, including a set of common procedural rules and a system of direct external supervision known as the "standards approach" (BCBS 1988).[31] The "standards approach" corresponds to the conceptualization of credit risk as centered on firms. The BCA strictly focused on the regulation of "credit risk capital requirements"—the amount of capital that must be set aside to insure banks' bottom lines against risks of credit defaults.

Only two years later the supervisory norms of the BCA had become outdated by the new investment practices, notably massive exchange-traded and over-the-counter (OTC) derivatives trading. The regular failures of compliance to mandatory and universal supervisory standards signaled the incipient problem of market risk precautionary capital, which refers to capital that serves as a guarantee for depositors (Izquierdo 2001: 75) from the risk of losses in on- and off-balance sheet positions arising from movements in market prices. The risks included in this term are those pertaining to interest rate related instruments and equities in the trading book, and foreign exchange risk and commodities risk throughout the bank. In 1996 a new supervisory regime was developed, the so-called 1996 Amendment to the BCA (ABCA), which came into force in January 1997. The new supervisory regime is important to my analysis as it has the effect of reinserting firms into trading markets and is one of the building blocks for arguing the importance of financial centers to the global financial system.

The new supervisory regime reinserts firms as crucial actors, but via the supervisory regime rather than the coordination functions of interfirm networks in producers markets.[32] Rather than charging external supervisors with establishing the adequacy of a firm's capital reserves, the new supervisory regime makes the firm itself responsible for demonstrating the adequacy of its risk assessment models, that is, how the firm itself evaluates the risk level of

---

[31] This required banks to raise their reserves to at least 8 percent of total assets weighted by risk class.

[32] From the perspective of the new economic sociology of finance it is also interesting in that it reintroduces firms in trading markets where the latter have been conceptualized (e.g. Cetina and Bruegger 2002) as centered on trading floors rather than firms, unlike producer markets. But firms are here reintroduced as sites for the external supervisory system, making for a qualification rather than a rebuttal of the trading markets model. This qualification contributes to a distinction within trading markets between spot (currency) trading and exchanges-centered trading (complex derivatives). See Sassen (2004) for an elaboration.

its trading. The target now is the financial services firm's own internal control systems, not its actual investment portfolio and capital reserves (as in credit risk management). The burden of proof is on the financial firm: it now needs to show that its model is sound, rather than simply that its reserves are adequate (BCBS 1996a: 8). Further, rather than continuously having to upgrade its capabilities to stay abreast of developments in firms, the new external supervisory model integrates the organizational know-how of the derivatives industry itself by asking firms to use their own internal risk measurement models and their own computerized systems of firm-wide risk management to determine for themselves the proper quantity of market risk capital reserves (BCBS 1996b: 38–50).[33] The advisory report contains a series of standard statistical countertrials or "backtests" for establishing the performance of a firm's internal model for risk assessment in relation to actual risk levels in the market (BCBS 1996a). These backtests consist of a periodic comparison of a bank's daily value-at-risk measures with the subsequent daily profit or loss (the trading outcome). In doing this, the bank essentially counts the number of times the trading outcome is not covered by the risk measure. The risk measure is designed to estimate the quantity that could be lost on a set of positions due to general market movements over a given holding period, measured using the specified confidence level of the ninety-ninth percentile (BCBS 1996a). This puts the responsibility for "external supervision" on the firm itself through the requirement to maintain and improve the effectiveness of the firm's internal model.[34] This new supervisory regime for market

[33] The 1996 BIS rules established a series of requirements for firms' internal risk management systems. These requirements call for initial validation by national external supervisors of a firm's model followed by periodic revisions. In addition, the 1996 amendment added a complementary advisory report with criteria for testing firms' value at risk internal models (BCBS 1996a), which were meant to strengthen the incentives for firms to adopt high quality and to raise the accuracy of their models. This adds costs to a firm's operations for the needed research and development and talent.

[34] Many of the internal risk control systems developed by firms active in global derivatives markets are based on the application of a class of generalized equilibrium asset-pricing econometric models known as Value-at-Risk models (VaR). These are proprietary risk management software, e.g., Riskmetrics originally codified by JPMorgan, or RaRoc2020 a computer application (Falloon 1998). These are two common procedures. The basic principle of VaR management is the daily calculation of a broad, aggregate figure of maximum potential losses. This model had been developed within the community of the biggest Wall Street investment banks since the October 1987 stock market crash. VaR models tackle a specific computational problem: how to determine the maximum financial loss, expected with a significant probability for a given confidence level, that could be suffered by a properly diversified asset portfolio during a given period of time as a consequence of an adverse and pronounced movement in financial prices coordinated across different markets, instruments, maturities, or countries (Jorion 1997: 86–93).

risk capital reserves is known as the "internal models approach" (Jorion 1997: 50). To complete the regulatory regime, national supervisory authorities are asked to conduct quarterly examinations of the forecasting performance of a firm's models.[35]

There is an interesting sociology of a collective action problem in this shift. On the one hand, the resources of firms themselves, rather than state or public sector resources, are deployed in the name of a public function (regulation). This public function is enabled and partly resourced through firms' private and proprietary information and models, as well as through the multiple resources firms need for functioning in highly competitive and speculative markets. These are all resources that firms have developed over often long periods of time for handling risk management. On the other hand, this public function derives its supervisory logic from the firm's own logic for trading—competitive advantage strengthened by raising the quality of its risk management system. There lies in this set of correspondences between actors on opposite sides of a regulatory divide an interesting, albeit partial, solution to a collective action problem. It also signals one way in which state authority—in this case a highly specialized type of authority—can use the resources of power and highly mobile global firms to do its work.

The Need for Technical Cultures of Interpretation

The limits of the academic embeddedness of derivatives trading become evident in two specific ways. One is the increasing recognition by both financial experts and traders that key mathematical and statistical assumptions built into standard neoclassical pricing models do not adequately represent the dynamics of derivatives trading markets (see note 36). The other is the fact of—and response by both firms and supervisors to—ambiguous results when testing the accuracy and effectiveness of firms' risk assessment models. This has led to the development of a particular type of interpretation of a model's failure to forecast a given outcome: interpretations that aim at

---

[35] The new supervisory system puts pressure on firms to adopt the often costly measures to improve the accuracy of their internal risk management systems. The central logic organizing supervision is guaranteeing that a firm's VaR figures of aggregate financial risk comply with some minimum econometric reliability requirements. In principle this requires firms continually to improve internal risk management systems by heavily investing in human capital and research and development (Dunbar 2000).

explaining away the outcome. In both cases there is a gap between a firm's model and market reality.

In what follows I examine the features of this gap and argue that the ways in which the gap is addressed point to the weight of cultures of interpretation as to what is acceptable risk and what is an acceptable level of deviation between models and market reality. But cultures of interpretation are not invented on the spot. They are complex formations with often thick histories. Financial centers are complex environments that have nurtured such cultures of interpretation and can intermediate between national cultures and the new global standards and norms.

The debate in the academic and trading community demonstrates the limits of technical modeling of a firm's value at risk.[36] Further, it shows that this holds no matter how sophisticated the academic economic knowledge deployed.[37] The debate divides along two lines on this point. One side accepts the assumptions as valid and explains failures in modeling risk assessments as resulting from exceptional events. The other side argues that the basic assumptions are faulty in that they fail to represent the dynamics of financial markets; hence the division between randomness, as captured in basic statistical assumptions, and exceptional events is a false one.

Which side is closer to the actual dynamics of derivatives trading markets is of less importance to my argument here than the fact that it has

---

[36] The debate is an important one, but this is not the place to analyze it. Very briefly, one assumption in equilibrium asset-pricing models is that markets are composed of autonomous firms, where no single firm can significantly shape aggregate market prices. In fact, the history of financial markets is full of instances of what are typically referred to as contagion and herd behavior (e.g., Bevir and Trentmann 2004). Further, very large investors can at times "move the markets"; perhaps the most notorious case in recent history is the Soros Fund's investments that brought down the English pound in the context of the EU's Exchange Rate Mechanism, the predecessor to the current European single currency regime. The speculative currency trading by a limited number of hedge funds that brought down the Thai currency in August 1997 is another dramatic example. Yet another example is MacKenzie's understanding that "LTCM's success led to widespread imitation, and the imitation led to a 'superportfolio' of partially overlapping arbitrage positions. Sales by some holders of the superportfolio moved prices against others, leading to a cascade of self-reinforcing adverse price movements" (2003: 353). A second critical issue is the assumption in common financial models that economic information is a public good, available out there, and one would assume in the context of information technologies (IT), characterized by distributed forms of access.

[37] While it is indeed possible that the issue is one of the quality of this knowledge, the additional high quality (that is, the growing incidence of academic financial economics) that has characterized the development of new models since the 1980s has not reduced the gap between models and market reality if we consider the financial crises of some of the top-level firms using some of the most sophisticated models.

become clear that academic financial economics cannot fully account for how financial markets actually work—whether that is because exceptional events are not infrequent in these markets or because the fundamental assumptions in equilibrium asset pricing models are inadequate.[38]

Whatever the genesis, this deficiency is of interest because it also helps explain the second feature that signals the limits of academic embeddedness: the need of both firms and supervisors for the construction of interpretations that explain away ambiguity in assessment results. This need for interpreting on grounds other than the features of the model can also be seen as an indicator of the limits of academic models. The unexplained gap needs to be recognized and rationalized to make the machinery of risk assessment and external supervision function properly. If it cannot be explained away, then the firm has to invest additional resources to raise the quality of its model, or even scrap it, which is both significant and costly.

Much of the effort of both the supervisor and the firm is due to the fact that the quality of the risk assessment models used by firms is a critical issue in the functioning of derivatives trading markets. It is not simply a technical matter that affects an individual firm's success, as would be the case in credit risk. A firm's decision about allocating resources for higher quality models is also part of a collective action problem since firms in derivatives trading markets are transferring risk to the market. In principle, the poorer their models, the more unnecessary risk they transfer. In this sense poor models can create conditions under which there is the potential for greater overall financial loss and market volatility and, at the limit, conditions under which shocks can be exacerbated.[39]

---

[38] Although for my purposes here the genesis of the deficiency does not matter, the implications of each explanation are significant for the role of academic financial economics in derivatives trading markets. In the first case, academic economics can be seen as crucial in that a refinement of the models might produce a closer fit with actual market functioning and, in principle, account for the occurrence, if not the characteristics, of exceptional events. The same would hold for supervisory testing of firms' models. In the second case, the gap between the fundamental assumptions of the models, i.e., statistically defined randomness, and the fundamental features of financial markets, i.e., wild randomness, cannot be bridged by the currently prevalent type of academic financial economics model, and would, furthermore, pose serious problems for both firms' risk assessment and external supervision.

[39] There is an interesting parallel here with the work and impact of credit rating agencies. Their fallibility is well-known and has become especially sharp with the globalizing of firms and markets. At the same time, even when their evaluation is incorrect, the effect of a positive rating seems to have a life of its own—often of about six months. One might see here a self-fulfilling prophecy at work (Merton 1968).

Within this process of risk assessment I want to single out two phases of interpretation. The first phase contains a set of interpretive processes in the functioning of, respectively, a firm's risk assessment and external supervision. These processes recover social action in what is represented as a technical operation. In this regard these processes can be conceived of as indicators of this need for interpretation.[40] One concerns the setting of a confidence level in the firm's risk assessment model and the establishment of the least probable outcomes; the other concerns the supervisory assessment's confidence level. These are both clearly technical issues, but they are shaped by notions of what is acceptable risk and these notions have, in turn, changed over time.[41] As I discussed briefly in the preceding section, theoretical VaR measures are meant to encompass all trading outcomes expected at the end of the day, allowing for a very limited number of exceptions considered the least probable outcomes.[42]

The second phase of interpretation kicks in when these various tests produce outcomes that cannot be accepted or rejected with certainty. These are outcomes where the exceptions are more than those allowed by the established confidence level and in that regard fail to fit the risk forecasts of the model but at the same time do not necessarily represent an evidently significant deviation. Thus an ambiguous result is one that shows more than two exceptions but not a particularly large number of them. The Basel Committee on Banking Supervision (BCBS) developed a series of quantitative criteria to address them. It identified three clusters of such criteria: a safety zone covering up to four exceptions (the green zone), a caution zone between five and nine exceptions (the yellow zone), and a danger zone of ten or more exceptions (the red zone). When the committee sets these three zones it is engaging in interpretation. There are, then, not only the problems of supervisory

---

[40] The BIS (BCBS 1999, 1996b) supplementary documents provide detailed information concerning the rules of conduct for firms in the elaboration of risk assessment models and interpretations of ambiguous results as well as supervisors' tests and their interpretations of ambiguous results (see also Jorion 1997; Smithson 1998).

[41] Pertinent here is also the literature on the changing contents of what is acceptable risk or procedure in highly technical domains, such as accounting for global corporate firms. In considering the evidence on the matter, it is quite clear that beginning in the 1980s we can see a transformation in some of the features of accounting practice at its most complex levels. (For a general overview, see Picciotto and Mayne 1999; for the case of banks, see Maxfield 1997.) This is particularly the case for U.S. firms.

[42] The extent of exceptions allowed by the model is a function of the confidence level a firm uses to calibrate its model. For the supervisory authorities this level of confidence is set at 99 percent—that is to say, out of a total of 200 trading sessions for the year, a daily VaR calibrated for a 99 percent confidence level should cover 198 of the 200 trading outcomes in a given year, allowing for only two exceptions (BCBS 1996a: 4).

models or criteria to establish the quality of a firm's internal risk assessment models, but also the need to develop criteria for ambiguous results. Both require interpretive work, albeit in a highly technical language.

Firms also engage in interpretation when explaining these types of results, and they are allowed to go beyond technical issues. While firms may frame this as explaining and as involving knowledge, we need to ask to what extent it is a matter of knowing or interpreting. Firms are asked to supply supplementary information about their models as well as trading outcomes their models failed to foresee. The burden of proof is on the firm to show that its model is sound (BCBS 1996a: 8). Firms are allowed to submit considerable additional information. They need not confine their supporting evidence to quantitative or technical material. They can, and do, submit information in the public domain, such as newspaper reports about a major social or policy change or a devastating explosion in any pertinent country. At the limit, firms are allowed to explain away every negative outcome on a case-by-case basis invoking exceptional events exogenous to financial markets. The technicalities of the model can thus escape blame and the firm's model can be "protected."[43] The objective is to demonstrate that the exception was completely unpredictable and hence could not have been factored into the model. Here we see the work inside firms of interpreting ambiguous test results, leaving behind the technicalities of their models and incorporating all types of information to explain the outcome in a way that does not disqualify the model or point to its shortcomings.[44]

If we use the concept of framing (Goffman 1974; Callon 1998) we can recognize these two phases as processes of interpretation (R. Harvey 2003). Within these phases framing occurs, first, in the construction of the

[43] A parallel logic can also be deployed regarding credit ratings.

[44] Depending on one's interpretation of the event, this can be well illustrated by what we now know as the perfect financial storm: the decision by LTCM to produce justificatory arguments to the U.S. government's inquiry after the private bailout of the fund. The partners argued that Russia's default on its ruble-denominated bonds triggered a "flight to quality" in financial markets. This was the exceptional event that explained the crisis at LTCM, an event they could not have foreseen. There are other interpretations than those produced by LTCM. One of these finds the partners were guilty of reckless risk taking. This led the fund to finance its positions too frequently through borrowing, rather than using its own capital. According to Dunbar, it was not the Russian bonds default in 1998 presented by LTCM as the exceptional event but the growing management prominence conceded to the firms' in-house VaR software, Risk Aggregator. While there is no consensus, we now know that it either did not work properly, was misused by the LTCM partners—none of whom now accepts responsibility—or, as Dunbar (2000) suggests, produced market effects outside the control of the firm itself. MacKenzie (2003: 352) explains the crisis in terms of a "superportfolio" effect. See also President's Working Group on Financial Markets (1999).

model itself given that the model frames the firm's risk. Second, framing also occurs when that model fails since an adjustment of the model's frame is required.[45] As Goffman notes (1974), social life is organized (both in terms of meaning and the actual material organization) so that a single event can be interpreted in multiple ways. This can be accomplished through framing as individuals use conventions (keys) to create various interpretations of actions.[46] Callon reminds us, however, that this framing is never complete as the elements used to construct the frame always have networks of connections to the outside world (1998: 249). This means that actors will constantly have to deal with the threat of overflow (or externalities in the language of economics) with their frames. The exceptions to the VaR models, therefore, can be seen as forms of overflow, which then require the work of interpretation in order to preserve and/or adjust the frame (that is, the model).

For both firms and supervisors the work of framing and interpreting the quality of a firm's model, especially given ambiguous results, is at least partly enabled by the existence of a broader interpretive financial culture that provides norms and authoritativeness. Such a culture can be conceived of as containing specialized narratives about what is and what is not safe, as well as what is and what is not appropriate behavior by firms and their employees (Abolafia 1996).[47] A reasonable counterfactual here would be to posit that given the catastrophic financial crises produced by highly speculative

[45] This idea of the model being a frame is supported by the fact of the considerable amount of resources that go into constructing these models. The setting up of qualitative and quantitative standards for producing these models is an example of the work required to bracket this form of risk (BCBS 1996b).

[46] Callon also uses this idea of framing and notes that a frame "establishes a boundary within which interactions—the significance and content of which are self-evident to the protagonists—take place more or less independently of their surrounding context" (1998: 249). Although he focuses more on the creation of calculative agents and how economists engage in framing, his understanding of framing can be applied to understanding how these models are social products of specific technical cultures of interpretation.

[47] Abolafia discusses these cultures in his chapter on bond traders. One possible explanation he gives for the opportunistic scripts in the bond market is that certain changes created an almost anomic situation. He suggests that with the floating of exchange rates in the 1980s, bond markets grew in volume and volatility and that the Reagan administration signaled a policy shift such that regulatory oversight was being reduced. This meant there was more trading and traders. More specifically, he notes, "The firms expanded their trading floor operations so rapidly that it became increasingly difficult to socialize trainees to the unwritten scripts and the institutional rules defining the limits of opportunism" (1996: 22). MacKenzie and Millo also draw attention to shifting norms in markets in their article on the Chicago Board Options Exchange. For instance, they note that when the Chicago Board of Trade began to promote the idea of options trading with the Securities and Exchange Commission, they encountered hostility toward this idea, "based upon corporate memory of the role options played in the malpractices of the 1920s" (2003: 114).

investments in the 1990s, the most speculative sectors of finance should not be allowed to continue to exist given their devastating effect on vast portions of the economy in many countries. One might argue that the equivalent level of destruction for a particular pharmaceutical product, for instance, would have led to its banning. Banning is, in fact, what many traditional financial sectors argued was the best way to proceed with some of the financial innovations of the 1980s, notably the so-called junk bonds. A similar response occurred when "vulture funds" made their appearance in the mid-1990s (IMF 1999; see appendix to chapter 5).

Enabling the development of innovative instruments and making their use acceptable requires both technical and cultural work. The innovativeness in the financial sector in the 1980s broke with old norms and rules: it represented a drastic wave of change in the traditions and common practices of the financial markets.[48] This eruption of new concepts and new rules beginning in the 1980s was decisively enabled by the existence of an increasingly transnationalized subculture of mostly young financial professionals who were knowledgeable about the pertinent mathematics and computer software and who were not rooted in older traditions in the financial sector.[49] They understood and developed the new formula for playing the financial markets; further, through their own global mobility or that of their firms, they helped these new instruments circulate, that is, they created a demand for them and found buyers. This global technical professional subculture is constituted both at the global scale and through the thick and complex environments of financial centers, a subject briefly developed in chapter 6 through the lens of global classes. Through their transactions and their new conceptions these professionals

---

[48] Questions of risk are not simply numerical and technical. They involve an entire set of understandings about the form and content of financial markets and their instruments. These understandings, furthermore, are not produced in a vacuum but instead involve debates between particular social groups with varying norms about what are legitimate financial instruments and practices. Finally, the eventual acceptance of many of the innovations initially greeted with disdain if not horror, points to the (at least partly) socially constructed character of definitions of acceptable risk.

[49] Abolafia's examination of conflicts between older and newer orders in financial markets points to these types of issues. He notes that traders of "low quality" bonds such as Michael Milliken, challenged existing norms in financial markets. These traders were "deviant" since they developed innovative means for financing that were outside the current accepted practices in markets. Abolafia argues that the case of junk bonds "is a story of deviant innovation and deep social conflict in the financial community . . . a conflict which the protagonists continue to offer competing and alternative interpretations of what happened" (1996: 155). MacKenzie and Millo note a similar process in the case of derivatives. In this case they recognize the role of economics in, "disembedding derivatives from the pervasive moral framework in which they were dangerously close to wagers" (2003: 139). They also stress that this disembedding did not leave a social vacuum. Instead, it helped create room for the emergence of new norms about financing methods.

contributed to a global technical culture that contained as key features new interpretations of what is acceptable financial practice. There is considerable evidence showing that top-level managers in the firms often lagged in knowledge and understanding of the mathematics and the algorithms involved, thereby giving this new stratum of financial professionals considerable room for implementing their innovations and rules of the game.[50] The developments of the 1990s in the derivatives trading financial markets represent yet another phase of new concepts and new rules. There were additional innovations in the design of instruments and finer risk calibrations enabling historically unprecedented levels of leveraging, which in turn mobilized another whole new class of financial professionals.

The issue I want to extricate from these microhistories of financial innovations and the formation of new concepts of what works is the need for specialized cultures that can construct the narratives as to what is and is not safe. This is a narrative that sharply widens the meaning of what is acceptable risk and does so not only through the technical apparatus of financial economics that is usually invoked but also through social systems.[51] The network of firms involved in derivatives trading markets becomes the institutional home for a formal global regulatory system and an informal global culture of interpretation. The macroscale gets constituted through global markets and the global systems at work in the functioning of these markets—the global supervisory system, as well as global professional technical (that is, neoclassical financial economics) and interpretive cultures in finance.

But each of these global formations is partially filtered through the specifics of the financial and business centers that are part of the global capital market. These centers are the local environments crucial for the operation of global derivatives trading markets, no matter how global and electronic

[50] This led to several major disasters. The most notorious case was that of one trader who brought the respectable Barings Bank down by overleveraging his investments. It is not necessarily the case that fraudulent intentions were at work but rather a speculative furor enabled by lack of senior supervisory capability.

[51] This holds not only for the particular complex derivatives trading markets; there are many different versions of such specialized cultures at the heart of markets. For instance, one study on the "making" of the EU single market captures the fact that it was a decisively sociopolitical process (Fligstein and Mara-Drita 1996). The shape of this market was not the product of abstract market forces but involved active work by social actors to create and mobilize support for a particular type of single market. Salzinger's (2003) study of peso-dollar traders draws attention to how trading, which traditionally is seen to be the domain of rational, utility maximizing actors engaging in a technical, cost-benefit analysis of different trading possibilities, is actually a form of social action. Although she does not focus on interpreting the results of "backtesting" VaR models, Salzinger draws attention to the importance of traders' nationality in interpreting current and future price movements in the peso-dollar market.

these markets are. In this way local social processes and practices at the sub-national level constitute one of the scales for the operation of global structures. Financial centers, to be distinguished from financial exchanges, ground and instantiate the global dimensions of trading and supervision. They are complex and thick environments containing systems of trust (e.g., Zaloom 2003; Martin 2002) and shared cultures of interpretation. Financial centers enable the local and global collaborations among firms that are a key part of many large financial transactions and often evolve into cooperative interfirm networks.[52]

A financial center is, therefore, more akin to a "production" center than a shopping mall. Where Harrison White emphasizes the gathering of information as an important part of producer markets, I emphasize the importance of "constructing" information in derivatives trading markets. Financial centers are the environments where this constructing of information can take place. Watching and constructing information is part of the constitutive dynamics of the cultures of interpretation that concern me here. What takes place and gets produced in individual firms can accumulate into a distinctive scale, a social form. Both the cultures of interpretation as well as what gets represented as authoritative information are examples of the dynamics of accumulation in financial centers. In this context, the financial center is a very particular enabling environment.

We can isolate three distinct sets of features of financial centers in the face of global electronic markets and international standardization. First, they facilitate the circulation of innovations and the production of new norms as to what is acceptable risk, and they can socialize firms and supervisors alike into both. Second, the financial center can ensure the operation (performativity) of global standards and rules pertinent to financial markets. The third feature concerns the national character of financial centers. The supervisory practices contain some elements that signal the importance of global dynamics and others that point to the weight of local or national dynamics. Among the first is the fact that insofar as these are global markets, then at least some of the specialized cultures that enable these complex and often innovative instruments to circulate must be global.[53] Among the second is the fact that the global supervisory system is in good part implemented through national supervisory authorities and personnel. The second feature

---

[52] There is a growing body of evidence that documents the importance of social networks for the efficient operation of electronic networks (Garcia [2002] provides a good overview).

[53] See, e.g., Sklair 2001; see also pp. 298–301 in this book.

interests me here, one magnified by the fact that the supervisors are also dealing largely, though not exclusively, with co-national managers and professionals in firms. Although supervisors and firms may represent opposite camps in
the process of supervision, this does not preclude a shared understanding
when it comes to interpreting ambiguous results. It may well help this work of
interpreting and of agreeing about these interpretations. This is particularly
true if we consider that financial centers are environments that can accommodate systems of trust and local specificities, no matter how global the firms
and exchanges in their midst.

These three features signal that the global network of financial centers can be shown to function as an aggregation of widely dispersed communities of practice within which these cultures of interpretation can be replicated
across the world even as each accommodates local features. We can conceive
of this process as a type of structural isomorphism that eventually produces a
global scale through recurrence—a networked global scale constituted hori-
zontally rather than through vertical integration. In turn, macrolevel structures (electronically linked markets, the global supervisory system, and global
technical and interpretive cultures in finance) enable this recurrence insofar
as these macrolevel structures partly instantiate in local environments. The
argument can be taken one step further. The quality of the interpretations of
ambiguous results by firms and supervisors is partly shaped by the larger environment of the financial center within which they function, but at the same
time the results of individual firms aggregate and partly produce the quality of
a center's culture of interpretation.[54] The evidence suggests that the degree of
liberties firms are allowed to take in explaining away negative outcomes
varies across centers and, within a center, across different times.[55] No matter
how globalized and electronic these markets are, there are variations across
centers as each center has a somewhat distinct subculture.

This type of analysis brings to the fore the importance of intermediary structures in the formation and functioning of global social forms such as

---

[54] This is evident in the design and implementation of international standards in
all financial centers integrated into the global markets, as well as in the growing international
pressure by BIS, often driven by U.S. regulators, to standardize criteria across the global network of centers.

[55] Thus Wall Street, New York's financial center, is generally recognized as having
high standards. Yet in the late 1980s and late 1990s it was home to some of the most flagrant
abuses in the interpretation of those standards. We are not referring to fraudulent abuse that represents a violation of the letter of the law but abuses of the spirit of the law that became normal
conduct across the board, engendering a culture of abuse that exploded when some of the firms
took it just one step too far. This points to the norm-making and circulation enabled by the thick
environment of a financial center.

electronic global markets. The particular intermediary structures here are nested cultures of interpretation and the thick environments that are financial centers.

A POLITICS OF PLACES ON GLOBAL CIRCUITS:

THE LOCAL AS MULTISCALAR

The issue I want to highlight here concerns the ways in which particular instantiations of the local can be constituted at multiple scales and thereby generate global formations that tend toward lateralized and horizontal networks rather than the vertical arrangements typical of entities such as the IMF or WTO. I examine this through a focus on diverse political practices and the technologies they use. Of particular interest is the possibility that local, often resource-poor organizations and individuals can become part of global networks and struggles. These practices are contributing to a specific type of global politics, one that runs through localities and is not predicated on the existence of global institutions. The engagement can be with global institutions, such as the IMF or WTO, or with local institutions, such as a particular government or local police force charged with human rights abuses. Theoretically these types of global politics illuminate the distinction between a global network and the actual transactions that constitute it: the global character of a network does not necessarily imply that its transactions are equally global. It shows the local to be multiscalar in a parallel to the preceding section, which showed the global to be multiscalar—that is, partly embedded in a network of localities, specifically, financial centers.

Computer-centered technologies have made all the difference here; in this case the particular form of these technologies is mostly the Internet.[56]

---

[56] While the Internet is a crucial medium in these political practices, it is important to emphasize that beginning in the 1990s, particularly since the mid-1990s we have entered a new phase in the history of digital networks in which powerful corporate actors and high-performance networks are strengthening the role of private digital space and altering the structure of public-access digital space (Sassen 2002). Digital space has emerged not simply as a means for communicating but as a major new theater for capital accumulation and the operations of global capital. Yet civil society—in all its various incarnations—is also an increasingly energetic presence in cyberspace. (For a variety of angles, see, e.g., Rimmer and Morris-Suzuki 1999; Poster 1997; Frederick 1993; Miller and Slater 2000.) The greater the diversity of cultures and groups the better for this larger political and civic potential of the Internet, and the more effective the resistance to the risk that the corporate world might set the standards. (For cases of information and communication technologies [ICT] use by different types of groups, see, e.g., APCWNSP 2000; Allison 2002; WomenAction 2000; Yang 2003; Camacho 2001; Esterhuysen 2000).

The Internet matters not only because of low-cost connectivity and the possibility of effective use (via e-mail) even with low bandwidth availability but
also because of some of its key features. Simultaneous decentralized access
can help local actors have a sense of participation in struggles that are not
necessarily global but are, rather, globally distributed in that they recur
across localities. In so doing these technologies can also help in the formation of cross-border public spheres for these types of actors and can do so
without the necessity of running through global institutions[57] and through
forms of recognition that do not depend on much direct interaction and
joint action on the ground. Among the implications of these options are the
possibility of forming global networks that bypass central authority and that
those who may never be able to travel can nonetheless be part of global
struggles and global publics. Distributed immobilities can actually come to
constitute a global public.

All of this is not historically new. Yet there are two specific matters
that signal the need for empirical and theoretical work on their ICT enabled
form. One is that much of the conceptualization of the local in the social sciences has assumed physical or geographic proximity and thereby a sharply defined territorial boundedness, with the associated implication of closure. The
other, partly a consequence of the first, is a strong tendency to conceive of the
local as part of a hierarchy of nested scales amounting to an institutionalized
hierarchy, especially once there are national states. To a very large extent
these conceptualizations hold for most of the instantiations of the local today,
more specifically, for most of the practices and formations, such as those examined in this chapter, likely to constitute the local in most of the world. But
there are also conditions that help destabilize these practices and formations
and hence invite a reconceptualization of the local that can accommodate a
set of instances that diverge from dominant patterns. Key among these current conditions are globalization and/or globality as constitutive not only of
cross-border institutional spaces but also of powerful imaginaries enabling aspirations to transboundary political practice even when the actors involved
are basically localized.

Computer-centered interactive technologies have played an important role, precisely in the context of globalization, including global imaginaries. These technologies facilitate multiscalar transactions and simultaneous interconnectivity among those largely confined to a locality. They can

[57] For instance, in centuries past organized religions had extensive, often global networks of missionaries and clerics. But these partly depended on the existence of a central
authority.

be used to further develop old strategies (e.g., Tsaliki 2002; Lannon 2002) and to develop new ways of organizing, notably electronic activism (Denning 1999; P. Smith 2001; Yang 2003). Internet media are the main type of ICT used. E-mail is perhaps the most widely used, partly because organizations in the global south often have little bandwidth and slow connections, making the Web a far less usable and effective option. To achieve the forms of globality that concern me in this chapter, it is important that there be a recognition of these constraints among major transnational organizations dealing with the global south: for instance, this means making text-only databases, with no visuals or HTML, no spreadsheets, and none of the other facilities that demand considerable bandwidth and fast connections (Pace and Panganiban 2002: 113; Sassen 2005).[58]

As has been widely recognized, new ICTs do not simply replace existing media techniques. The evidence is far from systematic and the object of study is continuously undergoing change. But we can basically identify two patterns. On the one hand it might mean no genuine need for these particular technologies given the nature of the organizing or it might come down to underutilization. (For studies of particular organizations, see, e.g., Tsaliki 2002; Lannon 2002).[59] For instance, a survey of local and grassroots human rights NGOs in several regions of the world found that the Internet makes information exchange easier and is helpful in developing other kinds of collaboration but that it did not help launch joint projects (Lannon 2002: 33). On the other hand, there is evidence of highly creative ways of using the new ICTs along with older media recognizing the needs of particular communities. A good example is using the Internet to send audio files that can then be broadcast over loudspeakers to groups who lack access to the Internet or are illiterate.

---

[58] There are several organizations that have taken on the work of adjusting to these constraints or providing adequate software and other facilities to disadvantaged NGOs. For instance, Bellanet (2002), a nonprofit set up in 1995, helps such NGOs gain access to online information and with information dissemination to the south. To that end it has set up Web-to-email servers that can deliver Web pages by e-mail to users confined to low bandwidth. It has developed multiple service lines. For example, Bellanet's Open Development service line seeks to enable collaboration among NGOs through the use of open source software, open content, and open standards; so it customized the Open Source PhP-Nuke software to set up an online collaborative space for the Medicinal Plants Network. Bellanet has adopted Open Content for all forms of contents on its Web site, freely available to the public, and supports the development of an open standard for project information (International Development Markup Language [IDML]). The value of such open standards is that they enable information sharing.

[59] In a study of the Web sites of international and national environmental NGOs in Finland, Britain, the Netherlands, Spain, and Greece, Tsaliki (2002: 102) concludes that the Internet is mainly useful for intra- and interorganizational collaboration and networking, mostly complementing existing media techniques for issue promotion and raising awareness.

The M. S. Swaminathan Research Foundation in southern India has supported this type of strategy by setting up Village Knowledge Centers catering to populations that although mostly illiterate, know exactly what types of information they need or want, for example, farmers and fishermen. When we consider mixed uses, it becomes clear that the Internet can often fulfill highly creative functions by being used with other technologies, whether old or new. Thus Amnesty International's International Secretariat has set up an infrastructure to collect electronic news feeds via satellite, which it then processes and redistributes to its staff workstations (Lebert 2002).

But there is also evidence that use of these technologies has led to the formation of new types of organizations and activism. For instance, Yang (2003) found that what were originally exclusively online discussions among groups and individuals in China concerned with the environment evolved into active NGOs. One result of this process of formation is that membership can almost automatically and from the start be national, distributed among different parts of the country. The diverse online hacktivisms examined by Denning (1999) are made up of mostly new types of activisms. To mention what is perhaps one of the most widely known cases of how the Internet made a strategic difference, the Zapatista movement became two organizational efforts, one a local rebellion in the mountains of Chiapas in Mexico, the other a transnational electronic civil society movement. The latter saw the participation of multiple NGOs concerned with peace, trade, human rights, and other social justice struggles. It functioned through both the Internet and conventional media (Cleaver 1998; Arquilla and Ronfeldt 2001), putting pressure on the Mexican government. It shaped a new concept for civil organizing: multiple rhizomatically connected autonomous groups (Cleaver 1998).

What is far less known is that the local rebellion of the Zapatistas operated basically without e-mail infrastructure (Cleaver 1998). Comandante Marcos was not on e-mail, let alone able to join collaborative workspaces on the Web. Messages had to be hand-carried, crossing military lines to bring them to others for uploading to the Internet; further, the solidarity networks themselves did not all have e-mail, and local communities sympathetic to the struggle often had problems with access (Mills 2002: 83). Yet Internet-based media did contribute enormously, in good part because of preexisting social networks, a fact that is important also in other contexts, including business (see Garcia 2002). Among the electronic networks involved, LaNeta played a crucial role in globalizing the struggle. LaNeta is a civil society network established with support of a San Francisco–based NGO, the Institute for Global Communication (IGC). In 1993 LaNeta became a member of the Association for Progressive Communications (APC) and began to function as a key connection between civil society organizations in and outside Mexico. In this regard, it is interesting to note that a local movement in a remote part of the country made LaNeta into a transnational information hub.

There is little doubt that gathering, storing, and disseminating information are crucial functions for these kinds of organizations (Meyer et al. 1997; Tuijl and Jordan 1999; Bach and Stark 2005). Human rights, large development, and environmental organizations are the leaders in the effort to build online databases and archives.[60] Oxfam has also set up knowledge centers on its Web site—specialized collections around particular issues, for example, the Land Rights in Africa site and its related resource bank (Warkentin 2001: 136). Specialized campaigns such as those against the WTO, for the banning of landmines, or for canceling the debt of the forty-one countries classified as hyper-indebted (the Jubilee 2000 campaign) have also been effective at this type of work since it is crucial for their campaigns. Special software can be designed to address the specific needs or organizations or campaigns. For example, the Human Rights Information and Documentation Systems International (HURIDOCS), a transnational network of human rights organizations, aims at improving access to, dissemination of, and use of human rights information. It runs a program to develop tools, standards, and techniques for documenting violations.

The evidence on NGO use of Internet media also shows the importance of institutional mechanisms and the use of appropriate software. Amnesty International has set up an institutional mechanism to help victims of human rights abuses use the Internet to contact transnational organizations for help: its Urgent Action Alert is a worldwide e-mail alerting system with seventy-five networks of letter-writing members who respond to urgent cases by immediate mailings to key and pertinent entities.[61]

All of this facilitates a new type of cross-border politics, deeply local yet intensely connected digitally. Adams (1996), among others, shows us how telecommunications create new linkages across space that emphasize the importance of networks of relations and partly bypass older hierarchies of scale.

---

[60] See, e.g., Human Rights Internet at *http://www.hri.ca*; Greenpeace's Web site at *http://www.greenpeace.org/usa*; and Oxfam's Web site at *http://www.oxfam.org*.

[61] Another, very different case is Oxfam America's effort to help its staff in the global south submit information quickly and effectively electronically, no easy aims in countries with unreliable, slow connections and other obstacles to working online. The aim was to help staff in the global south manage and publish information efficiently. To that end Oxfam adopted a server-side Content Management System and a client-side Article-Builder called Publ-X that allows end users to create or edit local XML articles while offline and submit them to the server when work has been completed; an editor on the server side is then promptly notified, ensuring that the information immediately becomes public.

Activists can develop networks for circulating place-based information (about local environmental, housing, political conditions) that can become part of political work and strategies addressing a global condition—the environment, growing poverty and unemployment worldwide, lack of accountability among multinationals, and so forth. The issue here is not so much the possibility of such political practices—they have long existed with other mediums and with other velocities. The issue is rather one of orders of magnitude, scope and simultaneity: the technologies, the institutions, and the imaginaries that mark the current global digital context inscribe local political practice with new meanings and new potentialities.[62] The dynamics are also at work in the constituting of global public spheres that may have little to do with specific political projects (Sack 2005); and they do not always work (Cederman and Kraus 2005).

There are many examples that illustrate the new possibilities and potentials for action. Besides some of the cases already discussed, there is the vastly expanded repertory of actions that can be taken when electronic activism is also an option. The New Tactics in Human Rights Project of the Center for Victims of Torture has compiled a workbook with 120 anti-torture tactics, including exclusively online forms of action (*www.newtactics.org/main.php*). The Web site of the New York–based Electronic Disturbance Theater, a group of cyberactivists and artists, contains detailed information about electronic repertories for action (*www.thing.net/~rdom/ecd/EDTECD.html*). The International Campaign to Ban Landmines, officially launched in 1992 by six NGOs from the United States, France, Britain, and Germany evolved into a coalition of over 1,000 NGOs in 60 countries. It succeeded when 130 countries signed the land mines ban treaty in 1997 (Williams and Goose 1998). The campaign used both traditional techniques and ICTs. Internet-based media provided mass distribution better and more cheaply than telephone and fax (Scott 2001; Rutherford 2002). Jubilee 2000 used the Internet to great effect. Its Web site brought together

---

[62] Elsewhere (Sassen 2002) I have posited that we can conceptualize these "alternative" networks as countergeographies of globalization because they are deeply implicated with some of the major dynamics and capabilities constitutive of, especially, economic globalization yet are not part of the formal apparatus or of the objectives of this apparatus, such as the formation of *global* markets. The existence of a global economic system and its associated institutional supports for cross-border flows of money, information, and people have enabled the intensifying of transnational and translocal networks and the development of communication technologies that can escape conventional surveillance practices. (Among the best critical and knowledgeable accounts, are WIO 2002; Nettime 1997; Lovink 2002; Rogers 2004) These countergeographies are dynamic and changing in their locational features. And they include a very broad range of activities, including a proliferation of criminal activities.

all the information on debt and campaign work considered necessary for the effort, and information was distributed via majordomo listserv, database, and e-mail address books.[63] Generally speaking preexisting online communication networks are important for these types of actions and for e-mail alerts aimed at quick mobilization. Distributed access is crucial: once an alert enters the network it spreads rapidly through the whole network. Amnesty's Urgent Action Alert described above is such a system. However, anonymous Web sites are definitely part of such communication networks: this was the case with S.11.org, a Web site that was used at the time for worldwide mobilizations as it was part of multiple online communication networks. The Melbourne mobilization against the regional Asian meeting of the World Economic Forum (WEF) (September 11–13, 2000) brought activist groups from around Australia together on this site to coordinate their actions, succeeding in paralyzing a good part of the gathering, a first in the history of the WEF meetings (Redden 2001). There are several much studied mobilizations that were organized online, for example, against the WTO in Seattle in 1999 and against Nike.[64]

An important feature of this type of multiscalar politics of the local is that it is not confined to moving through a set of nested scales from the local to the national to the international but can directly access other such local actors in the same country or across borders. One Internet-based technology that reflects this possibility of escaping nested hierarchies of scale is

---

[63] But, it must be noted that even in this campaign, centered as it was on the global south and determined as it was to communicate with global south organizations, the latter were often unable to access the sites (Kuntze, Rottmann, and Symons 2002).

[64] There are many other, somewhat less known campaigns. For instance, when Intel announced that it would include a unique personal serial number in its new PentiumIII processing chips, privacy advocacy groups objected to this invasion of privacy. Three groups in different locations set up a joint Web site called Big Brother Inside to provide an organizational space for advocacy groups operating in two different countries, thereby also enabling them to use the place-specific resources of the different localities (Leizerov 2000). The Washington, D.C.–based group Public Citizen put an early draft of the Multilateral Agreement on Investment (MAI) (a confidential document being negotiated by the OECD behind closed doors) on its Web site in 1997, launching a global campaign that brought these negotiations to a halt about eight months later. And these campaigns do not always directly engage questions of power. For instance, Reclaim the Streets started in London as a way to contest the Criminal Justice Act in England that granted the police broad powers to seize sound equipment and otherwise discipline ravers. One tactic was to hold street parties in cities across the world: through Internet media participants could exchange notes and tactics on how to deal with the police, and create a virtual space for coming together. Finally, perhaps one of the most significant developments is Indymedia, a broad global network of ICT-based alternative media groups located all around the world. Other such alternative media groups are MediaChannel.org, Zmag.org, Protest.net, and McSpotlight.org.

the online workspace, often used for Internet-based collaboration (Bach and Stark 2005). Such a space can constitute a community of practice (Sharp 1997) or knowledge network (Creech and Willard 2001). An example of an online workspace is the Sustainable Development Communications Network, also described as a knowledge space (Kuntze, Rottmann, and Symons 2002), set up by a group of civil society organizations in 1998; it is a virtual, open, and collaborative organization engaged in joint communications activities to inform broader audiences about sustainable development and build members' capacities to use ICT effectively. It has a trilingual Sustainable Development Gateway to integrate and showcase members' communication efforts. It contains links to thousands of member-contributed documents, a job bank, and mailing lists on sustainable development. It is one of several NGOs whose aim is to promote civil society collaboration through ICTs; others are the Association for Progressive Communications (APC), One World International, and Bellanet.

At the same time, the possibility of exiting or avoiding hierarchies of scale does not preclude the fact that powerful actors can use the existence of different jurisdictional scales to their advantage (Morrill 1999) and the fact that local resistance is constrained by how the state deploys scaling through jurisdictional, administrative, and regulatory orders (Judd 1998). On the contrary, it might well be that the conditions analyzed by Morrill and Judd, among others, force the issue, so to speak. Why work through the power relations shaped into state-centered hierarchies of scale? Why not jump ship if this is an option? This combination of conditions and choices is well illustrated by research showing how the power of the national government can subvert the legal claims of first-nation people (Howitt 1998; Silvern 1999), which has in turn led the latter increasingly to seek direct representation in international fora, bypassing the national state (Sassen 1996: chapter 3).[65] In this sense, then, my effort here is to recover a particular type of multiscalar context, one characterized by direct local-global transactions or by a multiplication of local transactions as part of global networks. Neither type is marked by nested scalings.

There are many examples of such types of cross-border political work. We can distinguish two forms of it, each of which captures a specific type of scalar interaction. In one the scale of struggle remains the locality and the object is to engage local actors, for example, a local housing or environmental

----

[65] Though with other objectives in mind, a similar mix of conditions can also partly explain the growth of transnational economic and political support networks among immigrants (e.g., M. Smith 1994; R. Smith 1997; Cordero-Guzmán, Smith, and Grosfoguel 2001).

agency, but with the knowledge and explicit or tacit invocation of the fact that multiple other localities around the world are engaged in similar localized struggles with equivalent local actors. This combination of multiplication and self-reflexivity contributes to constitute a global condition out of these localized practices and rhetorics. It means, in a sense, taking Cox's notion of scaled "spaces of engagement" constitutive of local politics and situating it in a specific type of context, not necessarily the one Cox himself might have had in mind. Beyond the fact of relations between scales as crucial to local politics, it is perhaps the social and political construction itself of scale as social action (Howitt 1993; Swyngedouw 1997; N. Brenner 1998) that needs emphasizing.[66] It is the actual thick and particularized content of the struggle or dynamic that gets instantiated.

These features can be illustrated with the case of the Society for the Promotion of Area Resources (SPARC). This organization began as an effort to organize slum dwellers in Bombay to get housing, as part of a larger project to organize urban and rural poor, especially women, to develop their organizing capabilities. The focus is local, as are the participants and those whom they seek to reach, usually local governments. But they have established multiple networks with other similar organizations and efforts in other Asian countries and now also some cities in Latin America and Africa. The various organizations making up the broader global network do not necessarily gain power or material resources from this global networking, but they gain strength vis-à-vis the agencies to which they make their demands.

The second form of multiscalar interaction is one where localized struggles try to engage global actors, for example, WTO, IMF, or multinational firms, either at the global scale or in multiple localities. Local initiatives can become part of a global network of activism without losing the focus on specific local struggles (e.g., Cleaver 1998; Espinoza 1999; Ronfeldt et al. 1998; Mele 1999). This is one of the key forms of critical politics that the Internet can make possible: a politics of the local with a big difference—these are localities that are connected with each other across a region, a country, or the world. From struggles around human rights and the environment to workers' strikes and AIDS campaigns against the large pharmaceutical firms, the Internet has emerged as a powerful medium for non-elites to communicate,

---

[66] Some of these issues are well developed in Adams's (1996) study of the Tiananmen Square uprisings of 1989, the popular movement for democracy in the Philippines in the mid-1980s, and the U.S. civil rights movement in the 1950s. Protest, resistance, autonomy, and consent can be constructed at scales that can escape the confines of territorially bounded jurisdictions.

support each other's struggles, and create the equivalent of insider groups at scales from the local to the global.[67] The possibility of doing so transnationally at a time when a growing set of issues are seen as escaping the bounds of nation-states makes this even more significant.[68]

Yet another key scalar element here is that digital networks can be used by political activists for global transactions, but they can also be used for strengthening local communications and transactions inside a city. The architecture of digital networks, primed to span the world, can intensify transactions among residents of a city or region, and it can make them aware of neighboring communities and gain an understanding of local issues that resonate positively or negatively with communities that are in the same city rather than with those that are at the other end of the world (Riemens and Lovink 2002). Recovering how the new digital technology can serve to support local initiatives and alliances inside a locality is conceptually important given the almost exclusive emphasis in the representation of these technologies of their global scope and deployment.[69]

Returning to Howitt's (1993) point about the constructing of the geographical scales at which social action can occur, cyberspace is, perhaps ironically, a far more concrete space for social struggles than is the national political system. As discussed in chapter 5, it becomes a place where nonformal political actors can be part of the political scene in a way that is much more difficult in national institutional channels. Nationally, politics needs to run through existing formal systems, whether the electoral political system or the judiciary (taking state agencies to court). Nonformal political actors are

---

[67] The Internet may continue to be a space for democratic practices, but it will be partly as a form of resistance against overarching powers of the economy and of hierarchical power (Calabrese and Burgelman 1999; see also Warf and Grimes 1997), rather than the space of unlimited freedom that is part of its romantic representation. The images we need to bring into this representation increasingly need to deal with contestation and resistance to commercial and military interests rather than simply freedom and interconnectivity (Sassen 2002).

[68] One might distinguish a third type of political practice along these lines, one that turns a single event into a global media event that then in turn serves to mobilize individuals and organizations around the world in support of that initial action or around similar such occurrences elsewhere. Among the most powerful of these actions, and now emblematic of this type of politics, are the Zapatistas' initial and several subsequent actions. The possibility of a single human rights abuse case becoming a global media event has been a powerful tool for human rights activists.

[69] One instance of the need to bring in the local is the issue of what databases are available to locals. Thus the World Bank's Knowledge Bank, a development gateway aimed at spurring ICT use and applications to build knowledge, is too large according to some (Wilks 2001). A good example of a type and size of database is Kubatana.net, an NGO in Zimbabwe that provides Web site content and ICT services to national NGOs. It focuses on national information in Zimbabwe rather than going global.

rendered invisible in the space of national politics. Cyberspace can accommodate a broad range of social struggles and facilitate the emergence of new types of political subjects that do not have to go through the formal political system. Individuals and groups that have historically been excluded from formal political systems and whose struggles can be partly enacted outside those systems can find in cyberspace an enabling environment both for their emergence as nonformal political actors and for their struggles.

The types of political practice discussed here are not the cosmopolitan route to the global. They are global through the knowing multiplication of local practices. These are types of sociability and struggle deeply embedded in people's actions and activities. These practices are also institution-building work with global scope that can come from localities and networks of localities with limited resources and from informal social actors. We see here the potential transformation of actors "confined" to domestic roles into actors in global networks without having to leave their work and roles in their communities. From being experienced as purely domestic and local, these "domestic" settings are transformed into microenvironments articulated with global circuits. They do not have to become cosmopolitan in this process; they may well remain domestic and particularistic in their orientation and remain engaged with their households and local community struggles, and yet they are participating in emergent global politics. A community of practice can emerge that creates multiple lateral, horizontal communications, collaborations, solidarities, and supports. I interpret these as microinstances of partial and incipient denationalization.

CONCLUSION

The two cases focused on above reveal two parallel developments associated with particular technical properties of the new ICTs that have become crucial for both financial markets and electronic activism. And they reveal a third, radically divergent outcome, one I interpret as signaling the weight of the specific social logics of the type of users in each case.

First, perhaps the most significant feature in both cases is the possibility of expanded decentralization and simultaneous integration. That local political initiatives can become part of a global network parallels the articulation of the capital market with a network of financial centers. That the former relies on public access networks and the second on private dedicated networks does not alter this technical outcome. Among the technical properties that produce the specific utility in each case is the possibility of being global without losing the focus on specific local conditions and resources. Comparing these very different cases allows us to see how global formations can be shaped through the multiscalar character of particular instances of either the local (electronic activist networks) or the global (the network of financial centers).

Second, once established, expanded decentralization and simultaneous integration enabled by global digital networks produce threshold effects. Today's global electronic capital market can be distinguished from earlier forms of international financial markets due to some of the technical properties of the new ICTs, notably the orders of magnitude that can be achieved through decentralized simultaneous access and interconnectivity and through the softwaring of increasingly complex instruments. In the second case, the threshold effect is the possibility of constituting transboundary publics and imaginaries rather than being confined to communication or information searches. Insofar as the new network technologies strengthen and create new types of cross-border activities among nonstate actors, they enable the constitution of a distinct and only partly digital condition variously referred to as global civil society, global publics, and commons.

Third, the significant difference lies in the substantive rationalities, values, objectives, and conditionings that organize the network transactions in each case. Once we introduce these issues, we can see a tendency toward cumulative causation in each case leading to a growing differentiation in outcomes. The constitutive capabilities of the new ICTs lie in a combination of digital and nondigital variables. It is not clear that the technology alone could have produced the outcome. The nondigital variables differ sharply between these two cases, even as digitization is crucial to constituting the specificity of each case. The divergence is evident in the fact that the same technical properties produced greater concentration of power in the case of the capital market and greater distribution of power in the second case.

These two cases illuminate specific aspects of the capacities of digital technologies to override existing relations of law to territory, notably the possibility even for resource-poor actors partly to exit national encasements and emerge as global political actors. But they also illuminate the conditionalities under which this takes place and thereby signal the formation of spatiotemporal orders that need to be distinguished from common understandings of the national and global as mutually exclusive, and from the global as exogenous. Both cases show there is an endogenous moment in the constituting of these global domains.

The mix of digital networks, platforms, and transactions, and their imbrications with the social logics guiding use of these technologies, signals the existence of complex assemblages, each constituting a specific spatio-temporal order. Yet these assemblages are basically informal in that they cannot be captured in terms of a specific legal persona; they are so even when the digital network is proprietary, and even when it is a powerful entity. The network or platform needs to be distinguished from the actual multiple transactions and actors that constitute the networked activity. At the same time, these assemblages can function as a type of political "actor," albeit an informal one. The technology is only one factor that facilitates political engagement on the part of "actors" arising out of or constituted as digital assemblages. In terms of the issues raised in this chapter and in chapter 5 concerning the notion that the global capital market functions as an informal political actor, it is clear these technologies are facilitators. Thus the additional power they have brought to financial markets can translate into added political power over governments, in good part through the technical properties of speed, interconnectivity, and simultaneity and the orders of magnitude these properties enable.

In this chapter I sought to elaborate a distinction between the formal persona that is an incorporated market or a firm or a not-for-profit organization, all entities in the private, not the political domain, and the far more complex notion of an assemblage constituted through the mix of networks, platforms, territorial insertions, and the multiple transactions and users in play. Such an assemblage is not a formal entity in the private domain. Nor is it a formal political entity as is the citizen or a registered lobby group. Yet it can function politically, for example, in the added political weight electronic financial markets and global activists can derive from the assemblages of networks and transactions they constitute. The technical properties of electronic networks are not sufficient, but they are a critical and necessary component of these distinct types of political "actors." In this sense, digital networks enable novel types of political actors, which while informal evince particular forms of power, and, in turn, these actors through their practices partly build and shape those assemblages. The specific types of spatio-temporal orders these assemblages entail and constitute are the subject of the next chapter.

8 ASSEMBLING MIXED SPATIAL AND

TEMPORAL ORDERS

Elements for a Theorization

A NEW SPATIO-TEMPORAL ORDER—digital networks—is beginning to inscribe specific components of the national. This alters microlevel features of the spatio-temporal order of the nation-state, an order constituted particularly through the bureaucratizing of time and space, and an orientation to a founding myth that lies in the past. Instead, the new order brings the experience of an instantaneously transnational time-space hinged on velocity and the future. How the insertion of this novel spatio-temporal order alters the national is a process in the making and can go in many different directions. Thus the denationalizing of particular state components can bring with it a sharp increase in velocity, which can disrupt the spatio-temporal order of the national but in an illegible way. Beyond digital networks, there is the variety of highly specialized cross-border domains and networks that have their own way of inserting different time-spaces in the national political economy. These are partly constituted through the assembling of specific national and global components into novel types of institutionalized entities that are neither "national" nor "global" and evince a variety of spatio-temporal features. In part 2 and chapter 7 I examined a range of instances in which these dynamics can be detected but did not specify the more abstract spatio-temporal dimensions involved. This chapter seeks to do so.

The spatialities and temporalities that are produced in these various networks and domains do not simply stand outside the national. They are partly inserted in, or arise from, the national and hence evince complex imbrications with the latter. Yet even when they arise from the national or are endogenized into the national, these spatialities and temporalities are not merely reproducing the national space-time as historically constructed. They need not be disruptive in a self-evident way, as is, for instance, forecast in the often wild scenarios on the consequences of the Internet for national state authority. But their inception does entail a bit of history in the making and thereby an unsettling of existing arrangements. One possible interpretation, albeit with different contents, is to see these moments of inception as instances of Sewell's concept of the "event" (1996), that is to say, a condition with the capacity to alter structures, or Barbara Adam's (2004) notion of the condition that exists between continuity and disruption. These formulations can help capture the particular types of unsettling brought about by these novel assemblages given the often disruptive effects of extreme velocities and interconnectivity on traditional institutional domains. The difficulty of interpreting the effects of these new technologies rests to some extent on the multiple and variable imbrications of the digital and the nondigital whereby the latter can distort the inferences we might make based on purely technical properties. Overlooking these "distortions" can easily lead to overlooking the mostly partial character of the digital in social formations. Digital domains cannot (at least for now) fully encompass the lived experience of users or the domain of institutional orders and cultural formations.

Although these new global assemblages are partial, albeit often strategic, neither can the national encompass the fullness of social life as it might once have. The national project of containment has always been imperfect given various cross-border flows—trade, travelers, capital. But today's novel assemblages can be a highly disruptive insertion into the national as container of social life. Further, the denationalizations examined in part 2 also help alter the historically constructed meaning of the national. States that participate in the global economy become one of the institutional homes for the multinational space of global firms and markets. Thus the national I juxtapose to the digital/global is itself a mixed condition. Neither the national nor the global represents a fully stabilized meaning today. To capture this mixed condition, an in-between type of spatio-temporal order, I develop the notion of analytic borderlands.

ANALYTIC BORDERLANDS: SPECIFICITY AND COMPLEXITY

In constructing the notion of analytic borderlands, my concern is to develop a heuristic device that allows one to take what is commonly represented as a line separating two differences, typically seen as mutually exclusive, into a conceptual field—a third entity—that requires its own empirical specification and theorization. The problem arises out of the intersection between systems of representation (that is, disciplinary forms of knowledge) sufficiently diverse to be seen as mutually exclusive so that their intersection is rendered analytically inconsequential for established disciplines or mainstream analysts.

Specifying analytic borderlands has, then, its own particular challenges: how to produce the contents and activities that mark a borderland and the needed theoretical tools to resist its collapse into a line that simply separates two differences. Put differently, how can we construct these sites analytically in ways that allow us to capture them as sites for spatial and temporal disruptions, or "events" in Sewell's terms?[1]

The analytic construction of these dynamics needs to accommodate both the national and the global as representing spatio-temporal orders with considerable internal differentiation and growing mutual imbrication. These internal differences may relate to each other in cumulative, conflictive, neutral, or disjunctive modes, both internally and across the national-global divide. The theoretical and methodological task entails detecting the social thickness and specificity of these various dimensions and intersections so as to produce a rich and textured understanding. Given the complexity and specificity within the global and the national, their overlaps and interactions may well produce a series of frontier zones where operations of power and domination, resistance and unsettlement, get enacted. We can construct each of these zones or their aggregate as an analytic borderland with its own theoretical and methodological specificity. Given the historically constructed meaning of the national as mutually exclusive with other nationals and as a dominant condition, one outcome of these interactions can be an incipient and partial denationalizing of specific national spatio-temporal orders. Researching this interaction in terms of the category of analytic borderlands does help us capture the specificity of this process and the possibility that the zone of interaction is part of the reconfiguration. This analytic stance does not confine the focus of research to establishing change on either side of a putative duality. Finally, it underlines the work of making, in this case, the making of change: the zones of interaction are dynamic and the outcomes vary. It is not simply a zero sum where either the national loses at the hands of the global or

---

[1] Interesting work on this issue can be found in fields other than the social sciences. For instance, Homi Bhabha's (1994) explorations and theorizations of spaces of intersection and the in-between forms of difference can be seen as contributing to the specifying of such analytic borderlands. I also read such an effort in the type of work done by, among others, Palumbo-Liu when he posits that the construction "Asian/American," at once implying both exclusion and inclusion, "marks both the distinction installed between 'Asian' and 'American' and a dynamic, unsettled, and inclusive movement" (1999: 1). In a different domain, I read Appadurai's (1996) global cultural disjunctures as a conception of the spaces and times of the global that captures this specificity of conditionings and contents, so much so that there can be disjuncture internal to the global (and the national). For questions concerning political economy, the analytics and the contents of such borderlands are of course quite different.

vice versa, nor is it simply a question of direct power. The matter cannot be reduced to the victimhood of the national at the hands of a powerful and invasive global.

Braudel's (1984) examination of the times and spaces of late medieval Europe illuminates some of these issues. His treatment of the distinctiveness of the major cities—his "supervilles"—of the fourteenth and fifteenth centuries compared with their surroundings—shows us the coexistence of diverse spatialities and temporalities. But a significant difference is that these were largely mutually exclusive zones, cores and peripheries articulated at best through relations of hierarchy. What I am positing is different from Braudel's mutually exclusive zones. For instance, in the case of the global economy, the capital fixity necessary to produce hypermobility can be seen as instantiating a spatiality/temporality that is distinct from that of the circulation of hypermobile dematerialized financial outputs yet it is one constitutive element in the possibility of the latter. This means that the spatiality of the global economic cannot be fully contained in either one, but inhabits both. The specificity of the global does not necessarily reside in being mutually exclusive with the national. The strategic spaces where many global processes are embedded are often national; the mechanisms through which new legal forms, necessary for globalization, are implemented are often part of state institutions. The infrastructure that enables the hypermobility of financial capital at the global scale is embedded in various national territories. But the processes that constitute this insertion partly denationalize the national. Here I want to extricate the implications for spatio-temporal orderings in this process.

This insertion of global projects, coming not only from the outside but also from inside the national, produces a partial unbundling of national space and hence potentially of the national spatio-temporal order. It is partial because these dynamics function through particular structures and institutions; and because the geography of globalization is itself partial—it is not diffuse nor is it an all-encompassing condition. Further, this unbundling is partial in the sense that national space was never a unitary condition, even though it was institutionally constructed as such. The doctrine of extraterritoriality was developed precisely to accommodate the fact that it was not a unitary spatial condition and to secure the extension of state authority beyond the geographic boundaries of national territory (Mattingly 1988).

Theoretically and operationally, these processes seem thus far to have become particularly legible in the global corporate economy, notably transnational corporations and financial markets, as well as in the types of global classes examined in chapter 6. But disciplines dealing with other subjects have made major theoretical contributions and broadened the range of foci for examination (e.g., Homi-Bhabha 1994; Appadurai 1996; Palumbo-Liu 1999). The global corporate economy has specificity in its spatio-temporal conditionalities and contents. In making legible the at least partial locational and institutional embeddedness of global economic processes and institutions in national systems it makes legible the specificity and social thickness of the global.[2] This in turn helps us track and detect the existence of interactions between different spatio-temporal orders of the national and the global. Using the category of analytic borderlands we can specify the features and variability of these in-between orders. The global economy needs to be implemented, reproduced, serviced, and financed. It cannot be taken simply as a given, or a set of markets, or merely as a function of the power of multinational corporations and financial markets. There is a vast array of highly specialized functions that need to be executed, infrastructures that need to be secured, and legislative environments that need to be rendered hospitable.

The spatio-temporal orders usually associated with the global economy are elementary—hypermobility and space-time compression. Much of the scholarship on economic globalization has confined its conceptualization to cross-border trade and capital flows, thereby denuding the global of much of its social thickness and its specific spatio-temporal orders. The tendency has been to understand the spatiality of economic globalization in terms of the hypermobility and neutralization of distance made possible by the new technologies. With this comes, inevitably, a notion about the compression of time: instantaneous integration and so-called real time simultaneity. What such an account tends to leave out of the analysis is the fact that hypermobility and time-space compression need to be produced and that this requires vast concentrations of material and not so mobile facilities and infrastructures.

The two cases in chapter 7 make it clear that we need to problematize the seamlessness often attributed to digital networks. Far from being seamless, these digital assemblages are "lumpy," partly due to their imbrications with nondigital conditions. And the lumpiness cannot be construed simply as resulting from or produced by the ongoing role of the national state

---

[2] William Sewell has developed the notion of "thickening the social." In a slight play on the terms, I argue for a thickening of the global that we need to bring social thickness to our analysis of globalization. This can be particularly helpful in identifying sites that allow for complexity in an inquiry about economic globalization.

in implementing and securing border controls, national standards, and other similar barriers to putatively seamless flows. The financial centers, which are after all located in national administrative territories, enable the global digital space for financial transactions and its new temporal order. The centers are themselves transformed by this imbrication with digital networks. Thus even though they continue to be parts of national administrative units they cannot be reduced to this fact. The second case examined in chapter 7 makes legible a second type of lumpiness. Localized struggles by actors who are not globally mobile are nonetheless critical for the organizational infrastructure of a globally networked politics: it is precisely the combination of localized practices and global networks that makes possible a new type of power for actors who would be seen as powerless in terms of conventional variables. While geographically immobile, these localized actors and their practices are also inflected by their participation and constitutive role in global civil society. They are contained within an administrative unit of a national state, but they cannot be seen as simply local. Both cases capture something about specific and partial unbundlings of national spatial and temporal orders even as key components of each case inhabit the national. These two cases are emblematic of how the multiple processes that constitute the new global digital assemblages partly inhabit and shape specific national structurations of the economic, the political, the cultural, and the subjective.

Thus the spatiality/temporality of globalization itself contains dynamics of mobility and fixity. While mobility and fixity may easily be classified as two mutually exclusive types of dynamics from the perspective of mainstream categories, they are not necessarily so. It is partly an empirical question: social practice as it develops will allow us to establish when they are and when they are not. The cases that concern me here—assemblages that mix the national and the global—signal that under some conditions one presupposes the other. This in turn raises a whole series of empirical, theoretical, and political questions about the spatiality/temporality of economic globalization that take us beyond the still common conception of a unitary space marked by a unitary time, hypermobility. The global city captures this mutual imbrication well, with its vast capacities for enabling hypermobile financial capital and the enormous concentrations of material and human, mostly place-bound resources that it takes to have the former circulating around the globe in a second. This is one way in which economic globalization, even in its most digitized components, can be said to be characterized by locational and institutional embeddedness.

Critical to this type of analytic strategy is detecting the specificity and complexity of these interactions. Part 2 of the book examined several such instances, even though the spatio-temporal dimensions were not fully extricated from the analysis at that point. The loss of functions by the legislature and the gain in functions and power by the executive branch of government examined in chapter 4 entail a shift of functions between two different space-times, from a slow space whose temporality is partly determined by the fact of public debate, to a fast space whose temporality is increasingly shaped by the growing secrecy through which the executive can partly function, with speed of action accelerating as secrecy grows. Much of this is predicated on and feeds into added executive powers, not all fully formalized and some contested, but all of them a fact that contrasts sharply with the growing ineffectiveness of the legislature compared to its role in the 1960s and 1970s. What this examination of the time-spaces of different components of the state illuminates is the partial unbundling of the bureaucratizing of time and space and of the aspiration to a unitary spatio-temporal order, which are both part of the development of the state. This unbundling, with its growing divergences in time-spaces inside the national state, is, in turn, an indicator of the fact that the state is itself one of the sites for producing the foundational changes that are constituting a new global phase.

Further, the privatization of once public sector activities is not only a change in property regime but also a change in velocity (Sassen 2001: chapter 5). When a public entity is privatized, its public regulatory functions do not simply disappear but are variously transferred to private domains. In the case of economic domains, particularly leading globalized sectors, these functions are often reconstituted as private legal and accounting services. This shift, I argue, is also a shift from a bureaucratized time-space to a private accelerated global time-space.[3] A similar interpretation can be made about the multiple privatized governance regimes for the corporate global economy: these regimes represent a shift from the bureaucratized time of public accountability

---

[3] Much scholarship on national public bureaucracies and public settlement mechanisms, notably courts, has given us good insights into how these institutional orders function, including their time cycles and duration of procedures. This is a scholarship guided by very different questions from those I am after, and it does not speak of temporalities. Yet they are unwittingly describing, without naming it, the temporal order within which these institutions operate. By giving content to the temporality of some of the institutional orders of the national, this scholarship can help specify how these shifts to the private and increasingly globalized sphere of leading sectors incorporates these privatized firms into a different type of temporal order. Thus in my past (1996) work I have emphasized the privatizing of "justice" that takes place through this type of arbitration. Revisiting this in the terms under discussion here brings to the fore the fact that this also entails a shift between temporal orders: avoiding national court systems also ensures quick adjudications and settlements. Generally, the temporal order of public bureaucracies is, in principle, subject to often slow-moving governmental processes of adherence to rules and subject to public accountability via legislatures and judiciaries.

to the accelerated time of private ordering, including outside the frame of national law. While this also holds increasingly for national corporate economic sectors, the matter becomes particularly significant for global firms insofar as they have to engage multiple national states. The accelerated and globally expanded time-space of private ordering regimes outside the frame of national law makes legible the fact that privatization is also a shift in spatio-temporal orders.

There are three elements that matter for the task of researching analytic borderlands. First, it is the actual constituting of the shift that is captured through the category of analytic borderland: what are the actual practices (material, organizational, discursive) involved in making that shift. The shift is not simply a result of new technological capacities to accelerate operations. The emergence of these time-space divergences is far more complex and involves a range of institutional domains. Most important for the analysis here is the fact that it takes making, and this dimension is easily lost in what remains a prevalent interpretation: that much of this shift is a function of the new technologies. Obversely, it is this emphasis on the work of constituting the shift that enables us to see that the line separating two different orders is actually a complex zone marked by specificity. In that sense, it requires its own research and theorization. Much of the analysis in this book has focused on this zone. The fact of the outcomes—the differences on either side of the putative line—were of less interest than the work itself of constituting the difference: the making of the tipping point that could take some old capabilities into a constitutive role for a new organizing logic. The process of denationalization is one thick category for capturing the shaping of the tipping that took us into the current global phase. It leads to a focus on how these processes get constituted in the interactions of historically constructed national dynamics and a whole series of new dynamics and possibilities, some self-evidently global and others coming from within the national itself.

Second, empirical specificity matters. For instance, we cannot assume that the global is by its nature faster than the national. Velocity is itself a constructed condition. The different temporalities we associate with the national and the global, or with advanced economic sectors and with backward ones, do largely correspond to empirical reality. But this is not sufficient ground to reify speed as the preserve of the global and the most advanced entities. Thus it matters to detect specific interactions—analytic borderlands—where actors or entities from two putatively different spatio-temporal orders intersect precisely on the question of velocity. Coming back to the new kinds of informal economy in global cities, we can find such an interaction in the street vendor grilling food at lunchtime on Wall Street and the hurried top-level professional for whom that street vendor provides lunch at the velocity he needs. They belong to different circuits of the economy, but they intersect precisely at that juncture of speed. This also is another way of showing that structurally the new informal economy of global cities is the low-cost equivalent of what we refer to as deregulation at the top of the system: both provide flexibility and thereby a greater relative speed of operations.

Third, the space we seek to capture with the category analytic borderland is not a no-man's-land. A good case in point is the earlier described divergence between the time-space of the legislature and the time-space of the executive. This is a divergence constituted in ways that are specific, complex, and consequential, including an array of formal state actions (even though some have been interpreted as bordering on illegality). Similarly, the new jurisdictional geographies discussed below do not exist by default. They are the product of deliberate action, notably by states and international courts. Thus, while novel, these formations are not anomalous or an accident. They are, in that regard, part of history in the making in that they capture the making of a structural shift.

Next I examine three distinct types of analytic borderlands.

MIXED SPATIO-TEMPORAL ASSEMBLAGES AS
TYPES OF TERRITORIALITY

I want to push the argument further and posit that among the cases discussed above and throughout the book we see the formation of particular types of territoriality assembled out of "national" and "global" elements, each individual or aggregate instance evincing distinct spatio-temporal features. These territorialities can be apprehended through the category of analytic borderlands.

A first type of territoriality can be detected in the formation of a global network of financial centers. We can conceive of financial centers that are part of global financial markets as constituting a distinct kind of territoriality, simultaneously pulled in by the larger networks and functioning as localized microinfrastructures for those networks. They inhabit national territories, but they cannot be seen as simply national in the historical sense, nor can they be reduced to the administrative unit encompassing the actual terrain, one that is part of a nation-state. In their aggregate they house significant components of the global, partly electronic market for capital. As localities they are denationalized in specific and partial ways. In this sense they can be seen as constituting the elements of a novel type of multisited territoriality, one that diverges sharply from the territoriality of the historic nation-state. As a capability, the territoriality that gets instantiated in these centers and localities has been relodged into new organizing logics.

We can detect a second type of territoriality in global networks of localized activists and, more generally, in the constituting of global civil society. Global civil society is enabled by global digital networks and the associated imaginaries. But this does not preclude that localized actors, organizations, and causes are key building blocks of global civil society as it is shaping up today. The localized involvements of activists are critical no matter how universal and planetary the aims of the various struggles—in their aggregate these localized involvements are constitutive. Global electronic networks actually push the possibility of this local-global dynamic further. One of the subjects addressed in chapter 7 is the possibility for even resource-poor localized organizations to become part of a type of horizontal globality centered on localities. When supplied with the key capabilities of the new technologies—decentralized access, interconnectivity, and simultaneity of transactions—localized, immobilized individuals and organizations can be part of a global public space. In principle we can posit that they might be more likely to experience their globality through this (abstract) space than individuals and organizations that have the resources and the options to travel across the globe. Thus even resource-poor localized organizations, too poor or persecuted to move internationally, can become microenvironments with global span. Sometimes these globalities can assume complex forms, as is the case with first-nation people demanding direct representation in international fora, bypassing national state authority—a longstanding cause that has been significantly enabled by global electronic networking. Other times they are more elementary, as is the case with various Forest Watch activists in rain forests around the world. We can see in this a particular type of interaction between placeless digital networks and deeply localized actors/users. These instances point to the emergence of a particular type of territoriality in the context of the imbrications of digital and nondigital conditions. This territoriality partly inhabits specific subnational spaces and partly gets constituted as a variety of somewhat specialized or partial global publics.

While these two types of territoriality might seem similar, they are actually distinct. The subnational spaces of these localized actors have not been denationalized, as is the case with the financial centers discussed earlier. It is the subjectivities of the actors involved that can become partly denationalized. Further, the global publics that get constituted are barely institutionalized and mostly informal, unlike the global capital market, which is a highly institutionalized space both through national and international law, and through private ordering. In their informality, however, these global publics can be seen as spaces for empowerment of the resource-poor or of not very powerful actors. In this sense the subjectivities that are emerging through these global publics constitute capabilities for new organizing logics.

A third type of territoriality is getting constituted through the development of new jurisdictional geographies. Legal frameworks for rights and guarantees, and more generally the rule of law, were largely developed in the context of the formation of national states. But now some of these instruments are strengthening a non-national organizing logic. As they become part of new types of transnational systems they alter the valence of older national state capabilities. Further, in so doing, they are often pushing these national states to go against the interests of national capital. A second type of instance is the formation of triangular cross-border jurisdictions for political action which once would have been confined to the national. Electronic activists often use global campaigns and international organizations to secure rights and guarantees from their national states. Furthermore, a variety of national legal actions involving multiple geographic sites across the globe can today be launched from national courts, producing a transnational geography for national lawsuits. A good example are the lawsuits launched by the Washington-based Center for Constitutional Rights against nine U.S. and foreign multinational corporations for abuses of workers' rights in their offshore industrial operations (Stephens 2002). Even if these lawsuits do not quite achieve their full goal, they signal it is possible to use the national judiciary for suing U.S. and foreign firms for operations outside the United States. Thus, in addition to novel courts and instruments, today we see components of the rule of law that once served to build the strength of the national state contributing to the formation of transnational jurisdictions. Finally, the U.S. practice of "exporting" prisoners it intends to torture to third countries to facilitate their torture (rendition) is yet another instance of a territoriality that is both national and non-national. Diverse jurisdictional geographies can also be used to manipulate temporal dimensions. Reinserting a conflict in the national legal system may ensure a slower progression than in the private jurisdiction of international commercial arbitration. In their aggregate these jurisdictional geographies contribute to produce an operational space that is partly embedded in particular components of national legal systems that have been subjected to specialized denationalizations (chapters 4 and 5); thereby they become capabilities of an organizing logic that is not part of the national state.

The category of analytic borderland can also be used to capture a variety of other, perhaps less defined but novel jurisdictional geographies. For instance, Stephan's (2002) notion of the stickiness of multilateral agreements clearly also points to the making of a particular, albeit elusive space. Once a matter for cross-border deliberation is inserted in this space of multilateral agreements, it will not be easy to dislodge it and address it in a different forum. Thus Stephan (2002) invites us to consider the possibility that some of the issues that are now part of the WTO agreement, such as TRIPS, might more usefully have been located in a different forum or system. And he points out how difficult, and perhaps quite impossible, this switch would now be no matter the flaws detected in the current system, notably that the state's access to international trade is now hostage to TRIPS specifications. Koh's (1997, 1998) notion of transnational legal process is yet another instance of a somewhat elusive space that mixes, in this case, international human rights norms with national law and institutions. He observes how these norms gradually get established and stabilize their meaning as part of federal law. What is interesting about both of these somewhat abstract applications of the notion of an analytic borderland is that they capture the process itself rather than merely the outcome, and in this case a very elusive one.

Although these three types of emergent territorialities are diverse, each containing multiple, often highly specialized and partial instances, all three evince specific features. First, they are not exclusively national or global but are assemblages of elements of each. Second, in this assembling they bring together what are often different spatio-temporal orders, that is, different velocities and different scopes. Third, this can produce an eventful engagement, including contestations and the frontier zone effect I alluded to above—a space that makes possible kinds of engagements for which there are no clear rules. The resolution of these encounters can become the occasion for playing out conflicts that cannot easily be engaged in other spaces. Those frontier zones may be the sites for Sewell's "events." Fourth, novel types of actors can emerge in this assembling, often with the option to access domains once exclusive to older established actors, notably national states. Finally, in the juxtaposition of the different temporal orders that come together in these novel territorialities, existing capabilities can get redeployed to domains with novel organizing logics.

These emergent assemblages begin to unbundle the traditional territoriality of the national, albeit in partial, often highly specialized ways. In cases where the global is rich in content or subject to multiple conditionalities, its insertion in an institutional world that has been historically constructed overwhelmingly as a national unitary spatio-temporal domain is eventful. It is the combination of this embeddedness of the global along with its specificity that gives meaning to the notion of overlap and interaction among the multiple spatialities and temporalities of the national and the global. Much of the enactment of these overlaps and interactions is in formation as the global is still in the process of producing the particular forms of its specificity as well as its social thickness. But this process is underway, and the global is already more complex today than it was only fifteen years ago.

These conditions suggest at least three distinct subjects for further research and theorization. One concerns the degree of specificity of these spaces where different orders interact and overlap through the variety of processes briefly described above. That is to say, what is the extent of their sociological and analytic legibility? The second concerns the level of complexity these interactions and overlaps can assume given the specificity and social thickness of the national and, though to a far lesser extent, now also the global. A third subject concerns the consequences of the combination of the embeddedness of the global and its specificity: generalizations will not help, and considerable variability of outcomes is likely. We might find that some instances of the national have a greater capacity for resistance to denationalization or, alternatively, for accommodation than others. A fourth subject, derived from the former, is that this variability suggests a move away from unitary spatio-temporal alignments inside nation-states and toward cross-border convergence of particular denationalized components of each nation-state involved. Getting to convergence is actually arduous work. It is partly enabled by a mix of conditions ranging from unequal power among states to the fact of emergent global publics among the powerless pushing for more social justice across nation-states. These developments entail a move toward centrifugal, and away from the centripetal dynamics that have marked the development of nation-states.[4]

JUXTAPOSED TEMPORALITIES AND NEW ECONOMIES

The temporalities constituted through advanced economic sectors can be construed as yet another kind of analytic borderland, one centered not so much on the formation of novel territorialities as on that of different velocities and durations. Seen through the lenses of advanced economic sectors, the

---

[4] I have developed this particular aspect in "Territory, Authority, and Rights: Emerging Assemblages/Specialized Normative Orders," 2004–05 Sherrill Lecture, Yale University School of Law.

question of duration and velocity in the economy can easily be reduced to the familiar issue of how technology has altered a variety of economic practices through acceleration and the often associated shortening of economic cycles. But it is not only acceleration. It is, I argue, the juxtaposition of sharply different rates of acceleration in different economic activities that is decisive for what are some of today's leading sectors. It is not a homogeneous or homogenizing process of overall acceleration, even though that is part of the trend. The differences engender the possibility of differing temporalities, and this is what matters. The ascendance of finance and the digitization of many economic activities assume their full meaning in the juxtaposition of different temporalities not in the fact of acceleration itself. These sectors are, then, an enactment in the economy of this sharpened differentiation—between their temporality as digitized activities and other sectors of the economy that still deal with the material and hence are going to be slower.

This strategic difference can be illustrated through the different temporalities of capital mobilized in the manufacturing of a car and in finance: the temporality of the first is about nine months; that of the second is significantly shorter—it could be a day or less. These are produced temporal orders, each embedded in a complex institutional world belonging to different spatio-temporal configurations. In the trade-off between the two lies a world of business opportunities that has shaped a whole new intermediate economy of specialized corporate services. This is not necessarily a new event per se. What is new is the scale and power of this intermediate economy; we can think of the parallel with medieval traders: trading was not new, but they built a whole new model of accumulation through their practices—merchant capital. The sharper the differentiation between the two temporalities has grown (with digitization), the more intense the world of new business opportunities will be. Finance can use the longer temporal cycles of other sectors to its advantage in a way that is not quite reversible. I have argued elsewhere that large-scale manufacturing is, however, a critical component not only through its longer temporal frame but also because it is one mechanism for producing massive levels of capital that can then be used by finance; mergers and acquisitions have further enabled massive concentrations of "slow" capital. Concentrating money and capitals in order to reach the increasingly high orders of magnitude that are part of the financial sector is no mean feat. This is one way in which economic globalization is constituted: large industrial firms secure the grist for the financial mill. The fact of this difference is consequential. Finance can subject other sectors of the economy to its rhythms, both at a national and a global scale.

The emergence of the new world of business activities at the interface of the distinct temporalities of different economic sectors in advanced economies brings with it new questions and agendas for theory and research. Insofar as many of these new activities tend to locate in cities and create new sources of growth and new hierarchies of profitability, it concentrates much of this new analytic effort on the city. The global city is an example of a dense and complex borderland marked by the intersection of multiple spatio-temporal (dis)orders. Analytically, the new world of business activities is itself a sort of border zone; it does not belong to either of the two or more sectors among which it negotiates its own existence and sources for profit. These are business opportunities that negotiate different temporalities and extract new types of profits from their coexistence.

These juxtapositions also produce novel presences in other domains. First, policy compliance can make legible some of these juxtapositions. Thus, insofar as globalization has contributed to a series of economic activities that get enacted in national contexts but are sufficiently novel in some of their features (for example, organizational or locational), they can render problematic the application of policy. They may not quite comply with extant regulatory frameworks yet cannot be said to be in violation either. I have named that in-between space "regulatory fractures." Certain financial operations are an example of this in that they have the power to destabilize national governments, as happened with the speculative attacks, especially by U.S. hedge funds, on the Thai currency in mid-1997. No regulations were violated, yet this was war on the Thai central bank. A very different instance is the already mentioned emergence of a new type of informal economy in global cities: it involves licit activities, and hence need not function underground. I see it as the counterpart of the intensively deregulated sectors at the top of the economic system. Its velocities and flexibilities are embedded in very different institutional domains. The proliferation of these new informal economies across the world are in good part an outcome of the new types of organizational, spatial, and temporal requirements, that is, greater flexibility and speed of execution, brought on by the implantation of global sectors in the city (Sassen 1998: chapter 8). The new informal economy meets an effective demand in these cities from firms, households, and the world of auxiliary services, such as hotels and restaurants, under conditions where providers cannot actually handle the regular costs of operation inside these cities even though it is here where the demand for their goods and services comes from. The new informal economy is a kind of infrastructure of flexible in situ firms and workforces that can overcome the obstacles to operating in these cities. Informalization raises the velocity at which they can be delivered—whether that is prepared food, a sudden demand for industrial services workers, or a renovation of a storefront on its way to becoming a luxury restaurant. In that sense, informalization is a systemic equivalent of deregulation in the national economy and of privatization of governance regimes in the global economy. The new informal economy can then be seen as another instance of an intermediary space for business activities that can profit from the different velocities, in this case of the leading sectors on the one hand, and the bureaucratized time of unionized or standardized ways of doing the same work on the other. In brief, while it seems backward, its velocities and spatial tactics belong to the world of leading sectors.[5]

A second issue concerns the level of complexity these interactions between the different velocities of economic sectors can assume given the specificity and social thickness of the national and the global. Though concerned with a different question, Appadurai's conceptualization of global cultural disjunctures (1996: chapter 2) is helpful here, as is his insistence that there is a dynamic and uncertain interaction among the various disjunctures he has famously identified in the language of scapes. Thus, for instance, he argues that the relationship between cultural and economic levels is not simply a one-way process "set wholly by, or confined wholly within, the vicissitudes of international flows of technology, labor, and finance," which would only call for a "modest modification of existing neo-Marxist models of uneven development and state formation" (1996: 39). On the contrary, these dynamics are producing distinct formations that need to be empirically specified and theorized on their own terms. He also posits that more than perhaps was the case in earlier periods, today an actor is likely to live, and an entity to operate, in overlapping domains of the national and the global.

A third issue concerns the formation of partly territorial and partly electronic geographies that cut across borders and the spatio-temporal orders of nation-states yet install themselves or get partly shaped in specific subnational terrains, notably cities. The earlier discussion of the network of financial centers captures one of the most acute instances of this dynamic. The networks of global cities, global commodity and value chains, the multisited organization of manufacturing production that firms have constructed—all of

---

[5] It is understood to be anachronistic, imported via immigrants from the Third World who replicate village practices from back home and as having nothing to do with the global economy. In brief, its representation locates it in a discursive domain that is radically unconnected to that through which we represent the global economy. The global city becomes the space where the interconnections are made legible and can be subjected to detailed empirical research, a further illustration of the point made earlier about the emergence of an urban analytic as part of research on today's leading economic sectors. It is a space that can be captured through the notion of analytic borderlands, which in turn prompts the researcher to look for the articulations between two domains that present themselves as radically different spatio-temporal orders.

these are instances of such novel geographies. They also function at the inter-face of different temporalities, a fact neglected in most of the research which has focused on the question of costs. The formalization and institutionaliza-tion of these geographies furthers the velocity of operations. This opens up new research questions about some of these conditions that have perhaps been excessively studied through the lens of costs and control, even though the latter may indeed be the critical factors. In brief, these novel geographies can be thought of as assemblages of cross-border networks among specific sites embedded partly in the national, elements of different spatio-temporal orders, and a variety of regulatory and institutional components. These are complex assemblages. While they contain components of the national—certain terri-tories, financial centers, particular regulations, laws, and institutions—they are partly constituted through spatial and temporal practices that distinguish them from those we might think of as emblematic national and global condi-tions. For instance, for the former we might think of highway construction, suburban development, and heavy manufacturing of the pre-outsourcing era. For the global, we might think of highly digitized sectors such as finance. The driving temporalities of the novel geographies are different from those of the national Fordist economy and of the public bureaucracies of national states. But they also differ from the temporalities of global electronic financial mar-kets, if only because they intersect with national states and national territo-ries. Further, these are geographies that explode the boundaries of contextual-ity and the traditional hierarchies of scale. Although inserted in the physical space of national territory, they may have little to do with the surrounding context. In brief, these novel geographies continuously fluctuate between the diverse spatio-temporal orders of the national and the global, and it is this juxtaposition that contributes to their economic utility.

These features also underscore the need to rethink what is often constructed as a duality: the distinction between the global and the local, no-tably the assumption about the necessity of territorial proximity in the consti-tution of the "local," and the placelessness of the global. This parallels our representations of backward and advanced economic sectors (for example, finance versus outsourced manufacturing). One of the tasks here has to do with rethinking spatial hierarchies that are usually taken as a given: local/national/global, where the local is seen as slow time and the global as fast time. For example, the new international professionals operate in contexts that are at the same time local and global, thereby overriding these conventional hierarchies of scale (chapter 6). The new professionals of finance are mem-bers of a cross-border culture that is in many ways embedded in a global net-work of "local" places—a set of particular international financial centers with much circulation of people, information, and capital among them. Further, as financial centers, London, New York, Zurich, Amsterdam, Frankfurt, and so on are all part of an international yet very localized work subculture. Here the "local" is the site where critical components for the velocity of the global are constituted and operated. Further, on the question of "proximity," this is indeed a feature, but it is not embedded in territorial space; it is a deterritorialized form of proximity.[6] This cross-border grid of strategic subnational sites connected via intense transactions and flows of professionals is one instantiation of a denationalized spatiality and temporality—they are neither national nor global.

Excavating the Temporality of the National

Here I want to focus on the temporality of the national, which runs through the issues discussed in the preceding section but demands explicit attention. The temporality of the national has been constructed historically through the expansion of bureaucratized systems and the associated standardizations. The national state project was to neutralize other temporalities and other spatialities. As a result the fact of a constructed temporality has to some extent remained submerged, an unnamed condition, partly because it is the given condition, the assumed built-in time of much social science. In contrast, the new accelerated time that has become a master image for globalization has been constructed as a distinct object of study. But as the cases examined in the preceding section signal, particular globalized economic sectors find often significant utilities in this temporality of the national, as they play precisely on the juxtaposing of different temporalities. The possibility of deriving economic utilities from juxtaposing different temporalities can then also be seen as one dynamic feeding into the denationalizing of the national as historically constructed.

The time of the national is slippery and requires excavation. It is constructed through a glance at the founding myths of a nation and at the future given the construction of the nation as a necessary condition for the

---

[6] This question of proximity also holds for other social groups, including groups we do not associate with these world-class mobilities. For instance, immigrants will tend to be part of a cross-border network that connects specific localities—their new communities and their localities of origin in home countries. Though in a manner different from the financiers, they nonetheless also have the experience of deterritorialized local cultures, not predicated on locational proximity. Both types of workers operate in labor markets that are local but not proximate; they are multisited networks of localities.

state, which reveals this future as an inherited project and hence also located partly in the past. In this regard I have found the work of scholars interrogating the past enormously compelling. The way in which John and Jean Comaroff locate their work against a broader set of conceptual and historiographic practices can help us understand something about the temporality of the national even though their focus is not on this issue particularly. "While, at least in one obvious sense, the making of the modern world has run its course, its grand narrative has been rendered all the more enigmatic by the sheer unexpectedness of its closing scenes . . . the jury is still very much out on some of the enduring issues of social theory." Theirs is "an account of a colonial past that reaches into the present—each chapter carries forward into this century—and contemplates the fashioning of the future" (1997: xiv). What I take out of that volume, pace the matter that it is a colonial past, is the notion that the past is unsettled, not in the sense of imperfect knowledge or data about it, but in the sense that it lives.

The past is not in a linear sequence where it can be left behind. Nor is it present simply in the sense of path dependence—the built-in constraints of what can be possible at subsequent stages. "The assumption that history requires a linear and cumulative sense of time that allows the observer to isolate the past as a distinct entity" (Trouillot 1995: 7) organizes the temporality of the national as constructed discourse; Trouillot observes how what is often called "the legacy of the past" may not be given to us by the past at all. Palumbo-Liu's (1999) proposition that the "American" in "Asian/American" is shown to be unsettled even though it is supposedly the settled part of an identity marker, unlike "Asian" in "Asian American," illuminates the possibility that what is meant to be settled, the past, may in fact be its resettling by a novel present in the shape of a newcomer. On the other hand, an explanation of some of the key dynamics necessary for the formation of today's global systems examined in this book allows us to detect some of the features of the temporality of the national and reveal it as unsettled.

Yet another dimension in these temporal dynamics can be found in the earlier discussion about how shifts from the public sector to the private sector, as in privatization, represent not only a change in property regime but also a shift in temporal orders. These shifts have the aggregate effect of constituting new temporal orders inside the national. This type of analysis, in turn, unsettles the proposition that national state authority is territorially exclusive and absolute insofar as we associate national authority with bureaucratized systems that operate with specific temporalities. To return to some of the issues raised earlier with other questions in mind, the encounter of a global actor such as a firm or a market with one or another instantiation of the national state can be thought of as a new frontier zone where two very different temporalities intersect and, at the limit, produce conflict. It is not merely a dividing line between the national and the global. It is a zone of politico-economic interactions that produce new institutional forms and alter some of the old ones. Nor is it just a matter of reducing regulations or the role of government generally, it may require more government but on different terms. In addition, the global economic may be enacted through a specific spatiality, which even though partly embedded in national territory has its own sociological reality. Economic globalization entails a set of practices that destabilize another set of practices, that is, some of the practices that came to constitute national state sovereignty. In their enactment these practices produce distinctive and complex spatialities that cannot simply be subsumed under the national. It also signals that the temporalities of the global cannot be confined to notions of hypermobility and space-time compression.

Specifying the processes that constitute economic globalization through this particular type of conceptualization brings to the fore how its strategic projects have emerged in the play between two master/monster space-times, within which we exist and transact (and enact all kinds of microtemporalities and spatialities). In the intersection of these two coexisting spatio-temporal orders we see the formation of new economic, political, subjective dynamics/opportunities that drive and constitute both denationalization and globalization. The organizing logic is one that accommodates a multiplication of orders, some inside the state and some not. This puts in play the temporality of the national as historically constructed in ways that are part of the new global phase rather than exogenous to it, as more traditional and common accounts suggest.

CONCLUSION

Examining the insertion of novel spatio-temporal orders into the national allows us to capture something about specific and partial unbundlings of national bureaucratized spatial and temporal orders. This holds whether that insertion arises out of denationalized conditions inside the national or external global factors. Yet even when they arise from the national or are endogenized into the national, these spatialities and temporalities are not merely reproducing the national as historically constructed.

The fact of overlapping and interacting spaces and times of the national and the digital/global has consequences for the work of theorization and research. Much of social science has proceeded on the explicit or implicit assumption of the nation-state as container and as representing a unified spatio-temporal unit. Most of history has not corresponded to these putative conditions; and even the modern nation-state failed to instantiate them fully. The particular structurations of the digital/global in the current era further undermine the efficacy and usefulness of those two propositions about the national state for a growing arena of sociological reality. Further, what has been constructed as the spatio-temporal unity of the national is itself constituted through multiple spatialities and temporalities organized at most into something approximating a spatio-temporal order that can, for instance, be distinguished from the digital/global.

The state's powers can be seen as historically coalescing into an overwhelming centripetal effect on a bundle of potentially disparate elements including spatio-temporal orders. That centripetal condition is today coming under multiple centrifugal effects. Although partial, this transformation begins to make legible the presence of diverse spatio-temporal orders within the putative unitary time-space of the national. In contrast to formal representations of the national, the global is both formally and in practice constituted through multiple specific domains going in often disparate and contradictory directions coalescing into an overwhelmingly centrifugal dynamic. This centrifugal dynamic is partly constituted through insertions in a growing number of the national systems of a growing number of nation-states. What this means is that in fact, at its most concrete, the national and the global each contain a whole array of dynamics of overlap and interaction among multiple spatio-temporal orders. In the case of the national this multiplication is in part a function of the unbundling of what was historically held together through the state's centripetal powers. In the case of the global this proliferation is in part a function of its own growing complexity and thickening; this includes as one of its more complex instances the partial denationalizing of the national, which in turn raises the complexity of the global.

Whether a national bureaucratized, centripetal, spatio-temporal order or an internally disparate and centrifugal "global" spatio-temporal order emerges triumphant out of this array of interactions is a question that cannot be clearly answered yet, nor do I think that that is the question to ask. Neither appears to be the case today; instead a mix of spatio-temporal orders is in the making. This in turn is producing a series of novel types of heterogeneity, inequalities, and imbalances. Two examples illustrate the tenor of what I sought to develop in this chapter. Bureaucratized time is not about to disappear; the question is rather whether it will be the national that is its master or critical institutional home. Similarly, the velocities that have been the preserve of resource-rich actors are not about to disappear—whether a horse where others walk or high-performance digital networks where others are confined to slow, low-bandwidth networks—but they may well be unsettled by the types of options that electronic activists can access.

IN CONCLUSION

9 CONCLUSION

FOUNDATIONAL CHANGE in complex systems is a complicated matter. Such change is only partly legible and hence interpretation becomes critical in the account of that change. The effort in this book was to examine the period of change beginning in the 1980s commonly referred to as globalization as an instance of foundational change. An organizing theme has been that today's epochal transformation of critical structures and discursive domains cannot be adequately grasped through what has become the standard account—growing interdependence and the formation of global systems. Both of these are indeed happening. However, if the change is foundational, these two processes are capturing only part of the transformation. A critical understanding of such change has to engage the enormous complexity, institutionalization, formalization, and centripetal force of the nation-state, the unit that has absorbed all major building blocks of society over several centuries. The nation-state is one of the major loci for the transformation, even when this is not easily legible and seems to contradict what is legible about the current epoch—that is, interdependence and globality. As the most formalized instantiation of the nation-state, the state apparatus itself is then, undergoing foundational change in one or another of its critical components, making this one of the constitutive changes of the new global era.

While suffused with history, this book does not trace the history of the national state. Mine are analytic incursions into specific periods as they have been constructed by particular disciplinary forms of knowledge—history, law, geography, political science, sociology, and technology. The result is a set of in-depth excavations of a few historical formations which I see as critical in illuminating the processes whereby the national gets assembled and then partly disassembled. I focus on periods when existing configurations and stabilized meanings become unsettled.

At the heart of the book is an examination of the partial and often highly specialized disassembling of the national as historically constructed in the West, and the emergence of novel types of assemblages at both the global and subnational scale. This period, beginning in the early 1980s, is marked by the coexistence of multiple dynamics—the incipient denationalizing of particular components of the national, the renationalizing of others, including ideological components, and the formation of self-evidently global entities. In some cases we see discontinuities surface that obscure critical continuities, and in others we see the obverse—surface continuities obscuring critical ruptures. Ultimately, the explanation for these multiple, partial, and frequently illegible dynamics is that the new does not invent itself. I interpret foundational change and the ascendance of novel formations as in good part a function of capabilities shaped and developed in the period preceding the one under examination—in this case, that of the formation and ascendance of the nation-state. The conditionality explaining the outcome—in this case partial denationalization of the national as historically constructed—is that at least some of those earlier capabilities become lodged in novel organizing logics. Critical to such an analysis is a need to distinguish between the whole and its parts, as well as deciphering the tipping points that mark the switch.

Under these conditions, history can function as a natural experiment—one that accommodates a mix of variables, potentials, and constraints and, at the same time, reveals the outcome. This helps develop an analytics through which to study the present. Looking at the present transformation through this lens takes the analysis beyond a privileging of the new and the self-evident global. Thus, even the global digital assemblages examined in part 3, which are an extreme instance of a novel type of emergent assemblage dependent on recently invented technologies, are not simply "new." In addition, these assemblages derive partly from older capabilities—for example, systems of trust in electronic financial trading floors or legal systems that ensure guarantees of contract in e-commerce.

The interpretive practices I use generate a form of grounded theory. Different temporal and spatial orders are shown to be wired into material practices, infrastructures, and institutional framings. Change can be shown as conditioned by capabilities developed in the period that is about to be left behind. Research strategies need to address thick environments, multisited localized domains, and small worlds in global systems. Grounded theory helps neutralize state capture of the major historiographies since the 1600s as well as capture by abstractions such as society or economy. Finally, these interpretive practices help deconstruct master categories such as the nation-state and the global economy.

In the following sections I focus on the transformations identified in parts 2 and 3 to understand emergent features in both the formal institutionalization of TAR, as well as informal features. The work in parts 2 and 3 used the analytics grounded in part 1 and hence already factors in the project of developing a complex grid to capture the details of the transformations afoot.

Ultimately the picture that arises from this work is one of emergent assemblages. The nation-state and interstate system remain critical building blocks but they are not alone, and are profoundly altered from the inside out, not just as a result of external forces, because they are one of the sites for today's foundational change. On the basis of this I then examine what we could conceive of as an emergent configuration whereby several specialized assemblages of TAR are in the making. They inhabit the nation-state, the formal state apparatus, and self-evidently global systems, such as the global corporate economy and the supranational system. Power and dominance are at work in this emergent configuration but so is the complexity of powerlessness, and the possibility that the disadvantaged also make history.

If there is one systemic feature that characterizes these diverse assemblages it is that they are denationalized, whether their origins lie in the nation-state or in self-evidently global systems. These emergent assemblages coexist with vast stretches of older historical formations constitutive of the modern nation-state. It is then, also in this sense, that they are emergent. The process of denationalization is in full swing. This does not mean that it will ever be absolute—nothing is in history. But it does mean that more is to come. The sections that follow hint at these dynamic, often as yet unstable formations, as well as the unsettlements of older forms they entail.

The first section discusses critical questions of method and interpretation developed in this book and the research and theorization agendas they open up. The second section brings together the various contributions of each chapter as filtered through the lens of territory, authority, and rights. The third and fourth sections focus, respectively, on the shift from borders to bordering capabilities, and the shift from centripetal scalings framed through the master normativity of the nation-state to centrifugal cross-border assemblages of territory, authority, and rights. Thus this third section takes the border as its anchoring element to examine how its unsettlement rearticulates territory, authority, and rights. And the fourth section examines the proliferation of specialized orders that bring with them multiple normative, temporal, and spatial framings of activity where once the project of the modern state was to organize its territory in terms of a single normative order, or raison d'état, and a unitary spatio-temporal order.

ON METHOD AND INTERPRETATION

The book develops two research strategies. One uses history as a series of natural experiments to raise the level of complexity through which to
understand our move into a global age, one that has tended to be simplified as
growing interdependence and space-time compression. A research strategy
that introduces greater detail and more options allows me to explore a key
substantive thesis, to wit, that major change in complex systems cannot happen *ad novo* but is generated at least partly on capabilities developed over earlier periods. This is a highly conditioned process as it entails tipping and new
organizing logics. The choice of particular historical conjunctures that capture such major changes in complex systems serves the purpose of developing
an analytics for examining such transitions and, secondly, understanding in
great detail one such transition, the current move into a global age.

The second research strategy aims at avoiding the endogeneity trap
common in the social sciences. It is predicated on the assumption that isolating foundational components present in major social and geopolitical wholes
allows for a critical perspective that differs from a focus on the wholes themselves. It allows us to capture the work of assembling these components according to specific organizing logics. In this book the pertinent wholes are the
nation-state and the world scale—examined through specific instances of
each. The pertinent components selected—territory, authority, and rights—
were isolated as critical to societies and geopolitics. They can then be conceived of as transhistorical even though they assume specific contents and
forms in each formation. It is in this combination of presence across time and
space with specificity of contents and institutional insertions that these three
components can be conceived of as analytic categories. The level of disaggregation they entail, compared with the wholes within which they are assembled, allows me to track how particular elements of each can get relodged into
new systems.

Building on and enabled by these two strategies for research, I constructed distinct analytic categories to get at the question of the formation of
complex systems and change in and of such systems. These categories are capability, tipping point, and organizing logic. A capability is a particular assemblage of specific institutionalizations of territory, authority, and rights—more
generally, of whatever the critical variables chosen by a researcher. A tipping
point is a particular combination of dynamics and resources that can usher a
new organizing logic; particular capabilities become dislodged from an older
organizing logic and get inserted, often as constitutive elements, in a novel

organizing logic, and new capabilities are formed. An organizing logic is, at its most abstract, the centrifugal/centripetal dynamic and the relational system that constitutes an order, in our case a social and geopolitical order. Of concern here are the three major orders usually designated as feudal, national, and global.

One of the assumptions guiding this book is that knowledge about the multiple dynamics shaping actual historical transitions helps us raise the level of complexity through which we examine and understand current transformations. The effort in this book was not to isolate a limited number of causal variables following the common criterion of the fewer the better. The effort was in the opposite direction: recovering the multifaceted rather than the monocausal and often multidirectional character of historical transitions. This helps in deciphering processes of disarticulation that produce multiple options, the capturing of a few of these options through tipping dynamics, and the subsequent closures that conform an organizing logic. Thereby we also recover the truncated histories that at their time might have been experienced as dominant conditions and dynamics but failed to get lodged in the path dependencies that contributed to the ensuing order. But we also capture the fact that capabilities significant to the older order can be critical to the formation of the new order, albeit subject to insertion into a new organizing logic that may alter the valence of these capabilities.

It is precisely these types of dynamics that are overlooked or evicted from social science accounts that dominate our understanding of the rise of territorial states. The feudal order and its capabilities represent the obstacle, that which needs to be overcome, that which works in the opposite direction of the centripetal dynamic of the nation-state. In turn, explanations and interpretations about the new global age tend to posit the mutual exclusivity of the national and the global—a kind of obverse state capture, in which the global is seen as the opposite of the national.

In recovering the multifaceted and multidirectional character of past transitions, notably from the feudal order to the national state, the transition from a national to a global age can also be shown to be far less defined than a national-global opposition. I used particular historical conjunctures as a type of natural experiment, and in this sense the use of history has theoretical and analytical aims. These are natural experiments that have been completed—to be distinguished from a notion of the past as completed. They can help us understand the character of social change in complex systems. In focusing on capabilities constitutive of a given order and tracking their movement or decay across major historic transitions, I can recover something about the making of critical elements of a new order. Capabilities can here be conceived of as intermediating in the move from one to another whole or master formation. This contrasts a focus on the attributes of the master formations themselves—feudal, national, and global order—or a focus on the "new"—as in technology-driven explanations of change. It helps one navigate both the ocean of details that is history and the representation of a transition as the elimination or overcoming of whatever is critical in specifying the preceding order. The transition from feudal to national state is far more marked by articulations than many stylized accounts suggest—though there are significant exceptions in the scholarship to this trend, and they helped me in developing my contrarian's analysis.

One of the critical hypotheses organizing the effort in this book is that we cannot understand the meaning of globalization by confining our study to the characteristics of self evidently global processes and institutions. There is nothing wrong with identifying these characteristics, but it is not enough. In many ways these are attributes of global systems; they do not explain the character of the transformation we seek to grasp with the concept of globalization.

TERRITORY, AUTHORITY, AND RIGHTS:

NATIONAL AND GLOBAL ASSEMBLAGES

The analytics and heuristics in this book hold that detailed in-depth examinations of the critical formal and de facto features of TAR allow us to grasp foundational change arising from inside complex systems rather than simply as a consequence of external forces. Thus transformations inside the nation-state are one foundational factor in the current global era. As filtered through the features of TAR, this transformation takes the form of particular elements of TAR becoming reassembled into novel denationalized configurations that may operate at the global, national, or subnational level. The disassembling, even if partial, denaturalizes what has often unwittingly become naturalized—the national constitution of territory, authority, and rights, and the global constitution of their undoing. Each, territory, authority, and rights, helps in dissecting the two master categories—the national and the global.

In part 1 I examined the formation of particular capabilities that eventually came to be foundational for the emergence of the nation-state. Among these were the elusive authority of the divine monarch as enabling the idea of secular sovereign authority, and the political economy of urban territoriality centered partly in the development of secular and constitutional forms of authority and rights. The development of industrial capitalism produced some of the foundational legal personae for the nation-state. Both as a historical actor and as a legal persona, the bourgeoisie is the historical subject for constituting a regime of private property of the means of production and the legal construction of a disadvantaged subject—the worker. As a legal persona, the worker is the subject that is bound by law to respect the private ownership of the means of production. These legal personae are a distinct departure from earlier notions of the monarch as the owner of the means of production and serfdom, as well as from more tribal notions of collective possession and usufruct, often centered in what is commonly referred to as folk law, that is, the folk law of the Germanic tribes (chapter 2). The British Parliament assumed its full historic role in the construction of these personae. With time it came to play a role in the teasing out of the tensions and contestations between these two subjects, resulting in the negotiation that is the emergence of the regulatory state and the welfare state. Chapter 3 briefly showed how this development was evident in all the major powers of the time, albeit under highly variable conditions producing somewhat different formalizations. Thus in the United States, the judiciary played a more critical role in shaping the disadvantage of the worker as a legal persona; yet in a parallel with the British case, it is Congress that eventually passed various legislative acts aimed at protecting workers and the disadvantaged, and, eventually, the welfare state.

Part 2 makes legible the partial, often specialized disassembling of the national that is critical for constituting the global. This underscores the need for analyses of partial, often highly specialized or particularized dynamics and their cross-country variability, rather than all-encompassing descriptions. Further, it also shows how the current global era consists partly of global systems evolving out of the capabilities that originally constituted the territorial sovereign state; some of the capabilities of the national sovereign state, with its territorial fixity and exclusivity, eventually came to enable the formation or evolution of particular global systems that require neither territoriality nor exclusivity. In contrast to the prevalent view in the literature, my interpretation does not construct the global and the national as mutually exclusive. Among others, the electronic global market for capital (chapters 5 and 7) and the changed relationship of citizens to their national states (chapters 6 and 7) evince new alignments in the assembling of constitutive elements of the global. Third, these chapters make legible the possibility of globalization as endogenous to the nation-state.

Each chapter in part 2 focuses on a particular site for this type of analytic and heuristic work. Chapter 4 addresses one of the critical dimensions in the heuristics developed in this book: the nation-state, especially the state

apparatus narrowly defined, as a crucial domain for some of the transformations ushering the global age. Though not the only one, the state apparatus is,
I argued, the most complex one. Hence its transformations are potentially
strategic and far-reaching in their scope. This is partly due to the institutional
weight of the state apparatus in the assembling of the social, and partly due to
the state centripetal dynamic of the last two centuries whereby vast stretches
of social life and geopolitics were absorbed by the state into its distinctive
structurations—that is, they were nationalized. Unlike what is the case in
much of the globalization literature, in this book's analysis the internal transformation of the state apparatus thus becomes critical, as does that of the
nation-state, a more diffuse and partly discursive category.

These various issues were explored in particular detail through a focus on the Bretton Woods system and on today's national state apparatus because these are two sites that have produced enormous confusion in the
analysis of the current era. The Bretton Woods system was, after all, an explicit effort to set up an international governance system and is, for many
globalization scholars, the beginning of today's global era. In chapter 4 I analyzed at length why the Bretton Woods system was not part of the organizing
logic of the global era: it was a system of global governance aimed at ensuring
the relative autonomy of national states from global forces. It was, thus, the
opposite of the current global governance system that aims at opening up
countries to global firms, markets, flows, and standards of all sorts, and, more
foundationally, install novel organizing logics that replace specific components of the state's logic. But Bretton Woods did develop capabilities for the
management of global dynamics, some of which became part of the new organizing logic of the global era. As for the state, it is usually seen as a victim of
the rise of global systems. The analysis developed in this book produces a far
more differentiated picture in that it focuses on the internal redistribution of
power in the state, which shows that the executive gains power over the
other branches of government partly because of globalization. The organizing
logic of each the national and global eras are then shown to be constituted by
both states and world political economies but with different alignments for
each of these components. The structuring of territory, authority, and rights
in each of these eras is one way of registering the differences.

Using the United States as the emblematic case, chapter 4 focused
on changes inside the state apparatus narrowly defined. Although not necessarily representative of statehood at this time, the U.S. state represents an
extreme instantiation of internal state transformation; among developed
countries, the British and Italian states, as well as global south states as varied
as Argentina and Malaysia, also are undergoing some of these changes, albeit

in a less extreme form. In the United States these changes are centered on two major shifts. One is the redistribution of power among the key branches, most notably the accelerated dominance of the executive taking off in the 1980s, and the loss of power by Congress after a rather innovative and assertive period in the 1960s and 1970s. I locate the reasons for this shift partly in the fact that policies such as privatization and deregulation hollow out the oversight and lawmaking functions of Congress. This asymmetry profoundly alters one of the constitutive rules of the liberal state. A second major shift is the reconstitution of the private-public divide, a divide that is foundational to the liberal state. This divide was historically constitutive for the ascendance and formation of a distinct subject—the bourgeoisie, a subject that embeds and embodies the legitimacy of private ownership of the means of production at a time when the state had long been the main economic actor.

The sharp loss of power of the legislature evident in the United States beginning in the 1980s contributed to a democratic deficit originating inside the liberal state rather than produced exclusively by globalization as is often claimed. Legislatures are the most open branch of government, centered as they are largely on public deliberation, and have played strategic roles at various times in the twentieth century to redress (partly) imbalances of power between workers and employers, and between the state and the citizenry. In chapter 4 I examined one of the critical dynamics facilitating the loss of power of the legislature: the deregulation, privatization, and marketization of public functions which all shift oversight responsibilities out of the legislature. While this has generally been grouped under such general categories as a loss of power by the state, chapter 4 shows how this is not an adequate representation. The executive branch gained some of the powers lost by the legislature as a proliferation of specialized agencies took over functions once in oversight committees of Congress. One of the key mechanisms for this shift has been the use of existing law to institute these at times foundational changes rather than making new law that would have involved the legislature. Using existing regulatory agencies to execute the various forms of deregulation and privatization meant that these changes stayed out of the public debate that is congressional deliberation in the making of new law. Chapter 4 contains a rather negative evaluation of this reinterpretation of old law: avoiding the making of new law meant avoiding a far larger public debate and it meant avoiding informing the citizenry. Further, although the proliferation of specialized government agencies that have taken on some of the regulatory and oversight functions once in the legislature would not necessarily mean a gain of power by the executive, this is what has happened insofar as the executive has taken the position that it has unitary power over the public administration.

This also has set the stage for the particular forms of expanded secrecy accumulated by the executive and its claims that the formalized erosions of citizens' privacy rights are lawful, with the Patriot Act merely the most extreme instance. Insofar as deregulation, privatization, and marketization of public functions are critical for expanded and novel forms of corporate economic globalization, these changes inside the state can be seen as part of the epochal transformation of the current age.

How do we theorize these erosions in two foundational propositions of the liberal state: the mutually balancing separation of powers inside the state, and the separation between a private domain with strong protections from incursions by the state, and a public domain subject to public scrutiny. The diminished power of Congress is consequential. It can hold the executive accountable and ensure a public moment in the making of major changes in the law dressed as executive reinterpretation of the law. These trends point to a partial but sharp privatization of key features of the executive that produce a sharp realignment inside the state and an erosion of privacy rights among the citizenry. This partial privatizing of executive power and erosion of citizens' privacy rights have reached their most pronounced form with the Bush administration. But rather than interpreting these shifts as the result of an abuse of power by the Bush administration, and in that sense as anomalous, I argued in chapter 4 that they are far deeper and systemic. These shifts began to take shape in the Reagan era and to some extent cut across party lines. Thus they continued under the Democratic presidency of Clinton, albeit in a less secretive and somewhat more public fashion given Clinton's strong public presence and engagement.

The character and often extreme form of these transformations makes the American state a heuristic space in that these changes allow us to discern limitations in the capacities of the liberal state to accommodate key features of the current global age: economic globalization and the new kinds of global wars the United States is fighting. The American state also functions as a heuristic space for understanding whether these shifts are a function of hegemonic status, or emblematic of the new age, even though not representative of all developed states. I am inclined to interpret this along the lines of the second—they are emblematic of the new age, and in this regard signal that this new age does not comfortably accommodate the liberal state as historically constituted. It is a question that remains to be settled. However, these changes do indicate the crossing of a line—a debordering of the liberal state. For the purposes of my analysis, this debordering is part of the constitutive elements of the new global age.

In chapters 5 and 6 I traced how this dynamic functions through two foundational personae or categories—capital and the citizenry—as these get constituted in far more elusive, diffuse, complex, multifaceted, and intermediated forms than even twenty years ago, let alone in earlier centuries. The examination sought to capture the changes in the division between the public and the private and in the relationship between the state and the citizen. Chapter 5 specifically posits a privatizing of norm-making capacities once in the public domain of the nation-state and once part of sovereign authority. Chapter 6 posits a transformation in the relationship between the state and the citizen or, more generally, in the architecture for political membership in a context where the executive pierces some of the foundational privacy rights of citizens and citizens in turn expand the meaning of citizenship beyond narrow forms of exclusive allegiance to the state. Some of these issues were revisited in part 3 through the lens of the new computer-centered interactive technologies that enable new forms of sociality.

I identified new geographies of power—the particular structurations of TAR that constitute forms of power. One of these geographies, examined in chapter 4, is internal to the state itself—the shift of power to the executive branch and away from the legislature, and the growing secrecy of executive branch. The other, the subject of chapter 5, is external; it includes a new private institutional order linked to the global economy, and it includes institutional orders such as the international network of NGOs and the international human rights regime. But critical to my analysis is that external here needs to be understood in more complex dimensions than the global as external and the national as mutually exclusive with the global. Even as it partly inhabits the national, including the state apparatus, this "external" geography does so by constituting a space that is distinct from the national and is thus predicated on, or productive of, a disarticulation of territory and authority when compared with the case of the nation-state. This external geography of power is a field of forces that includes a broad array of nonstate actors and alters the historically produced distinction between the private and public domains. Both the transformations inside the state and the novel "external" geography are partial and incipient but strategic.

Given my formulation, the processes identified evince high levels of complexity and specialization that at times required detailed examinations of specific domains either because they were emblematic of some of the novel trends, for example, the new forms of international commercial arbitration, or because they are the change, for example, global electronic markets for capital. Some of these processes are still largely represented in national terms. The effort was to detect foundational shifts that may as yet only operate at the edges or be a minor, even when strategic, component within each of several large routinized institutional sectors. I addressed these issues through an examination of particular, highly specialized dynamics in chapter 5. I posited that the marking features of the new, mostly but not exclusively, private institutional order in formation are its capacity to privatize what was heretofore public and to denationalize what were once national authorities and policy agendas. The capacity to privatize and denationalize is predicated on changes in specific components of territory, authority, and rights as these have been constituted historically in the national state. One critical instance I elaborated was that the new privatized institutional order for governing the corporate global economy has governance capabilities and a type of specialized and partial normative authority. That is to say, we see an emergent new normativity that has incorporated elements of what was once state authority. It is not embedded in what has been and to some extent remains the master normativity of modern times, raison d'état. At the same time, once constituted, this new normativity of the world of private power partly installs itself in the public realm where it reappears as public policy. In this particular process I see one of the dynamics that denationalize what had historically been constructed as national state agendas. I posit that particular institutional components of the national state begin to function as the institutional home for the operation of powerful dynamics constitutive of what we could describe as "global capital" and "global capital markets." In so doing, these state institutions reorient their particular policy work or, more broadly, state agendas toward the requirements of the global economy.

These types of dynamics unsettle the meaning of "national" in institutional components of states linked to the implementation and regulation of economic globalization, and they do so within the law, not in violation of the law. National territory and national state authority assume new meanings. The global electronic market for capital makes this unsettlement legible. The research literature has recognized this by focusing on the vast power of this market over governments. Less legible and less noted in the research literature on economic globalization, including on the capital market, is the denationalizing of state work involved in enabling the global economy, which I specify as one of the core dynamics in the functioning of this market and other critical components of economic globalization. By this I intend to specify foundational transformations brought about by the growing incidence of private interest logics circulating through the public domain where they then emerge as state policy. I see this as a different type of dynamic from what has commonly been described as state capture, a concept usually associated with violations of the law. The denationalizing of state work that I discussed in chapter 5 happens within the framing of the law, as do the

mutual shifts from the public to the private domain as historically constituted, discussed in chapters 4 and 6, notably the perforation of citizens' privacy rights. In this regard, an examination of the global market for capital
also allows us to understand particular shifts in the construction of the private and public domains.

A second major site where these dynamics get constituted and filtered through is political membership in the modern state. I examined formal
and informal changes in what remain the foundational institutions for membership in our societies, citizenship and alienage. I specified membership as an
incompletely theorized contract with the state. In this incompleteness I located the possibility of change in these institutions and hence my point of entry, my site for research. This type of research and theorization strategy allows
for the inclusion of informal practices by both citizens and aliens and the possibility of change that can begin with such informal practices; some of the
claims associated with such practices can get formalized into novel rights, often after decades of informal struggles.

Current foundational changes inside the state itself and in the state's
positioning in a broader field of forces (chapters 4 and 5) invite an inquiry as
to how that incompleteness can become activated today and push the institutions for membership in new directions, even if only in particular features. This
blurring entails a rearticulation, albeit it partial, of the way in which membership institutions articulate territory, authority, and rights. These changes are
perhaps most legible in specific formal transformations of particular features
of the institution of citizenship: the loss of social rights associated with the
scaling down of welfare entitlements, the loss of privacy rights, and the option of dual nationality with its associated weakening of notions of exclusive
allegiance. I interpret these and other such changes as lengthening the distance between the state and the citizen, a move away from what was the signal contribution of the French and American revolutions: the notion that
the people are the state, and the state is the people. The growing distance between state and citizenry, which I posited in chapter 6, allows for novel interventions, for example, suing one's government, and exit strategies, for example, imaginaries around transnational identities.

These transformations are not predicated necessarily on deterritorialization or locations for the institution outside the national state, as is crucial to conceptions of postnational citizenship. They are internal to the
national state. I refer to these transformations as a partial, often highly specialized denationalizing of particular features in the institution of citizenship.
At the other extreme, the case of unauthorized aliens, I emphasize micro-
transformations that make what is formally a non-persona into a carrier of

various legalities, often through judges' decisions in pertinent litigations or through the human rights regime. I interpret these trends as deeper in their capacity to produce new meanings around the question of political member-ship than the far more visible renationalizing of membership politics particu-larly evident in today's developed countries. It is difficult to establish the meaning of these divergent dynamics, partly because they are history in the making. I tend toward interpreting this renationalizing of membership poli-tics as rooted in older alignments of the nation-state which, as they weaken or operate in reduced domains, emerge in a kind of purified, that is, extreme, form, which can easily be seen as strength when it is in fact a diminished factor, or even systemically unsustainable—a last gasp. Use of religion and "culture," rather than citizenship, to construct membership may well be a function of the changed relationship of citizens to the state and the insecurities it pro-duces. In this regard, use of religion is not an anachronism but a formation arising out of particular changes in the current age.

Part 3 explored specific formations and dynamics that we might con-ceive of as extreme instances of the changes afoot, rather than the middle ground of change, or the instances of change that involve majorities—of people, of institutions, of actors. Among these are a variety of global digital assemblages, which refigure critical aspects of territory, authority, and rights in that they partly function outside the frames of state authority and the frames for various rights. No matter how powerful, they are largely informal, at least for now.

In chapter 7, I problematized the assumption about the autonomy of these global digital assemblages from the nation-state and its framings of TAR. I examined the relation, if any, of these assemblages to the nation-state and to the particular spaces inside the latter that have been newly de-nationalized. We cannot simply interpret these global digital assemblages as postnational, as disembedded from the nation-state, and as de facto global. These characterizations are too general and only partly correct. The variety of dynamics and practices that contribute to constitute these global digital assemblages are often deeply imbricated with nondigital factors that are likely to include multiple instances of the national but also the denational-ized. Even when they have global scope, some of these new digital assem-blages are profoundly rooted in local specifics and often derive much of their meaning from nondigital domains. But in so doing these assemblages can be shown to be powerful capabilities that constitute specific processes of dena-tionalization. Thereby they contribute to different meanings of territory, au-thority, and rights. In this regard, then, these global digital assemblages can be conceived of as a theoretical frontier zone for understanding the character of the global, even though the global is both more and less than the new electronic world.

To get at these types of questions and interpretations requires theoretical and methodological innovations. The social sciences are not yet fully equipped to study these new technical capabilities in ways that factor in the distinct character of these technologies without losing the complexity of a social science perspective, that is, avoiding technological determinism or reducing the technology to the independent variable in order to establish its impact on various extant socio-scientific objects of study, for example, work, family, and politics. Left out of these types of methodological framings for examining these technologies is the possibility that the digital helps constitute new domains that need to be constructed as objects of study, beyond the extant ones. The need to capture such new domains was part of the analytic effort in chapters 7 and 8. It includes the effort to embed the digital in more complex conceptual and practical fields than is typically done. Analytically this parallels the effort in part 2, which aimed at embedding the global in thicker and more complex national environments.

There are theoretical and political consequences: for instance, the complex assemblages examined throughout this book entail distinct spatio-temporal orderings. Chapter 8 examined a variety of practices, neither simply national nor global, which in their aggregate constitute new temporal orders inside the national. Thereby they go against the long term secular trend of the bureaucratizing and standardizing of national spatio-temporal orders. And it implies that even global electronic markets can be made accountable to national authorities because they are partly imbricated with a network of financial centers located inside nation-states. Some of the issues raised in chapters 6 and 7 get at this.

FROM NATIONAL BORDERS TO EMBEDDED BORDERINGS:

IMPLICATIONS FOR TERRITORIAL AUTHORITY

State sovereignty is usually conceived of as a monopoly of authority in a particular territory. Today it is becoming evident that state sovereignty articulates both its own and external conditions and norms. Sovereignty remains a systemic property but its institutional insertion and its capacity to legitimate and absorb all legitimating power, to be the source of law, have become unstable. The politics of contemporary sovereignties are far more complex than notions of mutually exclusive territorialities can capture.

The question of territory as a parameter for authority and rights has entered a new phase. State exclusive authority over its territory remains the prevalent mode of final authority in the global political economy. But it is less absolute formally than it once was meant to be and, as the examination in chapters 2 and 3 help make clear, prevalence is not to be confused with dominance. In addition, critical components of this authority that may still have a national institutional form and location are no longer national in the historically constructed sense of that term. One way of deciphering some of these issues and opening them up to a research agenda is by singling out the capability represented by the power of the geographic border in the modern nation-state project.

We are seeing the formation of global, partly territorial alignments that incorporate what were once protections encased in border regimes (chapter 5). Insofar as the state has historically had the capability to encase its territory through administrative and legal instruments, it also has the capability to change that encasement—for instance, deregulate its borders and open up to foreign firms and investment. The question that concerns me here is whether this signals that the capabilities entailed by territoriality, a form of exclusive and final authority, can be detached from geographic territory. Such detachment is conceivably partial and variable, depending on what is to be subjected to authority. This in turn raises a question about how the issue of borderings can function inside the nation-state.

Much of the material in parts 2 and 3 suggests that this detachment today assumes two forms broadly speaking. One is that the border is embedded in the product, the person, and the instrument: a mobile agent endogenizes critical features of the border. The other is that there are multiple locations for the border, whether inside firms or in long transnational chains of locations that can move deep inside national territorial and institutional domains. Global cities account for a disproportionate concentration of such border locations; the latter are mostly institutional locations that assume a territorial correlate, for example, the large concentration of international banking facilities in New York City. Institutional locations in principle need not have territorial correlates. The locations of bordering capabilities are in a phase of sharp unsettlement, which opens up a whole new research agenda. If there is one sector where we can begin to discern new stabilized bordering capabilities and their geographic and institutional locations it is in the corporate economy (chapters 5 and 7).

Thus, rather than conceiving of the much noted new mobilities as a function of globalization and the new information and communication technologies, I argue that these new types of mobilities also arise from a third critical dimension: the fact that state border capabilities centered on nineteenth- and twentieth-century geographic concepts of the border could switch into nongeographic bordering capabilities operating both transnationally and sub- nationally. In this process, particular legal protections get detached from their national territorial jurisdictions and become incorporated into a variety of of- ten highly specialized or partial global regimes and thereby often become transformed into far more specialized rights and obligations. I also see in this dynamic capabilities jumping tracks and becoming lodged into a novel organ- izing logic. One example is the bundle of rights granted by host states to for- eign firms under the WTO which unsettles older national regimes. Many of these rights and guarantees derive from what were once national rights and guarantees used precisely to distinguish national firms from foreign firms; these rights and guarantees were also one critical component in the building up of the state's exclusive authority over its national territory.

Such shifts from geographic borders to embedded bordering capabili- ties have been far more common and formalized in the case of major corpo- rate economic actors than they have, for example, for citizens and migrants. Firms and markets have seen their advantages shift toward new types of insti- tutionalized protections while for citizens this has not been the case. The in- ternational human rights regime is a weaker system of protections than the WTO provisions protecting the cross-border circulation of professionals (chapter 6). It is also weaker, though far broader, than the specialized visas for business people and the increasingly common visas for high-tech workers. As national states are directly and indirectly involved in both the human rights and these business regimes, one question this raises is how much divergence in critical regimes a system can accommodate.

While this detachment and re-embedding in new types of bordering regimes has been formalized and institutionalized for corporate economic ac- tors but not for citizenship, a systemic perspective would posit corresponding pressures on the institution of citizenship also moving toward particular types of detachments. This would be a type of pressure freeing citizenship from state capture—escaping the highly formalized and institutionalized relation be- tween the citizen and the state, one typically characterized as inevitable in much of the standard scholarship. In chapters 6 and 7 I discussed both formal and informal ways that signal such a partial shift out of the historically pro- duced correspondence between the nation-state and citizenship. I argued that such dynamics are taking place and that they are not confined to the much noted postnational and transnational citizenship identities but also include complex formalizations inside the state that partly denationalize various fea- tures of citizenship.

One of the modes in which the embedded borderings discussed above function is through specialized geographies that do involve particular forms of reterritorialization. For instance, some of the capabilities entailed by bordering operate through the variety of norms, standards, and subcultures of financial centers, as I examined in chapter 7. In the case of the new types of bordering for individual rights entailed by the international human rights regime, we can conceive of a national court (as distinct from an international court) using such instruments to adjudicate a case as also representing a particular type of reterritorializing of bordering functions. I identify a type of reterritorializing even in digital space, a transboundary space that in principle should be nongeographic and escape all territorial authority (chapter 7). Yet the state can also be shown to exercise authority over digital networks through the indirect venue of hardware standards and whatever regulations of content circulation and intellectual property rights might be involved.

Are these specialized types of reterritorializing a reinsertion into the exclusive territorial authority of the state? The processes presented above do not have the territorial parameters underlying territoriality but could, nonetheless, represent a form of state authority. Territoriality, understood as exclusive institutionalized authority over its territory, was foundational for the nation-state. It is not clear that the types of territorial insertions examined in parts 2 and 3 are constitutive of the state even though they do articulate state authority. My interpretation of the matter is that these territorial insertions—for instance, of electronic financial markets—do not necessarily entail subsumption under exclusive state authority because they are predicated on specific denationalizations in law and policy in the service of a global regime. While such circulate through the national institutional apparatus—or specific components of the latter—and hence are subject to state authority they cannot be seen as constitutive of the state's exclusive territoriality. This is a type of framing of the relationship between territory and state authority that comprises forms of globality constituted via localized actors encased in local places. The relationship between territory and state authority today can accommodate the existence inside national territory of denationalized spatialities. That relationship also encases the types of differential temporal orders discussed in chapter 8. This contrasts with the aims of the Bretton Woods regime. Bretton Woods illuminates a particular set of issues about territorial boundaries precisely because it was an international regime and as such aimed at strengthening national boundaries and state territorial authority, protecting national economies from external forces, and developing supranational authority. In the current period, the aim is the opposite—not to protect, but to open up, and, more significantly, to ensure strategic denationalizations.

Authority with territorial parameters can take many different forms: the historical territorial exclusivity associated with the nation-state should be conceived of as just one of these. In chapter 2 I posited that late medieval cities constituted a type of urban political economy of territoriality. Can we make this more abstract so as to accommodate particular forms of territorial authority we see emerge today? Some of these get constituted as denationalized territories inside ongoing national territorial regimes. Global cities are such entities as compared to electronic financial networks, which are not. Insofar as some components of historical borders are evolving into long chains with multiple locations inside national territories, the resulting denationalized domains inside those territories create a new type of internal bordering. One question for research is whether these internal borderings bring particular types of advantages to some actors and institutions—for instance, do they entail capacities akin to arbitraging in finance? These are all issues that complicate the question of state authority: it remains critical but corresponds less to its representation in national and international law than it did before the current transformation.

Another specific type of state territorial authority is extraterritoriality, an interesting capability in this context. It was and remains critical to an international system made up of nation-states, where the "community" of nation-states basically accounts for the system. What happens with extraterritoriality in a global context. Are the new global regimes a variant of extraterritorial authority, as some scholars posit? But even as this older form persists, the emergent dynamic is one whereby territorial insertions in a foreign country denationalize rather than produce an extension of national territorial authority.

It is interesting to recall that in feudal times, the capabilities for a future formation marked by unitary authority—the territorial sovereign— were being developed through organizational modes that would have seemed incompatible with those of the territorial state. We need to ask if today we might have a similar situation of ambiguity and illegibility—albeit moving in the opposite direction. The nation-state remains the prevalent organizational source of authority and to variable extents the dominant one. But, as I argued above and in this book generally, critical components of authority deployed in the making of the territorial state are shifting toward becoming strong capabilities for detaching that authority from its exclusive territory and onto multiple bordering systems. Insofar as many of these systems are operating inside the nation-state, they may be obscuring the fact that a significant switch has happened. It may take a while to become legible in its aggregate impact. At its most extreme this may entail a shift of capabilities historically associated with the nation-state onto global digital assemblages; given their extreme form, such assemblages may make the switch more visible than other types of transformations that might be foundational.

TOWARD A MULTIPLICATION OF SPECIALIZED ORDERS:

ASSEMBLAGES OF TAR

One of the arguments developed in the book is that much of the globalization literature has focused on what are at best bridging events in the process of foundational transformation, rather than the transformation itself or "the event," in Sewell's terms. Many of the global formations that have received much attention, such as the new roles of the IMF or the creation of the WTO are, from the perspective of this book, bridging events that function as indications of and capabilities for a foundational change. But the actual dynamics getting shaped are far deeper and more radical than such entities as the WTO or IMF per se. The latter are powerful capabilities for the making of a new order—they are instruments for, not the new order itself. Similarly, the Bretton Woods system was a powerful capability that facilitated some of the new global formations but was not itself the beginning of the new order as is so often asserted in the globalization literature. These are not the core of the transformation itself, no matter how powerful they are as foot soldiers. The transformation is partly an outcome of these powerful capabilities but is in itself far more complex and radical, albeit not all-encompassing. If anything, it is the new literature on empire (D. Harvey 2004; Hardt and Negri 2000), more so than those focusing on the IMF and WTO, that is closer to conveying the depth of the potential changes even when I have my disagreements with some of these analyses. Let us recall that even as industrial capitalism was becoming the dominant dynamic, most people, most firms, and most political debates were not centered on it. Objectively the prevalent condition remained agriculture and trade.

At the heart of this foundational transformation I see a sharp proliferation of subassemblages bringing together elements that used to be part of more diffuse institutional domains within the nation-state or, at times, the institutionalized supranational system. The novel types of bordering capabilities posited above play a critical role in the forming of these particularized assemblages. These are partial and often highly specialized formations centered in particular utilities and purposes. This trend brings with it several significant consequences even though it is a partial, not an all-encompassing development. While these are for now still mostly incipient formations, they are potentially profoundly unsettling of what are still the prevalent institutional arrangements—nation-states and the supranational system. In this regard, it is reminiscent in its analytic status of what I specified for the early development of industrial capitalism: even as it was the dominant form it was not (yet) the prevalent form (chapter 3).

One of the consequences of the sharpening differentiation among domains once suffused with the national, or the supranational, is that at the limit this can enable a proliferation of temporal and spatial framings and a proliferation of normative orders where once the dominant logic was toward producing unitary spatial, temporal, and normative framings. Even though this is a partial rather than all-encompassing development, its character is strategic.

There are, clearly, features of this development that resonate with the multiple systems of rule of the Middle Ages. But an interpretation of current developments along the lines posited above—the proliferation of particular kinds of specialized assemblages—points to a critical difference. At the heart of this difference is that these new assemblages produce a new type of segmentation that entails, in some of its components, a kind of inequality that can cut across every scale, nation-state, major city, and state apparatus. It is not the intrasystemic inequality that emerges out of a unitary, albeit highly differentiated system, such as is a nation-state. Nor is it the kind of inequality that exists among countries and among developed and less developed regions of the world. Those are two types of recognized and named inequalities and we have developed massive institutional and discursive domains to address them; although all this effort has only partly reduced those inequalities, they are a target for efforts and resources. The proliferation of specialized assemblages that cut across the master units that continue to organize our geopolity and that segment once unitary components produces a kind of inequality we might conceive of as multiplying intersystemic segmentations, where the systems are these particularized assemblages. It is then a kind of inequality that coexists with older forms of differentiation inside countries and across countries but is to be distinguished from these.

What distinguishes this multiplying intersystemic segmentation is both the possibility of exiting what are today still ruling normative orders and, equally important if not more so, the constituting of particularized novel normative orders internal to each assemblage. This is still a minor process in the larger scale of our geopolity. But it may well be the beginning of a multisited disruption of its existing formal architecture. This is not akin to the battles between old empires. It is multisited and often endogenous. It lifts territorial segments out of their unitary state normative framing. It is strategic and particular, and hence often illegible. For instance, I would include the internal transformation of the liberal state discussed in chapter 4—the growing inequality between the power of the executive and that of the legislature, and the trends toward the partial privatizing of particular components of executive authority—as one such emergent segmentation at the heart of an assemblage where there is not meant to be any.

Herein lies a foundational difference with the medieval period, when there were strong broadly encompassing normative orders (the church, the empire) and the disaggregations (the feuds, the cities) each contained within them a fairly complete structure involving many if not most aspects of life (different classes, norms, systems of justice, and so forth). Today these assemblages are not only highly specialized, partial, and without much internal differentiation, but not even the state can quite counteract the particularized normativities each contains. The norm-making power of the global capital market, examined in chapter 5, illustrates this well. Finally, these assemblages tend to have rules for governance wired into the structures of their system in a way reminiscent of how free markets function in that these are not explicated rules and norms, as distinct from formalized systems for governance, that are meant to be explicated and outside the system itself. Again, the new forms of unaccountable power within the executive (chapter 4) and the global market for capital (chapter 7) illustrate this; but so does the world of NGOs.

This type of analysis suggests a disaggregating of the glue that for a long time held possibly different normative orders together under the somewhat unitary dynamics of nation-states. I see in this proliferation of specialized assemblages a tendency toward a remixing of constitutive rules, for instance in the shifts of the private-public division (chapter 4) and in the microtransformations of the relationship of citizens to the state and vice versa (chapter 6). A second tendency is the multiplication of partial systems, each with a small set of sharply distinctive constitutive rules, amounting to a type of simple system. Not all of these new specialized assemblages contain such constitutive rules, but it is evident in a number of those that constitute themselves precisely as disembedded from state authority and normativity and as private systems of justice and authority (chapter 5). In contrast, the localized and limited world of the manor or the fief of the medieval lord was a complex world encompassing constitutive rules that addressed the full range of spheres of social life. This is, then, a very different formation from that of the Middle Ages, and it is a fallacy and a deeply erroneous—albeit it common—parallel. One synthesizing image we might use to capture these dynamics is that we see a movement from centripetal nation-state articulation to a centrifugal multiplication of specialized assemblages. We come to see how foundational the centripetal power of the nation-state has been, and to variable extents, remains. Thinking that this resembles feudalism is a genuine error of interpretation and far too easy a representation and explanation of the transformation.

The multiplication of partial, specialized, and applied normative orders is unsettling and produces distinct normative challenges in the context of a still prevalent world of nation-states. Just to mention one instance, I would induce from these trends that normative orders such as religion reassume great importance where they had been confined to distinct specialized spheres by the secular normative orders of states. I would posit that this is not a fallback on older cultures but is, on the contrary, a systemic outcome of cutting-edge developments. This is not pre-modern but a new type of modernity. It arises out of the partial unbundling of what had been dominant and centripetal normative orders into multiple particularized segmentations.

A second issue is, however, the considerable illegibility, ultimately, of this shift to a centrifugal logic. We cannot quite see that it has replaced important segments of the centripetal logic of the nation-state. This is partly because the administrative capability represented by the nation-state remains critical also for significant elements of the new centrifugal logic (chapters 4 and 5) and because war and militarized border controls mark the geopolitical landscape have mostly been sharpened rather than diluted in much of the world. The ongoing prevalence of strong state politics and policies may well increasingly be a matter more of raw power than the more complex category that is authority—as the new types of wars, whether "civil" or international, suggest. Even as the raw power of national states in many cases has increased, this may not necessarily mean that sovereign territorial authority has become more significant. This distinction is critical to the analysis in this book. It is grounded in the weight and gravitational pull of the centripetal logic that feeds the ascendance of the nation-state. As the unitary character of the nation-state disaggregates, even if only partially, sovereign authority is itself subject to partial disaggregations, which is exactly what the chapters in parts 2 and 3 show. As this centripetal dynamic of the nation-state becomes less significant, we also see exit options for the disadvantaged.

Denationalization is the category through which I attempt to capture this foundational difference. This is a historicizing categorization with the double intent of de-essentializing the national by confining it to a historically specific configuration and making it a reference point by positing that its enormous complexity and large capture of society and the geopolity make it a strategic site for the transformation—the latter cannot simply come from the outside. What this categorization does not entail is the notion that the nation-state as a major form will disappear but rather that, in addition to being the site for key transformations, it will itself be a profoundly changed entity.

Bibliography

Abbott, Andrew. 1992. "From Causes to Events: Notes on Narrative Positivism." *Sociological Methods and Research* 20(4): 428–55.

———. 2001. *Time Matters: On Theory and Method*. Chicago: University of Chicago Press.

Abbott, Kenneth W. 1996. "Economic Issues and Political Participation: The Evolving Boundaries of International Federalism." *Cardozo Law Review* 18(3): 971–1010.

Abolafia, Mitchel Y. 1996. *Making Markets: Opportunism and Restraint on Wall Street*. Cambridge, Mass.: Harvard University Press.

———. 2005. "Interpretive Politics at the Federal Reserve." In *The Sociology of Financial Markets*, ed. Karin Knorr Cetina and Alex Preda. New York: Oxford University Press.

Abu-Lughod, J. 1989. *Before European Hegemony: The World System A.D. 1250–1350*. New York: Oxford University Press.

Ackerman, Bruce. 2000. "The New Separation of Powers." *Harvard Law Review* 113(3): 633–729.

Adam, Barbara. 1990. *Time and Social Theory*. Philadelphia: Temple University Press.

———. 2004. *Time*. Cambridge: Polity.

Adams, Paul C. 1996. "Protest and the Scale Politics of Telecommunications." *Political Geography* 15:419–41.

Adilkno. 1998. *The Media Archive*. Brooklyn, N.Y.: Autonomedia.

Aksen, Gerald. 1990. "Arbitration and Other Means of Dispute Settlement." In *International Joint Ventures: A Practical Approach to Working with Foreign Investors in the U.S. and Abroad*, ed. David Goldsweig and Roger Cummings. Chicago: American Bar Association.

Alford, Roger P. 2003. "The American Influence on International Arbitration." *Ohio State Journal on Dispute Resolution* 19(69): 69–88.

Allen, Mike. 2004. "President Campaigns to Make Patriot Act Permanent." *Washington Post*, April 19.

———. 2005. "House Votes to Curb Patriot Act; FBI's Power to Seize Library Records Would Be Halted." *Washington Post*, June 16.

Allen, John, Doreen Massey, and Michael Pryke, eds. 1999. *Unsettling Cities*. London: Routledge.

Allison, Julianne Emmons, ed. 2002. *Technology, Development, and Democracy: International Conflict and Cooperation in the Information Age*. Albany: State University of New York Press.

Aman, Alfred C., Jr. 1992. *Administrative Law in a Global Era*. Ithaca: Cornell University Press.

———. 1995. "A Global Perspective on Current Regulatory Reform: Rejection, Relocation, or Reinvention?" *Indiana Journal of Global Legal Studies* 2(2): 429–64.

———. 1998. "The Globalizing State: A Future-Oriented Perspective on the Public /Private Distinction, Federalism, and Democracy." *Vanderbilt Journal of Transnational Law* 31(4): 769–870.

———. 2002. "Globalization, Democracy, and the Need for a New Administrative Law." *UCLA Law Review* 49(6): 1687–1716.

———. 2004. *The Democracy Deficit: Taming Globalization through Law Reform*. New York: New York University Press.

American Civil Liberties Union. 2005. "Science under Siege: The Bush Administration's Assault on Academic Freedom and Scientific Inquiry." June 20. Available at: http://www.aclu.org/Privacy/Privacy.cfm?ID=18536&c=39 (accessed June 22, 2005).

Amin, Samir. 1970. *L'Accumulation à L'Échelle Mondiale*. Paris: Anthropos.

———. 1980. *Class and Nation, Historically and the Current Crisis*. New York: Monthly Review Press.

Aminzade, Richard. 1992. "Historical Sociology and Time." *Sociological Methods and Research* 20(4): 463–80.

Anderson, Perry. 1974. *Passages from Antiquity to Feudalism*. London: Verso.

Andrew, D., M. C. Henning, and L. W. Pauly. 2002. *Governing the World's Money*. Ithaca: Cornell University Press.

Aouzu, Amazu. 2001. *International Commercial Arbitration and African States: Practice, Participation, and Institutional Development*. Cambridge: Cambridge University Press.

APCWNSP (Association for Progressive Communications Women's Networking Support Programme). 2000. "Women in Sync: Toolkit for Electronic Networking." *Acting Locally, Connecting Globally: Stories from the Regions*. Vol. 3. Available at: http://www.apcwomen.org/netsupport/sync/sync.html.

Appadurai, Arjun. 1996. *Modernity at Large: Cultural Dimensions of Globalization*. Minneapolis: University of Minnesota Press.

Archer, Robin. 1998. *Economic Democracy: The Politics of Feasible Socialism*. Oxford: Oxford University Press.

Aronson, M. 1997. "A Public Lawyer's Response to Privatization and Outsourcing." In *Province of Administrative Law*, ed. M. Taggart. Oxford: Hart Publishing.

Arquilla, John, and David F. Ronfeldt. 2001. *Networks and Netwars: The Future of Terror, Crime, and Militancy*. Santa Monica, Calif.: Rand.

Arrighi, Giovanni. 1994. *The Long Twentieth Century: Money, Power, and the Origins of Our Times*. London: Verso.

Arrighi, Giovanni, and Beverly Silver. 1999. *Chaos and Governance in the Modern World System*. Minneapolis: University of Minnesota Press.

Ashley, Maurice. 1961 [1952]. *England in the Seventeenth Century*. London: Penguin Books.

Ashton, T. S. 1948. *The Industrial Revolution, 1760–1830*. New York: Oxford University Press.

Assassi, Libby, Kees van der Pijl, and Duncan Wigan. 2004. *Global Regulation: Managing Crises after the Imperial Turn*. Basingstoke: Palgrave Macmillan.

Avgerou, Chrisanthi. 2002. *Information Systems and Global Diversity*. Oxford: Oxford University Press.

Axel, Brian K. 2004. "The Context of Diaspora." *Cultural Anthropology* 19(1): 26–60.

Axelrod, Robert, ed. 1997a. *The Complexity of Cooperation: Agent-Based Models of Competition and Collaboration*. Princeton: Princeton University Press.

Axelrod, Robert. 1997b. "The Dissemination of Culture: A Model with Local Convergence and Global Polarization." In *The Complexity of Cooperation: Agent-Based Models of Competition and Collaboration*, ed. Robert Axelrod. Princeton: Princeton University Press.

Ayers, Ian, and John Braithwaite. 1992. *Responsive Regulation: Transcending the Deregulation Debate*. New York: Oxford University Press.

Bach, Jonathan, and David Stark. 2005. "Recombinant Technology and New Geographies of Association." In *Digital Formations: IT and New Architecture in the Global Realm*, ed. Robert Latham and Saskia Sassen. Princeton: Princeton University Press.

Bairoch, Paul. 1964. *Révolution industrielle et sous-devéloppement*. Paris: Editions de L'école des Hautes Etudes en Sciences Sociales.

Baldwin, John W. 1986. *The Government of Philip Augustus: Foundations of French Royal Power in the Middle Ages*. Berkeley: University of California Press.

Bank for International Settlements (BIS). 1999. *Annual Report*. Basle: BIS.

Banisar, David. 2004. "Freedom of Information and Access to Government Records around the World." The FreedomInfo.org Global Survey. May 12. http://www.freedominfo.org.

Barlow, Andrew L. 2003. *Between Fear and Hope: Globalization and Race in the United States*. Lanham, Md.: Rowman & Littlefield.

Barraclough, Geoffrey. 1984. *The Origins of Modern Germany*. New York: W. W. Norton.

Barrington, Louise. 1997. "Arbitral Women: A Study of Women in International Commercial Arbitration." In *The Commercial Way to Justice*, ed. Geoffrey M. Beresdor Hartwell. The Hague: Kluwer Law International.

Barrington, Moore. 1966. *The Social Origins of Dictatorship and Democracy*. Boston: Beacon.

Basch, Linda G., Nina G. Schiller, and Cristine S. Blanc. 1993. *Nations Unbound: Transnational Projects, Postcolonial Predicaments, and Deterritorialized Nation-states*. Langhorne, PA: Gordon and Breach.

Basel Committee on Banking Supervision (BCBS). 1988. *International Convergence of Capital Management and Capital Standards*. Basel, Switzerland: Bank for International Settlements.

———. 1996a. *Supervisory Framework for the Use of "Backtesting" in Conjunction with the Internal Models Approach to Market Risk Capital Requirements*. Basel, Switzerland: Bank for International Settlements.

————. 1996b. *Amendment to the Capital Accord to Incorporated Market Risks*. Basel, Switzerland: Bank for International Settlements.

————. 1999. "Performance of Model-Based Capital Charges for Market Risk: 1 July–December 1998." Basel Committee Publications No. 57. Basel, Switzerland: Bank for International Settlements.

————. 2005a. *Quarterly Review*. Basel, Switzerland: Bank for Bank for International Settlements International Settlements.

————. 2005b. *Triennial Central Bank Survey: Foreign Exchange and Derivatives Market Activity in 2004*. Basel, Switzerland: Bank of International Settlements.

Bassioni, M. Cherif. 1997. "From Versailles to Rwanda in Seventy-five Years: The Need to Establish a Permanent International Criminal Court." *Harvard Human Rights Journal* 10:11–62.

Baudelot, D., R. Establet, and J. Malemort. 1974. *La petite bourgeoisie en France*. Paris: Maspero.

Baumont, Maurice. 1965. *L'Essor industriel et l'impérialisme colonial (1878–1904)*. Paris: Presses Universitaires de France.

Beaud, Michel. 1981. *Histoire du capitalisme: 1500–1980*. Paris: Editions du Seuil.

————. 1982. *Socialisme, a l'épreuve de l'histoire, 1800–1981*. Paris: Editions du Seuil.

Beaud, M., P. Danjou, and J. David. 1975. *Une multinationale française, Pechiney Ugine Kuhlmann*. Paris: Editions du Seuil.

Beck, Ulrich. 2001. *The Risk Society and Beyond: Critical Issues for Social Theory*. Thousand Oaks, Calif.: Sage.

Becker, Marvin B. 1981. *Medieval Italy: Constraints and Creativity*. Bloomington: Indiana University Press.

Bellanet. 2002. *Report on Activities 2001–2002*. Available at: http://home.bellanet.org.

Benedict, Michael Les. 1985. "Laissez-Faire and Liberty: A Re-Evaluation of the Meaning and Origins of Laissez-Faire Constitutionalism." *Law and History Review* 3:293–331.

Benhabib, Seyla. 2002. *Democratic Equality and Cultural Diversity: Political Identities in the Global Era*. Princeton: Princeton University Press.

Benhabib, Seyla, Judith Butler, Drucilla Cornell, and Nancy Fraser. 1995. *Feminist Contentions: A Philosophical Exchange*. New York: Routledge.

Berberoglu, Berch. *Globalization of Capital and the Nation-State: Imperialism, Class Struggle, and the State in the Age of Global Capitalism*. Lanham, Md.: Rowman and Littlefield.

Bergeron, Louis. 1978. *Les capitalistes en France, 1789–1914*. Paris: Archives Gallimard.

Berman, Harold J. 1983. *Law and Revolution: The Formation of the Western Legal Tradition*. Cambridge, Mass.: Harvard University Press.

Berman, Nathaniel. 1995. "Economic Consequences, Nationalist Passions: Keynes, Crisis, Culture, and Policy." *American University Journal of International Law and Policy* 10(2): 619–70.

Bermann, George A. 2000. "International Regulatory Cooperation and U.S. Federalism." In *Transatlantic Regulatory Cooperation: Legal Problems and Political Prospects*, ed. George A. Bermann, Matthias Herdegen, and Peter L. Lindseth. New York: Oxford University Press.

Bermann, George A., Matthias Herdegen, and Peter L. Lindseth, eds. 2000. *Transatlantic Regulatory Cooperation: Legal Problems and Political Prospects*. New York: Oxford University Press.

Bestor, Theodore. 2001. "Supply-Side Sushi: Commodity, Market, and the Global City." *American Anthropologist* 103(1): 76–95.

Beveridge, William. 1976. *Causes and Cures of Unemployment*. New York: AMS Press.

Bevir, Mark, and Frank Trentmann. 2004. "Markets in Historical Contexts: Ideas, Practices and Governance." In *Markets in Historical Contexts: Ideas and Politics in the Modern World*, ed. Mark Bevir and Frank Trentmann. Cambridge: Cambridge University Press.

Bevir, Mark, and Frank Trentmann, eds. 2004. *Markets in Historical Contexts: Ideas and Politics in the Modern World*. Cambridge: Cambridge University Press.

Bhabha, Homi K. 1994. *The Location of Culture*. London: Routledge.

Bhachu, Parminder. 1985. *Twice Migrants: East African Sikh Settlers in Britain*. London: Tavistock.

Bleiker, Roland. 2001. "The Aesthetic Turn in International Political Theory." *Millennium* 30(3): 509–34.

Bloch, Marc. 1961. *Feudal Society*. 2 vols. Chicago: University of Chicago Press.

Block, Fred. 1977. *The Origins of International Economic Disorder: A Study of United States International Monetary Policy from World War II to the Present*. Berkeley: University of California Press.

———. 1996. *The Vampire State and Other Myths of and Fallacies about the U.S. Economy*. New York: The New Press.

Bodin, Jean. 1568. *Response to the Paradoxes of M. de Malestroit, Regarding the Increasing Expense of Everything*. Publisher unknown.

———. 1576. *Les six livres de la Republique: Et se trouve à Paris, chez la veuve Quillau*. Publisher unknown.

Boggs, S. Whittemore. 1940. *International Boundaries: A Study of Boundary Functions and Problems*. New York: Columbia University Press.

Bok, Derek S. 1971. "Reflections on the Distinctive Character of American Labor Law." *Harvard Law Review* 84(6): 1394–1463.

Bollier, David. 2001. *Public Assets, Private Profits: Reclaiming the American Commons in an Age of Market Enclosure*. Washington, DC: New America Foundation.

Bonilla, Frank, Edwin Melendez, Rebecca Morales, and Maria de los Angeles Torres, eds. 1998. *Borderless Borders: U.S. Latinos, Latin Americans, and the Paradox of Interdependence*. Philadelphia: Temple University Press.

Bosniak, Linda. 1996. "'Nativism' the Concept: Some Reflections." In *Immigrants Out!: The New Nativism and the Anti-Immigrant Impulse in the United States*, ed. Juan Perea. New York: New York University Press.

———. 2000a. "Citizenship Denationalized. Symposium: The State of Citizenship." *Indian Journal of Global Legal Studies* 7(2): 447–510.

————. 2000b. "Universal Citizenship and the Problem of Alienage." *Northwestern University Law Review* 94(3): 963–84.

Bourdieu, Pierre. 1977. *Outline of a Theory of Practice*. Cambridge: Cambridge University Press.

————. 1987. "The Force of Law: Toward a Sociology of the Juridical Field." *Hastings Law Journal* 38:805–53.

Bouvier, Jean. 1973. *Un siècle de Banque Française*. Paris: Hatchette.

Boyd, M. 1989. "Family and Personal Networks in International Migration: Recent Developments and New Agendas." *International Migration Review* 23(3): 638–70.

Boyle, James. 1997. *Foucault in Cyberspace: Surveillance, Sovereignty, and Hardwired Censors*. Washington, DC: College of Law, American University.

————. 2000. "Governance of the Internet: A Nondelegation Doctrine for the Digital Age." *Duke Law Journal* 50(1): 5–16.

Bowker, Geoffrey C., and Susan Leigh Star. 1999. *Sorting Things Out: Classification and its Consequences*. Cambridge, Mass.: MIT Press.

Braro, G. M. 1970. *Les Socialistes avant Marx*. Vol. 1. Paris: Maspéro.

Braudel, Fernand. 1979. *Civilisation matérielle, économie et capitalisme: XVe–XVIIIe siècle*. Paris: A. Colin.

————. 1980. *On History*. Trans. Sarah Matthews. Chicago: University of Chicago Press.

————. 1984. *The Perspective of the World*. Vol. 3. London: Collins.

Braudel, F., and E. LaBrousse. 1976–1980. *Histoire économique et sociale de la France de 1850 à nos jours*. Vol. 6. Paris: Presses Universitaires de France.

Braun, Rudolf. 1975. "Taxation, Sociopolitical Structure, and State Building: Great Britain and Brandenburg-Prussia." In *The Formation of National States in Western Europe*, ed. Charles Tilly, pp. 243–327. Princeton, N.J.: Princeton University Press.

Brecher, Jeremy. 1972. *Strike!* San Francisco: Straight Arrow Books.

Brenner, Neil. 1998. "Global Cities, Global States: Global City Formation and State Territorial Restructuring in Contemporary Europe." *Review of International Political Economy* 5:1–37.

Brenner, Neil, and Nik Theodore. 2002. "Cities and the Geographies of 'Actually Existing Neoliberalism.'" *Antipode* 34: 349–79.

Brenner, Robert. 1977. "The Origins of Capitalist Development: A Critique of Neo-Smithian Marxism." *New Left Review* 104:25–92.

Bridge, Gary, and Sophie Watson, eds. 2001. *The Blackwell City Reader*. Malden, Mass., Blackwell.

Briggs, Asa. 1959. *The Making of Modern England 1783–1867: The Age of Improvement*. New York: Harper and Row.

————. 1984. *A Social History of England*. New York: Viking.

Brilmayer, Lea. 1989. *Justifying International Acts*. Ithaca: Cornell University Press.

Brinkley, Alan. 1995. *The End of Reform: New Deal Liberalism in Recession and War*. New York: Knopf.

Bron, Jean. 1970. *Histoire du mouvement ouvrier Français*. Vol. 3. Paris: Les Éditions Ouvrières, 1968–70.

Brysk, Alison, and Gershon Shafir, eds. 2004. *People Out of Place: Globalization, Human Rights, and the Citizenship Gap*. New York: Routledge.

Budd, Leslie. 1995. "Globalisation, Territory, and Strategic Alliances in Different Financial Centres." *Urban Studies* 32(2):345–60.

Bukharin, Nikolai. 1969. *L'economie mondiale et l'impérialisme, 1915–1917*. Paris: Anthropos.

Burgess, John W. 1890. *Political Science and the Comparative Constitutional Law*. 2 vols. Boston: Ginn and Company.

Bush, Jonathan A. "'Take This Job and Shove It: The Rise of Free Labor." *Michigan Law Review* 19:1382–1413.

Cabrera, Miguel A. 2001. *Postsocial History: An Introduction*. Oxford: Lexington Books.

Caglar, A. 1995. "German Turks in Berlin: Social Exclusion and Strategies for Social Mobility." *New Community* 21(3): 309–23.

Calabrese, Andrew, and Jean-Claude Burgelman, eds. 1999. *Communication, Citizenship and Social Policy: Rethinking the Limits of the Welfare State*. New York: Rowman and Littlefield.

Calabresi, Guido. 1982. *A Common Law for the Age of Statutes*. Cambridge, Mass.: Harvard University Press.

Caldeira, Teresa Pires do Rio. 2000. *City of Walls: Crime, Segregation, and Citizenship in São Paulo*. Berkeley: University of California Press.

Callon, Michel. 1998. *The Laws of the Markets*. Oxford: Blackwell.

Camacho, Kemly. 2001. "The Internet: A Great Challenge for Civil Society Organizations in Central America." *Fundacion Acceso*. Available at: http://www.acceso.or.cr/publica/challenges.shtml.

Cameron, R. E. 1961. *France and the Economic Development of Europe, 1800–1914*. Princeton: Princeton University Press.

Caprio, Gerard, Patrick Honohan, and Joseph E. Stiglitz, eds. 2001. *Financial Liberalization: How Far, How Fast?* Cambridge: Cambridge University Press.

Carbonneau, Thomas E. 2004. "Arbitral Law-Making." *Michigan Journal of International Law* 25(4): 1183–1208.

Carbonneau, Thomas, ed. 1990. *Lex Mercatoria and Arbitration: A Discussion of the New Law Merchant*. New York: Transnational Juris Publications.

———. 2004. *The Law and Practice of Arbitration*. Huntington, NJ: Juris Publications.

Carens, Joseph. 1989. "Membership and Morality." In *Immigration and the Politics of Citizenship in Europe and North America*, ed. William Roger Brubaker. Lanham, Md.: University Press of America.

———. 1996. *Culture, Citizenship, and Community: A Contextual Exploration of Justice as Evenhandedness*. New York: Oxford University Press.

Carrier, James G. 2005. *A Handbook of Economic Anthropology*. Northampton, Mass.: Edward Elgar Publishing.

Carrier, James, and Daniel Miller, eds. 1998. *Virtualism: A New Political Economy*. Oxford: Berg.

Carruthers, Bruce. 1996. *City of Capital: Politics and Markets in the English Financial Revolution*. Princeton: Princeton University Press.

Castells, Manuel. 1996. *The Networked Society*. Oxford: Blackwell.

———. 2001. *The Internet Galaxy: Reflections on the Internet, Business, and Society*. New York: Oxford University Press.

Cederman, Lars-Erik, and Peter A. Kraus. 2005. "Transnational Communication and the European Demos." In *Digital Formations: IT and New Architecture in the Global Realm*, ed. Robert Latham and Saskia Sassen. Princeton: Princeton University Press.

Cerny, Phillip G. 1996. "What Next for the State." In *Globalization: Theory and Practice*, ed. Eleonore Kofman and Gillian Youngs. New York: Printer.

———. 1997. "Paradoxes of the Competition State: The Dynamics of Political Globalization." *Government & Opposition* 32(2): 251–74.

———. 2000. "Structuring the Political Arena: Public Goods, States and Governance in a Globalizing World." In *Global Political Economy: Contemporary Theories*, ed. Ronen Palan. London: Routledge.

Cetina, Karin Knorr, and Urs Bruegger. 2002. "Global Microstructures: The Virtual Societies of Financial Markets." *American Journal Sociology* 107(4): 905–50.

Chabod, F. 1958. "Y a-t-il un état de la Renaissance?" In *Actes du Colloque sur la Renaissance*. Paris: Lib. Philosophique J. Vrin.

Chakrabarty, Dipesh. 2000. *Provincializing Europe*. Princeton, N.J.: Princeton University Press.

Chang, Ha-Joon, and Chul-Gyue Yoo. 2002. "The Triumph of Rentiers? The 1997 Korean Crisis in Historical Perspective." In *International Capital Markets: Systems in Transition*, ed. John Eatwell and Lance Taylor. Oxford: Oxford University Press.

Charny, David. 1991. "Competition among Jurisdictions in Formulating Corporate Law Rules: An American Perspective on the 'Race to the Bottom' in the European Communities." *Harvard International Law Journal* 32(2): 423–56.

Chatelain, J., and J. Bacot. 1978. *Développement du capitalisme et alliance de classes en France*. Grenoble: Ther.

Chatterjee, Partha. 1993. *The Nation and its Fragments*. Princeton, N.J.: Princeton University Press.

Chen, Xiangming. 2005. *As Borders Bend: Transnational Spaces on the Pacific Rim*. Oxford: Rowman and Littlefield.

Chevalier, Bernard. 1988. "L'état et les bonnes villes en France au temps de leur accord parfait." In *La ville, la Bourgeoisie at la Genèse de l'état moderne*, ed. Neithard Bulst and Jean-Philippe Gente. Paris: Centre Nationale de la Recherche Scientifique.

Chevalier, Louis. 1958. *Classes laborieuses et classes dangereuses à Paris pendant la première moitié du XIXᵉ siècle*. Paris: Plon.

Cheyette, Frederic, ed. 1975. *Lordship and Community in Medieval Europe*. New York: Robert E. Krieger.

Chomsky, Noam. 1999. *The New Military Humanism: Lessons from Kosovo*. London: Pluto.

Clarence-Smith, William. 1999. "The Modern Colonial State and Global Economic Integration, 1815–1945." In *States and Sovereignty in the Global Economy*, ed. David A. Smith, Dorothy J. Solinger, and Steven C. Topik. London: Routledge.

Clark, Colin. 1951. *The Conditions of Economic Progress.* 2nd ed. London: Macmillan.

Clark, Gordon L., and Nigel Thrift. "The Return of Bureaucracy: Managing Dispersed Knowledge in Global Finance." In *The Sociology of Financial Markets*, ed. Karin Knorr Cetina and Alex Preda. New York: Oxford University Press.

Clark, T., and V. Hoffman-Martinot, eds. 1998. *The New Public Culture.* Oxford: Westview Press.

Clark, John. 2003. "Turning Inside Out? Globalization, Neo-liberation, and Welfare States?" *Anthropologica* 45: 201–14.

Clarke, M. V. 1926. *The Medieval City State: An Essay on Tyranny and Federation in the Middle Ages.* London: Methuen.

Clawson, Dan. 1982. *Bureaucracy and the Labor Process.* New York: Monthly Review Press.

Cleaver, Harry. 1998. "The Zapatista Effect: The Internet and the Rise of an Alternative Political Fabric." *Journal of International Affairs* 51:621–40.

Clegg, Hugh A., Alan Fox, and A. F. Thompson.1964. *A History of British Trade Unions since 1889.* Oxford: Clarendon Press.

Clymer, Adam. 2003. "Bush Administration Most Secretive Ever." *New York Times*, January 3.

Cohen, Benjamin J. 1998. *The Geography of Money*, Ithaca: Cornell University Press.

Cohen, Jean. 1995. "Interpreting the Notion of Global Civil Society." In *Towards a Global Civil Society*, ed. M. Walzer. Providence, RI: Berghahn Books.

Cohen, Robin. 1996. "Diasporas and the Nation-State: From Victims to Challenges." *International Affairs* 72(3): 507–21.

Cole, A. 1969. *British Economic Growth, 1688–1959.* New York: Cambridge University Press.

Cole, David. 2003. *Enemy Aliens: Double Standards and Constitutional Freedoms in the War on Terrorism.* New York: New Press.

Collins, James B. 1988. *Fiscal Limits of Absolutism: Direct Taxation in Early Seventeenth-Century France.* Berkeley: University of California Press.

Comaroff, John L., and Jean Comaroff. 1997. *Of Revelation and Revolution: The Dialectics of Modernity on a South African Frontier.* Chicago: University of Chicago Press.

———. 2000. "Millennial Capitalism: First Thoughts on a Second Coming." *Public Culture* 12(2): 291–343.

Commons, John R. 1924. *Legal Foundations of Capitalism.* New York: Macmillan.

Conover, Pamela Johnston. 1995. "Citizen Identities and Conceptions of the Self." *Journal of Political Philosophy* 3(2): 133–66.

Contamine, Phillip. 1984. *War in the Middle Ages.* New York: Blackwell.

Cook, Brian J. 1996. *Bureaucracy and Self-Government: Reconsidering the Role of Public Administration in American Politics.* Baltimore: Johns Hopkins University Press.

Cooley, Thomas M. 1868. *A Treatise on the Constitutional Limits Which Rest upon the Legislative Power of the State of the American Union.* Boston: Little, Brown.

Cordero-Guzmán, Héctor R., Robert C. Smith, and Ramón Grosfoguel, eds. 2001. *Migration, Transnationalism, and Race in a Changing New York.* Philadelphia: Temple University Press.

Cornette, Joel. 1988. "Le 'point de Archimede': Le renouveau de la recherche sur l'Etat des Finances." *Revue d'histoire moderne et contemporaine* 35:614–29.

Council on Foreign Relations. 1999. "Safeguarding Prosperity in a Global Financial System: The Future International Financial Architecture." *Task Force Report*. New York: Institute for International Economics.

Coutin, Susan B. 2000. "Denationalization, Inclusion, and Exclusion: Negotiating the Boundaries of Belonging." *Indiana Journal of Global Legal Studies* 7(2): 585–94.

Cox, Archibald, el al. 2001. *Cases and Materials on Labor Law*. 13th ed. St. Paul, MN: West Publishing.

Cox, Robert W. 1979. "Ideologies and the New International Economic Order: Reflections on Some Recent Literature." *International Organization* 33(2): 267–302.

———. 1987. *Production, Power, and World Order*. New York: Columbia University Press.

———. 1996. "Social Forces, States, and World Orders: Beyond International Relations Theory." In *Approaches to World Orders*, ed. Robert Cox and Timothy Sinclair. Cambridge: Cambridge University Press.

———. 1997. "Economic Globalization and the Limits of Liberal Democracy." In *The Transformation of Democracy?* ed. A. McGrew. London: Open University Press.

Craig, Bruce. 2004. "Combating Government Secrecy—An Update." American Historical Association. http://www.historians.org/Perspectives/Issues/2004/0410/0410nch1.cfm.

Crane, Johnathan. 1991. "The Epidemic Theory of Ghettos and Neighborhood Effects on Dropping Out and Teenage Childbearing." *American Journal of Sociology* 96(5): 1226–59.

Creech, Heather, and Terry Willard. 2001. *Strategic Intentions: Managing Knowledge Networks for Sustainable Development*. Winnipeg: International Institute for Sustainable Development.

Crenshaw, Kimberlé, Neil Gotanda, Gary Peller, and Kendall Thomas, eds. 1996. *Critical Race Theory: The Key Writings That Formed the Movement*. New York: New Press.

Croly, Herbert. 1912. "State Political Reorganization." *American Political Science Review* 6:122–36.

Cronon, William. 1991. *Nature's Metropolis*. New York: W. W. Norton.

Crotty, James. 1999. "Was Keynes a Corporatist? Keynes's Radical Views on Industrial Policy and Macro Policy in the 1920s." *Journal of Economic Literature* 37(4): 555–78.

Cushman, Berry. 1998. *Rethinking the New Deal Court: The Structure of a Constitutional Revolution*. New York: Oxford University Press.

Cutler, A. Claire. 1997. "Artifice, Ideology, and Paradox: The Public/Private Distinction in International Law." *Review of International Political Economy* 4(2): 261–85.

———. 2001. "Globalization, the Rule of Law, and the Modern Law Merchant: Medieval or Late Capitalist Associations?" *Constellations* 8(4): 408–502.

———. 2002. "The Politics of 'Regulated Liberalism': A Historical Materialist Approach to European Integration." In *Historical Materialism and Globalization*, ed. Mark Rupert and Hazel Smith. London: Routledge.

Cutler, A. Claire, Virginia Haufler, and Tony Porter, eds. 1999. *Private Authority and International Affairs*. Sarasota Springs: State University of New York Press.

Czarniawska, Barbara. 2005. "Women in Financial Services: Fiction and More Fiction." In *The Sociology of Financial Markets*, ed. Karin Knorr Cetina and Alex Preda. New York: Oxford University Press.

Dahl, Robert A. 1989. *Democracy and Its Critics*. New Haven: Yale University Press.

Dam, Kenneth W. 1970. *The GATT, Law, and International Economic Organization*. Chicago: University of Chicago Press.

Davis, Diana E., ed. 1999. "Chaos and Governance." *Political Power and Social Theory*. Vol. 13, Part 4: *Scholarly Controversy*. Stamford, CT: JAI Press.

Dean, Jodi. 2002. *Publicity's Secret: How Technoculture Capitalizes on Democracy*. Ithaca, N.Y.: Cornell University Press.

Dean, John W. 2004. *Worse than Watergate: The Secret Presidency of George W. Bush*. New York: Little, Brown.

Deane, Phyllis, and William A. Cole. 1969. *British Economic Growth, 1688–1959*. New York: Cambridge University Press.

De Bondt, Werner. 2005. "The Values and Beliefs of European Investors." In *The Sociology of Financial Markets*, ed. Karin Knorr Cetina and Alex Preda. New York: Oxford University Press.

Debouzy, Marianne. 1972. *Le capitalisme sauvage aux États-Unis, 1860–1990*. Paris: Editions du Seuil.

Delanty, Gerard. 2000. "The Resurgence of the City in Europe?: The Spaces of European Citizenship." In *Democracy, Citizenship and the Global City*, ed. Engin Isin. London: Routledge.

Deleuze, Gilles, and Félix Guattari. 1987. *A Thousand Plateaus: Capitalism and Schizophrenia*. Minneapolis: University of Minnesota Press.

Delgado, Richard, and Jean Stefancic, eds. 1999. *Critical Race Theory: The Cutting Edge*. Philadelphia: Temple University Press.

De Ly, Filip. 1992. *International Business Law and Lex Mercatoria*. North Holland: Elsevier.

Demko, George J., and William B. Wood. 1994. *Reordering the World: Geopolitical Perspectives on the Twenty-first Century*. Boulder: Westview Press.

Dempsey, Paul S. 1989. "Market Failure and Regulatory Failure as Catalysts for Political Change: The Choice between Imperfect Regulation and Imperfect Competition." *Washington & Lee Law Review* 46(1): 1–40.

Denis, Henri. 1966. *Histoire de la pensée économique*. Paris: Presses Universitaires de France.

Denning, Dorothy. 1999. *Information Warfare and Security*. New York: Addison-Wesley.

Der Derian, James. 2001. *Virtuous War: Mapping the Military-Industrial-Media-Entertainment Network*. Boulder, CO: Westview Press.

de Souza Santos, Bonaventura. 1987. "Law: A Map of Misreading. Toward a Postmodern Conception of Law." *Journal of Law and Society* 14:279–302.

————. 2002. *Toward a New Legal Common Sense: Law, Globalization, and Emancipa-tion*. Cambridge: Cambridge University Press.

Deyon, P. 1969. *Le mercantilism*. Paris: Flammarion.

Dezalay, Yves. 1992. *Marchands de droit*. Paris: Fayard.

Dezalay, Yves, and Bryant Garth. 1996. *Dealing in Virtue: International Commercial Arbitration and the Construction of a Transnational Legal Order*. Chicago: University of Chicago Press.

————. 2002a. *The Internationalization of Palace Wars: Lawyers, Economists, and the Contest to Transform Latin American States*. Chicago Series in Law and Society. Chicago: University of Chicago Press.

————, eds. 2002b. *Global Prescriptions: The Production, Exportation, and Importation of a New Legal Orthodoxy*. Ann Arbor: University of Michigan Press.

Dicken, Peter. 2003. *Global Shift: Reshaping the Global Economic Map in the 21st Cen-tury*. New York: Guilford Press.

Dickinson, Laura A. 2003. "The Promise of Hybrid Courts." *American Journal of Inter-national Law* 97(2): 295–311.

Dinwoodie, Graeme B. 2000. "A New Copyright Order: Why National Courts Should Create Global Norms." *University of Pennsylvania Law Review* 149(2): 469–581.

Di Pietro, Domenico, and Martin Platte. 2001. *Enforcement of International Arbitration Awards: The New York Convention of 1958*. London: Cameron May.

Dobb, Maurice. 1969. *Political Economy and Capitalism*. London: Routledge.

Dodd, Randall. 2002. "The Role of Derivatives in the East Asian Financial Crisis." In *International Capital Markets: Systems in Transition*, ed. John Eatwell and Lance Taylor. Oxford: Oxford University Press.

Donohue, Laura. 2002. "Fear Itself: Counter-Terrorism, Individual Rights, and U.S. Foreign Relations Post 9-11." In *Terrorism and Counterterrorism: Understanding the New Security Environment, Readings and Interpretations*, ed. Russell D. Howard and Reid L. Sawyer. New York: McGraw-Hill.

Donohue, Laura, and Jim Walsh. 2001. "Patriot Act—A Remedy for an Unidentified Problem." *San Francisco Chronicle*, October 30.

Dowd, Maureen. 2005. "Bush's Barberini Faun." *New York Times*, February 17.

Drainville, Andre C. 2004. *Contesting Globalization: Space and Place in the World Econ-omy*. London and New York: Routledge.

Duara, Prasenjit. 1997. *Rescuing History from the Nation: Questioning Narratives of Mod-ern China*. Chicago: University of Chicago Press.

Duby, Georges. 1968. *Rural Economy and Country Life in the Medieval West*. Columbia: University of South Carolina Press.

————. 1974. *The Early Growth of the European Economy: Warriors and Peasants from the Seventh to the Twelfth Century*. Ithaca: Cornell University Press.

————. 1978. *The Three Orders*. Chicago: University of Chicago Press.

Duguit, Léon. 1917. "Law and the State." *Harvard Law Review* 31:1–185.

Dunbabin, Jean. 1985. *France in the Making*. Oxford: Oxford University Press.

Dunbar, Nicholas. 2000. *Inventing Money: The Story of Long-Term Capital Management and the Legends Behind It*. New York: Wiley.

Dunning, John H. 1992. *Multinational Enterprises and the Global Economy*. Wokingham: Addison-Wesley.

———. 1997. *Alliance Capitalism and Global Business*. London: Routledge.

Eastwood, David. 2004. "Tories and Markets: Britain 1800–1850." In *Markets in Historical Contexts: Ideas and Politics in the Modern World*, ed. Mark Bevir and Frank Trentmann. Cambridge: Cambridge University Press.

Eatwell, John, and Lance Taylor. 2002. *International Capital Markets: Systems in Transition*. Oxford: Oxford University Press.

Edelman, Bernard. 1978. *La légalisation de la classe ouvrière*. Paris: Bourgeois.

Edwards, Paul K. 1981. *Strikes in the United States, 1881–1974*. New York: St. Martin's Press.

Eggen, Dan. 2004. "Key Part of Patriot Act Ruled Unconstitutional." *Washington Post*, September 30.

Eichengreen, Barry. 2003. *Capital Flows and Crises*. Cambridge, Mass.: MIT Press.

Eichengreen, Barry, and Albert Fishlow. 1996. *Contending with Capital Flows: What Is Different about the 1990s?* New York: Council of Foreign Relations.

Eickelman, Dale, and Jon W. Anderson. 1999. *New Media in the Muslim World: The Emerging Public Sphere*. Bloomington: Indiana University Press.

Eisenstein, Zillah. 1996. "Stop Stomping on the Rest of Us: Retrieving Publicness from the Privatization of the Globe." *Indiana Journal of Global Legal Studies*. 4(1): 59–96.

Electronic Frontier Foundation (EFF). 2002. "Activist Training Manual," presented at the Ruckus Society Tech Toolbox Action Camp, June 24–July 2.

———. 2004. "Let the Sun Set on PATRIOT—Section 207: 'Duration of Surveillance of Non–United States Persons Who Are Agents of a Foreign Power.'" May 2. http://www.eff.org/patriot/sunset/207.php.

Electronic Privacy Information Center (EPIC). 2001. *Analysis of Provisions of the Proposed AntiTerrorism Act of 2001 Affecting the Privacy of Communications and Personal Information*. September 24. http://www.epic.org/privacy/terrorism/ata_analysis.html.

Elmer, Greg. 2004. *Profiling Machines: Mapping the Personal Information Economy*. Cambridge, Mass: MIT Press.

Ely, James W. Jr. 1992. *The Guardian of Every Other Right: A Constitutional History of Property Rights*. New York: Oxford University Press.

Engels, Friedrich. 1892. *The Condition of the Working Class in England*. London: Allen and Unwin.

Ernst, Daniel R. 1995. *Lawyers against Labor: From Individual Rights to Corporate Liberalism*. Urbana: University of Illinois Press.

Ernst, Dieter. 2005. "The New Mobility of Knowledge: Digital Information Systems and Global Flagship Networks." In *Digital Formations: IT and New Architecture in the Global Realm*, ed. Robert Latham and Saskia Sassen. Princeton: Princeton University Press.

Esping-Andersen, Gosta. 1990. *The Three Worlds of Welfare Capitalism.* Princeton: Princeton University Press.

Espinoza, V. 1999. "Social Networks among the Poor: Inequality and Integration in a Latin American City." In *Networks in the Global Village: Life in Contemporary Communities,* ed. Barry Wellman. Boulder, CO: Westview Press.

Esterhuysen, Anriette. 2000. "Networking for a Purpose: African NGOs Using ICT." *Rowing Upstream: Snapshots of Pioneers of the Information Age in Africa.* Available at: http://www.piac.org/rowing_upstream/chapter1/ full_chapter_1.html.

Evans, Peter. 1995. *Embedded Autonomy.* Princeton: Princeton University Press.

————. 1997. "The Eclipse of the State? Reflections on Stateness in an Era of Globalization." *World Politics* 50: 62–87.

Evans, Peter B., Dietrich Rueschemeyer, and Theda Skocpol, eds. 1985. *Bringing the State Back In.* New York: Cambridge University Press.

Fair Labor Association. 2003. "Towards Improving Workers' Lives." November 3. http://www.fairlabor.org.

Falk, Richard. 1992. "The Making of Global Citizenship." In *Global Visions: Beyond the New World Order,* ed. Jeremy Brecher et al. Montreal: Black Rose Books.

Falloon, William. 1998. "Rogue Models and Model Cops." *Risk* (September): 24–31.

Feinman, Jay M. 1976. "The Development of the Employment at Will Rule." *American Journal of Legal History* 118(20): 126–27.

Feis, Herbert. 1961. *Europe, the World's Banker, 1870–1914.* New York: Kelly.

Feldblum, Miriam. 1998. "Reconfiguring Citizenship in Western Europe." In *Challenge to the Nation-State: Immigration in Western Europe and the United States,* ed. Christian Joppke. Oxford: Oxford University Press.

Fennema, Meindert. 1982. *International Networks of Banks and Industries.* The Hague: Nijhoff.

Ferguson, Yale H., and R. J. Barry Jones, eds. 2002. *Political Space: Frontiers of Change and Governance in a Globalizing World.* Albany: State University of New York Press.

Ferguson, Yale H., and Richard W. Mansbach. 1996. *Polities: Authority, Identities, and Change.* New York: Columbia University Press.

Fernandez Kelly, Maria-Patricia. 1993. "Underclass and Immigrant Women as Economic Actors: Rethinking Citizenship in a Changing Global Economy." *American University International Law Review* 9(1): 151–69.

Fesler, James. 1962. "French Field Administration: The Beginnings." *Comparative Studies in Society and History* 5:76–111.

"Finance: Trick or Treat?" 1999. *The Economist,* October 21.

Fine, Sidney. 1956. *Laissez-Faire and the General-Welfare State: A Study of Conflict in American Thought, 1865–1901.* Ann Arbor: University of Michigan Press.

Finkin, Matthew W., Alvin L. Goldman, and Clyde W. Summers. 1989. *Legal Protection for the Individual Employee.* St. Paul, MN: West Publishing.

Fischer-Lescano, Andreas, and Gunther Teubner. 2004. "Regime-Collisions: The Vain Search for Legal Unity in the Fragmentation of Global Law." *Michigan Journal of International Law* 25(4): 999–1046.

Fisher, M. 2003. "Wall Street Women's 'Herstories' in Late Financial Capitalism." In *Constructing Corporate America: History, Politics, and Culture*, ed. K. Lipartito and D. Sicilia. New York: Oxford University Press.

Flamant, Maurice, and L. Singer-Kerel. 1968. *Crises et récessions économiques*. Paris: Presses Universitaires de France.

Fligstein, Neil. 1990. *The Transformation of Corporate Control*. Cambridge, Mass.: Harvard University Press.

Fligstein, Neil, and Iona Mara-Drita. 1996. "How to Make a Market: Reflections on the Attempts to Create a Single Market in the European Union." *American Journal of Sociology* 102:1–33.

Fohlen, Claude. 1956. *L'industrie textile au temps du Second Empire*. Paris: Plon.

Foner, Eric. 1978. "Class, Ethnicity, and Radicalism in the Gilded Age: Land League and Irish America." *Marxist Perspectives* 2(i): 6–55.

Forbath, William E. 1991. *Law and the Shaping of the American Labor Movement*. Cambridge, Mass.: Harvard University Press.

Foster, William A. 1996. *Registering the Domain Name System: An Exercise in Global Decision Making*. Kennedy School of Government, Harvard University. http://www.ksg.harvard.edu.

Fourcade-Gourinchas, Marion, and Sarah L. Babb. 2002. "The Rebirth of the Liberal Creed: Paths to Neoliberalism in Four Countries." *American Journal of Sociology* 108: 533–79.

Fourier, E. Poisson. 1932. *Le nouveau monde industriel et sociétaire*. Paris: Alcan.

Franck, Thomas M. 1992. "The Emerging Right to Democratic Governance." *American Journal of International Law* 86(1): 46–91.

Frank, Andre G. 1978. *World Accumulation, 1492–1789*. New York: Monthly Review Press.

———. 1966. *The Development of Underdevelopment*. Somerville, Mass.: New England Free Press.

———. 1969. *Latin America: Underdevelopment or Revolution: Essays on the Development of Underdevelopment and the Immediate Enemy*. New York: Monthly Review Press.

———. 1998. *Re-orient: Global Economy in the Asian Age*. Berkeley: University of California Press.

Frank, Thomas. 2000. *One Market under God: Extreme Capitalism, Market Populism and the End of Economic Democracy*. New York: Doubleday.

"Frederick II, Holy Roman Emperor and German King." 2004. *The Columbia Encyclopedia*, 6th ed. New York: Columbia University Press. www.bartleby.com/65/

Frederick, Howard. 1993. "Computer Networks and the Emergence of Global Civil Society." In *Global Networks: Computers and International Communications*, ed. Linda M. Harasim. Cambridge, Mass.: MIT Press.

Freeman, Linton C. 2000. "Visualizing Social Networks." Journal of Social Structure 1(1). http://www2.heinz.cmu.edu/project/INSNA/joss/vsn.html

Freund, Ernst. 1904. *The Police Power: Public Policy and Constitutional Rights*. Chicago: Callaghan and Company.

Friedman, Jonathan. 2003. "Globalization, Dis-integration, Re-organization: The Transformations of Violence." In *Globalization, the State, and Violence*, ed. Jonathan Friedman pp. 1–34. Walnut Creek, Calif. AltaMira Press.

Friedman, Lawrence M. 1973. *A History of American Law*. New York: Simon and Schuster.

Froomkin, Dan. 2005. "The Scandal That Keeps on Giving." *Washington Post*, February 18.

Fryde, E. B. 1983. "The Financial Policies of the Royal Governments and Popular Resistance to Them in France and England c. 1270–1420." In *Studies in Medieval Trade and Finance*, ed. E. B. Fryde. London: Hambledon Press.

Fuhrmann, Horst. 1986. *Germany in the High Middle Ages c. 1050–1200*. Cambridge: Cambridge University Press.

Furner, Mary O., and Barry Supple, eds. 1990. *The State and Economic Knowledge: The American and British Experiences*. New York: Cambridge University Press.

Galbraith, John K. 1972. *The Great Crash 1929*. Boston: Houghton Mifflin.

Garcia, Linda. 2002. "Architecture of Global Networking Technologies." In *Global Networks, Linked Cities*, ed. Saskia Sassen. London: Routledge.

Gao, Bai. 2001. *Japan's Economic Dilemma: The Institutional Origins of Prosperity and Stagnation*. Cambridge: Cambridge University Press.

GAWC. *Globalization and World Cities—Study Group and Network*. Available at: http://www.lboro.ac.uk/gawc.

Génicot, Leopold. 1966. "Crisis: From the Middle Ages to Modern Times." In *Cambridge Economic History of Europe: The Agrarian Life of the Middle Ages*, ed. M. M. Postan. 2nd ed. Cambridge: Cambridge University Press.

Georges, E. 1990. *The Making of a Transnational Community: Migration, Development, and Cultural Change in the Dominican Republic*. New York: Columbia University Press.

Gerth, H. H., and C. Wright Mills, eds. 1946. *From Max Weber*. New York: Oxford University Press.

Gibson-Asner, Rajna, François-Serge Lhabitant, Nathalie Pistre, and Denis Talay. 1998. "Interest Rate Model Risk." In *Asset and Liability Management: A Synthesis of New Methodologies*. London: Risk Books.

Giddens, Anthony. 1984. *The Constitution of Society*. Berkeley: University of California Press.

———. 1991. *Modernity and Self-Identity: Self and Society in the Late Modern Age*. Stanford: Stanford University Press.

Gierke, Otto Friedrich von. 1887. *Die Genossenschaftstheorie und die Deutsche Rechtsprechung*. Berlin: Weidmann.

———. 1900. *Political Theories of the Middle Age*. Translated by F. Maitland. Cambridge: Cambridge University Press.

Gilbert, E., and E. Helleiner. 1999. *Nation-States and Money: The Past, Present and Future of National Currencies*. London: Routledge.

Gill, Stephen, ed. 1993. *Gramsci, Historical Materialism, and International Relations*. Cambridge: Cambridge University Press.

Gill, Stephen. 1996. "Globalization, Democratization, and the Politics of Indifference." In *Globalization: Critical Reflections*, ed. James H. Mittelman. Boulder, CO: Lynne Rienner.

———. 2003. *Power and Resistance in the New World Order*. Basingstoke: Palgrave Macmillan.

Gille, Bertrand. 1959. *Recherches sur la formation de la grande entreprise capitaliste, 1815–1848*. Paris: SEVPEN.

Gillett, Sharon E., and Mitchell Kapor. 1996. "The Self-Governing Internet: Coordination by Design." http://ccs.mit.edu.

Gills, Barry, ed. 2000. *Globalization and the Politics of Resistance*. New York: St. Martin's Press.

Gilpin, Robert. 2000. *The Challenge of Global Capitalism: The World Economy in the 21st Century*. Princeton: Princeton University Press.

Given, James B. 1990. *State and Society in Medieval Europe: Gwynedd and Languedoc under Outside Rule*. Ithaca: Cornell University Press.

Gladwell, Malcolm. 2000. *The Tipping Point: How Little Things Can Make a Big Difference*. New York: Little, Brown.

Glaeser, Andreas. 2000. *Divided in Unity: Indentity, Germany and the Berlin Police*. Chicago: University of Chicago Press.

Global Civil Society Yearbook. 2002. Oxford: Oxford University Press.

Goffman, Irving. 1974. *Frame Analysis: An Essay on the Organization of Experience*. New York: Harper and Row.

Goldsmith, Oliver. 1770. *The Deserted Village*. London: Printed for W. Griffin.

Goldstein, Judith, and Robert O. Keohane. 1993. "Ideas and Foreign Policy: An Analytical Framework." In *Ideas and Foreign Policy: Beliefs, Institutions, and Policy Change*, ed. Judith Goldstein and Robert O. Keohane. Ithaca: Cornell University Press.

Goldwin, William. 1976. *Enquiry Concerning Political Justice*. Harmondsworth, Middlesex: Penguin.

Goodnow, Frank J. 1900. *Politics and Administration*. New York: Macmillan.

———. 1911. *Social Reform and the Constitution*. New York: Macmillan.

Gordon, Linda, ed. 1990. *Women, the State and Welfare*. Madison, WI: University of Wisconsin Press.

Gorz, Andre. 1976. *The Division of Labor*. Atlantic Highlands, NJ: Humanities Press.

Gottmann, Jean. 1952. *La politique: Des états et leur géographie*. Paris: Colin.

———. 1973. *The Significance of Territory*. Charlottesville: University Press of Virginia.

Gould, Mark. 1997. "Governance of the Internet: A UK Perspective." In *Coordinating the Internet*, ed. Brian Kahin and James H. Keller. Cambridge, Mass.: MIT Press.

Gourevitch, Peter. 1978. "The Second Image Reversed: The International Sources of Domestic Politics." *International Organization* 32(4): 881–912.

Graham, Mary. 2002. *Democracy by Disclosure: The Rise of Technopopulism*. Washington, DC: Brookings Institution.

Granovetter, Mark. 1978. "Threshold Models of Collective Behavior." *American Journal of Sociology* 83(6): 1420–43.

Greenfeld, Liah. 1992. *Nationalism: Five Roads to Modernity*. Cambridge, Mass.: Harvard University Press.

Griffin, Larry J. 1992. "Temporality, Events, and Explanation in Historical Sociology." *Sociological Methods and Research* 20(4): 407–27.

Group of Lisbon. 1995. *Limits to Competition*. Cambridge, Mass.: MIT Press.

Guérin, Daniel. 1936. *Fascisme et grand capital*. Paris: Gallimard.

Gurstein, Micheal, ed. 2000. *Community Informatics: Enabling Communities with Information and Communication Technologies*. Hershey, Pa.: Idea Group.

Gutman, Herbert. 1976. *Work, Culture, and Society in Industrializing America: Essays in American Working-class and Social History*. New York: Knopf.

Habermas, Jürgen. 1996. *Between Facts and Norms: Contributions to a Discourse Theory of Law and Democracy*. Trans. William Rehg. Cambridge, Mass.: MIT Press.

———. 1989. *The Structural Transformation of the Public Sphere: An Inquiry into a Category of Bourgeois Society*. Trans. Thomas Burger with Frederick Lawrence. Cambridge, Mass.: MIT Press.

Hadfield, Gillian K. 2001. "Privatizing Commercial Law." *Regulation* 24(1): 40–45.

Haggard, Stephan. 1990. *Pathways from the Periphery: The Politics of Growth in the Newly Industrializing Countries*. Ithaca: Cornell University Press.

Hales, John. 1659. *A Discourse of the Several Dignities, and Corruptions, of Man's Nature, since the Fall*. London: Printed for E. Curll.

———. 1929 [1581]. *Discourse of the Commonweal of This Realm of England*. Cambridge: The University Press.

Hall, John R., ed. 1997. *Reworking Class*. Ithaca, N.Y.: Cornell University Press

Hall, Rodney Bruce. 1999. *National Collective Identity*. New York: Columbia University Press.

Hall, Rodney Bruce, and Thomas J. Biersteker, eds. 2002. *The Emergence of Private Authority in Global Governance*. Cambridge: Cambridge University Press.

Hallam, Elizabeth. 1980. *Capetian France, 987–1328*. New York: Longman.

Haller, William, and Godfrey Davies, eds. 1944. *The Leveller Tracts, 1647–1653*. New York: Columbia University Press.

Handler, Joel. 1995. *The Poverty of Welfare Reform*. New Haven: Yale University Press.

Handlin, Oscar, and Mary Flug Handlin. 1947. *Commonwealth: A Study of the Role of Government in the American Economy: Massachusetts, 1774–1861*. Cambridge, Mass.: Harvard University Press.

Hansen, Randall and Patrick Weil, eds. 2002. *Dual Nationality, Social Rights and Federal Citizenship in the U.S. and Europe: The Reinvention of Citizenship*. New York: Berghahn Books.

Harden, Ian. 1992. "The Contracting State." In *Studies in Law and Politics*, ed. N. Lewis and C. Graham. Buckingham: Open University Press.

Hardt, Michael, and Antonio Negri. 2000. *Empire*. Cambridge, Mass.: Harvard University Press.

Hargittai, E. 1998. "Holes in the Net: Internet and International Stratification." Paper presented at INET Conference: The Internet Summit, Geneva, Switzerland, July 21–24.

Harris, Richard A., and Sidney M. Milkis. 1996. *The Politics of Regulatory Change: A Tale of Two Agencies.* 2nd ed. New York: Oxford University Press.

Hartwell, Roland M. 1971. *The Industrial Revolution and Economic Growth.* London: Methuen.

Hartz, Louis. 1948. *Economic Policy and Democratic Thought: Pennsylvania, 1776–1860.* Cambridge, Mass.: Harvard University Press.

Harvey, Andrew, and Paul A. MacNab. 2000. "Who's Up? Global Interpersonal Temporal Accessibility." In *Information, Place and Cyberspace: Issues in Accessibility,* ed. Donald G. Janelle and David C. Amsterdam: Elsevier.

Harvey, David. 1982. *The Limits to Capital.* Chicago: University of Chicago Press.

———. 1989. *The Condition of Postmodernity: An Enquiry into the Origins of Cultural Change.* Oxford: Basil Blackwell.

Harvey, Rachel. 2003. "London's Gold Fix: The Sub-National Constitution of Markets." Ph.D. diss., University of Chicago.

Hathaway, Oona. 2004. "Prisoner's Rights." *Newsday,* June 29.

Hathaway, Oona A., and Harold Hongju Koh. 2005. *Foundations of International Law and Politics.* New York: Foundation Press.

Haufler, Virginia. 1997. *Dangerous Commerce. Insurance and the Management of International Risk.* Ithaca: Cornell University Press.

Haupt, Heinz-Gerhard. 2004. "Guild Theory and Guild Organization in France and Germany during the Nineteenth Century." In *Markets in Historical Contexts: Ideas and Politics in the Modern World,* ed. Mark Bevir and Frank Trentmann. Cambridge: Cambridge University Press.

Hausner, Jerzy, Bob Jessop, and Klaus Nielsen. 1993. *Institutional Frameworks of Market Economies: Scandinavian and Eastern European Perspectives.* Aldershot: Avebury.

Havighurst, Alfred. 1976. *The Pirenne Thesis.* Lexington, Mass.: D.C. Heath.

Hawley, Ellis. 1966. *The New Deal and the Problem of Monopoly.* Princeton: Princeton University Press.

Hays, Samuel P. 1957. *The Response to Industrialism, 1885–1914.* Chicago: University of Chicago Press.

Held, David. 1995. *Democracy and the Global Order: From the Modern State to Cosmopolitan Governance.* Stanford, Calif.: Stanford University Press.

Helleiner, E. N. 1994. *The Reemergence of Global Finance.* Ithaca, New York: Cornell University Press.

———. 1995. "Explaining the Globalization of Financial Markets: Bringing States Back In." *Review of International Political Economy* 2: 315–41.

———. 1999. "Sovereignty, Territoriality, and the Globalization of Finance." In *States and Sovereignty in the Global Economy,* ed. David A. Smith, Dorothy J. Solinger, and Steven C. Topik. London: Routledge.

Hermann, Gerold. 1998. "The UNCITRAL Arbitration Law: A Good Model of a Model Law." *Uniform Law Review* 3(2): 483–500.

Hernández-Truyol, Berta Esperanza, ed. 2002. *A Critical Moral Imperialism Anthology.* New York: NYU Press.

Hertz, E. 1998. *The Trading Crowd. An Ethnography of the Shanghai Stock Market.* Cambridge: Cambridge University Press.

Hilferding, Rudolf. 1981. *Finance Capital.* Ed. T. Bottomore. London: Routledge.

Himanen, Pekka. 2001. *The Hacker Ethic and the Spirit of the Information Age.* New York: Random House.

Himmelfarb, Gertude. 2001. *One Nation, Two Cultures: A Searching Examination of American Society in the Aftermath of Our Cultural Revolution.* New York: Vintage Books.

Hirst, Paul, and Grahame Thompson. 1995. "Globalization and the Future of the Nation State." *Economy and Society* 24: 408–42.

———. 1996. *Globalization in Question.* Cambridge: Polity Press.

Hobsbawm, Eric. 1994. *The Age of Extremes: A History of the World, 1914–1991.* New York: Vintage Books.

Hobson, J. A. 1938. *Imperialism.* London: G. Allen and Unwin.

Hoerder, David. 2000. "Metropolitan Migration in the Past: Labour Markets, Commerce, and Cultural Interaction in Europe, 1600–1914." *Journal of International Migration and Integration* 1(1): 39–58.

Hoffman, Donna L., and Thomas P. Novak. 1998. "Bridging the Racial Divide on the Internet." *Science* 280(17): 390–91.

Hofstadter, Richard. 1955. *The Age of Reform: From Bryan to FDR.* New York: Knopf.

Hohenberg, Paul M., and Lynn H. Lees. 1985. *The Making of Urban Europe, 1000–1950.* Harvard Studies in Urban History. Cambridge, Mass.: Harvard University Press.

Holemans, Dirk. "Ecological Citizenship in a Dialogic Democracy." On file with author.

Hollifield, J. 2000. "Migration and the 'New' International Order: The Missing Regime." In *Managing Migration: Time for a New International Regime?*, ed. B. Ghosh. London: Oxford University Press.

Holloway, Sarah L., and Gill Valentine. 2001. *Youth Identities and Communities in an On-line World.* New York: Routledge.

Holzgrefe, J. L. 1989. "The Origins of Modern International Relations Theory." *Review of International Studies* 15:11–26.

Hondagneu-Sotelo, Pierrette. 1994. *Gendered Transitions: Mexican Experiences of Immigration.* Berkeley: University of California Press.

Horwitz, Morton J. 1992. *The Transformation of American Law, 1870–1860: The Crisis of Legal Orthodoxy.* New York: Oxford University Press.

Howard, Philip N., and Steve Jones, eds. 2004. *Society Online: The Internet in Context.* London: Sage.

Howe, Stephen. 1991. "Citizenship in the New Europe." In *Citizenship,* ed. Geoff Andrews. London: Lawrence and Wishart.

Howitt, Richard. 1993. "'A World in a Grain of Sand': Towards a Reconceptualisation of Geographical Scale." *The Australian Geographer* 24:33–44.

———. 1998. "Recognition, Respect and Reconciliation: Steps Towards Decolonisation?" *Australian Aboriginal Studies* 1:28–34.

Hudec, Robert E. 1987. *Developing Countries in the GATT Legal System*. Aldershot, UK: Gower.

Hull, N.E.H. 1997. *Roscoe Pound and Karl Llewellyn: Searching for an American Jurisprudence*. Chicago: University of Chicago Press.

Hume, David. 1955. "Essays on Economics." In *Writing on Economics*, ed. E. Rotwein. Madison: University of Wisconsin Press.

Hunter, David B. 1992. "Toward Global Citizenship in International Environmental Law." *Willamette Law Review* 28(3): 547–64.

Hurd, John C. 1881. *The Theory of Our National Existence, as Shown by the Action of the Government of the United States since 1861*. Boston: Little, Brown.

Hurst, James Willard. 1956. *Law and the Conditions of Freedom*. Madison: University of Wisconsin Press.

Ietto Gillies, Grazia. 2002. *Transnational Corporations: Fragmentation amidst Integration*. New York: Routledge.

Ignatieff, Michael. 2000. *Virtual War: Kosovo and Beyond*. New York: Vintage.

Ikenberry, J. 2000. *After Victory*. Princeton: Princeton University Press.

Indiana Journal of Global Legal Studies. 1996. Feminism and Globalization: The Impact of the Global Economy on Women and Feminist Theory. Vol. 4, issue 1.

———. 1998. Symposium: The Internet and the Sovereign State: The Role and Impact of Cyberspace on National and Global Governance. Vol. 5, issue 2.

Innis, Harold A. 2004. *Changing Concepts of Time*. Lanham, Md.: Rowman and Littlefield.

International Monetary Fund (IMF). 1999. *International Capital Markets: Developments, Prospects, and Key Policy Issues*. Washington, DC: IMF.

———. 2004. "Toward a Framework for Safeguarding Financial Stability." IMF Working Paper, WP/04/101, prepared by Aerdt Houben, Jan Kakes, and Garry Schinasi. Washington, DC: IMF.

International Telecommunications Union (ITU). 1998. *Challenges to the Network: Internet for Development*. Geneva: International Telecommunications Union.

Investment Company Institute. 2003. *2003 Mutual Fund Fact Book: A Guide to Trends and Statistics in the Mutual Fund Industry* 63. 43rd ed.

Isin, Engin. 2000. "Introduction: Democracy, Citizenship and the City." In *Democracy, Citizenship and the Global City*, ed. Engin Isin. New York: Routledge.

Izquierdo, Javier A. 2001. "Reliability at Risk: The Supervision of Financial Models as a Case Study for Reflexive Economic Sociology." *European Societies* 3:69–90.

Jackson, John Howard. 1997. *The World Trading System: Law and Policy of International Economic Relations*. 2nd ed. Cambridge, Mass.: MIT Press.

Jackson, Patrick, and Daniel Nexon. 1999. "Relations before States." *European Journal of International Relations* 5:291–332.

Jackson, R. H. 1941. *The Struggle for Judicial Supremacy: A Study of a Crisis in American Power Politics*. New York: Knopf.

Jacobson, David. 1996. *Rights across Borders: Immigration and the Decline of Citizenship*. Baltimore: Johns Hopkins University Press.

Jacobson, David, and Galya Ruffer. 2003. "Courts across Borders: The Implications of Judicial Agency for Human Rights and Democracy." *Human Rights Quarterly* 25(1): 74–93.

Jensen, M. 1998. *Internet Connectivity in Africa*. Report (January) available at: http://demiurge.wn.apc.org/africa/.

Jessop, Robert. 1999. "Reflections on Globalization and its Illogics." In *Globalization and the Asian Pacific: Contested Territories*, ed. Kris Olds, Peter Dicken, Philip F. Kelly, Lilly Kong, and Henry Wai-Chung Yeung. London: Routledge.

Jewell, Helen M. 1972. *English Local Administration in the Middle Ages*. New York: Barnes and Noble Books.

Johnson, David, and David Post. 1996. "Law and Borders—the Rise of Law in Cyberspace." Stanford Law Review 48(1367). http://www.cli.org/X0025_LBFIN.html.

Johnston, R. J., P. J. Taylor, and M. J. Watts. 2002. *Geographies of Global Change: Remapping the World*. Malden, Mass.: Rowman and Littlefield.

Jones, Katherine T. 1998. "Scale as Epistemology." *Political Geography* 17(1): 25–28.

Jorion, Philippe. 1997. *Value at Risk: The New Benchmark for Controlling Market Risk*. Chicago: Irwin Professional Publishers.

Joyce, Patrick. 1991. *Visions of the People: Industrial England and the Question of Class: 1840–1914*. Cambridge: Cambridge University Press.

———. 1994. *Democratic Subjects: The Self and the Social in Nineteenth Century England*. Cambridge: Cambridge University Press.

Judd, Denis R. 1998. "The Case of the Missing Scales: A Commentary on Cox." *Political Geography* 17(1): 29–34.

Kagan, Elena. 2001. "Presidential Administration." *Harvard Law Review* 114(8): 2245–2385.

Kantorowicz, Ernst Hartwig. 1957. *The King's Two Bodies: A Study in Mediaeval Political Theology*. Princeton: Princeton University Press.

Kaplan, Robert D. 2005. *Imperial Grunts: The American Military on the Ground*. New York: Random House.

Kapstein, Ethan. 1994. *Governing the Global Economy: International Finance and the State*. Cambridge, Mass.: Harvard University Press.

Kapstein, Ethan, and Branko Milanovic. 2003. *Income and Influence: Social Policy in Emerging Market Economies*. Kalamazoo, MI: W. E. Upjohn Institute for Employment Research.

Karl, Barry. 1983. *The Uneasy State: The United States from 1915–1945*. Chicago: University of Chicago Press.

Karst, Kenneth. 1997. "The Coming Crisis of Work in Constitutional Perspective." *Cornell Law Review* 82(3): 523–71.

———. 2000. "Citizenship, Law, and the American Nation." *Indiana Journal of Global Legal Studies* 7(2): 595–601.

Katz, Micheal B., ed. 1993. *The "Underclass" Debate: Views from History*. Princeton: Princeton University Press.

Katzenstein, Peter. 2001. "Japan, Asian-Pacific Security, and the Case for Analytic Eclecticism." *International Security* 26(3): 153–85.

Katznelson, Ira. 1985. "Working-Class Formation and the State: Nineteenth-Century England in American Perspective." In *Bringing the State Back*, ed. P. B. Evans, D. Rueschemeyer, and T. Skocpol. Cambridge: Cambridge University Press.

———. 1992. *Marxism and the City*. Oxford: Clarendon.

Katznelson, Ira, and Aristide R. Zolberg, eds. 1986. *Working-class Formation: Nineteenth-Century Patterns in Western Europe and the United States*. Princeton: Princeton University Press.

Kaufmann-Kohler, Gabrielle. 2003. "Globalization of Arbitral Procedures." *Vanderbilt Journal of Transnational Law* 36(4): 1313–34.

Kaul, I., and R. Mendoza. 2003. *Providing Global Public Goods: Managing Globalization*. New York: Oxford University Press.

Keck, Margarete E., and Kathryn Sikkink. 1998. *Activism beyond Borders: Advocacy Networks in International Politics*. Ithaca: Cornell University Press.

Keller, Morton. 1990. *Regulating a New Economy: Public Policy and Economic Change in America, 1900–1933*. Cambridge, Mass.: Harvard University Press.

Kelly, Philip F. 1999. "The Geographies and Politics of Globalization." *Progress in Human Geography* 23: 379–400.

Kennedy, David. 1995. "The International Style in Postwar Law and Policy: John Jackson and the Field of International Economic Law." *American University Journal of International Law and Policy* 10(2): 671–716.

Kennedy, Duncan. 1993. "The Stakes of Law, or Hale and Foucault." In *Sexy Dressing Etc.: Essays on the Power and Politics of Cultural Identity*. Cambridge, Mass.: Harvard University Press.

———. 1997. *A Critique of Adjudication: Fin de siècle*. Cambridge, Mass.: Harvard University Press.

Keohane, Robert O., Andrew Moravcsik, and Anne-Marie Slaughter. 2000. "Legalized Dispute Resolution: Interstate and Transnational." *International Organization* 54(3): 457–88.

Kenwood, A. G., and A. L. Lougheed. *The Growth of the International Economy, 1820–1960*. Albany: State University of New York Press.

Keynes, J. M. 1932. "The Economic Consequence of Mr. Churchill." In *Essays in Persuasion*. New York: Harcourt, Brace.

———. 1972 [1924]. *Monetary Reform*. New York: St. Martin's.

Khagram, Sanjeev. 2004. *Dams and Development: Transnational Struggles for Water and Power*. Ithaca, N.Y.: Cornell University Press.

Kindleberger, Charles P. 1973. *The World Depression, 1929–1939*. Berkeley: University of California Press.

———. 1978. *Manias, Panics and Crashes*. New York: Basic Books.

King, A. D. 1990. *Urbanism, Colonialism, and the World Economy: Culture and Spatial Foundations of the World Urban System*. The International Library of Sociology. London: Routledge.

King, Gary, Robert O. Keohane, and Sidney Verba. 1994. *Designing Social Inquiry.* Princeton: Princeton University Press.

Klare, Karl E. 1982. "The Public-Private Distinction in Labor Law." *University of Pennsylvania Law Review* 130(6): 1358–1422.

———. 1998. "Legal Culture and Transformative Constitutionalism." *South African Journal on Human Rights* 14(146): 156–72.

Knop, Karen. 2000. "Here and There: International Domestic Courts." *Journal of International Law and Politics* 32(2): 501–35.

———. 2002. *Diversity and Self-Determination in International Law.* Cambridge: Cambridge University Press.

Knorr Cetina, Karin. 2005. "How Are Global Markets Global? The Architecture of a Flow World." In *The Sociology of Financial Markets*, ed. Karin Knorr Cetina and Alex Preda. New York: Oxford University Press.

Koh, Harold Hongju. 1990. *The National Security Constitution: Sharing Power after the Iran-Contra Affair.* New Haven, CT: Yale University Press.

———. 1997. "How Is International Human Rights Law Enforced?" *Indiana Law Journal* 74(4): 1397–1417.

———. 1998. "The 1998 Frankel Lecture: Bringing International Law Home." *Honston Law Review* 35(3): 623–82.

Kolko, Joyce. 1988. *Restructuring the World Economy.* New York: Pantheon.

Kovacic, William E. 1998. "Merger Enforcement in Transition: Antitrust Controls on Acquisitions in Emerging Economies." *University of Cincinnati Law Review* 66:1075–1112.

Kozul-Wright, R., and R. Rowthorn, eds. 1998. *Transnational Corporations and the Global Economy.* London: Macmillan.

Krasner, Stephen D. 1999. *Sovereignty: Organized Hypocrisy.* Princeton: Princeton University Press.

———. 2004. "Globalization, Power, and Authority." In *The Evolution of Political Knowledge: Democracy, Autonomy, and Conflict in Comparative and International Politics*, ed. Edward D. Mansfield and Richard Sisson. Columbus: Ohio State University Press.

Kratochwil, Friedrich. 1986. "Of Systems, Boundaries and Territorialities." *World Politics* 30:27–52.

Kratochwil, Friedrich, and John Gerard Ruggie. 1986. "International Organization: A State of the Art on an Art of the State." *International Organization* 40(4): 753–75.

Krueger, Anne O. 1993. *Economic Policy at the Cross-Purposes: The United States and the Developing Countries.* Washington DC: Brookings Institute.

Kuntze, Marco, Sigrun Rottmann, and Jessica Symons. 2002. *Communications Strategies for World Bank- and IMF-Watchers: New Tools for Networking and Collaboration.* London: Bretton Woods Project and Ethical Media. Available at: http://www.brettonwoodsproject.org/strategy/commosrpt.pdf.

Kurland, Phillip B. 1986. "The Rise and Fall of the 'Doctrine' of Separation of Powers." Michigan Law Review 85(3): 592–631.

Kuttner, Robert. 1997. *Everything for Sale: The Virtues and Limits of Markets*. New York: Knopf.

Kymlicka, Will. 1995. *Multicultural Citizenship: A Liberal Theory of Minority Rights*. Oxford: Clarendon Press.

Kymlicka, Will, and Wayne Norman. 1994. "Return of the Citizen: A Survey of Recent Work on Citizenship Theory." *Ethics* 104:352–81.

Laguerre, Michel S. 2000. *The Global Ethnopolis: Chinatown, Japantown and Manilatown in American Society*. London: Macmillan.

Langewiesche, William. 2004. *The Outlaw Sea: A World of Freedom, Chaos, and Crime*. New York: North Point Press.

Lannon, John. 2002. *Technology and Ties That Bind: The Impact of the Internet on Non-Governmental Organizations Working to Combat Torture*. Master's thesis, University of Limerick. Available at: http://www.makeworlds.org/node/64.

Laski, Harold J. 1917. *Studies in the Problem of Sovereignty*. New Haven: Yale University Press.

Latour, Bruno. 1991. "Technology Is Society Made Durable." In *A Sociology of Monsters*, ed. John Laws. London: Routledge.

Lattimore, Owen. 1957. "Feudalism in History." *Past and Present* 12 (November): 47–57.

Laumann, Edward O., and David Knoke. 1987. *The Organizational State*. Madison: University of Wisconsin Press.

Laurie, Bruce. 1997. *Artisans into Workers: Labor in Nineteenth-Century America*. Champaign: University of Illinois Press.

Leavitt, Harold J. 2003. "Why Hierarchies Thrive." *Harvard Business Review* 81(3): 96–102.

Lebert, Joanne. 2002. "Information and Communication Technologies and Human Rights Advocacy: The Case of Amnesty International." In *Civil Society in the Information Age*, ed. Peter J. Hajnal. Aldershot, UK: Ashgate Publishing.

LeBlanc, Robin. 1999. *Bicycle Citizens: The Political World of the Japanese Housewife*. Berkeley: University of California Press.

Lee, Benjamin, and Edward LiPuma. 2002. "Cultures of Circulation: The Imaginations of Modernity." *Public Culture* 14(1): 191–213.

Le Goff, Jacques. 1989. *Medieval Civilization 400–1500*. Oxford: Blackwell.

Lehmkuhl, Dirk. 2002. "The Resolution of Domain Names vs. Trademark Conflicts: A Case Study on Regulation beyond the Nation-State and Related Problems." *Zeitschrift Für Rechtssoziolgie* 23(1): 61–78.

Leizerov, Sagi. 2000. "Privacy Advocacy Groups versus Intel: A Case Study of How Social Movements Are Tactically Using the Internet to Fight Corporations." *Social Science Computer Review* 18:461–83.

Lenin, Vladimir I. 1939. *Imperialism, the Highest Stage of Capitalism: A Popular Outline*. New York: International Publishers.

Leonnig, Carol D. 2004. "Energy Task Force Data Not Private: Agencies Ordered to Release Papers." *Washington Post*, April 2.

Lerner, Max. 1933. "The Supreme Court and American Capitalism." *Yale Law Journal* 42:668–701.

Leroy, Maxime. *Histoire des idées sociales en France*. Vol. 1. Paris: Gallimard.

Lessig, Lawrence. 2000. *Code and Other Laws of Cyberspace*. New York: Basic Books.

Lessig, Lawrence, and Cass Sunstein. 1994. "The President and the Administration." *Columbia Law Review* 41(1): 1–123.

Levasseur, Emile. 1900–1901. *Histoire des classes ouvrières et de l'industrie en France avant 1789*. Vol. 3. Paris: A. Rousseau.

Levitt, Peggy. 2001. *The Transnational Villagers*. Berkeley: University of California Press.

Levy, Robert. 2001. "The Patriot Act: We Deserve Better." Available at: http://www.cato.org/current/terrorism/pubs/levy-martial-law.html.

———. 2002. "Cato Handbook for Congress: Policy Recommendations for the 108th Congress." Washington, DC: Cato Institute. Available at: http://www.cato.org/pubs/handbook/hb108/hb108-12.pdf.

Levy-Leboyer, Maurice. 1964. *Les banques européennes et l'industrialisation internationale dans la première moitié du XIXe siècle*. Paris: Presses Universitaires de France.

Lewis, Anthony. 2003. "Un-American Activities." *New York Review of Books*. October 23. (Electronic copy).

2004. "A President beyond the Law." *New York Times*, May 7.

Lewis, Archibald. 1974. *Knights and Samurai*. London: Temple Smith.

Lewis, Charles. 2004a. *The Buying of the President 2004: Who's Really Bankrolling Bush and His Democratic Challengers—and What They Expect in Return*. New York: Perennial.

———. 2004b. *The Banking of the President*. New York: Perennial.

Lewis, P. S. 1962. "The Failure of the French Medieval Estates." *Past and Present* 23(November): 3–24.

Lewis, W. A. 1955. *The Theory of Economic Growth*. London: Allen and Unwin.

Leyshon, Andrew, and Nigel Thrift. 1997. *Money/Space: Geographies of Monetary Transformation*. London: Routledge.

Lhomme, Jean. 1964. *La grande bourgeoisie au pouvoir, 1830–1880*. Paris: Presses Universitaires de France.

Lichtenstein, Nelson, and Howell John Harris, eds. 1993. *Industrial Democracy in America: The Ambiguous Promise*. New York: Cambridge University Press.

Lipschutz, Ronnie, and Judith Mayer. 1996. *Global Civil Society and Global Environmental Governance: The Politics of Nature from Place to Planet*. Albany: State University of New York Press.

Lister, Ruth. 1997. *Citizenship: Feminist Perspective*. London: Macmillan.

Lively, Robert A. 1915. "The American System: A Review Article." *Business History Review* 29:81–96.

Livesey, James. 2004. "Improving Justice: Communities of Norms in the Great Transformation." In *Markets in Historical Contexts: Ideas and Politics in the Modern World*, ed. Mark Bevir and Frank Trentmann. Cambridge: Cambridge University Press.

Loader, B., ed. 1998. *Cyberspace Divide: Equality, Agency, and Policy in the Information Age*. London: Routledge.

Locke, John. 1924 [1690]. *Of Civil Government: Two Treatises*. New York: E. P. Dutton.

———. 1969. *Commission on Trade*. 1743. London: Printed for R. Willock.

———. 1988 [1690]. *Two Treatises of Government*. Ed. Peter Laslett. Cambridge: Cambridge University Press.

Lockwood, David. 1964. "Social Integration and System Integration." In *Explorations in Social Change*, ed. George K. Zollschan and Walter Hirsch. Boston: Houghton Mifflin.

Lomnitz, Larissa Adler, and Rodrigo Salazar. 2002. "Cultural Elements in the Practice of Law in Mexico: Informal Networks in a Formal System." In *Global Prescriptions: The Production, Exportation, and Importation of a New Legal Orthodoxy*, ed. Yves Dezalay and Bryant G. Garth. Ann Arbor: University of Michigan Press.

Lovink, Geert. 2002. *Dark Fiber: Tracking Critical Internet Culture*. Cambridge, Mass.: MIT Press.

Lovink, Geert, and Patrice Riemens. 2002. "Digital City Amsterdam: Local Uses of Global Networks." In *Global Networks/Linked Cities*, ed. Saskia Sassen. New York: Routledge.

Lowi, Theodore J. 1979. *The End of Liberalism: The Second Republic of the United States*. 2nd ed. New York: Norton.

Lyon, Bryce, and A. E. Verhulst. 1967. *Medieval Finance: A Comparison of Financial Institutions in Northwestern Europe*. Providence, RI: Brown University Press.

Machiavelli, Niccolò. 1981 [1516]. *The Prince*. Middlesex: Penguin Books.

MacKenzie, Donald. 1999. "Technological Determinism." In *Society on the Line: Information Politics in the Digital Age*, ed. William H. Dutton. Oxford: Oxford University Press.

———. 2003. "Long-Term Capital Management and the Sociology of Arbitrage." *Economy and Society* 32:349–80.

———. 2004. "Social Connectivities in Global Financial Markets." *Environment and Planning D: Society and Space* 22(1): 83–102.

———. 2005. "How a Superportfolio Emerges: Long-Term Capital Management and the Sociology of Arbitrage." In *The Sociology of Financial Markets*, ed. Karin Knorr Cetina and Alex Preda. New York: Oxford University Press.

MacKenzie, Donald, and Yuval Millo. 2003. "Constructing a Market, Performing Theory: The Historical Sociology of a Financial Derivatives Exchange." *American Journal of Sociology* 109(1): 107–46.

Mackenzie, D., and J. Wajcman. 1999. *The Social Shaping of Technology*. Milton Keynes, UK: Open University Press.

Magdoff, Harry. 1969. *The Age of Imperialism*. New York: Monthly Review Press.

Magnusson, Warren. 1990. "The Reification of Political Community." In *Contending Sovereignties: Redefining Political Community*, ed. R.B.J. Walker and Saul H. Mendlovitz. Boulder, CO: Lynne Rienner.

———. 1996. *The Search for Political Space: Globalization, Social Movements, and the Urban Political Experience*. Toronto: University of Toronto Press.

———. 2000. "Politicizing the Global City." In *Democracy, Citizenship, and the Global City*, ed. Isin F. Engin. London: Routledge.

Maclachlan, Patricia, and Frank Trentmann. 2004. "Civilizing Markets: Traditions of Consumer Politics in Twentieth-Century Britain, Japan, and the United States." In *Markets in Historical Contexts: Ideas and Politics in the Modern World*, ed. Mark Bevir and Frank Trentmann. Cambridge: Cambridge University Press.

Mahler, Sarah. 1995. *American Dreaming: Immigrant Life on the Margins*. Princeton: Princeton University Press.

Maitland, Frederic William. 1968. *Selected Essays*. Ed. H. D. Hazeltine, G. Lapsley, and P. H. Winfield. Freeport, N.Y.: Books for Libraries Press.

Malthus, Thomas Robert. 1826. *Essay on the Principle of Population*. London: John Murray.

———. 1959. *Population: The First Essay*. Ann Arbor: University of Michigan Press.

Mann, Michael. 1986. *The Sources of Social Power*. Cambridge: Cambridge University Press.

———. 1997. "Has Globalization. Ended the Rise of the Nation-State?" *Review of International Political Economy* 4: 472–96.

Manovich, Lev. 2001. *The Language of New Media*. Cambridge, Mass.: MIT Press.

Mansfield, Edward D., and Richard Sisson, eds. *The Evolution of Political Knowledge: Democracy, Autonomy, and Conflict in Comparative and International Politics*. Columbus, Ohio: The Ohio State University Press.

Mantilla-Serrano, Fernando. 2000. "Major Trends in International Commercial Arbitration in Latin America." *Journal of International Arbitration* 17(1): 139–42.

Mantoux, Paul. *La Révolution Industrielle au XVIIIᵉ siècle*. Paris: Presses Universitaires de France.

Marczewski, J. 1961. "Some Aspects of Economic Growth in France, 1660–1958." *Economic Development and Cultural Change* 9(3): 369–86.

Markusen, A. 2002. "The Case against Privatizing National Security." Council on Foreign Relations, rev. version.

Marres, Noortje, and Richard Rogers. 2000. "Depluralisin the Web, Repluralising Public Debate: The Case of GM Food on the Web." In *Preferred Placement: Knowledge Politics on the Web*, ed. Richard Rogers pp. 113–36. Maastricht: Jan van Eyck Editions.

Marrus, Michael R. 1985. *The Unwanted: European Refugees in the Twentieth Century*. New York: Oxford University Press.

Marshall, T. H. 1977 [1950]. "Citizenship and Social Class." In *Class Citizenship, and Social Development*. Chicago: University of Chicago Press.

Martin, David. 2002. "Dispositifs de défiance et fluidité des échanges sur les marches financiers de Gré a Gré" (Suspicion and the fluidity of mutual agreements on financial markets). *Sociologie du Travail* 44:55–74.

Marx, Karl. 1904. *A Contribution to the Critique of Political Economy*. Chicago: Charles Kerr.

———. 1977 [1867]. *Capital*. New York: Vintage Books.

Marx, Karl, and Friedrich Engels. 1949. *The Communist Manifesto*. New York: Monthly Review Press.

Marx, Roland. 1971. *L'Angleterre des révolutions*. Paris: Armand Colin.

———. 1972. *Le déclin de l'économie Britannique (1870–1929)*. Paris: Presses Universitaires de France.

Mathiason, John R., and Charles C. Kuhlman. 1998. *International Public Regulation of the Internet: Who Will Give You Your Domain Names?* Paper presented at International Studies Association, 21 March, Minneapolis.

Mattingly, Garrett. 1988. *Renaissance Diplomacy*. New York: Dover.

Maurer, Bill. 1999. "Forget Locke? From Proprietor to Risk-Bearer in New Logics of Finance." *Public Culture* 11:47–67.

Maxfield, Sylvia. 1997. *Gatekeepers of Growth*. Princeton: Princeton University Press.

Mayer, Pierre. 1995. "Le pouvoir des arbitres de régler la procédure: Une analyse comparative des systèmes de civil law et de common law." *Revue de L'Arbitrage* 2:163–84.

McConnaughay, Philip J., and Thomas B. Ginsburg, eds. 2002. *International Commercial Arbitration in Asia*. Huntington, NJ: Juris Publishing.

McKinnon, Ronald. 1993. "The Rules of the Game: International Money in Historical Perspective." *Journal of Economic Literature* 31(1): 1–43.

McNeill, William H. 1986 [1949]. *History of Western Civilization*. Chicago: University of Chicago Press.

McWilliam, Rohan. 1998. *Popular Politics in Nineteenth-Century England*. London: Routledge.

Mearsheimer, John J. 2001. *The Tragedy of Great Power Politics*. New York: Norton.

Mele, Christopher. 1999. "Cyberspace and Disadvantaged Communities: The Internet as a Tool for Collective Action." In *Communities in Cyberspace*, ed. Marc A. Smith and Peter Kollock. London: Routledge.

Merriam, C. Edward. 1915. *A History of American Political Theories*. New York: Macmillan.

Merton, Robert K. 1968. "The Self-Fulfilling Prophecy." In Robert K. Merton, ed., *Social Theory and Social Structure*. New York: The Free Press.

Meyer, John W., John Boli, George M. Thomas, and Francisco O. Ramirez. 1997. World Society and the Nation-State. *American Sociological Review* 103 (1): 144–81.

Michalet, Charles Albert. 1976. *Le Capitalisme Modial*. Paris: Presses Universitaires de France.

Miller, Daniel, and Don Slater. 2000. *The Internet: An Ethnographic Approach*. Oxford: Berg.

Mills, Kurt. 2002. "Cybernations: Identity, Self-Determination, Democracy, and the 'Internet Effect' in the Emerging Information Order." *Global Society* 16:69–87.

Minnow, Martha. 2002. "About Women, About Culture: About Them About Us." In *Engaging Cultural Differences: The Multicultural Challenge in Liberal Democracies*, ed. Richard Shweder, Martha Minnow, and Hazel Rose Markus. New York: Russell Sage Foundation.

Mitchell, W. C. 1913. *Business Cycles*. Berkeley: University of California Press.

Mittelman, James, ed. 1996. *Globalization: Critical Reflections*. Boulder, CO: Lynne Rienner.

Miyazaki, Hirokazu. 2002. "The Temporalities of the Market." *American Anthropologist* 105(2): 255–65.

Montesquieu, Charles de Secondat, baron de. 1949 [1758]. *L'esprit des lois*. Vol 1. Paris: Editions Garnier.

Montgomery, David. 1980. "Strikes in the Nineteenth Century." *Social Science History* 4(1): 81–104.

———. 1987. *The Fall of the House of Labor: The Workplace, the State, and American Labor Activism, 1865–1925*. New York: Cambridge University Press.

More, Thomas. 1516 [c. 1949]. *Utopia*. Trans. and ed. H.V.S. Ogden. Arlington Heights, IL: AHM/Harlan Davidson.

Morrall, John. 1980. *Political Thought in Medieval Times*. Toronto: University of Toronto Press.

Morrill, Richard. 1999. "Inequalities of Power, Costs and Benefits across Geographic Scales: The Future Uses of the Hanford Reservation." *Political Geography* 18:1–23.

Moyers, Bill. 2004. "Journalism under Fire." Address to the Society of Professional Journalists. September 11. Available at: http://www.commondreams.org/views04/0917-02.htm.

Mueller, Milton. 1998. "The 'Governance' Debacle: How the Ideal of Internetworking Got Buried by Politics." Paper presented at INET, Geneva, Switzerland. http://www.isoc.org/inet98/proceedings.

Mun, Thomas. 1664. *England's Treasure by Foreign Trade*. Glasgow: R. and A. Foulis.

Mundy, John H., and Peter Riesenberg. 1958. *The Medieval Town*. Princeton: Van Nostrand.

Munger, Frank, ed., 2002. *Laboring under the Line*. New York: Russell Sage Foundation.

Munker, Stefan, and Alexander Roesler, eds. 1997. *Mythos Internet*. Frankfurt: Suhrkamp.

Murphy, Craig N. 1994. *International Organization and Industrial Change: Global Governance since 1850*. New York: Oxford University Press.

Nadeau, J., C. Lointier, R. Morin, and M. A. Descoteaux. 1998. *"Information Highways and the Francophone World: Current Situation and Strategies for the Future."* Paper presented at INET Conference: The Internet Summit, Geneva, Switzerland, July 21–24.

Nakashima, Ellen. 2002. "Bush View of Secrecy Is Stirring Frustration." *Washington Post*, March 3.

Narula, Rajneesh, and Annelies Hogenbirk. 1998. "Dutch Manufacturing Mines in the United States, 1950–1995." In *Multinational Enterprises from the Netherlands*, ed. R. van Hoesel and R. Narula. London: Routledge.

Nash, June, ed. 2005. *Social Movements: An Anthropological Reader*. Malden, Mass. Blackwell.

Nelson, Jack. 2003a. "Government Secrecy: What Leaks Are Good Leaks?" *Los Angeles Times*, January 5.

———. 2003b. "U.S. Government Secrecy and the Current Crackdown on Leaks." Joan Shorestein Center on the Press, Politics and Public Policy. Working Paper 2003-1, Harvard University.

Nettime. 1997. *Net Critique*. Comp. Geert Lovink and Pit Schultz. Berlin: Edition ID-Archive.

Neumann, Iver B. 1996. *Russia and the Idea of Europe: A Study in Identity and International Relations*. New York: Routledge.

Ngai, Mae M. 2004. *Impossible Subjects: Illegal Aliens and the Making of Modern America*. Princeton: Princeton University Press.

Noble, David F. 1977. *America by Design: Science, Technology, and the Rise of Corporate Capitalism*. New York: Knopf.

Noble, Gregory W., and John Ravenhill, eds. 2000. *The Asian Financial Crisis and the Architecture of Global Finance*. Cambridge: Cambridge University Press.

Nonini, Donald M. 2003. "American Noeliberalism, 'Globalization,' and Violence: Reflections from the United States and Southeast Asia." In Globalization, the State, and Violence, ed. Jonathan Friedman, pp. 163–202. Walnut Creek, Calif.: AltaMira Press.

North, Douglass C. 1981. *Structure and Change in Economic History*. New York: W. W. Norton.

North, Douglass C., and Robert Thomas. 1973. *The Rise of the Western World: A New Economic History*. New York: Cambridge University Press.

North, Sir Dudley. 1691. "Discourse upon Trade, Principally, Directed to the Cases of the Interest, Coynage, Clipping, Increase of Money." In *A Selected Collection of Early English Tracts on Commerce*, ed. J. R. McCulloch. London, 1856.

Novak, William J. 1996. *The People's Welfare: Law and Regulation in Nineteenth-Century America*. Chapel Hill: University of North Carolina Press.

———. 2000. "Law, Capitalism and the Liberal State: The Historical Sociology of James Willard Hurst." *Law and History Review* 18: 97–145.

———. 2002. "The Legal Origins of the Modern American State." In *Looking Back at Law's Century*, ed. Austin Sarat, Bryan Garth, and Robert A. Kagan. Ithaca, N.Y.: Cornell University Press.

Novarese, Alex. 2004. "Commentary: Toothless Takeover Code Fails to Deliver." *Legal Week*, January 22.

NTIA (National Telecommunications and Information Administration). 1998. *Falling through the Net II: New Data on the Digital Divide* (July). Washington, DC: NTIA.

Nussbaum, Martha C. 2000. *Women and Human Development: The Capabilities Approach*. New York: Cambridge University Press.

Nyang'oro, Julius E. 1999. "Hemmed In? The State in Africa and Global Liberalization." In *States and Sovereignty in the Global Economy*, ed. David A. Smith, Dorothy J. Solinger, and Steven C. Topik. London: Routledge.

O'Connor, James. 1973. *The Fiscal Crisis of the State*. New York: St. Martin's Press.

Ōhmae, Ken'ichi. 1995. *The End of the Nation State: The Rise of Regional Economies*. New York: Free Press.

Olds, Kris, Peter Dicken, Philip E. Kelly, Lilly Kong, and Henry Wai-Chung Yeung, eds. 1999. *Globalization and the Asian Pacific: Contested Territories*. London: Routledge.

Ong, Aihwa. 1999. *Flexible Citizenship*. Durham: Duke University Press.

Ong, Aihwa, and Stephen J. Collier. 2005. *Global Assemblages: Technology, Politics, and Ethics as Anthropological Problems*. Malden, Mass.: Blackwell.

Organization for Economic Co-operation and Development. 2003. *OECD Institutional Investors Statistical Yearbook, 1992–2001*. Paris: OECD.

Overbeek, Henk. 2000. "Transnational Historical Materialism: Theories of Transnational Class Formation and World Order." In *Global Political Economy: Contemporary Theories*, ed. Ronen Palan. London: Routledge.

Pace, William R., and Rik Panganiban. 2002. "The Power of Global Activist Networks: The Campaign for an International Criminal Court." In *Civil Society in the Information Age*, ed. Peter I. Hajnal. Aldershot, UK: Ashgate.

Paddison, Ronan. 1983. *The Fragmented State: The Political Geography of Power*. New York: St. Martin's Press.

Paine, Thomas. 1792. *The Rights of Man*. Part 2. London.

Palan, R. 2003. *The Offshore World: Sovereign Markets, Virtual Places, and Nomad Millionaires*. Ithaca: Cornell University Press.

Palloix, Christian. 1973. *L'internationalisation du capital*. Paris: Maspero.

———. 1975. *L'économie mondiale capitaliste et les firmes multinationales*. 2 vols. Paris: Maspero.

Palumbo-Liu, David. 1999. *Asian/American: Historical Crossings of a Racial Frontier*. Stanford: Stanford University Press.

Panitch, Leo. 1996. "Rethinking the Role of the State in an Era of Globalization." In *Globalization: Critical Reflections*, ed. James Mittelman. Boulder, CO: Lynne Rienner.

Pare, Daniel J. 2003. *Internet Governance in Transition: Who Is the Master of This Domain?* Lanham, Md.: Rowman and Littlefield.

Parker School of Foreign and Comparative Law, Columbia University. 1992. *Guide to International Arbitration and Arbitrators*. 2nd ed. Ardsley-on-Hudson, N.Y.: Transnational Juris Publications.

Parnreiter, Christof, Andreas Novy, and Karin Fischer. 1999. *Globaliserung und Peripherie: Umstrukturierung ini Lateinamerika, Afrika und Asien*. Südwind: Brandes and Apsel.

Parr, John B., and Leslie Budd. 2000. "Financial Services and the Urban System: An Exploration." *Urban Studies* 37(3): 593–610.

Pastré, Oliver. 1979. *La stratégie internationale des groupes financiers américains*. Paris: Economica.

Pateman, Carole. 1989. *The Disorder of Women: Democracy, Feminism and Political Theory*. Cambridge: Polity.

Paul, Arnold M. 1960. *Conservative Crisis and the Rule of Law: Attitudes of Bar and Bench, 1887–1895*. Ithaca, N.Y.: Cornell University Press.

Paul, Joel. 1995. "Introduction: The New Movements in International Economic Law." *American University Journal of International Law and Policy* 10(2): 607–17.

Pauly, Louis W. 2002. "Global Finance, Political Authority, and the Problem of Legitimation." In *The Emergence of Private Authority in Global Governance*, ed. Rodney Bruce Hall and Thomas J. Biersteker. Cambridge: Cambridge University Press.

Peck, J., and N. Theodore. 2001. "Contingent Chicago: Restructuring the Spaces of Temporary Labor." *International Journal of Urban and Regional Research* 25(3): 471–96.

"Peering through the Monetary Mist." 1995. *The Economist*, October 7.

Perlman, Selig. 1928. *A Theory of the Labor Movement*. New York: Macmillan.

Perroux, Francois. 1948. *Le capitalisme*. Paris: Presses Universitaires de France.

Perroy, Edouard, et al. 1955. *Le Moyen Age*. Vol. 3 of *Histoire générale des civilisations*. Paris: Presses Universitaires de France.

Petrazzini, B., and M. Kibati. 1999. "The Internet in Developing Countries." *Communications of the ACM* 42(6): 31–36.

Picciotto, Sol. 1990. "The Internationalization of the State." *Review of Radical Political Economics* 22(1): 28–44.

Picciotto, Sol, and Ruth Mayne. 1999. *Regulating International Business: Beyond Liberalization*. London: Macmillan.

Pierson, Christopher. 1996. *The Modern State*. London: Routledge.

Pigou, A. C. 1968. *The Theory of Unemployment*. London: Franklin Cass.

Pirenne, Henri. 1925 [1952]. *Medieval Cities*. Princeton: Princeton University Press.

———. 1956. *Economic and Social History of Medieval Europe*. New York: Harcourt Brace Jovanovich.

Pizzorno, Alessandro. 1987. "Politics Unbound." In *Changing Boundaries of the Political*, ed. Charles Maier. Cambridge: Cambridge University Press.

Pocock, J.G.A. 1957. *The Ancient Constitution and the Feudal Law: A Study of English Historical Thought in the Seventeenth Century*. Cambridge: Cambridge University Press.

Pogge, Thomas. 1992. "Cosmopolitanism and Sovereignty." *Ethics* 103: 48–75.

Poggi, Gianfranco. 1978. *The Development of the Modern State: A Sociological Introduction*. Stanford: Stanford University Press.

Poidevin, Raymond. 1969. *Les relations économiques et financières entre la France et l'Allemagne de 1898 à 1914*. Paris: Armand Colin.

Polanyi, Karl. 1971. "Primitive Feudalism and the Feudalism of Decay." In *Economic Development and Social Change*, ed. George Dalton. New York: Natural History Press.

———. 2001 [1944]. *The Great Transformation: The Political and Economic Origins of Our Time*. Boston: Beacon Press.

Pollack, Mark A., and Gregory C. Chaffer, eds. 2001. *Transatlantic Governance in the Global Economy*. Lanham, Md.: Rowman and Littlefield.

Pomeranz, Kenneth. 1999. "Two Worlds of Trade, Two Worlds of Empire: European State-Making and Industrialization in a Chinese Mirror." In *States and Sovereignty in the Global Economy*, ed. David A. Smith, Dorothy J. Solinger, and Steven C. Topik. London: Routledge.

Poovey, Mary. 1998. *A History of the Modern Fact: Problems of Knowledge in the Sciences of Wealth and Society*. Chicago: University of Chicago Press.

Portes, A., ed. 1995. *The Economic Sociology of Immigration*. New York: Russell Sage Foundation.

Portnoy, Brian. 1999. "Constructing Competition: The Political Foundations of Alliance Capitalism." Ph.D. diss., University of Chicago.

Posner, Richard A. 1997. "Bad Faith." *The New Republic* June 9: 34–38.

Post, David. 1995. "Anarchy, State, and the Internet: An Essay on Law-Making in Cyberspace." *Journal of Online Law* Article 3.

Poster, Mark. 1997. "Cyberdemocracy: Internet and the Public Sphere." In D. Porter, ed., *Internet Culture*. London: Routledge.

———. 1999. "National Identities and Communications Technologies." *Information Society* 15(4): 235–40.

———. 2001. "What's the Matter with the Internet?" *Electronic Mediations*, 3. Minneapolis: University of Minnesota Press.

Postone, Moishe. 1993. *Labor, Time, and Social Domination: A Reinterpretation of Marx's Critical Theory*. Cambridge: Cambridge University Press.

Poulantzas, Nicos. 1968. *Pouvoir politique et classes sociales*. Paris: Maspero.

———. 1978. *L'état, le pouvoir, le socialisme*. Paris: Presses Universitaires de France.

Pound, Roscoe. 1911–12. "Scope and Purpose of Sociological Jurisprudence." *Harvard Law Review* 24: 591–619; 25: 140–68, 489–516.

Preda, Alex. 2004. "Informative Prices, Rational Investors: The Emergence of the Random Walk Hypothesis and the Nineteenth-Century 'Science of Financial Investments.'" *History of Political Economy* 36(2): 351–86.

———. 2005. "The Investor as a Cultural Figure of Global Capitalism." In *The Sociology of Financial Markets*, ed. Karin Knorr Cetina and Alex Preda. New York: Oxford University Press.

President's Working Group on Financial Markets. 1999. *Hedge Funds, Leverage, and the Lessons of Long-Term Capital Management*. Washington, DC: GPO.

Quadagno, Jill, and Stanley Knapp. 1992. "Have Historical Sociologists Forsaken Theory?" *Sociological Methods and Research* 20(4): 481–507.

Quesnay, "Grains." 1757. In *François Quesnay et la Physiocratie*. Paris: Institut National D'études Démographiques, 1958, vol. 2.

Radice, H. 1975. *International Firms and Modern Imperialism*. Harmondsworth: Penguin.

Rajagopal, Balakrishnan. 2003. *International Law from Below*. Cambridge: Cambridge University Press.

Rasmussen, Mikkel V. 2003. "The History of a Lesson: Versailles, Munich, and the Social Construction of the Past." *Review of International Studies* 29(4): 499–519.

Ray, Douglas E., Calvin William Sharpe, and Robert N. Strassfeld. 1999. *Understanding Labor Law*. New York: M. Bender.

Redden, Guy. 2001. "Networking Dissent: The Internet and the Anti-Globalisation Movement." *MotsPluriels* 18. Available at: *http://www.arts.uwa.edu.au/MotsPluriels/MP1801gr.html*.

Reidenberg, Joel, R. 1998. "Lex Informatica: The Formulation of Information Policy Rules through Technology." *Texas Law Review* 76(2): 553–94.

Reed, Lucy, and Jonathan Sutcliffe. 2001. "The Americanization of International Commercial Arbitration." *Mealey's International Arbitration Report* 16: 37.

Reich, Robert B. 1991. *The Work of Nations: Preparing Ourselves for 21st-Century Capitalism.* New York: Knopf.

Reidenberg, Joel R. 1998. "Lex Informatica: The Formulation of Information Policy Rules Through Technology." Texas Law Review 76(3): http://reidenberg.home.sprynet.com/lex_informatica.pdf.

Renouard, Yves. 1958. "1212–1216: Comment les traits durables de l'Europe Occidentale moderne se sont définis au début de XIIIᵉ siècle." *Annales de l'Université de Paris* 28(1): 5–21.

Rey, P. P. 1973. *Les alliances de classes.* Paris: Maspéro.

Reynolds, Susan. 1984. *Kingdoms and Communities in Western Europe, 900–1300.* Oxford: Clarendon.

Rheingold, Howard. 2003. *Smart Mobs.* Cambridge, Mass: Perseus.

Ricardo, Davis. 1951. *On the Principles of Political Economy and Taxation.* Vol. 1: *The Works and Correspondence of David Ricardo,* ed. Piero Sraffa. Cambridge: Cambridge University Press.

Riemens, Patrice, and Geert Lovink. 2002. "Local Networks: Digital City Amsterdam." In *Global Networks, Linked Cities,* ed. Saskia Sassen. London: Routledge.

Rifkin, Jeremy. 1987. *Time Wars: The Primary Conflict in Human History.* New York: Henry Holt & Co.

Rimmer, P. J., and T. Morris-Suzuki. 1999. "The Japanese Internet: Visionaries and Virtual Democracy." *Environment and Planning* 31: 1189–1206.

Rittich, Kerry. 2001. "Who's Afraid of the Critique of Adjudication?: Tracing the Discourse of Law in Development." *Cardozo Law Review* 22: 929–46.

Robbins, L. 1934. *The Great Depression, 1929–1934.* New York: Macmillan.

Robertson, Roland. 1991. "Social Theory, Cultural Relativity, and the Problem of Globality." In *Culture, Globalization, and the World-System: Contemporary Conditions for the Representation of Identity,* ed. Anthony D. King, pp. 69–90. Binghamton: Department of Art and History, State University of New York.

———. 1992. *Globalization: Social Theory and Global Culture.* Thousand Oaks, Calif.: Sage.

Robinson, William I. 2004. *A Theory of Global Capitalism: Production, Class, and State in a Transnational World.* Baltimore: Johns Hopkins University Press.

Rogers, Joel. 1990. "Divide and Conquer: Further Reflections in the Distinctive Character of American Labor Law." *Wisconsin Law Review* 1: 1–148.

Rogers, Richard. 2002. "Operating Issue Networks on the Web." *Science as Culture* 11(2): 191–213.

———. 2004. *Information Politics on the Web.* Cambridge, Mass. MIT Press.

Rohr, John A. 1986. *To Run a Constitution: The Legitimacy of the Administrative State.* Lawrence: University of Kansas Press.

Ronfeldt, David, John Arquilla, Graham Fuller, and Melissa Fuller. 1998. *The Zapatista "Social Netwar" in Mexico.* Santa Monica, Calif.: RAND, MR-994-A.

Rörig, Fritz. 1969. *The Medieval Town.* Berkeley: University of California Press.

Rosenau, James N. 1992. "Governance, Order, and Change in World Politics." In *Governance without Government: Order and Change in World Politics,* ed. J. N. Rosenau and E. O. Czempiel. Cambridge: Cambridge University Press.

Rosenau, James N., and J. P. Singh, eds. 2002. Information Technologies and Global Politics: The Changing Scope of Power and Governance. Albany, N.Y.: SUNY Press.

Ross, Edward Alsworth. 1969 [1901]. *Social Control: A Survey of the Foundations of Order.* Cleveland: Press of Case Western Reserve University.

Roulleau-Berger, Laurence, ed. 2002. *Youth and Work in the Postindustrial Cities of North America and Europe.* Leiden: Brill.

Rousseau, Jean-Jacques. *On the Social Control.* Ed. R. D. Masters. New York: St. Martin's.

Rubenstein, Kim, and Daniel Adler. 2000. "International Citizenship: The Future of Nationality in a Globalized World." *Indiana Journal of Global Legal Studies* 7(2): 519–48.

Rubinstein, W. D. 1998. *Britain's Century: A Political and Social History 1815–1905.* New York: Arnold Publishers.

Rueschemeyer, Dietrich, and Theda Skocpol, eds. 1996. *States, Social Knowledge, and the Origins of Modern Social Policies.* Princeton: Princeton University Press.

Ruggie, John Gerard. 1993. "Territoriality and Beyond: Problematizing Modernity in International Relations." *International Organization* 47: 139–74.

————. 1998. "Introduction: What Makes the World Hang Together? Neo-utilitarianism and the Social Constructivist Challenge." In *Constructing the World Polity: Essays on International Institutions.* London: Routledge.

Ruigrok, Winfried, and Rob van Tulder. 1995. *The Logic of International Restructuring.* London: Routledge.

Rupert, Mark. 2000. *Ideologies of Globalization: Contending Visions of a New World Order.* London: Routledge.

Rutherford, Kenneth R. 2002. "Essential Partners: Landmines-Related NGOs and Information Technologies." In *Civil Society in the Information Age,* ed. Peter I. Hajnal. Aldershot, UK: Ashgate.

Sabin, Cameron L. 2002. "The Adjudicatory Boat without a Keel: Private Arbitration and the Need for Public Oversight of Arbitration." *Iowa Law Review* 87(3): 1337–82.

Sack, Warren. 2005. "Discourse Architecture and Very Large-scale Conversation." In *Digital Formations: IT and New Architecture in the Global Realm,* ed. Robert Latham and Saskia Sassen. Princeton: Princeton University Press.

Sadat, Leila Nadya, and S. Richard Carden. 2000. "The New International Criminal Court." *Georgetown Law Journal* 88(3): 381–474.

Safire, William. 2003. "Behind Closed Doors." *New York Times,* December 17.

Sahlins, Marshall. 1972. *Stone Age Economics.* Chicago: Aldine-Atherton.

Salacuse, Jeswald. 1991. *Making Global Deals: Negotiating in the International Marketplace*. Boston: Houghton Mifflin.

Saltman, Michael. 1987. "Feudal Relationships and the Law: A Comparative Inquiry." *Comparative Studies in Society and History* 29(3): 514–32.

Salzinger, Leslie. 2003. "Market Subjects: Traders at Work in the Dollar/Peso Market." Paper presented at the annual meeting of the American Sociological Association, Wilder House Editorial Board Faculty Workshop, University of Chicago, July 6.

Sandel, Michael J. 1996. *Democracy's Discontent: America in Search of a Public Philosophy*. Cambridge, Mass.: Belknap Press of Harvard University Press.

Sandholtz, Wayne. 1999. "Globalization and the Evolution Rules." In *Globalization and Governance*, ed. A. Prakash and J. A. Hart. London: Routledge.

Sandholz, W., and A. Stone Sweet, eds. 1998. *European Integration and Supranational Governance*. New York: Oxford University Press.

Sarat, Austin, Lawrence Douglas, and Martha Merrill Umphrey. 2003. *The Place of Law*. Ann Arbor: University of Michigan Press.

Sassen, Saskia. 1988 [1997]. *The Mobility of Labor and Capital: A Study in International Investment and Labor Flow*. Cambridge: Cambridge University Press.

———. 1991. *The Global City*. Princeton: Princeton University Press.

———. 1996. *Losing Control?: Sovereignty in an Age of Globalization*. New York: Columbia University Press.

———. 1998. *Globalization and Its Discontents: Essays on the Mobility of People and Money*. New York: New Press.

———. 1999. *Guests and Aliens*. New York: New Press.

———. 2000. "Women's Burden: Countergeographies of Globalization and the Feminization of Survival." *Journal of International Affairs* 53(2): 503–24.

———. 2001. *The Global City*. 2nd ed. Princeton: Princeton University Press.

———. 2002. "Towards a Sociology of Information Technology." *Current Sociology* (Special Issue on the New Information Technologies) 50(3): 365–88.

———. 2003a. "The Participation of States and Citizens in Global Governance." *Indiana Journal of Global Legal Studies* 10(1): 5–28.

———. 2003b. "Global Cities and Survival Circuits." In *Global Woman: Nannies, Maids, and Sex Workers in the New Economy*, ed. Barbara Ehrenreich and Arlie R. Hochschild. New York: Metropolitan Books.

———. 2004. "The Role of Financial Centers in the Functioning of Complex Derivatives Trading." On file with author, Department of Sociology, University of Chicago.

Saunders, Peter. 1993. "Citizenship in a Liberal Society." In *Citizenship and Social Theory*, ed. Bryan Turner. London: Sage.

Saxonhouse, Arlene W. 1992. *Fear of Diversity: The Birth of Political Science in Ancient Greek Thought*. Chicago: University of Chicago Press.

Say, Jean-Baptiste. 1970. *Catechisme d'économie politique*. Paris: Mame.

Schafer, Axel R. 2004. "German Historicism, Progressive Social Thought, and the Interventionist State in the United State since the 1880s." In *Markets in Historical*

Contexts: Ideas and Politics in the Modern World, ed. Mark Bevir and Frank Trentmann. Cambridge: Cambridge University Press.

Schelling, Thomas C. 1971. "Dynamic Models of Segregation." *Journal of Mathematical Sociology* 1: 143–86.

Scheuerman, William E., ed. 1996. *The Rule of Law under Siege: Selected Essays of Franz L. Neumann and Otto Kirchheimer.* Berkeley: University of California Press.

Schiller, Nina Glick, and Georges Fouron. 2003. "Killing Me Softly: Violence, Globalization, and the Apparent State." In Globalization, the State, and Violence, ed. Jonathan Friedman pp. 203–48. Walnut Creek, Calif.: AltaMira Press.

Schlegel, John Henry. 1995. *American Legal Realism and Empirical Social Science.* Chapel Hill: University of North Carolina Press.

Schmidt, Vivien A. 1999. "Convergent Pressures, Divergent Responses: France, Great Britain, and Germany between Globalization and Europeanization." In *States and Sovereignty in the Global Economy*, ed. David A. Smith, Dorothy J. Solinger, and Steven C. Topik. London: Routledge.

Schuck, Peter, and Rogers Smith. 1985. *Citizenship without Consent: Illegal Aliens in the American Polity.* New Haven: Yale University Press.

Schuler, Doug. 1996. *New Community Networks: Wired for Change.* Boston: Addison-Wesley.

Schwarcz, Steven L. 2002. "Private Ordering." *Northwestern University Law Review* 97(1): 319–50.

Scott, Allen J., ed. 2001. *Global City-Regions: Trends, Theory, Policy.* Oxford: Oxford University Press.

Sée, Henri. 1928. *Modern Capitalism: Its Origins and Evolution.* New York: Adelphi.

Sell, Susan K. 2003. *Private Power, Public Law: The Globalization of Intellectual Property Rights.* New York: Cambridge University Press.

Sen, Amartya. 1999. *Development as Freedom.* New York: Anchor Books.

Sennett, Richard. 1980. *Authority.* New York: Random House.

Sewell, William H., Jr. 1980. *Work and Revolution in France: The Language of Labor from the Old Regime to 1848.* New York: Cambridge University Press.

———. 1994. *A Rhetoric of Bourgeois Revolution: The Abbé Sieyès and What Is the Third Estate?* Durham: Duke University Press.

———. 1996. "Three Temporalities: Toward an Eventful Sociology." In *The Historic Turn in the Human Sciences*, ed. Terence McDonald. Ann Arbor: University of Michigan Press.

Shade, Leslie Regan. 1998. "A Gendered Perspective on Access to the Information Infrastructure." *The Information Society* 14: 33–44.

"Shameful Revelations Will Haunt Bush." 2004. *The Economist.* June 18.

Shapiro, Ian, and Casiano Hacker-Cordón, eds. 1999. *Democracy's Edges.* Cambridge: Cambridge University Press.

Shapiro, Martin. 1993. "The Globalization of Law." *Indiana Journal of Global Legal Studies* 1: 37–64.

Sharp, John. 1997. "Communities of Practice: A Review of the Literature." Available at: http://www.tfriend.com/cop-lit.htm.

Shaw, David. 2004. "Reporters under Siege in Era of Government Secrecy." *Los Angeles Times*, November 28.

Shaw, Debora. 2001. "Playing the Links: Interactivity and Stickiness in .Com and 'Not.Com' Web Sites." *FirstMonday* 6(3): http://www.firstmonday.dk/issues/issue 6_3/shaw.

Shelton, Dinah. 1999. *Remedies in International Human Rights Law*. New York: Oxford University Press.

Shelton, Joanna. 1999. "Competition Policy: What Chance for International Rules?" (Print version of speech given in November 1998 at OECD conference on the global trade agenda). *OECD Journal of Competition Law and Policy* 1(2): 51–65.

Shklar, Judith N. 1964. *Legalism*. Cambridge, Mass.: Harvard University Press.

Shotter, John. 1993. "Psychology and Citizenship: Identity and Belonging." In *Citizenship and Social Theory*, ed. Bryan Turner. London: Sage.

Silver, Beverly J. 2003. *Forces of Labor: Workers' Movements and Globalization since 1870*. Cambridge: Cambridge University Press.

Silvern, Steven E. 1999. "Scales of Justice: Law, American Indian Treaty Rights and Political Construction of Scale." *Political Geography* 18: 639–68.

Simonson, R. 1963. *Historia Econômica do Brasil, 1500–1820*. São Paulo: Companhia Editora Nacional.

Sinclair, David. 2000. *The Pound: A Biography*. London: Century.

Sinclair, Timothy J. 1994. "Passing Judgment: Credit Rating Processes as Regulatory Mechanisms of Governance in the Emerging World Order." *Review of International Political Economy* 1: 133–59.

Siochrú, Seán O., and Bruce Girard with Amy Mahan. 2002. *Global Media Governance: A Beginner's Guide*. Lanham, Md.: Rowman & Littlefield.

Skeldon, R. 1997. "Hong Kong: Colonial City to Global City to Provincial City?" *Cities* 14(5): 265–71.

Skinner, Quentin. 1978. *The Foundations of Modern Political Thought*. 2 vols. New York: Cambridge University Press.

Sklair, Leslie. 2001. *The Transnational Capitalist Class*. Oxford: Blackwell.

Sklair, Leslie, and Peter T. Robbins. 2002. "Global Capitalism and Major Corporations from the Third World." *Third World Quarterly* 23(1): 81–100.

Sklar, Martin. 1988. *The Corporate Reconstruction of American Capitalism, 1890–1916*. New York: Cambridge University Press.

Skocpol, Theda. 1979. *States and Social Revolutions: A Comparative Analysis of France, Russia, and China*. New York: Cambridge University Press.

———. 1992. *Protecting Soldiers and Mothers: The Political Origins of Social Policy in the United States*. Cambridge, Mass.: Harvard University Press.

Skowronek, Stephen. 1982. *Building a New American State: The Expansion of National Administrative Capacities, 1877–1920*. New York: Cambridge University Press.

Slaughter, Anne-Marie. 1994. "A Typology of Transjudicial Communication." *University of Richmond Law Review* 29: 99–138.

———. 2004. *The Real New World Order*. Princeton: Princeton University Press.

Slawner, Karen, and Mark Denham. 1998. *Citizenship after Liberalism*. New York: Peter Lang.

Smit, H. and V. Pechota, eds. 2004. Smit's Guides to International Arbitration: The Roster of International Arbitrators. Huntington, N.Y.: Juirs Publishing.

Smith, Adam. 1759. *The Theory of Moral Sentiments*. London: Printed for A. Millar.

———. 1937. *An Enquiry into the Nature and Cause of the Wealth of Nations*. New York: Modern Library.

Smith, David A., Dorothy J. Solinger, and Steven C. Topik, eds. 1999. *States and Sovereignty in the Global Economy*. London: Routledge.

Smith, Michael Peter. 1994. "Can You Imagine? Transnational Migration and the Globalisation of Grassroots Politics." *Social Text* 39: 15–33.

Smith, Michael Peter, and Luis Eduardo Guarnizo, eds. 1998. *Transnationalism from Below*. New Brunswick, NJ: Transaction Publishers.

Smith, Peter J. 2001. "The Impact of Globalization on Citizenship: Decline or Renaissance." *Journal of Canadian Studies* 36: 116–40.

Smith, Robert C. 1997. "Transnational Migration, Assimilation and Political Community." In *The City and the World: New York's Global Future*, ed. Margaret Crahan and Alberto Vourvoulias-Bush. New York: Council of Foreign Relations.

Smithson, C. W. 1998. *Managing Financial Risks: A Guide to Derivative Products, Financial Engineering, and Value Maximization*. New York: McGraw-Hill.

Snyder, Francis, ed. 2001. *Regional and Global Regulation of International Trade*. Oxford: Hart Publishing.

Solow, R. M. 1971. "Growth Theory: An Exposition." *Revue Economique* 22(4): 685–86.

Sombart, Werner. 1928. *Der Moderne Kapitalismus*. Munich: Leipzig, Duncker, and Humblot.

Soros, George. 2002. *George Soros on Globalization*. New York: PublicAffairs.

Soysal, Yasemin Nuhoglu. 1994. *Limits of Citizenship: Migrants and Postnational Membership in Europe*. Chicago: University of Chicago Press.

———. 1997. "Changing Parameters of Citizenship and Claims-Making: Organized Islam in European Public Spheres." *Theory and Society* 26(4): 509–27.

Spinner-Halev, Jeff. 1994. *The Boundaries of Citizenship: Race, Ethnicity, and Nationality in the Liberal State*. Baltimore: Johns Hopkins University Press.

Spiro, Peter, J. 1997. "Dual Nationality and the Meaning of Citizenship." *Emory Law Journal* 46: 1411–87.

Spivak, Gayatri Chakravorty. 1994. "Can the Subaltern Speak?" In *Colonial Discourse and Post-Colonial Theory*, ed. Patrick Williams and Laura Chrisman. New York: Columbia University Press.

Spruyt, Hendrik. 1994. *The Sovereign State and Its Competitors: An Analysis of Systems Change*. Princeton: Princeton University Press.

Stanley, Amy Dru. 1998. *From Bondage to Contract: Wage Labor, Marriage, and the Market in the Age of Slave Emancipation*. Cambridge: Cambridge University Press.

Steinfeld, Robert J. 1991. *The Invention of Free Labor: The Employment Relation in English and American Law and Culture*. Chapel Hill: University of North Carolina Press.

———. 2001. *Coercion, Contract, and Free Labor in the Nineteenth Century*. New York: Cambridge University Press.

Stephan, Paul B. 1999. "Rationality and Corruption in the Post-Socialist World." *Connecticut Journal of International Law* 14(2):533–49.

———. 2002. "Institutions and Elites: Property, Contract, the State and Rights in Information in the Global Economy." *Cardozo Journal of International and Comparative Law* 10: 305–17.

Stephens, Beth. 2002. "Corporate Liability: Enforcing Human Rights through Domestic Litigation." *Hastings International and Comparative Law Review* 24: 401.

Stephenson, Carl. 1933. *Borough and Town: A Study of Urban Origins in England*. Cambridge, Mass.: Mediaeval Academy of America.

———. 1954. *Mediaeval Institutions*. Ithaca: Cornell University Press.

Stevenson, Richard W. 2004. "President Rejected Torture of Prisoners: Documents Show His Directive Ran Counter to Options Offered Later by Justice Dept." *New York Times*, June 23.

Stillman, Richard J. II. 1998. *Creating the American State: The Moral Reformers and the Modern Administrative World They Made*. Tuscaloosa: Alabama University Press.

Stix, Gary. 1998. "A Calculus of Risk." *Scientific American* 278(5): 92–97.

Strange, Susan. 1986. *Casino Capitalism*. Oxford: Oxford University Press.

Strayer, Joseph R. 1965. *Feudalism*. Huntington, N.Y.: R. E. Krieger.

———. 1970. *On the Medieval Origins of the Modern State*. Princeton: Princeton University Press.

———. 1980. *The Reign of Philip the Fair*. Princeton: Princeton University Press.

Sunstein, Cass R. 1993. "On Analogical Reasoning." *Harvard Law Review* 106: 741–67.

Suter, Christian. 1992. *Debt Cycles in the World Economy: Foreign Loans, Financial Crises, and Debt Settlements, 1820–1986*. Boulder, CO: Westview Press.

Swyngedouw, Erik A. 1992. "The Mammon Quest: 'Glocalization', Interspatial Competition and the Monetary Order: The Construction of New Scales." In *Cities and Regions in the New Europe: The Global-Local Interplay and Spatial Development Strategies*, ed. M. Dunford and G. Kafkalis. London: Belhaven Press.

———. 1997. "Neither Global nor Local: 'Globalization' and the Politics of Scale." In *Spaces of Globalization: Reasserting the Power of the Local*, ed. Kevin R. Cox. New York: Guilford.

Symons, Jeremy. 2003. "How Bush and Co. Obscure the Science." *Washington Post*, July 13.

Syre, Steven. 2005. "Fidelity, Exchange Cut E-Trade Pact: Regionals Face Turning Point amid Focus on Lower Costs, Fast Trading." *Boston Globe*, August 25.

Tabb, William K. 2004. *Economic Governance in the Age of Globalization*. New York: Columbia University Press.

Tarrow, Sidney G. 1994. *Power in Movement: Collective Action and Politics*. New York: Cambridge University Press.

Taylor, Benjamin, and Fred Witney. 1992. *U.S. Labor Relations Law: Historical Development*. Englewood Cliffs, NJ: Prentice Hall.

Taylor, Charles. 1994. "The Politics of Recognition." In *Multiculturalism: Examining the Politics of Recognition*, ed. Amy Gutmann. Princeton: Princeton University Press.

Taylor, Frederick W. 1967. *The Principles of Scientific Management*. New York: Norton.

Taylor, Peter. 1994. "The State as Container: Territoriality in the Modern Worldsystem." *Progress in Human Geography* 18(2): 151–62.

Taylor, Peter J., D.R.F. Walker, and J. V. Beaverstock. 2002. "Firms and Their Global Service Networks." In *Global Networks, Linked Cities*, ed. Saskia Sassen. New York: Routledge.

Taylor-Gooby, Peter. 2004. "Open Markets and Welfare Values: Welfare Values, Inequality, and Social Change in the Silver Age of the Welfare State." *European Societies* 6(1): 29–48.

Teubner, Gunther, ed. 1987. *Juridification of Social Spheres: A Comparative Analysis in the Areas of Labor, Corporate, Antitrust and Social Welfare Law*. Berlin: Walter de Gruyter.

———. 1988. *Dilemmas of Law in the Welfare State*. Berlin: Walter de Gruyter.

———. 2004. "Societal Constitutionalism: Alternatives to Sate-Centered Constitutional Theory." In *Transnational Governance and Constitutionalism*, ed. Christian Joerges, Inger-Johanne Sand, and Gunther Teubner. Portland, OR: Hartford Publishing.

———, ed. 1997. *Global Law without a State*. Aldershot, UK: Dartmouth Publishing.

Thomas, Chantal. 1999. "Transfer of Technology in the Contemporary International Order." *Fordham International Law Journal* 22(5): 2096–2111.

Thomas, R. 1995. "Access and Inequality." In *Information Technology and Society: A Reader*, ed. N. Heap, R. Thomas, G. Einon, R. Mason, and H. MacKay. Buckingham: Open University Press.

Thompson, E. P. 1963. *The Making of the English Working Class*. New York: Vintage Books.

Thompson, Walter. 1923. *Federal Centralization: A Study and Criticism of the Expanding Scope of Congressional Legislation*. New York: Harcourt, Brace.

Thrift, Nigel. 1987. "The Fixers: The Urban Geography of International Commercial Capital." In *Global Restructuring and Territorial Development*, ed. J. Henderson and M. Castells. London: Sage.

———. 1996. "New Urban Eras and Old Technical Fears: Reconfiguring the Goodwill of Electronic Things." *Urban Studies* 33(8): 1463–93.

———. 1996b. *Spatial Formations*. London: Sage.

Tierney, Brian. 1973. *The Middle Ages: Sources of Medieval History*. Vol. 1 New York: Knopf.

Tilly, Charles, ed., 1975. *The Formation of National States in Western Europe*. Princeton: Princeton University Press.

Tilly, Charles. 1990. *Coercion, Capital, and European States, AD 990–1992*. Oxford: Basil Blackwell.

———. 1995. "Globalization Threatens Labor Rights." *International Labor and Working-Class History* 47: 1–23.

Tomlins, Christopher L. 1985. *The State and the Union: Labor Relations, Law and Organized Labor Movements in America, 1880–1960*. New York: Cambridge University Press.

———. 1993. *Law, Labor, and Ideology in the Early American Republic*. New York: Cambridge University Press.

Tomlins, Christopher L., and Andrew J. King, eds. 1992. *Labor Law in America: Historical and Critical Essays*. Baltimore: Johns Hopkins University Press.

Torres, Maria de los Ángeles. 1998. "Transnational Political and Cultural Identities: Crossing Theoretical Borders." In *Borderless Borders*, ed. Frank Bonilla, Edwin Mélendez, Rebecca Morales, and Maria de los Ángeles Torres. Philadelphia: Temple University Press.

Trachtman, Joel. 1993. "International Regulatory Competition, Externalization, and Juridiction." *Harvard International Law Journal* 34: 47–104.

"Transcript: Bush Urges Reauthorization of Patriot Act: Gonzales Sworn as New Attorney General." 2005. *Washington Post*, February 14.

Trattner, Walter I. 1999 [1974]. *From Poor Law to Welfare State: A History of Social Welfare in America*. 6th ed. New York: Free Press.

Triffin, Robert. 1979. "The International Role and Fate of the Dollar." *Foreign Affairs* 51(2): 269–86.

Trouillot, Michel-Rolph. 1995. *Silencing the Past: Power and the Production of History*. Boston: Beacon Press.

Tsaliki, Liza. 2002. "Online Forums and the Enlargement of the Public Space: Research Findings from a European Project." *The Public* 9(2): 95–112.

Tsatsaronis, Kostas. 2000. "Special Features: Hedge Funds." *BIS Quarterly Review* (November): 61–71.

Tugan-Baranowsky, M. 1913. *Les crises industrielles en Angleterre*. Paris: Giard.

Tuijl, Peter van, and Lisa Jordan. 1999. *Political Responsibility in Transnational NGO Advocacy*. Washington, DC: Bank Information Center. Available at: http://www .bicusa.org.

Turgot, M. 1795. *Reflections on the Formation and Distribution of Wealth*. London: E. Spragg.

Turner, Bryan. 2000. "Cosmopolitan Virtue: Loyalty and the City." In *Democracy, Citizenship and the Global City*, ed. Engin Isin. New York: Routledge.

Turner, Bryan S., ed. 1993. *Citizenship and Social Theory*. London: Sage.

Turner, Terrence. 2003. "Class Projects, Social Consciousness, and the Contradictions of 'Globalization'." In *Globalization, the State, and Violence*, ed. Jonathan Friedman. Walnut Creek, Calif.: AltaMira Press.

United Nations Conference on Trade and Development (UNCTAD). 1998. *World Investment Report: Trends and Determinants*. New York: UNCTAD.

———. 2005. *World Investment Report 2004.* New York: UNCTAD.

Urry, John. 2000. *Sociology Beyond Societies: Mobilities for the Twenty-First Century.* New York and London: Routledge.

U.S. Department of Justice. 2001. "New Attorney General FOIA Memorandum Issued." Office of Information and Privacy. Available at: http://www.usdoj.gov/oip/foiapost/2001foiapost19.htm.

Van der Pijl, Kees. 1998. *Transnational Classes and International Relations.* London: Routledge.

Van Steenbergen, Bart, ed. 1994. *The Condition of Citizenship.* Thousand Oaks, Calif.: Sage.

Verhulst, Adriaan. 1989. "The Origins of Towns in the Low Countries and the Pirenne Thesis." *Choice* 51:3–35.

Viner, Jacob. 1958. *The Long View and the Short: Studies in Economic Theory and Policy.* Glencoe, IL: Free Press.

Vogel, David. 1986. *National Styles of Regulation: Environmental Policy in Great Britain and the United States.* Ithaca: Cornell University Press.

———. 1995. *Trading Up: Consumer and Environmental Regulation in a Global Economy.* Cambridge, Mass.: Harvard University Press.

Vogel, Ursula, and Michael Moran, eds. 1991. *The Frontiers of Citizenship.* New York: St. Martin's.

Wade, Robert. 1990. *Governing the Market: Economic Theory and the Role of Government in East Asian Industrialization.* Princeton: Princeton University Press.

Wajcman, Judy, ed. 2002. "Information Technologies and the Social Sciences." *Current Sociology* 50(3): 347–63.

Walker, R.B.J. 1993. *Inside/Outside: International Relations as Political Theory.* Cambridge: Cambridge University Press.

Wallerstein, Immanuel. 1974. *The Modern World System.* New York: Academic Press.

———. 1999. "State? Sovereignty? The Dilemmas of Capitalism in an Age of Transition." In *States and Sovereignty in the Global Economy*, ed. David A. Smith, Dorothy J. Solinger, and Steven C. Topik. New York: Routledge.

———. 2001. *Unthinking Social Science: The Limits of Nineteenth-Century Paradigms.* Philadelphia: Temple University Press.

Walzer, Michael. 1985. *Spheres of Justice: A Defense of Pluralism and Equality.* New York: Basic Books.

Wapner, Paul 1996. *Environment Activism and World Civic Politics.* Albany: SUNY Press.

Warf, B., and J. Grimes. 1997. "Counterhegemonic Discourses and the Internet." *Geographical Review* 87: 259–74.

Warkentin, Craig. 2001. *Reshaping World Politics: NGOs, the Internet, and Global Civil Society.* Lanham, Md.: Rowman and Littlefield.

Warner, Michael. 2002. Publics and Counterpublics. Cambridge, Mass.: MIT Press.

Warren, Charles. 1913. "A Bulwark to the State Police Power—The United States Supreme Court." *Columbia Law Review* 13: 667–713.

Watson, S., and G. Bridges, eds., 1999. *Spaces of Culture*. London: Sage.

Weber, Max. 1930. *The Protestant Ethic and the Spirit of Capitalism*. London: Routledge.

————. 1958. *The City*. New York: Free Press.

————. 1968. "General Characteristics of the City." In *Max Weber: On Charisma and Institution Building*, ed. S. N. Eisenstadt. Chicago: University of Chicago Press.

————. 1978. *Economy and Society*. Ed. Guenther Ross and Claus Wittich. 2 vols. Berkeley: University of California Press.

Weber, Steven. 2005. "The Political Economy of Open Source Software and Why It Matters." In *Digital Formations: IT and New Architecture in the Global Realm*, ed. Robert Latham and Saskia Sassen. Princeton: Princeton University Press.

Weberman, David. 1997. "The Non-fixity of the Historical Past." *Review of Metaphysics* 50(4): 749–68.

Weinstein, James. 1968. *The Corporate Ideal in the Liberal State, 1900–1918*. Boston: Beacon Press.

Weiss, L. 1997. "Globalization and the Myth of the Powerless State." *New Left Review* 225: 3–27.

————. 1998. *The Myth of the Powerless State*. Ithaca: Cornell University Press.

Weizsäcker, Ernst Ulrich von, Oran Young, and Matthias Finger, eds. 2005. *Limits to Privatization: How to Avoid Too Much of a Good Thing*. London: Earthscan.

Wendt, Alexander. 1995. "Constructing International Politics." *International Security* 20: 71–81.

————. 2001. "Driving with the Rear-view Mirror: On the Rational Science of Institutional Design." *International Organization* 55: 1021–51.

Wexler, Sadat. 1996. "The Proposed International Criminal Court: An Appraisal." *Cornell International Law Journal* 29: 665–726.

Whatmore, Richard. 2004. "The Politics of Political Economy in France from Rousseau to Constant." In *Markets in Historical Contexts: Ideas and Politics in the Modern World*, ed. Mark Bevir and Frank Trentmann. Cambridge: Cambridge University Press.

White, Harrison C. 1981. "Where Do Markets Come From?" *American Journal of Sociology* 87: 517–47.

————. 1993. "Markets in Production Networks." In *Explorations in Economic Sociology*, ed. Richard Swedberg. New York: Russell Sage Foundation.

Wiebe, Robert H. 1967. *The Search for Order, 1877–1920*. New York: Hill and Wang.

Wilentz, Sean. 1984. "Against Exceptionalism: Class Consciousness and the American Labor Movement, 1790–1920." *International Labor and Working Class History* 26: 1–24.

Wilks, Alex. 2001. "A Tower of Babel on the Internet? The World Bank's Development Gateway." Available at: http://www.brettonwoodsproject.org/topic/knowledgebank/k22gatewaybrief.pdf.

Williams, Eric. 1961. *Capitalism and Slavery*. New York: Russell and Russell.

Williams, Jody, and Stephen Goose. 1998. The International Campaign to Ban Landmines. In *To Walk without Fear: The Global Movement to Ban Landmines*, ed. M. A.

Cameron, R. J. Lawson, and Brian W. Tomlin. Ontario, Calif.: Oxford University Press.

Willoughby, Westel Woodbury. 1896. *An Examination of the Nature of the State: A Study in Political Philosophy*. New York: Macmillan.

Willrich, Michael. 1998. "The Two Percent Solution: Eugenic Jurisprudence and the Socialization of American Law, 1900–1930." *Law and History Review* 16: 63–111.

Wilson, Woodrow. 1890. *The State: Elements of Historical and Practical Politics*. Boston: D. C. Heath.

Winch, Donald. 2004. "Thinking Green, Nineteenth-Century Style: John Stuart Mill and John Ruskin." In *Markets in Historical Contexts: Ideas and Politics in the Modern World*, ed. Mark Bevir and Frank Trentmann. Cambridge: Cambridge University Press.

Witte, Edwin E. 1932. *The Government in Labor Disputes*. New York: McGraw Hill.

WomenAction. 2000. "Alternative Assessment of Women and Media Based on NGO Reviews of Section J, Beijing Platform for Action." Available at: http://www .womenaction.org/csw44/altrepeng.htm.

Wood, E. M. 2003. *Empire of Capital*. London: Verso.

Woods, D. C. 1982. "The Operation of the Master and Servant Acts in the Black Country, 1858–1875." Midland History 102(7): 93–115.

Woolgar, Steve, ed. 2002. *Virtual Society?: Technology, Cyberpole, Reality*. New York: Oxford University Press.

World Bank. 2001. "Making State Institutions More Responsive to Poor People." In *World Development Report 2000/2001: Attacking Poverty*. New York: Oxford University Press.

World Development Report. 1997. *The State in a Changing World*. Oxford: Oxford University Press.

World Federation of Exchanges. 2000. *Annual Report and Statistics*. Paris: World Federation of Exchanges.

———. 2001. *Annual Report and Statistics*. Paris: World Federation of Exchanges.

———. 2002. *Annual Report and Statistics*. Paris: World Federation of Exchanges.

———. 2003. *Annual Report and Statistics*. Paris: World Federation of Exchanges.

———. 2004. *Annual Report and Statistics*. Paris: World Federation of Exchanges.

World Information Order (WIO). 2002. *World-Information Files. The Politics of the Info Sphere*. Vienna: Institute for New Culture Technologies; Berlin: Center for Civic Education.

World Trade Organization (WTO). 2003. *World Trade Report*. Geneva: WTO.

———. 2005. *International Trade Statistics 2005*. Geneva: WTO.

———. 2004. *World Trade Report*. Geneva: WTO.

Yang, Guobin. 2003. "Weaving a Green Web: The Internet and Environmental Activism in China." China Environment Series, No. 6. Washington, DC: Woodrow Wilson International Centers for Scholars.

Young, Iris Marion. 1990. *Justice and the Politics of Difference*. Princeton: Princeton University Press.

———. 2002. *Inclusion and Democracy*. Oxford: Oxford University Press.

Yueh, Linda Y. 2003. "International Economic Law, WTO, and TRIPS: New Forms of Global Economic Regulation." Paper presented at Workshop on Globalisation and Diversity of Capitalism: New Concepts for a Post-Neoliberal Era. Centre for the Study of Global Governance, London School of Economics. June 23–24.

Yuval-Davis, N. 1999. "Ethnicity, Gender, Relations and Multiculturalism." In *Race, Identity, and Citizenship*, ed. R. Torres, L. Miron, and J. X. Inda. Oxford: Blackwell.

Zaloom, C. 2003. "Ambiguous Numbers: Trading Technologies and Interpretation in Financial Markets." *American Ethnologist* 30: 258–72.

Zelizer, Virginia A. 1988. "Beyond the Polemics on the Market: Establishing a Theoretical and Empirical Agenda." *Sociological Forum* 3:614–34.

Zerubavel, E. 1982. "The Standardization of Time: A Sociohistorical Perspective." *American Journal of Sociology* 88(1): 1–23.

Ziegler, Jean. 1978. *Main Basse sur L'Afrique*. Paris: Editions du Seuil.

Zelizer, Viviana. 1997. *The Social Meaning of Money: Pin Money, Paychecks, Poor Relief, and Other Currencies*. Princeton: Princeton University Press.

Index

Abbott, Andrew, 155
Abolafia, Mitchel, 360, 361n49
absolutism, 97–98
Abu-Lughod, J., 314
Ackerman, Bruce, 170–71, 173
activists, 3, 367–75
Adam, Barbara, 379
Adams, Paul C., 369, 373n66
Adler, Daniel, 283, 310–12
Aegean Islands, 55
Aftergood, Steve, 178n49
agriculture, 12, 94, 106, 111–12
AIDS, 200, 373–74
airline industry, 172n34
Aksen, Gerald, 244n28
Alford, Roger, 268
alienage, 22
allegiance, 33n4, 41
Allen, Mike, 314
alliances, 32
Allison, Julianne Emmons, 365n56
Aman, Alfred C., Jr., 170–76, 183, 191,
    197, 199
ambivalent allies, 78–79
American Arbitration Association, 243
American Bar Association, 239n16
American Civil Liberties Union (ACLU),
    178n48, 180n52
American Institute of Architects (AIA), 246
American Railway Union, 119
American Revolution, 61n75, 78n6, 100,
    113n69, 127
amore patria, 37, 41–42
analytic borderlands, 379–86
Anderson, Perry, 56n69, 348
Anglo-Saxon law, 47n45
Anti-Corn Law league, 106n62
antitrust laws, 119–20, 236–40
Appadurai, Arjun, 289, 380n1, 382
arbitration, 243–45, 384n3

Archer, Robin, 110
Argentina, 231n4, 262–63, 273–75, 306n20
arms control, 288
Arrighi, Giovanni, 42, 58, 76, 82, 135n112,
    232n8, 248n34, 249
Articles of Confederation, 109, 121n81
artisans, 94
Ashcroft, John D., 183
Ashley, Maurice, 93n37
assemblages, 5–6, 18, 401–402; digital, 23,
    325–27, 386 (*see also* digitization); emer-
    gence and, 403; global, 406–15; method-
    ological analysis of, 404–15; national,
    406–15 (*see also* national states); spatio-
    temporal order and, 386–90; special order
    multiplication and, 420–23
Association for Progressive Communications
    (APC), 372
authority, 1, 21–22, 403; *amore patria* and, 37,
    41–42; Bush administration violations of,
    204–21; Capetian kings and, 33, 39–41,
    44–45; central, 33, 49–53; city proliferation
    and, 53–71; class and, 35–36; crisscrossing
    jurisdictions and, 32–33; critical state role
    in, 76–82; decentralization and, 45–46,
    123; denationalization and, 230–42; digiti-
    zation and, 330–40; divergence in, 225;
    executive, 146, 168–84 (*see also* executive
    power); feudalism and, 27–28, 32–41; for-
    malizations and, 37n14; foundational
    changes in, 143; geographical, 41–53;
    Germanic chieftans and, 35n10; *Gibbons v.
    Ogden* and, 124; historical perspective and,
    3–6; homage and, 36n13; interdependen-
    cies and, 39–40; internationalism and,
    149–56; *McCulloch v. Maryland* and,
    123–24; merchants and, 87–88; method-
    ological analysis of, 404–15; monetary ma-
    nipulation and, 77–78; national states and,
    76–82, 222–23 (*see also* national states);